Further Praise for *A Great and Noble Scheme*

"The Acadians' doomed struggle for survival, recounted by the author in painstaking, even exhaustive detail, takes on the aura of inevitability as though the outcome had been inscribed by the gods on Olympus."

—William Grimes, *New York Times*

"A well-documented account th... ...ocess in which there were no winners.

— ...*)ispatch*

D0882018

"Manages to portray a huge an... ...arity and impartiality . . . entertainingly w...en and well illustrated . . . covers the ordinary human conflicts in the Acadian community with a sure hand and brings life to a vanished world." —John Wilson, *Quill and Quire*

"[A] fascinating account . . . recommended for anyone with a general interest in Colonial American history."

—James D. Fairbanks, *Houston Chronicle*

"Ambitious and provocative . . . a major new work intent on spicing up the prevailing thought on who the Acadians were, how they settled and thrived in what are now the Canadian Maritimes, why and how they were exiled from that homeland and what happened to them."

—Ron Thibodeaux, *New Orleans Times-Picayune*

"Powerful because of its concision and objectivity, and because of the voices from the past [Faragher] chooses to do the talking."

—Clive Doucet, *The Globe and Mail*

"*A Great and Noble Scheme* is one of those landmark books that everyone interested in American history will want to read and keep in his library for children and grandchildren to peruse. It delves deeply and with rueful wisdom into a terrible crime perpetrated by European imperialists and American colonists before they became a nation. John Mack Faragher has replaced the story of *Evangeline* with a narrative that makes all of us confront our flawed humanity."

—Thomas Fleming, author of *Liberty!: The American Revolution*

"Faragher's impressive account of the Acadian tragedy is notable for its narrative drive, drama, clarity, and comprehensive research. As an early American instance of ethnic cleansing, it brings the remote past into the present without being present-minded. Above all, in exposing numerous myths and romanticizations, the account is balanced because it is told from the perspective of all sides, including the British rationale for 'cruel necessity' and oppressive collaboration between British policy-makers and the maritime colonists." —Michael Kammen, professor of American history and culture, Cornell University

"From Acadia to zydeco, John Mack Faragher's extraordinary narrative of 'New France' unfolds with epic scope and vivid, novelistic detail. The 'removal' of the French Catholic Acadians from Nova Scotia to Louisiana and elsewhere has unnerving parallels to our own unsettled historical moment. Under Faragher's probing eye, 'American' history turns out to be a complex tangle of 'intercultural conversations,' something richer and stranger—and sadder—than the traditional (and wishful) melting pot." —Christopher Benfey, author of *Degas in New Orleans* and *The Great Wave*

"In the catalog of North American horrors, the destruction of Acadia can seem slight alongside the dispossession of Indian peoples and the enslavement of Africans, but it resonates deeply in our world of ethnic cleansings." —Richard White, Margaret Byrne Professor of American History, Stanford University

"This is the story of the making and unmaking of a Catholic people of French descent who tried to mind their own business on the edges of empires, something too anomalous to be tolerated by eighteenth-century British imperial officials and nearby New Englanders, who on the eve of the American Revolution successfully extirpated the Acadians. By extending the history of the colonies north to Nova Scotia, Faragher has recovered this dark and long-forgotten episode. We are indebted to him for his lively yet thorough and morally compelling account of it."
—Thomas Bender, University Professor of the Humanities and Professor of History, New York University

Also by John Mack Faragher

Women and Men on the Overland Trail (1979)

Sugar Creek:
Life on the Illinois Prairie (1986)

Daniel Boone:
The Life and Legend of an American Pioneer (1992)

The American West: A New Interpretive History (2000)
with Robert V. Hine

A Great and Noble Scheme

The Tragic Story of the Expulsion of the French Acadians from Their American Homeland

John Mack Faragher

W. W. NORTON & COMPANY
NEW YORK LONDON

Copyright © 2005 by John Mack Faragher

All rights reserved

Printed in the United States of America
First published as a Norton paperback 2006

For information about permission to reproduce selections from this book, write to Permissions, W. W. Norton & Company, Inc., 500 Fifth Avenue, New York, NY 10110

Manufacturing by R. R. Donnelley, Harrisonburg Division
Book design by Lovedog Studio
Production manager: Julia Druskin

LIBRARY OF CONGRESS CATALOGING-IN-PUBLICATION DATA
Faragher, John Mack, 1945–

A great and noble scheme : the tragic story of the expulsion of the French Acadians from their American Homeland / John Mack Faragher.— 1st ed.

p. cm.

Includes bibliographical references and index.

ISBN 0-393-05135-8 (hardcover)

1. Acadians—Migrations—History. 2. Acadians—Relocation—History. 3. Nova Scotia—History—To 1763. 4. Nova Scotia—Emigration and immigration—History—18th century. 5. Great Britain—Colonies—America—History—17th century. 6. France—Colonies—America—History—17th century. 7. Great Britain—Colonies—America—History—18th century. 8. France—Colonies—America—History—18th century. 9. North America—Historiography. 10. North America—Ethnic relations. I. Title.

F1038.F37 2005
971.6'01—dc22

2004013774

ISBN 0-393-32827-9 pbk.

W. W. Norton & Company, Inc., 500 Fifth Avenue, New York, N.Y. 10110
www.wwnorton.com

W. W. Norton & Company Ltd., Castle House, 75/76 Wells Street, London W1T 3QT

1 2 3 4 5 6 7 8 9 0

For my grandsons

Jeremy Daniel Garskof and Arthur Mack Aucoin

We are now upon a great and noble Scheme of sending the neutral French out of this Province, who have always been secret Enemies, and have encouraged our Savages to cut our throats. If we effect their Expulsion, it will be one of the greatest Things that ever the English did in America; for by all Accounts, that part of the Country they possess, is as good Land as any in the World: In case therefore we could get some good English Farmers in their Room, this Province would abound with all Kinds of Provisions.

—*Pennsylvania Gazette*, 4 September 1755

CONTENTS

ACKNOWLEDGMENTS

THE IDEA FOR THIS book first took shape during a visit my wife and I paid to our daughter, who was attending graduate school in Lafayette, Louisiana. On a memorable Sunday afternoon in November 1995 the three of us drove down Bayou Teche to Longfellow-Evangeline State Historic Site and in the reconstructed Acadian cabin there I first saw the poster "Acadian Odyssey," produced by Parks Canada, which details the expulsion of the Acadians. Aside from short discussions in histories of the French and Indian War, boyhood memories of reading Longfellow's *Evangeline*, and the plaintive chorus of the Band's "Acadian Driftwood," it was something I knew very little about. In the gift shop I bought Carl A. Brasseaux's little book on the expulsion, *Scattered to the Wind*, and before bed that night had learned enough to know that this awful episode, so strikingly similar to events of ethnic cleansing in our own time, was something about which I needed to know much more.

Many people and institutions provided support, assistance, and encouragement during the research and writing of this book. First and foremost, I owe a debt of gratitude to Yale University. The grant of a sabbatical leave from teaching in 1999–2000 gave me the chance to begin the project in earnest, and another leave in the fall of 2003 provided the opportunity to conclude it. The collections of Sterling Memorial Library and the Beinecke Rare Book and Manuscript Library at Yale supplied valuable materials and the staff generously offered their expertise and arranged for the loan or purchase of essential books and archival collections on microfilm. I especially want to thank Nancy Godleski, George Miles, Fred Musto, Margaret Powell, and Suzanne Roberts. Benjamin Parrish, in the Map Collection, helped prepare the original maps. I also benefited from the encouragement of my colleagues in the Department of History and the Program in American Studies, particularly the chairs, Professors Jon Butler and Jean-Christophe Agnew. Without the assistance and support of Victorine Shepard I would not have been able to move ahead with research and writing while performing my administrative duties, and I want to thank her specially.

This project was inspired by the intellectual community of the Howard R. Lamar Center for the Study of Frontiers and Borders at Yale, including my colleagues Howard R. Lamar, Jay Gitlin, George Miles, Gilbert Joseph, and Stephen J. Pitti, together with the senior scholars who have graced us with their presence over the past three years, Robert Utley, Melody Webb, Michael D. Quinn, Gerald Friesen, and Susan Armitage. Graduate students have been an essential part of this community. For what they have contributed I want to thank those who have participated over the past decade, many of whom are now professors and published scholars: Kenneth Orona, Catherine Corman, Elizabth A. Fenn, Raul A. Ramos, Benjamin H. Johnson, Thomas McCarthy, Andrew Lewis, Bettina Drew, J. C. Mutchler, Robert Campbell, Jon T. Coleman, James Kessenides, Michelle Nickerson, Aaron Sachs, Christian McMillen, Denise Bossy, Kristie Starr, Kari Main, Daniel Lanpher, Robert Morrissey, Roxanne Willis, Scott Kleeb, Melissa Stuckey, Angela Pulley Hudson, Karen Marrero, Paul Grant Costa, and Ashley Riley Sousa.

During my sabbatical leave in 1999–2000 the Huntington Library awarded me a Times-Mirror Fellowship, and during a year of residence the Huntington became my second intellectual home. For their hospitality I am indebted to Robert C. Ritchie, W. M. Keck Foundation Director of Research and Education, and his assistant Carolyn Powell. The Huntington allowed me months of uninterrupted research. But as important, it offered a wonderful group of smart and interested colleagues. In particular I want to thank Stephen Aron, Hal S. Barron, Richard Buel, William S. Deverell, Kathleen M. Donegan, Jonathan Earle, Richard Kaeuper, James Kessenides, Andrew Lewis, Karen Lystra, Charles Royster, Marguerite S. Shaffer, Leslie Tuttle, and the late Martin Ridge.

A number of individuals helped me locate important materials: A. J. B. Johnson and Wayne Kerr, Parks Canada; Brenda Lawson, Curator of Manuscripts, Massachusetts Historical Society; Jonathan Ralton, Historic Winslow House Association; Cynthia Krusell, Historical Research Associates of Plymouth County, Massachusetts; Scott Robson, Curator of the Historical Collection, Nova Scotia Museum; and Ilene Susan Fort, Curator of American Art, Los Angeles County Museum of Art. Michael Jo and Benjamin Johnson assisted me in finding documents at Yale. Paulina Alberto translated important French texts. Mary Litch, computer specialist at Yale, helped prepare digital images for publication.

Several institutions offered me an opportunity to present my work in progress, and the exchanges that took place on those occasions were critical in shaping my thinking. I want to thank the departments of history at the following universities: University of Southern California; California State University, Northridge; Claremont Graduate University; University of California, Los Angeles; University of California, Riverside; as well as the American Studies Symposium, Program in American Studies, Yale University; the Greater

American Histories Conference, the Huntington Library; the Center for Historical Studies, University of Maryland; and the Western History Workshop, Museum of the American West, Autry National Center.

The completed manuscript was read by Stephen Aron, Carl A. Brasseaux, Gerald Friesen, Jay Gitlin, Maurice Basque, George Miles, John G. Reid, and Harry S. Stout. They saved me from many errors and challenged me on many points. Although I did not take all of their advice, I value their criticism and thank them for their care. Maria Guarnaschelli at W. W. Norton edited the manuscript with attention to both the big picture and the fine detail, and the book is immeasurably better as a result. Her assistant, Erik Johnson, arranged for permissions and helped shepherd the book through the various stages of production. The manuscript benefited from the excellent copyediting of Ann Adelman. For connecting me with the fine people at Norton I thank Gerard McCauley, my literary agent and good friend.

My greatest debt is to Michele Hoffnung, my partner and life companion. Together we traveled through the New Acadia of Louisiana and the ancient l'Acadie of Nova Scotia and New Brunswick. During those trips she endured my stops at historical markers and used bookstores. Later she put up with the early mornings and the late evenings I spent writing. After the completion of each chapter she listened attentively as I read it aloud. And she gave me the confidence to go on to write the next one.

During the period I worked on this project, Michele and I were blessed with the arrival of two wonderful grandsons. This book is dedicated to them, in the hope that the world they inherit will be a better place than the one described in these pages.

INTRODUCTION

In the autumn of 1755, officers and troops from New England, acting under the authority of the colonial governors of Nova Scotia and Massachusetts, systematically rounded up more than seven thousand Acadians, the French-speaking, Catholic inhabitants who lived in communities along the shores of the Bay of Fundy. Men, women, and children alike were crowded into transport vessels and deported in small groups to other British colonies. Many families were separated, some never to meet again. Another ten to twelve thousand Acadians managed to escape and spent years as refugees. Hundreds of them were captured and deported, while others took up arms in resistance. Meanwhile, their property was plundered, their communities were torched, their lands were seized.

Le grand dérangement—the Acadian term for this "great upheaval" —continued until the end of the Seven Years War between Great Britain and France in 1763. It claimed thousands of lives and laid waste one of the oldest colonial homelands in North America. After the war the surviving Acadians settled again in the maritime region, but not on their former farms, for those had been turned over to Yankee settlers. Other Acadians sought refuge in the French colony of Louisiana, where they became the ancestors of today's Cajuns.

Although their descendants now number several hundred thousand persons in maritime Canada and southwestern Louisiana, most Americans are unfamiliar with the story of the Acadians. They are known—if known at all—as the unfortunate people of Henry Wadsworth Longfellow's epic poem *Evangeline*. For Americans of a certain age—myself included—Longfellow was required reading in public school. His Acadians, however, were a literary creation, little more than victims who endured other men's prejudice, hatred, and greed. What about the Acadians of history? They were largely illiterate, leaving few documents of their own, so telling their story is a bit daunting. But their voices may be found in the colonial records of France and Great Britain. They turn out to be fascinating subjects in their own right.

The founding generation of Acadians came from France in the early seventeenth century—contemporaries of the Puritan settlers of New England—to establish the French colony of l'Acadie. They developed a culture entirely their own, distinct not only from their Puritan neighbors to the southwest but their neighbors to the northwest, the inhabitants of the St. Lawrence River valley, known in early America as Canadiens, today as French-Canadians or Québecois. Intermarrying with the native Míkmaq people of the region, the Acadians forged an ethnic accord that was exceptional in the colonial settlement of early North America. Adapting to their environment, they learned to dike and farm the tidal marshlands, and perfected a farming system that was the envy of their neighbors. Living on the margins of the British and French empires, serving two masters, they declared themselves to be "neutrals" in the imperial contest. Neutrality was the Acadians' defining characteristic and their greatest asset. They pursued it for a century and prospered.

Like authentic tragic heroes, they insisted on defining themselves in their own way. And in the end they were overtaken by catastrophe.

The British government—and several generations of historians—defended their expulsion as a "cruel necessity" in the war against France. But the events of 1755 bear a striking similarity to more recent episodes of ethnic cleansing—the purposeful campaign of one ethnic or religious group to remove, by violent and terror-inspiring means, the civilian population of another ethnic or religious group from a certain geographic area. Reading in the history of colonial violence and warfare in eighteenth-century North America, the campaign to remove the Acadians brought me up short. Was their expulsion an early example of ethnic cleansing? Was ethnic cleansing a part of America's founding history? This book grew out of these questions.

As a historian of the American frontier, I have taught and written of the violent struggle between colonists and the indigenous inhabitants, as well as the bloody intercolonial conflicts that pitted English- and French-speaking colonists against one other. The removal of the Acadians was something different. In the words of a British colonial correspondent in 1755, it was "a great and noble Scheme, . . . one of the greatest Things that ever the English did in America." It was executed methodically by officers of the government in accordance with a carefully conceived plan many years in the making. It utilized all the available resources of the state. It included the seizure and destruction of Acadian records and registers, the arrest and isolation of community leaders, the separation of men from women and children. In the nineteenth century, operations of that kind would be directed at Indian peoples such as the Cherokees, but before 1755, nothing like it had been seen in North America. Today, the universal condemnation of ethnic cleansing by world opinion makes it difficult to defend what was done. In 2003, Queen Elizabeth II issued a Royal Proclamation acknowledging British responsibility for the decision to deport the Acadian people and regretting its "tragic consequences."

This is a tragic history, tragic not only because the undeserved suffering of the Acadians was brought on by their pursuit of independence, but also because it tells of the destruction of common hopes and dreams. It requires listening not only to the voices of the French-speaking, Catholic Acadians but to the English- speaking, Protestant Yankees who eventually removed them. It is a story of two peoples, of two paths, the ways they converged and diverged. It is premised on the conviction that American history is not exceptional but universal. It is an attempt at recounting a history of Greater America, the wider relations and connections that went into the making of the United States.

MAPS

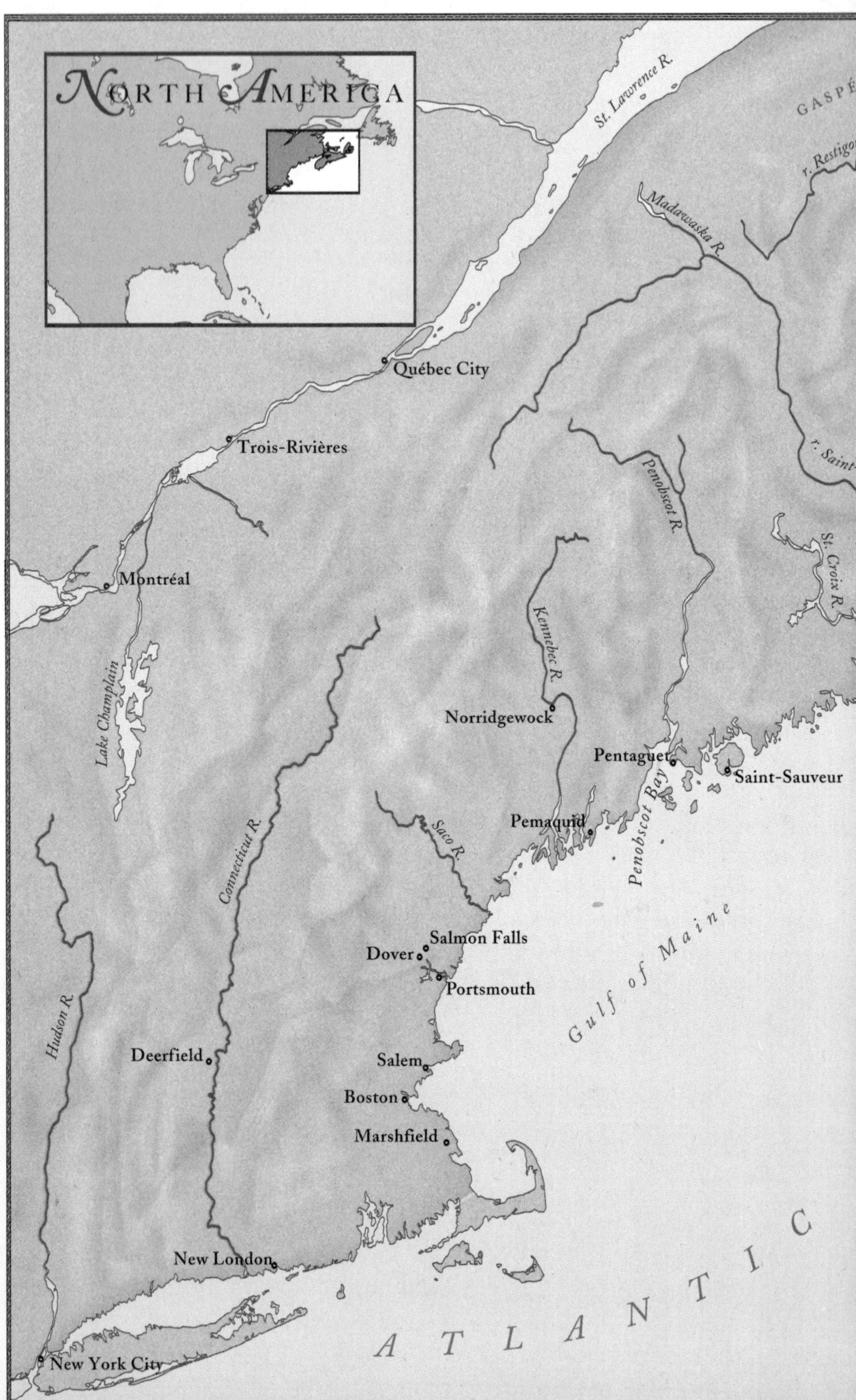
North America
St. Lawrence R.
Gaspé
r. Restigou
Madawaska R.
Québec City
Trois-Rivières
Penobscot R.
r. Saint-
St. Croix R.
Montréal
Kennebec R.
Lake Champlain
Norridgewock
Pentaguet
Saint-Sauveur
Connecticut R.
Saco R.
Pemaquid
Penobscot Bay
Salmon Falls
Dover
Portsmouth
Gulf of Maine
Hudson R.
Deerfield
Salem
Boston
Marshfield
New London
New York City
Atlantic

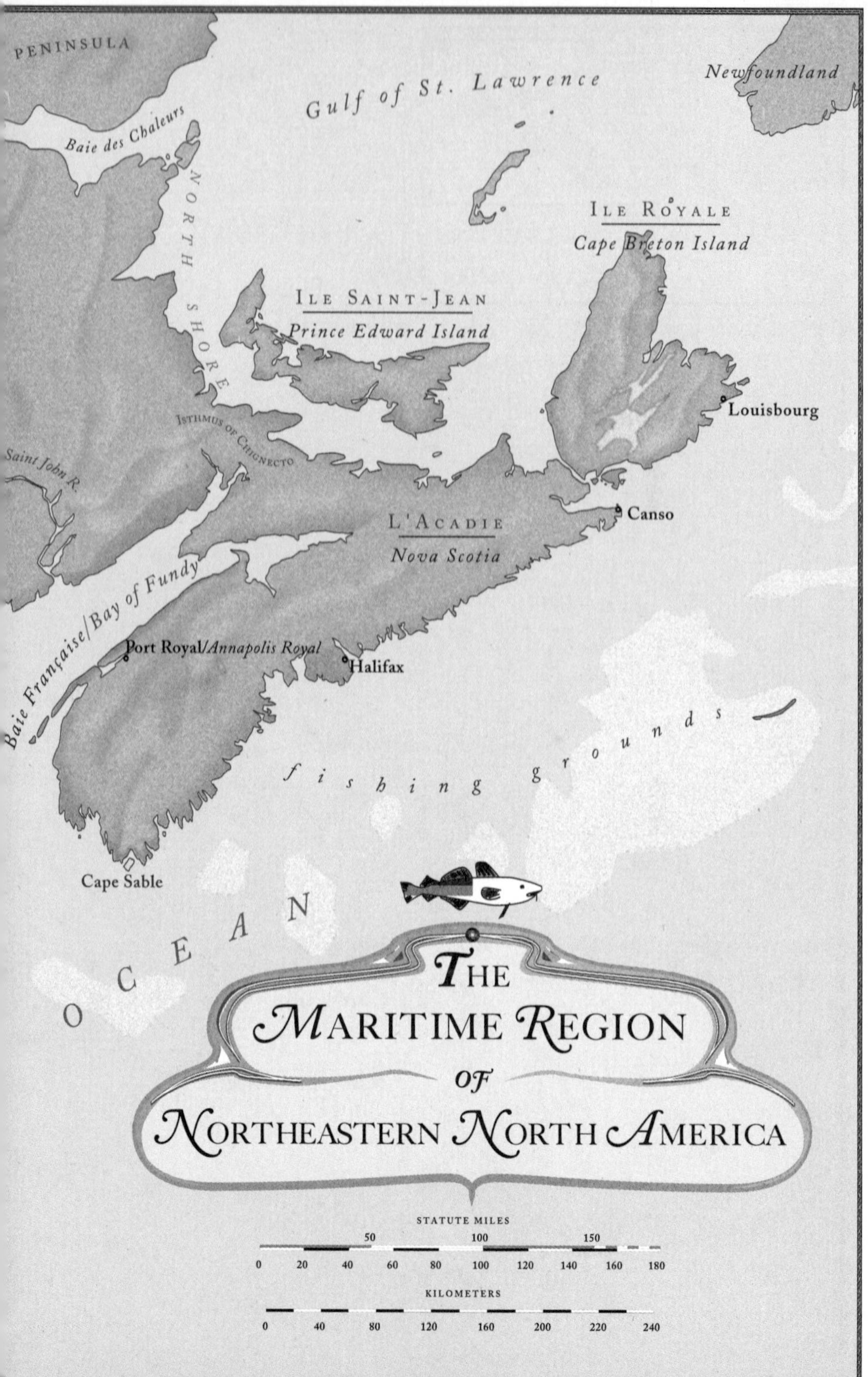

PENINSULA
Gulf of St. Lawrence
Newfoundland
Baie des Chaleurs
NORTH SHORE
ILE ROYALE
Cape Breton Island
ILE SAINT-JEAN
Prince Edward Island
Louisbourg
ISTHMUS OF CHIGNECTO
Saint John R.
Canso
L'ACADIE
Nova Scotia
Baie Française/Bay of Fundy
Port Royal/Annapolis Royal
Halifax
fishing grounds
Cape Sable
OCEAN
THE MARITIME REGION OF NORTHEASTERN NORTH AMERICA
STATUTE MILES
50
100
150
0
20
40
60
80
100
120
140
160
180
KILOMETERS
0
40
80
120
160
200
220
240

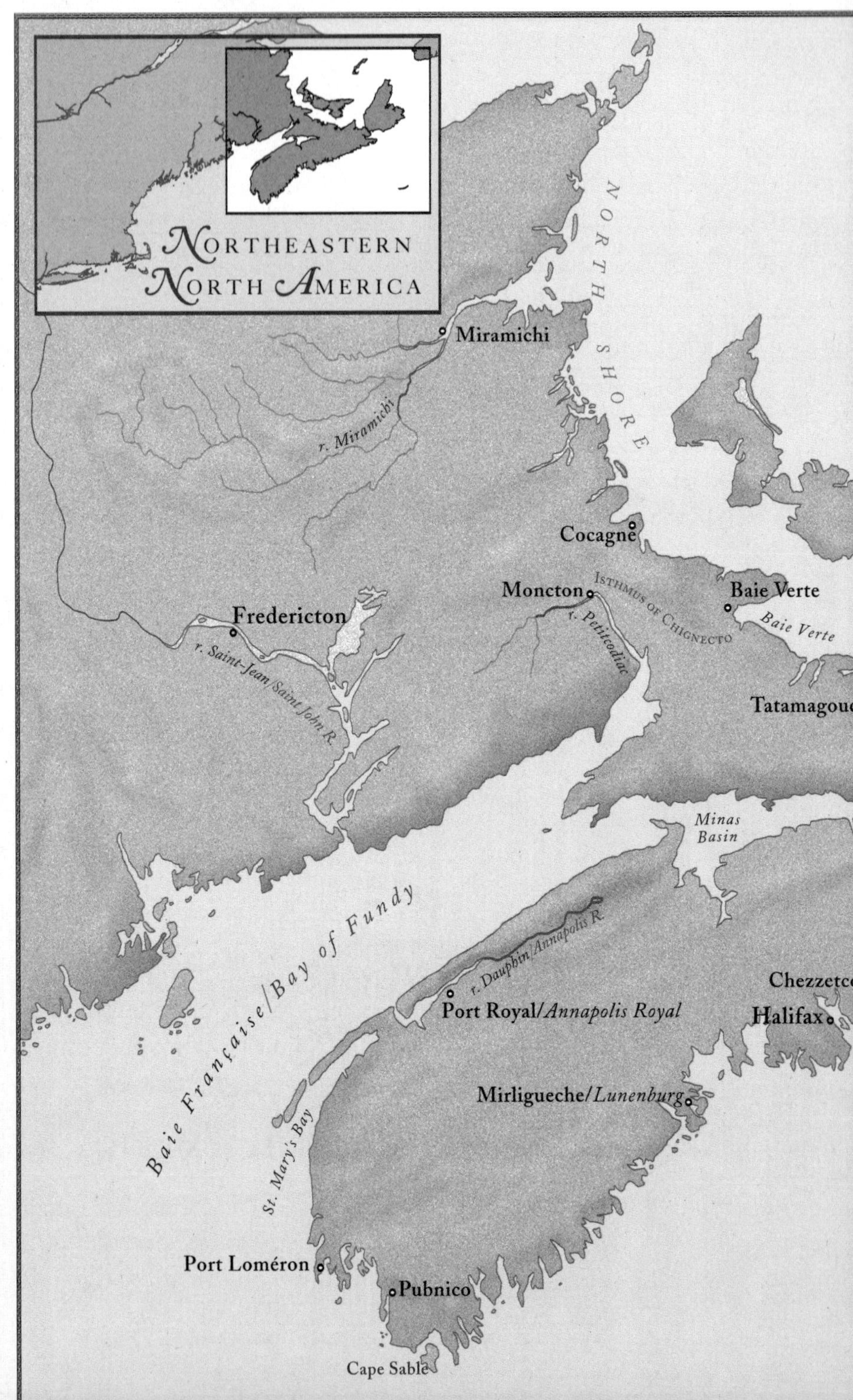

Northeastern
North America
North Shore
Miramichi
r. Miramichi
Cocagne
Moncton
Isthmus of Chignecto
r. Petitcodiac
Baie Verte
Baie Verte
Fredericton
r. Saint-Jean/Saint John R.
Tatamagouc
Minas
Basin
Baie Française/Bay of Fundy
r. Dauphin/Annapolis R.
Port Royal/Annapolis Royal
Chezzetco
Halifax
Mirligueche/Lunenburg
St. Mary's Bay
Port Loméron
Pubnico
Cape Sable

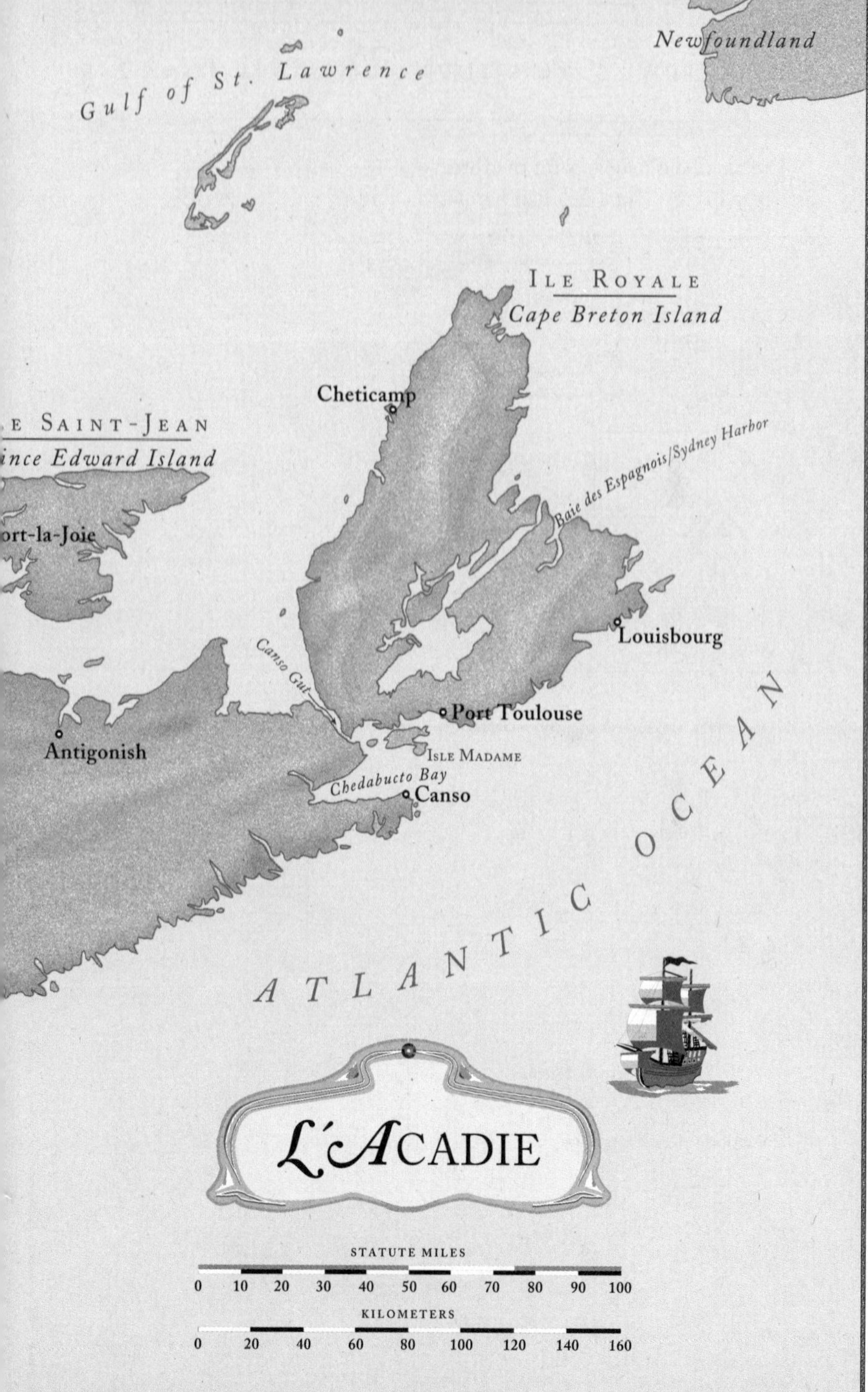
Newfoundland
Gulf of St. Lawrence
Ile Royale
Cape Breton Island
Cheticamp
e Saint-Jean
ince Edward Island
ort-la-Joie
Baie des Espagnois/Sydney Harbor
Louisbourg
Canso Gut
Port Toulouse
Antigonish
Isle Madame
Chedabucto Bay
Canso
Atlantic Ocean
L'Acadie
Statute Miles
0 10 20 30 40 50 60 70 80 90 100
Kilometers
0 20 40 60 80 100 120 140 160

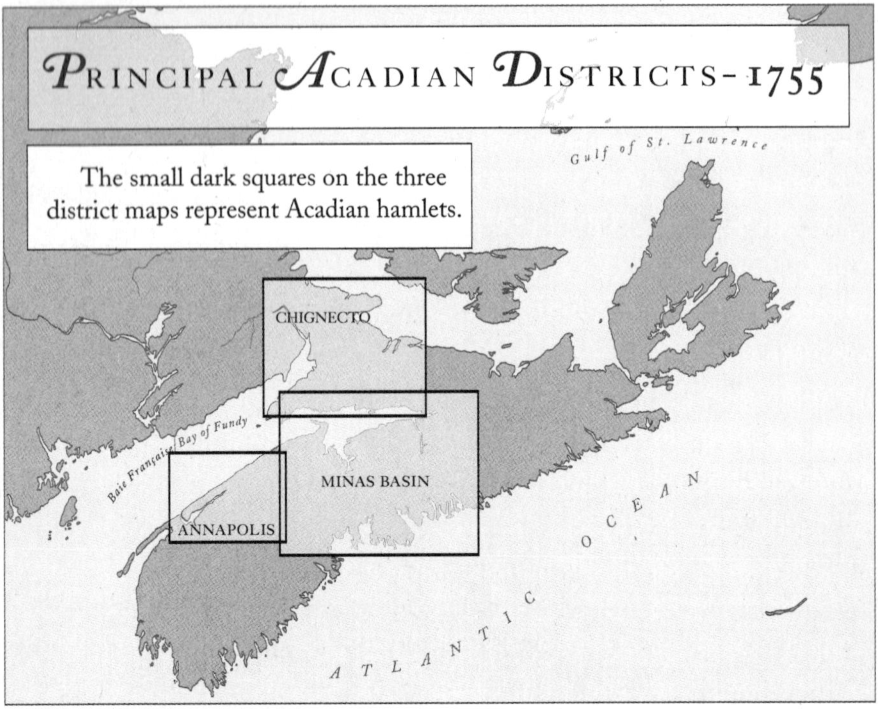

PRINCIPAL ACADIAN DISTRICTS-1755

The small dark squares on the three district maps represent Acadian hamlets.

Gulf of St. Lawrence
CHIGNECTO
Baie Française/Bay of Fundy
MINAS BASIN
ANNAPOLIS
ATLANTIC OCEAN

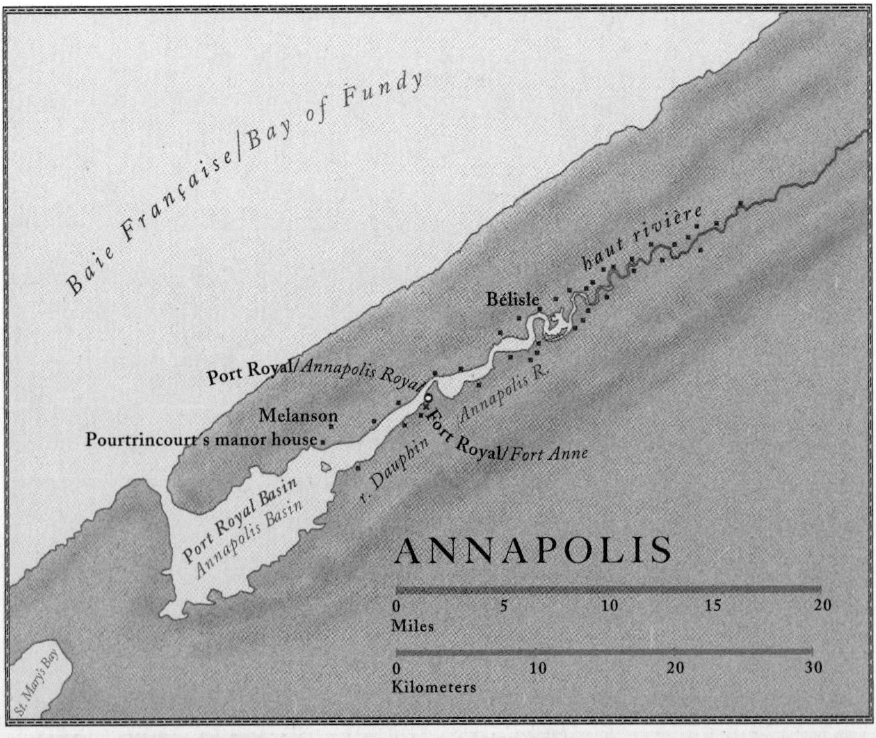

Baie Française/Bay of Fundy
haut rivière
Bélisle
Port Royal/*Annapolis Royal*
Melanson
Pourtrincourt's manor house
Fort Royal/*Fort Anne*
r. Dauphin/*Annapolis R.*
Port Royal Basin
Annapolis Basin
St. Mary's Bay

ANNAPOLIS

0 5 10 15 20
Miles

0 10 20 30
Kilometers

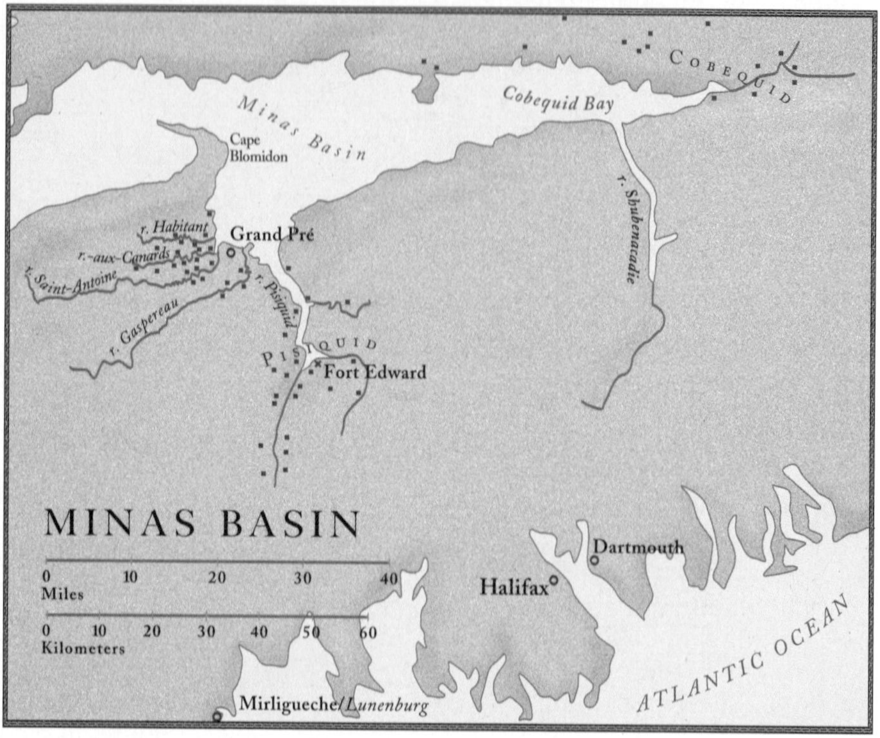

MINAS BASIN

Cobequid
Cobequid Bay
Minas Basin
Cape Blomidon
r. Shubenacadie
r. Habitant
Grand Pré
r.-aux-Canards
r. Saint-Antoine
r. Gaspereau
r. Pisiquid
Pisiquid
Fort Edward
Dartmouth
Halifax
Atlantic Ocean
Mirligueche/*Lunenburg*

0 10 20 30 40
Miles
0 10 20 30 40 50 60
Kilometers

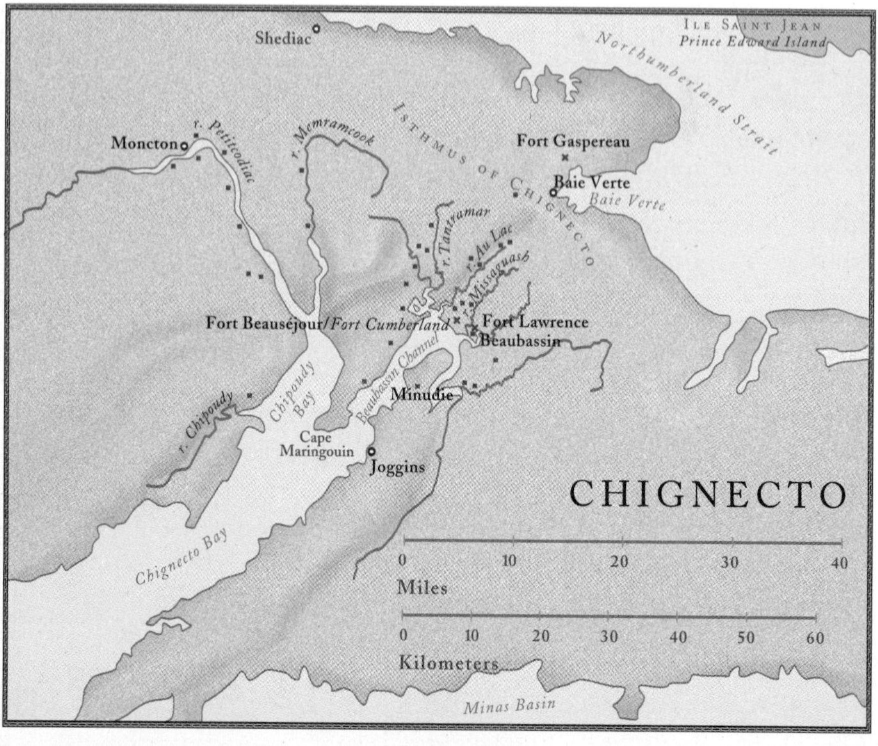

CHIGNECTO

Shediac
Ile Saint Jean
Prince Edward Island
Northumberland Strait
Isthmus of Chignecto
Moncton
r. Petitcodiac
r. Memramcook
Fort Gaspereau
Baie Verte
Baie Verte
r. Tantramar
r. Au Lac
r. Missaguash
r. La Planche
Fort Beauséjour/*Fort Cumberland*
Fort Lawrence
Beaubassin
Beaubassin Channel
Minudie
Chipoudy Bay
r. Chipoudy
Cape Maringouin
Joggins
Chignecto Bay
Minas Basin

0 10 20 30 40
Miles
0 10 20 30 40 50 60
Kilometers

A Great and Noble Scheme

CHAPTER 1

L'ORDRE DE BON-TEMPS

The French Arrival in l'Acadie, 1604–1616

THE FRENCH COLONIZATION OF l'Acadie began in earnest on 13 May 1606, when the *Jonas*, a vessel of 150 tons, loaded with provisions and carrying forty men, weighed anchor at the port of La Rochelle and sailed for the infant outpost of Port Royal on the far side of the Atlantic. This was seven months before the departure of English colonists for Jamestown in Virginia, and fourteen years before the landing of the *Mayflower* at Plymouth Rock. In fact, by 1606 Frenchmen had been fishing in North American waters for decades, landing along the shore of the North Atlantic coast to dry their catch, and trading with the native hunters for furs, particularly beaver pelts, which could be fashioned into a waterproof material for coats and hats. But this expedition, under the command of Jean de Biencourt, sieur de Poutrincourt, a fifty-year-old aristocrat from the barony of Saint-Just in the region of Champagne, would establish the first French agricultural colony on the North Atlantic coast of North America.[1]

Sieur de Poutrincourt was the associate of Pierre du Gua, sieur de Monts, viceroy and captain-general of New France, a vast swath of North America extending along the Atlantic coast from the fortieth to the forty-sixth degree of latitude, from Delaware Bay in the south to Newfoundland in the north. A veteran officer in the army of King Henri IV during the civil wars of religion fought between French Catholics and French Protestant Huguenots in the late sixteenth century, de Monts was described by one contemporary as a man of *le coeur porté à choses hautes*—literally, "high-hearted," which was to say, of daring and adventurous disposition. Think of him as a French Sir Walter Raleigh. His royal appointment provided him a monopoly of the lucrative fur trade of northeastern North America, but in turn required him, in the name of the king, to people and cultivate the region, to plant towns and build fortifications, "to establish, extend, and make known our name, power, and authority, and to subject, submit, and render obedient thereto all the tribes of this land . . . to summon and instruct them, provoke and rouse them to the knowledge of God and to the light of the Christian faith and religion, [and] to establish it among them." For de Monts, however, becoming the first of King Henri's subjects in America held no appeal. Like Raleigh, his interest lay less in settlement than in commerce, so the work of planting and converting he delegated to his associate Poutrincourt, who had lost much of his wealth during the religious wars and dreamed of recouping his fortune with the establishment of an agricultural colony. The idea was to transplant to the New World a version of the rural landscape of Champagne, a society of *seigneurs et roturiers*, lords who ruled the roost and commoners who worked the land. The start-up costs of this venture were to be supplied by the fur trade. There would be no subsidy from the royal treasury, which had been emptied by the religious wars.[2]

Two years before, in 1604, de Monts and Poutrincourt, with a company of seventy-five men, had crossed the Atlantic on an exploratory mission, guided by the accomplished navigator Samuel de Champlain and the merchant trader Francis Gravé, sieur du Pont (known as Pontgravé), both of whom possessed substantial experience in American waters. At a secluded harbor the explorers christened "Port Royal" (now Annapolis Royal), Poutrincourt selected alluvial lands along a salubrious river for his colony. Leaving de Monts and the others to continue their exploration, in the summer of 1604 he sailed back to France in one of the expedition's vessels to make arrangements for bringing over colonists. The following spring sieur de Monts returned to France as well, his vessel loaded with a rich cargo of furs. He told Poutrincourt that he and the company had spent the previous summer successfully trading along the coast, and in the fall had established a base camp on an island at the mouth of the St. Croix River, today's boundary between the state of Maine and the province of New Brunswick. But the winter had been disastrous. Thirty-five of the men, more than half the company, had perished from malnutrition and scurvy. In the spring de Monts had relocated the operation to Port Royal, where he hoped the winters would prove milder. They were welcomed by several hundred Míkmaw residents of the area, who permitted de Monts to construct a permanent headquarters, a "fort and habitation," modeled after the fortified manor houses of the French countryside. Champlain, Pontgravé, and some two dozen men were still there, continuing to trade for furs and holding the site in anticipation of Poutrincourt's arrival with the colonists.[3]

De Monts would remain in France, in charge of the commercial operation. But for Poutrincourt, the American adventure had just begun. It was the crucial first step in his plan to establish his fortune and his lineage in America. Although the advance force traveling on the *Jonas* was composed entirely of men, women and children were to follow later once the colony was established. Poutrincourt had picked men from his own homeland, relatives and associates including his fifteen-year-old son Charles de Biencourt de Saint-Just, who was to perpetuate the family name in New France; his relative by marriage, Louis Hébert, a young apothecary with a deep interest in horticulture, who was to conduct experiments in the cultivation of grapes and grain, and to supervise construction of the first winery and grist mill in North America; and his attorney, Marc Lescarbot, a forty-year-old Parisian bachelor assigned to act as the colony's notary and historian. When offered the position, Lescarbot later wrote in his engaging eyewitness account, *Histoire de la Nouvelle France* (1609), he jumped at the opportunity to exchange the tedious practice of the law for a chance to explore the New World "with my own eyes."[4]

It is difficult to exaggerate the physical and psychological distance that separated the Old World from the New in the seventeenth and eighteenth centuries. The typical voyage took six or seven weeks, but might last considerably longer depending on the season, the currents, the winds, and the fates. "I have been to Canada seven times," one French captain of the era testified, "and I venture to state that the most favorable of those voyages gave me more white hairs than all those that I have made elsewhere. It is a continual torment for mind and body." The voyage of the *Jonas* was to be Lescarbot's first crossing (it also proved to be his last), and he acknowledged his fear of traveling "over the unstable sea, every moment within two fingers of death [*à deux doigts de la morte*], as the saying goes." The voyage began pleasantly enough as the pilot steered the vessel into prevailing Atlantic currents taking them southwest to the Azores, where he hoped to pick up the trade winds. But in the vicinity of those islands, the weather turned foul. Gale-force westerlies bore down on the vessel, forcing the crew to close-haul the sails. Squalls rose up—"muttering, snorting, whistling, howling, storming, rumbling"—and violent seas tossed the vessel "aloft upon mountains of water, and thence down as it were into the most profound depths of the world." Fighting their way across the Atlantic the crew eventually caught the northward-coursing Gulf Stream, taking them into colder waters and impenetrable fogs. Finally, on 15 July, after more than eight hard weeks at sea, the men sighted the coastline of North America. "And while we held our course, lo! there came to us from the land odors of unrivalled sweetness, brought so abundantly by a warm breeze that all the Orient could not have produced more." They had reached another world.[5]

Despite the difficult voyage the pilot had brought them directly to the harbor known as Canso (Canseau), from *camsoak,* which in Míkmawísimk, the language of the Míkmaw people, means "rocks on the other side"—a reference to the cliffs of Cape Breton Island across the channel, visible to those arriving by sea, whether by canoe or by sailing vessel. In the early seventeenth century Canso was the most important stopping place on the North Atlantic coast for hundreds of European fishing vessels from Portugal, the Biscayan harbors of Spain and France, ports in Brittany and Normandy, and England's Bristol Channel. They were drawn by the proximity to *les grand bancs,* the broad continental shelf extending offshore, where the shallow waters teemed with "so great multitudes of certeyne bigge fysshes," as explorer Sebastian Cabot reported, "that they sumtymes stayed my shippes."[6]

For a century Europeans had been catching Atlantic cod here from spring to fall, salting them down, and shipping them back to Europe. Salt cod had become a staple in the Mediterranean diet, and over the next century would become a main provision of the slave plantations being established in the West Indies. European fishermen set up temporary fish-drying camps on the level beaches, and were soon exchanging European goods for animal pelts with the Míkmaq (the plural form of Míkmaw). This was the beginning of the North American fur trade. There was intense rivalry among fishermen, yet for the next fifty years the fishery remained open to all comers, and men from scores of ethnic backgrounds mingled amicably at places such as Canso. As for those who trucked and bartered with the natives of the country, however, it was precisely sieur de Monts's intention to curtail their commerce—or rather, to require them to redirect it through his operation at Port Royal. During his initial exploration in 1604, de Monts arrested a trader on the coast south of Canso, confiscating his goods as well as his vessel. But there were dozens more like him, and de Monts was now back in France, a long way from these shores.

The lands south of the Gulf of St. Lawrence—territory that today includes the Canadian provinces of Prince Edward Island, Nova Scotia, and New Brunswick, as well as the state of Maine—Lescarbot and Poutrincourt knew as *l'Acadie.* There are two accounts of the name's origins. In 1524 the Tuscan explorer Giovanni da Verrazano, sailing for the French crown, was so impressed by the beauty of the North American coast that he christened it "*Arcadia,*" after a prose pastorale of the same name published in 1502, a work that popularized the notion of a rural "golden age" among the ancients. On sixteenth-century French maps and charts *l'Arcadie* appeared as the place name for the northern Atlantic coastal region, and it was the name known and used by French sea captains and fishermen. According to this explanation, *l'Acadie* was simply a corruption of *l'Arcadie.* An alternate account notes the similarity in pronunciation between *Acadie* and the Míkmawísimk suffix *-akadie*, meaning "place of abundance," commonly used by the Míkmaq to mark important resource sites, as in *Shunakadie* (place of abundant cranberries) or *Shubenakadie* (place of abundant wild potatoes). These explanations are most compelling in combination—*l'Arcadie* mutating into *l'Acadie* as a result of the intercultural conversations between Míkmaw hunters and French traders.[7]

Intercultural conversation was something about which Lescarbot was to learn a good deal. As he stood on the deck of the *Jonas,* gazing toward the welcoming shore of Canso, he saw two Basque longboats rapidly approaching the vessel. The Basques had been among the first Europeans to exploit these waters, although like other fishermen they rarely established permanent residence in North America, but remained seasonal visitors. The first boat was manned by fishermen from the French port of Saint-Malo, the other by several Míkmaw seamen "who had a moose painted on their sail." By the early seventeenth century the natives of the Atlantic coast had mastered the art of sailing small European craft. They reached the vessel first and climbed aboard. These natives were "the first I had ever seen," Lescarbot wrote, "and I admired their fine shape and well-formed faces." The French called them *sauvages,* a term that did not have the same hard edge as the English "savage," yet was meant as a marker for the supposed primitivism of native culture compared to the sophistication of Europeans. Lescarbot employed the term, but with some skepticism. "We commonly call them *sauvages,* [but] they are anything but that." The leader of this group, for example, "wore only a piece of coarse red frieze, with *matachias* [beadwork] around his neck and wrists, above his elbows, and at his waist." Yet the Basque boat, the red cloth, even the tools used by native craftsmen to manufacture the wampum were all imported from Europe, and were evidence not of difference but of the connections between the continents.[8]

Using signs and a trade jargon including many French and Basque words ("indeed, they have been so long frequented by the Basques," Lescarbot joked, "that the language of the coast tribes is half Basque"), the Míkmaw captain told Poutrincourt what had taken place at Port Royal over the past winter. Another dozen Frenchmen, close to half the remaining company, had died of scurvy. The men were understandably desperate for the arrival of the supply vessel, and when it failed to appear by early summer, they feared being abandoned. Champlain and Pontgravé had ordered the construction of a small vessel in which they planned to sail to Canso, hoping to catch a ride back to France with a fishing vessel. They might already have left Port Royal.[9]

The *Jonas* departed from Canso the next morning, encountering more dense fog as it coasted southward. Rounding Cape Sable, the vessel sailed into Baie Française, the large body of water separating the Acadian peninsula from the mainland. At the end of the century, on the eve of the Anglo-American conquest of l'Acadie, New Englanders would rename it "Bay of Fundy," perhaps from the Portuguese *baia fonda*, or "deep bay." Indeed, it is exceptionally deep not only in fathoms but in nautical miles, a narrowing funnel that pushes and squeezes incoming tides to ever-increasing heights, reaching a maximum of fifty feet or more in the basins at the head of the bay, the greatest tidal variation in the world. As the crew of the *Jonas* soon discovered, the powerful surge of water creates dangerously strong currents that threatened to dash the vessel against what Lescarbot described as "the high, rocky, and precipitous" shore.[10]

On the evening of 26 July, the *Jonas* came to the entrance of Port Royal harbor, a narrow portal in the cliff wall. But so strong was the ebb of the tide through the gut that the vessel could not enter, and the crew had to cast anchor in the rough waters along the rocky coast. After passing an anxious night, late the next morning they entered with the flood tide, "though not without much difficulty," wrote Lescarbot, "for the wind was contrary, and gusts blew from the mountains which were like to carry us on the rocks. Amid all this our ship sailed stern-first, and more than once turned round, without it being possible to prevent it." Reaching the calm waters of the basin, however, the captain quickly regained control, and for the first time Lescarbot gazed out at the site of the new colony. He was charmed.[11]

"This Port Royal, the home of Sieur de Poutrincourt, is the most beautiful earthly habitation that God has ever made," he would later write. "It is fortified upon the North by a range of 12 or 15 leagues of mountains, upon which the Sun beats all day, and by hills on the Southern or Meridian shore, which forms a port that can securely harbor twenty thousand ships." Beautiful meadows at the mouth of what the French called rivière Dauphin offered grass for grazing livestock, making it a perfect place to establish a settlement. But what most impressed Lescarbot was the extent to which the site "remained wilderness." What a waste of resources, he thought, "seeing that so many folk are ill-off in this world who could make their profit of this land if they only had a leader to bring them thither." With Poutrincourt's guidance Port Royal could be the beginning of great things, truly a New France.[12]

As the *Jonas* sailed up the harbor toward the rivermouth, Lescarbot's reveries were interrupted by the sighting, to the larboard, of the French fort and habitation at the verge of forest and bay. It appeared abandoned. When the vessel drifted near to shore, Lescarbot saw a native man and woman suddenly emerge from the woods and run toward the building. The man "cried out like a madman," although no one on board could understand his words. The two then jumped into a birchbark canoe and began paddling swiftly toward the *Jonas*. Startled, the crew sprang to, but as the canoe drew closer the pair signaled their friendly intentions. They pulled alongside, and the young woman steadied the craft while the man climbed aboard.[13]

It was Membertou, *sagamore* or leader of the several hundred Míkmaq who regularly summered at Port Royal. He greeted Poutrincourt, and using signs and broken French explained that Champlain and Pontgravé had sailed away with most of the men a few days before, leaving only two soldiers behind to hold the post. The two men had been napping when Membertou came running, shouting orders at them: "Do you not see a great ship which is arriving? And we do not know who they are!" It certainly seemed that Membertou had assumed authority over these men. Champlain later told Poutrincourt that when he and Pontgravé left, Membertou agreed to look after them as if "they were his own children." Finishing his explanation, Membertou signaled to shore. One of the Frenchmen cautiously emerged from the gate with a lighted matchlock, and the other poked up from the parapet where a small cannon was positioned. Now recognizing the French ensign flying from the *Jonas*, he let loose a welcoming cannonade and the crew saluted back with three rounds from their own guns and a blast from the vessel's trumpet. "Soon we landed," wrote Lescarbot, "visited the house, and passed the day in returning thanks to God, in inspecting the wigwams of the *sauvages*, and in wandering through the meadows."[14]

Most histories of the Frenchmen's subsequent year at Port Royal fail to pay much attention to the Míkmaw village, which Lescarbot described as “a town surrounded with high palisades,” with dozens of large conical wigwams (from the Míkmawísimk *wikuom*—“dwelling”), as well as several impressive lodges, one “as big as a market-hall,” where the the community held their public gatherings and feasts. The village was a busy place, with women gossiping, children playing, and dogs everywhere underfoot. In the standard historical accounts, the Míkmaq appear fleetingly as occasional visitors to what Poutrincourt called his “manor house.” In fact, it was the French who were the visitors.[15]

The French built their outpost near Membertou's village, and they remained at the pleasure of the chief and his people. “I am the sagamore of this country,” Membertou declared at a ceremony of welcome held shortly after the *Jonas* arrived, and in the tradition of chiefs he graciously extended hospitality to the “Normans,” the name the Míkmaq used for the French, reflecting the fact that the first Frenchmen in the area hailed from Normandy. Membertou and Poutrincourt exchanged gifts. The French presented an assortment of trade goods—capes and jackets, kettles, hatchets, and knives—and the chief in turn declared that since the French “held metals in high regard, and since sagamores must be honorable and liberal toward the other,” he wished to grant the French king the right to mine at a place on the upper bay which Champlain had named Mines or Minas, because of copper deposits discovered there. Membertou declared Poutrincourt “his great friend, brother, companion, and equal,” Lescarbot noted, “showing this equality by joining together the fingers of each hand.” There was no mistaking the meaning of these words and gestures. “He considers himself the equal of the King and of all his lieutenants,” Lescarbot concluded. Impressed by the French custom of saluting visitors with their cannon, Membertou insisted on receiving a similar greeting whenever he came to call, “saying that this was due unto him, since he was a sagamore.”[16]

Membertou was an impressive character. Champlain reported he “had the reputation of being the worst and most treacherous man of his tribe"—adding condescendingly that nevertheless he had been "a good *sauvage* all the time we were there." Another Frenchman more generously described him as "the greatest, most renowned, and most formidable *sauvage* within the memory of man." Tall and long-limbed, with a splendid physique, the Míkmaw sachem wore a full beard, instantly distinguishing him from the other native men, none of whom displayed facial hair. His name (*Maupeltuk*, in proper phonetic Míkmawísimk) translates as "the game cock who commands many." He looked to be a man in his fifties, but Lescarbot understood him to say that he had been among his people when they met and traded with Jacques Cartier at Baie des Chaleurs on the Gulf of St. Lawrence in 1534, which would have made him a man in his eighties or nineties. Although Membertou may have been considerably older than he appeared, Lescarbot surely misinterpreted this remark. The Míkmaq often spoke figuratively rather than precisely. "Nothing enchants those people more than a style of metaphors and allegories in which even their common conversation abounds," wrote abbé Pierre Maillard, an eighteenth-century missionary with many years of experience among them. Moreover, while Membertou was renowned as a great war leader, he was also a shaman (what the Míkmaq called a *buoin*, which Lescarbot translated as a "soothsayer and medicine man"), who "from time immemorial has practiced this art among his followers." Not only did Membertou know when to fight, but when to compromise, and when to stretch the truth a little. By bringing up Cartier he was probably making the point that he was well acquainted with the French and their ways.[17]

Despite such linguistic misunderstandings (and there would be many), Lescarbot was a careful observer of the Míkmaq, and he offered an astute description of Membertou's authority among his people. "He has under him a number of families whom he rules, not with so much authority as does our King over his subjects, but with sufficient power to harangue, advise, and lead them to war, to render justice to one who has a grievance, and like matters. He does not impose taxes upon the people, but if there are any profits from the chase he has a share of them, without being obliged to take part in it." Except that Lescarbot was unfamiliar with a system of authority derived from recriprocity rather than power, he provided an excellent portrayal of the role of sagamore, one that is especially fascinating since it anticipates the kind of leadership that would develop among the Acadians, who were profoundly influenced by Míkmaw custom.[18]

Membertou's group was one of seven divisions of the Míkmaq, who collectively referred to themselves as *L'nu'k* (the people). The French took to calling them *Souriquois*, a name of indefinite origin. Gradually the term *Míkmaq* came into use by both groups, derived from the Míkmawísimk word *nikmak*, meaning "kith and kin." It is a good way to think of them, for they were more ethnic group than tribe, sharing extended kinship connections, common culture and language, but little political unity. Míkmaw family groups spent their winters dispersed in small camps, hunting for moose, caribou, and bear, but each spring and summer came together in large numbers in village communities at favored bays and rivers. The traditional summering site for Membertou's people was Port Royal, with its abundance of marine resources—smelt and herring, sturgeon and salmon, lobster, crab, and mussels, whales, seals, and porpoise—as well as geese, partridge, passenger pigeons, small game, supplemented with the abundant wild fruits and roots available in the adjacent meadows and woods. The native population at Port Royal during the summer of 1606 was at least three times greater than the French.

Sieur de Monts had relocated to Port Royal for the more tolerable climate. But the market potential of Membertou's Míkmaq proved an additional incentive. And the corresponding Míkmaw desire for European goods was precisely why Membertou welcomed him. The Míkmaq were among the first natives in North America to make contact with Europeans, and understanding immediately the value of iron and textiles, they became one of the first groups to develop a system of coastal barter. The imperial stereotype of first contact depicts explorers boldly stepping ashore while natives cower in the background. But in their 1534 encounter with Cartier at Baie des Chaleurs—an event well remembered by the Míkmaq, as Membertou made clear to Lescarbot—it was the Míkmaq who shouted and waved furs to encourage his vessel to land, the French who felt threatened. Even at that early date, the Míkmaq were experienced traders, having traded furs for goods with numerous European fishermen. "The *sauvages* showed a marvelously great pleasure in possessing and obtaining these iron wares and other commodities," Cartier wrote, "and so much at ease did [they] feel in our presence that at length we bartered with them, hand to hand, for everything they possessed, so that nothing was left to them but their naked bodies."[19]

In exchange for the pelts of beaver, otter, marten, seal, moose, and deer, the Míkmaq wanted needles, awls, knives, hatchets, and copper kettles, which they frequently cut up into arrowpoints and other implements of their own manufacture. "The things which come from us," wrote the French trader Nicolas Denys, "become to them an indispensable necessity. They have abandoned their own utensils. . . ." These goods made their lives easier and their work more productive. Míkmaw hunters soon were concentrating their attention on animals with commercial potential, trading pelts for cloaks and blankets, for beans, peas, and prunes, and for firearms, not only to hunt game more effectively but to extend their hunting territory at the expense of other native groups.[20]

Intensified violence among native peoples was one consequence of European contact, epidemic disease another. During the sixteenth and seventeenth centuries the Míkmaq were hit hard by maladies previously unknown to them—smallpox, measles, cholera, plague, whooping cough, syphilis, and gonorrhea. "They are astonished and often complain," one Frenchman reported, "that, since the French mingle with and carry on trade with them, they are dying fast and the population is thinning out." Asked about this, Membertou took hold of his scalp lock and declared that in his youth the Míkmaq were "as thickly planted as the hairs upon his head," but had thinned out "since the Normans have begun to frequent the country." The precise magnitude of Míkmaw losses is unknown, but an authoritative summary of the demographic evidence suggests a population decline over two centuries of 80 to 90 percent, bottoming out at about two thousand individuals in 1700, by which time most of the epidemics had run their course.[21]

Pointing to disease and increasing violence, as well as the growing problem of alcohol addiction, some of Membertou's Míkmaq argued against allowing Poutrincourt and the French to remain. "They have often been upon the point of breaking with us, and making war on us," one Frenchman wrote home. But Míkmaw rejectionists were in the minority. Most of the people wanted increased access to European trade. By the time de Monts and Poutrincourt arrived in Membertou's territory, European goods had already become necessities. By inviting the French to establish themselves at Port Royal, Membertou sought to institutionalize his connections with them and thereby guarantee his access to those powerful trade goods.[22]

Learning of the arrival of the *Jonas* from French fishermen at Canso, Champlain and Pontgravé soon returned to Port Royal, and in early September 1606, Poutrincourt and his lieutenants, with a majority of the men, sailed off to drum up trade at the numerous native villages along what Champlain called "the coast of Florida"—now the coast of Maine. ("Florida" would long persist as a place name for the entire coast, especially by the Spanish, seeking to deny English claims to regions they demarcated as "Virginia" and "New England.") Lescarbot was left in charge of those remaining at Port Royal, where Louis Hébert was conducting experiments in the cultivation of wheat, rye, and hemp. It was too late in the season to produce any food, however, so Lescarbot had to barter with the Míkmaq, and colonists had to learn indigenous methods of hunting, fishing, and foraging.[23]

In November, when Poutrincourt returned from the Maine coast with a load of furs—quickly dispatched to France on the *Jonas*—Lescarbot welcomed him back with a masque entitled *Neptune's*

Theater he had written himself, in which the god of the sea addresses Poutrincourt:

Prepare for France a flourishing Empire
In this New World, where ages will inspire
The immortal fame of de Monts and of thee,
Under the puissant reign of great Henri.

A banquet followed. Lescarbot's "jovial spectacle" gave Champlain an idea. Having spent two tough winters in America, with his men forced to survive on melted snow and salt meat, and knowing all too well the depression that could result from inactivity and outbreaks of scurvy, he proposed to Poutrincourt that each day over the coming season the leaders hold a similar banquet, thus keeping the company occupied, well fed, and in high spirits. It was the origin of the famous eating club, *L'Ordre de Bon-Temps,* perhaps the single best-remembered fact about the first French colony in America. For the next three months the leading men of the outpost—including Lescarbot, Hébert, Pontgravé, Champlain, and Poutrincourt himself—took their turn as maître d'hôtel, assuming responsibility for providing game and fish for the entire company. "This was so well carried out," Lescarbot wrote, that "as a rule we made as good cheer as we could have in *Rue aux Ours,*" a celebrated dining district of Paris. Lescarbot's description of the proceedings conjures up a most memorable image: the Grand Master for the day, shoulder draped with the ceremonial napkin, the staff of office in hand, entering the dining hall, aglow with the ruddy light of the roaring fire, the other leaders following, each bearing a great platter of food, the company passing flagons of wine, making toasts and quaffing liberally, song and laughter filling the air. Rich in the hearty colors of hedonism, with a hint of bacchanal, his image of the feasting among the colonists of l'Acadie makes a striking contrast to the drab piety of the New England Pilgrims' first Thanksgiving at Plymouth Colony.[24]

What is left out of this account is the participation of the Míkmaq. Most of the natives had dispersed to their winter hunting camps, but the chief and his extended family remained at Port Royal, and twenty or thirty Míkmaq were present for these banquets, Membertou and his lieutenants sharing the main table with the French leaders, "eating and drinking like ourselves," according to Lescarbot. Champlain, who consistently portrayed the Europeans as vastly superior to the natives, characteristically treated the Míkmaq presence as evidence of their weakness, claiming that Membertou had difficulty supplying sufficient game for his large family and that Poutrincourt generously fed them. Inexperienced Frenchmen able to provide what experienced Míkmaq could not? That seems unlikely. Almost certainly it was the Míkmaq who supplied most of the game for the feasting. Lescarbot wrote of native hunters coming from far and wide to Port Royal during winter with furs and skins to trade, often bearing gifts for the sagamore and his family, mostly fresh meat "on which they made many *tabagies* [banquets] and lived joyously as long as they had the wherewithal." It was the sagamore's responsibility to host those banquets, offering his guests plates of roasted and boiled game and bowls of steaming broth. The meal was punctuated by singing, storytelling, and tributes to the chief's hospitality. Afterward the "master of the feast" passed around "*calumets* filled with tobacco."[25]

This description of Míkmaw winter feasting sounds a great deal like the feasting at Poutrincourt's manor house, right down to the after-dinner ritual of smoking, a practice new to the French, but one that so bewitched them, wrote Lescarbot, that soon they could "no more be without it than without meat or drink." *L'Ordre de Bon-Temps* was a French variant on a Míkmaw custom, yet another marker of the extensive intercultural exchange taking place at Port Royal. What was truly distinctive about l'Acadie was this kind of mutual accommodation. Consuming the local fare of fresh game and forest gleanings, in addition to their own bread and wine, only four Frenchmen died of scurvy that winter, far less than the numbers for the two previous years. "We were not, as it were, marooned on an island," Lescarbot wrote, "for this tribe loves the French, and would at need take up arms, one and all, to aid them."[26]

Yet the French-Míkmaw relationship was less a love match than an alliance of mutual interest, and the Míkmaq expected to be able to call on French assistance. At winter's end in early 1607, the Míkmaq began reassembling at the village near the manor house, and by late spring there were nearly four hundred of them. Gradually it became apparent that the men were preparing for war, and when Poutrincourt inquired about it, Membertou told him that his son-in-law had been killed near the Saco River on the mainland by a hostile group of Abenakis, a loose ethnic confederation that inhabited the coastal and interior regions of Maine. He insisted that the French provide supplies and muskets, as well as casks of wine so he could entertain his men, and Poutrincourt grew worried at the number of *sauvages en armes* surrounding his manor house—men with metal-tipped arrows in their quivers and muskets on their shoulders—many of them drunk and arrogant. These fears were fed by one of Membertou's rivals, who whispered to Poutrincourt that the old leader was plotting against the French. This was almost certainly untrue. Membertou had acquired considerable prestige and power from his close association with the French, something Lescarbot understood full well. "He has been a very great and cruel warrior in his youth and during his life," he wrote. "He has many enemies, and is well content to keep close to the French, in order to live in safety." One day Membertou and his men set out in their canoes, and several weeks later they returned celebrating a great victory over the Abenakis of the Saco River. This may have been the first time native fighters used firearms against other natives along the North Atlantic coast.[27]

Meanwhile the French anxiously awaited the arrival of the annual supply vessel from France. Again it was the Míkmaq who saw it first, and Membertou who came with the report, although none but the old chief could see the vessel across the shimmering water until it drew near to shore. The captain brought bad news. In response to protests from independent merchants and traders, the king had revoked de Monts's royal monopoly. Moreover, the return from the furs sent back the previous fall had been insufficient to offset the cost of maintaining the outpost at Port Royal. De Monts was pulling out of the Acadian enterprise, leaving Poutrincourt to fend for himself. To pursue his vision of a feudal society in New France, Poutrincourt would require new backers. He resolved to return to France, remaining only long enough for Hébert to complete his crop experiments. Finally, at summer's end, Poutrincourt pulled up a sample of the wheat "to show in France its beauty, richness, and exceeding height," crucial evidence that l'Acadie could be settled.[28]

The last of the French left Port Royal in August 1607. Poutrincourt had been unable to convince any of his men to remain behind to maintain a French presence. Lescarbot wrote that the Míkmaq shed tears at their departure, and Poutrincourt promised that "next year we should send households and families to dwell permanently in their land, and to teach them trades in order to help them to live like us, which promise did in some sort comfort them." Lescarbot's description of Míkmaw sorrow at the French departure was intended to demonstrate the good work Poutrincourt had done in building a strong relationship with the native people. He did not understand that tears at farewells were a mandatory gesture for well-mannered Míkmaq, nor did he suggest that they might be lamenting the loss of French company less than the loss of French commerce. Poutrincourt gifted Membertou with the remaining trade goods (it made no sense to transport them back to France) and offered him the possession of the manor house. The Míkmaq found the French quarters dark, dank, and repugnant, and preferred to live in wigwams that could be opened to the fresh air or broken down and moved. As the French missionary Chrétien Le Clercq later wrote, "they ridicule and laugh at the most sumptuous and magnificent of our buildings." Yet Membertou and his people would carefully watch over the French quarters, and when Poutrincourt returned in 1610 he would find everything exactly as he had left it, powerful evidence of the trusting relationship that had been established between the French and the Míkmaq.[29]

JEAN DE BIENCOURT, sieur de Poutrincourt, spent nearly two years attempting to attract investors for his Acadian colony. But without the promise of a royal monopoly he had little to offer, since merchants could simply outfit North American trading ventures of their own, bypassing the expense of maintaining a base of operations at Port Royal. Gaining an audience with King Henri, Poutrincourt found him intransigent on the subject of the monopoly, but willing to offer a royal subsidy for the work of Catholic missions. With that slender thread of support Poutrincourt decided to finance the Acadian venture himself, securing loans against his properties and those of his wife. At the port of Dieppe he purchased a vessel, the *Grâce de Dieu*, assembled a crew, and hired a firm of Huguenot merchants to outfit the expedition.

Poutrincourt had no objection to doing business with Huguenots, for although he was a Catholic, in the context of the times he was a practical one. During the wars of religion he fought for the Church, but came over to the side of Henri of Navarre in 1593 when the king converted to Catholicism in order to ensure his succession to the throne—allegedly remarking, "Paris is well worth a Mass." This kind of pragmatism—also embodied in Henri's Edict of Nantes (1598), which provided a measure of toleration for French Protestants—was part of the initial project of Acadian colonization. De Monts was a Protestant, Poutrincourt a Catholic, but they united in their enthusiasm for l'Acadie. Henri's patent called for Catholic instruction and conversion of the *sauvages*, but he raised no objection to the inclusion of Huguenot ministers in the expeditions of 1604 and 1606. Undeniably, religious difference introduced an element of discord. "I have seen our *curé* and the minister fall to with their fists on questions of faith," Champlain observed impatiently. "That was their way of settling points of controversy." But the company was not particularly pious. According to Lescarbot, when both clergymen succumbed to scurvy, the men "put them into the same grave, to see whether dead they would live in peace, since living they had never been able to agree." The early Acadian enterprise differed from "the Roman Catholic colonization of Canada, on the one hand, or the Puritan colonization of Massachusetts, on the other," the historian Francis Parkman has noted, "for it did not attempt to enforce religious exclusion." Protestants would continue to be important in l'Acadie, although the colony was always officially Catholic, and Huguenots kept their religious identity hidden.[30]

Both Catholics and Huguenots were aboard the *Grâce de Dieu* when she departed Dieppe in late February 1610. They suffered through another long and nasty crossing, forcing them to consume supplies intended to support the colony. The cooperation of the Míkmaq would be essential to their survival, and since Poutrincourt had been out of contact with them for more than two years, he was justifiably anxious as the vessel approached its destination. The enthusiastic welcome of Membertou's Míkmaq came as a relief. "Anxious about their old friends," wrote Lescarbot, the Míkmaq "asked how they were all getting along, calling each individual by his name, and asking why such and such a one had not come back." Lescarbot himself was among the absentees, choosing to remain in Paris after the publication of his history. He continued to act, however, as the colony's chronicler—perhaps Poutrincourt's mouthpiece would be a more apt description—receiving reports when vessels returned to France. Champlain and Pontgravé were also missing, both now involved in the founding of Québec on the St. Lawrence. The returnees included Poutrincourt's son Charles de Biencourt, now nineteen, as well as his younger brother Jacques de Salazar, and the horticulturalist Louis Hébert. Two important new recruits were Claude de Saint-Etienne de La Tour and his fourteen-year-old son Charles, Poutrincourt's kinsmen and associates from Champagne. The party totaled only twenty-three men, and all Poutrincourt could reasonably expect from such a small expedition was the reestablishment of a colonial beachhead at Port Royal.[31]

Yet he needed tangible and immediate results, something that would persuade the king to authorize a trade monopoly to subsidize the infant colony. Henri had shown considerable interest in the Christian conversion of the *sauvages*, and Poutrincourt grasped at that straw. Probably reflecting that hope, Lescarbot wrote that de Monts lost his monopoly because "he had not made any Christians," even though the available evidence indicates that the revocation had been entirely due to the opposition of powerful merchants. But such wishful thinking had led Poutrincourt to a plan. He would convert Míkmaq in large numbers as quickly as possible, then rush a report of his accomplishment back to the royal court.[32]

Membertou was easily convinced to convert. He had sorely missed the presence of the French in his territory. Access to trade goods notched up his prestige and enhanced his authority. Coming from a kin-ordered society, it surely struck him that a logical way to strengthen connections with strangers was to turn them into kinsmen. Baptism, after all, was an adoption ceremony of sorts. Moreover, the Míkmaq were believers in a world infused with spirit, a force they called *manitou.* Every living thing had a measure of this spiritual power. Special *manitou* looked after the Míkmaq, and Membertou assumed that the Normans as well had their own guardian *manitou.* Alliance and kinship required that the Míkmaq welcome those spirits. Lescarbot's way of describing it—that Membertou and his family "wish for nothing better than to enroll themselves under the banner of Jesus Christ"—put a colonialist spin on Membertou's decision, missing its pantheistic character. Yet it seems clear the two leaders enjoyed a conspiracy of interests.[33]

The baptism of the Míkmaq presented a problem, however, for Father Jessé Fléché, the priest Poutrincourt recruited for the expedition. Fléché spoke no Míkmawísimk and the Míkmaq little French, with the result that there could be no effective instruction in the Catholic faith. Defending Poutrincourt against charges he forced Fléché to violate church standards, Lescarbot argued that the pressure for the baptisms came entirely from the Míkmaq. "What was M. de Poutrincourt to do," he asked, "for he was importuned by the *sauvages*, who would have felt themselves scorned had he refused." It was a matter of security, he argued, and Fléché did what was required of a loyal Frenchman. "It is necessary in such matters to establish the State first of all, for without it the church cannot exist." Within a few days of the French return to Port Royal, with Poutrincourt and his son Biencourt standing as patrons and godfathers, Membertou and twenty members of his family accepted baptism, each individual taking the Christian name of some illustrious French person—Membertou became Henri, after the king, his wife Marie, after the queen—thus underlining the kin-making character of the ritual. Membertou "promises to have the others baptized—or else make war upon them," a Huguenot colonist wrote home with a touch of irony. Over the next few months more than a hundred more members of Membertou's community would follow his example, but Poutrincourt had already sent his son Charles de Biencourt back to France in the *Grâce de Dieu* to deliver the good news to the king.[34]

Stopping at Canso on his way out, Biencourt learned from French fishermen that Henri had been assassinated by a Catholic fanatic earlier that spring. The French state was now in the hands of a harder-edged Catholic, the royal widow, Marie de Médicis, acting as regent for her nine-year-old son, Louis XIII. Reaching France, Biencourt traveled to Paris and in October was granted a royal audience. But word of the Míkmaw baptisms, the first in New France, had preceded him, and the queen's religious advisers were appalled by their superficiality. Marie welcomed the young Biencourt but insisted he return to Port Royal with two Jesuits from her court, principled men who would ensure the missionary work was properly conducted. As for a royal monopoly of the fur trade, that remained out of the question.

The fate of Poutrincourt's settlement now rested in the hands of this inexperienced young man, who quickly demonstrated the requisite cunning. The Jesuit missionaries, Pierre Biard and Enemond Massé, had waited several years for an assignment in North America and were anxious to depart. Turning the situation to his advantage, Biencourt impressed on them his need for funds, and talked them into loaning what they could from the alms collected to support their mission. Father Massé persuaded his patroness—the queen's maid of honor, Antoinette de Pons, marquise de Guercheville, a devout and militant Catholic—to invest in the expedition. With funds secured, Biencourt was able to outfit the vessel with provisions. He sailed at the end of January 1611. His arrangement had kept the colony alive, but at a cost. When the *Grâce de Dieu* landed at Port Royal in May, after yet another lengthy, storm-tossed crossing, Poutrincourt was surprised by the presence of two Jesuit missionaries claiming that their order was to be his partner for a half share of the profits.[35]

POUTRINCOURT and the Jesuits immediately fell into serious conflict. Father Pierre Biard was a brilliant man with a keen sense of observation, evident in the fascinating descriptions of the Míkmaq he included in his reports. But he was also insufferably arrogant. As Lescarbot put it, reflecting Poutrincourt's perspective, Biard wanted "a finger in too many pies." Poutrincourt bristled particularly at the priest's interventions in what he considered matters of his own authority. "I pray to you leave me to do my duty, which I know very well," he testily told Biard after one confrontation. "Show me the path to heaven—I will give you good guidance on earth." But it was precisely the colony's religious policy that was most at issue. Biard was pleased to see the Míkmaw converts "carrying the candles, bells, holy water and other things, marching in good order in the processions," but he could find little substance behind the appearance of piety. He understood that the Míkmaq had "accepted baptism as a sort of sacred pledge of friendship and alliance with the French," but was disturbed that of "the commandments of God, prayer and the Sacraments, they knew almost nothing." The Míkmaq needed instruction, and "in order to catechize we must first know the language."[36]

Newcomers and natives were already communicating through a jargon composed of French and Míkmawísimk. But Father Biard was shocked by the kinds of exchange it facilitated. The colonists, drawn from the ranks of sailors and dockworkers from Dieppe and other French port towns, he found brutish and blasphemous. From the beginning there were numerous casual sexual liaisons between French men and Míkmaw women. "The first things the poor *sauvages* learn [from them] are oaths and vile and insulting words," Biard lamented, "and you will often hear the women *sauvages* (who otherwise are very timid and modest), hurl vulgar, vile, and shameless epithets at our people in the French language—not that they know the meaning of them, but only because they see that when such words are used there is generally a great deal of laughter and amusement." The joking ran both ways. Biard complained that when he and Massé asked their converts to supply them with translations of Bible passages, "they often ridiculed instead of teaching us, [and] sometimes palmed off on us indecent words, which we went about innocently preaching for beautiful sentences from the Gospels."[37]

Gradually the missionaries gained some fluency in Míkmawísimk, but this facility only emphasized for them the divide between the two cultures. As Biard attempted to teach Membertou his *Pater Noster,* the chief puzzled over the line, "Give us this day our daily bread." "If I did not ask Him for anything but bread, I would be without moose-meat or fish." Biard was impressed with Membertou's wit, but found himself hard-pressed to explain how bread, an exotic item to the Míkmaq, could be a metaphor for food of all kinds. It was part of a larger problem. He found the abstract concepts of Christianity extremely difficult to explain. "All their conceptions are limited to sensible and material things," Biard complained. "*Good, strong, red, black*—they will repeat to you in their language;

goodness, strength, redness, blackness—they do not know what they are." Rather than abstracting from reality to essence, as the Jesuits were trained to do, the Míkmaq sought to express reality in its particularity and specificity.[38]

Míkmawísimk—part of the Algonquian family of languages, which continues to be spoken by an estimated ten thousand Míkmaq today—is a verb-based language that takes its structure from the relationships among things. It becomes increasingly complicated with the variety of components, conditions, relations, and feelings affecting perception and requiring expression. To illustrate how sophisticated such modes could become, one student of the language tells of the Míkmaw hunter who in a single word was able to convey his state of mind as he stalked a bear in the middle of the woods: the hope he would meet his prey, the fear he would be killed in the encounter, and the love he felt for his wife and children, for whom he was hunting. Biard believed that the specificity of native language was evidence that the Míkmaq remained in "perpetual infancy as to language and reason"—but he mistook cultural difference for ignorance. There was an existential immediacy to Míkmaw cultural perception that was lost on the Jesuits.[39]

Biard was also frustrated by the cultural conservatism of the Míkmaq. "There is scarcely any change in them after their baptism," he wrote. "They keep up the same manners and traditions and mode of life, the same dances and rites and songs and sorcery; in fact, all their previous customs." The Míkmaq "willingly came to Church, but it was to mutter there their ancient idolatries. They observed the appointed saints' days, but it was while carrying on their ancient sacrifices, dances, and superstitions. They went to holy Communion, if it was desired, but without knowing either the *Creed* or *Confession*, and emerging from there, they went off to get drunk and to sing to the Devil their usual sorceries." For their part, the Míkmaq believed they could incorporate Christian perspectives within their established traditions. Baird attempted to "rouse the conscience" of one man with several wives by preaching on the prohibition of adultery.

"That is all well enough for you Normans," the man responded, but as for the Míkmaq, the more wives the better. "I asked him how many wives he had," Baird continued, and "he answered that he had eight, and in fact he counted off seven to me who were there present, pointing them out with as much pride, instead of an equal degree of shame, as if I had asked him the number of his legitimate children."[40]

In the late summer of 1611, Membertou fell mortally ill. The cause is unknown, but it is likely that he had been infected by one of the diseases introduced by the French. Biard nursed him in his final hours and after his death preached on the meaning of his conversion. "Learn our language quickly," he quoted the old sachem saying near the end, "for as soon as thou knowest it and has taught me well, I wish to become a preacher like thee." Biard was just beginning to learn Míkmawísimk, so this translation is best taken with a grain of salt. Yet it may have contained a kernel of truth. Membertou was a respected *buoin,* and as a fellow spiritual practitioner he acknowledged Biard's power. The Jesuit returned the compliment by paying tribute to Membertou's spirituality, noting that "God impressed upon his soul a greater idea of Christianity than he had been able to form from hearing about it."[41]

The lesson to be learned here was the importance of mutual accommodation. Eventually the Jesuits and other Catholic missionaries in New France would learn to tailor their teachings to fit native culture. "One must be very careful before condemning a thousand things among their customs, which greatly offend minds brought up and nourished in another world," one Jesuit wrote. "It is easy to call irreligion what is merely stupidity, and to take for diabolical working something that is nothing more than human; and then, one thinks he is obliged to forbid as impious certain things that are done in all innocence, or, at most, are still not criminal customs. . . . I have no hestiation is saying that we have been too severe in this point." In response to missionary tolerance of their customs, the Míkmaq would accept Catholic saints as guardian *manitou* and Jesus as an incarnation of their culture hero Gluskabe, incorporating Christian teaching into their spiritual system.[42]

Biard left a description of one occasion that is powerfully suggestive of the way cultural mixing worked. He accompanied Biencourt and a contingent of the colonists on a trading mission along the mainland coast, and they were invited to attend an Abenaki ritual ceremony. "All night," he wrote, "there was continual haranging, singing, and dancing, for such is the kind of life all these people lead when they are together." Horrified at the thought that "probably their songs and dances were invocations to the devil," as Biard put it, he asked the Frenchmen to sing some of their sacred songs, to purify the air, so to speak. They offered up the *Salve Regina* and the *Ave Maris Stella*, hymns to the Blessed Virgin. "But when they once got into the way of singing, the spiritual songs being exhausted, they took up others with which they were familiar," wrote Biard, and "when they came to the end of these, as the French are natural mimics, they began to mimic the [Abenakis'] singing and dancing." The native dancers stopped and watched for a time, then took up the chants again, and soon all were dancing and singing together. Even the humorless Biard was delighted. "It was really very comical," he wrote, "for you would have said that they were two choirs which had a thorough understanding of each other." Religion and ritual would become a powerful bond between the French colonists and the Míkmaq.[43]

Biard and Massé as yet only dimly glimpsed the accommodations that would be necessary. What they did perceive clearly, however, was their urge to better understand the things that needed doing. After Membertou's death they announced a moratorium on conversions and baptisms. Biard would continue ministering to the French colonists and Míkmaw converts at Port Royal, while Massé undertook a mission of cultural immersion, resolving to "live with the natives, wandering and roving about as they did through the mountains and valleys, and adopting their ways, civil as well as physical," learning not only their language but also "the usages, habits, and life of the country." Doing otherwise, continuing to baptize the uninstructed, Biard declared, "would not only be a profanation of Christianity, but also an injustice towards the *sauvages*." Later, in his memoir of his years in l'Acadie, Biard acknowledged that "many complaints arose among our French people because no one was being baptized." Charles de Biencourt—leading the colony in the absence of his father, who had gone to France to secure additional support from the marquise de Guercheville—protested the moratorium. What use were missionaries if they refused to perform the rituals that tied the Míkmaq to the French interest? "This is not to be tolerated," he sputtered. "These people are useless here; we must write to France about them."[44]

Affairs quickly went from bad to worse. In January 1612, a supply vessel outfitted by the marquise arrived at Port Royal. On board was a Jesuit lay brother, Gilbert du Thet, who had been told to keep an eye on the goods intended for the missionaries, a task he carried out with relish, even questioning the distribution of hardtack to the crew during the voyage. The sailors were upset, and when the vessel landed, one of them claimed to have overheard du Thet say that the king's death was a blessing from heaven. This was an explosive charge, since many Frenchmen, Catholic and Huguenot alike, suspected the Jesuits of complicity in the recent regicide. Biencourt prepared a formal accusation against du Thet and included it with the packet of letters being sent back with the supply vessel. For Biard and Massé, this was the last straw. Concluding that they could work no longer in the poisoned atmosphere, they packed their bags and secretly boarded the vessel the night before it was to sail. But learning of their plan, Biencourt had them forcibly removed. The Jesuits were troublesome, but allowing them to return would mean the certain loss of assistance from their patroness, dooming the colony.

Frightened and angry, the Jesuits shut themselves up in their quarters, declared the colony under interdict, and refused to say mass or take confession. "Instead of a Christian stronghold," as Father

Biard put it, Port Royal had become "a den of thieves, a nest of brigands, a haven for parasites, a refuge for rogues, a hotbed of scandal and all sorts of wickedness." Biencourt wrote his father, begging him "to do everything you can to reveal the wickedness of these Jesuits." But when news of the confrontation reached the French court, the marquise took the side of the missionaries and cut off support. Unable to pay his creditors, Poutrincourt was thrown into debtors' prison, and in an attempt to preserve her own properties, his wife sued him for legal separation. For more than a year Port Royal received no supplies of any kind from France, and over the winter of 1612–13 Biencourt and his men had no choice but to disperse with the Míkmaq into their winter hunting camps.[45]

The following spring, while most of the colonists were still in the woods, two French vessels finally arrived at Port Royal. Outfitted by the marquise, they had come not to resupply the colony but to rescue the Jesuits. The few men present at the manor house were powerless to prevent the marquise's men from commandeering tools, furnishings, and church ornaments, then sailing across Baie Française to Mount Desert Island on the Maine coast, near today's Bar Harbor, where the Jesuits established an outpost and mission station called Saint-Sauveur.

The Jesuit mission would be short-lived. Soon after they arrived, the missionaries were attacked by Samuel Argall, a Welsh privateer with a commission from Governor Thomas Dale of Jamestown, the struggling colony of the Virginia Company of London. Argall worked as Dale's troubleshooter. Earlier that year, on the governor's orders, he had led a raid on one of the principal native towns in the Chesapeake, abducting the chief's daughter Pocahontas and holding her hostage against the return of English prisoners. Fresh from that success, Governor Dale sent him to search out rumored French intruders along the North Atlantic coast. Just as the grandiose bounds of New France in theory stretched south to Delaware Bay, so the northern limits of English Viriginia were supposed to encompass the Grand Banks. At Penobscot Bay, Argall met a group of Abenakis anxious to trade who greeted him with French phrases. They were unaware of any hostility between the French and the English and Argall was able to pose as a friend of the "Normans" and convince one of them to guide him to Mount Desert. The French were still unloading supplies from their two vessels when Argall's vessel emerged suddenly out of a dense early summer fog, blasting them with a hail of musket fire that killed the Jesuit Gilbert du Thet. Plundering the infant settlement, Argall set half the colonists adrift in two open boats (later to be rescued by French fishermen), but Father Biard and the rest he took back to Jamestown, along with the captured vessels and a load of booty that included "apparel, victuals, and many other necessaries." When Governor Dale learned of the Port Royal colony from his interrogation of the prisoners, he sent Argall back to finish the work of destruction, with Father Biard ordered to show the way.[46]

On the evening of All Saints Day—1 November 1613—Argall entered Port Royal Basin by moonlight and dropped anchor within sight of the French settlement, unable to land because of the low tide. When dawn brought no apparent stirring from the manor house, he came ashore and entered, finding shoes, clothes, and personal possessions scattered about—bachelor's quarters, after all—but no colonists. As it happened, they were all off with the Míkmaq, or working in the fields at the "great meadow" upriver, near Hébert's grist mill. Argall had his men load the vessels with everything they could carry, even ordering them to strip iron hinges, locks, bolts, nails, and floorboards from the place before torching it. To remove all evidence of the French presence, he had them deface a massive stone monument near the landing, on which the colonists had chiseled the names of the sieurs de Monts and Poutrincourt, as well as the French fleur-de-lis. "In an hour or two," Biard wrote in his memoir, "the work of several worthy people, during a number of years, was reduced to ashes." And he added, spitefully: "May our Lord grant that this same fire has so completely destroyed all sins, which may have been committed in this place, that they may never again arise in any other place, nor ever provoke the just and dreadful vengeance of our God."[47]

Biard's role in Argall's attack became a matter of considerable controversy. Charles de Biencourt swore that the Jesuit had "driven on and guided" the English because of his hatred for the Poutrincourts. Surely it was Biard who directed Argall to the great meadow where the colonists were working, since he alone would have known that. When the French saw the approach of the English vessels, Biencourt testified, they withdrew to the safety of a hill, but Biard hailed them from Argall's deck. The English offered safe passage to Jamestown, he shouted, subsistence for those willing to work, and safe return to France after a year's service. "What did they expect to do here with their penniless captain, with whom they would be constrained to live like beasts." But the French scorned the offer, said Biencourt, and the English departed. In his account, Father Biard not surprisingly denied rendering any assistance to the English. Argall "demanded that I lead them," he wrote, and "I did all I could to evade and refuse." But the English "grew very angry and my peril became imminent—when suddenly they found the place without my help, and plundered and burned it." Far from seeking the colonists' destruction, he begged his captor to take pity on them, "to leave them some food, their boat, and other means of passing the winter," but to no avail. In fact, he wrote, it was Biencourt who had betrayed him, warning Argall that Biard had been nothing but trouble at Port Royal "and there could not be the slightest doubt that he would do something still worse to the English," and promising that if the English would turn the priest over, he and his comrades would "rid the world" of him, saving everyone a great deal of trouble. But Argall declined, Biard testified, vowing personally to see the Jesuit severely punished when they returned to Jamestown.[48]

In their respective histories of New France, Champlain credited Father Biard's story, while Lescarbot characteristically sided with the Poutrincourts. An English report, reputedly based on the testimony of Captain Argall, offered a third perspective that supports some of the details in both accounts, but to the credit of neither. Argall confirmed Biencourt's charge that Biard had guided him to Port Royal. "Out of the indigestible malice that he conceived against Biencourt," he reported, Biard "did inform him where [Biencourt] had planted himselfe, offering (as he did) to conduct him there." He also confirmed Biard's charge that Biencourt wanted the priest killed, "labouring earnestly to have the Jesuit, as he confessed, with a purpose to hang him." Argall added another interesting detail. In his meeting with Biencourt, the Frenchman had proposed that were he allowed to continue his trading unmolested, he would share the profits with Argall, and even switch his allegiance from the French to the English king. Argall told him, however, that his commission was to "displant" the French from the jurisdiction of the Virginia Company, and he advised that they clear out as soon as possible, for "if hee found [them] there thereafter hee would use [them] as an enemy." Although it is impossible at this remove to sort out the conflicting details in these accounts, both Biard's treachery and Biencourt's desire for revenge and his willingness to change sides are credible. It was the conflict among the Frenchmen that provided the English with their opportunity.[49]

In England, Captain Argall was greatly celebrated for his "conquest" of Port Royal, which vindicated the extensive territorial claims of the Virginia Company. The Privy Council—the private council of the British monarch, consisting of all current and former ministers of the crown—refused the marquise de Guercheville's demand for restitution for her lost vessels, declaring that they had "enter'd by force the territory of the Virginia colony to settle there and to trade without their permission." Argall returned to Jamestown, where he later became deputy governor, ruling "with a rod of iron," in the words of Francis Parkman. But Father Biard was able to avoid learning anything more about Argall's temperament. Departing Port Royal on a separate vessel that fortuitiously was blown off course, and by a circuitous route eventually finding his way back home, he spent his last years writing a justification of his failed mission to North America.[50]

Before Biard's return, and before news of the English attack reached France, sieur de Poutrincourt had left La Rochelle on his fourth and final voyage to l'Acadie. He arrived at Port Royal in March 1614 to find his manor house in ashes and his men living among the Míkmaq. His hopes for a world of *seigneurs et roturiers* in l'Acadie had been dashed. He returned to France with most of the colonists, including his son Jacques de Salazar and his kinsman Louis Hébert. Poutrincourt was a broken man. The project had cost him his reputation, his fortune, his marriage, and perhaps his mental balance. The next year, when civil violence once again broke out within France, he took up arms in defense of the crown, and in December 1615 he was killed in a suicidal charge at the conclusion of the siege at Méry-sur-Seine, a town not far from the Poutrincourt manor in Champagne.

Internal conflict and English violence put an end to the first French colony at Port Royal. But those were only the proximate causes. Fundamentally the colony failed because the French state had refused to support it, and it proved unable to support itself. Lescarbot attributed the collapse to the competition of independent fur traders, writing that Poutrincourt would "have been sure of prompt advancement in his work had he not been hindered by the greed of those who robbed him of the fat of his lands without making any settlement there." But if Poutrincourt had been granted the royal monopoly, what then? How could he have enforced it? Father Biard was closer to the mark when he cast doubt on the premise that the fur trade could ever generate sufficient revenue to support a settlement colony. "It is a great folly," he wrote, and he ridiculed Frenchmen in America "who picture to themselves Baronies, and I know not what great fiefs and demesnes." A colony required "a sufficiency of means to maintain it," and such means could be developed only with the active assistance of the state. Preoccupied with continuing struggles over religion and empire in Europe, however, France was in no position to provide the necessary support.[51]

The first decade of French experience nonetheless was important, for it established a strong and lasting connection with the Míkmaq. That would prove the foundation of the distinctive colonization of l'Acadie. Mikmaw "friendship and fidelity," wrote Father Biard, "was especially noticeable after our rout by the English." The colonists survived because of the assistance of the Míkmaq, who desired continuing commercial connections. When Poutrincourt returned to France, his son Biencourt decided to remain behind with Claude and Charles de La Tour and some twenty of the men. Feudal l'Acadie might be a fool's dream, but commercial l'Acadie was already a reality.[52]

CHAPTER 2

Seigneurs et Roturiers

The Birth of the Acadian People, 1614–1688

THE FRENCH FUR TRADE of the early seventeenth century might not be able to support a colonial settlement, but it certainly could produce handsome profits. On his last visit to Port Royal in 1614 Poutrincourt was accompanied by David Loméron, a merchant associated with the prominent Huguenot firm of Georges et Macain in La Rochelle, who arranged with Charles de Biencourt to be suppliers and marketers for the trade of l'Acadie. With this association Biencourt established a highly profitable business that over the next dozen years delivered tens of thousands of beaver pelts to France. He shifted operations from Port Royal to Cape Sable, the southern extremity of the Acadian peninsula, and established his headquarters at a site that became known as Port Loméron (near the present town of Yarmouth). Across the Gulf of Maine, on Penobscot Bay, Claude de Saint-Etienne de La Tour established a highly profitable trading post among the Abenakis, while his son Charles maintained another outpost at the mouth of rivière Saint-Jean, tapping the trade of the Maliseets, "cousins" of the Míkmaq, who inhabited a vast country extending north to the St. Lawrence. Rather than the agricultural colony Poutrincourt had envisioned, l'Acadie became a source of natural resources for the merchants and entrepreneurs of La Rochelle.[1]

Both Charles Biencourt and Charles de La Tour had been boys when they first came to l'Acadie, and had grown up among the Míkmaq. They spoke Míkmawísimk and were accustomed to living in the native manner. Their *engagés* (employees) knew how to use birchbark canoes and snowshoes, to snare moose in early winter and spear salmon at nightfall by the lure of burning pitch pine, to dress in moccasins, leggings of moose, deer, or seal skin, with a fur or blanket cape. It may not be too much to assume that they also began to think and feel Míkmaw. With Poutrincourt's final return to France, except for the occasional visit of trading vessels at Port Loméron to deliver trade goods and pick up furs, the remaining *engagés* had almost no contact with Frenchmen. After the Jesuits abandoned Port Royal in 1613, Catholic missionaries did not reestablish a presence for nearly twenty years. The cultural ties to Europe wore thin. Although Biencourt's men left few traces in the slim historical record of those years, there are intriguing hints of the extent to which they "went native." In his memoirs, Samuel de Champlain reported without skepticism the stories of *engagés* who told of hearing, on long winter nights in the deep woods, the "strange hissings" of the giant cannibals of Míkmaw legend, and Champlain himself believed in the existence of "some devil that torments them." Frenchmen came to accept many Míkmaw beliefs. One legend warned against setting foot on a certain island off the Atlantic coast harbor of La Hève, lest a fire instantly seize upon the privy parts of the trespasser. After the French established a colony at La Hève in the early 1630s, the commandant scoffed when told that story, and to demonstrate its foolishness he asked for some experienced *engagés* to accompany him there. There was not a single volunteer. The history of colonization is usually written as the process of native assimilation to European culture. It may be more accurate to think of the men who remained in l'Acadie as assimilated to the customs of the Míkmaq.[2]

There were as yet no French women in l'Acadie, and sexual relations with Míkmaw women greatly facilitated the assimilation of the *engagés* to native culture. Lescarbot saw no evidence of prostitution among the Míkmaq when he first arrived, but he noted a custom of sexual freedom among young, unmarried women that was eagerly exploited by fishermen and traders. The Míkmaq did not consider an illegitimate child a stigma but rather a measure of a young woman's fertility, and bearing a child early out of wedlock tended to enhance rather than compromise her chances for marriage. While girls were free to accept or reject lovers, however, the Míkmaq had no patience with forced sexual relations or rape. "It is dangerous to dally with them," wrote Lescarbot. After one French colonist "meddled" with a Míkmaw woman, the men of her family came to Biencourt in a rage, warning him that "anyone who attempted to do that again would not stand much of a chance, that they would kill him on the spot." Marriage, too, was a serious business. If a young man with marriage on his mind found his attentions encouraged by a young woman, he was expected to ask her father for permission to take up residence in the family's lodge. The father agreeing, the suitor entered the service of the bride's household, hunting and trapping exclusively for them. During this period—which could last up to a year—intimate relations between the prospective partners were strictly forbidden. Only after the groom had demonstrated his capacity to support a wife and children was the couple allowed to marry.[3]

Despite these rather stringent rules, within a few years most of Biencourt's *engagés* were living in Míkmaw communities with native wives and *métis* (mixed-ancestry) children. In the words of a genealogist as familiar with Míkmaw as Acadian lineages, the majority of French traders "married to Indian women and passed the remainder of their days with the Indians, adopting their manner of living." The gradual conversion of the Míkmaq to Catholicism may have made this easier for the French. When Catholic missionaries returned to l'Acadie in the 1630s, they found a large backlog of marriages to solemnize and baptisms to perform. Charles de La Tour himself had married a native woman according to Míkmaw custom (her name went unrecorded), and they had three daughters and perhaps two sons. Some *engagés* returned to France with their *métis* offspring, as did Louis Lasnier of Dieppe, who arranged for the baptism of his twelve-year-old son André, the register noting that the mother was a "*femme canadienne*." But the records of most marriages and births were lost, or went unrecorded.[4]

It is not known whether Charles de Biencourt married. He died prematurely in 1623 or 1624, several years before the missionaries began keeping records. Charles de La Tour assumed leadership of the commercial operation on the peninsula, laying claim as well to the title *seigneur de Port-Royal*, which he maintained Biencourt had bequeathed to him in a deathbed testament, and backed up his claim by forming a partnership with Biencourt's surviving brother, Jacques de Salazar, heir to the Poutrincourt titles and properties in France. Huguenot merchants from La Rochelle continued to handle marketing and supply. That connection was threatened, however, by the continuing confrontation between the Catholic center and the Huguenot periphery in France. When French royal forces besieged and closed the port of La Rochelle in 1627, La Tour was left stranded. In remarkable letters to Louis XIII and the king's principal minister Cardinal Richelieu, he complained of his isolation, and warned that the English—who had sent a fleet to relieve the Huguenots of La Rochelle—would use the occasion to attempt a seizure of l'Acadie with its lucrative fisheries and fur trade. He requested material support, as well as a royal commission naming him protector "of the coast of l'Acadie, with all others forbidden to disturb me." For twenty years, he wrote, he had lived in this "beautiful and good country" with his "little band of resolute Frenchmen," and he would defend the country in the name of the king, supported by his friends the Míkmaq, whom he described as "*les gens du pays.*" La Tour's use of this unusual phrase—"the people of the country"—rather than the more typical *sauvages,* reflected his close association with his native kinsmen.[5]

LA TOUR'S request for support coincided with the founding in France of the *Compagnie de la Nouvelle-France* (also known as *Compagnie des Cent Associés*—the Company of One Hundred Associates), a consortium of private investors who accepted responsibility for establishing and maintaining settlers in French North America in exchange for a royal monopoly of the fur trade. Yet another attempt at the old idea of financing colonization by means of private capital. The company's charter, which Richelieu signed as he prepared for the year-long siege of La Rochelle, explicitly forbade Huguenot participation in the settlement or commercial exploitation of New France. Charles de La Tour's Protestant suppliers were cut out, but the company members decided they had to keep La Tour himself in the loop. In 1628 they outfitted a fleet of vessels to resupply Canada and l'Acadie, including one bound for Cape Sable. On board was La Tour's father Claude, who in 1626 had returned to France—evicted by English traders from the newly established Plymouth Colony—and was now acting as his son's agent.[6]

None of these vessels reached their destinations. They were captured by English privateers—the three Kirke brothers of London sailing armed frigates manned by more than two hundred fightingmen—who took a great quantity of booty and many prisoners, including Claude de La Tour. The Kirkes were financed by Sir William Alexander, a Scottish poet who had served as tutor to the eldest son of King James VI of Scotland, and continued as one of his student's favorite courtiers after he became James I of England in 1603, at the death of Elizabeth I. Alexander was one of the scholars whom the king assigned to work on a new English translation of the Bible (the King James Version), published in 1611, and in 1621 he rewarded his former tutor with a royal grant of exclusive right to develop the lands "lying between our Colonies of New England and Newfoundland, to be known as New Scotland," or *Nova Scotia*, following the Latin text of the royal charter issued in 1621. The grant was part of a scheme to make Sir William's fortune. Over the preceding decade King James had raised considerable cash by the sale of Irish baronetcies—tracts of land accompanied with the honorary title of baronet—and he invited Sir William to do the same. But the distance to Nova Scotia and the uncertainty of colonization made for a weak market, and by 1626 Sir William had raised a mere £18,000. Hence his turn to more tried and true methods of accumulation—plunder and conquest. The outbreak of war with France provided the opportunity, just as Charles de La Tour had feared.[7]

The Kirke brothers, sons of a Scottish merchant and a French Huguenot woman of Dieppe, found a good deal in common with their captive Claude de La Tour, who also had been raised a Huguenot. The Kirkes introduced him to the extensive network of expatriate Huguenots in London. Although he had been careful not to make an issue of his religious background in France, La Tour found that it provided him with access to influence in England. Throughout his life the elder La Tour was renowned as a charmer, but even so, it is astounding how much he was able to accomplish in less than a year in London. Using his considerable personal appeal, he won an introduction at court, where he soon became a favorite. Within a few months of his capture he formally renounced his allegiance to Louis XIII and swore loyalty to Charles I, who ascended the English and Scottish thrones at the death of his father, James I, in 1625. La Tour then wooed and married an English noblewoman, maid of honor to the queen, and a relative of Sir William Alexander, with whom La Tour struck up a relationship. The two men shared an interest in l'Acadie. Perhaps Sir William could assist La Tour's return there to rejoin his son, and perhaps La Tour could persuade the Míkmaq to come over to the aid of the British.

In the spring of 1629—only a year after he had sailed for l'Acadie as an agent for the explicitly Catholic Compagnie de la Nouvelle-

France—Claude de Saint-Etienne de La Tour sailed for l'Acadie again, this time as part of an expedition of seventy Scottish Presbyterians under the command of William Alexander the younger, Sir William's son. Claude and Charles de La Tour were named baronets of Nova Scotia, with extensive grants of land at Cape Sable, "upon condition that the said knight de la Tour, and his said sonne . . . doth promise to be good and faithful vassals of the Sovereign lord of the king of *Scotland*, and their heires and successors, and to give unto him all obedience and assistance to the reducing of the people of the country."[8]

The expedition anchored at Port Royal, which had been abandoned by the French traders, and selected a defensible point of land several miles upriver, near the old Hébert mill and the great meadow. Richard Guthry, the expedition's chronicler, marveled at the abundance of wildlife. "We eat lobsters as bige as little children," he raved, "plenty of salmons and salmon trouts, birds of strange and diverse kinds, haukes of all sorts, doves, turtles, pheasents, partridges, blacke birds, a kind also of hens, wild turkies, crannes, herones, infinit store of geese, and three or foure kinds of ducks, Snyps, Cormorants, and many Sea fouls, whales, seales, castors, otters." He was also enthusiastic about the potential for farming, noting that "by God's grace we expect a rich crope of whatsoever we trust to the earth." The Scots planned an agricultural colony, and Guthry drew a contrast between their intentions and those of "Monsieur Latour [and] his sonne . . . who live in the country a savage kind of life traveling, trucking, and marrying with the savages." But in truth, neither Sir William nor his son was much interested in settlement, which served merely to anchor their tenancy. Their focus was firmly fixed on the fur trade, which promised immediate profits. And for that they were dependent on good relations with the Míkmaq, and especially with Charles de La Tour, whose support was critical to their success.[9]

Several days after their arrival, the Scots were visited by a party of Míkmaq whom Guthry described as "naked people with mantles, either of beaver, blanket, or deer leather curiously wrought, tyed over there left shoulder with a poynt, without shirts, with clouts covering there secret parts." In broken French the native residents welcomed the Scottish colonists with gifts, impressing Guthry as a "fair cariaged people among whom [we] may live verry well." But the hope of establishing good relations was dashed when Charles de La Tour rejected out of hand his father's appeal to come over to the English. Without La Tour's support, the Scots suffered a typically hard first winter, thirty of their number dying from scurvy and other diseases.[10]

The next spring, April 1630, Compagnie de la Nouvelle-France finally succeeded in getting supply vessels with reinforcements and missionaries of the Récollect order of the Franciscans to Port Loméron. Charles de La Tour's request for support of five years before was answered with a royal commission naming him "grand master, chief and superintendent of navigation and commerce" in l'Acadie—or as La Tour described himself, in his own indigenous formulation, *"Grand Sagamos des Souriquois, Etcherines, Pantegois, et Quiniban, et Lieutenant Général pour le Roy en la coste de l'Acadie*—Great Sagamore of the Míkmaq, Maliseet, Pentagouets, and Kennebecs, and Lieutenant General of the King on the coast of l'Acadie." Again shifting with the tides, Claude de La Tour abandoned the Scots and joined his son at Port Loméron, where in 1636 he died in considerable comfort.[11]

With the failure of the Scots' colony, William Alexander the younger returned to England, frustrated that his efforts to seduce the La Tours had come to naught. The Scottish colonists were left to fend for themselves. Sir William's only remaining option was military conquest, but England and France had already signed a truce, closing that window of opportunity, and in early 1632 they concluded a treaty formally returning l'Acadie to French control. Sir William was ordered "to remove all the people, goods, ordnance, ammunition, cattle and other things belonging unto that colonie." The scheme to make his fortune had driven him to bankruptcy, and in 1644 he died in poverty.[12]

FOR imperial-minded French officials, the brief occupation l'Acadie by the Scots was a warning. One high-ranking naval officer, Isaac de Razilly, Catholic hero at the blockade of La Rochelle, argued that France must act forcefully in North America to "limit the Scots and English as much as possible." In response, Cardinal Richelieu authorized the Compagnie de la Nouvelle-France to commit itself to a significant effort to build up New France and appointed Razilly as *lieutenant-général* of l'Acadie. In the summer of 1632, Razilly crossed the Atlantic with a small fleet loaded with supplies, three hundred *hommes d'élite* (handpicked men), and six Capuchin Franciscan missionaries. He took possession of Port Royal and repatriated the remaining Scots, but established his own outpost at the harbor of La Hève (now La Have) on the Atlantic coast. He was "looking for others to join them soon," Razilly announced, and he boasted of the vitality of his newly planted vineyards, on the hillsides overlooking the Atlantic. One of Razilly's lieutenants, Nićolas Denys, claimed that his commander's principal object was "to people this land" and that "he had brought here as many people as he possibly could for this purpose." Although La Hève provided a secure base for French fishermen, the climate and soil in fact were far from ideal for agriculture, and there were very few families among the recruits, strongly suggesting that Razilly's actual intention was to establish a resource colony—fish, furs, and other forest products—rather than a settlement. Understanding that commercial success depended on the cooperation of the Míkmaq, Razilly and Charles de La Tour negotiated an agreement allowing La Tour to continue his operations at Cape Sable and across the bay at rivière Saint-Jean. Razilly was to control commerce with the Míkmaq at La Hève and Port Royal on the peninsula, as well as with the Abenakis at Penobscot Bay, where he tossed out the Plymouth traders and reestablished French authority. The two men agreed to share the profits of their respective operations equally, each with the right to inspect the other's warehouse of furs.[13]

But the company found the revenues of Razilly's new venture dis-

the expenses were far greater than anticipated. fishing and timbering operations, the colony profit. When Razilly died unexpectedly in 1636, seized the opportunity to shift direction. They revived ncourt's old plan for an agricultural colony, with farmers producing surpluses that would support the commercial operations of fur traders. Razilly's successor, Charles de Menou d'Aulnay de Charnizay—the younger son of an aristocratic family with extensive estates in the Loire Valley—shifted the center of operations back to Port Royal, where he established administrative headquarters and built a small fort on the foundations of one abandoned by the Scots. D'Aulnay recruited settlers from his own native region, planning to assign them tracts of land on the nearby great meadow, the best site for farming in l'Acadie, the place Louis Hébert had conducted his crop experiments.

The passenger list for the transport *Saint-Jehan,* which sailed from La Rochelle in April 1636, offers evidence of the colony's shifting direction. It included not only a group of *engagés* from Dijon bound for the fishery at Canso, and a party of ship's carpenters from the Basque country, but also a group of nineteen *paysans* from the wine-making villages of Bourgueil and Chinon near the Razilly estate in d'Anjou, several of them accompanied by their wives and children. Farming meant families. Poutrincourt had intended to recruit families once his colony was well established, but it failed before he could do so. These were the first French families to journey to l'Acadie, and a number of them would lay down roots, including Guillaume Trahan, *maréchal de tranchant* (steelsmith), with his wife Françoise Charbonneau, their two daughters, and a servant; Louis Blanchard, *vigneron* (vineyardist), who came alone but soon sent for his family; and Pierre Martin, *laboureur* (plowman), with his young son and wife Catherine Vigneau, who soon after landing delivered their second son, Mathieu Martin, the first child of French parents born in l'Acadie.[14]

D'Aulnay remained in charge at Port Royal for the next fourteen years. Over that time he continued to recruit colonists, many of them from the vast seigneuries he owned with his mother in Poitou, most notably the villages of Martaizé and La Chaussée. These migrants were both pushed from their homeland and pulled to l'Acadie. Pushed out by the religious wars and accompanying epidemics that devastated their region into the 1630s—there were many Huguenots in both the cities and villages of Poitou, and it is likely that some of the colonists were Protestants. And pulled abroad by the hope of a more peaceful and prosperous life. Single men, and a few married men with their families, came for terms of three or four years to work as craftsmen or farmers. *L'esprit de retour* (the spirit of return) proved strong for the majority of French migrants, and fewer than one in ten remained in l'Acadie.[15]

But those who stayed became the founding generation of the Acadians: Pierre Lejeune and his wife (her name unknown), with their three young children; Jean Thériot and Perrine Rau, she pregnant with their first child; Vincent Brun and Renée Breau with two infants; the widower Jean Gaudet with his three children; Martin Aucoin, his wife Marie Sallé, and their four children; Michel Boudrot, who married the Aucoins' daughter Michelle; Robert Cormier and his wife Marie Péraud; and a large party of interrelated Bourgs and Landrys, including the siblings Perrine, René, and Antoinette Landry, and the cousins Antoine and Perrine Bourg. Of the many unattached young men arriving in the province, most returned, but those who remained married the daughters of settlers and raised families of their own: François Gautrot, Abraham Dugas, Antoine and Etienne Hébert, François Savoie, François Girouard, Daniel Leblanc, Michel Dupuis, Pierre Comeau, Antoine Belliveau, Vincent Breau, Antoine Babin, and Pierre Thibodeau. A fair number of French garrison soldiers stayed on after completing their terms of service, including Jean Poirier and Michel Richard, and the offspring of a few French officials and military officers established family lines at Port Royal, among them Claude Petitpas, whose father was *syndic* (chief civil officer) of the settlement; Pierre, Marguerite, and Germain Doucet, the children of the commander of the Port Royal garrison; and Jacques Bourgeois, the commander's nephew and a military surgeon. By 1650 some fifty families, linked by kinship and culture, were living and farming at Port Royal. There were "two hundred people under his care," d'Aulnay reported, "soldiers, farmers, artisans, without counting their wives and children, nor the Capuchin Fathers nor the Indian children."[16]

THE "Indian children" belonged to the interethnic families of the settlement. Most of the *engagés* with native wives and *métis* children remained in the vicinity of La Hève or Cape Sable, where several small fishing and trading communities developed, but a number relocated to Port Royal. Their presence helped maintain good relations with the Míkmaq and introduced colonists to the practice of *métissage.* Dozens of church-registered interethnic unions were a significant factor in the making of the Acadian community. One of the first such marriages took place in 1635, when twenty-two-year-old François Gatrot married Marie, a Míkmaw woman. In the 1640s, several years after Marie Sallé lost her husband Martin Aucoin, she married Jean Claude, of a family of Christian Míkmaq who resided at Port Royal. When Pierre Martin came of age in the 1650s, he married Anne Ouestnorouest, a Míkmaw woman, and two decades later their eldest son Pierre married Anne Godin, a *métis.* In the 1680s Guillaume Bourgeois married Marrianne d'Aprendistigny, the *métis* granddaughter of Charles de La Tour. The Acadians "were a mixed breed," wrote an eighteenth-century observer. One modern historian, noting the number of mixed marriages in the genealogies Acadians themselves compiled after the expulsion, argues for "the influence that life *à l'Indienne et métissage* exerted among the first European immigrants." Settler children at Port Royal grew up with Míkmaw neighbors and *métis* playmates, intimate connections that distinguished l'Acadie not only from New England, where settlers had very little friendly contact with natives, but from French Canada, where interethnic marriage was rare.[17]

In part, *métissage* is explained by demographic realities. The emigration of unmarried Frenchmen, as well as the maintenance of a small French garrison, meant that colonist men outnumbered colonist women by about three to two throughout the seventeenth century, while among the Míkmaq, perhaps because of the toll of intertribal warfare, marriageable women outnumbered marriageable men. Compare that with New England, where the number of men and women was much closer to parity. But demographics alone cannot explain the sympathy and sociability that prevailed among newcomers and natives in l'Acadie. The French colonists, writes the historian Emile Lauvrière, established amiable relations with the Míkmaq, "approaching them with sympathetic curiosity, pleasing them by the gentleness of their manner, conquering them through good nature and trust, justice and religion, in brief, making of them loyal friends and good neighbors." This description is a bit romantic, but certainly the record of friendly interethnic relations in l'Acadie contrasts sharply with the dismal history of violence and dispossession in neighboring New England.[18]

A number of factors help explain the difference. One is the contrasting material circumstances. Unlike the Míkmaq, who were principally hunters and gatherers, the native peoples of coastal New England were farmers, which put them in direct conflict with English colonists, who were more interested in agriculture than the fur trade. But contrasting policies and attitudes were of equal importance. French colonial doctrine was that baptized natives would be considered French subjects. Speaking to one group of natives, Champlain promised that "our sons will marry your daughters and we will be a single people." No Puritan ever said anything vaguely similar. And for the most part the Puritans were uninterested in the kind of missionary work to which the Catholics, and particularly the Jesuits, were so dedicated. The Catholic missionary effort created a bond of sympathy between native and colonist in l'Acadie, and made possible genuinely intimate personal relations. It is likely that many of the colonists who chose to remain in l'Acadie rather than return to France had reasons to feel alienated from their homeland, and they may have been open to close relationships with the native people of the new land. As a result, *métissage* played a prominent part in the prevailing climate of cooperation during the early years of the settlement.[19]

Living in a mixed community, settlers more readily adopted indigenous ways. From the Míkmaq they learned the indigenous arts of fishing and hunting, methods of making clothing and moccasins from skins, furs, and animal sinew, and the many uses of birchbark. A jargon composed of Míkmawísimk and French became the lingua franca of the countryside, and many settlers learned to communicate at least a little with their Míkmaw cousins. All this made Acadian culture unique among the settler traditions that developed on the Atlantic coast of North America. In the judgment of the distinguished historian Francis Jennings, "of all European colonials in North America they seem to have accommodated most wholeheartedly with the Indians of their vicinity. In this respect the calamity that befell the Acadians holds significance transcending themselves, for it aborted a promising experiment in ethnic reconciliation."[20]

Perhaps in the spirit of mutual accommodation, the colonists found ways to farm the land without infringing on Míkmaq territory. Ceding the *hautes* or uplands to native people for their migratory hunting, fishing, and gathering, they confined their settlements to the *terres basses,* the lowlands along the coast. Because these consisted of tidal salt marsh, however, the colonists required a strategy for reclaiming them to agriculture. In one of the most remarkable developments of seventeenth-century North American colonization, French settlers in l'Acadie developed a distinctive agricultural economy based on the farming and grazing of reclaimed marshland, diked in from the tides by communal effort. Emigrants from the Loire Valley may well have been familiar with the use of dikes to drain riverine wetlands. Moreover, in the 1630s, d'Aulnay, hoping to produce his own salt for curing fish, brought over a group of experienced *sauniers* or saltmakers. It was an experiment that failed, but the attempt to construct tidal salt pans may have suggested the value of diking for reclamation. Indeed, the Acadian diking spade, used to cut the sod from which dikes were constructed, bears a strong resemblance to the French saltmakers' *fraye,* used for maintaining the earthen walls surrounding salt pans. Despite these possible influences, however, the Acadian diking system was of genuinely original design. Its key feature, the *aboiteau*—a sluice fitted with a clapet that was forced shut by the rising tide on the seaward side, then pushed open as the tide fell by water draining from the fields—is found neither on *saunier* dikes nor in the drainage systems of Poitou, and the word *aboiteau* itself has no equivalent in continental French. The colonists developed this system during the 1640s, and it was in full operation by the early 1650s, when Nicolas Denys was impressed with the "great extent of meadows which the sea used to cover and which the Sieur d'Aulnay has drained."[21]

Although Denys attributed the diking to d'Aulnay, it is doubtful that the lieutenant-governor had much to do with it. In fact, throughout the era of French administrative control in l'Acadie, local officials remained consistently negative about diking, ridiculing the *habitants* as *défricheurs d'eau* (water clearers). In the critical opinion of one official, they diked the marshlands because they were "unwilling to clear the uplands [where] the work is too hard." But the charge that the inhabitants avoided hard work was ridiculous. Not only did they fell trees from the forests for fuel and lumber, and clear plots of upland for their orchards, but officials greatly underestimated the labor that dike construction and maintenance required. Sieur de Dièreville, a young French surgeon who spent several months at Port Royal in 1699–1700, was among the few who actually paid attention. "The marshes which are inundated by the sea at high tide must be drained, [and] what labor is need to make them fit for cultivation!" he exclaimed. "The ebb and flow of the sea cannot easily be stopped, but the Acadians succeed in doing so." The construction of a major dike demanded that the men of the neighborhood work together quickly and efficiently, and the maintenance of established dikes required the cooperation of neighboring farmers. Antoine de Lamothe, sieur de Cadillac, who served in the Port Royal garrison in the 1680s, noted that the "creoles or natives of the country" worked with "great affection among themselves, assisting each other with pleasure." The dikes not only made it possible for settlers to share the country with the Míkmaq—creating new land rather than moving into lands already claimed—they proved to be a significant factor in building a strong sense of community.[22]

Marshland farming was also much more productive than farming the uplands would have been. Once a dike was constructed, farmers grazed their livestock on the luxuriant marsh grass, which they also used to make salt hay, enabling them to maintain their herds throughout the winter—something New Englanders were not able to do until the introduction of clover and grass crops in the mid-eighteenth century. As a result, Acadian herds were notably large and robust. Moreover, after the desalination of the reclaimed marsh (a process that required several years of rainfall and drainage), the fields proved exceptionally fertile, the result of the rich silt deposited by the tides of many centuries. Denys noted that the reclaimed fields of the inhabitants "bear wheat in much greater abundance than those which they cultivated round the fort, good though those were." After a decade or so, the diked lands began to suffer from compaction and settling, and crop yields declined; but this problem was remedied by the periodic breech of the dikes by neglect, nor'easters, or invading New Englanders, renewing the marshes with new deposits of silt.[23]

D'Aulnay saw farming as a means to an end. It was intended to support the traders and provide surpluses that could be exchanged with the Míkmaq, who were encouraged to become full-time hunters of game. With headquarters at Port Royal on Baie Française, he was better positioned to capture the commerce of the mainland, where the action had moved by the mid-seventeenth century. Charles de La Tour, fifty miles west across Baie Française at the mouth of rivière Saint-Jean, clearly felt threatened by d'Aulnay's relocation. His division of territory and profits with Razilly had gone smoothly enough, but in 1637 d'Aulnay went back to France, seeking a revision of the old arrangement that would make him the superior officer in l'Acadie, with authority over La Tour. Although the king's ministers declined to change the status quo, confirming both men as lieutenant-governors in their respective spheres and urging them to come to "a good understanding," La Tour continued to feel aggrieved. By rights, he told Governor John Winthrop of Massachusetts several years later, Port Royal should have succeeded to his control after Razilly's death. "D'Aulnay had dispossessed him of it by force," Winthrop reported La Tour exclaiming. By that time the rivalry between the two lieutenant-governors of l'Acadie had erupted into open warfare.[24]

While he was in France, d'Aulnay consolidated his position by marrying Jeanne Motin de Reux, a woman of noble birth he had met when she came to l'Acadie two years earlier as the companion of her sister Anne, bride of one of his lieutenants. This may not have been d'Aulnay's first marriage. New England traders reported that "Monsieur Dony" (as they called him) had contracted a "country marriage" with an Abenaki woman from Penobscot Bay who bore him several *métis* children. It was, perhaps, a *mariage de convenance* furthering d'Aulnay's commercial prospects on the Maine coast. His marriage with Jeanne Motin was also politically motivated. Her father was Louis Motin, sieur de Courcelles, a wealthy shareholder in the Compagnie de la Nouvelle-France, and she brought to her marriage a significant dowry, including a number of shares in the company, which for the first time gave her husband a direct voice not just in operations but in management. His wife was no *"femme du monde,"* no society woman, d'Aulnay wrote with a touch of condescension—

she was merely a "very humble and modest little servant of God." Jeanne Motin would prove far shrewder than d'Aulnay imagined.[25]

At about the same time d'Aulnay's rival Charles de La Tour contracted for a similarly advantageous marriage to Françoise-Marie Jacquelin, a young Huguenot woman from a town southwest of Paris. The marriage settlement made no mention of a dowry, but the Jacquelin family, members of the lesser nobility, must have added to La Tour's network of support within the French Huguenot community. La Tour promised his bride a small fortune in jewels, a new wardrobe, and a retinue of servants. (The contract also detailed a number of provisions for his *métis* children, although it failed to mention their Míkmaw mother.) These negotiations were handled by La Tour's representatives in France, and while it is possible that he met Françoise-Marie Jacquelin on an earlier trip to the continent, it is more likely that he first laid eyes on her after she arrived at rivière Saint-Jean in 1640. By all accounts strikingly handsome, Françoise-Marie became La Tour's invaluable partner in his struggle with d'Aulnay. Certainly she did not fit conventional seventeenth-century notions of womanhood. D'Aulnay thought her a virago, writing to Governor Winthrop of Massachusetts that in order to understand La Tour one must consider his wife, "the cause of his contempt and rebellion."[26]

It is true that Madame La Tour placed herself at the center of the struggle between her husband and d'Aulnay. She was with La Tour in the summer of 1640 when he sailed from rivière Saint-Jean to Port Royal with two armed vessels, demanding his right to inspect the furs stored in d'Aulnay's warehouse—a deliberately provocative act. Refused permission to land, La Tour opened fire on d'Aulnay's fort, but in an ensuing sea battle in Port Royal Basin he was outmaneuvered, outgunned, and forced to surrender. He secured the release of his wife and men from d'Aulnay's dungeons only after signing a deposition in which he admitted to firing the first shot. When the king's ministers read that statement, they revoked La Tour's trading rights on the grounds of "misconduct" and ordered his return to France. And when he failed to comply, they ordered d'Aulnay to "seize his person . . . employing all the means and forces you can." D'Aulnay didn't need to be told twice. He immediately attacked and sacked La Tour's outpost at Cape Sable, then blockaded his headquarters on rivière Saint-Jean. Once again it was Frenchman versus Frenchman. Over the previous decade, French settlers had proved that they could live in l'Acadie "with as much satisfaction as in France itself," trader Nicolas Denys observed, "provided that the envy of the French, one against another, does not ruin the best intentioned plans."[27]

Indeed, while La Tour and d'Aulnay preoccupied themselves with fighting each other, the title of strongest along the North Atlantic coast was rapidly shifting to the English. It is doubtful, however, that had the two seigneurs found a way to cooperate they could have done anything to slow the advance of New England. During the 1630s English colonists at Massachusetts Bay (*Grande Baie* in French parlance) established a density of settlement that the French could not hope to match. By 1640, the population of New England was nearly five times greater than the entire population of New France, and soon Boston traders and Salem fishermen were active in Acadian waters. With his access to French markets closed, La Tour turned to them for help. Throughout the preceding decade he had been doing an intermittent and illegal business with the Puritans, although their commerce was sometimes punctuated by conflict. During one confrontation with a Plymouth trader, La Tour shot and killed two men and seized a large quantity of trade goods, declaring it "lawful prize" since his French commission named him master of the Atlantic coast as far south as Cape Cod. When the incredulous trader demanded to see that document, La Tour drew his rapier, asserting that his "sword was commission sufficient." But under challenge by d'Aulnay he was compelled to adopt a milder approach. He sent envoys to Boston promising "liberty of free commerce" for Puritan traders at rivière Saint-Jean and proposing to lease Boston vessels in order to ship his furs to England. A number of prominent merchants saw profit in the plan; but when Massachusetts authorities received word of the fact that La Tour was "under displeasure and censure in France," they resolved "to have no further to do with him."[28]

In 1642, Madame La Tour succeeded in breaking the blockade with a vessel loaded with furs, which then sailed to La Rochelle and her husband's Huguenot backers. She outfitted a return with supplies, munitions, and 140 Huguenot fightingmen, but unable to break the blockade a second time, she landed instead at a secluded inlet up the coast, sent for her husband, and together they sailed to Boston to make a personal appeal for support. The arrival of "Monsieur Delatore and lady" with a large contingent of troops in the spring of 1643 created quite a stir. But La Tour calmed fears by putting himself in the hands of the authorities. He attended Puritan services with the magistrates, and requested permission to drill his troops on the commons. "They were all very expert in their postures and motions," noted Governor Winthrop, who ordered a comparable drill of the Boston militia. La Tour complimented Winthrop on the discipline of his men, exclaiming that "he could not have believed it if he had not seen it." Like his father, he could be charming. Meeting with the Massachusetts Council of Magistrates, he displayed his French commission (the document this time, not the sword) and asked for authorization to hire vessels and men to break d'Aulnay's blockade. The magistrates were divided. Some took the position that the struggle among the French was none of their business. But the council was finally persuaded by Winthrop's argument that d'Aulnay was likely to prove "a dangerous neighbor to us," and that it was therefore politic to treat his enemy as a friend.[29]

Despite his best efforts, La Tour would find himself outmaneuvered and outgunned by d'Aulnay. He sailed north in the late spring of 1643 with a fleet of five armed vessels and 270 men, broke the blockade, and chased d'Aulnay's vessels back across Baie Française. In June he led a joint force of Puritan and Huguenot troops in an assault on the outskirts of Port Royal, killing three of d'Aulnay's defenders and wounding seven others, slaughtering cattle, burning a mill, and seizing a transport loaded with furs valued at 18,000 *livres*. "Sieur de La Tour [is] a very evil Frenchman who attends Protestant services when he is in *Grande Baie*," the outraged Capuchin missionaries of Port Royal wrote to the king. La Tour and the English mercenaries split the booty between them before leaving, wrote the Capuchins, "*les Bastonnais* keeping two-thirds and La Tour one-third." This was the first attack on l'Acadie by New Englanders.[30]

To avoid another, d'Aulnay swiftly negotiated a non-aggression pact with the Massachusetts Bay Colony, sweetening the deal by offering New Englanders permission to fish and trade in the waters of l'Acadie. "I engage my word from this hour," he pledged in a letter to Massachusetts officials, "that whatever troubles may fall out between the two crownes of France and England (which I heartily pray God not to permit), to keep inviolably with you that peace and intelligence which is requisite in these beginnings." Desperate to maintain his support in Massachusetts, La Tour was forced to return there during the winter of 1644–45. D'Aulnay "is a cunning man who tries to make you believe that it is your duty to abandon me," he warned the magistrates, "but does not tell you that this is to strengthen himself through my downfall." La Tour was still in Boston in the spring of 1645 when word arrived that d'Aulnay had captured his fort and habitation on rivière Saint-Jean "by assault and scalado."[31]

Récollect missionaries, disgusted with the increasingly Protestant character of La Tour's men and supporters, had gone over to d'Aulnay, informing him of La Tour's absence and the weak state of his garrison. D'Aulnay attacked during Holy Week, expecting a quick capitulation, but was surprised by the stout defense organized by Madame La Tour, who acted as *La Commandante* through the battle. After three days of fighting, and fearful of the losses he might suffer in a final assault, d'Aulnay proposed a capitulation, which she accepted, according to Nicolas Denys, the French trader, "under the condition that d'Aulnay should give quarter to all." But upon taking possession of the fort, d'Aulnay abrogated the agreement and ordered all the defenders hanged, save one who agreed to serve as executioner of the rest. Madame La Tour herself was forced to endure a mock execution. "The Lady Commandant accompanied them at the gallows," wrote Denys, "with a cord around her neck as though she had been the greatest villain." Afterwards she was clamped in irons and informed she would be sent to France to stand trial for treason. According to Governor Winthrop, she died three weeks later—of "chagrin," some said; poisoned by d'Aulnay, according to others. D'Aulnay now took command of the fort on the rivière Saint-Jean and the commerce of the mainland, which brought him a fortune in beaver, otter, and other furs.[32]

Charles de Menou d'Aulnay de Charnizay did not long enjoy his undisputed rule in l'Acadie. In the spring of 1650, five years after this triumph, he overturned his canoe while conducting an inspection of his seigneurie along rivière Dauphin and died from exposure to the icy water. When Charles de La Tour learned of his enemy's death, he left Québec, where he had been living, and hurried to Paris to appeal for reinstatement as governor of l'Acadie. It seems absurd that the French court would entertain such a request from a man it had previously declared an agent of "foreign sectaries" in New England who had engaged in "open rebellion" against the state. But France was in turmoil as nobles seeking greater political power challenged the authority of the crown. La Tour deftly exploited the chaos, and swayed the king's advisers with his argument that he could bring stability to l'Acadie. With his old commission reconfirmed, he outfitted an expedition in France and by late 1651 had reestablished control at Cape Sable and rivière Saint-Jean.[33]

Jeanne Motin, the widow d'Aulnay, filling in for her late husband, was powerless to prevent La Tour's return. She was vulnerable as well to the assault of Emmanuel Le Borgne, a wealthy merchant of La Rochelle, with whom her husband had run up enormous debts during his struggle with La Tour. When Le Borgne failed to collect from the d'Aulnay family at Charnizay, he raised an armed force and sailed to l'Acadie, seized Port Royal, installed himself as commandant, and evicted the widow d'Aulnay and her eight children from the governor's quarters, leaving them with only two small farms for their support. With the political chaos in France, neither the state nor the Compagnie de la Nouvelle-France was able to prevent Le Borgne from taking charge. The man "surprised me," wrote Jeanne Motin, "and maliciously wrenched from me the transactions and papers which concern the little property I have ever had in my life."[34]

In desperation, she turned to La Tour. After several weeks of negotiation, they married in February 1653, signing artlcles in which they declared their intention to unite to assure "the peace and tranquility of the country, and concord and union between the two families." It was a calculated political move for both. La Tour agreed to endow Motin with 30,000 *livres* and the lifetime use of his fort and habitation on rivière Saint-Jean, "with all the rights of trading, fruits, revenues, emoluments thence proceeding"—providing her with a way of evading Le Borgne's humiliating domination. La Tour's marriage to Françoise-Marie Jacquelin had not produced any heirs, and he must have looked forward to bearing children with Motin, a woman of noble lineage. She agreed to accept responsibility for La Tour's minor *métis* children, pledging that they should share rights of inheritance equally with any offspring of the new marriage. As for the children she had borne with d'Aulnay, their care was to be her sole responsibility, not La Tour's. Soon they were sent to France to be raised by her relations. "My children," she later wrote them, "you will remain ruined and poor your entire life because of the trickery and meanness of Sieur Le Borgne." It was a fate that Jeanne Motin did not intend to share.[35]

When he learned of the La Tour–Motin alliance, Le Borgne made plans for an assault on rivière Saint-Jean, with the intention of eliminating his rivals and consolidating the entire fur trade in his own hands. He was preempted by the intervention of Massachusetts. Since d'Aulnay's death the French had feared the New Englanders would try to take advantage of the turmoil in l'Acadie. In 1651, acting in her late husband's stead, Motin wrote Governor John Endicott of Massachusetts asking for his assurance of "good and perfect alliance, friendship and confederation" in the relations of the two colonies. His colony did not intend "any thing but all neighbourly, loving and friendly compliance with you," Endicott replied, "unless ought shall proceed from yourselves towards us." Despite his words, Massachusetts awaited only the means and the opportunity to strike north.[36]

In 1654, during England's naval war with Holland, authorities in London commissioned Major Robert Sedgwick of Boston to raise an expedition to strike at New Amsterdam to the south. By the time the Massachusetts General Court issued a call for volunteers, however, the war with Holland had been settled by treaty. Sedgwick—prosperous Massachusetts merchant and captain of the town militia La Tour had so admired—decided to steer his heavily armed fleet north instead of south. Their aim, he wrote, was to establish Puritan dominance in "tradinge and fishinge" to the eastward. Captain John Leverett—Sedgwick's son-in-law, a man prominent in the Maine and Acadian trade, and a future governor of Massachusetts—offered a more grandiose justification, writing to the English government that their expedition was designed to enlarge the nation's "Dominions in these Westerne American parts." Sedgwick's summer campaign of conquest was swiftly concluded. He forced La Tour's surrender after a three-day siege and Le Borgne's after a single bloody skirmish, seizing booty estimated at £10,000 and capturing 220 French soldiers. When news of the victory reached Boston, the General Court ordered "a publick and solemn thanksgiving to the Lord for his gracious working."[37]

Le Borgne and the troops were sent to France, but Sedgwick sailed to London with La Tour, who had a final card to play. Resurrecting his old Nova Scotia baronetcy, he convinced his captors that the title might be useful as a legal cover for the conquest, which had been undertaken without bothering about a formal declaration of war with France. In exchange for the settlement of his outstanding debts with Massachusetts merchants, as well as a small annual share of the profits in the commerce of l'Acadie, La Tour transferred his title and grant to Thomas Temple, the agent for a group of English investors, who was then given a royal appointment as governor of "Nova Scotia or l'Acadie." La Tour pledged his loyalty to the English and retired to his estate at Cape Sable, where over the next decade Jeanne Motin bore him five children. There in 1663 Charles de Saint-Etienne de La Tour died at the age of seventy, fifty-seven years after first arriving in l'Acadie.[38]

FOR the next sixteen years—from 1654 to 1670, the year France regained possession of the colony in exchange for territorial concessions in the West Indies—l'Acadie remained under nominal English control. It is not clear how the inhabitants of Port Royal regarded this period. They may have seen it as a tragedy, or perhaps as an opportunity. In the absence of any documentary evidence there is no way of knowing what they thought. But what they *did* marked a crucial turning point in Acadian history. As French officials and soldiers prepared for repatriation to France, Sedgwick offered the inhabitants, who numbered several hundred, the choice either of returning to their mother country or of remaining "unmolested" on their marshland farms with "liberty of conscience allowed to religion." They chose to stay, taking an oath "that they would no longer bear arms against the English nation, and in the event that they did declaring themselves worthy of death."[39]

For two decades on rivière Dauphin the inhabitants had been putting down roots, constructing dikes, planting orchards, building homes, and raising families. And the fact was, for the inhabitants life in l'Acadie was certainly better than life had been in France, where peasants lived under the domination of seigneurs, farmed small plots, paid *cens et rentes* (feudal tribute and rent), endured famines, epidemics, and religious warfare, and suffered high mortality. In

France, scarcity was the rule. In Acadia, there was abundance. The inhabitants sowed wheat, rye, peas, and flax on their marshland fields, grazed cattle and sheep on their meadows, and allowed hogs to forage in the forests beyond their dwellings. "The region is quite fertile," wrote the French surgeon sieur de Dièreville, "and produces all kinds of vegetables, enough fruit, and a sufficient amount of wheat; there is meat and fish and poultry, and every variety of game." The inhabitants lavished attention on their gardens, which one observer described as overflowing with "cabbages, beets, onions, carrots, chives, shallots, turnips, parsnips, and all kinds of salad greens." They consumed fresh fruits and vegetables with fish in the summer, and in the winter relished their *soupe de la toussaint*, made from cabbage and turnips. "Neither of these vegetables goes into the pot without the other," Dièreville noted, and "nourishing soups are made of them, with a large slice of pork." The inhabitants impressed him with their self-sufficiency. "There's nothing which they cannot produce," he wrote. "They make the things they lack," not only raising all their own food but spinning their own yarn from homegrown flax and wool, weaving their own cloth on looms of their own construction, and cutting their own clothing in the old French manner, in "no way distinguished by new fashions . . . [but] made for comfort."[40]

Dièreville's first impression of Port Royal had been not so positive. Its frontier backwardness horrified him. "To what a wild country, oh heaven, have I come! Nothing before my eyes but streams and forests, huts of mud and cottages. . . . How one can live here I don't know. What a scene of poverty! With but a taste, already I have had enough of *Nouvelle France.*" But after several months residence he developed a fondness for the directness and simplicity of life in l'Acadie, and when he returned to France, his sentiments blossomed into fulsome nostalgia.

. . . Each one in peace beneath a rustic roof,
Empties his breadbox and his cask;
And, in the winter, keeps himself quite warm

Without a farthing spent on wood; where else
Could such advantages be found? . . .
This country from a thousand vexing cares
Has set them free; no taxes burden them,
And so they only work that they may live.
They take things as they come;
When times are good, then they rejoice,
They suffer when the times are hard,
Each keeps himself as best he can,
And without envy or ambition, waits
Until his modest labor bears its fruit. . . .

In Dièreville's memory, Acadia *was* Arcadia, a land whose residents were thankfully isolated from the currents of cultural change coursing through the Atlantic world. His one lament was that the climate could not support the viniculture of the day, forcing the inhabitants to wash down their meals with spruce beer instead of wine. "If but a hillside of *champagne* were there," he wrote, "better than any other land it would be."[41]

Dièreville's account was a great success when published in France in 1708. His book went through three editions and was translated into English and German. His sentimental portrayal would have considerable influence after the later expulsion of 1755. But his contention that the inhabitants were isolated from the larger Atlantic world was considerably off the mark. They indeed were remarkably productive on their farms, more than meeting the hopes of the Compagnie de la Nouvelle-France. Yet the company sponsored agricultural development to facilitate commerce, not subsistence. Conquest by New England put an end to the company's commercial relationship with l'Acadie, leading to its bankruptcy and dissolution in 1663. But there was no pause in local commerce. In fact, it expanded, with La Rochelle companies quickly replaced by Boston merchants trading to the eastward.[42]

New Englanders proved far more proficient than the French in supplying local needs, bringing the essential commodities farmers could not make for themselves—gunpowder and firearms, cooking pots and farm tools, fancy fabric and ribbon, spices, molasses, and rum. They were also far more opportunistic in what they were willing to take in trade—not merely fish and furs but grain from the fertile marshlands, cattle fattened on salt hay, pine logs and lumber from the forests. London refused to place the province directly under the de jure authority of Massachusetts, but de facto it made little difference, since Governor Temple established his primary residence in Boston. He built close working relations with the merchants there, and in turn Massachusetts authorities enforced his trade monopoly, authorizing him "to seize and confiscate the vessels and goods of all persons trading peltry or furs with Indians without his license, as also to burne, kill, and destroy all such as shall resist him." Temple collected a fee from each New England vessel engaged in fishing or trade, and during his tenure an important triangular trade developed: cargoes of fish and furs dispatched to European ports in exchange for wines and other commodities marketable in Boston, cloth and manufactured goods shipped from New England. After 1654 l'Acadie swung into Boston's commercial orbit, where it would remain even after the restoration of French authority. Sieur de Dièreville simply closed his eyes to the active participation of inhabitants in the economy of greater New England. Peripheral yet connected—that would be the Acadian situation.[43]

Conquest by New England meant isolation from old France. It meant an end to the small but steady stream of French migrants who came to the colony from the 1630s to the 1650s. Although Governor Temple brought over several shiploads of workers, including a number of families, he made relatively little effort to recruit settlers since he considered l'Acadie mainly a site for commerce. A French official later commented on "the lack of attention paid by the English to establishing themselves in these parts" and noted that "they sent settlers only on a token basis, and without making the slightest improvement." Cutting off immigration at this early stage of social development, when the population of Port Royal included but a few hundred souls, helped to shape a culture notably self-contained and clannish.[44]

Isolation also created real social problems. Young people had increasing difficulty finding suitable marriage partners, other than blood relatives, among their neighbors. Missionaries and priests did a steady business issuing dispensations of consanguinity. In the early years of the settlement the problem had been resolved in part by intermarriage with the Míkmaq, but *métissage* declined as colonists spent more time farming and less time trading. It was replaced by the recuitment of wayfaring Europeans. The inhabitants did what they could to encourage sailors, fishermen, and other seasonal workers who passed through Port Royal to stay on and marry in. The surviving records suggest that about a third of all marriages in the late seventeenth century united a local woman with a man from the outside, often a man of contrasting ethnic background. Marie Pesseley married John Peters, a blacksmith from the Channel Islands, and Marie Landry married Lawrence Granger, a sailor from Plymouth, after both men renounced Protestantism; Marie-Françoise Poirier married Roger Casey, a laborer from Ireland, who having been raised Catholic had nothing to renounce. Jehan Pitre, Laurent Granger, and Roger Caissie (as these grooms' names were rendered *en français*) would have numerous descendants. Before 1654, such wayfaring men had come from France; during the English period they came mostly from the British Isles or New England, but also from Portugal, Spain, the Azores, the Basque country, and a scattering of other places. Their presence at Port Royal was testimony to connections with the wider Atlantic world. With all their diversity, the newcomers were folded into the arms of a traditional farming culture that focused on family and locality.[45]

The settlement patterns of inhabitant families suggest a culture in which elders enjoyed considerable power and prestige. Several dozen families lived in the village of Port Royal, next to the fort, but most sited their dwellings on land overlooking their reclaimed fields along both sides of rivière Dauphin. "The houses are built rather far apart," Dièreville noted, "more or less separated from one another." As children came of age and married, they raised houses of their own nearby those of their parents, resulting in the development of little *hameaux* or hamlets of interrelated and extended families. In 1667 Marie Landry and her husband Laurent Granger set up housekeeping near her parents in a small cluster of Bourg and Landry households on the north side of rivière Dauphin, across from Fort Royal. Marie's near neighbor was young Marguerite Martin, who married Jean Bourg that same year. Marguerite was raised at the hamlet of Bélisle upriver, named for Alexandre Le Borgne de Bélisle, who inherited seigneurial title to the land at Port Royal and Minas Basin from his father, the merchant Emmanuel Le Borgne. The land there had been pioneered in the 1640s by her parents, Pierre Martin and Catherine Vigneau, who built their house at the edge of a large tidal marsh and over the years diked and reclaimed several acres of farmland. By 1671, when newly returned French authorities assigned a Franciscan missionary, Laurent Molins, the task of conducting a census along the river, all of the adult Martin children except Marguerite lived near their parents, including both sons and the two daughters, married to wayfaring men. But as was his practice, abbé Molins listed all the Martin offspring under the heading of the elder:

> Ploughman Pierre Martin 70, his wife Catherine Vigneau 68, and their five children, four of them married, a boy and three girls, Pierre 45, Marie 35, Marguerite 32, Andrée 30, the unmarried Mathieu 35. Seven horned cattle, eight sheep, and two arpents of arable land.

These *hameaux* were "patriarchal enclaves," in the historian Emile Lauvrière's phrase, and Molins's language and method of classification suggests that contemporaries thought of them precisely that way.[46]

Certainly the lives of women were circumscribed by the traditional constraints of marriage and childbearing. Daughters married at an average age of twenty-one (compared to twenty-five in France), and nearly a third married in their teens. Dièreville put his observations into verse:

A father and a mother do not keep
A nubile daughter long at home, although
She causes them no care, and to their will
Submits in registering her vows. If when
Some tender suitor comes, to urge his love,
His sweetheart favors him, wedlock
Unites them both and they are free
To populate the world; which is,
Moreover, that which they do best. . . .

Early marriage meant large families for those women who survived through their childbearing years. Françoise Brun was seventeen when she married twenty-two-year-old Bernard Bourg, and over the next twenty-two years she bore thirteen children, two of whom died in infancy. Marie-Madeleine Girouard was only fourteen when she married Thomas Cormier, who at thirty-two was more than twice her age; she bore ten children over the next twenty years, ending her reproductive years at the relatively young age of thirty-four. "In almost every family five or six children are to be found, and often many more," wrote Dièreville; "the swarming of brats is a sight to behold." He provided a good estimate. The typical Acadian woman of the second generation bore six or seven children, a birth rate as high as it gets. And those children, and their parents, ate very well, and suffered from very little epidemic disease—unlike the peasants back in France. So the population grew rapidly, despite the absence of any significant immigration. The five hundred inhabitants of the 1670s had grown to more than fifteen hundred by the end of the century.[47]

In other ways, however, Acadian culture was not traditional at all. Several important supports of the *ancien régime* failed to survive the New England interregnum. In 1654, Major Sedgwick granted the inhabitants religious liberty, and agreed to allow the Capuchin missionaries to remain in l'Acadie. But they left the following year, and there is no evidence of any priest residing at Port Royal during the sixteen years of English control. For the next twenty years the inhabitants were served by the occasional visits of Catholic missionaries. Devout Catholics in the community practiced *la messe blanche* (the white mass), in which an elder led liturgical chants and prayers. In 1670, the year French authorities returned, a group of inhabitants began a subscription for the construction of a new church building at Port Royal, but it was not until 1674 that the bishop of Québec sent Récollect missionary Claude Moireau to take up the post there. He was succeeded two years later by abbé Louis Petit. The inhabitants "come in groups to church Sundays and holy days, and they partake well of the sacraments," Petit reported to the bishop, "even though they were fifteen years without a priest when under English government." Catholicism was important, but it was by no means the foundation of Acadian culture. That notion developed in the nineteenth century, when the Catholic Church was practically the only social institution in the Acadian community. But it ignores the years when priests were absent or scarce, and disregards the substantial participation of Protestants in the making of the seventeenth-century Acadian community.[48]

If the Church was weak in late seventeenth-century l'Acadie, seigneurialism was moribund. The seigneurial grants made by royal charter and the authority of the Compagnie de la Nouvelle-France, as well as the corresponding grants of land by seigneurs to individual inhabitants, continued to be the legal basis for land tenure. But after 1654 there was no substance to Poutrincourt's ideal of a transplanted feudal world of *seigneurs et roturiers.* According to Nicolas Denys, d'Aulnay had treated his tenants "like slaves, without letting them make any profit." After the English conquest, many inhabitants took the opportunity to migrate further up rivière Dauphin, where they settled land without seigneurial authorization. "Since the English became masters of the country," wrote Denys, "the inhabitants who lived near the fort have for the most part abandoned their houses and gone to settle on the *haute rivière*." Seigneur Alexandre Le Borgne de Bélisle, son of the merchant Emmanuel Le Borgne, who resided at Port Royal after the restoration of French rule, attempted to lure them back by offering grants with very few seigneurial obligations. Most of these grants were poorly described, and often overlapped, which led to conflicts over boundaries. Bélisle accepted no responsibility for such problems, focusing solely on the collection of rents, which were infrequently and grudgingly paid.[49]

The first generation of leaders—Poutrincourt, Razilly, d'Aulnay, even La Tour—operated under the presumption of *noblesse oblige*, and built homes and displayed goods appropriate to their class. The inventory of Razilly's estate, for example, included upholstered furniture, a silver table service, and thirteen suits of velvet, satin, or taffeta—suggesting that he expected to live in the same elegant style on the frontier as a gentleman of his rank in France. But the New England interregnum changed all that. For sixteen years no French colonial officials or military officers resided at Port Royal, and the descendants of former officials and officers who remained lived much like everyone else. There is little evidence that Le Borgne, or the handful of other seigneurs in l'Acadie, had the resources to live in a style that significantly distinguished them from more prosperous inhabitants. "A great social leveling had taken place," writes the historian Birgitta Wallace. "The children of the original elite married the children of those who worked for their fathers, a situation that would have been unlikely in France." The conquest by the English, and the departure of French officials, had helped this process along. But it was also an aspect of the general frontier equality that prevailed in l'Acadie. As Dièreville put it, "here more than elsewhere mesalliances occur. . . . And so the nobleman to extend his line leads to his couch, or rather to his hut, the peasant maid."[50]

Under d'Aulnay, local governance was the responsibility of the seigneur; but the New Englander Major Sedgwick created an inhabitants' council, presided over by Guillaume Trahan, *syndic* of Port Royal. The council was to administer the colony under the watchful eye of Captain John Leverett and a small garrison of Massachusetts troops. Governor Thomas Temple did not arrive until 1657, and aside from an initial visit to Port Royal he conducted his administration from Boston and Penobscot Bay, content to leave local matters in local hands. The New England idea of self-government took hold, and was noted by French officials when they returned in 1670, after the agreement with England that returned l'Acadie to their control. Governor-General Louis de Buade de Frontenac of New France complained to the king that the inhabitants were reluctant to obey orders without first having a full discussion among themselves, something he attributed to "a certain English and Parliamentary inclination which is inspired by the frequent contact and commerce they have with those from Boston." But the inhabitants also must have drawn on their own traditions of governance, their experience in communal management of the dikes, for example, as well as the example of consensus decision making in Míkmaw society, to which they were so closely bound.[51]

Upon the resumption of French control, the crown assumed the responsibility for appointing provincial governors, no longer confident to rely solely on seigneurial leadership, as it had before 1654. Governor Hector d'Andigné de Grandfontaine arrived in 1670 with a garrison of thirty men. Over the next two years scores of new settlers arrived, including men with names that would become familiar over the coming century—Broussard, Bastarache, Dorion, Arseneau. Following the example of Governor Temple, Grandfontaine established his headquarters on the mainland at Penobscot Bay, where he could be close to the source of the fur trade. He dissolved the inhabitants' council at Port Royal and delegated local authority to sieur Le Borgne de Bélisle. But with imperious decrees and impetuous demands, Bélisle quickly alienated the inhabitants, who had grown accustomed to governing themselves, and Grandfontaine was forced to dismiss him. Nor was abbé Molins, closely associated with Bélisle, always treated with respect. When he conducted his census in 1671, several inhabitants refused to cooperate. Etienne Robichaud would not open his door, and Pierre Melanson "refused to give his age and the number of his livestock or lands," Molins noted, "and his wife told me that I was crazy to run through the streets asking for these things."[52]

A few years later M. de Gargas, chief clerk of New France, sent to Port Royal to conduct another census, also found the inhabitants "rebellious and independent." He was unfortunate enough to fall into dispute with one of the Bourgs—probably one of the five adult brothers from the Bourg settlement—from whom he had borrowed a canoe, and to whom he had not (in the opinion of Bourg) paid proper respect. "He grew so angry that he insulted us in terms which my respect for you presents me from inserting here," Gargas wrote in his report. "Now this man possesses more relations than almost anyone else in Port Royal, and without looking into the matter all his relations took his side." Surrounded by a threatening group of irate kinsmen, Gargas promised to return the canoe as soon as he had finished his enumeration of the inhabitants along rivière Dauphin, and even offered to pay rent for its use, but "two or three of his brothers treated me very insolently, adding that they desired neither the canoe nor the money." As they would later say in Québec, *"en tête comme un Acadien"*—he has the head of an Acadian, which was something like saying the man was as stubborn as a mule.[53]

During the period of English interregnum a distinctive Acadian ethnic culture took shape. The inhabitants had come from a variety of backgrounds—Catholic but also Huguenot, French but also Míkmaq, English, Irish, even Spanish. Their culture was a combination of old and new. Their families were patriarchial and extended, and although some were better off than others, their society essentially egalitarian. They were peripheral to the main currents of the Atlantic, but deeply connected to it through trade and commerce.

They identified weakly with the distant mother country, but enjoyed close and amicable attachments to the native people. They had ceased to think of themselves as colonists and begun to develop a *perspective indigène.* As sieur de Cadillac noted, they were "creoles"—a transplanted people that saw themselves as *natifs.* Dièreville, who lived with them, and surely knew the name they used for themselves, called them *les Acadiens.*[54]

CHAPTER 3

Cunning Is Better than Force

Life in the Borderland, 1671–1696

Soon after Port Royal returned to French hands, Acadians began leaving their farms on rivière Dauphin and settling the tidelands at the head of Baie Française. In 1671, a prominent local inhabitant, Jacques Bourgeois—surgeon, shipbuilder, son-in-law of Guillaume Trahan, and president of the inhabitants' council during the preceding years of English control—moved his large extended family to *Chignecto* ("great marsh" in Míkmawísimk), an isthmus ten miles long and seventeen miles wide at its narrowest point, connecting the Acadian peninsula to the Canadian mainland and marking the northernmost extension of Baie Française. Chignecto was ideal country for Acadian pioneers: 50,000 acres of salt marsh, drained by four tidal rivers and interspersed with forested uplands. Fifty feet or more of tidal variation had left deep deposits of rich sediment in the lowlands. Bourgeois and his sons selected land on an extended channel of Baie Française the French called *Beaubassin*, clearing homesteads on the hillsides, diking the lowlands for pasture, and introducing livestock. The location proved perfect for cattle grazing, and over the next few years Beaubassin attracted dozens of young families from Port Royal. The place names they left on the land suggests the diversity of their origins. *Butte à Roger*, on Beauséjour ridge to the north of rivière Missaguash, was named for Irishman Roger Caissy and his wife Marie Poirier, who planted the community's first orchards. *Butte à Mirande*, on Beaubassin ridge to the south, was the homeplace of Emmanuel Mirande, emigrant from Portugal by way of Québec, who prospered, and after a few years married the young widow Marguerite Boudrot, daughter of Jacques Bourgeois.[1]

Throughout colonial North America, movement outward from the original hearth of settlement was part of the typical process of growth, new communities hiving off as older ones filled with farms. But by the late seventeenth century the inhabitants of rivière Dauphin had diked only a few hundred of the more than five thousand acres of marshland, suggesting that something other than population pressure may have been behind this migration. François-Marie Perrot, governor of the colony in the late 1680s, complained of the tendency of the inhabitants to scatter themselves "very far one from the other," and thought it indicated their preference for a wandering life of frontier trading over a settled life of marshland farming. The *coureurs de bois* (literally, "runners of the woods") were "a species of savage" and their profligacy was boundless, another official wrote. "They Lavish, Eat, Drink, and Play all away as long as the Goods hold out; and when these are gone, they e'en sell their Embroidery, their Lace, and their Clothes." In the imperial scheme of things, colonists were expected to live in settled communities, industriously producing sustenance for officials, soldiers, and licensed traders. After a trip to l'Acadie, a bureaucrat from Canada advised that inhabitants should be compelled to live at Port Royal, "for scattered as they are they are neither useful nor profitable." The colony could never be put on a paying basis as long as "the governor allows the young sons of the colonists to go and settle elsewhere along the coast, where they do nothing but hunt or negotiate with the natives."

But a succession of governors found it impossible to prevent colonists from relocating to the frontier, despite royal commands "for the prevention of licentiousness and ranging in the woods." As Governor Perrot put it, young men evaded the constraints imposed by colonial officials in order to spend their time in "*la débauche avec les sauvagesses*."[2]

Perrot, like other colonial officials, was uncomfortable with the close relations between Míkmaq and Acadians—and especially uncomfortable with the intimate connections between Míkmaw women and Acadian men. At places such as Beaubassin, the Míkmaw and Acadian communities were closely connected, with natives outnumbering inhabitants until the first decades of the eighteenth century. But the lure of the frontier was principally about commerce, and the commerce Acadians most desired was not with natives but New Englanders. Before his move to Beaubassin, Jacques Bourgeois had prospered as a trader at Port Royal. He learned to speak English and developed close commercial connections with several Boston merchants, particularly John Nelson, a cosmopolitan Londoner and nephew of Governor Thomas Temple, who spoke perfect French and some Algonquian. The return to French control threatened the commercial connections of men such as Bourgeois and Nelson. It would be necessary, wrote Intendant Jean Talon of New France, "to break off, without violence, the trade which the English conduct with the king's subjects living at Port Royal." At remote places such as Chignecto, Acadians and New Englanders found a way around the problem. Bourgeois set up grist and sawmills with equipment imported from Boston and began a lucrative trade with Nelson and other New Englanders in flour and lumber, beef and furs.[3]

Such clandestine arrangements—violating the mercantilist regulations of both England and France—angered French traders who were attempting to break into the Acadian market. "The English are at present trading on our lands," one of them wrote to Canadien authorities in 1675. "If no one interferes with them this year they will think that we are abandoning this coast, which is worth a great deal." He requested a commission granting him the authority to prevent the inhabitants from trading illegally. "Even if it were only an old contract in parchment, with a large seal of yellow or red wax," he wrote, "it will be sufficient to dazzle the scum of this country."[4]

But local French authorities in l'Acadie were no more willing to clamp down on the illegal trading than were English authorities in New England. The English traders offered the inhabitants better goods at lower prices. According to Louis Armand, baron de Lahontan, a French garrison officer who served in the maritime region for a number of years, "the French prize their Goods too high, though they are not so good as those of the English." Rather than attempting to suppress the illegal trade, officials sought instead to profit from it. French governors contracted with John Nelson—who after 1670 succeeded his uncle Thomas Temple as the most important Englishman in l'Acadie—to continue the practice of licensing New England fishing vessels. Nelson became a kind of de facto agent for Acadian officials at Boston, allowed to operate a large warehouse at Port Royal, and in turn passing a portion of the fees back to Acadian officials in the form of credit. "He had always traded to this coast," Governor Perrot wrote, "and greatly benefited the settlers by the large loans he made them in seasons of their greatest necessity." Presents and secret dealings became a way of life. The governors "look upon their place as a Gold Mine given 'em in order to enrich themselves," Lahontan noted.[5]

French officers in charge at frontier trading posts followed the example set by the governors of the province. Pierre de Joybert de Soulanges et de Marson, who served a term as provincial governor in the mid-1670s, accepted kickbacks from English traders whom he allowed to do business at rivière Saint-Jean. At Cape Sable, the descendants of Charles de La Tour and Philippe Mius d'Entremont (who as La Tour's adjutant had been granted a seigneurie there) intermarried and established themselves as a local ruling clan through their control of smuggling with New Englanders. The most notorious of these officers was Jean-Vincent d'Abbadie de Saint-Castin, who did an extensive business with John Nelson, exchanging large cargoes of furs for trade goods at Pentagouet, his outpost on Penobscot Bay. The second son of a French baron from the Béarne region, Saint-Castin was a career military officer assigned to l'Acadie, where he accumulated a huge fortune of "two or three hundred thousand Crowns," according to Lahontan. But rather than sending his profits back to France, as did most officers, Saint-Castin used them "to buy up Goods for Presents to his Fellow *Sauvages*," built a semi-feudal principality at Pentagouet, and became the most powerful *capitaine de sauvages* in l'Acadie.[6]

Following the Abenaki custom for a powerful man, he took two wives, Marie and Mathilde, the daughters of Matakando, a prominent Abenaki war chief, and after Marie's death in the mid-1680s, he married Mathilde in a formal Catholic ceremony. The Saint-Castin children were raised in the Abenaki community at Pentagouet, and when they were sent to be educated at Port Royal were described as "speaking nothing but the native language [*ne sachant que parler sauvage*]." They grew up with an identity both Abenaki and Acadian. The historian Jean Daigle suggests that the phrase on the Saint-Castin family crest—"*ni trop près, ni trop loin* (neither too near, nor too far)"—encapsulated the Acadian experience. French in background but no longer French in nationality, they were truly becoming a people in between.[7]

At Beaubassin, the illegal trade with New Englanders was dominated by Michel Leneuf de La Vallière—the son-in-law of fur trader Nicolas Denys, who had retired to the Canadien village of Trois-Rivières on the St. Lawrence. In 1676, Governor-General Frontenac of New France assigned La Vallière to patrol the Acadian coast for smugglers. When La Vallière succeeded in seizing three New England vessels engaged in illegal commerce on the coast of Cape Breton Island, Frontenac rewarded him with the title *seigneur de Beaubassin,* and in 1678 named him commandant of l'Acadie, in effect, acting governor. Despite this, La Vallière continued the practice of his predecessors. From his estate at Beaubassin he cultivated the cooperation of local residents, built the chapel of Notre-Dame-du-Bon-Secours, supervised the construction of an extensive dike system that allowed more livestock grazing, and established himself as majordomo of illegal trading on the upper bay. Under La Vallière's auspices Beaubassin grew into a hearty and prosperous smuggling center with more than two hundred residents.[8]

Beaubassin was not the only new settlement to hive off the original Acadian community at Port Royal. During La Vallière's tenure as commandant pioneers also began to settle the shores of Minas Basin, the eastern extension of upper Baie Française. In 1682 a group of extended families settled on rivière Gaspereau at *le grand pré,* the "great meadow" stretching eighteen miles along the southern shore of Minas. They were led by Pierre Melanson dit Laverdure, who like many Acadians was known by his *dit nom,* or nickname, names that were frequently passed on to descendants. Laverdure was authorized to act as agent for the seigneur Alexandre Le Borgne de Bélisle, making grants of land at Grand Pré to encourage settlement. About the same time, several miles to the west on rivière Saint-Antoine (today's Cornwallis River), Pierre Thériot and Cécile Landry, accompanied by the families of Cécile's brothers, Antoine and Claude Landry, were breaking land and building homes. These were kinship migrations, in which extended family groups moved together and founded new hamlets. According to one French official, the house of Pierre Thériot, "the most important resident at Minas," was a shelter for nephews, widows, orphans, "and other needy people," while their own dwellings were being built. Dike construction, abundant harvests, and lucrative trade with New Englanders led to rapid expansion of the settlement. New hamlets were founded east of Grand Pré at the mouth of a river the Míkmaq called *Pisiquid* ("flowing into the sea"), and at the eastern terminus of Minas Basin at *Cobequid* ("end of the tidal water"). By 1700, with six hundred residents, Minas Basin had grown into the largest of the three main Acadian districts—served by three churches, Saint-Charles-des-Mines at Grand Pré, Saint-

Joseph on rivière-aux-Canards, and Sainte-Famille at Pisiquid—and had become the breadbasket of the province.[9]

In the early 1680s, in an attempt to wrest economic control of the colony from the grip of the New Englanders and corrupt local officials, the French resorted to an old strategy, the grant of a trade monopoly to a commercial combine. The Compagnie de la Nouvelle-France had been disbanded in 1663, but another took its place, the *Compagnie Sédentaire de Pêche de l'Acadie,* better known simply as *Compagnie d'Acadie*, headed by Clerbaud Bergier, a Huguenot merchant adventurer from La Rochelle. Determined to drive the English from Acadian waters, in 1683 Bergier seized a number of New England fishing and trading vessels, and in retaliation, Massachusetts privateers commandeered several French vessels. The Acadian inhabitants, however, were adamantly opposed to the company's imposition of a trading monopoly and openly sympathized with the New Englanders. Commandant La Vallière, whose authority and livelihood were threatened by Bergier, condemned the seizure in a letter to the governor of Massachusetts, and did all he could to interfere with company operations, which resulted in his dismissal by French authorities. But his replacement, François-Marie Perrot, proved an inauspicious choice. The previous year Perrot had been sacked from his position as governor of Montréal for illegal trading, and according to Lahontan, in l'Acadie he continued the same practice, making it "his chief business to enrich himself" by striking illegal trading deals with New Englanders. After less than two years in office, he "was broke with disgrace."[10]

In 1685–86, Jacques de Meulles, Intendant of New France, paid an extended visit to the troubled colony in order to advise French authorities on reforms. De Meulles was impressed with the spirit and industry of the inhabitants, but he calculated that the product of their labor did little or nothing to enrich the mother country. He was correct in his analysis. Acadian farming had been intended to support the French fur trade, but at each of the settlements de Meulles watched as Acadians engaged in lively exchanges with New England, not French traders. "The English of Boston regard themselves as lords of all these coasts," he wrote. "They do all their commerce here, and . . . are better liked by the inhabitants than the French themselves." If this continued, he warned, *les Bastonnais* "will carry away all of our land's profit." But de Meulles expressed some sympathy for the inhabitants. "The people of l'Acadie may be excused for their inclination toward the English," he wrote, "never having heard of France, nor ever receiving any aid from her. It is only the English who every year furnish these people with their necessities." It was an important observation. The generation of American-born Acadians had grown up with tenuous connections to old France, growing commercial relations with New England, and deepening roots in l'Acadie.[11]

Their language reflected this history. French officials of the late seventeenth century thought Acadian speech was amusingly quaint and old-fashioned. In the nineteenth and twentieth centuries those impressions were confirmed by linguists who discovered that the speech of maritime Acadians uniquely preserved vocabulary, pronunciation, syntax, and idioms of early modern French. Without schools, the great majority of Acadians were illiterate—although some acquired reading and writing skills through tutoring by the priests—and had no access to the language of written French. More important, when immigration from the mother country was cut off by the English occupation in the mid-seventeenth century, the colonists were insulated from the currents of linguistic change in France. Some of their most common aphorisms, for example, echoed sayings recorded in sixteenth-century French literature: *Le temps mauvais passe quand on mange et s'amuse*—Bad times pass when one eats and is merry. *On ne fait pas comme on veut, mais comme on peut*—One doesn't do what one wants, but what one can. *La moitié du monde se moque de l'autre moitié*—Half the world laughs at the other half.[12]

Yet their language did not remain static, for it liberally included both Algonquian and English elements. Inhabitants commonly communicated with their Míkmaw cousins in a composite trade jargon and some men who could not sign their names used native-style ideograms as personal marks on documents. While it is difficult to know what effect Míkmawísimk had on their speech, the ease with which they resorted to Míkmaw terms is suggested by how often they used native place names for their own settlements. Documentary evidence does exist, however, for the curious combinations of English and French that peppered the Acadian language—*vous too* instead of *vous aussi*, *pas yet* rather than *pas encore*. It was something New Englanders found quite amusing. Fond of linguistic joking themselves, the Acadians ironically referred to their trading English-speaking partners as *nos amis les ennemis*—our friends the enemy. The phrase captured something essential about their situation. They lived in a world on the margins, a world of ambiguities, a world where by necessity people had to learn to play both sides, a world where, as the inhabitants put it, *ruse vaut mieux que force*—cunning was worth more than strength.[13]

Representatives of England and France signed the Treaty of Whitehall in 1686, the same year Jacques de Meulles, Intendant of New France, filed his report on l'Acadie at Versailles. Also known as the Treaty of American Neutrality, the document bound the respective kingdoms to a pledge that "if ever any rupture shall occur in Europe between the said crowns (which God forbid)," their "colonies in America shall continue in peace and neutrality." Louis XIV of France sought to prevent any colonial conflict that might disrupt his plan to take the Rhineland for France and place his own man on the throne of Spain. James II of England hoped that France might be an ally in his attempt to reintroduce Catholicism and absolutism into England. In early 1687 the text of the treaty arrived in l'Acadie and Massachusetts, where it was welcomed by men such as La Vallière and John Nelson, who made their livings crossing borders. Such an arrangement long had been the aim of local officials, both English and French. Even the language of the treaty harked back to the agreement between Charles de Menou d'Aulnay of l'Acadie and the province of Massachusetts Bay in 1644. While calling on colonists to abstain from fishing or trading in the territory of "the other party in America," the treaty also affirmed "freedom of navigation." Neutrality—especially a neutrality that winked at violations of mercantilist restrictions on intercolonial trade—perfectly suited the needs of Acadian inhabitants and New England traders.[14]

Independent merchant interests might favor neutrality, but imperial agents from both France and England began testing the treaty's limits in the months following its ratification. In 1687 a French royal frigate patrolling the waters off Cape Sable in the interests of the Compagnie d'Acadie seized a New England fishing ketch and escorted it under arms to Port Royal. Governor Edmund Andros at Boston sent Captain Francis Nicholson to l'Acadie to protest, maintaining that the fishermen had been in neutral waters. Although the French commander refused to back down, local Acadian officials were apologetic and promised Nicholson that New Englanders could continue to fish so long as they refrained from landing to dry their catch. The new Acadian governor, Louis Alexandre des Friches de Meneval, made a show of warning off English trading vessels—an action which, he admitted, "angered the inhabitants"—but he quietly continued the practice of his predecessors, allowing New England traders to do business in the colony, and even striking deals himself with John Nelson. For the moment local interests trumped imperial ones.[15]

The next year a more serious challenge to neutrality came from Governor Andros himself. Many in New England believed that clandestine trade with the French strengthened the warmaking ability of the native tribes. For several years Andros—commissioned by the English king to strengthen royal authority in New England—had maintained a small garrison and naval force at Pemaquid on the Maine coast, where he attempted to intercept New England traders on their way to Saint-Castin's outpost at Pentagouet, some fifty nautical miles to the northeast. Finding those efforts ineffective, Andros decided on a bolder strategy. In late 1688 he sailed a royal English frigate into Penobscot Bay and summoned Saint-Castin to parlay, declaring that the Frenchman would be allowed to maintain his post only if he swore an oath of allegiance to the English king. Several years earlier Saint-Castin had been abducted by a group of New Englanders who attempted to coerce him into declaring for their side by using a burning fuse on his fingers. It was not something the Frenchman was likely to forget, and he fled into the woods with his family and his men. Andros then ordered the plunder and destruction of his post. According to merchant John Nelson, writing a decade later, this raid marked the beginning of the war "with which we have ever since been infested." Although there were deeper causes for the conflict than Nelson's assessment admitted, the English raid at Penobscot Bay opened a generation of warfare that would transform the lives of the Acadians.[16]

Governor Andros's attack on Pentagouet came at a time of increasing tensions between New Englanders and the native Abenaki people of Maine. The Abenakis depended upon English trade, but complained bitterly about the abuses of English traders—price-gouging, cheating, and especially the traffic in alcohol, which ravaged their communities. Even more upsetting was the movement of English settlers into their homeland. Like the Acadians, New Englanders were "hiving off" from their original settlement communities on Massachusetts Bay, founding new towns in the western interior of the province and along the coast of Maine. But unlike the Acadians, New Englanders clashed violently with native people. Their experience with the Abenakis makes a telling contrast with the accommodation that was simultaneously taking place between Acadian inhabitants and native Míkmaq in l'Acadie.

The English colonization of what became known as the province of Maine began under the auspices of proprietors with grants issued by the Council for New England, a group of British officials charged with managing the region. By the mid-seventeenth century approximately a thousand settlers were living in half a dozen towns on the Maine coast, but none had negotiated the purchase of their lands from the Abenakis, whose homeland it was. In the 1650s, Massachusetts asserted jurisdiction over the Maine settlements and began issuing patents and titles to the settlers, but again, no one bothered to obtain permission. The Abenakis "were greatly enraged," wrote the Puritan minister and New England historian Cotton Mather, "threatening the Surveyor to knock him on the Head if he came to lay out any Lands there." The Abenakis were culturally quite similar to the Míkmaq and were no more prone to violence. They would likely have been quite content to live in peaceful neutrality with the English, whose trade goods they much preferred to those of the French. But they demanded an acknowledgment of their sovereign rights. "We are the owners of this country, and it is wide and full of Indians, and we can drive you out," a group of Abenaki leaders wrote the governor of Massachusetts, "but our desire is to be quiet." Massachusetts authorities, however, ignored their complaints and the settlers treated them with utter contempt.[17]

The breaking point came, as it so often did, with an act of despicable brutality. In 1675, two New England seamen in a dory on the Saco River overtook the canoe of a native woman, the wife of Squando, sachem of the Abenakis of Saco, a leader who long had counseled patience and negotiation with the English. In the words of a contemporary account, the seamen conducted themselves in a "rude and indiscreet" manner with the woman, and when she attempted to avoid their advances they began rocking her canoe, finally overturning it and sending her infant son into the river. As the men watched impassively, the desperate mother dove to the bottom and rescued her baby, but several days later he died. When asked to explain their conduct, the seamen declared they merely had been trying "to see if young Indians could swim naturally like animals of the brute creation, as some had reported." With the murder of his son, Squando became an implacable foe of the English, leading his fellow Abenakis into war. They burned Saco and other towns along the coast, and settlers fled back to Massachusetts Bay in panic. These attacks coincided with King Philip's War (1675–77) in southern New England, a conflict that cost the lives of hundreds of colonists and natives. In Massachusetts, Connecticut, and Rhode Island the tribes were eventually crushed, but in New Hampshire and Maine, where colonial settlement was scattered, the Abenakis prevailed, and in 1678 Massachusetts found it necessary to sign a treaty acknowledging Abenaki sovereignty over their homeland in order to obtain peace.[18]

After the war the English returned to their settlements and rebuilt their homes, and soon the Abenakis once again felt the pressure of encroachment. Their leaders complained that the English were destroying their livelihood by clearing the forests and spoiling their hunting, by spreading nets across the mouths of rivers and preventing their fishing, by grazing cattle on native fields and ruining their crops. In the summer of 1688 a group of outraged young Abenaki men slaughtered several head of cattle at Casco Bay. A subsequent confrontation between settlers and natives ended with casualties on both sides, and when local English authorities seized twenty native men, women, and children and packed them off to Boston in chains, the Abenakis retaliated by capturing a similar number of settlers.[19]

Governor Andros dramatically intervened in this conflict with his sack of Saint-Castin's post at Pentagouet. His assault not only took the conflict deeper into Abenaki territory but transformed it from a local to an imperial struggle. Supplied by an outraged Saint-Castin, and accompanied by abbé Louis-Perry Thury, their Catholic missionary, in 1689 the Abenakis hit the English settlements along the coast, razing the post at Pemaquid and in June attacking the town of Dover, upriver from Portsmouth, killing twenty-three settlers and taking twenty-nine captives. This raid raised the alarm throughout

New England, in part because of widely circulated reports of Abenaki atrocities. During the fighting a number of Abenakis had taken the opportunity to settle scores with Richard Waldron, Dover's most prominent resident. Waldron had begun his career as a frontier trader, developing a reputation as a notorious cheat, a man who reportedly used his finger to tip the scales against the Abenakis when he weighed their pelts or supplies. Such behavior was expected and tolerated. The intense hatred of Waldron by the Abenakis, however, dated from 1676, when with promises of pacific surrender he lured to his post a large group of refugees from southern New England, then seized and sold them into slavery in the West Indies. When Abenaki fighters burst into his garrison house at Dover, Waldron put up a fierce fight with his broadsword; but stunned by a blow from a hatchet, he was bound into an armchair and methodically tortured, his cheating fingers cut off one by one before he was finally dispatched.[20]

Stories such as this created an indelible image of the native as terrorist. Indeed, to offset the tremendous odds against them, homeland defenders frequently resorted to the tactics of terror—painting their bodies and masking their faces for battle, operating by stealth and ambush, and employing torture in ways, as one historian puts it, that "would have taxed the sadistic ingenuity of Europe's most ruthless despots." Captives were bound to the stake and skinned alive, or covered with honey that they might be stung to death by wasps and other venomous insects. In the aftermath of battle, native fighters took care to arrange the bodies of their victims in grotesque positions intended to test the nerve of the most battle-hardened veterans. Yet New Englanders required little instruction in brutal warfare. In the wars of the seventeenth century, colonial militia slaughtered native people indiscriminately, attacking combatants and noncombatants alike with guns, swords, and dogs, burning them in their homes, and enslaving the survivors. "Horrified at being unable to prevent the butchering of their people," writes another historian, colonists "exploded in spasms of uncontrolled violence when they finally did manage to get their devilish tormentors into their power."[21]

Getting the Abenakis into their power—that was precisely the problem. Native combatants proved an elusive enemy, and English colonial militia could not match their woodland skills. So New Englanders transferred their fury to an easier target. Ignoring the legitimate complaints of native people, they interpreted the struggle in traditional anti-French and anti-Catholic terms. The Abenakis, they argued, were under the control of the French. Saint-Castin had supplied them and it was reported that abbé Thury directed their raids and even celebrated mass in the midst of the slaughter. The natives and the French blurred into a common enemy, one Cotton Mather stigmatized as "Half Indianized French and Half Frenchified Indians." But it was the French, he wrote, who were the "chief Source of New-England's Miseries."[22]

Developments in Europe encouraged this imperial perspective on local events. In the fall of 1688 Louis XIV's troops invaded the Rhineland, precipitating a war with most of the rest of Europe. To prevent James II, a Catholic, from allying with France, the English Parliament invited the Protestant Dutch prince William of Orange—son-in-law of James by virtue of his marriage to Mary Stuart, the king's daughter—to invade England with a sizable army. James fled the country; Parliament proclaimed William and Mary rulers over England and Scotland; and the new monarchs declared war against France. Although the events along the Maine coast had nothing whatsoever to do with events in Europe, to New Englanders, the disaster at Dover and the loss of Pemaquid were now seen as the opening shots of this imperial conflict. What had been "Castin's War" became "King William's War." Tossing aside any thought of New World neutrality in Old World disputes, in late 1689 the Massachusetts Assembly or House of Representatives, the popularly elected legislature, resolved to raise a force "for the Reduceing of the French on the Coast of Acadia or elsewhere to the obedience of their

Majesties of Great Britain." At Port Royal there were incendiary priests, Míkmaw fighters, French garrison soldiers, and the Acadian farmers who supplied them all with provisions. What did it matter that not a single Míkmaw had been involved in the Abenaki raids, or that not a single inhabitant of Port Royal had anything to do with events on the Maine coast?[23]

The colonial officers of New France held a similarly imperial view of the conflict. In the fall of 1689, Governor Frontenac returned from a sojourn in France with plans for an offensive against the English colonies, including a plan for the conquest of New York. As an initial step he offered active encouragement to the Abenakis in their struggle with the English. For the French too, the Treaty of Neutrality was a dead letter. When Canada was hit by a devastating Iroquois attack, Frontenac reacted in much the same way as New Englanders had. Early in 1690 he struck back with joint attacks by Canadien militia and native warriors, under the command of French officers, on the village of Schenectady in New York, Salmon Falls in New Hampshire, and Falmouth on Casco Bay in Maine. More than two hundred colonists were killed or captured. New Englanders were no more connected with the Iroquois campaign than Acadian inhabitants had been with the raids of the Abenakis, but local conflicts were folded into the general state of warfare between France and England. King William's War marked an important turning point in North American history, raising both the stakes and the risks. Semi-autonomous settlements and colonies were now to be incorporated into colonial empires.[24]

In the spring of 1690 Massachusetts impressed a force of several hundred men for an expedition against Port Royal. John Nelson was named to the committee planning the mission. According to one of his associates, there was widespread expectation in Boston that the Massachusetts Governor's Council—the group of magistrates that advised the governor, and acted with both judicial and executive authority—would name Nelson "generalissimo," since he was widely acknowledged to be "the fittest person for the enterprise" because of his experience in l'Acadie. It was not to be. Councilors from outside the city objected that Nelson "was a Merchant and not to be trusted." They suspected that he preferred trading to fighting. Instead, the council appointed Sir William Phips from frontier Maine, a veteran of the brutal fighting there, who had made his fortune exploring for sunken treasure in the Bahamas, an accomplishment for which he had been knighted. Nelson might have pursued a course of accommodation with the Acadian inhabitants, but Phips could be expected to deal with them in a harsher manner. In a last-minute gesture of inclusion, the council offered Nelson the position of second in command, but he rejected it "with scorn and contempt."[25]

On 9 May 1690, Phips's fleet departed Boston Harbor—seven vessels bristling with 64 cannon and carrying 736 men and boys, far outnumbering the Acadian population of Port Royal. Ten days later the fleet passed through the narrow gut to Port Royal Basin. "What I have always had reason to fear as long as I have been here has finally taken place," Governor Meneval wrote. Attacks on New England, he had predicted, would be followed by massive retaliation against his nearly defenseless colony. His views reflected those of the inhabitants, who expressed the fear that the French use of native fighters against the English colonists would result in their own destruction. With only seventy-some men in his garrison, insignificant and decrepit fortifications, and tepid support from the inhabitants, Meneval was powerless to put up an adequate defense. He fired a cannon round, a signal for the inhabitants' militia to assemble at Fort Royal, but few men responded, most taking flight with their families into the woods, carrying whatever possessions they could.[26]

Phips anchored his vessels at the mouth of rivière Dauphin and sent a sloop up the current to the fort with a summons demanding Meneval's surrender "at discretion"—that is, without terms. Meneval appointed parish priest Louis Petit as his representative, and it took Petit only half an hour to negotiate a capitulation. Meneval described the terms as "pretty advantageous." The Acadian inhabitants were to remain secure in their persons and possessions, free to exercise their religion, with their church neither plundered nor burned. The garrison was to be granted the "honors of war," the right to march out unmolested with their arms and baggage, drums beating and colors flying, then transported by vessel to Québec or France. This ritual, part of the European etiquette of siege and surrender, had been devised to regulate the conduct of armies and prevent the slaughter or enslavement of surrendering troops. Sir William declined to commit the agreement to writing, however, saying that "his word was worth more than all the writing in the world," and abbé Petit advised Meneval not to insist on a signed document from Phips, "for fear of irritating him."[27]

Phips, however, had no intention of honoring the agreement. He was gracious in his first meeting with Meneval, but once his men took possession of Fort Royal, his manner changed dramatically. Using angry and abusive language he demanded Meneval's sword, ordered the French garrison disarmed, and imprisoned the French troops. Phips was infamous in Massachusetts for his vulgar tongue and violent temper, which many attributed to his frontier upbringing. He loathed upper-class pretense, and the aristocratic bearing of the French governor presented a tempting target. The New Englanders, Meneval wrote from confinement, were "very angry people, from whom I have little expectation of either mercy or good treatment." Once the French were locked up, Phips unleashed his men. They burned the fort, looted the warehouses, and as Meneval reported, "made a point particularly to pull down and destroy the church and all emblems of Religion." The official chronicler of Phips's expedition boasted of the desecration: "We cut down the cross, rifled the Church, [and] pull'd down the High-Altar, breaking their Images." As the church burned, the Puritan chaplain preached a sermon of thanksgiving.[28]

Over several days the New Englanders methodically slaughtered livestock, burned barns, and ransacked the homes of inhabitants, digging in their gardens for buried treasure—for it was common practice among the Acadians to bury for safekeeping whatever specie they accumulated. An employee of the Compagnie d'Acadie had buried the cashbox, and Phips had him tortured until he revealed its location. The company later estimated its losses at 50,000 *écus* (approximately 300,000 *livres*), surely an exaggeration, perhaps for insurance purposes. The New Englanders also confiscated some 4,000 *livres* from the colonial treasury. It turned out there were additional funds, several thousand *livres* stashed in a pot, buried in the corner of a garden, but Mathieu des Goutin, the provincial treasurer, had cooked the books, and was able to convince the barely literate Phips that he got the whole of it. Phips himself seized Meneval's personal possessions, for safekeeping, he said, although he refused to return them until forced to do so months later by a New England court. The outraged French governor tallied up his losses: "Two dressing gowns of linen, trimmed with lace. A gray vest, entirely new. Three new wigs. Three pair of new shoes. Four pair of silk garters. Twelve cravats of lace. Four nightcaps, with lace edgings. Twelve pair of new socks. Six silver spoons. Six silver forks. Two large silver tumblers." And approximately 1,000 *livres* of his own money. Phips and the New England volunteers carried away everything that wasn't nailed down; yet in the end the expedition reportedly cost Massachusetts £3,000 or £4,000 more than the value of the plunder.[29]

As the looting continued, Phips summoned the inhabitants hiding in the woods "forthwith to come in, and subject yourselves to the Crown of England . . . swearing allegiance to their Majesties, William and Mary of England, Scotland, France and Ireland, King and Queen." Otherwise, he declared, "you must expect no other Quarter, than what the Law of Arms will allow you." Fearing slaughter, the frightened residents cautiously returned to their homes. On 24 May, Phips administered the oath of allegiance to the adult males. The English chronicle of the event recorded their demonstrations of "great Joy" and their "great Acclamations and Rejoicings," while the French account claimed that they obliged only after Phips threatened to burn their houses and make them all "prisoners of war." Summoned by military messenger, representatives arrived from Chignecto and Minas, and they too took the oath of allegiance to the English monarchs.[30]

Then, in a return to the practice that prevailed during the period of English control from 1654 to 1670, Phips appointed an inhabitants' council, approving six prominent individuals chosen by the inhabitants themselves—seigneur Alexandre Le Borgne de Bélisle; treasurer and provincial judge Mathieu des Goutin; king's attorney Pierre Dubreuil; and elderly inhabitants René Landry and Daniel Leblanc, both of whom had resided at Port Royal for nearly half a century. As president of the council, Phips picked Charles Chevalier dit La Tourasse, first sergeant of the French garrison. "Remember the oath which you have taken before God, of allegiance and fidelity to the Crown of England," Phips instructed the councilors, "lest you draw down upon yourself the wrath of the King by your unfaithfulness." He then ordered John Alden, one of his captains, to sail "to all places on the Coast of Nova-Scotia, to parley with the French and Indians, and cause them to submit and subject themselves to the Crown of England, and to swear Allegiance; and upon refusal hereof, to burn, kill, and destroy them." And with those bellicose instructions, Phips reembarked his men and sailed his fleet back to Boston, taking as hostages the officers and men of the French garrison, the Catholic priests from Port Royal and Beaubassin, and a poorly clad Governor Meneval. He took a personal hostage as well, the young daughter of Saint-Castin, kidnapped from the chapel school at Port Royal. Established procedure was to treat elite hostages with a good deal of respect, as guests under house arrest. But in Boston Phips put the Saint-Castin girl to work as a servant in his household, perhaps another not so subtle sign of his contempt for aristocratic trappings.[31]

In Boston it was generally thought that the city of Québec could be had "upon as easy termes" as Port Royal, in the words of one New Englander. "The English boast they will reduce Québec as easily as they have taken Port Royal," a spy informed Frontenac. Massachusetts sent Phips to Canada with another flotilla of 34 vessels and 2,300 men. Sailing up the St. Lawrence, he reached the bluffs of Québec in August 1690, and demanded Frontenac's surrender much as he had demanded Meneval's. But denouncing Phips as the "man who did not honor the capitulation he had agreed upon with the governor of Port Royal," Frontenac sent back a defiant answer: "I have no reply to make to your general except from the mouths of my cannons." Unlike Port Royal, Québec was impressively fortified. Phips spent several weeks ineffectively shelling the fortress city from his vessels, and when his troops were struck by an epidemic of smallpox, he retreated back to Boston, with losses of more than four hundred men.[32]

Despite the disaster at Québec, Massachusetts continued to assert its claim to l'Acadie by right of conquest. In 1691 Phips was in London, where he persuaded the king and queen's ministers that a windfall trade in furs, naval stores, and agricultural surpluses would result from the extension of the colony's jurisdiction to the eastward. The authorities rewarded Phips by naming him governor of Massachusetts and issuing a new royal charter that included l'Acadie within the colony's territorial domain. Yet aside from sending an occasional armed vessel to Port Royal, Massachusetts did little to enforce its sovereignty. For the most part, the Acadian inhabitants were left to their own devices, and a system of live and let live characterized relations for the next several years. As John Nelson noted, "the inhabitants of Port Royal have accepted as magistrates such as the Government of Boston from time to time placed over them," while for their part the New Englanders had chosen "men who were most agreeable to the French inhabitants."[33]

The illegal intercolonial trade quickly resumed. Captain John Alden of Plymouth, charged with enforcing Phips's demands, was a man who had plied Acadian waters for nearly thirty years, doing business with inhabitants and natives alike. There was little chance he would "burn, kill, and destroy" his best customers. He made four voyages around Baie Française in the year after the conquest, but his real purpose was trade. A New Englander redeemed from captivity among the Abenakis in 1691 told authorities that Alden had paid a visit to the coastal camp of his captives, but there had been no talk of submission and subjection, only commerce. Alden brought the Abenakis "food and ammunition, without which they would have perished," the man testified, and he accused Alden of refusing to pay his ransom, quoting the old trader as declaring that "he came to trade, not to redeem captives." For New Englanders caught up in the Abenaki raids, this kind of fraternization was intolerable. During the 1692 witchcraft crisis in Salem, a town crowded with refugees from Maine, a young woman pointed an accusing finger at John Alden. "There stands Alden," she told investigators. "He sells powder and shot to the Indians and French, and lies with the Indian squaws, and has Indian papooses." Commercial intercourse was thus conflated with sexual. Alden was imprisoned on suspicion of witchcraft, but he succeeded in breaking out of jail and avoiding the hangman's noose.[34]

The French response to Phips's conquest was equally conflicted, for while they continued to claim sovereignty over Port Royal, in practice they left the inhabitants free to act as they chose. With Meneval's incarceration in Boston, regional authority fell upon Joseph Robineau de Villebon, native of Canada, officer in the French *troupes de la marine* (regulars recruited in France and led by Canadien officers), and commandant of the garrison at Port Royal. Villebon had been returning from a visit to France when Phips attacked, and when he arrived he found Fort Royal a smoking ruin. The frightened inhabitants begged him to establish a new garrison, one adequately armed and commanded by officers who could organize the local militia and Míkmaq fighters into an effective force for home defense. Were that done, they would do all they could to assist in holding the colony for France; but without support, they would be vulnerable to further attacks. Indeed, within weeks Port Royal was raided again, by English and Dutch freebooters from New York.

Finding the settlement stripped of plunder, they grew so enraged that they hanged two men, torching the house of one of them while his wife and children hid inside.[35]

By that time, however, Villebon had gone, relocating the seat of French authority, such as it was, across Baie Française to an outpost fifty miles up rivière Saint-Jean. From this protected location he used whatever resources he could muster to wage war on New England by proxy, supporting privateer attacks on fishing and shipping vessels, and coordinating ruinous raids on frontier settlements by combined forces of Abenaki, Maliseet, and Míkmaw fighters. Villebon had no troops of his own, and since he could offer no protection to the Acadians, he had no choice but to accede to their request that local authority at Port Royal remain in the hands of the inhabitants' council in order that the New Englanders be given "no ground for suspicion." He ordered the president of the council, La Tourasse, to "take no steps save those which I should prescribe." But that was mere pretense, and Villebon knew it.[36]

In Villebon's phrase, the Acadian inhabitants found themselves "between the hammer and the anvil." Perilous as their situation was, however, it was not unfamiliar, and their leaders proved adept at playing both ends against the middle. Visits by English and French armed vessels to Port Royal in the early fall of 1691 gave them the opportunity to demonstrate their skill. The New Englanders arrived first, in late August, in an armed sloop captained by John Alden. On board was John Nelson with a lading of trade goods and Colonel Edward Tyng of Maine commanding a company of twenty armed men. In a deal with the General Court, Nelson and a group of Massachusetts merchants had agreed to establish a garrison at Port Royal at their own expense in exchange for a monopoly of the Acadian trade. Starved for English commodities, the inhabitants welcomed Nelson enthusiastically, and soon he accumulated a valuable cargo of furs. But they warned Tyng they could offer no guarantees for his safety, that he would be at the mercy of the Míkmaq. The colonel took the hint, and when Alden's sloop departed Port Royal a few days later to do some more trading at other Acadian communities, Tyng and his men were on board.[37]

Soon after the New Englanders departed Villebon arrived in an impressive French frigate of 30 guns and 150 men, sent by the governor of New France to patrol Baie Française. Finding the English colors flying above the ruined fort, the frigate's commander, Simon-Pierre Denys de Bonaventure, a member of the influential Denys family of Trois-Rivières, tore down the flag, hoisted the fleur-de-lis, and reprimanded the councilors for their display of disloyalty to their king. The inhabitants listened respectfully, and according to Villebon seemed "very well disposed" to French authority, but they appealed for an appreciation of their position. They would have "reason to repent" any excessive show of attachment to the mother country because they were at the mercy of the New Englanders. The inhabitants proved themselves very good at telling people precisely what they did *not* want to hear. Bonaventure and Villebon left Port Royal and sailed west for rivière Saint-Jean, where they found Alden and Nelson trading and succeeded in capturing them. Villebon sent Alden and the crew back to Boston to arrange a swap of prisoners—the hostages Phips had taken from Port Royal the year before in exchange for Tyng and Nelson.[38]

John Nelson was admired and respected by the French. In pointed contrast to Sir William's boorish treatment of Meneval, Nelson had invited the Acadian govenor to stay in his Boston home, supported his claim for the return of the personal possessions stolen by Phips, and helped arrange his safe passage to France. Nelson made no secret of his contempt for Phips's conduct, referring to the capture of Port Royal as "that Late foolish and unhappie Expedition." Nelson's political posture was summarized in the report of his captivity sent by Governor Frontenac of New France to Versailles. "Possessing influence in Boston, where his friends have always been opposed to those of Sir William Phips," Nelson "has ever distinguished himself by kind treatment of the French, as well in peace as during the War." But Nelson's friends were not in power at Boston. His enemy William Phips was, and Nelson's captivity conveniently eliminated one of the governor's most powerful and hated rivals. Phips refused to release any of the remaining French hostages, a decision Nelson later described as a "malicious contrivance" designed to keep him imprisoned. Nelson and Tyng were conveyed first to Québec, then to France, where they suffered what Nelson described as "hard usage." Tyng "dyed miserably" in French custody; Nelson was locked up in a filthy cell for more than two years before finally being moved to better accommodations at the Bastille in Paris.[39]

Nelson's absence provided Phips with the opportunity to pursue his own economic ventures to the eastward. During Phips's tenure as governor from 1691 to 1695, there was a substantial increase in the trade with l'Acadie. In addition to New England traders such as John Alden, a number of Acadian merchants traded directly with Boston. Jacques Bourgeois of Beaubassin and Louis Allain of Port Royal sent lumber and flour in their own sloops, and brought back trade goods to sell to their Acadian customers. Charles de Saint-Etienne de La Tour frequently procured supplies for his trading post at Cape Sable, clearing Boston Harbor with cargoes that included fabric and thread, iron tools, brass and copper kettles, vermilion, soap, tobacco, and rum. Acadian Abraham Boudrot of Port Royal formed a trading partnership with Belgian-born Huguenot André Faneuil of Boston. Because l'Acadie was now under the jurisdiction of Massachusetts, and men such as Boudrot had taken the oath of allegiance to the English monarchs, Phips argued that this trade was no longer illegal. Not everyone agreed. When the Boston customs collector attempted to impound a cargo of furs that Boudrot brought to port in 1693, Phips rushed to their defense. Those men were "as good or better English men than the Collector is," he declared, and he challenged the official to "seize them if he dare, and if he doth, I will break his head."[40]

Phips claimed that through Boudrot and others he received

important intelligence on French operations in Baie Française. Unbeknownst to Phips, however, Boudrot had proposed to commandant Villebon that if allowed to carry on his business in New England, he would bring back reliable intelligence. Boudrot had "made a pretence of attaching himself to William Phips," Villebon wrote to his superiors. In fact, Boudrot seems to have provided the French with important information about the state of English defenses. Villebon thus managed to find certain advantages in the illegal intercolonial commerce he was powerless to prevent.[41]

The Acadians consistently acted in what they considered their own best interest, exploiting their location at the intersection of empires. A confrontation with New Englanders in 1692 gave them the opportunity to put their own understanding of their position on the record. In the late spring of that year Governor Phips ordered Captain Richard Short to sail north with a warship of 36 guns and 150 men to destroy Villebon's outpost on rivière Saint-Jean. But low tides and uncooperative winds made ascent of the river impossible, so Short turned eastward and crossed the bay to Port Royal. Assembling the inhabitants' council, he announced the intention of his province to rebuild the fort and establish a garrison there, and demanded that the councilors pledge themselves to assist in resisting an attack by the French or their native allies. According to council president La Tourasse, who reported to Villebon, the members told Short that they could make no such commitment, that they "would be the first victims if the Indians came to regard them as friends of the English." They welcomed his protection, they declared, but in the struggle between the English and the French, "*they themselves would remain neutral.*"[42]

When in 1654 the New Englanders had insisted on an oath, the inhabitants had sworn not to bear arms against the English. That was what they promised now. Neutrality was an ideal for them, and it would remain so throughout their history, proving a constant source of tension between the Acadians and their colonial rulers, whether English or French. Villebon considered the report good news, but he knew it would displease his superiors, who expected absolute Acadian loyalty and unambiguous assistance. Neutrality was not part of their imperial plan. But, Villebon advised Versailles, it was something France would be required to tolerate. "Without these compromises, it would be impossible to exist in this country."[43]

CHAPTER 4

Nos Amis les Ennemis
The English Conquest, 1696–1710

NEUTRALITY SERVED THE ACADIAN inhabitants well for most of King William's War. But repeated attacks by the combined force of native warriors and Canadien militia eventually drove New England to take severe measures that threatened Acadian life and property. In 1696, the Massachusetts General Court criminalized the intercolonial trade—declaring it "very evident that the French and Indian Enemy are relieved and succoured by the supplyes transmitted from hence unto Port Royal and other places"—and offered a bounty of £50 on the scalps of native enemies. The practice of scalping originated in the customs of native warfare, but it was Europeans who converted it into a ghastly commerce by setting scalp bounties. Governor-General Frontenac of New France established the first in 1688, but the 1696 Massachusetts bounty was the largest offered to that date. It attracted Major Benjamin Church of Rhode Island, famous as the man who had led New England to victory in King Philip's War. Church requested and received authorization from

Massachusetts lieutenant-governor William Stoughton (Governor Phips had died prematurely during a trip to London in 1695) to recruit four hundred fightingmen, including fifty Iroquois warriors, and sail to l'Acadie in pursuit of the enemy.[1]

Church and his men arrived at Beaubassin in the early daylight of 20 September 1696, but had to await the afternoon high tide before they could land, giving the inhabitants plenty of time to flee into the wood with their goods, some taking the opportunity of firing a few potshots in the direction of Church's vessels. By the time Church led the New Englanders up the trail from the landing toward the Acadian settlement, his men were spoiling for a fight. Ahead they spied a lone figure coming toward them, a musket in one hand and a paper in the other. Thinking it might be a trick, Church ordered his men to keep on, and the frightened Acadian turned to run. Halt or be shot, Church shouted, and with that the man stopped, laid down his musket, and waited as Church's men came up. He identified himself as Germain Bourgeois, oldest son of Jacques Bourgeois, Beaubassin's founder, and he handed Church the paper which he described as "a treaty of neutrality," attesting to the oath of fidelity the inhabitants had sworn to the English monarchs but apparently containing as well a declaration of their intention to remain neutral. Church glanced at the document. "In that case the people had nothing to fear," he declared.[2]

Bourgeois invited the major into his home to meet his parents and take refreshment. But as Church sat drinking, his lieutenants were outside surpervising the slaughter of livestock, the plunder of homes, the burning of houses and barns. After a short time Church joined them and personally ordered the torching of the chapel of Notre-Dame-du-Bon-Secours. The men "carried off and pillaged all the moveables belonging to several settlers," Commandant Joseph Robineau de Villebon reported, "burning the houses of those that had fled into the woods, and killing all their cattle that they could catch, although a treaty of Neutrality had been signed between the poor people and the Governors of Boston."[3]

Where were the Míkmaq? Church demanded. According to the major's account, Bourgeois "shaked his head and said he durst not tell, for if he did they would take an opportunity and kill him and his." Frustrated in his hunt for scalps, Church made it clear that he held the inhabitants themselves accountable for Míkmaw attacks. Doubtless they were "troubled to see their cattle, sheep, hogs and dogs lying dead about their houses, chopped and hacked with hatchets," he told the assembled inhabitants. But this was "nothing to what our poor English, in our frontier towns, were forced to look upon. For men, women and children were chopped and hacked so, and left half dead, with all their scalps taken off." The Acadian inhabitants may not have committed those crimes, but their communities were "the root from whence all the branches came that hurt us." If the raids on New England continued, Church vowed, he would return to "kill, scalp, and carry away every French person." Before leaving Beaubassin, Church exacted a new oath of allegiance from the inhabitants.[4]

After Church's raid the Acadians were certainly on their guard. According to the local agent of the Compagnie d'Acadie, with the approach of every English sail the inhabitants were torn between the fear "that they would be subjected to similar treatment," and the hope that the vessel might be a Boston merchantman bringing "trade-goods, sugar cane from Barbadoes, molasses, and the utensils which are needed, taking in exchange pelts and grain." Their greatest concern was not New England violence, a group of inhabitants told the new French governor of l'Acadie shortly after the war, but French regulation—not Church's threat of destruction but the company's threat of restricting trade. If French rule meant the end of free trade, they declared, "they would rather belong to the English."[5]

THE Acadians were a people of the borderlands, at the crossroads of native, French, and English cultures, with complicated loyalties and interests. Consider the brothers Charles and Pierre Melanson, among the most successful and prominent of Acadian inhabitants. As vessels entered Port Royal Basin and headed for the docks on rivière Dauphin, the Melanson hamlet was the first cluster of farms passing on the north shore. It was founded in 1663 by Charles Melanson and his bride Marie Dugas, daughter of one of the first French colonists of l'Acadie. Over the next thirty years Marie bore fourteen children, and a number of them built homes of their own near their parents. By the 1690s, the parents household had been joined by those of three married children with a total of twenty-one grandchildren. Charles Melanson, by then a man in his fifties, possessed the largest herd of cattle in the colony, and was a respected leader of the Port Royal community. His older brother Pierre held a similarly prominent position at Minas. In 1665 Pierre Melanson dit Laverdure married Marie Mius d'Entremont, daughter of the seigneur at Cape Sable, and in 1682 the couple removed to Grand Pré, settling on the banks of rivière Gaspereau, where they raised a family of eleven children. Laverdure's neighbors chose him as commander of the Minas militia, and eventually one of his daughters married Captain Louis-Simon Le Poupet de La Boularderie, son of a French aristocratic family and second in command at the Port Royal garrison.[6]

Though these were solid Acadian credentials, the Melanson brothers were in fact English immigrants and not French by birth. Both converted to Catholicism when they married, yet they had been raised Protestant by their parents—Priscilla Melanson, a woman from Yorkshire, and Pierre Melanson dit Laverdure, a Huguenot refugee who fled from La Rochelle to England in the aftermath of the siege of 1627. The couple married in 1631, raised three sons, and in midlife emigrated to l'Acadie with Governor Thomas Temple and his entourage, settling at rivière Saint-Jean. When the province was restored to France in 1670, the Melansons and their youngest son Jean removed to Boston, seeking refuge from what Priscilla feared would be "the wrath of the Countrymen Papists at John's fort and thereabouts." But her two married sons remained in l'Acadie with their wives and growing families.[7]

In 1676 the Melanson's youngest son, Jean, who in Boston took the name John Laverdure, hired onto a privateering expedition that intended using King Philip's War as cover for slave raiding along the Maine coast. Posing as an Acadian trader, Laverdure successfully lured twenty-six Abenakis aboard the vessel. The men and women were bound, transported to the Azores, and sold into bondage. Two New England traders who witnessed that auction filed a complaint with Massachusetts authorities, who arrested Laverdure and his associates when they returned to Boston. His parents borrowed £100 and posted bond to secure his release, but Laverdure jumped bail and fled the province. According to Priscilla Melanson, who filed an unsuccessful petition for remission of the forfeited bond, her elderly husband traveled to Port Royal in search of his son, "the staff of his age," but the stress and strain of the search "went to his heart" and he died, leaving her an impoverished widow. While in Port Royal, Laverdure the elder would have stayed with his son Charles Melanson, who was in close contact with his parents. Charles's daughter Marie was living with them in Boston, where grandmother Priscilla raised the girl as a Protestant. In 1682 eighteen-year-old Marie married David Basset, a Huguenot merchant of Boston who was active in the Acadian trade. Cécile, another of Charles Melanson's daughters, married the Acadian merchant Abraham Boudrot of Port Royal, and accompanied him on his business trips to Massachusetts, where she stayed with her sister and brother-in-law. Eventually the prodigal brother Jean returned to Boston under the name John Melleson, married a New England woman, and raised a family of five children.[8]

The Acadians were not the isolated people they sometimes appeared to be. Connections of commerce, kinship, and politics linked the extended Melanson family and others like them to a wider world. In 1690, Charles Melanson's son-in-law David Basset was a participant in the Phips expedition, outfitting a vessel of his own as part of the armada. Early on the first morning of the fleet's arrival at Port Royal Basin, Phips sent a company of men under a flag of truce "to Mr. Laverdure's house to command him on board." Surely this refers to Charles Melanson, whose house was in the Melanson hamlet on the north shore of the basin. Melanson came aboard "and gave a full account of the strength of Port-Royal." Perhaps Basset had arranged that meeting with his father-in-law, and perhaps the information Melanson provided bought the protection of his family and property during the subsequent episode of pillage and plunder. In his summons Phips promised that in exchange for his cooperation, Melanson and his people would have the enjoyment of their "Lives, Liberties, and Properties under the Privilege of the English Government."[9]

Through the 1690s Charles Melanson continued to operate as a secret informant for Massachusetts authorities, even as his brother Pierre Melanson dit Laverdure served as "captain of the coast" for the French. Pierre wrote reports in French detailing for Commandant Villebon of l'Acadie the comings and goings of English vessels at Minas Basin, while Charles wrote letters in English informing Governor William Stoughton of Massachusetts "how all things doth pass" at Port Royal. On 5 February 1695 he promised to send Stoughton additional information by his son-in-law Abraham Boudrot and one of his brothers-in-law (perhaps Claude Dugas, his wife's brother, who was married to the daughter of merchant Jacques Bourgeois of Beaubassin). "I darst not Right more at present," Melanson closed his letter, "for if it should be knowne it is Death for me." Such were the tangled webs the Acadians wove.[10]

At the end of 1697 word arrived in America of the Treaty of Ryswick, signed by France and England in The Hague, ending King William's War. The settlement would make the Acadians' desire to remain neutral in French-English conflicts increasingly problematic.

During the peace negotiations with the Netherlands, England, and Spain, there had been some talk of renewing the agreement on the neutrality of the American colonies. The French first broached the subject through John Nelson, whom they asked to act as an intermediary with the English. Released from custody at the Bastille in 1696, he traveled to London and met with English officials. To the members of the Board of Trade—the body advising king and Parliament on matters of colonial policy—Nelson recounted conversations he had had with representatives of the French Colonial Office "about Canada, New York and New England, in which we all agreed as to the woeful condition those countries were in, on both sides." The French had "proposed the setting on foot, if possible, the late Treaty of Neutrality for those parts." To be sure, French officials believed that colonial neutrality would serve their own interests, encouraging the autonomy of leading provinces such as New York and Massachusetts and weakening the English alliance with the Iroquois.[11]

But Nelson argued that in fact neutrality would favor England. As long as the English pursued a colonial policy based solely on "the improvement of lands," he wrote to the Board of Trade, the native people would forever remain allies of the French. Such a policy did not take advantage of England's commercial superiority. "We can and always do supply them cheaper and give them better prices for their peltry than the French." Thus zones of neutrality on the frontiers of New England and New France—areas where traders from both countries could freely compete—would inevitably result in England's advantage. As the natives became dependant on English commerce, their ties to the French would weaken, for they were "a people that love and study their own interest as much as others." To maintain the peace between the French and English colonies, Nelson suggested that French and English provincial governors exchange envoys to negotiate points of dispute and attest to the good faith of the other side. With such an arrangement not only would New England grow more prosperous but more secure.[12]

Nelson's assessment was remarkable for his deft comparison of the English and French experience in North America and particularly for his realistic understanding of native peoples as important players in the colonial drama. His proposal reflected his worldview: cosmopolitan and genteel, with a faith in the power of commerce to build bridges and make connections between peoples acting in their own self-interest. With attention to "justice and equality" in commercial relations, he wrote, "love and inclination will follow, even among Indians." But among English colonial officials there was little sympathy for these views, which were considered subversive enough to call Nelson's loyalty into question. At one point in 1697 he was arrested and held on suspicion of being a French agent. "If he be not a renegade and spy," one official wrote, "he carries a good many marks of it." The charges were baseless, and Nelson was soon released, but by that time the French had decided that colonial neutrality was not in their interest either. Reflecting the dominant imperial and military view of the world, the two sides eventually concluded an agreement that returned their North American possessions to the status quo ante, prohibiting intercolonial trade and commerce, and continuing the linkage between Old World and New World rivalries. Nelson returned to Massachusetts after an absence of nearly six years, rejoining his wife and children in Boston. He was not yet fifty years old, and would live another thirty-five years, but never again would he participate actively in the Acadian trade. His trading business, he wrote toward the end of his life, had been "crusht between the two Crownes."[13]

The inhabitants, who made clear their desire for free trade with New England, were equally unhappy with the outcome of the war. When French officials renewed their demand that inhabitants conduct all their business through the Compagnie d'Acadie, a group of prominent Port Royal residents wrote Lieutenant-Governor Stoughton of Massachusetts, imploring him "to continue his protection of them, and to allow trade with them." Villebon was outraged, and sent a letter to Stoughton himself, writing that "you must expect that I shall cause all Englishmen caught trading or fishing to be arrested." But the French inability to supply his garrison forced Villebon to reverse himself and contract directly with Massachusetts merchants for provisions. Similarly, although he protested the incursions of New England fishermen in Acadian waters, Villebon gave serious consideration to a proposal from Salem and Marblehead captains that he renew the old licensing system. He advised his superiors to approve the plan, since an expansion of fishing would employ large numbers of New England seamen who otherwise would be available for expeditions against New France. Moreover, he wrote, "during summer it would deprive the coast near Boston of its best men, and enable the Indians to attack their settlements more boldly." Clearly Villebon expected a resumption of the imperial fighting. He insisted on the importance of rebuilding and strengthening Fort Royal, and suggested that a battery of cannon be installed at the entrance to Port Royal Basin, making it impossible for enemy warships to enter.[14]

Villebon died in 1700, but the next year his successor arrived with orders to refortify Port Royal. Governor Jacques-François de Monbeton de Brouillon expected the Acadians to provide both labor and materials for the project. He found the inhabitants near the fort cooperative, but those at Minas and Chignecto defiant, even "mutinous." Those Acadians lived very comfortably, he reported, with great herds of cattle and surpluses of wheat; yet they "are so little accustomed to subjection that it seems to me that they live as true republicans, recognizing neither royal nor judicial authority." Brouillon intended to change that. For the several years of his tenure he ruled harshly, acquiring real property through intimidation and padding his own pockets with the proceeds of illegal trade. "Everyone trembles and no one dares to speak," Claude Trouvé, the resident priest at Beaubassin, wrote in a letter to authorities in France. So many complaints piled up against Brouillon, he was eventually recalled to answer them. Rebuked and fined, he was ordered back, but died on his return voyage. According to Mathieu des Goutin, when Brouillon's remains were interred at Port Royal, the inhabitants "were unable to conceal their joy at his loss."[15]

Brouillon was different in degree but not in kind from his predecessors. Jean-Chrysostome Loppinot, a Frenchman who served as notary at Port Royal for nearly thirty years and married into an Acadian family, giving him an intimate understanding of local culture, wrote of the mutual animosity that existed between inhabitants and officials. Treated contemptuously, the Acadians returned the favor by generally ignoring official ordinances and decrees: working on the Sabbath, supplying rum and brandy to the Míkmaq, and trading freely with New Englanders. French authorities railed about their disobedience, but to no effect. Baron Lahontan was so struck by the disaffection of the inhabitants and the corruption of officials that he predicted l'Acadie would not long remain in French hands. "To be plain," he wrote in 1703, "the knowledge I have of that Country, makes me foresee that the *English* will be masters of it some time or other."[16]

International hostilities resumed in 1702 when the Grand Alliance (England, Holland, Denmark, Portugal, and the German states of the League of Augsburg) declared war on France to prevent Louis XIV from placing his heir on the Spanish throne, which would have given him control not only of continental Spain but the Spanish Empire in America. What was called the War of the Spanish Succession—which the English colonists knew as Queen Anne's War, since it took place during her reign—renewed the struggle for control of the imperial borderlands in North America. Moderate Abenaki leaders at first declared their desire "to be as Neuters," but tribal factions in favor of war with the English seized the initiative. The fighting began in the northeast in August 1703 with Abenaki raids on English settlements in Maine, attacks coordinated and supported by colonial officials of New France. Anticipating swift retaliation from New England, Governor Brouillon announced plans to call the Acadian militia from outlying settlements to assist in the defense of Port Royal. This produced a minor rebellion at Minas, where the inhabitants declared their intention to remain neutral in the event of attack, and even threatened to ally themselves with the New Englanders if Brouillon called for their mobilization. The governor dispatched garrison troops under the command of Captain La Boularderie, who quashed the revolt with the assistance of his father-in-law, militia commander Pierre Melanson dit Laverdure. The governor then declared a *corvée*, ordering all the men of Minas to provide twelve days of labor on the rebuilding of Fort Royal.[17]

In light of the considerable antagonism that existed between Acadians and French officials, as well as the inhabitants' preference for doing business with the English, it should have been possible for New England to encourage Acadian neutrality during the conflict, as it had done successfully during the previous war, or perhaps even to persuade the Acadians to break with the mother country. But that opportunity was lost when, in February 1704, a party composed of Abenaki fighters and Canadien militia hit the western Massachusetts community of Deerfield, destroying much of the town and killing or capturing more than half of its 291 residents. It was the most destructive raid in memory, and New Englanders were shocked and outraged. Governor Joseph Dudley of Massachusetts declared a day of fasting and his council raised the bounty on native scalps to an astounding £100. That drew the attention of Benjamin Church, who volunteered "to put an end to those barbarities" by returning to l'Acadie and punishing the inhabitants. Massachusetts authorities knew full well that the Acadians had nothing to do with the attack on Deerfield. But it was not possible to strike at Canada, and Acadia was a vulnerable target. Dudley quickly authorized an expedition of destruction and terror. "Use all possible methods for the burning and destroying of the enemies houses and breaking the dams of their corn grounds," he instructed Church, "and make what other spoil you can upon them, and bring away the prisoners." It was hoped that Acadian prisoners might be exchanged for those taken at Deerfield.[18]

Church sailed from Boston in June 1704 in command of a fleet of 14 transports and three men-of-war manned with a total of 550 fightingmen. Their first assault, on Saint-Castin's establishment at Penobscot Bay, set the terms of engagement. "We killed and took every one," declared Church, "both French and Indians." Saint-Castin himself was absent, having gone to France in 1701 to take care of family affairs (he would die there in 1707). But Church's captives included another of Saint-Castin's daughters, a woman known to history only as "Madame Chateauneuf," who was taken prisoner to Boston with her children. Massachusetts documents record she was soon ransomed and returned home, but the fate of her sister, kidnapped by Phips in 1690, is unknown.[19]

Church took the majority of his force on to Minas, sending two of the men-of-war to Port Royal, where it was hoped they would intercept transport vessels expected from France. On 1 July 1704 the two vessels entered the basin undetected, and landing a force on the north shore they attacked the Melanson settlement without warning. Houses and crops were burned, livestock were slaughtered, and a woman and four of her children were taken hostage. Pierre Leblanc, commander of the Port Royal militia, agreed to deliver to Fort Royal a demand for the capitulation of the garrison; but Governor Brouillon refused to surrender and dispatched parties of soldiers, inhabitants' militia, and Míkmaq fighters along the banks of the river to fire at the English vessels, keeping them at bay. Church, meanwhile, had arrived at Minas, where he detailed a French-speaking lieutenant to carry the same demand to Grand Pré, giving the inhabitants only a short interval to respond. When they did not, he made an attempt to land his men, but the rapidly ebbing tide kept them from reaching the shore, and Church anchored the transports on the back side of a wooded island, where he thought they could remain concealed until morning. He did not realize the tide would lift his vessels so high that his men would be exposed to the guns of the Acadian militia.

At first light the inhabitants began firing from the woods, and several New Englanders were killed before Church was able to disembark the rest. Enraged, he ordered the destruction of the Minas settlements. The residents had abandoned their homes but their possessions remained for the New Englanders to ransack. The pillage went on for a full day. At Grand Pré the invaders found a cache of brandy and claret, and soon were roaring drunk and out of control, firing at every pig or turkey, torching houses and barns. Church eventually reestablished order and directed his men to "dig down the dams, and let the tide in, to destroy all their corn and everything that was good." Late on the evening of the second day, under cover of darkness, a large group of inhabitants attempted to repair the damage, but the New Englanders were lying in wait and ambushed them. Church's history included no count of casualties, but he boasted of seizing more than a hundred prisoners, at least a third of them women.[20]

Leaving Minas, Church burned dozens of houses and barns at Pisiquid and Cobequid before sailing for Chignecto, where eight years before he had threatened to return to "kill, scalp, and carry away every French person." The Acadian militia was waiting to receive him. As they disembarked, the New Englanders came under fire. On the ridge before them they saw the Acadian commander, possibly one of La Vallière's sons, waving his sword over his head and challenging them to come on. The inhabitants specially targeted Church, who at more than 250 pounds could scarcely be missed, but although the major was described as "ancient and unwieldy," he somehow got through unscathed, which he attributed to God's grace rather than the poor aim of his enemies. As the New Englanders advanced, the inhabitants fell back into the woods, leaving nothing of value behind. By his own account, Church once again burned and wasted the village. Many of the residents fled overland to distant missionary outposts, and a number died of exposure, including their priest Trouvé, who had been at Beaubassin since 1688, excepting the year he spent at Boston as Phips's prisoner.[21]

"The forces and vessells I sent Eastward into Nova Scotia and l'Accadia are all returned with a good booty and have destroyed and burnt all the Coast," Governor Dudley reported to the Board of

Trade. With much of the annual grain crop destroyed, the inhabitants suffered famine the following winter. Church's destruction of the Acadian settlements could not have been better calculated to turn neutrals into implacable enemies. They were "a nest of hornets provoked to fly out upon us," wrote Cotton Mather, and he worried that Church's expedition would be "a shame cast upon us that will never be forgotten." It marked a significant turn in Acadian history, for not only did Church destroy the settlements at Minas and Chignecto but also much of the former friendly feeling for *nos amis les ennemis*. Indeed, Acadians would long remember Major Benjamin Church's assault. As late as the mid-1740s, they expressed a "Dred of having their Dykes cut down and their Estates by that Means ruined by the English, [a] Practice they felt the severe effects of about forty Years ago, when their Lands were thus exposed by the New England Forces, the Remembrance of which is pretty strongly impressed on the old Inhabitants."[22]

The commerce between New England traders and Acadian inhabitants continued after 1704, but there was less tolerance for it by both sides. In 1706 an enterprising Scot named Samuel Vetch, who for several years had been involved in trading and smuggling between the English and French colonies, returned to Boston from l'Acadie with a cargo of furs. The year before, Governor Dudley had sent him to New France in hopes of arranging for the exchange of the Deerfield captives. The diplomatic mission was a failure, but at Port Royal Vetch purchased several hundred pounds of furs from the new governor, Daniel d'Auger de Subercase, paying him with his personal bills of exchange. When members of the Massachusetts General Court learned of this, Vetch and his associates were punished with stiff fines. Dudley himself, who had been involved with Vetch in several Canadien trading ventures, came under suspicion of "private treacherous correspondence with Her Majesty's enemies."

The controversy put a damper on the enthusiasm of New England merchants for intercolonial trading with the French.[23]

The traders came under even more serious assault from the French. Governor Subercase continued Villebon's policy of waging war against New England by proxy, using presents and promises to persuade the Maliseets and Míkmaq to join the Abenakis in their attacks. But he put considerably more emphasis than his predecessor on the use of French privateers to disrupt English shipping and fishing. After Subercase's arrival in 1706, attacks on English vessels greatly increased, and in 1707 French freebooters even raided a number of New England coastal towns. The Acadians, still suffering from the effects of Church's devastating raid, were enthusiastic about these strikes against the New Englanders, and the prize cargoes privateers brought into Port Royal helped the governor cope with a shortage of supplies from France. Two of the most celebrated and feared of the corsairs were Bernard-Anselme d'Abbadie de Saint-Castin, who avenged his captive sisters by taking dozens of English vessels, and Louis-Pierre Morpain, a French privateer from the West Indies, who found such rich pickings in northeastern waters that he heeded Governor Subercase's plea to remain in l'Acadie, "and even to take a wife there." Morpain and Saint-Castin married prominent Acadian sisters, the daughters of Louis d'Amours de Chauffours, seigneur and fur trader from rivière Saint-Jean, adding romantic luster to their celebrity.[24]

Subercase's privateering campaign had a devastating effect on the New England economy. English vessels operating in the Grand Banks fishery fell from 234 before the war to only 46 in 1707, and there was a similar reduction in the Atlantic carrying trade. Inhabitants celebrated freebooters like Saint-Castin and Morpain, yet their success had a drastic impact on l'Acadie, dependent as it was on New England commerce. Severe shortages developed. The colony had "no pots, no ovens, no scythes, no knives, no iron, no axes, no kettles for the Indians, and no salt for the inhabitants," complained Mathieu des Goutin. The inhabitants would not be able to cultivate their fields or harvest their crops the following year, and would be forced "to pull up grass by the roots in order to make hay." Trading with the enemy was surely a bad business, yet des Goutin admitted he would be delighted if "our enemies would bring us the necessary items in exchange for beaver pelts which we have in abundance." But the risks from French privateers were simply too great. L'Acadie became even more dependent on the captured supplies, and Boston merchants who had previously been advocates of moderation began to call for the reduction of Port Royal. In the spring of 1707, Governor Dudley, in part to quiet his critics, proposed an expedition. "I am of opinion," he wrote, "that a thousand men, with two or three ships of strength, besides transports, may drive all their country into their fort, and in a short time starve them out." The Massachusetts General Court voted support for the governor's plan "to make a General Ravage of that Country and to insult [attack] the fort at Port Royal."[25]

In late May 1707, a thousand men under the command of Colonel John March of Newbury, the most senior militia officer in the province, set sail from Boston Harbor aboard some two dozen vessels. They arrived at Port Royal on the evening of 17 June and the next morning disembarked with the tide. Subercase was taken by surprise, and according to his second in command, the garrison was "very intimidated" by the size of the enemy force, which outnumbered the French by at least four to one. But Colonel March's inept leadership quickly lost the New Englanders the advantage. Had he immediately opened a siege of Fort Royal, the garrison could have been isolated from the inhabitants. Neither March nor his officers were familiar with the techniques of siege warfare, however, and instead he landed his men in dispersed groups several miles away. The inhabitants, fearing another episode of plunder and destruction, fled to the safety of the fort. The following day, as the New Englanders collected before the fort, Governor Subercase led his troops, the Acadian militia, and a number of Míkmaw fighters in an attack which drove the invaders back, killing many. With his enemy in complete disarray, Subercase repaired to the fort and prepared for a siege that never came. After a few days of ineffectual bombardment, March decided to risk a direct assault. It was a disaster. Eighty New Englanders were killed and the rest of the men retreated back to their vessels in disorder. On 28 June, after burning all the houses in the vicinity of the fort and desecrating the Port Royal graveyard, disinterring Governor Brouillon's bones, the New Englanders reembarked and sailed for Casco Bay.[26]

While his troops rested on the Maine coast, Colonel March and his lieutenants sailed to Boston to consult with Governor Dudley. Word of their failure had preceded them, and they were greeted at the wharf by a crowd of scornful women, waving wooden swords and shouting abuse. John Winthrop, grandson of the Puritan governor, recorded the confrontation. "For shame!" the women cried. "Pull off those iron spitts which hang by your sides, for wooden ones is all the fashion now." As the commanders made their way down the narrow streets to the governor's house they were trailed by the women, who called out to housewives in the homes along the way: "Holloo neighbor, hallo. Is your piss-pot charged? So-ho, souse the cowards. Salute Port Royal!"[27]

In the face of this public clamor, Dudley demanded that another attempt be made on the French fort. The second assault was even more disastrous. Under the command of Colonel Francis Wainwright, who replaced a dispirited March, the New Englanders arrived on 20 August. They were slow in deploying, giving Subercase the opportunity to encircle their encampment with Acadians and Míkmaq. Bombardment from the fort and sniper fire from the surrounding woods kept the invaders pinned down. He was "surrounded with enemies," Wainwright wrote home. A company of his hungry troops had raided an inhabitant's garden in search of cabbages. "They were no sooner at their plunder but they were surrounded by at least one hundred French and Indians who, in a few minutes, killed every one of them, their bodies being mangled in a frightful manner."[28]

Wainwright was understandably gloomy. "It is truly astonishing to behold the miserable posture and temper that most of the army are in," he added. "Most of the forces are in a distressed state, some in body and some in mind, and the longer they are kept here on the cold ground the longer it will grow upon them. And, I fear, the further we proceed, the worse the event. God help us." On 31 August he ordered a final direct assault. Subercase came out to meet him and in fierce close-quarter fighting the New Englanders lost sixteen men killed, the French but three. The invaders retreated in confusion. Their return to Boston in early September was marked by another public protest and demands for the resignation of Colonel March, who complied and soon afterward moved his family to New Jersey in disgrace.[29]

The assistance of the Acadian and Míkmaw fighters was critical to Subercase's victory. The invaders "did not fail to commit great damage, having burnt several settlements," the governor reported, and he promised the inhabitants and natives that the king would reimburse their losses. It never happened. The French, who were doing badly in the European theater, sent no reinforcements and few provisions to l'Acadie, and by the end of the year the colony was in even more desperate straits. "It is of the utmost importance that we receive help as soon as possible," Subercase wrote to Versailles. Des Goutin appealed for supplies. "There could not be greater need here, the country is denuded of everything." But France sent no fresh troops and no supplies, the comte de Pontchartrain, minister of marine, writing Subercase that the state treasury was empty, and that "the king would abandon the colony if it continues to be such a burden." For the next three years privateers were the colony's only source of supplies.[30]

Meanwhile a series of poor harvests from 1708 to 1710 depleted grain reserves. To feed his garrison, Subercase expropriated what he could from the inhabitants of Minas, paying them with the bills of exchange Samuel Vetch had left him in 1706. (They were essentially worthless, since there was no way they could be redeemed, but the Acadians carefully stowed them away.) The greater the need at Port

Royal, the more the governor stepped up the privateer war. The more New England suffered, the louder merchants and traders cried for the "reduction" of l'Acadie. "Boston hath been a place of great trade," reported an agent of the Board of Trade, "but the war have extremely impoverished them, so that the trade is not now one-third of what it was." There was little likelihood that the New Englanders themselves had the wherewithal to take care of the problem. Without assistance from England, the whole region would be ruined. "If some effectual means be not used [in] this war to remove the French, it will be too late afterward."[31]

EARLY in 1709, the British government pledged itself to providing military and naval support for an invasion of New France. Responding to appeals from colonists and officials in New England, Queen Anne's ministers approved a plan for a military campaign proposed by Samuel Vetch, who after his humiliation by the Massachusetts General Court had gone to London, where he successfully appealed his sentence. An inveterate schemer, Vetch used his colonial connections—not only with Massachusetts governor Dudley but also with the powerful New York merchant Robert Livingston, his father-in-law—to gain access to important British officials such as Charles Spencer, Earl of Sunderland, who as secretary of state for the Southern Department was the minister most responsible for British colonial policy. His aim in doing business with the French, Vetch told Sunderland, had been "to make such observations as might render me Capable of being an Instrument of serving my native Sovereign and country."[32]

In a detailed proposal to the Board of Trade, Vetch argued that Great Britain could no longer tolerate the existence of New France. "It cannot but be wondered att by all thinking men," he wrote, "that a nation so powerful in shipping, so numerous in subjects, and other ways so wisely jealous of their trade, shou'd so tamely allow such a troublesome neighbor as the French . . . to possess a country of above 4,000 miles extent." Neither Port Royal nor Québec would present a formidable challenge to a military expedition supported by British forces and led by British officers. Vetch's outline of his "glorious enterprise for the conquest of French Canada" called for Vetch himself and his associate Francis Nicholson—who had risen from the rank of garrison officer at Boston to the governorship of both Virginia and Maryland, and was a favorite of the Board of Trade—to share joint command of the invasion, with Vetch appointed governor of l'Acadie and Canada after the conquest.[33]

Vetch did not envision *governing* the inhabitants of Acadia, but *removing* them. "The greatest part of the inhabitants being removed from thence is absolutely necessary," he argued, both "for the security of our own people in case of an attempt from France to recover it, as [well as] to make the natives come over entirely to the interest and obedience of the Crown." He suggested dispatching the Acadians "in their own small barks" to the French island of Martinique in the West Indies. In any event, they should be replaced with Protestant settlers, preferably families from his native Scotland, whom Vetch thought would be best suited to the country, being accustomed to northern climes.[34]

The strategy of removing one people and replacing them with another did not originate with Vetch, of course. In the Old World, such forced removals were a characteristic feature during the brutal religious wars of the sixteenth and seventeenth centuries. After the English conquest of Ireland under Elizabeth I, great areas were confiscated and the former owners forceably removed in favor of "planters" from England. There were also some precedents in the colonial history of the New World. After the English seized Jamaica in 1655, they expelled the small population of Spanish colonists and confiscated their property, including their slaves; and when the French conquered the British island of St. Kitts in 1666, they ordered the deportation of approximately 2,500 colonists, an event celebrated in Paris by the striking of a commemorative medallion. In 1673, England's Council for Trade and Plantations planned "to expel all the Dutch" from New Amsterdam, although once the English had taken possession, the removal of the inhabitants was judged to be too expensive. In turn, when in 1689 French colonial authorities proposed the conquest of the province of New York, they instructed Governor-General Frontenac that all Protestants, men, women, and children alike, "should be put out of the colony and sent to New England, Pennsylvania and other such quarters." That conquest never took place, but when French forces captured Newfoundland during the winter of 1696–97, they destroyed all English settlements and deported all the settlers. The idea was certainly not new. But Samuel Vetch had the distinction of being the first to propose cleansing the French inhabitants from l'Acadie and Canada. The queen's ministers would later reject his plan as impractical.[35]

Through the spring and summer of 1709, as French privateer attacks escalated in intensity, Vetch and Nicholson worked with the governors of New England and New York, raising troops and provisions for the anticipated invasion of Canada. Nicholson had visited Port Royal in 1686 on a mission for the late Governor Andros, and had not been impressed with the fortifications there. The commanders judged that with British support, Port Royal would easily fall. But British support never materialized. Word came in October that the promised naval force had been sent instead to Spanish waters, where the queen's ministers determined that more vital British interests were at stake. A group of prominent Boston residents wrote the queen, protesting that with the cancelation of the expedition, New England had been "reduced to a great distress, our enemies having their fears scattered, and being flushed with success, doe looke on us, as a people forsaken of your Majesty, and as left to be a prey to their teeth."[36]

Scaling back their ambitions, Vetch and Nicholson developed a plan for a smaller assault, directed only at "reducing that nest of privateers" at Port Royal, and Nicholson sailed to London, where he presented it to the queen's ministers. His efforts were rewarded with royal approval in March 1710. "We have resolved to fitt out an

Expedition under your Command," read Nicholson's instructions, and if Port Royal fell to his assault, "it is our pleasure that Col. Vetch have the command of it." To encourage the support of the New England colonies, Nicholson was authorized to promise the reward of lands in the conquered territory. "You shall assure them in our Name that such of them as contribute to the reduction of Port Royal, and any of the Country and Places adjacent belonging to the enemy, shall have a preference, both with regard to the soil and trade of the country." The men who conquered and removed the Acadian inhabitants would have first crack at their farms.[37]

A fleet of thirty-six vessels and two thousand men, under the command of Nicholson, with Vetch acting as adjutant general, sailed on 29 September 1710. The expedition was three times the size of March's force of 1707, a significant escalation. They arrived at noon, 5 October, and anchored before the narrow entrance to Port Royal Basin. One of the first vessels to attempt passage through the gut ran aground, drowning nineteen men, but the remainder of the fleet entered the basin without incident. Governor Subercase had been warned of their coming by his privateers. He fired off a beacon and the inhabitants fled to the safety of Fort Royal, as they had in 1707. But this time provisions were desperately short and morale bad. "I have every reason to fear an impending disaster for both the inhabitants as well as the soldiers," Subercase reported to Pontchartrain. "I shall do all that I can, but truly my lord, please understand that I cannot accomplish the impossible." His men, less than three hundred strong, were frightened and whispering among themselves. A number had already deserted, "and I am sure that if I had not caused the canoes to be removed, there would have been thirty by this time."[38]

In contrast to Colonel John March's expedition of 1707, this invasion force was under experienced command. Nicholson sent a message to Subercase demanding capitulation. Receiving no reply, he landed his men on the morning of 6 October and marched them directly toward the fort. Bombardment from Subercase's cannon drove them back to the shelter of a small ridge where, without panic or disorder, they struck their encampment. Nicholson immediately ordered entrenchments dug and batteries constructed, and the bombardment soon began, spreading terror among both inhabitants and soldiers within Fort Royal.

On 10 October, Subercase sent out an officer under a flag of truce requesting shelter for the women, who did "flatter themselves that they could hear and bear the noise of your bombs without fear, but now find themselves a little mistaken." Nicholson agreed to take under his protection those who were pregnant or caring for young children, declaring that his queen "hath not sent me hither to make War with Women." Once the women had left the fort the bombardment resumed, and the next day the leaders of the Acadians told Subercase they feared that if he held out any longer, Nicholson would refuse them quarter. Subercase resisted; but that night one of his senior staff officers was seriously wounded by an explosive shell, an event that "turned the heads" of his officers, forcing him to call a council of war. His staff quickly voted to request terms, and Subercase sent Nicholson a message: "I now write to you to tell you, Sir, that for to prevent the spilling of both English and French blood, I am ready to hold up both hands for a capitulation that will be honorable to both of us."[39]

The articles of capitulation, signed on 13 October 1710, granted the French garrison the honors of war. But three days later, after Governor Subercase delivered the keys to the fort, his 156 soldiers did not march out but dragged themselves through the gates wearing tatters and rags. Entirely without provisions, Nicholson was forced to feed them with his own stores. Later that month, 258 people—soldiers, French officials, and their dependants—boarded British transports for France, supplied by Nicholson with provisions and several kegs of beer. Subercase offered his thanks, and expressed the hope that the New Englanders would "do Justice to those French that remain behind, as has been done to those that now are going away."[40]

A small but unknown number of Acadians took advantage of

Nicholson's offer of free passage out of the province for all who wanted it by the first available transport. But the considerably larger proportion—some five hundred, according to Nicholson's estimate—chose to remain. Vetch's initial plan had called for the deportation of all the inhabitants, but last-minute instructions from British authorities directed Nicholson to "give all encouragement to such of the French inhabitants as shall come over to us, or to make a timely submission, by offering them the continuance of all such lands, estates and privileges, as they do at present possess under the French Government." Consequently, the terms of capitulation granted those Acadians living "within cannon shot of the Fort"—a district known as the *banlieu* of Fort Royal—the right to remain "on their Estates, with their Corn, Cattle and Furniture, during two years," providing they took an oath of allegiance to the British queen. The fact was, an English garrison, like the French one, would require provisions from local farmers. As long as the inhabitants of the *banlieu* behaved themselves they would meet with "all the good treatment imaginable," Nicholson and Vetch declared in a proclamation to those choosing to remain. As for the Acadians living more distant from the fort, they were considered "prisoners at discretion," and would have to wait to learn of their fate "until Her Majesty's Royal pleasure shall be more particularly notifyed with regard to them and their Country."[41]

The commanders had already written to the queen's ministers with their own recommendations. They had "reduced to your Royall obedience the fort of Port Royal, the only fortified place in all the vast territorys of l'Acadie and Nova Scotia." They had renamed the place Annapolis Royal, in the queen's honor. The crown now had access to a vast country with fertile fields, a productive fishery, forests abundant in naval stores, and a climate much better suited to "the British constitution" than either the southern colonies of North America or the West Indies. The problem that remained, however, was what to do with the Acadian inhabitants. The queen had promised the soil and trade of the colony to the New Englanders who participated in the conquest, and soon the officers and men would expect to claim their spoils. Notwithstanding the instructions to offer the inhabitants continued possession of their estates, the commanders pressed for their removal. "With all possible expedition," they wrote, it was "necessary to transport all the French from the Country," and they asked the queen's ministers to send the men and vessels necessary to do the job.[42]

In the meantime the Acadian inhabitants would be useful to the British as pawns in the larger struggle. Nicholson and Vetch made this clear in a letter carried to Québec and delivered to Governor-General Philippe de Rigaud de Vaudreuil of New France by the corsair Saint-Castin the younger, whom they had captured during the siege. "Your people in this Country l'Accadie or Nova Scotia," the British commanders wrote to Vaudreuil, were "absolutely at our discretion," and if his forces continued to raid the British colonies, "we will upon notice thereof make the same Military Execution upon the chief of your people in this Country." Moreover, if the New England captives in Canadien hands were not released without delay, the inhabitants "would be made slaves." The Acadians were about to learn how difficult it would be to maintain their ideal of peaceful neutrality under the rule of such conquerors.[43]

CHAPTER 5

The Meadows of l'Acadie

Imperial Designs and Acadian Desires, 1710–1718

The Acadian Jean Landry boarded his little sloop the *Mar* at midday on 11 November 1710, caught the outgoing tide from the landing at the mouth of rivière Gaspereau, and sailed into Minas Basin, past the looming cliffs marking the passage to Baie Française, which the English called the Bay of Fundy. According to Míkmaw storytellers, the forest on the bluff was home to the giant Gluskabe, spirit protector of the natives. It was Gluskabe who cleared the strait, allowing the tides to rush into the basin, bringing the bounty of salmon, shad, and smelt. In 1604, Champlain named this projecting escarpment *Cap Poutrincourt*—which English seamen corrupted into "Cape Porcupine"—but the Acadian inhabitants knew it as *Cap Baptiste*, in reference to the many sailors who received rough baptism in the violent whirlpools of the surging tidal current and the strong gusts at the point. Later in the century Yankee sailors would call this place "Blow-me-down," the origin of its present name, the more elegant-sounding Cape Blomidon.[1]

Landry steered his sloop through the passage, keeping close to the north shore, where the channel was deeper and the current calmer. He knew these waters well, having made the voyage to Port Royal many times, carrying grain and bringing back country produce or Boston goods. On this trip he carried a small cargo of furs and pelts, a gift for Samuel Vetch, the new British governor at Annapolis Royal, the name the conquerors insisted on using since their victory over the French the month before. A week or two earlier Acadian leaders from Minas had traveled there to pay their respects, but Vetch summarily sent them home, declaring he would deliver his demands to them at a time and place of his own choosing. The inhabitants remembered Vetch as the English trader who several years before had done business with Governor Subercase, purchasing a substantial cargo of furs and paying with personal bills of exchange that proved unredeemable during the escalating warfare between the French and British. The Acadians regularly traded with their Míkmaw kinsmen, doing a regular business in beaver pelts and other furs, and the ones Landry was carrying on board the *Mar* were intended as a peace offering to Governor Vetch from the inhabitants of Minas.[2]

Passing through the strait, Landry made for the shelter of a cove on the northeast shore, dropping anchor and preparing for early nightfall on the landward side of an island the Míkmaq called *Wochuk* (little kettle). Known to English pilots as Spencers Island, it was the traditional way station on the voyage in or out of Minas. New Englanders had been stopping here for a half century, so it was not unusual that as Landry rode at anchor he spied the approach of another vessel from the southwest. It was an armed brigantine, the *Betty*, captained by British commodore Nathaniel Blackmore, carrying sixty officers and men under the command of Major Paul Mascarene, a man who would play a critical role in the lives of the Acadian inhabitants for the next forty years.[3]

Mascarene was a young Huguenot from the South of France, the son of a Protestant father and a Catholic mother. When he was yet a babe in arms his father had been exiled to Holland for his Protestant faith, and Mascarene spent his first years with his mother at the family home in Languedoc. At the age of ten, his paternal relatives spirited the boy away to join his ailing father, who died shortly before the son's arrival. Mascarene never returned to France and never saw his mother again. Reared by Dutch relatives, he received a classic humanist education at Utrecht, and came under the influence of uncles who served as officers in the army of King William of Holland and England. In 1706, when he turned twenty-one, Mascarene crossed the Channel, became a naturalized British subject, and with the assistance of family and friends won a lieutenant's commission in the British army. Three years later he signed on as captain of a company of grenadiers in Samuel Vetch's "glorious enterprise," the proposed expedition against Canada and l'Acadie. After distinguishing himself at the siege of Fort Royal, Mascarene was brevetted to the rank of major and given the honor of taking possession of the fort and mounting its first British guard. With his French linguistic skills, he quickly became Governor Vetch's principal intermediary with the inhabitants. Mascarene would later lead the province himself, and the talent for diplomacy he developed in the years following the conquest would be the hallmark of his administration.[4]

The *Betty* drew up and Mascarene hailed Jean Landry to come aboard. "He told me that he came out of Minas that same day having on board some few furrs for a present to the Governor," Mascarene reported. The *Betty* had departed that morning as well, from Annapolis Royal, to deliver Governor Vetch's demands to the Minas inhabitants. Mascarene proposed to Landry that he "go back again into Minas with me, when he might learn what the Governor's Orders to me were, to which he gave his consent." Not that Landry had much choice in the matter. The next morning, on the rising tide, the two vessels sailed back through the passage, dropping anchor at Minas Road, the deep anchorage under the sheltering arm of Cap Baptiste, some six miles from the landing place at Grand Pré. As Landry waited, Mascarene prepared a proclamation in French addressed to the "People of Minas," calling on them to assemble and meet him at the landing the following morning. "I let them further know," he wrote, "that they need not to take an umbrage at my landing with some forces." Memories of Benjamin Church's ruinous attack of four years before were still fresh. The inhabitants had nothing to fear, Mascarene wrote, "so long as they shall do their duty." Landry was dispatched with the document.[5]

Jean Landry proved a fortuitous choice as messenger. A native-born Acadian in his mid-forties, he was raised on rivière Dauphin, but had lived his entire adult life at Minas. He married at Saint-Charles-des-Mines at Grand Pré and his seven children were baptized there. He was connected by kinship to the leading men of the community. His elder brother Antoine Landry and his uncle Pierre Thériot were co-founders of the western Minas settlements on rivière Saint-Antoine, and as one French official noted, their extended family network "embraced two-thirds of the colony." Landry's wife, Cécile Melanson, was daughter of Pierre Melanson dit Laverdure, captain of the Minas militia, and chief inhabitant of Grand Pré. So Landry's news spread quickly, and the next morning, 14 November, 150 Acadian men and boys were at the landing to cheer as Mascarene and 42 of his men disembarked and marched the mile and a half to Grand Pré village, where they were offered refreshment and several houses for their use.[6]

It was Mascarene's first visit to Grand Pré, and he took careful note of the landscape. The dwellings, he found, were not clustered, but formed "a kind of scattering town" on rising ground, looking down on the wheat fields and pastureland that stretched to the dikes holding back the waters of Minas Basin. "This place has a great Store of Cattle and other conveniences of life," Mascarene wrote, "and in the road they catch white porpoises, a kind of fish, the blubber of which turned into oil, yields a good profit." Minas was prosperous, the breadbasket of l'Acadie, and Mascarene thought it might become the granary of neighboring colonies as well.[7]

After he settled his men and posted a guard, Mascarene sat down with the assembled heads of household. They began with a request. Since most lived some distance from Grand Pré, they wished for the liberty "to choose some particular number of men amongst them who should represent the whole." The New Englanders had introduced the representative system during their previous term as controlling power in l'Acadie, and Mascarene readily agreed. The representatives the inhabitants selected suggest the importance of kinship to them. The first chosen, and leader of the delegation, was Pierre Melanson dit Laverdure, at seventy-eight an elder statesman. Raised a Huguenot in England, and speaking English as well as French, Laverdure made an excellent counterpart to Mascarene. Joining him were three younger men from his clan: his son-in-law Jean Landry, captain of the *Mar*; Landry's younger brother, Pierre; and Alexandre Bourg dit Bellehumeur, *procurateur-général* (surveyor, notary, and judge) for the Minas settlements, member of an extended family long associated with the Landrys, and another of Laverdure's sons-in-law. Three additional deputies came from the extended Bourgeois clan: Charles Bourgeois, grandson of pioneer Acadian merchant Jacques Bourgeois; his uncle, Antoine Leblanc; and his cousin, Michel Poirier. Rounding out the delegation was Mathieu Martin, the first child of French parents born in l'Acadie, seigneur of the land at the water's end at Cobequid. Collectively these men owned herds of livestock and cultivated plots of marshland approximately a third larger than the average at Minas.[8]

Mascarene sat down with them and, as he put it, went over the governor's orders "particularly and plainly." Vetch had been perfectly plain in his written instructions to Mascarene. "You are in my name to acquaint them [that] by the fate of war they are become prisoners at discretion and that both their persons and effects are absolutely at the disposal of the Conquerors. Had I not interposed to protect them, the army would have plundered, ravaged, carried awaye, destroyed all they now have hence. But as out of pitty, I have hitherto saved them." Vetch hoped to save them yet, but believed he deserved a reward for doing so. "I expect of right due to me a very good present." Vetch thought 6,000 *livres* in money or peltry an appropriate sum, in addition to a continuing monthly stipend of 20 *pistoles* (200 *livres*) "towards maintaining my Table." Pay me or face the consequences. It was blackmail, pure and simple.[9]

The deputies reacted predictably. How could they raise such a sum, the equivalent of £600? Over the previous few years they had suffered poor harvests, and what little surplus they produced Subercase had expropriated for the garrison at Port Royal. A third of their neighbors were actually beggars, "not worth a groat." But through two days of negotiations Mascarene kept up the pressure while his men drilled on the road before the church of Saint-Charles, and finally he and Laverdure struck a deal. Mascarene agreed to ask Governor Vetch to reduce the size of the "present" by half, while the inhabitants agreed to pay a portion of it immediately, the rest over time. But in order to do so, the deputies told Mascarene, they needed "some show of power" from him, something authorizing them to compel "the meaner part of the inhabitations to contribute to the best of their power." Otherwise, they feared, the whole burden would fall upon the most "public-spirited" (and well-off), "and so draw them into a total ruin and under obligation of entirely deserting the country." Mascarene drew up an order naming the deputies as "receivers," empowered to require the inhabitants to "contribute proportionally according to Each's capacity" under threat of "military execution"—that is, the ravage and destruction of their homes and property. The deputies then levied on their neighbors a tax payable in beaver pelts, a typical medium of exchange, which duly was collected and loaded onto Landry's sloop.[10]

On the morning of 19 November, after Mascarene paid 16 *livres* to cover the costs of lodging his men, the *Betty* and the *Mar* departed together for Annapolis Royal, arriving the afternoon of the following day. Vetch happily received the furs—which Mascarene valued at 500 or 600 *livres*—and readily agreed to lower the amount of the "present." But "so far as I know," Mascarene later wrote, the inhabitants of Minas "never paid the full sum." Instead, they fulfilled their obligation by sending Vetch the bills of exchange Subercase had paid them for the expropriated grain, the same bills Subercase had received for a boatload of Acadian furs, the bills issued and signed by Samuel Vetch himself. *Ruse vaut mieux que force*—cunning is worth more than strength.[11]

Some years later, in language that echoed the criticisms of the French authorities who preceded him, Paul Mascarene cautioned his superiors about the difficulties of dealing with the Minas inhabitants. "As they never had any force near them to bridle them," he wrote, they were "less tractable and subject to command" than the inhabitants of the *banlieu*, which included Port Royal village and its surrounding hamlets. "All the orders sent to them, if not suiting to their humours, are scoffed and laughed at, and they put themselves upon the footing of obeying no Government." That surely was the pose the Acadians struck with Mascarene, as they had with previous French officials; yet nothing in the negotiations of 1710 suggested that they thought they could avoid British authority. On the contrary, they skillfully used Vetch's attempt at extortion to win important concessions—the right to select their own deputies and the power to levy their own taxes—creating a limited yet significant role for themselves in the political life of the colony. It was an important indication of things to come.[12]

Governor Samuel Vetch considered the inhabitants a resource to be exploited. In his view, these Catholic French were incapable of loyalty to the British crown. The profitable development of l'Acadie required Protestant settlers, preferably from Scotland, but possibly from New England or even Europe. Vetch recommended locating them on the lands of the Acadians, who would be dispossessed and "sent hence to Martinico and Placentia"—the French colonies of Martinique in the West Indies and Plaisance in Newfoundland. But l'Acadie was not a priority of the queen's ministers, and Vetch's request was ignored. In the meantime the inhabitants remained "prisoners at discretion," subject to the whims of their conqueror.[13]

Vetch had been left in charge at Annapolis Royal in late October 1710 when Francis Nicholson departed for Boston to organize a British assault on New France, scheduled for the following summer. Vetch was to hold Fort Anne (the new name for Fort Royal) over the winter with a garrison of 450 men—250 "country troops" from New England and 200 Royal Marines, mostly Irish, organized into four independent companies. The place was in wretched condition, bombed out and half-destroyed, and Vetch set the men to work converting the chapel into a barracks, unclogging the wells and the "necessary house," and beginning the reconstruction of bridges, magazines, and earthworks. But provisions were dangerously short. "We began to be pincht," Mascarene remembered, "nothing but pease and beefe and little or no pork." There was also a serious shortage of grain for baking bread. Undernourished and underclothed, shivering through long winter nights, soldiers began to fall sick and die. Desertion became a serious problem, especially among the Irish Marines, Catholics who were seduced by the French missionary priests. Despite desperate pleas to Boston, no supply vessels were forthcoming.[14]

So Vetch resorted to the ancient methods of the conqueror, levying what he needed from the conquered. The inhabitants of Port Royal village wrote to Governor Vaudreuil of New France, complaining of "the harsh manner in which M. Weische [Vetch] treats us, keeping us like negroes, and wishing to persuade us that we are under great obligation to him for not treating us much worse"—the same line Vetch had instructed Mascarene to use at Minas. One of Vetch's officers corroborated their complaints in a letter to London in which he objected that the governor "had raised Excessive contributions and committed [an] abondance of Extortions, using the people more like slaves than anything else." According to Mascarene, the seizures "caused a great deal of clamour and noise," and he warned that the inhabitants, "like any new conquered people," had begun "to flatter themselves with the hopes of recovering what they had lost."[15]

The first sign of Acadian resistance came in January 1711. Vetch had sent the garrison's commissary, a Huguenot from Bordeaux named Peter Capon, to negotiate the purchase of grain from Pierre Leblanc, captain of the Port Royal militia and chief inhabitant of the *haute rivière*, the collection of a dozen or more hamlets along the upper strech of rivière Dauphin, which the British renamed the Annapolis River. As the two men sat talking in Leblanc's house one evening, a group of armed Acadians burst in "with their firelocks cocked," seized Capon, and dragged him out into the night. Leblanc quickly put an end to the incident by going after them and arranging for Capon's release, paying a ransom of 20 *pistoles*; but Vetch kept the pot boiling by sending an officer and fifty armed men to Saint-Laurent chapel in the *haute rivière* the following Sunday morning to arrest Father Justinien Durand, priest of the parish of Saint-Jean-Baptiste, as well as a score of leading inhabitants—merchants Louis Allain and Germain Bourgeois along with their eldest sons; wealthy inhabitant Jean Comeau; François Broussard; and Captain Pierre Leblanc himself. "This was done in reprizal of what they had done Mr. Capon," Vetch announced. There is no evidence that any of them had anything to do with planning the incident, and Leblanc had been the one to rescue Capon. But Bourgeois was well known as the man who had bravely confronted Major Benjamin Church and his invaders at Beaubassin in 1696, and Broussard was acknowledged to be a dissident, and would raise two sons who would later be prominent leaders of the resistance to British rule. The hostages would not be released, Vetch declared, until the Acadians delivered the persons responsible for Capon's abduction.[16]

The men remained in the dungeon for several weeks, and Bourgeois died soon after his release, according to his family, as the direct result of his sufferings. Durand was sent to Boston, where he languished in jail for nearly a year before being released in a prisoner exchange with French authorities in Québec. But although numerous inhabitants surely knew the identity of the men responsible, no one informed the British. A few months later, Christophe Cahouet, an Acadian merchant and officer in the Port Royal militia, told French authorities that the group who seized Capon had been led by Abraham Gaudet of Beaubassin, and included "three mulattoes from the coast" (*métis* living in Míkmaw communities), as well as two Irish deserters from the British garrison.[17]

Gaudet was not the only anti-British inhabitant, but he and other militants were a distinct minority. Most Acadians were willing to do business with the garrison. Trading with the English, after all, was a tradition of long standing. Inhabitants of the *banlieu* supplied the garrison with fresh produce and firewood, and those of the *haute rivière* sent logs downriver for the reconstruction of the fort's battlements. (The English verb "to log" was incorporated into Acadian French as *loguer*, and the spring river log drive as *le draive.*) Prudent Robichaud, nephew of merchant Abraham Boudrot, became the principal intermediary between the British and inhabitants who wished to sell their surpluses. But the War of the Spanish Succession between Great Britain and France continued, and in the spring of 1711 it resumed in l'Acadie when Bernard-Anselme d'Abbadie de Saint-Castin returned from Québec with orders to organize resistance to the British occupation. In May, small parties of Abenakis and Míkmaq threatened and harassed inhabitants who had traded with the British—the first recorded instance of violent conflict between Acadians and Míkmaq—while Father Antoine Gaulin, a Canadien-born missionary to the Abenakis, and Saint-Castin's principal agent provocateur, along with Father Félix Pain, the former chaplain of the Port Royal garrison, circulated through the countryside railing against anyone who cooperated with "heretics." The intimidation had its intended effect, and by the end of May supplies had stopped flowing to Fort Anne.[18]

Vetch responded in a typically hotheaded manner, sending a company of seventy officers and men, mostly New Englanders, to the *haute rivière*, with orders to threaten the inhabitants there "with severity." The expedition was a disaster. On 14 June 1711, at a narrowing of rivière Dauphin, near the mouth of a stream afterward called Bloody Creek, the New Englanders were ambushed by a party of several dozen Abenakis outfitted by Saint-Castin. Sixteen men were killed, nine wounded, and the rest taken prisoner by the native fighters, who themselves suffered no casualties. No local residents were involved in this attack, Mascarene later testified, but in its aftermath, fearing British retaliation, most inhabitants of the *banlieu* abandoned their homes and withdrew upriver.[19]

Over the summer of 1711 Fort Anne was besieged by a force of several hundred Abenakis, Maliseets, and Míkmaq—loosely joined as partners in what became known as the Wabanaki Confederacy—as well as an unknown number of militant anti-British Acadians. They "block'd us closely up," wrote Mascarene, and so short-handed was Vetch—the number of able-bodied men in the garrison had fallen to less than two hundred—he did not dare put defenders on the ramparts. Yet without siege guns or ammunition the besiegers were unable to make any headway, and all hope of expelling the conquerors was dashed when two hundred New England volunteers arrived in the fall. "When these were come," wrote Mascarene, "there was no keeping of the Soldiers within the walls." The siege was broken.[20]

It proved the end of the uprising. The Abenakis went home and gradually the Acadians returned to their homes in the *banlieu*. Vetch, following the orders of his superiors, circulated a proclamation offering to all who agreed to swear loyalty the peaceable enjoyment of their estates and "the privileges as the English themselves" for the duration of the war. In November a delegation of "principal inhabitants," led by merchant Prudent Robichaud, accepted the offer and signed an agreement to resume supplying the garrison. A number of British deserters were returned, and Vetch had one of them executed as an example to the rest. Within the walls of Fort Anne conditions remained miserable, especially over the winter when supplies once again fell dangerously low. The enlisted men were seldom paid, their clothing was "slight and thin," and they were so mutinous that the officers dared only issue arms to those mounting guard. Among the officers personal and partisan conflict was endemic, and eventually Vetch was recalled to London to answer complaints that he had acted intemperately and used his position for private gain. But despite these troubles, relations between the British and the Acadian inhabitants began to settle into something resembling stability.[21]

The War of the Spanish Succession, of which these conflicts were local manifestations, ended in April 1713 with the signing of the Treaty of Utrecht. The war had gone badly for the French, and they were forced to cede to Great Britain dominion over the American colonies of St. Kitts, Hudson Bay, Newfoundland, and "all *Nova Scotia or l'Acadie*, comprehended within its antient Boundaries." The subjects of Louis XIV were to be given the choice of removing themselves and their movable effects from the province within a year, or remaining on their lands as subjects of the British crown, enjoying "the free exercise of their Religion, according to the Usage of the Church of *Rome*, as far as the Laws of Great Britain do allow the same."[22]

There were considerable problems with the language of this treaty. What were the ancient boundaries of l'Acadie? For decades the French had insisted on an expansive definition, from the southern shore of the Gulf of St. Lawrence to Penobscot Bay on the Maine coast. In the negotiations with the British at Utrecht, however, they understandably argued that the colony consisted of nothing more than the Acadian peninsula itself. The two sides agreed to exclude Cape Breton and other islands in the Gulf from the cession, but other territorial questions were delegated to a joint commission. The attempt to reach agreement was unsuccessful, however, leaving the issues to be settled at another time. Also problematic was the treaty's promise of religious freedom "as far as the Laws of Great Britain do allow," for those laws seriously restricted the freedom of Catholics. The activities of Catholic priests in England were highly circumscribed, and the Test Act, passed by Parliament in 1673, required public officials to swear a "test oath" denouncing Catholicism as "superstition and idolatry." The missionary priests made certain that the inhabitants were fully aware of these restrictions, especially emphasizing the situation in Ireland, where the notorious Penal Laws had banished the Catholic hierarchy and prohibited Catholics from holding office or practicing law, as well as severely limiting their ability to freely acquire or dispose of real property. The Acadians took the British promise for what it was—hollow.[23]

In a royal letter of 23 June 1713 addressed to Francis Nicholson, Vetch's replacement as governor of Nova Scotia or l'Acadie, the queen's ministers attended to the concerns over the Acadian right to hold property. Inhabitants who were willing to "Continue our Subjects," the letter instructed, would have the right "to retain and Enjoy their said Lands and Tenements without any Lett or Molestation as fully and freely as other our Subjects do," or "to sell the same if they shall rather Chuse to remove elsewhere." As Vetch recognized, this amounted to a rejection of his plan for removing the Acadians. By these instructions the inhabitants had been restored "to the full possession of all their Lands and Estates," he complained, "tho' at the same time these lands had been promis'd by Her Majesty to the Captors in the first place, to Encourage them to reduce the same." Former promises and commitments notwithstanding, British authorities seemed committed to the Acadian inhabitants remaining in l'Acadie. This had nothing to do with protecting the interests or well-being of the inhabitants. The British simply had no intention of investing in the development of the province, and they needed the Acadians to provide support for the garrison at Annapolis Royal.[24]

Ironically, it was the French who insisted on Acadian relocation. As early as 1711, anticipating the loss of the colony, the Ministry of

Marine was developing a plan for the construction of a substantial military port and fortification, to be called Louisbourg, on the North Atlantic coast of Cape Breton Island, renamed Ile Royale. The plan called for the relocation of the Acadians to Ile Royale, where they would establish farms and provide provisions for the garrison. Governor Philippe Pastour de Costebelle had first raised this possibility with Father Antoine Gaulin at Plaisance in 1711, but he found the priest's reaction less than encouraging. "His inhabitants will not go out until they see an assured succor," Costebelle reported to comte de Pontchartrain, French minister of marine, and until then "they will remain on their lands with the English." He believed that Acadian loyalty to France was weak. "Without money one can expect nothing from the good will of these people, who will always be much disposed to go back into foreign territory on the smallest discontent, than to be subjected to the nation from which they draw their origin, which they have for the most part forgotten." The inhabitants were unreliable, "half-Indian" in their disposition. It would be better to import slaves to work the new colony. But Pontchartrain, in charge of the Louisbourg project, continued to insist on Acadian relocation. The inhabitants would be much better than green colonists from France, and he was counting on them to supply the new garrison. "The important thing," he wrote, "is that the Acadians must leave l'Acadie."[25]

Pontchartrain's letter marked the first recorded usage of the term *Acadien* by a French official, and it suggested the extent to which the inhabitants were taking an independent position, emphasizing the distinction between their interests and those of the French. In the summer of 1713, after supervising the transfer of the approximately 150 permanent residents of Plaisance to Ile Royale, Governor Costebelle entertained several large delegations of Acadian leaders from Minas and Beaubassin. They looked over a number of potential farming sites before returning home to consult with their neighbors. A month later they laid out their position in a letter to missionary Félix Pain, who forwarded it to Costebelle. They did not like what they saw on Ile Royale. "There is not in all the island land suitable for the maintenance of our families, since there are no meadows sufficient to feed our cattle, which are our principal means of subsistence. . . . To leave our residences and our cleared lands to take new waste lands, which must be cleared without assistance or subsidy, would expose us to die of starvation." Moving to Ile Royale, in fact, would almost certainly have reduced them to the status of the inhabitants along the St. Lawrence, who were required to pay *cens et rentes*. They kept silent about that fact, but it was surely something they knew.[26]

The Acadians' reluctance to leave their homeland was not merely circumstantial. It was a deeply held value that originated in the peasant traditions of France. For the present, they wrote, they would remain on "*les prés d'Acadie*"—the meadows of Acadie—in their ancient homes and communities. But concerned lest they offend their former French masters, they added a few encouraging words. "We do not yet know in what manner the English will use us. If they burden us in respect of our religion, or cut up our settlements to divide the land with people of their nation, we will abandon them absolutely." They wished to be clear about their priorities. "We will never take the oath of fidelity to the Queen of Great Britain, to the prejudice of what we owe to our king, to our country, and to our religion."[27]

The matter of an oath of fidelity or allegiance had come up only a few weeks before, when British authorities summoned Acadian deputies to Annapolis Royal to hear the terms of the cession. Those choosing to exercise their right to remain would be required to take an unconditional oath of allegiance. While neither the treaty nor the queen's letter mentioned such an oath, from the British point of view there was nothing extraordinary about such a requirement. It followed a ruling by the English Lord Chief Justice in 1608 that whenever the crown acquired a new possession, whether by discovery, conquest, or cession, the local inhabitants were eligible to become subjects with rights and duties in no way inferior to those who were native-born. But they first were required to make formal expression of their subordination by swearing an oath of allegiance. Allegiance carried with it the right to own and convey real property, a right historically derived from the sovereign's guarantee of peaceful possession to his subjects. No oath, no protection of possessory rights. When given a similar choice, after the English conquest of New Netherlands, the Dutch residents took the oath. The Dutch were Protestants, however, and could expect to be admitted to all the civil rights of Englishmen, while the Acadians knew that their Catholicism would mark them for serious restrictions. Yet over the previous sixty years of back-and-forth between England and France, groups of Acadians themselves had taken various oaths of allegiance to the English crown.[28]

What was different this time was the British insistence that the oath be unconditional. The inhabitants had previously taken oaths, but they had also added conditions, particularly the exemption from participating in the imperial contest. "They would no longer bear arms against the English nation," they swore in 1654. "They themselves would remain neutral," they declared in 1691. They did not object to an oath itself, but to an unconditional one. The Acadians were very careful about what they pledged to French governor Costebelle. They did not say they would refuse to take an oath to the British king. They said they would not take an oath "to the prejudice" of the French king, to the country, or to their religion. This is a subtle reading, perhaps, but the use of subtlety with imperial officials was a highly developed Acadian art. They were protecting their own interests, playing both ends against the middle.[29]

The Acadian dilemma was not one of their own making. It was created by imperial rivalry. The French pressed the inhabitants to move from communities in which they had lived for generations. The British pressed them to swear an unconditional oath of loyalty in a borderland world in which there were very few unconditional truths.

Perhaps it goes without saying that neither the French nor the British acted out of concern for the peace and security of the inhabitants themselves. On the contrary, to both imperial powers the Acadians were merely pawns. "Nothing must be spared in getting the inhabitants to leave," one French official wrote, for "it is certain that if they leave, the English will not be able to keep the lands." Not only would the inhabitants lend material aid to French plans for the development of Ile Royale, their removal would seriously undermine British control of l'Acadie. The British reached the same conclusion. An Acadian exodus would leave the province "intirely destitute of inhabitants," while making Ile Royale "at once a very populous Colony." So advised Samuel Vetch, who abandoned his original proposal for deporting the Acadians and provided the Board of Trade with firsthand testimony of the danger of losing them to the French. "It is to be considered, that one hundred of the French [Acadians], who were born upon that continent, are perfectly known in the woods, can march upon snow shoes, and understand the use of Birch Canoes, are of more value and service than five times their number of raw men, newly come from Europe. So their skill in the fishery, as well as the cultivating of the soil, must inevitably make that Island, by such an accession of people, and French, at once the most powerful colony the French have in America." The Board of Trade adopted Vetch's position as its own, even incorporating his language into its advisory report. Both the French and the British needed the inhabitants.[30]

By the spring of 1714 only a few dozen Acadian households—many of them closely associated with the former colonial regime—had left l'Acadie for Ile Royale. French authorities dispatched Captain Louis Denys de La Ronde, formerly an officer in the Port Royal garrison, and nephew of the late seigneur of Beaubassin, Michel Leneuf de La Vallière, to encourage more inhabitants to emigrate. With the permission of Governor Francis Nicholson, who was following the queen's orders to cooperate fully with the French, La Ronde and his delegation, accompanied by Major Paul Mascarene and other British officers, held assemblies at Annapolis Royal, Grand Pré, Cobequid, and Beaubassin. The meetings were conducted with diplomatic pomp and ceremony, but behind the scenes La Ronde warned the inhabitants that swearing allegiance to the British crown would make them rebels in the eyes of French authorities. "To a man," according to Mascarene, the Acadians signed declarations stating their intention of removing themselves from the province. Accompanied by twenty-four heads of household, La Ronde returned to Ile Royale with Nicholson's assurance that the British would not stand in the way of those who wished to relocate.[31]

In fact, the British were deeply concerned, for if a majority of the Acadians departed it would be nearly impossible for the garrison to hold out through the winter. Among those who left with La Ronde for Louisbourg were individuals from some notable Acadian families—including navigator and carpenter Jean Landry of Minas, who settled at Port Toulouse on the Atlantic coast of Ile Royale, where Acadians founded a new settlement. Governor Nicholson, infamous for his hot temper and erratic conduct, flew into a rage. The Acadians "were all rebels," he railed, and warning his men that the inhabitants "would certainly cutt their throats if they went into their houses," he ordered an end to all friendly correspondence between the garrison and the residents of the *banlieu*, reinstating a regime of tribute and seizure to supply the fort's needs. Despite his pledge to La Ronde, he did everything in his power to frustrate Acadian emigration from Annapolis Royal, refusing the naval stores and equipment they needed to outfit their vessels, prohibiting them from shipping goods and livestock, and barring British subjects from purchasing their property.[32]

The British could restrict movement at Annapolis Royal, but could do little or nothing to prevent the departure of inhabitants from the *haute rivière*, from Minas or Chignecto, where they had no forces. Yet there was no mass exodus. Despite their declaration to La Ronde, most Acadians remained in their hamlets and communities. Since they had not been much troubled by the French in the past, perhaps they would not be much troubled by the British in the future. Moving to Ile Royale, on the other hand, would place them under direct French supervision. The inhabitants who returned with La Ronde were witness to the great efforts being put into the construction of the fortress at Louisbourg, which would make it the most heavily fortified garrison town in North America. The men met with Governor Costebelle and assured him that there was "not one among them who did not wish to give His Majesty proof of loyalty." They wanted the king to know they were not rebels. But like other Acadian visitors, most were unenthusiastic about the land on Ile Royale. Costebelle concluded that most of these inhabitants would "remain with the English," and indeed, of the twenty-four, only eight relocated permanently. The British certainly attempted to prevent the inhabitants from leaving, but the majority had no intention of moving anyway.[33]

Swearing unconditional allegiance to the British crown, however, was another matter. In August 1714 Queen Anne died, George I became king of Great Britain, and a new government came to power in London. Governor Francis Nicholson was recalled to answer complaints lodged against him, and new orders were issued to Lieutenant-Governor Thomas Caulfeild, a Protestant Irishman who had served in the conquering expedition of 1710, instructing him "to use his endeavours to persuade the French inhabitants to remain." Caulfeild was to reestablish friendly connections, lift restrictions on commerce, and provide "all fitting encouragement," in an effort to convince them to swear allegiance to the new king. The Acadians welcomed the change in policy, but not the invitation to take the oath. Caulfeild stressed the advantages of becoming subjects—freedom of religious practice and clear title to property "as if they were native English." In response, the inhabitants of Annapolis Royal told him they were willing to promise "not to take up arms as long as they should be under English dominion," but "could not pledge themselves to anything else." The inhabitants of Minas and Beaubassin responded similarly, in a letter heavy with irony. "We could not be any more grateful than we are for the kindness shown us by King George, whom we recognize to be the legitimate sovereign of Great Britain, and under whose domination it would give us great pleasure to remain, for he is such a good Prince, had we not taken since last summer, before knowing of his ascent to the throne, the resolution to return under the domination of our Prince, the King of France." This was the kind of response the British labeled "insolent." There would be many more like it over the years.[34]

After considerable negotiation, Caulfeild and leaders from the *banlieu* worked out a compromise. To the original language of the oath—"I sincerely promise and swear, that I will be faithful and maintain a true allegiance to His Majesty, King George"—Caulfeild allowed them to append a significant condition: ". . . as long as I shall remain in l'Acadie or Nova Scotia. And that I shall be permitted to withdraw wheresoever I shall think fit, with all my movable goods and effects, without any one being able to hinder me." This oath was signed by Prudent Robichaud and thirty-five heads of household.[35]

When the authorities in London received this document—which amounted to little more than an acknowledgment of British sovereignty—they were shocked. Reprimanded and pressed to justify his conduct, Caulfeild pointed out that if the inhabitants quit the colony, "we would not be able to make it through the winter without dying of misery," that without the material support of the Acadians, "we have no other way of living." He believed that by encouraging the inhabitants to remain he had been acting in His Majesty's service, and that generational change would eventually bring them more firmly into the British camp. "Tho' we may not expect much benefitt from them [now], yet their children in process of time may be brought to our constitution." Indeed, Caulfeild's approach had already paid dividends, for most of the Acadians remained in the province. "I am persuaded it will be with reluctancy they leave the Country," he wrote the following year, "most of those who had formerly gone being again returned." By the time Caulfeild died in 1717, only fifty or so of the approximately five hundred Acadian families living in l'Acadie had relocated to Ile Royale, and even some of those eventually returned to the meadows of Acadie. Yet the British did not revise their expectations, and continued to push for an unconditional oath from the Acadians.[36]

THE French and British were also intent on winning over the native peoples of the North Atlantic coast. "The French and Indians of l'Acadie must look up to the Sun and the Stars from the same land," Pontchartrain wrote to Saint-Castin. "They must stand shoulder to shoulder on the battlefield; when the hatchet is buried, live together in peace and harmony; and when the time comes, sleep side by side beneath the sod of their common country." The Míkmaq, in other words, were expected to relocate to Ile Royale along with the Acadians. They were even less enthusiastic. "The Indians say that to shut them up in the island of Cape Breton would be to damage their liberty, and that it would be a thing inconsistent with their natural freedom and the means of providing for their subsistence," Félix Pain wrote to Costebelle from Minas in 1713. The British might gain control of the Acadian meadows, the Míkmaq declared, but "they, the Indians, had the woods, out of which no one could ever dislodge them."[37]

At Penobscot Bay in the spring of 1714, Paul Mascarene and a delegation of British officers negotiated a truce with the Abenaki, Maliseet, and Míkmaw leaders of the French-supported Wabanaki Confederacy. But the native allies rejected the demand that they subject themselves to the British crown. "I have my own kings and governors, my chief and my elders," one of their leaders declared. "I am strong enough to occupy the land on my own." The British argued that the French cession encompassed not only all the lands but all the peoples of the region, including the natives. But the native leaders saw things very differently. While they professed the greatest esteem for the French king—"who was their father, and had placed them on the true paths of salvation and of the gospel"—they had never considered themselves his subjects. The Míkmaq later angrily protested to French authorities at Louisbourg that the king had no authority to transfer their homelands to the British. "He never had the intention of taking them from you," the governor responded. The king "knew full well that the lands on which he trod, you possess for all time." But this was merely expedient talk. The Treaty of Utrecht made no mention of any reserved rights of native peoples to their homelands, and the French made no such case with the British.[38]

The French at Ile Royale certainly encouraged ongoing Míkmaw hostility to the British, but the natives determined their own course, often diverging from the path the French charted for them. Decision making was vested in the leaders of the separate Míkmaw communities, of which there were some fifteen, each identified with a particular district. In 1714 and 1715, as the French attempted to arrange the relocation of the Acadians, Míkmaw fighters from Minas and Chignecto attacked English merchant vessels, plundering their cargoes, and in one incident killing a crewman—an act they justified by claiming that the English had sold their people poisoned goods. When Father Gaulin protested that such violent actions put the inhabitants at risk and were likely to result in greater British intransigence, the Míkmaq responded angrily. Their attacks were intended as a reminder that they were sovereign in l'Acadie, they told him, deeply opposed to British efforts to win Acadian submission. "These animals are very difficult to lead," Costebelle wrote in his report of the incident.[39]

The British, however, remained convinced that the Míkmaq—indeed, all the tribes of the Wabanaki Confederacy—were mere French puppets. In November 1717, after newly arrived Lieutenant-Governor John Doucette (another Huguenot, the English-born son of French exiles) demanded that they take the oath, the inhabitants of the *banlieu* presented him with a soiled document that had been passed from hand to hand and signed by each head of household. It

"The Embarkation of the Acadians," engraving by French illustrator Émile Bayard from William Cullen Bryant and Sydney Howard Gay, *A Popular History of the United States* (1884). This image conveys the frenzy of the violent expulsion of the French-speaking Catholic Acadians from the village of Grand Pré. During the late summer and fall of 1755, two thousand troops from Massachusetts, acting under the authority of British colonial officials in Nova Scotia, systematically rounded up approximately seven thousand Acadians, crowding them into the holds of transport vessels and dispersing them in small groups throughout the British North American colonies. The embarkation was carried out "with so little regard to our necessities and the tenderest ties of nature," one group of Acadian exiles wrote several years later, that "parents were separated from children and husbands from wives, some of whom have not to this day met again."

"European Vessel," a seventeenth-century Míkmaq rock carving photographed in 1946 at Kejimkujik National Park, Nova Scotia, by Arthur and Olive Kelsall, who enhanced the lines of the carving with white ink. The vessel closely resembles a small pinnace with lanteen sails, similar to those used by French explorers and traders, and the native artist depicted the crew as welcoming, with open arms. The Míkmaq were among the first native North Americans to make contact with Europeans, and they quickly developed a system of barter and exchange. Amicable relations between the Míkmaq and the French made possible the unique colonization of l'Acadie.

"Homme Acadien" [Acadian man] and "Femme Acadienne" [Acadian woman], engravings from Jacques Grasset de Saint-Sauveur, *Encyclopédie des voyages* (1796). In these first published images of the Míkmaq, the hunter holds his prey and the woman smokes a fanciful pipe. Although the artist depicted the couple with European features, the man's tattoos are consistent with French missionaries' descriptions of native body markings, and the woman wears a traditional Míkmaw peaked cap.

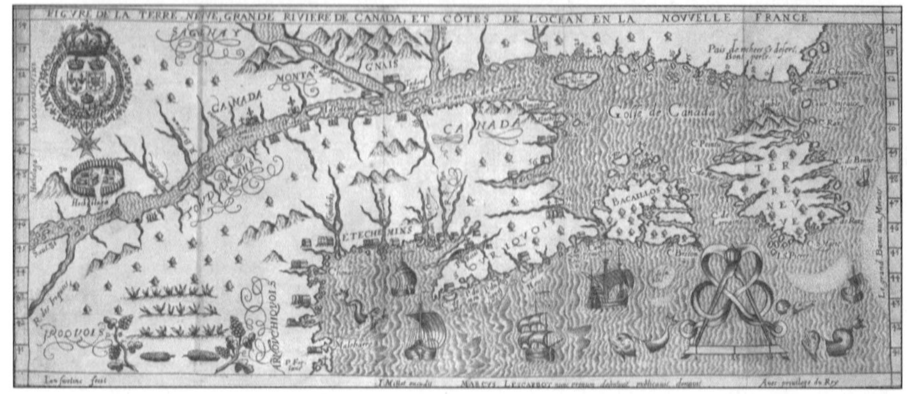

"Figure de la Terre Neuve, Grande Riviere de Canada, et Cotes de l'Ocean en la Nouvelle France" [Map of the New World, the Great River of Canada, and the Ocean Coasts of New France], from Marc Lescarbot, *Histoire de la Nouvelle France* [History of New France] (1609), showing the broad expanse of northeastern North America on the eve of its colonization.

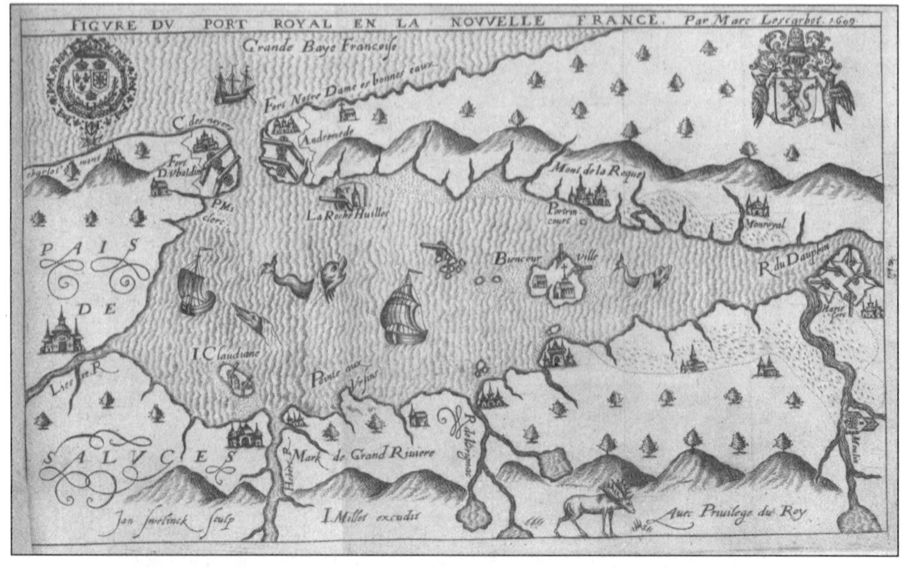

"Figure du Port Royal en la Nouvelle France" [Map of Port Royal in New France], also from Lescarbot, *Histoire de la Nouvelle France*. Lescarbot, a member of the initial French colonization party of 1606, depicted oceans filled with European vessels and lands populated by native peoples, a reminder of the human encounter at the center of colonization. The map shows the location of Poutrincourt's manor house (pictured on the next page), but the other installations, including the batteries artillery, are creations of Lescarbot's fancy—propaganda of the real estate developer.

"Habitation de Port Royal" [Dwelling at Port Royal], from Samuel de Champlain's *Les voyages du sieur de Champlain* (1613), the so-called "manor house" of Jean de Biencourt, Sieur de Poutrincourt, commander of the first French colonization effort in l'Acadie. Features include: the dormitory of the workmen (*A*), the battery of artillery (*B*), the storehouse (*C*), the rooms of the gentlemen (*D*), the gardens where the French first experimented with growing European crops (*I*), and the cemetery (*K*).

"L'Ordre de Bon-Temps" [The Order of Good Cheer] (1926), by historical illustrator Charles William Jefferys. These daily banquets, intended to keep the French colonists in high spirits over the first winter of 1606–07, were patterned on the Míkmaw custom of winter feasting, and included the participation of Míkmaw chief Membertou and his entourage, although Jefferys relegates the native diners to a marginal position.

"Repairing a Dike" (above) and "Saltmarsh Haying" (c. 1981) (below), watercolors by artist Azor Vienneau depicting seventeenth-century Acadian life. In the absence of historic images of the Acadians, the Nova Scotia Museum commissioned a set of illustrations based on evidence from two Acadian archaeological sites near Port Royal. The unique diking system developed by the Acadians along the shores of the Bay of Fundy, which features the greatest tidal variation in the world, created some of the most fertile farmland in North America, and provided the inhabitants with the means to live well without infringing on Míkmaw territory or resources. Salt hay harvested on these meadows allowed the Acadians to feed their livestock through the winter and supported large herds of cattle.

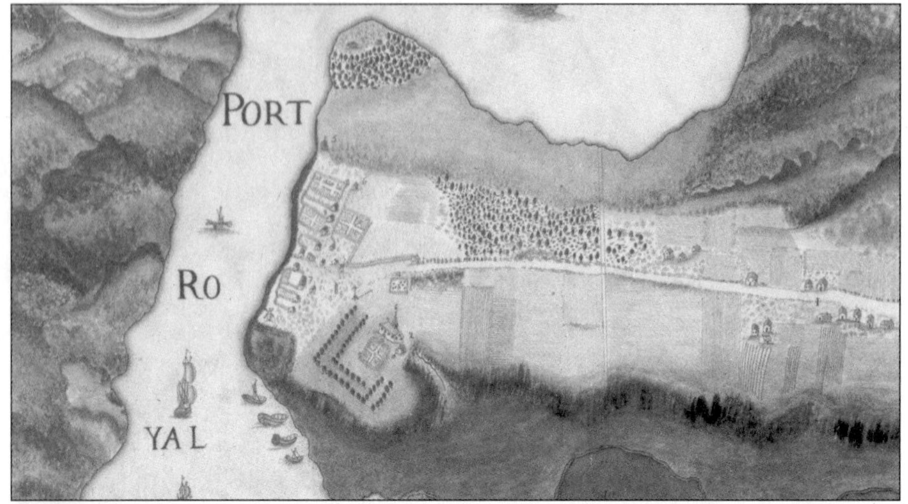

"PLAN TRES EXACT DV Terrain où sont sçituées les maisons du Port Royal" [Very Exact Plan of the Ground where the Houses of Royal Port are located] (1686), detail of a map by French cartographer Jean-Baptiste-Louis Franquelin, showing the village of Port Royal, including the church of Saint-Jean-Baptiste (*2*) and the site of the "ruined fort" (*3*), soon to be rebuilt, only to be destroyed by invading New Englanders in 1690.

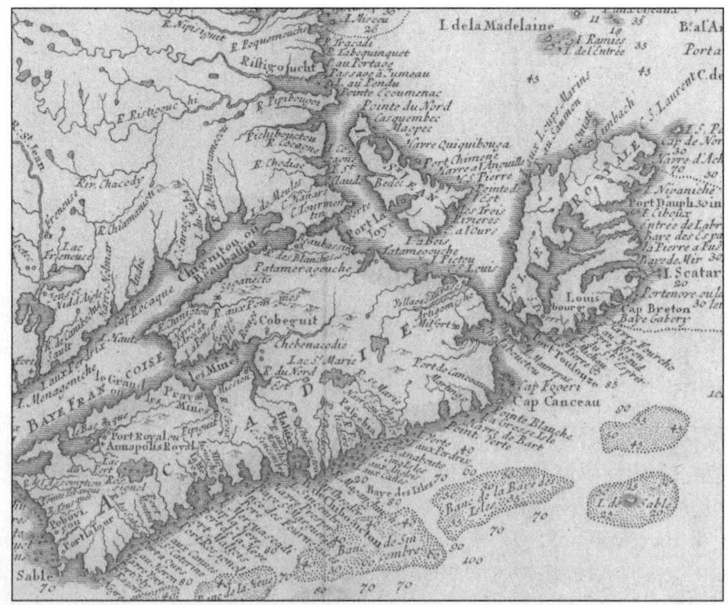

Detail from *A New and Accurate Map of the Islands of Newfoundland, Cape Breton, St. John and Anticosta; Together with the Neighbouring Countries of Nova Scotia, Canada &c.* (1747), by Emanuel Bowen, depicting the region before the construction of the military port of Halifax on Chebucto Bay ("Chibucto") in 1749.

Detail from *Map of Nova Scotia, or Acadia* (1768), by British military engineer John Montressor, showing the Acadian settlements at Minas shortly before the expulsion, including the roads to Annapolis (left) and Halifax (bottom right). The highly productive farms of this district made it the breadbasket of l'Acadie, and highly coveted by New Englanders.

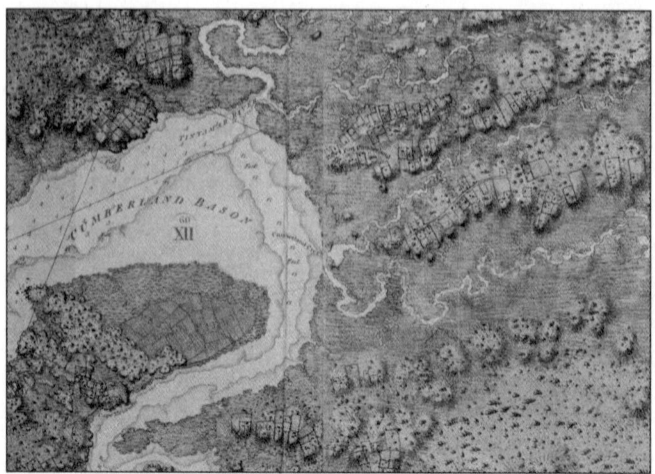

"Chignecto," detail of a map in J. F. W. Des Barres, *Atlantic Neptune* (1781). Although it portrays the district some years after the expulsion, the map shows that the new British residents continued the old Acadian settlement pattern—home lots on the ridges, with diked valley lowlands used for farming and pasture. By the 1770s a number of Acadians had returned from exile to take up their old way of life at Chignecto, but as tenants rather than owners, obliged to provide up to a third of their annual produce to English landlords.

PROCLAMATION

Par Son Excellence

Richard Philipps Efcuyer,

Capitaine General et Gouverneur en Chef de la Province de fa Majefte' La *Nouvelle Efcoffe* ou *Accadie*, Gouverneur d'*Annapolis-Royalle* dans la ditte Province et de *Plaifance* en *Terre Neuve*, et Collonell d'un des Regiments d'Infanterie de fa Majefte'.

Par la Grace de Dieu

A Sacre'e Majefte' GEORGE Roy de la *Grande Bretagne* et d'*Ireland*, &c. Duc de *Brunfwick* et *Lunnenbourg*, Seigneur de *Bremen*, Souverain Prince d'*Hannover*, Electeur du Saint Empire, Seigneur de plufieurs Vaftes Domaines en *Amerique*, et en particulier l'Inconteftable Souverain Seigneur de toute la *Nouvelle Efcoffe* ou *Accadie* auffy bien par Traite' que par Conquefte; ESTANT informe' que les Habitants *Francois* de cette ditte Province ou la plus grande Partie d'entreux ont neglige' Jufques icy de fatisfaire a leur Obligation de Jurer Veritable et Fidelle Allegiance a fa Majefte', quoy qu'ils ayent Jufques icy Joui des Influences de fon Gouvernement doux et benign (comme ils le confeffent eux mefmes:) M'a Commande' de Declarer [illegible] mon Arrive'e dans cette Sienne PROVINCE, que fon VOULOIR ET BON PLAISIR ROYALL eft, que quoy que les dits Habitants *Francois* ayent par leur Obftination ou Negligence efcoule' le tems, Stipule' pour eux dans le Traite' de Paix conclu a *Utrecht* pour prefter le dit Serment ou fe retirer de ce pays avec leurs Effets, Sa Majefte' cependant par la grande Indulgence qu'il a pour eux, eft porte'e a ne prendre aucun advantage de leur tel deportement, et Veut de Sa Grace leur donner une autre Occafion d'obtenir Sa Faveur Royalle en leur accordant quatre mois de plus, a commencer de la datte de cette Proclamation, pour prendre le dit Serment, Promettant a touts ceux qui S'y Conformeront le libre Excercice de leur Religion et qu'ils Jouiront des Droits et Privileges Civils comme S'ils eftoient *Anglois* auffy long tems qu'ils fe comporteront comme Bons et Fidelles Subjects de Sa Majefte', et que leurs Biens et Poffeffions defcendront a leurs Heritiers: Mais il eft Pofitivement defendu a ceux qui Choifiront de fortir du Pais de faire aucune forte de degaft ou dommage a leurs Maifons ou Poffeffions, ou d'Alienner difpofer ou emporter avec eux aucuns de leurs Effets. DE QUOY toutes Perfonnes qui y font Intereffe'es doivent prendre Connoiffance a leur Peril. Donne' a *Annapolis Royalle* le dix n.me Jour de Avril dans l'anne'e de notre Seigneur 1720. et dans la Sixieme anne'e du Regne de Sa Majefte'.

Vive le Roy.

Par Ordre de Son Excellence,

"Proclamation Par Son Excellence Richard Philipps Escuyer" [Proclamation By His Excellency Richard Philipps Esquire], 10 April 1720, which gave the Acadians four months to swear an unconditional oath to the British king, on pain of expulsion. The inhabitants resisted, and did not finally swear to the oath until 1730, when Governor Philipps gave them verbal assurances that they would not be required to bear arms against either the French or the Míkmaq. The oath controversy was renewed in 1749 when the British began militarizing the province in preparation for an expected war with France.

was so dirty and disgusting, "I blush to send [it to] your honour," Doucette informed Joseph Addison, the English poet and essayist who was serving as secretary of state for the Southern Department, "and I would not have done it had I more time to gett another Signed." In the document the Acadians offered an explanation of their refusal to swear allegiance. "Unless we are protected from *les sauvages*," it read, "we cannot take the oath demanded of us without exposing ourselves to have our throats cut in our houses at any time, which they have already threatened to do." The inhabitants of the outlying settlements similarly argued that taking the oath "would expose ourselves to the rage and the fury of *les sauvages*, who have so to speak acquired an Empire over us from the time that the English have taken possession of this Country." Doucette was scornful. The argument was counterfeit, he wrote, and he would not accept it, "for the Indians here are intirely ruled by the French, and are used by them in no other manner but like slaves."[40]

The Acadians were willing to take the oath, they declared, but only with the addition of a condition: "That we will take up arms neither against his Britannic Majesty, nor against France, nor against any of their subjects or allies." This statement marked an important turn in their history, for as the Acadian historian Edouard Richard was the first to note (in 1895), with these deft words the inhabitants refined their position on neutrality into a declaration of principle, one they would reiterate for years to come. Richard's reflections on their declaration are worth considering.

> It might have been disagreeable to have conditions imposed by poor peasants, but either this must be endured or the inconveniences which their departure entailed, at least if justice should regulate the relations between the high and the low, between the weak and the strong. Their conditions were certainly not frivolous. Nothing was more reasonable than the exemption which they claimed, especially when they were deprived of the right of going away; and those who treat their claim as frivolous have evi-

dently never sounded their innermost hearts to see what would be their sentiments in a similar situation.

Doucette, of course, rejected the Acadian condition out of hand. He had little choice in the matter. He was only the lieutenant-governor, and his predecessor in that office had lost the confidence of his superiors by agreeing to a compromise with the inhabitants. Soon his government would send a military governor with forces sufficient to deal with their insolence, Doucette told the inhabitants. In the meantime, he declared an embargo on all Acadian trade through Annapolis Royal.[41]

Not long afterward word reached the inhabitants through Fathers Gaulin and Pain that there was a new governor at Louisbourg as well, and that he had received a message from the French king expressing his disappointment that more Acadians had not relocated to his domain on Ile Royale. In the spring of 1718 the leaders of the three principal Acadian districts prepared a "memorial"—an ancient term for a document in which subjects present their case to the authorities—and selected Prudent Robichaud of Annapolis Royal to carry it to Governor Joseph de Monbeton de Brouillon, dit Saint-Ovide. For seven years Robichaud had attempted to arrange an accord with the British. His mission was now to reach an accord with the French as well. "Our situation is harsh," read the document he presented to Saint-Ovide, "and the conjuncture in which we find ourselves is very thorny." They could neither take the oath of allegiance to the British nor remove to the territory of the French. "They were bound to their legitimate sovereign by double ties which they could not betray"—ties of culture and religion. Yet without material support from France, and facing the opposition of their Míkmaw relations, neither could they withdraw. "We entreat you, Sir," the petition closed, "to honor us with your charitable counsels."[42]

Saint-Ovide was no newcomer to the region. The nephew of a former French governor of l'Acadie, he had served as a garrison officer at Plaisance on Newfoundland for more than twenty years before it was transferred to the British and renamed Placentia. He understood that the main obstacle to Acadian relocation was—in the words of a report on "the present situation of the Acadians" which Saint-Ovide had ordered prepared for his council of advisers—the inhabitants' "grief at abandoning the hereditary estates of their fathers, their own work and their children's." An important signal of this new sensitivity to the inhabitants' attachment to their homeland was the report's use of the term *Acadien*. Saint-Ovide also appreciated the opposition to Acadian removal among the Míkmaq, who "experience the abandonment of l'Acadie with grief and impatience" and who "will never consent to the inhabitants' withdrawal." The emergence of the Acadians and the transformations in the lives of the Míkmaq were intimately interconnected. They were kindred peoples, actors in the same history. Since it was imperative that the Míkmaq be kept on "the side of our interests," the members of Saint-Ovide's council advised retreating from the insistence on the emigration of either inhabitants or natives to the new colony. Instead, they recommended increasing the annual budget for gifts and presents and supporting the construction of permanent mission stations in l'Acadie, first at Antigonish in the far northeast of the peninsula, later at rivière Shubenacadie in the interior heart of the province. By remaining in l'Acadie the Míkmaq could prove a useful counter to British power, and their influence might prevent the Acadians from leaning too much in the British direction. Saint-Ovide continued to pay lip service to relocation, but he acted on the assumption that British l'Acadie would be populated by Acadian farmers and Míkmaw hunters.[43]

This adjustment of policy would not have been possible without the implicit cooperation of New Englanders. In the original design for Louisbourg, Acadians relocated to Ile Royale were to supply grain and livestock for the French garrison. By 1718, however, it was clear this would not be necessary. Closed out of the market at Annapolis Royal by an angry Governor Nicholson in 1714, the inhabitants of Minas and Beaubassin developed a series of trails across the isthmus of Chignecto to small ports on the sound of Ile Saint-Jean (later known as the Northumberland Strait), where Yankee shipmasters were eager to trade for their livestock and surplus grain. The New Englanders sailed their Acadian cargoes through the gut of Canso to Louisbourg, where they exchanged them for fancy French goods and wine, as well as French West Indian molasses, to supply the insatiable rum distilleries of Boston. The French garrison at Ile Royale came to depend and rely on Acadian livestock and grain supplied by New England vessels, and like his predecessors in l'Acadie, Governor Saint-Ovide maintained a monetary interest in this illegal trade. British officials in l'Acadie complained to New England authorities, and in 1715 the Massachusetts Governor's Council expressly forbade the commerce, but it would have taken a fleet of customs inspectors to prevent it.[44]

This phenomenon was not created by Lieutenant-Governor Doucette's 1718 embargo on Acadian commerce through Annapolis Royal, but surely it was strengthened by his decree. If Doucette allowed his order to stand, the resident English traders protested, it "will certainly terminate in our Ruin." His restrictions were ultimately self-defeating, as was so much of British policy in l'Acadie, undercutting the merchants who sought to tap the Acadian market at Annapolis Royal and thus make the colony profitable for the empire. The French had lost the war and the province; but five years after the treaty they had devised a strategy that garnered the economic support of the Acadians, leaving the British with the difficult task of governing those spirited people.[45]

CHAPTER 6

To Gett Them Over by Degrees

Controversy Over the Oath, 1718–1730

Responding to the French buildup at Louisbourg, in 1717 the British began reorganizing their forces in the maritime region. The independent companies garrisoned at Annapolis Royal and Placentia were merged under unified command and their strength increased from less than 200 to a total of 434 men and officers. Colonel Richard Philipps, a career officer in his mid-fifties who had distinguished himself fighting in Ireland for King William III and in Flanders and Spain for Queen Anne, was persuaded to exchange command of the 12th Regiment of Foot—a commission he purchased for £7,000 in 1712—for that of this newly formed regiment, later known as the 40th. What made the swap attractive for Philipps was his additional appointment as "Governor of Placentia in Newfoundland and Captain General and Governor in Chief of the Province of Nova Scotia," a position that paid a handsome £1,000 per annum, and carried no expectation of residence—after an initial visit to set things right, he could return to England and govern in absentia. Philipps began making the necessary arrangements immediately, but it was nearly two years before the Board of Trade issued his final instructions, and he did not sail for America until the fall of 1719. He wintered at Boston, as Vetch and Nicholson had done, finally reaching Annapolis Royal on 17 April 1720.[1]

There is no contemporary description of his landing, but Philipps would have made as much of the occasion as possible. His most important task was to secure the allegiance of the Acadians—whom he considered the "neutral subjects of another prince"—and he believed his best strategy was to awe them with a decisive display of power. He arrived with fresh reinforcements, impressively decked out in new uniforms designed for the regiment. Red coats with ample skirts, buff lining showing broadly on turned-up sleeves and buttoned-back lapels; white lace with a woven blue and yellow stripe on the lapels, sleeves, cuffs, pocket flaps, and waistcoats; long white leggings or "spatter dashes," with black garters below the knees; cocked hats, bound with white lace and bearing a black cockade on the left side; swords and bayonets suspended from brass-buckled waist belts, with broad shoulder belts supporting ammunition pouches on the right hip; long, heavy, brass-mounted flintlock muskets shouldered by the enlisted men, spontoons carried by the officers.[2]

The military pomp contrasted dramatically with the threadbare uniforms of the independent companies garrisoned at Fort Anne, and must have struck the Acadians forcibly. Philipps thought they had been "very much surprised at the arrival of a Chief Governor which they never expected." He was told how the inhabitants had laughed scornfully when Lieutenant-Governor John Doucette warned them of the new governor's imminent coming, responding that the man who could govern them had not yet been born, which sounds very much like Acadian humor. But the inhabitants may have been less surprised than Philipps thought. They might bluster with Doucette but still acknowledge among themselves that the day of reckoning would come. Shortly after Philipps landed, the inhabitants of the *banlieu* wrote Governor Saint-Ovide of Ile Royale to report that "the

English general whom we have been expecting for a long time has arrived armed."[3]

The Acadians wasted no time in responding. On Philipps's third day at Annapolis Royal, Father Justinien Durand of Saint-Jean-Baptiste parish came to the fort with a large group of inhabitants—"fifty lusty young Men," was how Philipps described Durand's entourage, "as if he meant to appear formidable." A little intimidation to match the governor's, perhaps. After introductions, Durand asked Governor Philipps about his plans. The Board of Trade had instructed him to take a conciliatory approach, to invite the Acadians to swear allegiance to the crown "in the most friendly manner," and to offer "all civil and friendly treatment to the Indian Nations or Clans." Philipps assured Durand of his intention to treat the inhabitants with "mildness." The priest responded curtly. "The people were not at liberty to swear Allegiance," he declared. "They were sure of having their throats cut by the Indians whenever they became Englishmen." During Governor Nicholson's term the inhabitants had formally chosen to remain subjects of the French king, Durand continued, and if necessary they would remove to Ile Royale to keep their promise. Philipps attempted to argue the necessity and advantage of the inhabitants becoming British subjects, but as he put it in his report to London, "arguments prevaile little without a power of enforcing." For years the garrison at Annapolis Royal had been so weak that the inhabitants no longer gave it much mind. The Acadians had begun to think that "they had as much *right* here as any other," Philipps wrote. Interpreting this extraordinary statement requires considering what he meant by "right." Not the right that comes from generations of living and dying in a country, nor the right that inheres in the emotional attachment to a homeland. What Philipps had in mind, of course, was the right of conquest and lordship.[4]

Following this unsatisfactory interview, Philipps immediately released a printed proclamation in French, brought from England, and sent copies to the priests at each of the principal settlements, instructing them to read it aloud to the inhabitants. What the Acadians heard could hardly be termed conciliatory. Despite their "obstinacy" in failing to comply with the time limit specified by the treaty of cession, King George would give them four additional months in which to swear unconditional allegiance and "obtain His Royal Favour." Those who agreed to become his faithful subjects were promised "the free exercise of their religion [*le libre Exercise de leur Religion*]" and the enjoyment of "civil rights and privileges as if they were English [*de Droits et Privileges Civils comme s'ils estoint Anglois*]," including the ownership of real property. Those who refused could expect to be removed from their homes and forced from the province, without any of their goods or effects.[5]

The leaders of the principal settlements replied promptly with predictable arguments that were nonetheless stunning to Philipps, inexperienced as he was with the Acadians. They dared not accept his offer, they explained, because the Míkmaq threatened violence if they did. Neutrality was something their native kinsmen would tolerate, but that was as far as they would go. "This is why, Sir, we cannot take any other oath than the following, which is to be loyal to King George without being compelled to bear arms against anyone, and which we very humbly entreat you to accept." If, however, he could not accept this, "we very humbly beseech you to grant us some more time for ourselves and our families to withdraw." The four-month deadline would expire at the end of August 1720. Wouldn't he allow them to remain through the harvest—for without the products of their labor, how were they to survive the winter? Wouldn't he allow them to take their clothing and tools—for without these necessities how were they to establish themselves in a new country? And without vessels or carts how were they to transport their families? "Sir, if you think that what we have had the honour to represent is not justice and equity, we beg that you will have the goodness to tell us so."[6]

Philipps did not respond directly—he was not about to enter into negotiations with a conquered people—but instead ordered them to choose deputies to meet with him and the Governor's Council of Nova Scotia, a body he appointed soon after arriving at Annapolis

Royal as the first step in regularizing provincial governance. In addition to Lieutenant-Governor Doucette, Major Paul Mascarene, and staff officer Major Lawrence Armstrong, the Governor's Council included the garrison chaplain and surgeon, the provincial secretary and customs collector, and several merchants, representatives of the community of traders who lived in the English *faubourg* (neighborhood) next to Fort Anne. The inhabitants themselves—who outnumbered the British by at least ten to one—went unrepresented. For one thing, they had not yet sworn allegiance; but even if they had, their Catholicism made them ineligible to hold civil office. But the deputy system, a continuation of the practice approved by Paul Mascarene at Minas ten years before, at least provided the Acadians a forum for making their voices heard. Philipps certainly did not envision council sessions with the deputies as deliberative, but rather as directive, and he expected the deputies to display an attitude that he termed "thankful complyance." At the first meeting he made his point by immediately objecting to the qualifications of two men from Annapolis Royal—one of them Prudent Robichaud, probably the most important leader of the *banlieu*—demanding that they be replaced. The Acadians did not respond as Philipps anticipated. This was "something we cannot do," they told him. The men they had selected were "the most appropriate ones we have found among us," and if the governor was going to veto their choices, they might as well send no deputies at all. Philipps was outraged. The Acadians had used the meeting as an occasion for "shewing their Contempt of His Majesty's Government."[7]

Surely, he thought, the priests were behind this insolence. The council heard reports that Félix Pain and Vincent Cocuet, serving at Grand Pré and Beaubassin respectively, had denounced the British promise of religious freedom as a ruse, warning the inhabitants that if they became British subjects they would suffer the fate of the Irish. Those priests were outside the range of Philipp's authority, so he ordered the arrest of Justinien Durand of Annapolis Royal, but the man was nowhere to be found. In a letter to Philipps delivered to the fort several days later, Durand explained that he had left for Ile Royale with a memorial from the inhabitants requesting Governor Saint-Ovide's assistance. But he wished to make it clear that the Acadians were acting on their own. "I left them in complete liberty to take whichever side they found most advantageous," he wrote, and could "not be held responsible for the troubles that may arrive." This was disingenuous, for as Durand reported to Saint-Ovide, he anticipated big troubles. His Acadian parishioners had told him that if Governor Philipps moved to expel them, they would leave their homes and join forces with the Míkmaq, and he feared "a revolution on the part of the inhabitants and *sauvages* together against the English." Durand sought to remove himself from harm's way. Ten years earlier, during Samuel Vetch's term as governor, he had been arrested and held hostage against the good behavior of the Acadians. He wasn't going to let that happen again. "In a country such as this, open to all pillagers and wrongdoers," he wrote Philipps, "the simplest method is to leave promptly." Although he continued to perform missionary work in New France for another twenty years, Durand never returned to l'Acadie.[8]

Governor Philipps had few options open to him. His plan had been to impose his will on a population of docile peasants and he was not prepared for the sophistication of the Acadian strategy of refusal and resistance. Not only did he lack the force necessary to carry through on his threat to remove them, he had to doubt the wisdom of such a course, which would create "a great inconveniency to the garrison," dependant as it was on a supply of fresh provisions from the inhabitants. He decided on a waiting game. "For the sake of gaining time and keeping all things quiet," Philipps wrote the Board of Trade, he would "send home the Deputys with smooth words," reassuring them that he would take no action while he submitted their requests to the King and waited for a response. As long as peace prevailed, he thought it was "very probable that they will be obedient." In the event of war, however, they would be "so many enemyes in our bosom."[9]

In fact, warfare between the British and the Míkmaq was just around the corner. The Board of Trade had instructed Governor Philipps to do what he could to befriend the natives, even authorizing him to make awards of land and money to encourage British subjects to marry among them, noting that "nothing has so much contributed to Strengthen the hands of the French in those parts, as the Friendship they maintain and the Intermarriages they make with the Indians." Philipps pretty much disregarded those instructions. Following the precedent of his predecessors Vetch and Nicholson, he ignored the diplomatic protocols and rituals that had developed during the century of relations between the French and their Míkmaw hosts—neglecting, for example, the tradition of gift exchange—and conducted negotiations that were, at best, ham-handed. Míkmaw and Maliseet leaders who met with Philipps at Annapolis Royal told him of their grave concerns about the fate of the Acadians. They "do not like to hear of the French goeing off," he acknowledged. Nevertheless, he insisted on declaring to them that unless the Acadians became British subjects, "the king will not permit them to reside much longer in this country." It would have been difficult for any British official to overcome Míkmaw hostility, but Philipps hardly made an attempt.[10]

The Míkmaq who resided in the vicinity of Canso were the most aggrieved. For more than a century they had welcomed the fishing vessels of many nations to that site, which they considered part of their territorial domain. But in 1718 Massachusetts authorities, acting on the premise that Canso was included in the French cession of 1713, sent a man-of-war to evict all French fishermen, claiming exclusive British rights to the site. The Míkmaq were outraged. Philipps visited Canso in July 1720 and attempted to mollify the leaders of the local native community with presents. But on 8 August, only a few days after he returned to Annapolis Royal, a large force of Míkmaq, joined by a number of French fishermen, struck at the British fishing camps there, killing at least one Englishman and forcing the rest to retreat in their vessels. The following day Prudent Robichaud the younger, on a trading voyage for his father in nearby Chedabucto Bay, was overtaken by a shallop manned by fifteen Míkmaw sailors. They told him they were fresh from the fighting at Canso and provided details. Robichaud's maternal aunt, Marie-Thérèse Petitpas, was a Mikmaw woman, and the boy grew up with a basic conversational ability in Míkmawísimk. He enjoyed good relations with his native kin. Yet like his father, his prosperity depended on cooperative relations with the British, so upon his return to Annapolis Royal, Robichaud did not hesitate to report to Philipps what he had learned from the men, whom he identified as from the Minas area. They told him they were at war with the British and planned an attack on Annapolis Royal. But they sailed off to the northwest in their stolen sloop, toward the north shore of the Chignecto isthmus.[11]

Later that month a group of Míkmaq, very likely the same men, boarded Captain John Alden's sloop as he did business with the inhabitants of Grand Pré at Minas, and in an aggressive manner demanded 50 *livres* from him "for the liberty to trade." Alden, who like his late father was an old hand in Acadian waters, quickly came up with the money. But the Míkmaq plundered his vessel anyway, robbing him of trade goods he valued at more than £200. Minas was Míkmaq country, declared one of their leaders, a man Alden identified as Peter Nunquadden, and "every English Trader should pay Tribute" to the natives. On the shore a large group of several hundred inhabitants stood and watched. Some spoke up in his defense, Alden reported, but then joined their neighbors in buying his stolen goods from the Míkmaq, joking that this was "*bon marché*." When he learned of the incident, Governor Philipps wrote to the Minas deputies. He suspected that the inhabitants were directly involved in the robbery, and he demanded that the Minas deputies come to Annapolis Royal immediately with an explanation.[12]

It was several months before Philippe Melanson and Antoine Landry appeared before the Governor's Council of Nova Scotia, representing the inhabitants of Grand Pré. They presented a letter from two men identifying themselves as the Míkmaw chiefs of Minas. "We believe that this land God gave to us," the chiefs declared, and "on it we reckon we have lived since before the trees were born." Why had they attacked the British? "We tell you that you are the cause. It is you who have taken Canso." Before the British came, there had been peace. Now there was war because the British threatened to seize lands bequeathed to them by their fathers. "If we wished to go to England to live, what would we be told, if not that we should withdraw?" The Míkmaq felt the same way about the British invaders. "We are masters, and dependents of no one," they concluded. "We wish to have our country free."[13]

This remarkable letter expressed sentiments widely shared by native people throughout the region. In 1714, Paul Mascarene had negotiated a treaty with the Abenakis, Maliseets, and Míkmaq of the Wabanaki Confederacy which obligated both sides to live peacefully. But in the intervening years the British had fortified sites on tribal land in Maine, just as they fortified Canso, and soon thereafter settlers crowded in, cutting forests and damming rivers. In the summer of 1721 Abenaki leaders sent a warning to the governor of Massachusetts. "Is it living peacefully with me to take my land away from me against my will?" Their lands had been given to them by God, and no one could take them without the collective agreement of the nation. "The king of France, sayst thou, gave thee it. But could he give thee it? Am I his subject? The savages, sayest thou, gave thee it. Could a few savages whom thou caughtest by surprise by getting them drunk give thee it to the detriment of their entire nation?" If the British did not pull back in Maine, they would be burned out, just as they had been at Canso.[14]

In their letter to Philipps the Míkmaw chiefs responded to the suggestion that the inhabitants—"our brothers"—were involved in the assault on Alden. "We tell you that this is not true," they declared. But Philipps rejected the entirety of the chiefs' statement, dismissing it as "an insolent letter signed by one or two savages, but dictated by the French." Like other British officials, he believed the Míkmaq were incapable of acting independently. "It is very well known that the savages have never, or at least very rarely, committed any depredations upon the English except at the instigation of the French," he wrote. The inhabitants and the priests imposed their wicked designs upon "these ignorant people" and were "making them bear the blame." Interrogated about the Acadian role in the incident at Minas, Melanson and Landry admitted that inhabitants had purchased stolen goods, and that the community should compensate Alden for his losses; but they insisted that they had no intention of challenging British rule and denied any complicity in the robbery.[15]

Distinguishing Acadian from Míkmaw, however, was sometimes difficult. The Míkmaw chiefs who wrote to Philipps signed their letter with marks that identified them as Antoine and Pierre Couaret. "Couaret" was an alternate spelling of "Charet," the *dit nom* of their father, a Frenchman named Cellier who emigrated to l'Acadie with his brother about 1680. The Cellier brothers soon married—one to Marie, a Míkmaw woman, the other to Marie-Josèph Lejeune, a *métis*. Both families appeared on the enumerations of French census takers, but while Antoine, Pierre, and their siblings were part of the Míkmaw community of Minas, their cousins grew up in the Acadian settlement of Grand Pré. The Míkmaw branch of the extended family was known as Charet, or Memcharet, or sometimes Nemcharet, names that appeared in the record in a variety of spellings. (It is likely that Pierre Couaret and Peter Nunquadden, the man who led the assault on Alden, were one and the same individual.) The Celliers illustrate that while Acadians and Míkmaq maintained separate identities and separate communities, they were connected in ways that made them "brothers." Philipps and the council worried that the Acadians supported and encouraged the Míkmaq—but in some cases the Acadians *were* the Míkmaq, and vice versa.[16]

Philipps reestablished British control at Canso, and the Minas inhabitants paid Alden for his losses, apologizing for their role in the plunder of his vessel. But the incidents convinced Philipps and his council that the Acadians were so troublesome that they should be removed. In September 1720, Paul Mascarene, the councilor with the most experienced knowledge of the province, wrote a report for the Board of Trade laying out this perspective in considerable detail. Since 1714, British policy had been to secure Acadian loyalty by requiring an oath, but Mascarene argued that even if they were persuaded to swear allegiance it would make little difference, for the inhabitants would remain "enemies to the English Government." They would continue to use "all the means they can to keep the Indians from dealing with the British subjects" and would be "forever inciting the savages to some mischief or other." Their priests—who would remain in the province as part of the agreement to allow the free exercise of Catholicism—would continue taking orders directly from Louisbourg and Québec. Thus would the French continue to rule indirectly.[17]

Revealingly, the French authorities at Louisbourg no longer pressed for the relocation of the Acadians to Ile Royale. Why should they, so long as the inhabitants remained in l'Acadie "under a kind of allegiance to France"? Keeping the inhabitants in l'Acadie also ensured that the French at Louisbourg would continue to benefit from the illegal commerce that amply supplied them with grain and beef from Acadian farms—something the British garrison at Annapolis Royal was too weak to prevent. Altogether this was an intolerable situation. It was necessary "for the interest of Great Britain," Mascarene concluded, "that the French Inhabitants may not be tolerated any longer in their non-allegiance, but may have the test put to them without granting them any further delay." An additional force of six hundred men would be sufficient to carry out their removal and protect the new Protestant emigrants who must "come to settle in the room of the French." To encourage this emigration, the government should offer free transportation, free grants of land, and free stocks of cattle, drawn from herds forfeited by the departing Acadians.[18]

In a letter endorsing Mascarene's report, Governor Philipps acknowledged that the transportation of the Acadians would require the commitment of substantial resources, but argued that the need was critical. "The inhabitants seem determined not to swear allegiance," he wrote, yet "at the same time I observe them goeing on with their tillage and building as if they had no thoughts of leaveing their habitations. It is likely they flatter themselves that the King's affaires here will allwayes continue in the same feeble state." Philipps was frustrated. "This has been, hitherto, no more than a mock government, its authority having never yet extended beyond the cannon reach of this fort." If the home government was not prepared to commit to removal and resettlement, he concluded, it would be better "to give the country back to the French."[19]

The reply from the members of the Board of Trade reached Philipps the following winter. They shared his concern that the French inhabitants "will never become good subjects." For that reason, they wrote, "we are of opinion they ought to be removed as soon as the forces which we have proposed to be sent to you shall arrive in Nova Scotia." The Acadians were to be cleansed from the province. The board recommended to the king that additional troops and a man-of-war should be sent, and that "all due encouragement should be given to such of your Majesty's subjects as shall be willing to settle in this province." Several resettlement proposals were already on the table. Former Governor Samuel Vetch petitioned for a grant of land on behalf of himself and the officers "who were in the actuall service in the late expedition by which Port Royall and Nova Scotia were reduced." Thomas Coram, a wealthy retired sea captain, concerned with the plight of refugee Protestants, proposed the settlement of a large group of Palatine Germans. And the directors of the South Sea Company argued for the transfer of Acadian lands into their hands so that they might "people, cultivate, and improve the same." The board had yet to approve one scheme or another, and in the meantime urged Philipps to "continue the same prudent and cautious conduct" toward the inhabitants, and particularly "not to attempt their removal without His Majesty's positive order."[20]

In the early spring of 1721, a few weeks after Philipps received this letter, the inhabitants of the *banlieu* requested his assurance that if they sowed their lands they would be able to harvest their crops in the fall. Prudently, Philipps told them he was still awaiting definite word from London, and that only "positive orders" from the king would induce him to disturb them in their possession of their farms. Believing that the Acadians were likely to be removed, he began to make plans to return to England. In fact, no such order would be forthcoming. In England the economic panic that accompanied the collapse of the speculative South Sea Company brought to power a new government under the leadership of Chancellor of the Exchequer Robert Walpole, who believed that stability and prosperity required the avoidance of conflict with France. Plans for Acadian removal were shelved. They would not be revived for a quarter century.[21]

In the fall of 1721 the Abenakis delivered on their threat to destroy the settlements of New Englanders, burning farms and killing livestock in the settlements at Casco Bay. The settlers struck back, taking hostages (including yet another member of the Saint-Castin family) and sending an expedition deep into the interior to attack and burn the mission community of Norridgewock on the Kennebec River. This began a war between the English and the native peoples of the North Atlantic coast that would continue for the next three years. In the spring of 1722 the Míkmaq, who counted among their number many experienced sailors, opened a campaign of seaborne warfare in l'Acadie, seizing scores of English vessels and assembling a flotilla at Minas Basin in preparation for an attack on Annapolis Royal. In the absence of Governor Philipps—who was at Canso on his way back to England—Lieutenant-Governor Doucette responded by seizing two dozen hostages, mostly women and children, from the Míkmaw community summering on the shores of Annapolis Basin, justifying this conduct with a declaration that the Míkmaq were "a people of no faith, nor honour, but common enemies to all mankind." Although the Míkmaq fleet sailed into Annapolis Basin, they called off their attack, probably out of concern for those hostages. At Canso, Philipps outfitted and manned two sloops to go in search of Míkmaw pirates along the Atlantic coast, and many natives were killed in fierce ship-to-ship fighting. New Englanders brought a number of enemy heads back to Canso, mounting them on pikes surrounding the village.[22]

It was but one terrifying episode in a war waged with the tactics of terror. Native fighters carried off dozens of captives, most intended as hostages, but some as candidates for torture. Rangers in Maine found the dismembered bodies of settlers tied to trees. Massachusetts authorities authorized a scalp bounty of £100, encouraging the indiscriminate murder of native people, regardless of tribal affiliation, gender, or age. The leader of one group of bounty hunters wore a wig made of scalps as he led his men triumphantly through the streets of Boston. Native fighters struck back mercilessly when they found the opportunity.[23]

In the spring of 1724 a war party of Abenakis and Míkmaq ambushed and slaughtered a company of Massachusetts volunteers led by Captain Josiah Winslow, great-grandson of Pilgrim father Edward Winslow. New England sent a retaliatory expedition of more than two hundred men up the Kennebec, surprising the Abenakis at Norridgewock. According to their own account, the troops slaughtered women and children as well as men and brought back twenty-eight scalps, including that of the Abenakis' Jesuit missionary, Sébastien Rasle. Rasle's fellow Jesuit, Pierre-François-Xavier de Charlevoix, said that Abenakis who returned to the burned-out village found the priest's broken body, his mouth and eyes filled with dirt, "and all his members mutilated in a hundred different ways." There would be other engagements in the war, but the destruction of Norridgewock and the death of Rasle dispirited the Abenakis and convinced many of them to relocate further north and eastward.[24]

For British authorities in Annapolis Royal the worst moment of the war came in early July 1724, when a group of some sixty Míkmaq and Maliseets fell upon Fort Anne. Surprising a patrol outside the fort's walls, the attackers killed and scalped a sergeant and a private, wounded four more soldiers, and terrorized the dozen or so families in the English *faubourg*, burning houses and seizing hostages, before slipping back into the woods. Shocked and outraged, Doucette and the Governor's Council ordered one of the Míkmaw hostages taken to the spot the soldiers had died, where he was shot in cold blood and scalped. Although the Acadians of the *banlieu* arranged for the ransom of the English hostages, who were returned unharmed, Doucette also ordered three Acadian houses in the *banlieu* selected at random and burned.[25]

Investigating, the council learned that before striking Annapolis Royal the native army had grouped at Minas, where the men attended a mass and meeting conducted by the French missionaries, including Félix Pain, Antoine Gaulin, and Charlemagne Cuvier, a Récollect who had replaced Justinien Durand. Doucette ordered the priests to appear before the council, but only Father Cuvier showed up. In a grueling interrogation he refused to give an inch. Didn't everyone under the protection of the government have the duty to report any design against it? He admitted as much, but added, "I would not do it at the risque of my own person, for I love my skin better than my shirt, and I had rather have wars with the English than the Indians." The council's investigation also revealed the presence of several inhabitants at the native mass in Minas. Jacques Michel and Joseph Broussard dit Beausoleil, two young unmarried men from the *haute rivière,* admitted they had been there and heard the native fighters planning the attack, but said nothing because Father Pain threatened that if they did, "their Brains Should be beat out." The three missionaries were ordered banished, but the council decided against punishment for Michel and Broussard, fearing that it "might Occasion the Inhabitants to Rebell and Joyn perhaps with the Indians as formerly." Lacking the power to keep the Acadians "under Due Subjection," the council members released the young men with a stern warning that if they were caught in a similar situation again, they would be severely punished.[26]

The Governor's Council had issued standing orders prohibiting anyone in the province from trading, provisioning, or in any way supporting the natives while the conflict continued. A number of inhabitants certainly violated these orders, some willingly, some not. But there were also Acadians who were targeted by the Míkmaq for cooperating with the British. Alexandre Bourg dit Bellehumeur, notary at Minas, petitioned French authorities at Québec to compensate him and his neighbors for cattle and other provisions the Míkmaq had taken from them by force. In Bourg's account, Acadians were not of one mind. A number took a militantly anti-British stand, while others "openly declared themselves for the English." Most attempted to remain neutral. If Doucette and the council were aware of political divisions among the Acadians, however, they made no attempt to exploit them. "As to the Inhabitants who desire to live as neuter," the lieutenant-governor wrote, "I must say they never will, for tho' they don't take up arms with the Indians att this Juncture, we have great reason to believe they incite the Indians to disturb us."

There was no doubt that the inhabitants' militia at Minas and Chignecto had mobilized. Three young English sailors, captured by the Míkmaq, ransomed by Acadians, and brought to Annapolis Royal by the Huguenot merchant James Blin, told the council that during a stay of several weeks at Minas, "they saw a great many of the inhabitants under Arms, who keept Guard, pretending to be afraid the English would come and Attack them," and that many of them "had Removed their Goods from the houses in Expectation the English would Come." But preparing for an English attack—something that had happened before—was not the same thing as inciting the Míkmaq.[27]

To British authorities, however, all Acadians were equally suspect. In 1725 the council learned that a prominent inhabitant of the *banlieu* had "entertained an Indian in his house." The man was ordered suspended in chains by his wrists for several hours on a platform near the base of the fort, facing the village, "in Order to terrify the other Inhabitants from Clandestine Practices of betraying the English Subjects into the Indians' hands." The offender had Míkmaw relatives, and had stood as godfather at a number of Míkmaw baptisms. He was Prudent Robichaud, whose record of cooperation and accommodation with the British was unmatched. Later that year, when the war finally sputtered to a close, and Doucette needed a translator for negotiations with the Míkmaq at Annapolis Royal, he chose Robichaud.[28]

In December 1725 leaders of the native peoples of the North Atlantic coast signed a treaty of "Peace and Friendship" with delegates from Massachusetts, New Hampshire, and Nova Scotia, which was represented by Paul Mascarene. Leaders of the several Míkmaw communities ratified the agreement at Annapolis Royal in June 1726. "They seem to be quite tired of the Warr and are extreamly well pleas'd with the peace," Lieutenant-Governor Doucette reported. The Míkmaq acknowledged British "jurisdiction and dominion over the territories" and promised not to molest any British subjects "in their settlements already made or lawfully to be made," while in turn the British pledged "that the Indians shall not be molested in their persons, Hunting, Fishing and planting grounds." The contradiction between the prospect of future British settlements and the promise to protect Míkmaw territory was not addressed, but the treaty established a peace that would last for the next eighteen years.[29]

Once again the British turned to the problem of the Acadians. The duty of securing their allegiance fell to Major Lawrence Armstrong, who became lieutenant-governor shortly after the death of John Doucette in mid-1726. Armstrong—a career officer in his mid-sixties who had served in the garrison at Fort Anne since 1711—was a man with pronounced views, thin skin, and violent temper. He once flew into a rage at the remarks of a young captain at officers' mess and clobbered the man over the head with a full decanter of wine, which nearly "sent him to the other world." In 1715 a group of Acadians formally complained of Armstrong's "frequent misbehavior" toward them. Indeed, he argued that the British ought to "strike such a terror" among the inhabitants that they would feel compelled to become "true and lawfull subjects or be obliged to Quitt the Government interely." In fact, he continued, the deportation of the inhabitants remained the best option, "for we never shall be safe or secure so long as they are permitted to be Snakes in our Bosoms, that would cutt our Throats on all occasions." Armstrong was a man particularly ill-suited for a task that, as Governor Philipps had learned, called for "smooth words."[30]

Yet Armstrong began his tenure by employing persuasion rather than force. Soon after taking office, he called in the Annapolis deputies—Abraham Bourg, Guillaume Bourgeois, and Charles Landry—and once again put before them the question of the oath of allegiance, making no mention of the threat of removal. The deputies consulted with their neighbors, and on 25 September 1726 they returned to the fort, joining Armstrong and the councilors at the flag bastion, where the swearing ceremony was to take place. There was a problem, they told Armstrong. The inhabitants were ready to take the oath, but desired the insertion of an exception, specifying that "they might not be Obliged to Carry Arms." Armstrong, with long experience in l'Acadie, had to know this was coming. They had no reason to fear any such thing, he told them, since it was "Contrary to the Laws of Great Britain that a Roman Catholick Should Serve in the Army"—an interesting attempt to turn Acadian concerns over religious discrimination to British advantage. But it was a lame argument, for not only had Fort Anne been garrisoned by Irish Catholic troops but every British commander since 1710 had held out the possibility of enlisting the inhabitants' militia in the defense against the Míkmaq, and it was to prevent precisely such a possibility that the inhabitants sought the protection of an officially sanctioned neutrality.

The deputies insisted on the exception. Armstrong wanted a success with the Acadians to match the recent success with the Míkmaq, and he knew that empty threats of violence would get him nowhere. The minutes of the meeting record the compromise he proposed and the deputies accepted on the exception from bearing arms: "The Governor with the Advice of the Council Granted the Same to be writt upon the Margent of the French Translation in order to gett them over by Degrees. Whereupon they took and Subscribed the same both in French and English."[31]

"To gett them over by Degrees." It was essentially the same strategy Thomas Caulfeild had resorted to nearly a decade before—addressing the Acadians' reservations in the expectation that gradually they would become loyal subjects, "in process of time." But Armstrong did not make Caulfeild's mistake of reporting the details of the compromise to London. The inhabitants of Annapolis Royal "had lately taken the Oaths of fidelity to his most gracious Majesty," he wrote, "which they never would be brought to before by any former Commander." He did not mention the exception written on the margin of the French text. That copy went with the Acadian deputies. The English text, without it, went to London.[32]

The Acadians of the upper bay were less cooperative. That had been true during the French period (Governor Brouillon, for example, had condemned the Minas inhabitants as "true republicans"), and it remained so during the British era. Paul Mascarene described them as "less tractable and subject to command," because of their distance from the garrison. In the spring of 1727, Armstrong dispatched Captain James Bennett and Ensign Erasmus Philipps (Governor Philipps's nephew) to Grand Pré and Beaubassin with orders to administer oaths under the same conditions, but the inhabitants greeted them with what the lieutenant-governor characterized as rebellious and insolent behavior. More civil, but no less negative, was the letter of explanation to the Governor's Council from Alexandre Bourg, notary of Grand Pré. "We will always remain true to *Notre Bon Roy de France* [our good French king]," he wrote, but the inhabitants would "promise to continue in obedience to your government without taking the oath." The officers reported that Acadian opposition had been incited by a group of "antimonarchical traders" from

New England who told them that Armstrong had neither the authority nor the power to administer the oath.[33]

These men were likely concerned over the prospect of an accommodation that might redirect the lucrative trade of the upper bay through Annapolis Royal. But the presence of Yankees was not necessary to explain the resistance of the inhabitants at Minas and Chignecto to imperial authority—that had been a steady feature of Acadian life for many decades. With few options open to him, Armstrong did what Doucette had done, declaring an embargo on all commerce outside of Annapolis Royal. The order nearly caused a rebellion—not among the Acadians, who had ample opportunity to market their surpluses to Yankee or French traders on the northern Chignecto coast, but among the English traders at Annapolis Royal. James Blin, one of the leading merchants, publicly confronted Armstrong, and using "disrespectful language and unmannerly gestures" announced "he would not give him two pence for his commission." Armstrong ordered Blin tossed in jail. But as it became clear that the embargo would mean starvation for the garrison over the winter, the lieutenant-governor had to relent, and once the council exempted traders who were licensed to provision Fort Anne, the embargo was effectively broken.[34]

By September 1727, when Armstrong received news of the death of George I and the accession of George II, as well as instructions to secure an oath of allegiance to the new monarch, he was in no mood to compromise. He might not be able to effect his will on Yankee traders, or on the insolent Acadians of the upper bay, but he would now insist that the Acadians of Annapolis Royal swear an oath without conditions. There would be no informal exemptions written in the margin. The inhabitants came to the same conclusion, responding to Armstrong with a memorial signed by seventy-one heads of household, patiently explaining once again the necessity for a neutrality clause, and insisting that it be included as part of the official text. Condemning them as "insolent, rebellious, and highly disrespectful to His Majesty's Authority and Government," the council ordered deputies Guillaume Bourgeois and Charles Landry "remanded to prison, laid in irons, and there remain until His Majesty's pleasure shall be known concerning them." In consideration of his age, Abraham Bourg's property was forfeited and he was deported—likely to Ile Royale, where he would have joined his children and grandchildren who had previously relocated to Port Toulouse. Bourgeois had been imprisoned before, in 1711 with his father, who died as a result. Now his cellmate Charles Landry fell dangerously ill in the miserable conditions of the dungeon. Landry's wife, Cathérine-Josèphe Broussard, appealed to the council for his release, but it denied her request, calling Landry "a very Great Offender." Within a month he was dead.[35]

Things would go from bad to worse at Annapolis Royal. But in the meantime something of a comedy was played out at Beaubassin and Grand Pré. In an attempt to secure oaths from the inhabitants of the upper bay, in early October 1727 Armstrong sent a company of men under the command of Ensign Robert Wroth, a young officer who came to l'Acadie in 1720 as Governor Philipps's adjutant. Wroth's instructions were to proclaim the accession of George II "with all the Ceremonys and Solemnity usual in Such Occasions," supplying ample food and spirits that the inhabitants "may taste of the general joy of His Majesty's happy accession." After the feasting Wroth was to ask the deputies to sign the proclamation, and only then to raise the requirement of the oath. "You are to behave your self seemingly with an air of Indifference," Armstrong wrote, "yet to Engage them to their Duty." As the historian Edouard Richard read the instructions, Armstrong seemed to be hoping that Wroth would be able to "slip in" the oath of allegiance.[36]

Arriving at the landing place at Beaubassin, Wroth was greeted by the deputies, who escorted his company to the vacated priest's house and placed it at their disposal. At an assembly of more than one hundred inhabitants Wroth read the official proclamation and invited the Acadians to join him in drinking the health of the new king. There was music and song, Wroth and the deputies offered toasts, the inhabitants' militia fired several volleys, and the crew of Wroth's schooner replied with three rounds from the small cannon. "The Solemnity was as decent as the Country and People could possibly admitt of," Wroth reported, "everyone shewing their Loyalty and Affection in loud husas of 'God Preserve King George the Second.'" He told the deputies that he required their signatures or marks on the proclamation, and they signed, although only after Jean-Baptiste Vécot, a Canadien who served as notary for the community, insisted that they attest merely as "witnesses."[37]

Vécot's intervention threw something of a damper on the festivities, and with the afternoon growing long, the Acadians requested permission to return to their homes. Sensing his opportunity slipping away, Wroth then produced a copy of the oath and asked the deputies to sign that as well. Vécot insisted on seeing the French text, and with that in hand he went off to consult with the deputies in private. They returned about sunset with the demand that Wroth include three additional articles: that the inhabitants be "exempted from taking up arms against anyone"; that they be "free to withdraw to wherever they may desire, and will be released from the [oath] as soon as they are beyond the dominions of the King of Great Britain"; and that they be guaranteed "the liberty to their Religion, and to having Catholic, Apostolic, and Roman priests." The precise language of the last article suggested that one of the missionaries—who kept discreetly out of sight—was involved. The inhabitants were "ready to take the Oath," deputy Pierre Hébert told Wroth, "provided their demands could be granted."[38]

"I turned my selfe at once upon my Heel," Wroth wrote in his report, "telling them that the most favourable construction I could conceive was the Lyquor had prompted their Imprudence in daring to propose any conditions to so Indulgent an Oath. I hoped after they had slept they would be sensible of their bad conduct." But the sober light of morning did not alter the deputies' resolve. Wroth faced the same dilemma that had confronted every British official, for he was powerless to command the Acadians to swear and powerless to punish them if they did not. He made an executive decision. He looked closely at the articles, "and not judging them Repugnant to Treatys, Acts of Parliament and Trade, I Granted them as an Indulgence." The deputies insisted that their conditions be written down and signed by Wroth, having learned from the experience of the inhabitants of the *banlieu*, with whom they were in regular communication, that they could not trust additions scribbled onto the margins of the French text only.[39]

Wroth went on to Grand Pré, where word of his concessions preceded him. He and the inhabitants of Minas went through the same rituals, the reading and signing of the proclamation, the feasting, the drinking, the toasting, the volleys of arms. And when it came to the swearing, the inhabitants added a fourth condition of their own to the other three: that they "remain in veritable possession of the goods granted to them and to their heirs," and that, if they decided to remove from the province, they "be able to sell their possessions and transport the resulting revenue without any trouble." Wroth agreed, drew up another document, and signed that as well.[40]

When Lieutenant-Governor Armstrong received Wroth's report, he was flabbergasted. "The gentleman has acted very well as far as the proclaiming of His Majesty," he wrote to London, "but in tendering the oaths he has fallen into very great errors by making some unwarrantable concessions." Subjected to a humiliating examination, the young ensign's only defense was that he believed he was acting "for the good of His Majesty's service." The Governor's Council pronounced his conduct "dishonourable" and declared his agreements with the Acadians "null and void." But desperate to close the book on this frustrating exercise, its members decided that since the inhabitants had signed the proclamation of King George's accession, and "thereby acknowledged his title and authority to and over this Province," they would henceforth be considered as having "the liberties and privileges of English subjects." The Acadians were never told that the exemptions they won were unacceptable. Many times over the subsequent decades, they would refer to the agreement that they had made with Ensign Wroth, believing that they had gained everything they had asked for.[41]

LAWRENCE ARMSTRONG was confronted by trials on every hand. He had effectively cut off all communication with the inhabitants of the *banlieu* by banishing one deputy and imprisoning another. He had alienated the community of English traders with his attempt to enforce an embargo on Acadian commerce. And in the fall of 1727 his power was seriously undercut by a direct challenge from a fellow officer of the regiment. Major Alexander Cosby, twenty years Armstrong's junior, was Richard Philipps's brother-in-law and enjoyed a close personal relationship with the governor. When Philipps announced his departure for England, Cosby expected to be appointed lieutenant-governor, and was bitterly disappointed when the Board of Trade named Armstrong to the position. From the beginning of Armstrong's tenure, Cosby resisted his authority. In 1726 Cosby married fourteen-year-old Anne Winniett, eldest child of William Winniett, a Huguenot merchant who came to Annapolis Royal with the British in 1710, married Marie-Madeleine Maisonnat, an Acadian woman with connections to several prominent families, and through pluck and influence rose to become the colony's most important trader. Through his association with the Winnietts and Governor Philipps, Cosby developed close connections with both the Acadian and merchant communities, placing him in an excellent position to exploit their hostility to Armstrong. The lieutenant-governor accused Cosby of association with the "anti-monarchical traders" who encouraged Acadian resistance to taking the unconditional oath. The conflict between the two men remained mostly personal until October 1727, when Philipps (from his estate in Wales) appointed Cosby to be lieutenant-governor of the town of Annapolis Royal, a position that also placed him on the

Governor's Council. From that point the feud between Armstrong and Cosby turned political, with neither man recognizing the authority of the other. By 1728 the council had ceased to function and provincial government was largely inoperative.[42]

The confrontation between the two men escalated into a crisis over the status of René-Charles de Breslay, a Sulpician missionary who in 1724 replaced Charlemagne Cuvier as the priest at the parish of Saint-Jean-Baptiste in Annapolis Royal. In September 1728, Breslay wrote his superiors complaining of continuous harassment by Armstrong. The lieutenant-governor had intervened in church affairs, several times insisting that Breslay "render accounts of the confessions of my parishioners." Armstrong's men had disrupted the priest's celebration of mass, marching to the foot of the altar and shouting that he was a "false apostle." They had seized church funds, taking a strongbox with gold and silver jewelry that a late widow of the *banlieu* entrusted to Breslay, that he might pay her debts and endow her children after her death. About a month after writing this letter of complaint, fearing that Armstrong was about to have him arrested and thrown into the dungeon, Breslay fled into the woods, where he remained in hiding for more than a year. During his absence, he later testified, Armstrong's men entered the presbytery and "rifled through my most secret papers," taking away personal and sacred possessions, and even stealing his cows and pigs. In an attempt to discover Breslay's hiding place, Armstrong had the priest's young servant boy whipped and threatened with hanging.[43]

Not surprisingly, Armstrong told a different story, which he laid out in his own letter of complaint to the Board of Trade in the spring of 1729. Breslay had used his priestly office to punish parishioners who cooperated with the British, "assuming to himself the authority of a Judge in Civil Affairs." When at last "his insolence and tyranny" grew insupportable, Armstrong sent an officer "to speak to him," but Breslay had fled and taken refuge among the Míkmaq. The story was neither surprising nor unusual. The British had been in conflict with the missionary priests from the beginning. Armstrong's complaint was not so much with Breslay, however, as with Major Alexander Cosby, whom he believed had conspired with and encouraged the priest. Cosby's continued support of the inhabitants, he wrote, makes it "impossible His Majesty's service can be advanced or promoted while he remains in the station he is in, and this province at last must be rent and torn by parties and factions." Cosby had stirred up the traders and the inhabitants, and now was attempting "to wrest my authority and command of the troops from me." Armstrong urged that Cosby be removed from office and tried for mutiny. This letter, with its complicated and conspiratorial story, was testimony to the wreck provincial government had become under Armstrong's tenure. Even as he wrote urging Cosby's court-martial, Governor Philipps was on his way back to l'Acadie, to set things right, and once and for all to resolve the problem of Acadian allegiance.[44]

After spending the summer at Canso, Philipps returned to Annapolis Royal in November 1729 and immediately called a meeting of the Governor's Council. Although he did not take a public position on what he described as the "disagreement between the two Lieutenant Governours about the right of power and command," he made it perfectly clear where he stood. He announced that Father Breslay was free to return to his post at Saint-Jean-Baptiste, and he appointed William Winniett, Cosby's father-in-law, to the council, praising him as "eminent in his zeal for His Majesty's service." The lieutenant-governor's complete repudiation came several months later, when Philipps named Cosby president of the council. Soon thereafter Armstrong left the province for England.[45]

The inhabitants of Annapolis Royal joyfully welcomed Governor Philipps's return. "We have unfortunately experienced," they wrote him, "the very great difference that exists between your mild and just administration and that from which we presently emerge." Father Breslay's persecution had "made us apprehensive lest we should not have our religion safe and free," but now that Philipps had consented to the restoration of their "good pastor," they offered their sincere thanks. "We only await your orders to appear before your Excellency in order to give the last proofs of our obedience to His Britannic Majesty by taking the oath of fidelity." It was an unexpected but welcome turn of events, and within three weeks of his arrival Philipps claimed to have administered the oath to every man over sixteen in both the *banlieu* and the *haute rivière.* "They are pleas'd to express that the good likeing they have of my Government in comparison of what they experienc'd afterward did not a little contribute," he reported to London. He enjoyed playing good governor to Armstrong's bad. Early the following spring he sailed up the bay to Minas and Chignecto, and returned a few weeks later to inform the council of "the entire submission of all those so long obstinate people." Only a handful of the inhabitants up the bay "persist in their obstinacy," and he promised to go after those "recusants." The thing had finally been done.[46]

But how? "I have had no occasion to make use of threats or compulsion," Philipps wrote to Thomas Pelham-Holles, Duke of Newcastle, secretary of state for the Southern Department, the king's minister responsible for North American affairs. "Nor have I prostituted the King's honour in making a scandalous capitulation in his name and contrary to His Majesty's express orders, as has been done by one Ensign Wroth of my regiment." What Philipps did not report was that he had made an oral concession to the Acadians, granting them the neutral status for which they had held out so long. Alexandre Bourg, notary at Minas, made a record of his concession, which was witnessed by Charles de la Goudalie and Noël-Alexandre de Noinville de Gléfen, missionary priests at Grand Pré and Pisiquid. "We . . . certify to whom this may concern," read Bourg's affidavit, "that His Excellency Richard Philipps Esquire, Captain-in-Chief and Governor-General of the Province of His Majesty, Nova Scotia or l'Acadie, has promised to the inhabitants of Minas and other rivers dependant thereon, that he exempts them from bearing arms and fighting in war against the French and the Indians, and that the said inhabitants have only accepted allegiance on the promise never to take up arms in the event of war against the Kingdom of England and its government." A copy was sent to French authorities and another kept by Bourg, "to be put into the hands of the inhabitants wherever there shall be a need or reason for it."[47]

Philipps had returned to l'Acadie knowing he would not be able to convince the Acadians to take an unconditional oath. He also knew that the British government would consider any written amendments to the oath a "shameful capitulation." His achievement lay in convincing the Acadians to accept his oral concession. Paul Mascarene provided a firsthand account of the negotiations that took place between Philipps and the Acadians. When the governor asked them to swear to the unconditional oath, "they at first absolutely refused," Mascarene wrote. But following earnest discussion, "they at last swore allegiance, after having extorted the same assurance from under the General's hand, that they should not be obliged to bear arms." The French Foreign Ministry later ridiculed the Acadian naïveté in not demanding that Philipps give them a written document. They did not seem to understand that the concession "was devoid of value" without the governor's signature. "This verbal promise seemed sufficient to a simple people, who were loyal and therefore trusting, and for whom a given word was the most sacred pledge." But this was a criticism written from hindsight. In fact, the concession of 1730 seemed to settle a troubling question. The Acadians had held out and finally had won from the British governor a recognition of their neutrality.[48]

CHAPTER 7

The French Neutrals

Years of Acadian Prosperity, 1730–1739

The Acadians were not timid about declaring their newly won status, asserting that the oath of allegiance "binds them no further than to keep a neutrality." In his 1730 report Governor Richard Philipps suppressed mention of the oral concession he allowed them, but over the next few years the Acadian insistence on neutrality became well known to British officials both in the province and in London, and was reflected in the name commonly assigned to the inhabitants. "They were usually stiled *French neutrals*," remembered Richard Bulkeley, who for many years served as Nova Scotia's provincial secretary, "and so called themselves." *Les français neutres.* Neutrality was shorthand for the Acadians' complex relationship to the colonial world. It stood for their intimate and cooperative connection to the Míkmaq, with whom they shared the land. It stood for their cultural identity, one that retained its French origins in custom, language, and religion, yet was at the same time something new, something *American* in its attachment to place, local practice, and newly developed traditions. And it stood for their problematic relationship to empire, their desire to participate wholeheartedly in the opportunities for wider connections, but their insistence on an exemption from the intercolonial struggle for conquest and hegemony.[1]

Rather than picking sides, the Acadians attempted to maintain connections with both. They had developed this position during the period of shifting imperial control which required understanding the conflict between the empires, knowing the character of the combatants, and practicing the fine political arts of equivocation and compromise. Under unambiguous British rule this position became more difficult to manage, but it was not something the Acadians could simply give up—it was an essential part of the conception they had of themselves, part of their identity. Neutrality would eventually lead the Acadians to catastrophe, but that was not at all apparent in 1730. Neutrality had provided the space for their development as a people, and for the next two decades it would continue to serve them extremely well. The period from the 1720s to the 1740s was a good time for the Acadian people, possibly the best time of all, "a golden age," at least in their own memory of it, looking back in the aftermath of removal.

A good indication of Acadian prosperity was the stunning growth of their numbers. In 1730, Governor Philipps marveled at "the great increase of those people, who are at this day a formidable body and like Noah's progeny spreading themselves over the face of the Province." Between Annapolis Royal, Minas, and Chignecto, he counted eight hundred households—probably more than six thousand inhabitants—considerably more than twice the number of twenty years before. By 1750, the population would more than double again, reaching at least thirteen thousand, possibly as high as fifteen thousand. The best demographic estimate is that through the first half of the eighteenth century Acadian population grew at a mean annual rate of 4.5 percent, one of the highest rates of growth recorded anywhere, any time, greater even than that of the colony of Pennsylvania, which is usually ranked as the fastest-growing colony in eighteenth-century North America. This was quite extraordinary, since immigration was the driving force in Pennsylvania, and played no role at all in l'Acadie.[2]

The population explosion was the result of exceptionally high fertility and relatively low mortality. Acadian women of the early eighteenth century married in their early twenties and bore large numbers of children—nearly two thirds of the mothers had at least six offspring. And they were blessed with remarkably low infant and child mortality—three quarters of their children reached adulthood, compared to considerably less than half those of France or Canada. Acadian communities were youthful, which made them dynamic and restless, but low mortality meant that there was also a large number of grandparents and even great-grandparents. "They were a very healthy people, generally living to a very advanced age," wrote Moses Delesdernier, a French-speaking immigrant from Switzerland who worked as a trader at Pisiquid in the early 1750s and left a memoir of Acadian life.[3]

One explanation for the low mortality is that before the middle of the eighteenth century l'Acadie did not experience the outbreaks of epidemic disease that plagued most North American colonies. Although smallpox and other killers had devastated the Míkmaq of l'Acadie in the seventeenth century, those epidemics did not spread to the first generation of Acadian settlers, presumably because, as emigrants from areas of France where the infectious diseases were endemic, the men and women were protected by a degree of immunity through childhood exposure. Second- and third-generation Acadians had no such acquired immunities, and would have been highly susceptible to infection; but by 1700 the epidemic cycle among the Míkmaq had abated, and indeed their numbers grew through the first half of the eighteenth century. Moreover, although Acadians of the eighteenth century were part of the Atlantic network of trade, they had little direct exposure to seamen from Europe or the Caribbean, the principal germinating sites for epidemics in the Atlantic world. Nearly all Acadian commercial intercourse was with traders from New England, particularly from Massachusetts, where colonial authorities enforced strict quarantine regulations, in effect maintaining a protective barrier against the spread of infectious disease to l'Acadie. Compare the disease history of Louisbourg—the French fortress and port on Ile Royale which had a great deal of direct contact with Europe and the West Indies—where during the first half of the eighteenth century the residents suffered through periodic epidemics that claimed hundreds, perhaps thousands of lives. Louisbourg was crowded and densely populated, l'Acadie decentralized, and that too made a difference.[4]

Another important factor in the health of the Acadians was their substantial and diverse diet, a direct consequence of their dikeland farming system. They grew wheat and peas, cabbages and turnips, and all sorts of vegetables on their reclaimed fields. They grazed cattle and sheep on their pastures, and raised hogs and poultry around their farmsteads. They pulled cod, bass, salmon, and shad from the waters surrounding them. They ate well, especially compared to the diets of European farmers. Inhabitants took an early breakfast of bread or pancakes, fried pork, and milk, consumed a light supper of bread and milk in the evening, and like farming people everywhere, sat down to a main meal at midday. When Robert Hale of Massachusetts was in Beaubassin on a trading venture in July 1731, he recorded his daily routine in his journal. Boarding at a little inn run by Guillaume Cyr and his wife Marguerite Bourg, he joined the family in a Sunday dinner of bonnyclabber (thickly curdled milk), soup, salad, roast shad, bread and butter. The next day, at the home of inhabitant Abraham Arseneau, he dined on roast mutton and a salad dressed with bonnyclabber and molasses prepared by Arseneau's wife, Jeanne Gaudet. These were typical Acadian dinners. Their diet was rich in protein and fat as well as stone-ground whole grains, and included plenty of cabbage, turnips, and fresh fruit and vegetables in season.[5]

Theirs was an agrarian world of household production. Men worked the fields from spring to harvest, cut timber for firewood and lumber in winter, tended livestock, repaired and extended the dikes.

At planting and harvest time they were joined in the fields by women, but otherwise work was divided strictly by gender. Women kept house, ran the dairy, fed the hogs and chickens, maintained the garden and the orchard. Acadian apple orchards, renowned throughout the North Atlantic for the superiority of their fruit, were the special province of women. Andrew Brown, a young Presbyterian minister who in the 1790s studied the surviving Acadians, remarked on the importance of the orchard as a cultural space. When a young couple first set up housekeeping, he wrote, it was the bride's duty to begin the family orchard, often with cuttings provided by her mother. The orchard was a site of repose and sociability. While women pruned or picked, children played beneath the boughs. Many scenes of early childhood memory were set there. "On Sunday evenings during the summer it was the chosen scene of family devotion . . . by a very natural law the charge of the orchard fell early under the direction of the daughters of the family, and became the resort of their youthful companions of the other sex. Many of their social amusements passed within this soft shelter." Despite the rosy glow of this description, Brown's account suggests some of the ways in which the orchard extended women's influence into the wider world.[6]

"These French Acadians are hard-working by nature," an official at Louisbourg wrote; "they are born smiths, joiners, coopers, carpenters, and builders. They themselves make the cloth and the fabrics in which they are dressed." For their husbands and sons, women made loose-fitting collarless shirts of unbleached linen, breeches of wool, and straw or knitted hats. They dressed themselves and their daughters in linen chemises, woolen skirts, vests, aprons, neck scarves, and caps. "The women's cloaths are good eno'," Robert Hale noted in his journal, although he thought their dresses "look as if they were pitched on with pitchforks, and very often their stockings are down about their heels." He was surprised to find both men and women wearing wooden shoes, something he had never seen in New England. For special occasions Acadians dressed in more colorful and showy clothing—moccasins embroidered with trade beads and ribbons, jackets and shirts of imported calico, red-striped skirts cut from cloth made by teasing out the yarn of English scarlet duffel and reweaving it with homespun wool blackened with vegetable dye. "They were fond of black and red," recalled Moses Delesdernier, "and liked to have stripes on their legs, with knots of ribbons and flowing bows."[7]

The Acadian economy had to accommodate the desire for ribbons and bows—as well as buttons, buckles, straight pins, needles, awls, scissors, stoneware, earthenware, glassware, drawer pulls, nails, knives, haying forks, fishhooks, muskets, gun flints, clay pipes, and jew's harps, all objects turned up in archeological digs conducted at the sites of the Bélisle and Melanson settlements on the Annapolis River in the late twentieth century. These items were manufactured in Europe or New England, and indicate that Acadians were participants in the consumer revolution of the eighteenth-century Atlantic world. Other important trade goods—cloth, sugar, and rum—left no trace in the archeological record, but the study of ancient Acadian garbage produces a great deal of interesting evidence. Analysis of hundreds of animal bones discarded from thousands of dinner plates reveals that they dined on domestic animals rather than game, slaughtered the oldest and least productive of their sheep and cattle, probably saving the best cuts of meat for sale or trade. There was certainly a steady demand for Acadian provisions at Fort Anne in Annapolis Royal. The garrison was so desperate for supplies, in fact, that the inhabitants could name their price—a source of considerable frustration to British officials. "The inhabitants, by a mutual consent, are contriving all the ways and means possible to distress His Majesty's Garrison by raising the price of all eatables, firewood, &c.," the Governor's Council complained in 1732. But what the British interpreted as conspiracy was actually the free operation of the market. When officials attempted to regulate the price of provisions, they only succeeded in driving business away.[8]

The Acadians found another ready market with New England traders. Robert Hale learned something about this booming business during his visit to Beaubassin in 1731. The frontier trader Pierre Arseneau of Ile Saint-Jean (brother of Abraham Arseneau) with whom Hale dined told him that the Acadians kept themselves very well informed about commodity prices in New England, and would "give no more (or scarce so much) for our goods as they cost in Boston." Unable to make much of a profit selling commodities for cash, Yankee traders exchanged their merchandise for Acadian produce—cattle, sheep, beef, pork, eggs, poultry, wheat, flour, corn, potatoes, turnips, onions, apples, and cider—which they were able to sell at Louisbourg at considerable markup. The French there willingly paid inflated prices because supplies from France or Canada were even more expensive. In this "clandestine manner," complained Hibbert Newton, provincial collector of customs, the Acadians supplied the French garrison on Ile Royale while "our garrison at Annapolis Royal and Canso, which is in their neighbourhood, are in great want, and can gett neither beef nor mutton but at great Expences from New England." The mercantilist regulations of both Great Britain and France defined this trade as smuggling. In 1731, Governor Philipps issued a proclamation forbidding all commercial transactions between Acadians and seaborne traders except at Annapolis Royal, where it could be scrutinized and supervised by British officials; but the regulation was ignored, just as previous ones had been. At Louisbourg, Governor Saint-Ovide and his subordinates encouraged and protected the trade, since it was a source of personal profit for them. A number of French merchants there sent vessels to Acadian ports on the north shore of Chignecto—to Tatamagouche, which served the inhabitants of Minas, and to Baie Verte, less than fifteen miles from Beaubassin—but they were outnumbered and outbargained by the Yankees, who greatly expanded their Acadian business in the 1730s. By the early 1740s more than a hundred New England vessels were trading each year at Louisbourg, many of them loaded with Acadian provisions.[9]

Acadian society was notable for what in the eighteenth century was referred to as "equality of rank." After the demise of the seigneurial system in the mid-seventeenth century, there was relatively little stratification along economic or social lines. But in the booming commercial economy of the 1730s some Acadians did better than others, and class differences began to emerge. The leading Acadian merchant in the province was Joseph-Nicolas Gautier, whom the Governor's Council in 1732 ranked as "most considerable in lands and possessions" among all the inhabitants. The son of a French garrison officer at Port Royal, young Gautier remained in l'Acadie when his father returned to France in 1710, entering into business with Louis Allain, the former privateer and successful entrepreneur. Gautier married his partner's daughter Marie, said to be a capable businesswoman in her own right, and when Allain retired in the 1720s, the couple took over the family business at Bélair, a commercial compound at the head of navigation on the Annapolis River that included grist and sawmills and a docking facility for two *goelettes* or schooners of "fair tonnage."[10]

The Gautiers made a fortune shipping cattle to Louisbourg from Minas. That operation was coordinated at Louisbourg by Michel Dupont de Gourville—a member of Ile Royale's most prestigious military family, whose marriage to the Gautiers' daughter in 1737 brought him a generous 10,000-*livre* dowry—and by Pierre Allain, Marie's brother, who lived at Grand Pré, and was the brother-in-law of Joseph Leblanc dit Le Maigre, foremost cattle broker in l'Acadie. Le Maigre—"the Thin One," a joking Acadian nickname for a fat man—was well connected, through the prominent Leblanc family as well as his marriage to Anne Bourg, daughter of notary Alexandre Bourg dit Bellehumeur and his wife Marguerite Melanson. Leblanc was reported to be wealthier even than Gautier, with lands and properties at Minas worth more than £10,000. Another merchant of importance was Jacques Maurice Vigneau, a native of Port Royal whose family left for Ile Royale after the conquest when he was yet a boy, but who returned in the 1720s to make his fortune. Like Gautier, Vigneau began his ascent by allying himself to a family of traders, marrying Marguerite Arseneau of Beaubassin, whose father was involved in shipping and trade. Vigneau acquired a vessel and by 1735 had become the most prominent merchant at Baie Verte, principal entrepôt for Acadian provisions bound for Louisbourg. Gautier, Leblanc, and Vigneau were big fish, but there were dozens of small fry, Acadian *petit bourgeois* who invested profits from the sale of their provisions in the construction of little sloops and *goelettes* so they too could grab a piece of the flourishing carrying trade.

Contempory observers were generally more impressed with Acadian vessels than Acadian homes. In 1688, French governor Meneval characterized the Acadian houses as nothing but "wretched dwellings of mud and wood," an opinion echoed several decades later by the British officer John Knox, who thought the inhabitants lived in "miserable structures." Because all their buildings were destroyed during the removal in 1755, the best evidence for testing these judgments comes from archeology. Historians once assumed that Acadians built in the French *piquet* style, log posts driven into the ground to form crude walls. But the discovery of numerous relic fieldstone foundations at the sites of the former *hameaux* of Bélisle and Melanson shows that they constructed their houses in the tradition known as *charpente*, in which massive post-and-beam house frames are anchored on substantial courses of foundation stone.[11]

Amid the excavated rubble archeologists also found quantities of fabricated material made of local clay and marsh hay—the remains of the insulation known as *bousillage,* used to fill the spaces between the upright posts of the frame. Examples from the Bélisle site retain an impression of wood grain on one side, while the other is covered with a smooth white clay slip, suggesting that the Acadians clad their houses in weather-tight clapboard siding and plastered the interior walls to make their rooms bright and pleasant. Also discovered at the sites were pieces of bundled marsh hay (probably used to thatch the roofs), broken window glass, iron door hinges, and even a well-preserved door lock. The foundations at Bélisle and Melanson range from small to moderate in size (350 to 1,000 square feet), but share common proportions and orientation, and include a combination fireplace and bake oven on the west gable end. These distinctive features constitute the basics of an Acadian building tradition that developed and flourished in the seventeenth and eighteenth centuries. It exists today only in replica. A layer of ash and charred thatch uncovered in the excavations offers poignant evidence that the houses of the Bélisle and Melanson hamlets were destroyed by fire, presumably in 1755.

Acadian houses were built to last and required considerable investments of labor and money—a tangible evidence of Acadian prosperity. Yet the inhabitants seem to have furnished them sparsely. "They have not above 2 or 3 chairs in a house, and those wooden ones, bottom and all," Robert Hale noted. To these the inhabitants added table, benches, bedsteads, and cupboard, all of local manufacture. Residents stored their clothes, personal items, and papers in chests, and displayed their small possessions on shelves built along the walls. "They have but one Room in their Houses besides a Cockloft [a small attic], Cellar, and Sometimes a Closet," wrote Hale. "Their Bedrooms are made something after the Manner of a Sailor's Cabbin, but boarded all round about the bigness of the Bed, except one little hole on the foreside, just beg eno' to crawl into, before which is a Curtain drawn, and as a Step to get into it, there stands a Chest." This was what was called a *cabinet à coucher,* a sleeping space divided off from the main room by means of movable partitions, providing a little privacy for the husband and wife, a rare commodity in Acadian homes, where the whole family—and generally a very large family at that—shared the one-room space.[12]

As in the household, so in the *hameaux.* Acadian life was largely communal. A British survey of 1733 mapped more than three dozen hamlets along the northern and southern shores of the Annapolis River, from the Melanson settlement at the river's mouth to a cluster of Bastarache family households at the head of navigation. There may have been as many as sixty *hameaux* at Minas, another dozen at the water's end on Cobequid Bay, and at least thirty more at Chignecto. A typical hamlet might include half a dozen to a dozen houses and fifty to seventy-five persons. Newlyweds were welcomed into the community with the old custom of charivari—which Acadians called *raccroc*—established residents gathering outside the couple's house on the wedding night, beating kettles and blowing horns, until invited in for refreshment. Typically the bride and groom lived with one of their families until they were able to assemble the materials for a neighborhood house-raising. "The whole village worked to help settle the newly-weds," one English observer remembered. "They built them a house, they cleared a plot of land sufficient for its immediate use, they provided them with cattle, pigs, fowl; and nature, aided by their own industry, soon placed them in a position to begin helping others."[13]

Individual families tended their own gardens and fields, but Acadian life was characterized by a good deal of collective work. An inhabitant chosen by his neighbors as *sourd des marais*—inspector of the marsh—had responsibility for calling the men of the district together to maintain and repair the dikes. "The inhabitants make a joint business of dyking-in several large tracts," a colonist from New England wrote in the 1740s, "which serve first as common fields, being afterwards subdivided into smaller allotments." The balance between individual and collective effort is suggested by the arrangement of the relic foundations at the Melanson and Bélisle sites: each house near tracings suggesting enclosed gardens and outbuildings, with large communal barns located centrally. Circular mounds on the hillocks are likely the remains of community windmills, where inhabitants ground their grain into flour, positioned to take advantage of the prevailing breeze blowing downriver. "In all their public works," wrote Hugh Graham, a Protestant minister who lived at Halifax in the 1780s, "everyone did as much as he could—as in building aboiteau and dikes, in erecting chapels, and in enclosing burying grounds and the like. The interest of the community had ever its due preponderancy over the interest of the individual."[14]

The favorite forms of entertainment were public. Inhabitants gathered frequently together to tell stories and share gossip. The Acadians loved mimicry, and inhabitants took great pleasure in lampooning each other, and especially the Yankees, whom they considered hard-nosed and standoffish. According to the modern Canadian folklorist and playwright Antonine Maillet, the leading authority on Acadian traditional culture, their stories reveled in irony, heroic tales often ending with the champion stuck in an inextricable situation. A favorite motif concerned the adventures of the "young giant," a boy born with superstrength who might have been a hero of the people, but who was so clumsy and hungry that he caused havoc whereever he went. Instead of "happily ever after," Acadian storytellers might conclude with a rhetorical shrug of the shoulders: "He'll never pull himself out of that one." Villains were punished with a *bain-de-mer*, an unexpected cold dunk in the sea. Acadians preferred a laugh at the scoundrel's expense to the cold comfort of narrative justice. As they put it, *c'est pour rire*—these stories are for laughing. Many tales took the form of *chansons* or ballads. According to Andrew Brown, theirs was a culture "where everything was sung." They loved music, violin-playing, and dancing. The worst torture in the world, Acadians joked, would be to tie up a man's feet while music was playing.[15]

Saints' days and holidays were excuses for community feasting, drinking, and dancing, and the calendar was punctuated with dozens of festivals, some uniquely Acadian. The celebration of the New Year included a processional in which men and boys went from house to house embracing and kissing the women, symbolizing the end to old arguments between neighbors and the beginning of a new season of harmony and peace. One of the most striking holidays was the spring fête known as *le retour des oies*, celebrating the return of the geese. Andrew Brown, who observed the festivities at the Acadian village of Chezzetcook later in the century, believed it combined both Míkmaw and Catholic traditions. "In the Algonquin ritual," he wrote, "this was the festival of dreams and riddles, all fools' day," a occasion of joy on being delivered from the storms and cold of winter. Onto this the rituals of Catholic Easter were "engrafted on with some dexterity."[16]

The church played an important role in Acadian cultural life. During his visit to Beaubassin, Robert Hale watched as Father Jacques de Lesclaches, accompanied by a sexton ringing a small handbell, circulated through the village each day on his way to celebrate mass at the chapel of Notre-Dame-du-Bon-Secour, which had been rebuilt after Benjamin Church burned it in 1696. Hale was surprised to see his hosts, the Cyr family, on their knees each morning and evening, saying their prayers. But Antonine Maillet insists that eighteenth-century inhabitants were profane as well as pious, and more sensual than ascetic. The missionary Pierre Maillard, who spent many years with the Míkmaq, wrote that his native communicants were better Catholics than the inhabitants. The majority of the Acadians, he maintained, "lead a life that is completely discordant with the Evangelical maxims." He believed that missionaries should as much as possible keep natives separate from inhabitants. Priests complained that Acadian inns and taverns remained open on Sundays, doing business during the celebration of mass. One missionary reported that not only were men and women seen dancing after sunset but they could be heard singing *chansons lascives*—lascivious songs.[17]

Antonine Maillet believes such songs and stories were very popular in the eighteenth century, but that most failed to survive the devout Catholicism that characterized the more recent era of Acadian history. One of the few ribald tales she collected in its entirety—interestingly, she heard it from a priest—related the story of a "saucy" Acadian woman. Her husband and a young devil get into a dispute over the ownership of a certain field, and to settle the matter they agree to a clawing contest. The one who can inflict the deepest scratches will win the land. Catching a glimpse of the devil's frightening claws, the man despairs, but his wife devises a plan to save the day. When the devil arrives at the couple's house on the day appointed for the contest, he finds the woman crying. Just look at the horrible wound my husband gave me last night, she sobs, and lifting her skirts she shows the naive young devil something he has never seen before. "I surrender the field," he cries.[18]

Maillet's earthy story helps balance the accounts of late eighteenth-century observers who depicted the inhabitants in terms both idyllic and condescending. "The Acadians were the most innocent and virtuous people I have ever known or read of in any history," wrote the Swiss trader Moses Delesdernier some four decades after the removal, an operation in which he had played a critical role, and for which he felt an old man's remorse. "They were very remarkable for their inviolable purity of morals. I do not remember a single instance of illegitimate birth among them." But the inhabitants experienced their fair share of the passions and failings of all mortals, and fell into as much conflict as any people. From 1730 to 1755, nearly half the marriages at Annapolis Royal required dispensations for consanguinity. The pattern of cross-cousin marriage had developed in the previous century, perhaps a cultural invention born of necessity because of the limited number of unrelated persons. But historians have demonstrated that in Europe and elsewhere, the pattern tends to be an indicator of premarital pregnancy, the result of intimate relations among "kissing" cousins. Historians of the Acadians have generally rejected that interpretation because of statements such as Delesdernier's and because there is little documentary evidence to the contrary.[19]

But rare or not, illegitimacy was a fact of life in l'Acadie, as it was everywhere. Consider the case of Marie Daigre, the young widow of Pierre Sibilau, who at the turn of the eighteenth century lived near her parents in the Daigre hamlet on the *haute rivière*. In 1703, when she was twenty-six, Marie bore *un enfant naturel,* an illegitimate daughter (also named Marie), whose father she steadfastly refused to name. Five years later she bore another daughter out of wedlock, and once again refused to reveal the father's identity. There is no record of any public outcry about this. In 1711 Madame Daigre married Jacques Gouzil, who adopted her two girls, and together the couple had four children more. The pattern of illegitimacy repeated itself in the next generation. In 1726 Gouzil complained to British provincial authorities that Joseph Broussard dit Beausoleil, a twenty-four-year-old resident of a neighboring hamlet, had fathered the bastard child of his stepdaughter Marie. Broussard, who had recently married, was summoned by the Governor's Council—before whom he had appeared two years earlier to answer a charge of fraternization with the Míkmaq—and testified that he "never had any Carnall Deallings" with the young woman. But after hearing from the midwife, who testified under oath that during the most violent phase of Marie's labor she called out for Broussard, the council ordered him to pay child support or be jailed.[20]

L'affaire Beausoleil offers an example of the kind of ordinary human conflict that characterized the Acadian community. During the French regime the inhabitants had taken such matters to provincial judge Mathieu des Goutin, and after the British conquest in 1710 they expected the British to provide the same adjudication. In 1711, in order to "ease himself of the perpetualle Complaints of the French against one another in their private Feuds and Quarrells," Governor Vetch appointed an informal committee of officers and prominent Acadians to hear them, but that system proved inadequate to the task at hand. The British balked at the creation of a formal court system; but noting that "the dayly cry here is for Justice by many of the Inhabitants and residents," in 1721 Governor Philipps decreed that the council sit periodically as a "Court of Judicature." Over the next three decades this court heard hundreds of cases, generally attempting to follow the precedent of what Paul Mascarene described as "the Antient laws and customs established with the inhabitants," which required that councilors have at least some familiarity with the *Coutume de Paris,* the legal code governing the province before 1710.

Many of the cases were prepared and presented by Prudent Robichaud, acting in his capacity as *syndic* at Annapolis Royal.[21]

Before 1730, however, the council refused to consider disputes involving real property, insisting that it could not rule on such questions until the problem of the oath had been resolved. Under the French regime, land tenure had been part of the seigneurial system. In 1703, after reviewing the documents in their archives, French authorities confirmed several dozen seigneuries in l'Acadie, issuing *arrêts du roi* to the heirs of the original grantees. When the British assumed control, they promised that seigneurs willing to take the oath of loyalty would "retain and Enjoy their said Lands and Tenements without any Lett or Molestation." Most seigneurial families chose not to stay, but left for France or Ile Royale; yet the inhabitants continued to remit their annual quitrents, thinking they had better pay someone if they were to retain possessory rights. The British made no attempt to prevent this, although Governor Philipps believed the continuing relationship between inhabitants and absentee French landlords was an obstacle to winning Acadian loyalty, and he was surely right. They should "hold their lands of the King by a new Tenure," he argued in a letter to the Board of Trade, "instead of holding them as at present from the Lords of Mannors who are now at Cape Breton, where at this day [the inhabitants] pay their rents." This transfer of authority awaited the settlement of the loyalty question, but shortly thereafter Philipps issued an order that henceforth the inhabitants were to remit their quitrents to the provincial government, as representative in l'Acadie of the British king, "the only lord paramount and sole and only seigneur of the province."[22]

His order was immediately challenged by one of the few seigneurial heirs who had remained in the province, Marie-Agathe de Saint-Etienne de La Tour, one of the granddaughters of Charles de La Tour. Madame La Tour, as one later commentator wrote, was an extraordinary Acadian woman who had inherited "a good deal of her grandfather's cleverness." In contrast to most of the seigneurial heirs, she had chosen to identify herself closely with the British regime.

She was the widow of two British officers of the garrison—Lieutenant Edmund Bradstreet, with whom she had two sons before his untimely death; and Ensign Hugh Campbell, who also died after only a few years of marriage, but left her with three more children. Her children had been baptized in the Anglican chapel of Fort Anne (although for good measure at least two of them were also baptized at the Catholic church of Saint-Jean-Baptiste). Indeed, in her own account of her history she told of growing up in the Melanson hamlet, where she had "embraced the principles of the Protestant religion." This was not as improbable as it might have seemed to those who did not know the complicated Melanson history. Madame La Tour's mother Anne-Marie Melanson—wife of Jacques de Saint-Etienne de La Tour, the eldest son of Charles de La Tour and Jeanne Motin—was the daughter of Charles Melanson, who had been raised a Huguenot. Although the family was officially Catholic, it is possible young Agathe was affected not only by her grandfather's lingering sympathy for Protestantism but by the Calvinism of her maternal aunt Marie, who had been raised in Boston and for a time lived in the extended family hamlet with her husband, Huguenot trader David Basset.[23]

After the death of her second husband, Madame La Tour was left with a modest military pension, but she had no intention of settling for that. Although she shared her rights to the La Tour seigneuries at Cape Sable, Annapolis Royal, and Minas with numerous siblings and cousins, she presented Governor Philipps with a claim to the entirety, arguing that her relations had agreed to convey their shares to her. Philipps scornfully rejected her petition. "She has by cunning address got the others to make over their pretensions to her on promise of small consideration," he reported, and warned that she was on her way to London to lay a memorial before the Board of Trade. "A small addition to her pension as an officer's widow would content her," he advised, "and put an end to that affair."[24]

Philipps seriously misjudged both the ambition and the ability of Madame La Tour. Her memorial to the Board of Trade was a masterpiece of pleading. She had been "a most dutiful and Loyal Subject to the Crown of Great Britain ever since the conquest," she began. She had been widowed by two British officers in the service of the king, and her two oldest sons were now serving His Majesty in the British army. She had relied on the monarch's promise that inhabitants who remained and became loyal subjects would be guaranteed "the quiet possession and full enjoyment of the rights, properties, and privileges they had before." But Governor Philipps had "forcibly dispossessed her, by ordering his steward to receive her rents for the Governor's own use." There was "no prospect of justice in that distant part of His Majesty's dominions, where there is no civil Government to protect the inhabitants from the unreasonable, arbitrary and terrifying practices of the Military Governors." So Madame La Tour had been forced to undertake "a dangerous and tedious voyage to implore His Majesty's justice and protection." She was but a poor widow with orphan children whose need was pressing, and she prayed "to be allowed to enjoy the estate of her ancestors in Nova Scotia, or for compensation if resumed to the Crown."[25]

The memorial was accompanied by a parcel of documents—conveyances of seigneurial title from two aunts and an uncle and depositions from several residents of the English *faubourg* at Annapolis Royal, including the Anglican chaplain at Fort Anne, who attested that Madame La Tour had been a "constant communicant of the Church of England" and was generally acknowledged "sole Lady of the Manour, Lands, and Premises of all the Inhabited Part of that Province . . . greatly beloved by the Inhabitants, her Tenants." This rhetorical flourish conveyed a wholly false impression of Acadian social relations.[26]

The Board of Trade was impressed—less with Madame La Tour's rhetorical style than with the problem her claim presented for the creation of a stable property system. "Mrs. Campbell [Madame La Tour] is in a very weak state of health," wrote the board's secretary,

Alured Popple. "Should she Dye, her Right might then devolve on her Children with whom it might not be possible for many years to compleat any Bargain." Although both Governor Philipps and Lieutenant-Governor Armstrong (sent back to the province by the Board of Trade when Philipps retired to his estate in Wales in 1731) doubted that the heirs had actually agreed to cede their claims, British officials found it convenient to assume they had. The board recommended and the Privy Council approved paying the handsome sum of £2,000 sterling to quiet Madame La Tour's title. It was considered in "His Majesty's Service that the Right of Mrs. Campbell should be purchased and extinguished," wrote Popple, for "it will remain a doubt whether without this Purchase, His Majesty can grant any Land in Nova Scotia."[27]

With this transaction the British declared King George to be *grand seigneur* of all the lands of l'Acadie. The energies of colonial administration in the province had already been turned to the standardization of the property system. With the authorization of the Board of Trade an official survey of the colony had begun, and Armstrong ordered the inhabitants to "plant poles at their Respective Boundarys" to assist in the preparation of metes and bounds plats of their lots, in which boundaries are described by courses, directions, and distances. Lieutenant-Governor Armstrong appointed Prudent Robichaud at Annapolis Royal and Alexandre Bourg dit Bellehumeur at Minas *procureurs du roi* (king's attorneys), empowered to record titles, sales, inheritances, and other transfers, as well as collect quitrents. Armstrong expected the inhabitants to resist paying, but they proved him wrong. Eager to have their rights confirmed, they were not about to raise a fuss over rents which, as Paul Mascarene observed, "seldom amount to more than one bushell of wheat and a couple of capons for every plantation." It was not the revenue but the principle that counted. The quitrents, he wrote, were "claim'd of the Inhabitants more to show them their dependence on the Crown than for any profit that accrued."[28]

It was an important moment in the history of British-Acadian relations. Armstrong, whose experience in l'Acadie was second only to Mascarene's, understood the long-term advantages of tethering Acadian interests to colonial government. He named numerous inhabitants to minor offices and established procedures for the annual election of an expanded number of deputies. He led the Governor's Council through the tedious process of hearing and sorting out the property disputes among the inhabitants. "They are a litigious sort of people," he wrote, "and so ill-natured to one another as daily to encroach upon their neighbour's properties, which occasions continual complaints." But Armstrong knew that the cases brought before the council had less to do with the Acadian character than with the restrictions imposed by his superiors. Despite the rapidly growing population, the British Colonial Office had consistently refused to authorize any new settlements or even to approve the reclamation of any additional marshland in established hamlets. The Acadians found themselves, in Paul Mascarene's words, "pincht for want of room from the subdivisions of their improv'd lands amongst their children." As lands were divided, conflicts erupted among neighbors over the location of property lines. "Either they must be made to Starve," Mascarene warned, "or they will, as they have done for many years past, go contrary to repeated orders, [and] settle themselves on some of the unappropriated lands, from whence it has been reckon'd very difficult to dispossess them."[29]

So Armstrong pressed the Board of Trade to permit the inhabitants to establish new settlements in order to relieve crowding, and in addition to authorize the creation of a popular assembly like the one in Massachusetts and other British colonies, a body that could levy local taxes to support the cost of colonial administration. By such measures, he argued, the Acadians "in time may be perhaps brought through their own free and voluntary acts to pay a greater obedience to the Government, and contribute to its greater support." It was a solid argument, similar to the one advanced by Lieutenant-Governor Thomas Caulfeild some fifteen years before. And British colonial officials responded in much the same way they had then: with horror. Catholics were prohibited from holding public office, they reminded Armstrong. Only those men willing to swear to "the usual oaths appointed by Act of Parliament to be taken by all officers and magistrates"—as established by the anti-Catholic Test Act of 1673—could serve as delegates in an elected assembly. Moreover, they would allow no extension of Acadian holdings. Armstrong was instructed to inform the inhabitants that as Catholics, they were ineligible for any further grants of land. All unclaimed lands in l'Acadie were to be "reserv'd for Protestant Subjects." The window of opportunity closed. It was a fateful turn. British policy and Acadian interests were set in opposition.[30]

In London, the Board of Trade was already soliciting proposals for the settlement of Protestant groups on lands adjacent to those of the Acadians. Among others, Thomas Coram renewed his plan to settle Germans or Scots Irish. No proposal got beyond the talking stage, but the talking was important, for it kept alive the idea of a Protestant Nova Scotia. At Annapolis Royal, meanwhile, provincial authorities embarked on a scheme of their own cooked up by Paul Mascarene. The plan called for the development of a colliery at a place called Joggins on the eastern shore of the Chignecto Basin where there were substantial deposits of bituminous coal, and the settlement of a community of French Huguenots in the vicinity. Presumably the Huguenots would serve as a buffer against possible Míkmaw attacks on the mine.[31]

Mascarene had developed this proposal at a point of crisis in his own life. Although he had served in the 40th Regiment, garrisoned at Fort Anne, since the conquest of 1710, and had been a member of the Governor's Council since 1720, he made his permanent residence in Boston, where he spent most winters, developing close personal and business ties to the merchant community there, especially with men trading to the eastward. He married Elizabeth Perry, daughter of a well-connected family (and a cousin of both John Nelson and former Massachusetts governor Joseph Dudley). Judging by Mascarene's affectionate letters to Elizabeth, it was a love match; but the marriage also brought him social standing and a moderate fortune. Guided by his wife's connections and her business acumen—she was "the sole manager of all my cash, of all my bills, of all my business," he later wrote—Mascarene prospered in trade, built a fine brick house, and joined King's Chapel, religious home to Boston's Anglican elite.[32]

Mascarene's world was shattered when Elizabeth died prematurely in 1729, leaving him not only disconsolate but deprived of her valuable assistance. With four young children, and only an officer's modest stipend to support them, he concocted the mining scheme with the assistance of Major Henry Cope, a retired British army officer and merchant trader of Boston, and succeeded in pushing it through the council with the support of Lieutenant-Governor Armstrong. Cope seems to have been in charge of raising the capital, and in 1730 he relocated to Annapolis Royal, where he joined the council and was able to supervise the mine's construction. The colliery opened in the spring of 1731 and appears to have been a successful operation. In the fall of that year Robert Hale docked there and "hawl'd off" sixty tons of coal. Meanwhile Mascarene remained at Boston, where he took responsibility for recruiting settlers. The project was endorsed by André Le Mercier, pastor of Boston's Huguenot church, but neither Mascarene nor Le Mercier could drum up any enthusiasm among the small Huguenot community. With Armstrong's authorization, Mascarene attempted to recruit more widely. "As it is the intention of the British government to settle the province with Protestant inhabitants," read an advertisement he prepared for the local papers, "notice is given that large tracts of land are to be granted in fee-simple." There were no takers. As Mascarene's friend Governor Jonathan Belcher of Massachusetts wrote in a letter to Thomas Coram, he saw no reason why settlers should go to Nova Scotia when they might live better in New England. "God deliver me and mine from the government of soldiers."[33]

Despite the failure of all these various plans, the idea of settling Protestants on lands that were closed to them was deeply disturbing to the Acadians. Many young couples left Annapolis and Minas for settlements elsewhere. Some relocated to French-administered Ile Saint-Jean (today's Prince Edward Island), a short voyage across the narrow strait from the isthmus of Chignecto, where by 1740 a population of about five hundred inhabitants had established a number of farming and fishing villages under French auspices. Others settled where no government could control them, on the salt marshes and tidal flats of Chipoudy Bay, the western terminus of the Bay of Fundy, where by 1730 several hundred inhabitants were spread thinly along the western shore of the bay and its three tidal rivers—the Chipoudy, Petitcodiac, and Memramcook. British authorities at Annapolis Royal asserted that the district was part of the province, but had no power to enforce their claim. In fact, the Acadians there were under the jurisdiction of neither Great Britain nor France. In the 1730s, migration to the Chipoudy area picked up considerably. Shortly after his paternity trial, Joseph Broussard dit Beausoleil and his older brother Alexandre settled there with their wives, the sisters Agnès and Marguerite Thibodeau; and in 1740, they relocated their families to the middle reaches of the Petitcodiac, founding a village they christened Beausoleil, after the hamlet of their birth.[34]

At Annapolis and Minas tensions arose over the ongoing survey of provincial lands, the chief surveyor reporting that a number of Acadians had refused to cooperate, and that a party of Míkmaq had interrupted his work, warning him against surveying the so-called unclaimed land, for it belonged to them and was "unalienable." Compelled to dispatch troops to protect the surveyors, Armstrong decided it was time to extend British authority to the upper reaches of the bay. In the spring of 1732, "for the better government of those more remote parts in the Bay of Fundy," he appointed Henry Cope to supervise the construction at Minas of a blockhouse where he could lodge a company of troops in order "to Curb the Insolence of these unruly people." The job was contracted to René Leblanc of

Grand Pré, who previously had served as a deputy and was known to be cooperative. But fearful of provoking a hostile reaction from the Acadians and Míkmaq, Armstrong told Leblanc that the building was intended as a storage facility.[35]

One day in early July 1732, as work on the blockhouse was getting underway, three Míkmaw men came to Leblanc's house where Henry Cope and another British officer were boarding. "In a most villainous manner," Cope reported to Armstrong, the men threatened Leblanc and his brother Pierre. They knew Leblanc had been ordered to build "a fort for the English," one of the men announced. "All the Leblancs were dogs and villains except François, and as for René. . . ." He reached for a knife hidden under his cloak, but Cope intervened. The Leblancs had been given no such instructions, he declared. "But suppose the King of Great Britain thought it convenient to build a fort there, who had anything to say against it?" Another of the Míkmaq immediately picked up the dare. King George may have conquered Annapolis Royal but not Minas, he replied angrily, and he would not suffer the British to build there, for he was "King of that country." After further harangues the men left, and Cope sent a runner to Armstrong, who in turn dispatched a message to the Acadians at Minas, assuring them that in undertaking the project he had "the Wellfare of the Province and the freedom of Trade only at heart," and expressly forbidding any of them from hindering its completion. But the construction got no further, probably because neither Leblanc nor anyone else was willing to test the Míkmaw threats. In the meantime, a party of Míkmaq overran the colliery at Chignecto, destroying the mineworks and scattering the miners. There would be no further production at the site before the nineteenth century.[36]

Armstrong suspected that the French at Louisbourg had incited the "rebellious spirits" at Minas, and there is evidence to suggest that he was right. Although the governor attempted to keep his plans for the blockhouse secret—even keeping them hidden from his council—the Míkmaq had learned of them by the spring of 1732, when they reported the details to Governor Saint-Ovide, who in turn encouraged them to do what they could to frustrate Armstrong. At about the same time Acadian merchant Joseph-Nicholas Gautier reported the plans to his Louisbourg business partners, Michel Dupont de Gourville and his brothers, great-grandsons of Charles de La Tour. The news stoked a smoldering resentment kindled by the British refusal to recognize their seigneurial rights. When King Louis ceded l'Acadie, Captain François Dupont Duvivier, adjutant of the Louisbourg garrison, wrote to Governor Saint-Ovide, he gave only what belonged to him, "not the property of his subjects." The Dupont family had the right to prevent the British from taking possession of what was not rightfully theirs. The Míkmaw action at Minas, he claimed, "had been secretly stirred up" by three of his uncles who still resided there.[37]

It is doubtful, however, that either the Míkmaq or the Acadians needed any stirring up. Both had reasons of their own to be angry about the direction of British policy in l'Acadie. The Acadians had sworn allegiance to the British crown only to find that they continued to be denied what they most wanted, the right to claim new land and establish new settlements. But the Leblancs and presumably other inhabitants nevertheless saw advantage in working with the British. The Míkmaq believed such cooperation was a dire threat to their future. Acadians and Míkmaq were no longer as close as they once had been. *Métissage* was increasingly rare, and the missionary Pierre Maillard pursued a course that kept natives separate from inhabitants. Both groups continued to occupy common spiritual ground, and the kinship between the two communities was remembered and honored by elders on each side. But there were evident fractures in the old alliance.[38]

FROM his estate in Wales Governor Richard Philipps periodically weighed in with reports and proposals to the Board of Trade; but it was Lieutenant-Governor Lawrence Armstrong who administered the colony through the 1730s. Armstrong had warned of the danger of excluding the Acadians from British plans for the province. Nonetheless, he was a military officer, in charge of the administration of a military government, and when his superiors rejected his proposals for creating an inhabitants' council and appointing more Acadians to local office, he followed orders. Isolated in a filthy, crumbling fort on the fringe of the British Empire, Armstrong faced a thankless task. The situation brought out his worst, although as he entered his seventies his explosive temper gave way to melancholy and sullen depression. Armstrong was an Irish Protestant, whose family had been, in his phrase, "great sufferers for the Protestant Interest," which explains perhaps why the most troublesome issue for him continued to be his relations with the missionary Catholic priests.[39]

To be fair, the British had a legitimate concern over the role of the priests who ministered to the Acadians and Míkmaq. They were Frenchmen, for the most part, appointed by the bishop of Québec and paid by the French crown, which of course made them suspect as foreign agents and spies. Governor Philipps attempted to gain some control by requiring them, upon their arrival in the province, to appear before the council and obtain written permission before taking up their stations. But the limits of British authority were constantly being tested by priestly independence, as they had been in the conflict between Armstrong and Father René-Charles de Breslay in 1728. After his return in 1731, Armstrong found numerous occasions to complain to Governor Saint-Ovide about the interference of priests in secular affairs. When Saint-Ovide sent two candidates to fill vacancies at Annapolis Royal and Minas in 1732, he assured Armstrong that he had strongly advised the men—Claude-Jean-Baptiste Chauvreulx and Claude de La Vernède de Saint-Poncy—to devote themselves solely to their "spiritual duties" and "not to meddle directly or indirectly in matters concerning the temporal power." The two dutifully reported to the council in Annapolis Royal, received their papers, and took up duties at their respective posts, Saint Poncy at Saint-Jean-Baptiste in Annapolis, Chauvreulx at Saint-Charles-des-Mines in Grand Pré.[40]

Trouble did not develop until the spring of 1736, when Armstrong summoned both men to appear before the Governor's Council. A British vessel had shipwrecked off the coast of Cape Sable and been stripped of all its valuables. Certain that Acadians and Míkmaq had been involved in the looting, Armstrong ordered the priests to accompany a British patrol to the area "to admonish and exhort both French and Indians to make a Discovery of what they knew and to make Restitution and satisfaction for the Injuries they had Committed." His order illustrated one of the most persistent dilemmas for the British. While insisting that priests abstain from meddling in secular affairs, provincial officials were frequently forced to turn to them when they needed to communicate or negotiate with the Míkmaq, so unpracticed and unskilled were they at native diplomatic protocol.[41]

Understandably, Chauvreulx and Saint-Poncy took exception to Armstrong's order, which he delivered in a brusque and aggressive fashion; and in what the secretary of the council characterized as "a most insolent, audacious, and disrespectful manner," the priests announced that "they would not go, and that they would have nothing to do with the affair." When Armstrong insisted that the two men "obey the just and lawful orders of His Majesty's Government," Chauvreulx responded impertinently. "I am here on behalf of the King of France," he declared, to which Saint-Poncy added, "we are not here to receive commands." Armstrong turned livid. In that case, he declared, they would be sent back to France forthwith. Hearing that, the two priests turned on their heels and stomped out of the chamber, in the words of the minutes, "slamming and throwing the doors in a most rude and insolent manner." The council voted unanimously that they be deported, but before it could be arranged, the men fled to Louisbourg.[42]

Armstrong had generated another religious crisis. The parishioners of Saint-Jean-Baptiste at Annapolis Royal wrote to French authorities complaining that "Contrary to the articles of the peace treaty of Utrecht, and contrary to all the promises made to us when we had taken the oath of loyalty to His British Majesty King George II," the lieutenant-governor had prohibited their priest "from saying Holy Mass, from entering the church, hearing our confessions, administering us the other sacraments, and carrying out any of their ecclesiastical functions." They asked for a ruling on "the conditions to which our missionaries should be bound, so that we will not be deprived of our spiritual succor *at the slightest whim* of those who command." When Saint-Ovide asked Armstrong for an explanation, he received a defensive reply. "It was not so much for Affronting myself and His Majesty's Council," Armstrong wrote back, "as their affecting an Independency and disowning His Majesty's Authority in his own Dominions." The inhabitants had the right to freely practice their religion, he agreed, but their priests were obliged to obey the lawful orders of the king's representatives.[43]

Saint-Ovide disagreed. The treaty "does not say that the missionaries sent to instruct the French inhabitants in their religion should be regarded as subjects of the King of Great Britain and subject to the orders of those in command in the Province," he responded. Priests ought not to fall under the same obligation as the inhabitants, who "remain by choice and their own free will." Saint-Ovide did not respond, however, to Armstrong's most telling argument. "I am Convinced," Armstrong had written, "that the French Government would not have been so mild on such an Occasion, if I may Suppose, that any priest would have dared to disobey their lawful Commands. Disobedience in Spiritual Pastors is always of a Contagious nature." The comte de Maurepas, French minister of the marine, agreed with Armstrong, and corrected Saint-Ovide on precisely this point a few months later, using the same analogy. "You were mistaken," he wrote, "that the French missionaries residing in l'Acadie are not subject to the English government. That is not reasonable, and you yourself would surely be far from adopting it, if by chance English ministers were to be tolerated within the expanse of your government."[44]

Governor Saint-Ovide never made this admission to Armstrong, for by then he had been recalled to France by officials who had grown tired of his flagrant disregard for mercantilist regulations. Before he left, however, he sent the fugitive missionaries back to l'Acadie. There was little Armstrong could do. Chauvreulx became resident priest at Pisiquid, and after the council succeeded in getting Saint-Poncy to agree to certain restrictions on his movements, he was allowed to return to Saint-Jean-Baptiste. Lieutenant-Governor Armstrong expressed his frustration in a letter to the Board of Trade. Beyond the *banlieu*, the British were powerless. He could control neither the Míkmaq nor the Acadians, and could not prevent the priests from doing whatever they pleased. The French at Louisbourg commanded loyalty from the priests, natives, and inhabitants outside Annapolis Royal, he wrote; "how dangerous this may prove in time to His Majesty's authority and the peace and tranquility of the Province I believe your Lordships can easily foresee. And how to prevent the ill consequences, I know not."[45]

In the ten years since his conflict with Father Breslay, little had changed for Armstrong. With fewer than two hundred men in the garrison, he was able to exercise very little authority outside the *banlieu*. Moreover, his conflict with with British and New England merchants continued apace at Annapolis Royal. Armstrong's feud with Major Alexander Cosby and William Winniett, Cosby's father-in-law, grew even more intense. Deeply implicated in the illegal Acadian trade, the power and influence of these two men grew in proportion to the increase in commercial traffic to Louisbourg. From their position on the Governor's Council the pair took every opportunity to criticize the conduct of the lieutenant-governor. Many times Armstrong appealed to the Board of Trade to have them removed, but his request was always denied. "You must wholly consider yourself as a civil magistrate when you sit in Council," the board instructed him, "where, by the Constitution of the Plantations, full liberty of debate, assent, or dissent, is allowed to every councilor. . . . Where they are so few civil inhabitants [that is, Protestants], one would not part too lightly with one of them out of the Council." Responding with typical imperiousness, Armstrong ran council meetings with such a heavy hand that Winniett eventually resigned, while Cosby and several other councilors refused to attend. By 1738, the council had ceased meeting altogether. Armstrong's authoritarian streak extended as well to the officers and soldiers in the garrison, many of whom came to hate and shun him. The end of the decade was a high point in Acadian prosperity but the nadir of British authority in l'Acadie.[46]

On 6 December 1739, Armstrong was found dead in his chambers, "five Wounds in his Breast and his sword Lying carelessly by him in his bed." It surely was a lonely and bitter conclusion to the old man's long military career and nearly thirty years in His Majesty's service in America. An inquest chaired by his nemesis, Major Cosby, ruled that the lieutenant-governor had "put a Period to his life with his own Hands," and attributed his suicide to "Lunacy." A number of later commentators found the verdict suspect—how does a man extract a sword from his chest after a final fatal thrust? There were certainly those with sufficient motive for murder, all of them officials at the inquest. Yet the grisly means of Armstrong's death may simply have been a measure of his desperation to exit what had become an intolerable life. "Governor Armstrong has been for a long time frequently Afflicted with melancholy fitts," one of the councilors wrote to the Board of Trade, "the Consequence of which none ever Suspected till they found him Dead." There was no mourning for Lawrence Armstrong's passing among the Acadians. But who would replace him?[47]

CHAPTER 8

Plac'd Between Two Fires

Paul Mascarene and Imperial War, 1739–1747

In April 1740 the Acadian deputies received a letter from Major Paul Mascarene at Fort Anne. As a result of the death of Lieutenant-Governor Armstrong, he wrote, provincial authority had devolved "on me as Eldest Councilor and President." He promised a smooth transition. "The Regulations made for the Administration of Justice" would remain in effect. But with pointed reference to the arbitrary conduct of his predecessor, he pledged to enforce them "with gentleness." His intention was to do justice to all and preserve the peace.[1]

Peace and war were very much on Mascarene's mind. Seeking maritime and commercial advantage in the West Indies, Britain had declared war on Spain the previous October and the conflict was expected to spread through the entangling alliances of Europe's royal families and kingdoms, and force the resumption of the violent conflict between Great Britain and France. Mascarene knew that for every Briton in l'Acadie, including garrison soldiers, there were thirty French-speaking inhabitants. The British hold on the province, he was convinced, would depend on the Acadians keeping to their promise "never to take up arms in the event of war." War would be the acid test of Acadian neutrality, he warned the deputies, and the least tincture of disloyalty would be disastrous to their interests. "The people of New England," he wrote with chilling prescience, "would ask nothing better than to take possession of lands cleared and ready to receive them."[2]

As a longtime resident of Boston and a famliar figure among the leading circles of merchants and public servants in Massachusetts, Mascarene was well acquainted with New England's views. For years he had actively sought a military or civil appointment that would keep him in Boston with his motherless children. When that effort failed—his French origins may have been the reason—he reluctantly accepted an assignment as commander of the small garrison of some eighty men at the British fishing station of Canso, only a half-day's sail from Louisbourg, the center of the flourishing intercolonial smuggling trade. Evidence suggests Mascarene used this position, which he occupied from 1735 until 1739, to further the trading interests of his friend and patron, Governor Jonathan Belcher of Massachusetts, negotiating deals of dubious legality with French Governor Saint-Ovide of Ile Royale. During his posting at Canso, Mascarene continued to winter in Boston, and it was there in February 1740 that word reached him of Armstrong's suicide.[3]

As senior member of the Governor's Council, Mascarene stood first in line to be selected by the members as their next president, which would make him in effect acting governor, as well as presumptive candidate as the Board of Trade's official replacement. A career officer in his mid-fifties, he knew this was likely his final opportunity for distinction, and he hurried to Annapolis Royal by the first available packet, even though it meant a painful separation from his children. His bid for the presidency was opposed, however, by the second most senior member of the council, a crusty old Puritan merchant named John Adams, a permanent resident of Annapolis Royal since his move from Massachusetts in 1710. Adams put himself forward as the more appropriate candidate since Mascarene had never made his permanent residence in the province. Mascarene always claimed he was conducting official business in Massachusetts, Adams wrote, but in fact "he was building his Great Brick house in Boston and getting his picture drawn at full length." His reference was to a life-size portrait of Mascarene, resplendent in white linen and black armor, painted by the English artist John Smibert in the summer of 1729, the moment when Mascarene and Major Henry Cope proposed their project to settle Huguenots at Chignecto.[4]

In the painting, Mascarene rests his left hand on a map of l'Acadie, while with his right he gestures to an idealized landscape of Annapolis Royal and Fort Anne in the background. Adams claimed the portrait showed Mascarene holding the baton of a French officer (it does not), and the old man wrote that it struck him as a "Piece of Vanity for a Captain of thirty men in Col. Philipps's Regiment to exalt himself to the highest dignity of the French Nation." There was more than a hint in that comment of the prejudice that stymied Mascarene's appointment to office in Massachusetts. But the slur carried little weight in Annapolis Royal, where Huguenots played important roles in British administration, and where a succession of governors and lieutenant-governors had put Mascarene's multilingual and diplomatic talents to good use. The council unanimously selected him as president (with Adams recusing himself), and some months later the Board of Trade appointed him lieutenant-governor. Adams resigned from the council and removed to Boston.[5]

Mascarene assumed office with a clear view of the task before him, one based on three decades of experience in l'Acadie. British interests in the region, he argued, were best advanced by encouraging the Acadians to be good subjects and emphasizing to them the advantages of British rule. In the short run, that offered the best prospect of dissuading them from supporting the French, and over time they might even become loyal British subjects. Mascarene had not always taken this position. Twenty years before, he had argued for the removal of the Acadians and the recruitment of Protestant settlers. He had been a skeptic about their pledge of neutrality when they took the oath of allegiance in 1730, and had proposed his own scheme of settling Huguenots at Chignecto. But over the subsequent decade he had gradually become convinced that the vast majority wished "to live at peace and in submission to the King." Eventually he came around to the position advocated by his predecessors Thomas Caulfeild and Lawrence Armstrong, which Mascarene summarized as making the inhabitants "sensible of the advantage and ease they enjoy under the British Government, whereby to wean them from their old masters," although he recognized that "to do this effectually, a considerable time will be required." This policy would require the active participation of Acadians in civil society, and Mascarene committed himself to recruiting responsible deputies and utilizing them to the limits of their capacity. "Must try to get the inhabitants to choose for Deputies men of good sense," he reminded himself soon after his selection as council president. "Upright men of property, having the good of the community at heart, and sensible to the duty to which they are bound by their oath of allegiance."[6]

This approach called for goodwill, tolerance, and patience, traits Paul Mascarene possessed in abundance. The strength of his character was clearly evident in his response to the death of the Huguenot trader William Winniett, who drowned in Boston Harbor while on a business trip there in 1741. Winniett and his wife Marie-Madeleine Maisonnat, an important trader in her own right, were deeply involved in the illegal commerce with Louisbourg, and as a matter of course they came into considerable conflict with the lieutenant-governor. Winniett and his son-in-law Major Alexander Cosby opposed Mascarene just as they had Lawrence Armstrong. Yet after Winniett's death, no one did more than Mascarene to assist his widow, who was left with six minor children. He helped collect money owed to her husband and wrote letters on behalf of the family, despite the continued obstruction of Cosby, who died suddenly and unexpectedly in 1742, much to Mascarene's relief. "My speaking so much to the advantage of the widow may occasion some wagg to think I am actuated by other motives," Mascarene wrote a friend in Boston, "butt you may rest assur'd that I am prompted by no other sentiments than those of Christian Charity, humanity and good will."[7]

Mascarene's biographer argues that much the same attitude governed his approach to the Acadians. During the first four years of his tenure, in striking contrast to his predecessor, he worked to cultivate friendships with the inhabitants and with their priests. An intellectual at heart—his papers include his personal translations of Molière's plays into English—the priests provided him with a rare opportunity for stimulating conversation. He and Claude de La Vernède de Saint-Poncy, curé at Annapolis Royal, engaged in a fascinating correspondence over the relative merits of Protestantism and Catholicism. While Mascarene would not admit the validity of Saint-Poncy's arguments, he was prepared to hear them. "As long as there are men," he closed one of his letters, "there will always be different opinions and sentiments on certain points." Yet Mascarene did not hesitate to enforce the rule of temporal over religious authority. When Saint-Poncy violated the orders of the council, leaving Annapolis Royal on the instructions of the bishop of Québec to take up duties at Chignecto, Mascarene put an abrupt end to their friendly exchange. "M. Saint-Poncy persists in his Slighting the Orders of this Government," Mascarene noted after the priest ignored his order to return. "Tho this government is slow in executing what belongs to Severity, be assur'd that sooner or later those who disobey the orders of it and are within its reach will feel the weight of its resentment."[8]

Saint-Poncy attempted to repair the breech with a conciliatory note, but Mascarene refused to open it. Father Charles de la Goudalie of Grand Pré attempted to mediate, but Mascarene was adamant. Officially it was necessary for the lieutenant-governor to demonstrate his resentment, he wrote, but unofficially he hoped Goudalie would communicate to Saint-Poncy that as a man he held no hard personal feelings. "In all our actions," Mascarene once wrote to his daughter, "the Intention is what ought principally to be lookt at. All the devotion we pay to God if not done with a Sincere intention to please him can not be acceptable; and all our offices toward men if void of the same good intention are butt meer gremace and shew."[9]

The armed conflict Mascarene feared began in 1744. For three years France had been allied with Spain and Prussia in an invasion of Austria's central European dominions. Great Britain supported Austria and was at war with Spain. Neither Britain nor France wanted war, but it became impossible to avoid. Pressed by Spain, France declared war on Great Britain on 15 March 1744, and Britain responded with its own declaration three weeks later. During what Europeans knew as the War of the Austrian Succession (which British North Americans called King George's War) the maritime region would be the most important colonial theater. The news of war arrived at Louisbourg on 3 May, and French governor Jean-Baptiste-Louis Le Prévost Duquesnel—who had replaced Saint-Ovide—immediately ordered Captain François Dupont Duvivier, adjutant of the garrison, to organize an assault on the British outpost at Canso. Duvivier saw the war as the opportunity to win back the province lost thirty years before. With 350 *troupes de la marine* he sailed into Canso harbor with a small fleet of vessels on 13 May and announced his presence by hurling a salvo toward the British blockhouse. The small garrison surrendered without resistance, and after burning the buildings at the site, Duvivier carried the British soldiers back to Louisbourg in good cheer. More ominous was the attack by Míkmaq on a New England fishing vessel anchored in the harbor. Fired up by the recent kidnapping of one of their chiefs and his family by a privateer sailing out of Massachusetts, native fighters overwhelmed the vessel and killed nearly the entire crew.[10]

Mascarene learned of the attacks within days. He knew an assault on Fort Anne soon would follow and he considered his prospects "dismal." The 40th Regiment was seriously understrength. "I had butt one hundred [men]," he later wrote, "twenty or thirty whereof were utter Invalides, [and] of ten or a dozen of Officers not above two or three who had ever seen a gunn fir'd in anger, and who for the most part were tainted by Republican principles"—that is to say, they were New Englanders, accustomed to electing their own officers. The fort itself was in terrible condition. Built by the French more than thirty years before, it had not been substantially improved by the British and was "mouldering away," as Mascarene put it. There were no bomb-proof casements or shelters for protection during a siege, and according to an official report prepared for the British Board of Ordnance, the palisade was "of no use in the world but to keep the cattle out of the ditch." By contrast, Louisbourg was one of the most heavily fortified places in all North America, and its garrison numbered some eighteen hundred men and officers. Moreover, a French census of 1739 counted six hundred Míkmaw fighters available for service. Mascarene had regularly appealed to London for additional men and the resources to reinforce Fort Anne, but there had been no reply to his requests. "Without some assistance of a Sea force, an augmentation of the Garrison, or a good healthy and lively recruit, it cannot be expected that the place when attacked can hold out long," he wrote.[11]

In the emergency, Mascarene turned to the governor of Massachusetts, William Shirley, who in 1741 had been named to succeed Jonathan Belcher. Shirley was an ambitious lawyer who as a young man left England and relocated to Boston. With the support of his patron, the Duke of Newcastle, secretary of state for the Southern Department, he won appointment as Advocate General in the Court of the Vice-Admiralty, which dealt with the enforcement of the maritime and mercantile laws, and as "Surveyor of the King's Woods," a position requiring him to travel extensively on the frontiers of the province. His work introduced him to prominent advocates of a war of conquest against New France, and Shirley soon became their political spokesman. Governor Belcher had tended to take a more mercantile, less military view of intercolonial affairs, favoring the interests of men trading to the eastward. The division between expansionist and mercantile factions long had been a defining conflict in Massachusetts politics, and when the king's ministers sacked Belcher and appointed Shirley to the governorship, it strongly suggested a drift toward war.[12]

Shirley responded eagerly to Mascarene's call for help in late May 1744. In contrast to the Board of Trade, he believed the maritime region was the key to success in the struggle with France for supremacy in North America. The loss of l'Acadie, he feared, would directly threaten the security of Massachusetts and New England. He instructed John Henry Bastide, the colony's chief military engineer, to organize a force of several dozen workers and proceed immediately to Annapolis Royal to assist in the repair and refortification of Fort Anne. News of the official declaration of war against France arrived from England before the provincial galley departed, providing Shirley with the justification for doing even more. Calling the Massachusetts Assembly into session, he urged the authorization of two companies of volunteers for the defense of Annapolis Royal. "I believe you will judge it a Piece of Service that will be highly acceptable to His Majesty, and tend to secure some of the most valuable Interests of this Province, to send some Recruits for that Garrison to continue there for a few Months." Despite considerable opposition from the mercantile faction, with the support of the expansionists Shirley won the Assembly's authorization of funds to recruit and outfit the troops. Using this funding authority to distribute contracts to both his political supporters and his critics, Shirley began to assemble a powerful political machine in Massachusetts.[13]

At Annapolis Royal, meanwhile, the small British community was reeling in panic. Rumors of imminent attack by French privateers and Míkmaw fighters swept through the English *faubourg*, and terrified families fled into the fort, hauling their goods and possessions behind them in great confusion. Although the rumors proved false, Mascarene wrote, "the impression it had made would not however be taken off from most people's minds." The arrival of the Massachusetts galley in early June brought a little calm, but panic returned as soon as Mascarene posted news of the official declaration of war. When the galley returned to Boston a few days later, it was loaded with women and children, and soon the few remaining dependants departed on other vessels.[14]

As Bastide and his work crews set to strengthening the decrepit fortifications, Mascarene received a visit from the Annapolis deputies. They pledged their loyalty and offered assistance, but also reiterated their position of strict neutrality—they would bear arms for neither side. "It is certain we can never force them to take up arms against the French," Mascarene reported to the Board of Trade after the meeting, "but if I can succeed in what I have labour'd for these four years past, that is to wean them so far from the French as to prevent their joining with or assisting them and hinder by their means the Indians about us giving us any disturbance here, it will make it more difficult for the French of Cape Breton to attack us." All through the month of June and into the second week of July the Acadians of the *banlieu* brought timbers, hauled stone, and labored on the fortifications alongside the workmen from Massachusetts.[15]

On 11 July the deputies reported to Mascarene that three hundred Míkmaq and Maliseets were on their way from Minas and would soon attack. The inhabitants working on the fort immediately left, and all the Acadians of the *banlieu* swiftly barricaded themselves in their homes. Although the assault force included no French or Canadien troops, it had been assembled on the orders of Governor Duquesnel of Ile Royale by Pierre Maillard, the missionary who for the previous decade had lived and worked among the Míkmaq, learning their language and gaining considerable influence in their councils. The assault came the following morning. The attackers killed two soldiers tending their gardens outside the fort, and hiding themselves behind fences and barns, took potshots at the defenders whenever they took the chance of looking over the ramparts. But aside from torching the abandoned English *faubourg* and indiscriminately slaughtering the livestock of the inhabitants, the Míkmaq were unable to do any serious damage. The affair came to an end with the arrival on 15 July of vessels from Boston with Shirley's two companies. The next morning, the Míkmaq and Maliseets were gone.[16]

Within hours the Acadians returned to the fort with fresh provisions and supplies. Mascarene was pleased. They had kept faithful to their promise of neutrality, he reported, "and no ways join'd with the Enemy, who has kill'd most of their cattle." Native fighters had targeted the farms of Acadians known as friends of the British. A few days later two deputies arrived from Minas with a letter signed by the leading inhabitants there, pledging to do their best to prevent livestock from being driven to Louisbourg to supply the French garrison. Mascarene was appreciative, and he wrote sympathetically to Shirley of the Acadians' plight: "The French inhabitants are certainly in a very perilous Situation, those who pretend to be their Friends and old Masters having let loose a parcell of Banditti to plunder them, whilst on the other hand they see themselves threatened with ruin and destruction if they fail in their allegiance to the British government."[17]

The native army retreated to Minas, where in late August 1744 it was joined by Captain Duvivier with a company of fifty French troops from Louisbourg. The great-grandson of Charles de La Tour and an Acadian by birth, François Dupont Duvivier had great expectations of support from his countrymen. Since the British conquest in 1710, he wrote in a *mémoire,* the inhabitants had "preserved the hope of returning to their allegiance to the king." So strong was their zeal that "with one hundred men only from the garrison of Louisbourg, and a certain quantity of arms and ammunition to distribute to the inhabitants, the Sieur Duvivier puts his head on the line [*s'engagerait sur sa tête*] to make the conquest of this part of

North America." This was the plan Governor Duquesnel approved. Duvivier was to foment an uprising among the Acadians, and with a combined force of inhabitants and natives was to march on Annapolis Royal, where he would be met by two French warships carrying siege guns and additional troops. The fort would be taken, the British expelled, and l'Acadie returned to France.[18]

Duvivier was to be bitterly disappointed. Although a number of Acadians assisted the French—the merchant Joseph-Nicholas Gautier, related to Duvivier by marriage, offered Bélair, his *haute rivière* estate, as French headquarters, and transported Duvivier's men and equipment in his schooners—the overwhelming majority did not. The Acadians of Minas and the *haute rivière* did not greet him as a liberator. Duvivier, who had planned to live off the country, was forced to requisition the supplies he needed. The inhabitants resisted by hiding their stores, and in frustration Duvivier issued draconian commands, ordering them to furnish horses, cattle, grain, tools, and boats under penalty of severe punishment. He required the deputies to swear loyalty to the French king, threatening that those who refused would be "left to the discretion of *les sauvages* to be punished by death." The Acadians obeyed reluctantly and bitterly, and not one of them agreed to shoulder arms. On the morning of 8 September, when Duvivier arrayed his forces before Fort Anne, there were no Acadians among them.[19]

The French vessels with the siege guns had not yet arrived, so Duvivier could do little more than the natives had done several weeks earlier, pinning down the British with small-arms fire. The standoff continued until 26 September, when the sails of two vessels were sighted entering the basin. To Duvivier's disappointment and Mascarene's great relief they proved to be an armed brigantine and a sloop from Boston, carrying a company of seventy Abenakis of the Pigwacket band, who had hired on as mercenaries to fight under the command of Captain John Gorham of Maine. A few days later Gorham led his native rangers in a surprise attack on the Míkmaw encampment, killing women and children and mutilating their bodies. Demoralized by this assault, the Míkmaq retreated, and the following day, 5 October, Duvivier withdrew as well. The French vessels finally arrived three weeks later, but beat a quick retreat when their commander learned Duvivier had already gone.[20]

The French, Míkmaq, and Maliseets arrived at Minas totally bereft of provisions, and Duvivier sent them out to forage what they could from the inhabitants. The Acadians were outraged and the Minas deputies, "in the name of their communities," pleaded with him to desist. "We hope," they petitioned, "that you will not plunge both ourselves and our families into a state of total loss, and that this consideration will cause you to withdraw your *sauvages* and troops from our districts. We live under a mild and tranquil government, and we have good reason to be faithful to it. We hope, therefore, that you will have the goodness not to separate us from it; and that you will grant us the favour not to plunge us into utter misery." This remarkable statement amounted to an explicit rejection of Duvivier's claim of Acadian zeal for France and an all but explicit ratification of Mascarene's policy. Three days later Duvivier pulled out of Minas and returned to Louisbourg.[21]

WHEN some time afterward Captain Duvivier was charged with leading an incompetent campaign, he defended himself by producing a copy of that petition, lamenting that the Acadians had "observed the neutrality they had promised." He blamed the priests. Abbé Desenclaves at Annapolis Royal had "fully informed the English governor of all he could learn of the French plans and exhorted his parishioners to remain faithful to the King of England," Duvivier testified, and Chauvreulx at Pisiquid had "pronounced excommunications against those of his parishioners who took arms in favor of the French." Lieutenant-Governor Mascarene reported much the same thing. The conduct of the parish priests, he wrote Shirley, had been "farr better than could have been expected." Indeed, the Catholic clergy in l'Acadie maintained this position throughout the war, despite considerable pressure from Québec. Mascarene's policy of *rapprochement* had paid off.[22]

Soon after Duvivier's departure the Acadians deputies detailed for Mascarene the oppression they had suffered under French occupation. According to Louis Robichaud, the son of Prudent Robichaud and an Annapolis deputy, he and his family "ran the risk of our lives" by providing intelligence of French movements to the British. Native fighters had plundered their household goods and livestock and he had suffered a bad beating because of his loyalties. "They assur'd me," Mascarene reported to Shirley, "that notwithstanding the entreaties and threats of M. Duvivier, none of the inhabitants could be persuaded to take up Arms and Joyn the Enemy." But Shirley received a contradictory report from John Henry Bastide, his military engineer, who wrote from Annapolis Royal criticizing the wavering loyalty of the inhabitants, arguing that only the vigorous use of military power would keep them in "proper awe and attachment to the Garrison," and suggesting that Shirley order the Massachusetts troops to seize Acadian hostages in order "to deterr the inhabitants from taking arms."[23]

Shirley considered this an excellent idea. In the last days of October he ordered Captain Edward Tyng, of the Massachusetts militia, to fit out several vessels for an assault on the Acadians of the upper bay. The purpose of the expedition, Shirley informed the Board of Trade, was "to take satisfaction of such of the French Inhabitants as have already revolted from their allegiance and join'd the French Enemy, by destroying and burning their Settlements and taking them prisoners, and to take hostages from among them, who have not yet revolted to be deliver'd to the Garrison as pledges for the fidelity of the Country." Shirley simultaneously declared war on the Abenakis, Maliseets, and Míkmaq, setting a bounty of £100 on the scalps of males, £50 for those of women and children. Because Acadians and Míkmaq were interrelated, it amounted to placing a price on the heads of inhabitants as well.[24]

Concerned that four years of patient work was about to be

wrecked, Lieutenant-Governor Mascarene sent a friendly but forceful warning to the Acadian deputies. While he was much pleased that most of them had remained true to the allegiance they owed the king, he knew there were men among them who had supported the French, and unless those rebels surrendered themselves immediately, he feared the whole community would suffer the consequences of an attack by the forces of Massachusetts. "Those who have done their duty, and for whom we have great consideration," he wrote, "must unavoidably share in the trouble that military people bring with them, and which I should like to prevent as much as possible." The Acadians were granted a temporary respite by fortuitous storms in the Bay of Fundy that prevented Captain Tyng from sailing north. In late December, however, after reporting to the council that a great body of native fighters had assembled at Minas and Chignecto, "supported by the assistance of the French inhabitants," Captain Gorham began planning another assault by his much-feared Abenaki rangers.[25]

In January 1745 the deputies of Minas wrote to Mascarene, pledging their loyalty and promising to deliver to Annapolis Royal the inhabitants who had supported the French. In turn they appealed for Mascarene's protection from the New Englanders, who were planning "to destroy all the inhabitants that had any Indian blood in them and scalp them." Since they counted "a great number of mulattoes amongst them who had taken the Oath and who were allied to the greatest families, it had Caused a terrible Alarm which made many put themselves on their Guard being very much frighten'd." Mascarene could only offer his assurance that the bounty had not been intended to include Acadians of mixed ancestry. If that had been the policy, he wrote, "the inhabitants of this river, many of whom have Indian blood in them, and some even who live within reach of the cannon, would not be suffered to live peaceably as they do." As it happened, bad weather once again postponed the planned expedition. But Mascarene's words were cold comfort. For the duration of the war the Acadians remained under constant threat from bounty hunters.[26]

Shortly thereafter the deputies of Minas and Chignecto delivered to Annapolis Royal a number of inhabitants suspected of supporting the French, and they were subjected to questioning by the council. Typical was the interrogation of Louis-Amand Bugeaud, a merchant trader of Grand Pré. Bugeaud was evasive in his answers, at first claiming the French had confiscated his vessel, then admitting he had transported arms from Beaubassin to Minas, although contending he had been forced do so at gunpoint. At first he denied, then acknowledged, an eyewitness report—which could only have come from another Acadian—that he had been "dancing and making merry in Company with the Enemy." On one point, however, he was clear and insistent: "I did not bear weapons against this Government." Witnesses provided corroboration of his denial, testifying that they had seen a French officer command Bugeaud to arm himself, and heard Bugeaud respond that he would not touch any weapons—"*ne toucherait aucun armes*." It was a consistent feature of the testimony of all the Acadians the council questioned. While they may have consorted with the enemy and provided them with succor, they had done all they could to avoid violating the pledge not to bear arms. In fact, with the exception of Joseph-Nicholas Gautier, a collaborator whom Mascarene ordered arrested, the council uncovered no evidence that any Acadian had willingly violated the neutrality agreement. "The French inhabitants have in general behav'd well," Mascarene wrote Shirley after completing the investigation, "tho' it can not be surprising the Enemy has creatures amongst them."[27]

Determined to make another try at retaking l'Acadie, in January 1745 French authorities in Québec sent three hundred militia to join a similar number of Míkmaw fighters at Chignecto, all under the command of Lieutenant Pierre-Paul Marin de la Malgue, a Montréal native with considerable experience in frontier warfare. When he learned of their presence at Beaubassin, Mascarene ordered the arrest of a score of inhabitants he considered French supporters. Joseph-Nicolas Gautier, who headed the list, successfully evaded capture, but Mascarene seized his wife Marie Allain and his youngest son Pierre, clamped them in irons, and confined them to the fort's dungeon. This ought to have provided the French with an opportunity to exploit Acadian resentment at harsh British conduct. But when Marin and his small army moved to Grand Pré, then on to Annapolis Royal in mid-May, they treated the inhabitants with contempt. Unlike Duvivier, Marin had no illusion that the Acadians would provide assistance, and he simply took what he wanted from them by force. Inhabitants later told Mascarene of being rousted from their sleep by Canadien militia and threatened with death at the hands of the Míkmaq if they protested the ransacking of their homes. The Canadien occupation "had been very harsh," they declared. For three weeks Marin kept Mascarene and his garrison bottled up in Fort Anne. He succeeded in capturing two supply vessels from Boston, taking their crews hostage. But again the French vessels with siege implements failed to appear. The reason became apparent on 3 June when a runner arrived from Ile Royale with orders for Marin to come "as quickly as possible with the Canadien and Indian force that you command." Louisbourg was under siege by an expeditionary army of several thousand New Englanders.[28]

Neither the French nor the British had thought this possible. The audacious idea of assaulting the great fortress was the brainchild of John Bradstreet, one of the sons of Agathe de La Tour and another of Charles de La Tour's great-grandsons. But Bradstreet was enlisted in the service of the British rather than the French. He was a young lieutenant serving in the 40th Regiment, garrisoned at Canso, when in the spring of 1744 his cousin, François Dupont Duvivier, forced their surrender and carried them prisoner to Louisbourg. Bradstreet had been there numerous times before, to visit his uncle and the captain of the fort, Pierre Rousseau de Souvigny, or to see any of several cousins, officers of the garrison. Usually he went to conduct business, for like most British and French officers in the maritime region, Bradstreet was engaged in smuggling on the side. So he was well known at Louisbourg, and during his captivity was allowed the run of the fortress. Studying the lay of the harbor, fortifications, and defensive batteries, he came to the conclusion that the place might be captured by a relatively small force.[29]

In September 1745, when Governor Duquesnel asked Bradstreet to act as an intermediary in the negotiation of a prisoner exchange with Governor Shirley, he got an opportunity to present his idea. Shirley was enthusiastic and convinced the Massachusetts Assembly to provide funds. Although others were involved in drawing up the actual plan of attack, according to William Pepperrell, the wealthy merchant and Maine landowner Shirley appointed as commander of the expedition, it was Bradstreet, the Acadian, who was the "first projector of the project."[30]

Shirley and Pepperrell succeeded in recruiting more than three thousand men, organized into two regiments. The province of Massachusetts promised them 25 shillings per month (the first month in advance), a two-year exemption from further military service, and the suspension of personal debt repayment until their return from the campaign. Massachusetts was in the midst of an economic depression and these proved attractive inducements. But religious fervor also played an important role in recruitment. Some fourteen ministers accompanied the troops, and the journals kept by soldiers suggest that many of them followed their pastors. Reverend Samuel Moody, minister of Pepperrell's church, had been chaplain on Colonel John March's disastrous Port Royal campaign thirty-eight years before. Now in his eighties, he joined in the Louisbourg expedition, which he described as a "crusade." Reverend John Barnard proclaimed that "the cause is God's." The Puritan hatred of Catholics was considerably more intense than that of the English generally. New England's religious certitude would provide effective cover for a good deal of gratuitous violence and pillage.[31]

The expedition, in eighty vessels, with naval support provided by four British men-of-war under the command of Commodore Peter Warren of the Royal Navy, came ashore at Gabarus Bay a few miles from the fortress on 11 May 1745. Louisbourg's commander, Louis Dupont Duchambon—uncle of both François Duvivier and John Bradstreet—had never been tested in battle and provided poor leadership. He hesitated in deploying his men and failed to prevent the landing, then panicked and abandoned the battery defending the harbor entrance, a fateful error that proved the key to the New England victory. The French managed to hold out for six weeks, but finally surrendered on 28 June. Few of the New Englanders had been directly involved in the siege—most were out plundering the surrounding villages. According to Colonel Samuel Waldo, in command of the 2nd Massachusetts Regiment, three quarters of his men were "employed in ravaging the country." One contingent attacked and destroyed the fishing village at Port Toulouse, a community of several hundred Acadians, driving the men into the woods and seizing the women and children. Other companies sailed along the coast, plundering and burning whatever hamlets they found. "One captain's company went up into the woods and took a small village," a soldier noted in his journal. "They kill'd 20ty and Brought away 25 prisoners." Another man reported that his company had found "one more camp with 2 Pritty Gurls in it [and] 3 Boys." The troops "had no particular orders," a diarist noted. "Everyone did what was right in his own eyes."[32]

When news of the surrender reached Boston, there was joyous celebration. The victory inspired enormous confidence in the impending fall of New France. God had "triumphed gloriously over his and our antichristian enemies," Reverend Thomas Prince declared from his pulpit at South Church in Boston, and he predicted the coming of a British Protestant empire "from the *Eastern* to the *Western* sea, and from the River of Canada to the Ends of America." Shirley had his sights set closer to home. The time had come, he believed, to move decisively against the Acadians. "It grieves me much," he wrote Pepperrell shortly before the French surrender at Louisbourg, "that I have it not in my power to send a party of 500 men forthwith to Menis, and burn Grand Pré, their chief town, and open all their sluices, and lay their country waste at the back of their camp, which might be done with such a number in a night's time. But if it pleases God that we succeed at Cape Breton, I doubt not but we shall settle Nova Scotia upon a better foot for the future."[33]

Shirley's bold stroke against Louisbourg and his decisive interventions at Annapolis Royal gave him considerable influence among the members of the Nova Scotia Governor's Council, and his aggressive views dominated their discourse. But with several thousand New England troops still at Louisbourg enduring a nasty winter, as well as a scourge of epidemic disease that was taking an awful toll, Shirley was unable to convince the Massachusetts Assembly to authorize yet another force to strike at the Acadians. Inevitably, however, the Annapolis deputies—Jean-Simon Leblanc, Jean-Baptiste Pellerin, Jean Melanson, Charles Girouard, Claude Granger, Joseph and Louis Robichaud—caught wind of the threatening talk from garrison officers and soldiers, and in late June they presented Mascarene with a memorial expressing their concerns. "You know the condition in which we are placed both by the French and the Indians in all their operations," they appealed. "The latter ravage, plunder, and kill us; the former overwhelm us with work and trouble, not giving us a moment to breathe. And now from another side we are made to understand that out of Boston will come those intent on destroying us entirely, which would not be difficult, since we are already crushed in all ways."[34]

It was true that the inhabitants had supplied the French invaders with provisions. "We bring them what they demand in order to shelter ourselves from greater harm. And despite all that, they call us Englishmen and cause us a thousand sorrows." It was true that "a few among us have been unfaithful in their conduct and discretion. But would you damn the innocent many for the guilty few?" They had denounced the offenders and provided evidence against them. "To what test have we not submitted our loyalty, aside from having not shouldered arms?" And that they would not do, for surely it would result in their complete destruction. They appealed to Mascarene's sense of justice. "In mercy prevent our alarms by promising your protection, which we will strive to deserve more and more by our attention to following your command to be faithful to the government."[35]

The terms of the capitulation imposed on the French at Louisbourg provided for the transportation of all officers, soldiers, and civilian inhabitants. During the summer of 1745 the British arranged for the deportation to France of more than four thousand residents of Ile Royale, including nearly two thousand inhabitants, mostly Acadians who had relocated there in the aftermath of British conquest in 1710. The people asked to be taken to Canada, but Commodore Warren, in charge of the operation, refused unequivocally. This was the opportunity to begin the extirpation of the French from North America, and he intended to make the most of it. In July, Warren ordered the transportation of the inhabitants of Ile Saint-Jean, where the emigrant Acadian population had grown to nearly one thousand. Yankee troops landed on the east coast of the island, burned settlements, and attacked the small garrison town of Port-la-Joie on the south shore. The French soldiers retreated into the interior; but joined by inhabitants and natives they rallied, counterattacked, and drove the invaders back to their vessels, inflicting heavy losses. Following this engagement the island Acadians sent deputies to Louisbourg with an offer to become British subjects and take the oath of allegiance if they might remain in their homes and communities. Warren was unwilling to agree to a long-term arrangement, but he knew the New Englanders were in no mood for another fight, and lacking the troops necessary to enforce the removal, he was forced to negotiate. "We have made a treaty with them to be neuter, and to remain there during our pleasure," he reported to Newcastle, the colonial secretary. But, he added, "I hope they will be sent away next spring, as we see the ill consequences in Nova Scotia that attend in keeping any of them in our territories. And indeed it would be a good thing if those now at Annapolis could be remov'd."[36]

As his comment indicated, the victory at Louisbourg had put the removal of the Acadians on the agenda once again. At Annapolis Royal the Nova Scotia Governor's Council voted to form a special committee to investigate the question, and in November 1745 the members delivered their report, which amounted to a complete repudiation of Mascarene's policy. The Acadians, they wrote, had been coddled and indulged, but in the end had still failed to be faithful to their oath of allegiance. Instead, they proved themselves to be "entirely devoted to the Interest of France." They had refused to supply the British with adequate warning and intelligence. They had furnished the invaders with provisions, horses, boats, and even guides. They had embraced the French. "Both men, women and children frequented the Enemies Quarters at their Mass, prayers, dancing and all other ordinary occasions." In short, "it appears that their actions in favour of the Enemy proceeded rather from a Natural disposition than force." As for those "terrifying orders of Duvivier and Marin," the committee supposed they had been "purposely contriv'd" as a cover for treasonous conduct. There was no hope of the Acadians ever becoming loyal British subjects. "Upon the whole," the report concluded, "it is most humbly submitted whether the said French Inhabitants may not be transported out of the Province of Nova Scotia and be replac'd by good Protestant Subjects."[37]

The council voted to adopt the report. For Mascarene it was a stinging rebuke, and he waited almost a month before forwarding the document on to Shirley and Newcastle, accompanying it with letters of his own. He found the report slanted too much in one direction. Considering the matter carefully, he thought, "it was less to be wonder'd att, that the Enemy has had so much influence on this People lately as that he has not had much more." The report made the worst possible case against the Acadians, "so as to make them all equally guilty and involved in the same threatened ruin." He included a copy of the Annapolis deputies' June memorial, which he characterized as "showing the dangers they incur, whichever side they take." His policy had been to carefully distinguish between those inhabitants who were faithful to the government and deserving of commendation, and those who were not and deserving of punishment.[38]

Nevertheless, he would not argue with the report's conclusion. It might indeed be time for a change in policy. "If new measures are to be taken and these Inhabitants can be remov'd and good Protestant Subjects transplanted in their room, nothing can be of greater advantage to the Brittish interest in general and to that of the Northern Colonies in particular and especially to that of this Province." But there were practical problems to be considered. How were the Acadians to be rounded up? He estimated their number at not less than twenty thousand souls, which would "make that removal to be attended with great difficulties." Here Mascarene alluded to the violence accompanying the attempt to remove the Acadians on Ile Saint-Jean only months before. Once the inhabitants had been arrested, how would they be transported and where would they be sent? These problems required careful planning, although Mascarene cautioned it be done in confidence, "for fear of throwing the Inhabitants into despair." Pronouncements about the removal of the island Acadians had been closely attended to by the inhabitants of the peninsula, presenting a very real danger of driving them into the arms of the French. If, after careful consideration, it was determined that it was in His Majesty's service to remove them all, it would be up to the authorities in London and Massachusetts to set the scheme in operation. "Any revolution in this Province cannot be brought about butt by means of the neighbouring Colonies, in which your Province will always bear the greatest Share," he wrote to Shirley. If Mascarene's policy was to be overthrown, if Shirley chose to make a revolution in l'Acadie by removing the Acadians, he would have to do it himself.[39]

Governor Shirley welcomed the opportunity to take charge and turn policy in a different direction. He had, in fact, already requested that Newcastle add the governorship of Nova Scotia to his portfolio as governor of Massachusetts, arguing that Richard Philipps could not adequately do the job "on account of his great Age." Since

Shirley was the man most responsible for defending the maritime region, it was reasonable that he be rewarded with the governorship. He criticized Mascarene's Acadian policy, arguing that there was "danger of too much tenderness towards 'em on his part." The Acadians, he believed, were merely waiting for an opportune moment to join with the French. "If a thousand French troops should land in Nova Scotia all the people would rise to join them, besides all the Indians." Overwhelming the small garrison at Annapolis Royal, the French—in combination with the inhabitants and natives—would then sweep down on New England. This would provide them with "such an hold of the Continent as to make 'em think in time of pushing with the assistance of the Indians for the Mastery of it." While this chain of events might "seem remote," he admitted, it was "not impossible." Moving decisively against the Acadians thus was a "matter of the highest consequence," and he urged "the immediate removal of some at least of the French inhabitants of Nova Scotia" and the settlement of English families "in their room."[40]

The events of the subsequent year forced William Shirley to move much closer to Mascarene's position. London's rejection of his request for the Nova Scotia governorship—instructing him to wait patiently until Philipps died in office—may have dampened his aggressive enthusiasms. But much more important were the French plans for a massive counterattack. In June 1746 the Annapolis deputies came to Mascarene with rumors that "a great Armament is coming from France to retake Louisbourg and this place." A month later Mascarene reported that Captain Jean-Baptiste-Nicolas Roch de Ramezay with six hundred troops from Canada had occupied Beaubassin and Grand Pré in preparation for an attack on Fort Anne. The truly shocking news, however, arrived at Boston in early September. British naval vessels in the Atlantic had captured two French gunships and learned they were part of a French fleet of more than fifty armed vessels transporting some three thousand regular troops across the Atlantic to retake Louisbourg, capture Annapolis Royal, and strike at Boston.[41]

The people of Massachusetts were terror-stricken. Shirley immediately requested authorization to raise fifteen hundred troops, but he knew it would be weeks if not months before such a force could be mustered and sent to the eastward. In the meantime, by the logic of his own analysis, the Acadians would tip the balance in the success or failure of the French campaign. Despite Mascarene's advice to soften talk of removal, British officials at Louisbourg continued to issue bellicose pronouncements threatening the island Acadians. Shirley now had to take seriously Mascarene's warning that such loose gossip was alienating the Acadians of the peninsula.[42]

Early in October, Mascarene received a packet from Massachusetts containing multiple copies of a proclamation, dated 16 September 1746, which Shirley requested be posted in and around Annapolis Royal. Written in French, and addressed to the Acadians, the proclamation was intended as a gesture of reassurance. The governor of Massachusetts had been informed, it read, of rumors circulating that a great force was coming from New England to remove the inhabitants from their estates and transport them to France or elsewhere. He wished to assure them that "their Fears are without Foundation." Furthermore, he pledged his best effort to lay their case before the king in order "to obtain the Continuation of His Royal Favour and Protection to such of them as shall behave dutifully and peaceably, and refuse to hold any Correspondence with his Enemies."[43]

Shirley explained his changed thinking in a series of letters to Newcastle. The attempt to remove the Acadians on Ile Saint-Jean had convinced him that the inhabitants would resist. Many would escape into the woods and join with the natives. Others would retreat to Canada, and later would return with Canadien troops to make war on the British garrison. Under such circumstances it would be extremely difficult to introduce new settlers. The garrison, wholly dependent upon provisions supplied by local farms, would be unable to survive. In other words, "an attempt to drive all the French inhabitants from their settlements, should it succeed, would in effect be driving 5 or 6,000 men to take up Arms against his Majesty's Government there every Year during the War."[44]

There was no doubt that the British ought to have removed the Acadians when they conquered the province in 1710. But having allowed them to remain in the country all these years, it was doubtful whether their transportation now could be considered "just usage." There was neither any doubt that the Acadian notion of neutrality was inconvenient, even dangerous. But having explicitly granted them the exemption from bearing arms on their consenting to take the oath, British officials themselves were responsible for their mistaken belief. Simple justice required that some allowance be made for the inhabitants' unfortunate situation, "continually plac'd between two fires, the force and Menaces of the Canadeans and Indians plundering 'em of whatever they wanted, and deterring 'em in the strongest manner from having any communication with his Majesty's Garrison, on the one hand, and the Resentments of the Garrison for their withholding their Intelligence and Supplies on the other, tho's at the same time it was not in a condition to protect 'em from the Enemy."[45]

It now struck Shirley as "too rigorous a Punishment" for the innocent as well as the guilty to suffer "the loss of their estates and the expulsion of their families out of the country." Instead, he proposed the apprehension and expulsion of those judged to be "most obnoxious and dangerous to His Majesty's Government," while "keeping the rest in the country and endeavouring to make them and their posterity useful members of society under his Majesty's Government." In order to do this, small garrisons of British soldiers should be deployed at Grand Pré and Beaubassin, Catholic priests should be expelled and replaced with French-speaking Huguenot ministers, and a system of English schools established so that the "next generation in a great measure become true Protestant Subjects." Hearty settlers from frontier New England, and perhaps from northern Ireland and Germany as well, should be encouraged to settle in the province to counterbalance the Acadians.[46]

While there were some new ideas here—including some, such as the expulsion of the priests, which would have so alienated the Acadians as to undercut the rest of the scheme—in essence Shirley had adopted Mascarene's policy as his own. Mascarene interpreted the proclamation as a vindication, noting in the council minutes that the text was "conformable to what his Honor the President has frequently told the Said Inhabitants." Convinced that the only thing that could precipitate an Acadian uprising was their fear of removal, Mascarene immediately called in the Annapolis deputies and read the proclamation to them, "and thereby prevented any mischief accruing from that notion, and defeated the hopes Mr. Ramezay might have from it."[47]

Mascarene's contention was proved by the experience of Captain Ramezay's Canadien militia, who were waiting at Chignecto. According to Major Daniel-Hyacinthe-Marie Liénard de Beaujeu, a young Canadien officer who kept a journal during the campaign, although Ramezay relied on support from a small group of "trustworthy Acadians [*Acadiens de confiance*]"—including Joseph-Nicolas Gautier of the *haute rivière*, Joseph Leblanc dit Le Maigre of Minas, and Joseph Broussard dit Beausoleil of Chipoudy Bay—he regarded the majority of the inhabitants with deep suspicion. At Minas, and later at Annapolis Royal, Ramezay assembled the deputies and warned them against communicating with the British in any way. He issued written orders demanding that the inhabitants provide provisions for his troops, their refusal punishable by death. When the Acadians pled poverty, he ordered his officers into the countryside to requisition what they needed. Beaujeu, who had the misfortune to draw that duty, wrote of the anger of the Acadian women from whom he seized cattle and sheep, and the shame he felt at playing the thief. When Ramezay moved his force to Annapolis Royal, Beaujeu noted, he situated his encampment so as "to cut off communication between the Acadians and the English, and to take provisions more easily from the inhabitants."[48]

Ramezay had been told to expect the arrival of the French fleet in July, but the first vessels did not appear at Chebucto harbor on l'Acadie's Atlantic coast until late September. Horrible storms in the mid-Atlantic had dispersed the fleet and thrown them off course. As the vessels straggled in one by one it became clear that a number had gone down with the loss of some twelve hundred men. To make matters worse, the surviving troops and crews were suffering an epidemic of some unknown deadly disease. Within a month another several hundred men perished, including the commander, M. de Rochefoucald, duc d'Anville. His second in command, Vice Admiral d'Estournelle, fell into such despair that he took his own life. Jacques-Pierre de Taffanel, marquis de La Jonquière, accompanying the fleet on his way to assume the office of governor-general of New France, took command and issued orders to proceed to Annapolis Royal. Word was sent to Ramezay to take up entrenchments around Fort Anne, which he did on 12 October 1746. But the epidemic spread to the Míkmaw fighters, most of whom returned to their villages, leaving the Canadiens to fight alone, and Ramezay could do little more than keep the British garrison pinned down with harassing fire while he awaited the arrival of the fleet. Then, on 3 November, he received word that La Jonquière had returned to France. At Cape Sable the fleet had encountered more severe storms and the governor had decided to abandon the ill-fated enterprise.[49]

"This unfortunate piece of news [was] announced immediately to the Acadians by the sadness painted on our faces," Beaujeu wrote in his journal that day. The pent-up resentment and rage of the inhabitants burst forth, and they railed at the Canadiens, charging that "we had come only to place a knife at their throats," and that it "would finally crown their misfortunes, that they would fall victim to British rage and relentlessness." Unmoved, Ramezay demanded that they deliver up their horses for the transport of his men—several score of whom were sick and dying—and ordered an immediate retreat to

Minas. But fearful lest the Acadians betray him, he reserved one company to remain behind to keep them under guard, preventing them from going to the British for at least a few hours. The Canadiens later learned that all through the campaign Mascarene had been fed intelligence by a number of inhabitants, "even by the Acadians who had appeared most faithful to us." Beaujeu was not surprised by this news. "People quite frequently take the side of the strongest," he noted stoically.[50]

Mascarene was naturally pleased with the way things had gone. "I cannot see the inhabitants of this river have acted anything that can justly be taken amiss in this last affair," he wrote, although he suspected that there had been "a pretty deal of delinquency at Minas," and told Shirley that he wished "the season and the means here could allow me to call them to account." Plagued by mutinous troops and rebellious officers, however, he felt unable to divide his forces. Mascarene's inaction disgusted Shirley. "He seems indifferent about pursuing the advantageous Turn," the governor wrote Newcastle in frustration. By this time the Massachusetts Assembly had approved the recruitment of an additional five hundred men. Bypassing Mascarene completely, Shirley decided to dispatch them under the command of Colonel Arthur Noble, a freeholder and fur trader from Maine who had distinguished himself during the attack on Louisbourg. Noble was to advance to Minas and form a line of defense at Grand Pré, with the aim of preventing the French from using it as a staging area for further attacks down the Annapolis Valley. "This seems to be the critical conjuncture," Shirley declared, "whilst the Nova-Scotians are chagrin'd and dispirited at their late disappointment from the French, and before their deluded hopes shall be revived by fresh promises from Canada and France, and whilst a most ravaging sickness prevails among the Cape-Sable and St. John's Indians."[51]

Colonel Noble and his regiment arrived at Annapolis Royal in two vessels in mid-December and immediately proceeded to Minas in two contingents—a force of one hundred men by land up the Annapolis Valley, the rest by sea with the supplies, cannon, and two prefabricated blockhouses Shirley wanted installed, one at Grand Pré and the other at Beaubassin. After hard travel through heavy winter storms, the two contingents joined at Grand Pré in the second week of January 1747. Mascarene, who at this point was little more than an onlooker of what had become an independent Massachusetts operation, urged the officers "to treat with all tenderness and kindness those of the Inhabitants who have remain'd in their Duty," but like all such campaigns this one was expected to "subsist of the produce of the country," expropriating provisions from the inhabitants. The Acadian deputies begged Noble and his men to leave, saying, "they were entirely incapable of nourishing them and of supplying them with firewood, that they had already burned all their fences, and that the militia was inflicting nearly irreparable damages upon them," but of course it made no difference. Noble roused further resentment by ordering the deputies to clear twenty houses for his use, including the community mill, an octagonal stone building located on the highest point of land, where he established his headquarters. Later there also were vague reports that his soldiers had taunted the inhabitants with threats of "extirpation."[52]

None of this inclined the Acadians to think favorably of this occupying army of Yankees. Nevertheless, a number of them warned Colonel Noble that Ramezay was likely to attack during the winter. That prospect struck Noble as highly unlikely. There had been an unusually heavy snowfall and the Canadien militia were at Chignecto, a good distance away. "There was no reason to believe that they would make new attempts upon Acadia," Noble responded. He seems to have considered the warnings part of the inhabitants' attempt to convince him to withdraw. Instead, he ordered the vessels tied down at the landing, not bothering to unload either the materials for building the blockhouse or the cannon, and settled in for the winter.[53]

It was a disastrous error. The war in the maritime region had gone about as badly for the French as it could have, and they were eager for a victory. Receiving the news that the New Englanders had occupied Grand Pré, Ramezay decided that his best opportunity for a salvaging victory was a difficult overland march and surprise attack in the dead of winter. Suffering from a wounded knee, he assigned the mission to Captain Nicolas-Antoine Coulon de Villiers, a tough Canadien who had served in the Mississippi Valley. On 23 January 1747, 240 Canadiens and 60 Maliseets and Míkmaq set out on snowshoes, pulling their provisions on wickerwork sleighs. They were accompanied by a few militant anti-British Acadians, including Joseph Broussard dit Beausoleil and a handful of his followers.[54]

Moving along the north shore of the isthmus of Chignecto, over the well-traveled cattle trail to Minas Basin, the trek required seventeen days, a grueling journey through deep snow and across icy rivers. Zédore Gould, one of the Acadians among the party, later told of camping among the evergreens on those frigid nights, the men sleeping fitfully, huddled together around great fires in scooped hollows of snow. They were welcomed by the inhabitants at Cobequid and Pisiquid, but de Villiers set guards on the road to Grand Pré while the others rested, "for fear they might be betrayed by the Acadians." Late in the evening of 10 February they arrived at a hamlet on the east side of rivière Gaspereau. They found a wedding party in progress, and Gould remembered how the Acadian girls "handed round black bread and cheese and hard cider, a satisfying ration for exhausted men." The New Englanders were in the houses across the river, the Acadians told Captain de Villiers, and several of them agreed to join in the attack. "They had enrolled as combatants," Beaujeu wrote in his journal, but "they served only as guides."[55]

The Canadien assault began at three the following morning, in the midst of a raging snowstorm. "We attacked sharply, despite the enemy's fire, and forced the houses by axe-blows, and in a very short time took possession of them," reported Captain Louis de La Corne, second in command. Colonel Noble died fighting in his nightshirt, and many Yankees were shot or bludgeoned in their beds. Casualty figures vary by source, but at least one hundred New Englanders were killed, another twenty or thirty seriously wounded, and more than fifty taken prisoner; the attackers suffered only six killed and fourteen wounded, including de Villiers, whose left arm was so badly shattered by a musket blast he later died of his injuries. "The night was so black, the wind so violent, and the snow so thick," the eighteen-year-old Canadien ensign Charles Deschamps de Boishébert testified, "that the noise of the attack was not heard by the two small vessels which were a gun shot away, near the shore." Boishébert and a small company overwhelmed the guard at the landing and seized the vessels, thus cutting off any possibility of reinforcement or retreat. It was the key to victory. The surviving New Englanders, perhaps 250 men, fought their way to the stone millhouse, but without snowshoes—which remained unpacked on the vessels—they found it impossible to escape. They surrendered at midday. La Corne, who had assumed command, allowed them the honors of war on their promise to return to New England and not fight in l'Acadie for the next six months.[56]

When Ramezay received the news of the victory, he issued a proclamation addressed to all the inhabitants of the upper bay. "We consider ourself as master of Beaubassin and Mines, since we have driven off the English," he declared. The Acadians now owed their allegiance to the king of France, and he ordered them to arm themselves against the return of the enemy. The proclamation meant very little at Minas. While they were "charmed" to be French subjects, the deputies told La Corne, they hoped he and his men soon would depart, since supplying Yankee and Canadien troops had left them in a "pitiful state." The Míkmaq had already dispersed to their winter camps, and in late February the Canadiens also departed for Chignecto.[57]

The bloody battle at Minas had changed nothing for the Acadians. Six weeks later, in mid-April, three hundred New Englanders under the command of Captain John Winslow of Massachusetts landed at Grand Pré and raised the British flag above the stone mill-house. His men had "taken repossession of Minas," Shirley reported to Newcastle, and the deputies "thereupon renewed their oath of fidelity to His Majesty." Even at Beaubassin, where Ramezay remained until he returned to Canada in June, the Acadians equivocated. As French subjects they would be required to bear arms against the British "on pain of death, confiscation of all their goods, burning of their houses, and the punishment due to rebels against the King." But in response the Acadians begged for recognition of their neutrality, arguing that once the Canadiens returned home they would be left unprotected and vulnerable. An attack by New Englanders, they wrote, was "a disaster that daily threatens us, that keeps us in continual fear."[58]

The reports raised concern in London. Newcastle worried that Acadian fears of removal and destruction at the hands of New Englanders had induced them "to withdraw themselves from their Allegiance to His Majesty and to take part with the Enemy." It was necessary, he wrote to Shirley in the late spring of 1747, "that proper Measures should be taken to remove any such ill-founded suggestions; and for that Purpose it is the King's Pleasure that you should declare in some publick and Authentick manner to His Majesty's Subjects, Inhabitants of that Province, that there is not the least Foundation for any apprehension of that nature." He instructed Shirley to issue a proclamation reassuring the inhabitants in the king's name.[59]

Shirley demurred. While he had made just such assurances in his own proclamation of the previous year, he believed the significant Acadian collusion in the Canadien attack on Massachusetts troops demanded a tough response, not a mollifying one. Singling out theinhabitants of Chignecto, who "seem to have ever been so deeply engaged on the Side of the Enemy as to make 'em forfeit all pretense of right to hold their Posessions," he proposed that a force of one thousand New Englanders be sent to secure the isthmus. The inhabitants of Beaubassin and its surrounding hamlets should "be transplanted into New England and distributed among the four governments there," and their lands divided among the troops, "upon condition of their settling there with their families." This bold act would put an end to problems with the remaining Acadians at Minas and Annapolis Royal, "lock'd between the settlement in Chignecto at one end and His Majesty's Garrison at the other, and aw'd by the removal of the French inhabitants from Chignecto from off their Lands." Through growth and intermarriage the entire province would eventually become overwhelmingly English and Protestant.[60]

Before Shirley's proposal reached London, the news arrived that the Royal Navy had destroyed a French convoy transporting troops for a campaign to retake Louisbourg. Four or five thousand French soldiers were taken prisoner of war, in addition to La Jonquière, admiral of the fleet and governor-elect of New France. Now there was talk of a cease-fire. With the urgency removed, the king's ministers decided that Shirley's plan was too expensive. "His Majesty therefore, upon the whole, thinks it right to postpone anything of this kind for the present," Newcastle wrote Shirley in October, but added a significant postscript—"tho' His Majesty would have you consider, in what manner such a Scheme may be executed, at a proper Time, and What Precautions may be necessary to be taken, to obviate the Inconveniences that are apprehended from it." Quintessentially bureaucratic language, but with chilling implications.[61]

With this note of encouragement, Shirley proceeded to issue the proclamation dated 21 October 1747, which was published in French and forwarded to Mascarene for posting at Annapolis Royal. It offered both a carrot and a stick. Those Acadians who remained loyal to their oath were promised royal protection. "It is His Majesty's Resolution to protect and maintain all such as have adher'd to, and shall continue in their duty and allegiance to him, in the quiet and peaceable possession of their respective Habitations and Settlements, and in the Enjoyment of all their Rights and Privileges as his Subjects."

Those who had violated their pledge of neutrality and actively assisted the French, however, were to be prosecuted as traitors. Shirley listed twelve men as most-wanted—including Joseph-Nicolas Gautier, his sons Joseph and Pierre, Joseph Leblanc dit Le Maigre, Louis-Amand Bugeaud, and Joseph Broussard dit Beausoleil—and placed a bounty of £50 sterling on their heads. Broussard lived on the middle reaches of rivière Petitcodiac, well outside the area of British control. The others fled to Ile Saint-Jean with numerous members of their extended families, and in their absence the British destroyed and burned their homes as an object lesson for their neighbors.[62]

On 30 April 1748 the belligerents in the European war agreed to a general cease-fire. That same month Mascarene wrote a long letter to Shirley in which he reflected on what had been learned during the conflict in l'Acadie. The Acadians, he concluded, had effectively demonstrated their loyalty and had shown they were capable of being "good subjects." They had refused numerous opportunities to rise up against British authorities. "Their plea with the French, who pressed them to take up arms, was their oath, their living easy under the government, and their having no complaint to make against it." It was not the inhabitants who presented the greatest problem for provincial government. Rather, it was the members of the Governor's Council and the officers of the garrison, who were incapable of grasping the essential requirements for governing in the borderlands of the empire. They were "prejudic'd against the French Inhabitants." They held "an imbibed notion that all who bear the name of French must be natural Ennemies of Great Britain." They were "ever talking of ousting them, transplanting or destroying them, without considering the Circumstances this Province has lately been and still is in, and the fatal consequences that might have insued from any Violent measures." The future stability and prosperity of the colony, Mascarene argued, depended on finding men with broader views.[63]

Shirley ignored Mascarene's advice. He was, after all, one of the foremost advocates of ousting, transplanting, and destroying the Acadians. Instead, acting on Newcastle's suggestion that he explore the manner in which a scheme of explusion and transportation might best be executed, he ordered a comprehensive survey of the province, that detailed plans might be made for the best locations to introduce Protestant emigrants "in the room" of the Acadians. Removal and resettlement were now at the top of the agenda. Those who doubted the efficacy and morality of the scheme were cast aside, Paul Mascarene among them. "Being too old and crazy to act my part," as he put it in a letter to an old Huguenot friend, he soon retired to Boston.[64]

"I am now after these tossings," he wrote, "in my own house amongst my children and a numerous offspring of grand children, there by God's grace to pass the remainder of my days in quiett and in peace." Looking back over his record as lieutenant-governor, he was justly proud. "I us'd our French Inhabitants with so much mildness, administered Justice so impartially, and employ'd all the skill I was master of in managing them to so good purpose, that tho' the Ennemy brought near two thousand men in Arms in the midst of them and us'd all the means of cajoling and threatening to make them take up arms . . . they could not prevail upon above twenty to joyn." It was a significant accomplishment. Despite the bonds of common language, cultural tradition, and religious faith with the French, the overwhelming majority of the inhabitants had refused to be enlisted in the armed struggle for control of the province. But Mascarene's legacy of mild government and goodwill would soon be forgotten in a horrifying cascade of events that would threaten the complete destruction of the Acadians.[65]

CHAPTER 9

DISCORD AND DESOLATION

The British Buildup, 1748–1753

THE WAR OF THE Austrian Succession—King George's War—formally ended on 18 October 1748 with the signing of the Treaty of Aix-la-Chapelle. In Europe the war had gone very badly for Great Britain and its allies, but in North America France had been humiliated. Convinced that the permanent loss of Louisbourg severely threatened the security of its North American empire, the French government offered the British a settlement they could not refuse: a return to the status quo ante. The French would abandon gains made by their armies in Europe and elsewhere in exchange for the return of Ile Royale. For the British there was really no alternative, for otherwise it meant the destruction of their army in Europe. Despite angry protests from New England, they accepted the proposal. The king's ministers responsible for colonial and foreign policy, however, had no intention of abandoning the maritime region. The Duke of Newcastle and John Russell, Duke of Bedford, secretaries of state for the Northern and Southern departments respectively, and George Montagu Dunk, Earl of Halifax, first lord commissioner of the Board of Trade, all advocated an aggressive policy toward France. Even as they arranged for the return of Louisbourg, they planned an unprecedented buildup in Nova Scotia. The question before us, Halifax wrote, is "whether we shall settle or whether we shall lose the Province."[1]

Newcastle, Bedford, and Halifax were driven by fears of French aggression, convinced that Versailles sought to confine the British in North America to the Atlantic coast, and that an important part of the French plan was their insistence on the smallest possible definition for the "antient limits" of l'Acadie. Should France succeed in winning the argument over boundaries, Newcastle wrote his brother, Prime Minister Henry Pelham, "you may not only lose that province, but from what I have heard from Halifax and Governor Shirley, endanger all your Northern Colonies, which are inestimable to us." Lord Halifax and Governor William Shirley were both committed imperialists. During the war Shirley had written Newcastle regularly, arguing that the security of the British colonies depended upon the effective defense of l'Acadie, which in turn meant suppression of any Acadian support for French imperial ambitions. After the war he provided Bedford with a summary of his thinking. Previously he had favored the wholesale removal of the Acadians, he wrote, but their resistance to the attempt to remove them from Ile Saint-Jean demonstrated that such a campaign "would be attended with very hazardous consequences." A much safer and more effective approach, Shirley had come to believe, was a program to settle Protestants in the room of the Acadians, which would require the relocation of a smaller and selective number of inhabitants. He proposed transforming l'Acadie into a fully British colony by encouraging the emigration of New Englanders with "their knowledge of cultivating new lands, well rooted allegiance, and fondness for the Protestant religion," although he allowed that emigrants from northern Ireland or the German provinces might do equally well.[2]

Shirley forwarded to London a survey of the province that identified those places where Protestants might "speedily settle themselves" and recorded in impressive detail the location of every significant Acadian village and hamlet. Shirley had commissioned the survey from Captain Charles Morris, an officer of the Massachusetts militia who had been with the late Colonel Arthur Noble at Grand Pré when the Canadien militia attacked in 1747. The inhabitants, Morris found, controlled all the best land in the province, and a program of Protestant colonization would require the confiscation of hundreds of acres of their farms. "Without that, I am sure it would be impossible any large number of Protestants can ever be settled in the Country," he wrote. In order to legally accomplish this, Shirley suggested that those Acadians who had refused to defend the province against the French in the late war might be stripped of their titles. Once a sufficient number of Protestants had been settled, Shirley continued, a civil government could be organized. But the Acadians who remained would be barred from participation until they were "acquainted in some Degree with the English Language, Customs and Government and are qualify'd for serving upon Juries or in the Assembly, and other posts"—that is, until they converted to Protestantism.[3]

Shirley would not remove the Acadians, but he was intent on their destruction. His proposal envisioned their virtual imprisonment in a burgeoning Protestant province. That objective was made even clearer in an argumentative treatise, published in London in 1748, that Shirley commissioned from Otis Little, a Massachusetts attorney who before the war had resided in the English *faubourg* at Annapolis Royal and who, like Charles Morris, had served as an officer of the Massachusetts forces dispatched to the province to turn back the French invasion. Little brought Shirley's proposals to the attention of politically engaged Britons. "It must surely be deemed impolitic," he wrote, "to suffer such a Colony of French Bigots to be reared up under the kindly Influences of a British Administration, to cut our own People's Throats whenever the Priest shall consecrate the Knife." Yet it would be impossible to effect their removal without a great deal of bloodshed. Moreover, "if they were dispossessed, they would be a very great additional strength to Canada and Cape Breton."[4]

The only workable solution was the colonization of the province by Protestant emigrants. The Acadians could remain in their communities, but would be required to relinquish sufficient improved lands for the emigrants. There was justice in this, "for 'tis beyond Dispute but they claim much larger Tracts than they have any Right to." Little was confident that a strong force could manage the Acadians, but anticipated a great deal of trouble from the Míkmaq, whom the British must hammer "till they are wholly extirpated." Little's proposal—which in fact was Shirley's—required the presence of a substantial British military force in the province, and he argued for the construction of new forts and permanent garrisons at Chignecto, Minas, and Chebucto harbor on the Atlantic coast (the rendezvous of the ill-fated French fleet of 1746), which should be built up as a great British stronghold, offsetting the loss of Louisbourg.[5]

In March 1749, Lord Halifax, in his capacity as first lord commissioner of the Board of Trade, placed before the board a plan for the "Settlement of His Majesty's Colony of Nova Scotia." Approved by the board, endorsed by Newcastle and the cabinet of ministers, and quickly authorized by Parliament, the plan offered free passage to the province for up to three thousand Protestant emigrants, a year's subsistence, provisions, arms, and tools for them, and grants of land free from rents or taxes for ten years, along with a promise that a civilian government would be established as soon as possible. In essence, Nova Scotia had become the fourteenth British colony on the North American mainland. The emigrants were to depart as a group for Chebucto harbor, where they would lay out and construct a garrison town at the expense of the crown. This was essentially William Shirley's proposal—with the difference that instead of Yankees, Lord Halifax's plan relied on English emigrants, including discharged soldiers and sailors, which turned out to be a mistake, for they would prove thoroughly unreliable. Parliament voted an annual budget of £50,000 to support the venture, which proved a serious underestimate, for in the end the plan to convert the province into a Protestant colony would cost the British government at least twice that much per annum.[6]

THIRTEEN transports and an armed sloop departed from London in late May 1749, carrying 2,576 men, women, and children, along with all the necessary provisions and a complete civil organization—governor, administrative officials, as well as merchants, artisans, and clerks. Young Colonel Edward Cornwallis, named as the new governor of Nova Scotia or l'Acadie, replaced elderly Sir Richard Philipps, who had not been in the province since 1731. Cornwallis was a member of a wealthy and influential family with large estates in Suffolk and a fine house and retinue in London, and the uncle of Charles Cornwallis, who was to become famous in American history as the general who surrendered the British army to Washington at Yorktown in 1781. In 1725, at the age of twelve, Edward and his twin brother Frederick were appointed royal pages, and afterward both attended Eton, where Frederick suffered a injury on the playing fields that paralyzed his right arm. Disqualified for military service, he entered the church and eventually became archbishop of Canterbury.

It was Edward who pursued the military career, was gazetted ensign at eighteen, and at twenty-one appointed to the personal staff of William Augustus, Duke of Cumberland, second-born son of George II. Cornwallis was at Cumberland's side in 1745–46 when he turned back the French-supported invasion of Charles Stuart, Catholic pretender to the British throne. In April 1746, Cornwallis led his regiment at the Battle of Culloden, brutally crushing Stuart's Scottish supporters. And in the aftermath of the battle, on Cumberland's order, he commanded raiding parties sent into the remotest parts of the Highlands to "pacify" the population, raids legendary for their brutality and bloodlust. Cornwallis had supervised the burning of Catholic chapels and the torture of Catholic priests. This was the man the British selected to handle the Acadian problem.[7]

Cornwallis's instructions, prepared by Halifax, directed him to settle the majority of the Protestant emigrants at the new garrison town to be constructed at Chebucto, but also to survey townships at Minas and Chignecto, in preparation for settling several hundred Protestants near existing Acadian hamlets. "To the end," Halifax wrote, "that the said French Inhabitants may be subjected to such Rules and Orders as may hereafter be made for . . . better ordering and governing." Those "Rules and Orders" referred to the organization of a civil government, from participation in which the Acadians were to be excluded. British supervision of the inhabitants was also to be tightened. Halifax noted that the Acadian "exemption that they should not be obliged to bear arms" had been the source of great inconvenience and trouble during the war, and Cornwallis's first order of business was to require the inhabitants to swear to a new, unconditional oath. Those inhabitants who did so, read his instructions, "shall continue in the free exercise of their Religion, as far as the Laws of Great Britain shall admit of the same, as also the Peaceable Possession of such Lands as are under their cultivation." But those who did not would be forced to vacate the province, forfeiting all their property, although there was no actual plan to effect their removal, since both Halifax and Cornwallis fully expected the Acadians to bend to pressure. The revival of the oath controversy was part of a program to subject the Catholic Acadians to the rule of a new Protestant civil authority.[8]

The transports arrived at Chebucto the first week of July 1749. Cornwallis, seeing America for the first time, marveled at the abundant marine life of the harbor and the heavily wooded hills ashore. He visited a small Acadian village down the coast. "They seem to be very peaceable, [and] say they always looked upon themselves as English Subjects," he wrote. But he was not counting on the peaceful intentions of the Acadians. He planned to build forts and garrison troops at Cobequid, Grand Pré, and Beaubassin, in the belief that it was "necessary to shew them that 'tis in our power to master them." Once the transports were unloaded, he sent them off to Louisbourg to collect the British garrison there, more than five hundred men and officers of the 29th and 45th regiments. After the transfer of that fortress to the French was completed on 23 July, the British men and officers departed for Chebucto, where they greatly strengthened the armed force available to Cornwallis.[9]

On 23 July, Paul Mascarene and the members of the Nova Scotia Governor's Council arrived at Chebucto from Annapolis Royal. If he was true to form, Mascarene would have been gracious, yet not hesitant to offer his own perspectives on the province, views based on forty years of experience. Cornwallis, whom an associate characterized as cool and ceremonious in demeanor, responded scornfully. He believed the management of the province had been "scandalous," and Mascarene at fault "to suffer so many abuses." Two days later, on the deck of the transport *Beauford*—temporary headquarters while government house was being constructed ashore—Cornwallis officially assumed command of the province and, as the minutes record, read to the councilors and staff officers his commission and instructions, "particularly the Instructions relating to His Majesty's French Subjects."[10]

While this ceremony took place, three Acadian deputies waited in the wings. Claude Leblanc, Jean Melanson, and Philippe Melanson had come down from Minas Basin to find a great swarm of English settlers engaged in raising the town Cornwallis christened Halifax, for the first lord commissioner of the Board of Trade. Identifying themselves to military authorities, they were ferried out to the *Beauford*, and following the formalities were called before the council. Cornwallis immediately got down to business, asking the clerk to read a French translation of a royal declaration, written by Halifax, and addressed to the Acadians.

> I doe hereby declare in His Majesty's Name, that . . . the many indulgences, which, He and His Royall Predecessors have shewn to the said Inhabitants in allowing them the entirely free exercise of their Religion and the quiet and peaceable Possession of their Lands, have not met with a dutifull Return. But on the contrary, divers of the said Inhabitants have openly abetted or privately assisted His Majesty's Enemies in their attempts, by furnishing them with quarters, provisions and intelligence, and concealing their designs from His Majesty's Governor, insomuch that the Enemy more than once appeared under the walls of Annapolis Royall, before the Garrison had any notice of their being within the Province.
>
> Yet His Majesty being Desireous of showing further marks of his Royall Grace to the said French, in hopes thereby to induce them to become for the future True and Loyall Subjects, is Graciously pleased to allow that the said Inhabitants shall continue in the free exercise of their Religion, as far as the Laws of Great Brittain doe allow the same, as also the peaceable possession of such lands as are under their cultivation. Provided that the said Inhabitants do within three months from the date of this Declaration [25 July 1749] take the oaths of Allegiance appointed to be taken by the Laws of Great Britain and likewise submit to such Rules and Orders as may hereafter be thought proper to be made for the maintaining and supporting His Majestys Government. And Provided likewise they doe give all possible countenance and assistance to such Persons as His Majesty shall think proper to settle in this Province.

The deputies were taken by surprise. Yet they immediately indicated their opposition to an unconditional oath. "They pretend their only difficulty is from fear of the Indians in case of a French War," Cornwallis noted. He sent them home with printed broadsides of the declaration (in French), and orders that all the deputies were to appear before the council in a fortnight.[11]

Deputies representing the districts of Annapolis Royal, Minas, and Chignecto returned on 11 August with a letter addressed to Cornwallis asking for a guarantee of religious freedom and for an exemption from bearing arms in time of war. These concerns went to the heart of the conflict. The British planned to convert Nova Scotia into a Protestant colony—raising a justifiable concern among the inhabitants about their status as Catholics. They worried that the British promise of "free exercise" might be a cover for serious restrictions and limitations, on their right to have priests reside in their communities, for example, or on the right of parish authorities to collect tithes. The fact that Halifax was to be a military fortress raised an equally justifiable concern among the inhabitants about their rights as neutrals. The British demand, the Acadian leaders wrote about the same time in a memorial to the French king, would deprive them of their religion and force them to take up arms against the Míkmaq. Their right to their faith and to their neutrality "cannot be separated from the oath," they argued, "and both the inhabitants in accepting them, and the [British] government in granting them, in the name of King George the Second, have done nothing but what was a natural consequence of the Treaty of Utrecht, and at the same time conformable to the laws of Great Britain, where acts proposed by the people acquire, when they are approved by Royal authority, a force which the king himself cannot take away from them." This was a brilliant and original formulation. Their Catholicism and their neutrality, they seemed to be saying, had become part of the customary common law of l'Acadie. Their identity as Acadians was protected by the common-law rights of Englishmen.[12]

Cornwallis was willing to reassure them on the first point concerning religious liberty, but he would not bend on the second. "His Majesty is not willing that any of His subjects, who enjoy the privileges and advantages of His Government, and who possess habitations and lands in this province, shall be exempted from an entire allegiance, or from the natural obligation to defend themselves, their habitations, their lands, and the government under which they enjoy so many advantages." What would be the consequence, the Acadians asked him, of their refusing to subscribe to an unconditional oath? They had until 25 October to swear or "quit the province," he told them. If they chose to depart, they wondered, would they have his permission to sell their lands and effects? They would not be allowed to sell or carry off anything, Cornwallis responded. With this exchange, the deputies begged leave to return to their districts and consult with their neighbors.[13]

They were back on 18 September with a letter signed by one thousand inhabitants. "We are very grateful, Sir, when we consider the privileges which were granted to us by General Philipps, after we had taken the oath of allegiance to his Majesty . . . the full enjoyment of our property, and the free exercise of our religion." For twenty years they had been good subjects and had counted on those privileges. Only two years before, in 1747, British authorities had issued a proclamation in the king's name promising to "protect and maintain" all inhabitants who continued to adhere to their oath. "We have received all these promises as coming from His Majesty. We have encouragingly relied upon them, and have rendered service to the Government of his Majesty, never having had the wish to violate our oath." They would happily renew it, as long as it continued to include "an exemption for ourselves and for our heirs from taking up arms." An unconditional oath, however, would place them at great risk. Agreeing to bear arms for the British would infuriate their Míkmaw neighbors, and "we should assuredly become the victims of their barbarous cruelty." It had been a generation since Acadians were required to make these arguments, but here they appeared again, their logic unaltered. "Monsignor," the letter concluded, "the inhabitants in general over the whole extent of this country, have resolved not to take the oath which Your Excellency requires of us. . . . We are resolved, every one of us, to leave the country."[14]

Cornwallis, like other British officials before him, was astounded at the "insolence" of the Acadians. "You declare openly that you will be the subjects of His Britannic Majesty only on such and such conditions. It appears to me that you think yourselves independent of any government, and you wish to treat with the King as if you were so." He read the implications correctly. Born on the boundaries of empire, the Acadians considered themselves to be a distinct people with distinct political rights, including the right to be exempted from the struggle between the British and the French. To these implications, Cornwallis responded with incredulity. "You deceive yourselves if you think that you are at liberty to choose whether you will be subject to the King or not," he pronounced. "You tell me that General Philipps granted you the reservation which you demand; and I tell you, Gentlemen, that the General who granted you such reservations, did not do his duty." The conditional oath "has never in the slightest degree lessened your obligations to act always and in all circumstances, as a subject ought to act, according to the laws of God and of your King."[15]

Such matters ought not to require explanation, Cornwallis declared in frustration. "It is only out of pity to your situation, and to your inexperience in the affairs of government, that we condescend to reason with you. Otherwise, Gentlemen, the question would not be reasoning, but commanding and being obeyed." But there would be no commanding and obeying that day. Instead, Cornwallis shifted ground. The Acadians boasted of the service they had rendered to the government over the years, but what, he asked, had they done to assist British efforts at settling the Protestant emigrants at Chebucto? He would make this the test of their loyalty. "Let me have here in ten days, fifty of your inhabitants whom I shall employ in assisting the poor to build their houses, to shelter them from the bad weather. They shall be paid in ready money, and fed on the king's provisions."[16]

Like Governor Philipps before him, Cornwallis arrived with the intention of intimidating these peasants into submission, and was not prepared for the sophistication of their response or the strength of their resistance. Not only was there no plan for the expulsion of the Acadians, Cornwallis did not have the force necessary for such an operation. Moreover, driving the Acadians out of the province and into the arms of the French—who would immediately put them under arms and utilize them against the British—was obviously counterproductive. The situation called for a reassessment of tactics. "My view is to make them as useful as possible to His Majesty while they do stay," he wrote the Board of Trade. "If, afterwards, they are still obstinate, and refuse the Oath, I shall receive in Spring His Majesty's further Instructions from your Lordships."[17]

In fact, Cornwallis was in great need of assistance from the inhabitants. Things were not going well at Halifax. No sooner had the Protestant emigrants disembarked than New England shipmasters were among them, recruiting them for settlements elsewhere. Vessels were departing daily for points south, loaded with emigrants intended for Nova Scotia. The majority of them, Cornwallis reported, had proven to be "poor, idle, worthless vagabonds" who had "only wanted a passage to New England." He issued a proclamation forbidding anyone from quitting the colony without permission, but did not have the means to enforce it. After less than a month the number of emigrants at Chebucto was down to fourteen hundred, meaning that more than a thousand had gone elsewhere. By September, Cornwallis counted no more than three hundred able-bodied men, not enough to construct the shelter necessary for the coming winter. Thus he was forced to turn to the Acadians for help. A group of several dozen inhabitants soon arrived and were put to work; nevertheless, many emigrants endured their first winter in America in canvas tents. "Many unfortunate People died of Cold," one of them later wrote. "This indeed may be imputed to the Want of Houses, which only such as could build were able to obtain; and to see the vast Flakes of Snow lying about the Tents of those who had been accustomed to warm fires about Newcastle and London, was enough to move the Heart of Stone."[18]

The buildup of British forces in l'Acadie "can be nothing but very dangerous for us," wrote French colonial minister Antoine-Louis

Rouillé. It fell to Roland-Michel Barrin de La Galissonière, serving as "commander-in-chief" of New France in the absence of Governor-General La Jonquière, to develop a plan to stop "the undertakings of the English." A career naval officer and a man of letters, La Galissonière was a committed imperialist with a capacity much like William Shirley's for interpreting local events in strategic perspective. British ambitions in North America were boundless, he argued, and they sought nothing less than the conquest of the entire continent, including France's rich sugar colonies in the West Indies. Although Canada was not strictly profitable to France, it was the "bulwark of America," the Canadiens and their native allies constituting "the strongest barrier that can be opposed to the ambition of the English." It is remarkable, the similarity of French and British fears. "What mattered most," writes the historian Patrice Higonnet, "was the suspicion with which each side considered what it *supposed* were the tangible goals and purpose of the other." To an extent their fears were the result of conflicting strategic interests, but both considered the other the aggressor, and saw themselves taking appropriate defensive measures—measures that in turn were interpreted by the other side as further signs of aggressive intent.[19]

For La Galissonière, holding the line against the British was critical to French strategic interests. Already British traders were moving beyond the Appalachians, so he sent a detachment, led by the French officer Pierre-Joseph Céloron de Blainville, coursing down the Ohio River to reinforce French claims, map the country, and warn off the intruders. British plans to settle Protestants at Chignecto would give the enemy a foothold on the southern shore of the Gulf of St. Lawrence, gateway to Canada, and should be prevented at all costs, so he sent to rivière Saint-Jean another detachment commanded by the young Canadien officer Charles Deschamps de Boishébert, one of the heroes of the Canadien attack on Grand Pré. When La Jonquière finally reached Québec in the late summer of 1749, he enthusiastically endorsed La Galissonière's strategy. He ordered further contingents of Canadien militia to the northern shore of the Bay of Fundy, to Chignecto, and Ile Saint-Jean. The officers were to do all they could to assist the Míkmaq in resisting British expansion and encouraging the Acadians to abandon the peninsula and establish new agricultural settlements inside French-controlled territory. Because France and Great Britain were officially at peace, Rouillé cautioned La Jonquière not to intervene directly, but rather to "provide as many indirect obstacles as possible, without compromising ourselves," principally by encouraging and supporting native opposition to British expansion. La Jonquière understood. "It is to be desired that these Indians should succeed in thwarting the designs of the English," he acknowledged, but "without showing that I have any knowledge of the matter."[20]

Catholic missionaries in l'Acadie, taking orders directly from French officials, were to be the instruments of this policy. The most important of those "incendiary priests," as the British labeled them, was abbé Jean-Louis Le Loutre, who had arrived in America a dozen years before as a twenty-eight-year-old graduate of the Séminaire des Missions-Etrangères in Paris. Posted to the mission station on rivière Shubenacadie, he proved a tireless worker, traveling widely through the region and ministering to both natives and inhabitants. He found the Míkmaq more receptive to his message than the Acadians, whose customs often clashed with his puritanical version of Catholicism. "I have never seen a more abandoned people," he wrote to a friend in France. "They live in total ignorance of the Christian virtues. The evil seems incurable." His lack of empathy with the Acadians would have dreadful consequences.[21]

Le Loutre's passion for the Míkmaq and his disdain for the inhabitants developed further during the warfare of the 1740s, when he was appointed chaplain to Míkmaw fighters, accompanying them on their expeditions. He became the most important intermediary between the natives and authorities in Québec. Fiercely partisan and rigidly ideological, Le Loutre found it impossible to understand the equivocation and compromise of the inhabitants. In 1746, disheartened by the disaster of the d'Anville expedition to l'Acadie, he retreated to France with Governor La Jonquière, and on his return the following year was captured by the British and spent several months in an English prison. "Such misfortunes and hardships, far from diminishing his zeal," Le Loutre wrote in a third-person autobiographical account, "only served the more to stimulate his desire to rejoin his scattered flock, abandoned and without spiritual sustenance." He returned to Louisbourg with Charles Desherbiers de La Ralière, new governor of Ile Royale; by the fall of 1749 he had been sent to Chignecto with instructions to do what he could to encourage both Míkmaq and Acadians to leave peninsular Acadia and relocate there, or further west on Chipoudy Bay or the North Shore, the coast of the Gulf of St. Lawrence.[22]

Over the winter of 1749–50 Le Loutre retraced his former missionary rounds, but this time as military and political commissar. He had convinced many of his Míkmaw congregants to relocate to Chignecto, but had more difficulty with the Acadians. Most of them took a wait-and-see attitude regarding the demands of the new British governor, a typical Acadian approach, and Le Loutre condemned it. "A dominating spirit was his main characteristic," wrote Louis de Courville, a Canadien notary who knew the priest well, "and he never lost an opportunity to exhibit it." Le Loutre argued the advantages of relocation: in French territory the inhabitants would be among compatriots and Catholics. But when they told him that "the love of their homes would not permit them to take the final step," he flew into a rage. If they remained, he threatened, he would turn the Míkmaq on them. "Their homes would be plundered, and their wives and children carried off and even massacred before their very eyes." Although it would take more than threats to move the Acadians, Le Loutre's tirades were a forecast of disaster. "Indeed," noted de Courville, "no one was more fit to carry discord and desolation into a country."[23]

Le Loutre's efforts at organizing were soon known to the British through the reports of supporters among the Acadians. The intelligence reinforced the long-standing assumption that the Míkmaq were merely pawns in the hands of the French. "The Savages are neither intelligent nor brutish enough to meddle of their own will in affairs that in no way concern them," Cornwallis wrote. Such condescension revealed a serious inability to consider the Míkmaq as the independent actors they were. They could accept the support of the French, yet have reasons of their own for opposing the British. Observing the rapid buildup at Halifax, the Míkmaq grew increasingly concerned. A council of their leaders succinctly and eloquently laid out those concerns in a document they sent to Cornwallis in late September.

> . . . The place where you are, where you build, where you fortify, where you think to make yourself master—that place belongs to me. I have sprung from this land as surely as the grass. I was born here and my fathers before me. Yes, I swear, it is God who has given it to me, to be my country forever. . . . What you are doing at Chebucto cannot but alarm me. . . . Where will the Indian live? When you drive me away, where will I seek refuge? . . . You glory in your great numbers. The Indian, with his small numbers, glories in nothing but God, who knows very well what is happening. Even an earth worm knows when it is attacked. I may be worth little more than an earth worm, but I know how to defend myself when I am attacked. . . .

Two weeks later, Míkmaw fighters attacked a group of Protestant emigrants working at a sawmill at Dartmouth on the outskirts of Halifax, killing four men and taking another prisoner. Cornwallis had already made clear his intention of crushing the Míkmaq at the first sign of violence. "We ought never to make Peace with them again," he wrote, but "root them out entirely." In the aftermath of this attack he issued a proclamation calling on the emigrants to form ranger companies to hunt Míkmaq, offering a bounty of £10 on scalps.[24]

In this context the deadline for the Acadians to take the unconditional oath came and passed. "As we are at war with the Indians," a member of the Nova Scotia Governor's Council noted in his journal, "we did not think proper to press the Oath to them—least they might refuse, and we have not force to Compell them. Force is requisite and nothing can be done Effectuall without it." It was not surprising that Cornwallis and his council would see the solution of the Acadian problem in military terms. Nothing but "severity or greater power [will] awe and bring them to their duty and allegiance," Cornwallis argued in his report to the Board of Trade. "With two Regiments more, I will venture to make Nova Scotia in four years His Majesty's to all intents and purposes, great and more flourishing than any part of North America." He would require additional troops in order to carry out his original instructions.[25]

Faced with the British determination to force their submission, and pressured by the French to emigrate, Acadians began moving out of the province as early as the fall of 1749. Among the first to depart was a group of about one hundred inhabitants from the vicinity of Chebucto, who petitioned Governor Desherbiers of Ile Royale for a grant of land. He agreed to settle them at Baie des Espagnols (today's Sydney Harbor) and asked that they spread the word of the free land awaiting any inhabitant who moved to French territory. A group from Beaubassin wrote Governor-General La Jonquière at Québec asking for concessions of land in French territory, and another group from Annapolis Royal beseeched him to send boats and supplies that they might "withdraw down the St. Lawrence River to any settlement that you may judge comfortable for farmers and fishermen." The governor "need only read the history of Father Charlevoix," the Annapolis inhabitants wrote, "to know how we have resisted the instances and even the violence to compel us to take the oath, and that we took it only after the Governor of Louisbourg had told us that it was necessary to seek to accommodate ourselves with these people." In fact, in his *Histoire et description générale de la Nouvelle France,* published in 1744, Pierre-François-Xavier de

Charlevoix had written that when pressed to take the oath by Governor Richard Philipps, the Acadians had warned that "if he undertook to drive them to extremes, he would have the Indians on his hands," forcing Philipps to agree to their claim of neutrality. That they mischaracterized Charlevoix's interpretation is less remarkable than that the Acadians would cite a fashionable history, published in Paris only five years before. By year's end, several hundred Acadians had made their way to Baie Verte, where La Jonquière provided for passage to Ile Saint-Jean. A British naval patrol intercepted one such vessel, whose passengers declared "they chose rather to quit their lands and estates than possess them upon the terms propos'd by the English governor." Fearing a mass defection to the French, Cornwallis ordered two companies of troops from Fort Anne in Annapolis Royal to Minas with instructions to patrol the roads and prevent any more Acadians from leaving. Captain John Handfield marched the troops to Grand Pré, where he commandeered several houses and established a makeshift barracks for his men.[26]

In December 1749 the British at Minas were attacked by a large force of Abenakis, Maliseets, and Míkmaq, armed and provisioned by abbé Le Loutre. The native fighters captured nineteen soldiers and kept the others bottled up for more than a week before breaking off the siege. They left for Chignecto, taking not only their military prisoners but also René Leblanc, notary at Minas, a longtime supporter of the British. These men would spent several years in captivity before being ransomed. The British soon learned from the Minas deputies that a number of inhabitants had joined in the attack, pressed into service by the Míkmaq "on pain of death." But Cornwallis would accept no explanations. "Secret enemies" among the inhabitants, many of them "of Indian blood" themselves, and indistinguishable from the Míkmaq, had taken up arms, he maintained. He ordered the arrest of a dozen inhabitants, but the men and their families had already fled to French territory.[27]

"If I could have spared three hundred men I should have sent and attacked them at Chignecto," Cornwallis declared. But he needed his troops at Halifax, where several hundred Protestant emigrants were hunkered down for the winter in log houses and tents, protected by little more than a rough barricade of felled trees and logs. Intent on striking a blow, however, he commissioned Sylvanus Cobb, a New England privateer, to raise a company in Boston, sail to Beaubassin, and mount an attack. Cobb had worked with Charles Morris on his survey of the province, and according to Cornwallis was "thoroughly acquainted with every harbour and creek in the Bay, and knows every house in Chignecto." In addition to the standard bounty of £10 for native scalps, he was promised £100 for the capture of Le Loutre, and was instructed "to seize and secure as many of the Inhabitants as you can; or in case they quit their houses upon your approach . . . as many of their Wives and Children as you think proper . . . to remain Hostages of their better behaviour." By foolishly placing an announcement in the Boston press, however, Cobb compromised the secrecy of the expedition, and Cornwallis called it off. But the plan suggested the intensification of violence accompanying the wholesale militarization of the province.[28]

Arbitrary military rule was on display a few weeks later when Cornwallis dispatched a company of rangers to Cobequid to check on the disappearance of an Acadian carrying messages for the British. Captain Joseph Gorham (brother of John Gorham, both commanders of much-feared ranger companies composed largely of native fighters from New England) learned from the Cobequid inhabitants that Le Loutre and an entourage of Míkmaq had been at the village when the courier arrived, and had seized and taken him to Chignecto. Le Loutre had stood in the doorway of the chapel as the inhabitants left after mass, the Acadians told Gorham, threatening them with death if they dared to return to Halifax to trade or work, and demanding that they relocate to French territory. But rather than take advantage of what was clearly the inhabitants' resentment at such treatment, Gorham instead held them personally responsible for the courier's capture. He led his rangers on a rough house-to-house search for arms, and arrested the Cobequid deputies as well as the parish priest, Jacques Girard, taking them back to Halifax, where they were jailed.[29]

After the rangers departed, the leaders of the Cobequid Acadians sent a message to their compatriots at Beaubassin. Captain Gorham "came furtively during the night to take our pastor and our four deputies," they wrote. "He read the orders by which he was authorized to seize all the muskets in our houses, thereby reducing us to the condition of the Irish." He told them to remain in their homes and stay off the roads. He had orders to build a blockhouse at Pisiquid, on the Minas road, and henceforth would be conducting regular patrols of all their hamlets. "Thus we see ourselves on the brink of destruction, liable to be captured and transported to the English islands and to lose our religion." If the Beaubassin inhabitants would come armed, together they could drive Gorham and his rangers out of Minas. That would give them the opportunity to pack their things and flee. "We have no desire to make war. If the country is English, we wish them to have it. But being our own masters, we are absolutely determined to leave it." Nothing seems to have come of this appeal, but like Cornwallis's plan for hostage taking at Chignecto, it is revealing. Despite the disclaimer, it was remarkably martial, suggestive how profoundly everything was changing.[30]

There was a good deal of truth in the contention that the Acadians were being reduced "to the condition of the Irish." Consider Cornwallis's response to a petition from the Annapolis and Minas inhabitants that he allow them to emigrate peacefully from the province. "It is a demand I can by no means grant," the governor told them, and "in the present state of the province, we are astonished that you thought of asking." Less than a year before he had insisted that if the Acadians did not swear an unconditional oath, they must "quit the province." Now he was refusing their request to depart, fearful of the danger of their joining the French and Míkmaq enemy. Indeed, so insolent did he find their request, he ordered the arrest and detention of their deputies. The time had come, he announced, to put an end to the pretense that the inhabitants might exercise the privilege of petition or the right to representation. Now that military authorities were installed in each district—with the significant exception of Chignecto—the deputy system was outmoded and "it would be better to put an end to such a useless custom." Henceforth, Cornwallis declared, the inhabitants were to communicate with the government exclusively through the commanding officer in their district. Furthermore, there would be no more public meetings. "As we are not ignorant of the bad consequence of those frequent assemblies, where often the most honest people are led astray by some seditious persons, we hereby positively forbid, for the future, all assemblies of the inhabitants, except for some important business when they shall have the permission of the commander, and when he or someone for him shall be present." Inhabitants were to supply the commanders with provisions and labor on demand, and at prices set by regulation. With the announcement of such rules and restrictions, it is not surprising that by the summer of 1750 Acadians by the hundreds were in flight from the province.[31]

Cornwallis then took the next logical step: establishing a British military presence at Chignecto. In late April 1750, Lieutenant-Colonel Charles Lawrence marched four hundred troops from Halifax to Grand Pré, where they embarked in a small fleet of armed sloops headed for Beaubassin. As the British force entered Chignecto Basin, they were greeted by the light of signal fires along the shore. Runners with news of their approach soon reached Captain Louis de La Corne, another hero of the Canadien triumph at Grand Pré in 1747. In the event of a British assault, La Corne had standing orders to hold the territory north of rivière Missaguash, but also to secure the inhabitants of the *hameaux* on the south side. Not knowing the size of the British force, and fearing his own troops might be outnumbered, he decided the Acadians south of the river must be evacuated, and dispatched Le Loutre and the Míkmaq to Beaubassin to do the job.

It was a fateful decision. The Acadians were reluctant to abandon their village, and Le Loutre proved willing to take drastic measures. "Seeing that the Acadians were in no hurry to abandon their homes," Louis de Courville wrote, Le Loutre "set fire to their church himself, and made others whom he had gained to his side burn their houses." Sailing into Beaubassin channel on the cold, wet morning of 2 May, Lawrence and his men saw the village erupt in flames. By the time they landed at midday, it had been "reduced to ashes." Several hundred inhabitants lost all their possessions in the conflagration, and were left with no choice but to flee north across the river.[32]

Gathering his men amid the smoking ruins of Beaubassin, Lawrence and his lieutenants spied a group of inhabitants atop the dike that ran along the north side of the Missaguash, planting what proved to be a French flag, which the Acadians defiantly declared marked the "boundary of the French King's territory." After communicating through couriers, Lawrence and La Corne met on the riverbank to hold a parlay. On whose authority did La Corne dare trespass on British territory? Lawrence demanded. On the orders of Governor-General La Jonquière of New France, La Corne responded. Lawrence surveyed the terrain, which he was viewing for the first time, and saw Míkmaw, Acadian, and Canadien troops posted in all the most advantageous positions. They numbered upward of a thousand men, he thought, which was a gross overestimate. Nervously concluding that his force was "strongly surrounded on every side," Lawrence elected to retire and reembark his men. La Corne's "confident air of superiority," he reported, suggested that "the inhabitants to a man had rebelliously joined him." Indeed, La Corne's own account reflects that same self-assurance. The British colonel took his men and fled, he noted scornfully in his report, apparently not wishing "to have their scalps lifted." Lawrence returned to Pisiquid, where he spent the next few weeks strengthening the blockhouse Captain Gorham had constructed, which he named Fort Edward for Cornwallis, a small way of currying favor, perhaps, in the wake of a military humiliation.[33]

When Cornwallis's report of the confrontation at Chignecto arrived in London, the foreign minister protested to the French ambassador, who after inquiring of his government responded that the Míkmaq and the Acadians were the "sole authors" of what had transpired there, that the French had nothing whatsoever to do with it. What did the British expect, he continued, after their governor had publicly declared in the Boston press his intention of crushing the inhabitants of Chignecto? "General Cornwallis proceeds as if he were in an open and declared war against the Indians, against the inhabitants of his Government, and even against the French, who are the subjects of the [British] King." It was a fair charge, although the French were blatantly lying about their own responsibility, which extended from Captain La Corne at Chignecto to Governor-General La Jonquière at Québec to Colonial Minister Rouillé at Versailles. For his part, Cornwallis smarted under the humiliation of the affair. If only he had sufficient forces, he wrote the Board of Trade, he would push the Canadiens off the isthmus. Then the inhabitants and natives would either have to submit to British authority or be pushed out themselves. In June the Board of Trade recommended, and the British cabinet approved, offensive action to expel the French from Chignecto. While cautioning Cornwallis to moderate his fervor and keep open the possibility of a settlement, the board wrote that the king had authorized the dispatch of another regiment, which was to be used to gain a foothold at Chignecto. The militarization of the province was further intensified.[34]

On 15 September 1750, Lieutenant-Colonel Lawrence returned to Chignecto in an impressive fleet of seventeen armed vessels carrying seven hundred men. Opposing his landing was a force of some five hundred Canadien, French, Míkmaq, and Acadians, led by La Corne and Captain Louis de La Vallière, grandson of Chignecto's original seignior, who was sent from Louisbourg in command of a company of fifty French *troupes de la marine*. The British force succeeded in gaining the shore in sharp fighting, driving the defenders across the Missaguash to Beauséjour ridge, where they took up previously established defensive positions. Lawrence made no attempt to follow, but began the construction of an armed encampment of his own near the site of the burned village of Beaubassin. Over the next few days Míkmaw fighters, acting on orders from Le Loutre, torched many of the buildings in the other hamlets on the British side of the Missaguash, leaving another several hundred refugees homeless, destitute, and stranded in French territory. With that, the opposing forces settled in for the winter.[35]

By the following year the British encampment had grown into a picketed enclosure known as Fort Lawrence, while across on the ridge across the river the French proceeded with the construction of a much more substantial fortress known as Fort Beauséjour, as well as Fort Gaspereau, a smaller picketed bastion seventeen miles northwest at the port of Baie Verte. The Missaguash had became a fortified border between empires.

Cornwallis sent troops to Chignecto to push the Canadiens out, but also to prevent the flight of Acadians. Inhabitants from Minas and Annapolis Royal, however, continued to find their way to French-controlled territory by sailing across the Bay of Fundy in their small vessels and slipping into Chipoudy Bay. Most of these refugees went directly to Baie Verte, where they boarded vessels for transport to Ile Saint-Jean, a fifty-mile voyage across the sound. A French census of the island in the fall of 1752 counted 2,223 persons, an increase of nearly 1,500 in little more than two years. Among the first refugees to arrive were the extended families of Joseph-Nicolas Gautier, Joseph Leblanc, Louis-Amand Bugeaud, and the others who had been outlawed for high treason by Governor Shirley at the end of the last war. They were followed by the group of inhabitants who had joined the Míkmaq in the attack on Captain Handfield's company at Grand Pré, including the brothers Jean and Joseph Vincent, their cousin François Lavache, Joseph

Vincent's brother-in-law Charles Hébert, Hérbert's neighbor René Aucoin, and Aucoin's nephew Charles Guérin.[36]

Within two years those men and their immediate families had been followed by approximately 750 men, women, and children belonging to their clans. Indeed, most of the refugees came in family groups. Augustin Doucet, his wife Cécile Mius d'Azy, and their four children fled Annapolis Royal in company with the families of her two married sisters, Marie-Madeleine and Marguerite Mius d'Azy. Doucet wrote to an aunt in Canada, informing her of his move. "I was settled in l'Acadie, I lived contented on my land. But that did not last long, for we were compelled to leave all our property and flee from under the domination of the English. . . . If l'Acadie is not restored to France I hope to take my little family and bring it to Canada. I beg you to let me know the state of things in that country. I assure you that we are in poor condition, for we are like Indians in the woods."[37]

Doucet did not exaggerate. The limited marshland on Ile Saint-Jean had been colonized by Acadian settlers in the 1720s and '30s, and French officials placed the refugees of the early 1750s on the heavily timbered uplands, an environment with which they were unfamiliar. Their distress was compounded by a series of plagues that struck the island. In 1749, swarms of black field mice totally destroyed that years' crop, and the refugees survived on emergency rations sent from Louisbourg. A plague of locusts followed the year after, a blistering drought the next. Sieur de la Roque, the official in charge of the 1752 census, noted that "the greater number amongst them had not even bread to eat"; many refugees "subsisted on the shell fish they gathered on the shores of the harbor when the tide was out." Father Jacques Girard of Cobequid, who fled to the island in the fall of 1753 with most of his parishioners, found many families without sufficient clothing for the impending winter. "Most of the children are entirely naked, and when I go into a house they are all crouched in the ashes, close to the fire."[38]

Conditions were no better for refugees in the French-controlled territory north of rivière Missaguash, where some fifteen hundred refugees from Beaubassin crowded into the hamlets northwest of Fort Beauséjour or in the shanty village that grew up in the shadow of the fort itself. Most of the refugees were former residents of Beaubassin and surrounding hamlets, homeless as the result of Le Loutre's calculated campaign of arson. They too survived on rations that the French distributed in exchange for work performed on the construction of their forts. "They ought not to work for nothing," the refugees and inhabitants complained to the French commander, and lacking any other source of labor he had no choice but to comply. The Acadians, Governor Desherbiers of Louisbourg noted, were "not accustomed to obey their superiors."[39]

Obstinacy became an issue of major importance when Governor La Jonquière ordered the inhabitants in his jurisdiction to take an oath of allegiance. The French no less than the British insisted on the absolute loyalty of their subjects. La Corne and Le Loutre were instructed to exact an oath of allegiance from both inhabitants and refugees and "make them bear arms and to form companies of militia—all for the purpose of opposing invasions of the English." Just as the Acadians had resisted similar British demands for years, many resisted La Jonquière's order, enough of them that the governor felt compelled to issue an official proclamation threatening dire consequences. He made a point of blaming the prominent merchant Jacques Maurice Vigneau of Baie Verte—a man skilled at playing both British and French sides against the middle—as one of the leaders of those inhabitants "wishing to make themselves independent." Such independence or neutrality was impossible. "The considerable expense which His Majesty has undertaken," La Jonquière announced,

> does not permit us to entertain doubts as to the zeal and faithfulness of the Acadians. . . . And since we must punish such subjects WE DECLARE by the present ordinance that all Acadians who

> within eight days of the publication of this have not taken the oath of fidelity, and are not incorporated with the militia companies which we have created, will be declared rebels to the orders of the King and as such expelled from the lands which he holds.

Resistance seems to have faded in the face of this declaration, although Vigneau was so embittered by the experience he later became a spy for the British. By the early summer of 1751, La Vallière reported, approximately 250 Acadians had enrolled in the local militia. But that number represented less than half the men listed as capable of bearing arms in the French census of the district. Some Acadians apparently fled northwest to settlements at Shediac and Cocagne on the North Shore, where there were no French authorities. Others sailed to Ile Saint-Jean, which was under the administration of Governor Desherbiers of Louisbourg, who seems to have issued no similar orders for an oath.[40]

The Acadian militia at Chignecto, meanwhile, was encouraged to join the Míkmaq in attacks on the British. "Allow the Acadians to be mixed in among the Indians," La Jonquière advised. "Should they be caught, we could say that they acted purely out of their own initiative. Besides, it will contribute in no small way toward drawing other Acadian families to our lands." A small number of militant partisans, led by Joseph and Alexandre Broussard dit Beausoleil of Petitcodiac, painted and dressed themselves as native fighters and participated in Míkmaw attacks on British patrols or ambuscades of English or Yankee vessels blown ashore by the frequent storms that troubled the waters of Chignecto Basin. "The Indians and Acadians continue to harry the English and frequently kill some of their men," reported La Vallière, and he provided his superiors with a detailed summary of their operations. Their most daring assault took place in June 1751, when a mixed party of Míkmaq and inhabitants struck the British village of Dartmouth across Chebucto harbor from Halifax, killing men, women, and children, taking captives, and thoroughly terrorizing the residents. The British retaliated with a raid of several armed companies across the Missaguash. Few of the French defenders were killed, but the invaders suceeded in breeching the dikes that protected the land at the base of Beauséjour ridge. Hundreds of acres were inundated with seawater, ruining the crops intended for refugees and troops.[41]

The destruction of the Missaguash dike convinced Le Loutre of the necessity of laying a permanent foundation for the relocation of all the Acadians to secure areas on the north side of the Missaguash. In the summer of 1752 he left Chignecto for Québec, where he presented Governor-General Ange Duquesne de Menneville, the marquis Duquesne (successor to La Jonquière, who had died earlier that year) with a plan for a massive new project on rivière Au Lac, north of Beauséjour, designed to reclaim sufficient land to support the entire Acadian population. Securing Duquesne's endorsement, Le Loutre sailed for France to win a subsidy from the crown to support his project, which he described as nothing less than the creation of *Nouvelle-Acadie*.[42]

THE British government, meanwhile, was having second thoughts about its own project of Protestant emigration. Alarmed at the expense—which was running well in excess of the amount approved by Parliament—the Board of Trade instructed Governor Cornwallis to economize. Taking those instructions as a personal criticism, Cornwallis responded defensively; there followed a testy exchange of letters, and in the summer of 1752 he resigned. His successor, Colonel Peregrine Thomas Hopson, who arrived at Halifax that August, established a strikingly different administration. He was determined, he announced, to govern the province "by the most moderate measures."[43]

A career officer with nearly fifty years of service in the military, Hopson had spent several years at Louisbourg, including a term as the last British governor of the fortress from 1747 to 1749. Whether it was this experience or personal inclination that made the difference is not known, but within weeks he was negotiating peace with one of the few Míkmaw leaders who had declined to accompany Le Loutre to Chignecto. The French reacted in horror, although they needn't have worried, for Hopson's peace was short-lived, wiped out by an atrocity. Shipwrecked English sailors, rescued by a Míkmaw family, murdered and mutilated their hosts (including a mother and her two children) in order to collect the scalp bounty, unaware that Hopson had abolished that ghastly commerce. The family was part of the group whose leader had negotiated the peace, and he reacted understandably, burning the treaty and leading his community to Chignecto, where they joined the French. The episode demonstrated the limits on Hopson's power, but it also illustrated his intentions.[44]

Hopson was more successful in pursuing accommodation with the Acadians. Within a few weeks of his arrival, he realized "how useful and necessary these people are to us, how impossible it is to do without them, or to replace them even if we had other settlers to put in their places." The demand for an unconditional oath, he argued in a letter to the Board of Trade, was counterproductive. "Mr. Cornwallis can thoroughly inform your Lordships," he wrote, "how difficult, if not impossible, it may be to force such a thing upon them, and what ill consequences may attend it." The board agreed to put the decision off until "the circumstances of the province are such, as it may safely be done," leaving it to Hopson "to determine the time and manner."[45]

This was the first of several steps the governor took to improve relations with the Acadians. In response to a memorial from the Minas inhabitants, he persuaded the council to repeal its requirement of an oath from resident priests. And when the Acadians of Pisiquid complained that Captain Alexander Murray, commanding officer at Fort Edward, had commandeered livestock and poultry, impressed Acadian workers, and jailed resisters, Hopson immediately issued a general order that officers were "to look on the French Inhabitants in the same light with the rest of His Majesty's Subjects, as to the protection of the Laws and Government." All commodities, including labor, he decreed, must be purchased at fair market prices, and "no officer, non-commissioned officer, or soldier shall presume to insult or otherwise abuse any of the Inhabitants of the Country." The governor ordered that these rules be printed in French and posted in the public parts of every fort, which made it plain that he was intent on reversing the authoritarian trend of Cornwallis's rule.[46]

The new governor also moved to resolve the messy situation that had developed with the Protestant emigrants in Halifax. Shirley's original proposal and Cornwallis's instructions had envisioned settling them in the midst of existing Acadian communities, but the armed conflict with the Míkmaq that began in 1749 made that course highly imprudent. Nevertheless, the authorities in London continued to recruit needy emigrants, nearly three thousand of them from 1750 to 1752, mostly Protestants of German background. Hundreds of them slipped away to New England; but when Hopson arrived, the population of Halifax included nearly two thousand frustrated settlers—terrorized by Míkmaw attacks and angry over the British failure to fulfill the promise of free land. Scores of them had already gone over to the French, who promised grants of land on Ile Saint-Jean and Ile Royale. Such desertions, Hopson wrote, "not only disgrace and weaken our settlement, but at the same time will strengthen our neighbours," and he issued orders prohibiting any emigrant from leaving Halifax without written permission. But understanding that the situation called for more positive action, he wrote the Board of Trade requesting an immediate suspension of further emigration and an authorization of a change of plans for settling those emigrants already in the province.[47]

"I hope," he wrote, "that I may not be directed to send out those we have to settle any where among the French Inhabitants, for I have sufficient reason to be assured was that to be done, the latter would immediately quit the Province." Instead, he proposed a separate Protestant settlement at Mirligueche, an Atlantic harbor sixty-five miles southwest of Halifax, and far from any of the main

Acadian settlements. In the summer of 1753, Hopson instructed Lieutenant-Colonel Charles Lawrence to supervise the transportation of two thousand Germans to the new settlement, which he named "Lunenburg," a variation on one of the German titles claimed by the Hanovers, the British royal family. Lawrence was an imperious commander, who treated the German emigrants contemptuously, and they in turn came to despise him. But they adored Hopson, whom they considered their benefactor. The new governor's leadership did much to ease tensions at Halifax, and by planting the new Protestant town a good distance from the existing Acadian communities, soothed relations with the inhabitants as well.[48]

By the summer of 1753, Captain George Scott, commander at Fort Lawrence, was receiving discreet inquiries from refugee Acadians about the possibility of returning to the province. In September, the leaders of a group who had formerly lived in a hamlet near Beaubassin sent a memorial to Hopson. They were willing to take the same oath as the one administered to them in 1727 by Ensign Robert Wroth, the young officer sent by Lieutenant-Governor Lawrence Armstrong. That oath contained a set of specific exemptions, which the Acadians cited specifically: "That we shall be exempt from taking up arms against anyone. . . . That we shall be free, we and our descendants, to withdraw whenever we shall think proper, with heads raised high [*la tête levée*]. . . . That we shall have the full and entire enjoyment of our religion, and as many priests Catholic, Apostolic, and Roman as shall be thought necessary. . . . [And] that we shall have the entire enjoyment of our property without being disturbed by any one in the world. . . ." The refugees prayed that Hopson allow them to return on those terms, and that their oath would be endorsed by the authorities in London, "so that those who may succeed your Excellency shall not make the pretext that His Excellency Cornwallis made in saying that Mr. Philipps had no authority from the court of England for the oath which he granted us."[49]

The memorial was certainly impressive for its tone of self-assurance, what British officials labeled as "insolence." It was even more impressive for its command of historical detail. Certainly it impressed Governor Hopson, and it was a measure of his character that he ignored the insolence and focused on the history. With Paul Mascarene retired and living in Boston, and a new set of councilors in place, there was almost no institutional memory among officials at Halifax. Could it be true, Hopson wondered, that the Acadians had never taken an unconditional oath? He asked William Cotterell, the provincial secretary, to inspect the written record. It proved spotty, but from Cotterell's survey Hopson concluded that the history recounted by the refugee Acadians was probably correct.[50]

Neither Hopson nor the council, however, was willing to allow the "deserted inhabitants," as they called the refugee Acadians, to return without swearing an unconditional oath. But Hopson offered them his solemn assurance that they would not be expected to bear arms, since "the nature of our constitution makes it both unsafe and unprecedented to trust our cause in the hands of people of their [religious] persuasion." The refugees would not budge from their terms, yet Hopson was encouraged. "Since I have been here the French Inhabitants have behaved tolerably well, tho' their apprehensions from the French and Indians have entirely prevented their taking any step to shew themselves attached to us," he reported to the Board of Trade. Further progress, he was convinced, would require forcing the French from their entrenched position at Chignecto; but were that accomplished, he had hopes that "the French inhabitants will take the Oaths, and, giving over all hopes of any change, enjoy the benefit of English laws and Liberty." It was Paul Mascarene's vision of a settlement reincarnate.[51]

Hopson did not have the opportunity to test his assumptions. Suffering from a severe ocular infection, he left Halifax for treatment in London in the fall of 1753, putting the leadership of the province in the hands of Lieutenant-Colonel Lawrence, president of the Governor's Council, a man cast in the mold of Cornwallis rather than Mascarene. Charles Lawrence's temperament echoed that of abbé Jean-Louis Le Loutre, who returned to Chignecto with a royal subsidy, eager to begin supervising the construction of his great diking project on rivière Au Lac. Over the next two years the intransigence of Lawrence and Le Loutre would frustrate all attempts at accommodation. The tenure of Governor Peregrine Thomas Hopson proved but a brief interlude—yet an important one, if only as a demonstration that there was nothing inevitable about the subsequent course of events. The removal of the Acadians would not be determined by inexorable forces or ancient hatreds, but by the immediate choices made by men.

CHAPTER 10

BY FIRE AND SWORD

The Siege of Beauséjour, December 1753–July 1755

LIEUTENANT-COLONEL LAWRENCE PREPARED his first report on the state of the province in early December 1753, a few weeks after the departure of Governor Hopson. The Míkmaq and Acadians were "tolerably quiet," he wrote, although "French emissaries" continued to keep alive the issue of the oath, despite Hopson's decision not to press the issue. The inhabitants seemed convinced that "we only wait a convenient opportunity to force it upon them." Lawrence did not say so, but the Acadians were absolutely correct. The Board of Trade had instructed Hopson to determine "the time and manner" in which getting them to swear to the unconditional oath "may safely be done." Lawrence drew a conclusion from the fact. Since this was what they expected, there seemed little point in waiting. The council had already reiterated its demand for the unconditional oath from the refugee Acadians, and Lawrence endorsed that decision. "They will never have my consent to return," he declared, "until they comply without any reservation whatever." Why then exempt those Acadians still residing in the province? "It would be of great advantage, both to them and us, that this matter was, one way or other, cleared up as soon as possible."[1]

The board's reply, which Lawrence did not receive until the following summer, urged caution. While a resolution of the Acadian question was greatly to be desired, the members agreed, he ought to consider the dilemma the situation presented for policy.

> The more we consider this point the more nice and difficult it appears to us. For, as on the one hand great caution ought to be used to avoid giving any alarm, and creating such a diffidence in their minds as might induce them to quit the province, so on the other hand we should be equally cautious of creating an improper and false confidence in them, that by a perseverance in refusing to take the Oath of Allegiance, they may gradually work out in their own way a Right to their Lands, and to the Benefit and Protection of the Law, which they are not entitled to but on that condition.[2]

The predicament called for subtlety, for the tact of a Hopson or the diplomacy of a Mascarene. But Charles Lawrence was not a subtle man. At the German settlement of Lunenburg the year before, encountering the resistance of emigrants who objected to his insistence that they labor on military and government facilities before building shelters for their families, he responded with condemnations of their "sloth" and their "unwillingness to do any part of what they call the King's work." Lawrence lacked any capacity for empathy, which placed severe limits on his political leadership. Once Governor Hopson left the province, a minor rebellion broke out at Lunenburg. Quickly suppressed without violence by British troops, the uprising was clearly prompted by the privation and suffering of the settlers. But Lawrence saw conspiracy. The Germans had been incited by "French emissaries," he asserted, and had hoped "to affect the same kind of Independency that the French Inhabitants have done." There was no evidence for the charge, but that was the way he saw the world—right and wrong, black and white, without shading.[3]

Lawrence was, in the words of the historian John Bartlet Brebner, "almost purely the soldier." If one motive drove him, it was his ambition to succeed as an officer. From humble origins, his rise through the ranks of the class-bound British military would not have been possible without the patronage of Lord Halifax, a distant relation. But Lawrence was also a striver, and his was a remarkable ascent. Commissioned ensign in 1727 at the age of eighteen, he was posted to the West Indies for several years. Promoted lieutenant, he worked as military attaché in the War Office in London. Advanced to captain, he commanded a company of foot during the War of the Austrian Succession and was wounded leading his men against French forces at the Battle of Fontenoy, an experience that certainly contributed to his harsh view of all things French. Gazetted major and sent to Louisbourg to join Hopson's regiment, he landed in Halifax when France regained possession of the fortress in 1749, following the Treaty of Aix-la-Chapelle.[4]

Cornwallis, veteran of the Highland clearances, immediately recognized Lawrence as a fellow "military man," a kindred militarist. He appointed the young officer to his council, helped him procure the lieutenant-colonelcy of the 40th Regiment, the position vacated by Mascarene, and honored him with command of the British assault at Chignecto. In 1752 he elevated Lawrence to the council presidency and recommended that he be named lieutenant-governor, an appointment approved by the Board of Trade in 1754. According to Richard Bulkeley, aide-de-camp to Cornwallis, Lawrence was a large man, standing six feet two, of prepossessing appearance, a perfect picture of strength and virility. He was both admired and feared for his assertive and direct methods. He had no tolerance for indeterminacy, no penchant for compromise or accommodation. He neither understood nor appreciated the tangled situation of the inhabitants, and was incapable of handling the problem of Acadian allegiance with any imagination. He was Mascarene's opposite, precisely the right man to orchestrate Acadian removal.[5]

Lawrence responded to the Board of Trade's note of caution with an assertive letter in which he announced his intentions. The Acadians "have been long the object of my most serious attention," he wrote.

> The frequent experience I have had of them in the course of my duty has enabled me to form an opinion of them and their circumstances that I shall now take the liberty to lay before your Lordships, together with such measures as appear to me to be the most practicable and effectual for putting a stop to the many inconveniences we have long laboured under from their obstinacy, treachery, partiality to their own countrymen, and their ingratitude for the favor, indulgence and protection they have at all times so undeservedly received from His Majesty's Government.

Believing that "the mildness of an English Government would by degrees have fixed them in our interest," provincial authorities for years had sought to avoid the use of violent measures with them. It had been a foolish policy. "This lenity has not had the least good effect." Although the Acadians "affected a neutrality," in truth they always had been French partisans. Hundreds had abandoned their communities to join the French on the frontier, and were now diking new land and making settlements on the rivers of Chipoudy Bay. Those inhabitants remaining at Minas and the *haute rivière* of Annapolis continued to send provisions to Louisbourg. In short, there were "no hopes of their amendment." So long as the Acadians remained in possession of the best lands, and were supported by the Míkmaq, effective Protestant settlement was impossible. The situation called for drastic measures. "Tho' I would be very far from attempting such a step without your Lordship's approbation," Lawrence concluded, "I cannot help being of the opinion that it would be much better, if they refuse the oaths, *that they were away*."[6]

About the same time Lawrence assumed control in Halifax, Governor William Shirley of Massachusetts returned to Boston after an absence of nearly four years. He had been serving on the joint British-French commission established by the Treaty of Aix-la-Chapelle to resolve the conflicting territorial claims of the two powers in America. Shirley and his French counterpart, Roland-Michel Barrin de La Galissonière, former commander in chief of New France and architect of French grand strategy in North America, countered each other demand for demand, both absolutely convinced of the aggressive intentions of the other's government. Indeed, Shirley's position was so uncompromising he became an embarrassment to the British government and was recalled. His departure failed to improve the negotiations, which in the end produced no result, other than two multivolume folio sets, published simultaneously in French and English, in which the powers laid out their respective cases. Back in Massachusetts, Shirley found his power considerably diminished. The Assembly rebuffed him on policy matters and refused his request for increased salary. It was a fall from the heights. During King George's War, Shirley had used patronage to construct one of the most powerful political machines in the British colonies, building a network of political supporters by strategically distributing recruitment and supply contracts as well as military commissions. Since his power had come as a war governor, it was natural that he would see war as an avenue to reviving it. "War had increased his political capital," writes Shirley's biographer, "the discontinuance of war threatened to reduce it. He had motives to avoid peace."[7]

Rising conflict between Britain and France in North America provided Shirley with his opportunity. During the summer of 1753 the colonial press was filled with alarming reports that "an army of French and Indians" had invaded the frontiers of western Pennsylvania and Virginia. Marquis Duquesne, governor-general of New France, sent fifteen hundred *troupes de la marine* and Canadien militia, under the command of Pierre-Paul Marin de la Malgue—the Canadien officer who had laid siege to Annapolis Royal in 1745—

to construct a string of forts from the southern shore of Lake Erie to the junction of the Allegheny and Monongahela rivers, known as the Forks of the Ohio, the future site of Pittsburgh. The effort cost the lives of four hundred men, including Marin himself, but it succeeded in blocking the westward passage of British traders, competitors of the French for the lucrative fur trade of the Ohio country.[8]

Duquesne had instructions to protect French interests, but the size of this operation went well beyond the expectations of Versailles—perhaps because he was also protecting his own interests as an investor in the western trade. Meanwhile, a group of Virginians interested in western lands formed the Ohio Company. In his reports to London, Governor Robert Dinwiddie of Virginia, a prominent investor in the company, represented the incursion of the French as "an impending invasion" of his colony, claiming that British subjects had "abandoned their settlements in great Panick." In fact there were no settlements to abandon, only the huts of Ohio Company traders at the Forks. But the British cabinet reacted in alarm, and the minister dispatched letters to all the governors of Britain's North American colonies, including William Shirley in Massachusetts, directing them to "resist any hostile attempts that may be made upon any parts of His Majesty's Dominions within your Government." Dinwiddie took this directive as the authorization for an armed challenge to the French, and dispatched a company of Virginia militia to the Ohio under the young officer George Washington.[9]

Like Dinwiddie, Shirley had reasons of his own for interpreting the directive from London as a general authorization for the use of military force. French aggression on the Ohio, he wrote back, was matched by French aggression at Chignecto and rivière Saint-Jean, areas clearly within His Majesty's domain. He had hopes of persuading the Massachusetts Assembly to authorize its "just quota of men and money" in an effort to expel the invaders. But Shirley knew he would have a difficult time building support for a Massachusetts expedition against Chignecto. What he needed was a French encroachment closer to home, and several weeks later he uncovered one. He had received intelligence, he reported to the General Court in late March 1754, that "rebel inhabitants" were settling on the upper reaches of the Kennebec River and that Jesuit priests were stirring up the native tribes against New England. Their intention, he wrote to Sir Thomas Robinson, secretary of state for the Southern Department, was "to break up all the Eastern Settlements of this province," and if they were not thrown back, "there may be a Danger of their soon becoming Masters of the whole River Kennebeck, which Event would prove destructive to His Majesty's Subjects within this Province, and greatly Affect the Security of His Territories within the other Colonies of New England."[10]

Appealing to his political base—frontier landowners and entrepreneurs—Shirley won Assembly approval for an expedition of five hundred men to establish fortified outposts and expel any French or French allies found in the Kennebec country. The plan proved popular among the Massachusetts electorate, resulting in the selection of more Shirley supporters in the May elections, and in turn the Assembly's authorization of another three hundred troops in June. To command them, Shirley turned to Captain John Winslow, an Assembly deputy and officer in the provincial militia, promoting him to the rank of major general. Winslow and his men, accompanied by Shirley himself, left in July and moved up the middle reaches of the Kennebec in August, building two forts and leaving small garrisons behind. They found neither armed Canadiens, rebel Acadians, nor hostile Abenakis. There was, in fact, no substance to the reports of invasion. Yet when the expedition returned to Boston, Winslow was greeted with popular acclaim and Shirley hailed as a brilliant strategist. The "success" of the Kennebec expedition contrasted with news reports of the defeat suffered by the Virginia militia under Washington's command, in a skirmish with French forces near the Ohio River.[11]

That fall, the Boston press featured numerous essays and opinion pieces in favor of further action against the French to the eastward. Correspondents in Halifax argued that the French encroachments at

Chignecto and rivière Saint-Jean would have what one characterized as "fatal Consequences to all the rest of the British colonies in North America." The only way to save Massachusetts, another wrote, was to expel the French from Beauséjour immediately, before the next war was officially declared. "Should the French make themselves Masters of Nova Scotia, which is a Country fruitful of all kinds of Grain and Provisions, they would be in a Condition to introduce and subsist a Body of Troops strong enough with the French *Acadians*, and inhabitants of *Cape-Breton* and *Canada*, together with the *Indians*, to reduce all the English Colonies." These were Shirley's views, and there is strong suspicion that he was behind the propaganda offensive.[12]

But there was something much larger than propaganda at work here. The early 1750s had been very hard years for New Englanders. The region was stricken by drought, depression, unemployment, and high taxes, as well as by continuing frontier violence with the native tribes allied to the French. The Puritan ministry of New England interpreted the bad times as signs of the "final days" before the great struggle between the forces of good and evil. Priests filled their sermons with the virulent rhetoric of anti-Catholicism. The Catholic religion, declared Jonathan Mayhew, liberal minister of Boston's West Church, was "calculated rather to make men wicked than to keep them from being so." He was echoed by Reverend Samuel Checkley of Boston's conservative New South Church. French Catholics were "enemies of the Son of Man and His cause," members of the "Antichristian Romish Church, spoken of in the Book of Revelations, the downfall of which is clearly foretold." According to Jonathan Edwards, the distinguished Puritan theologian, French Catholics were the "open enemies of God's church" and "members of the kingdom of Antichrist." The final struggle was coming, in which they would be totally destroyed.[13]

These were not just abstract notions but calls to action. Mayhew made that point explicit in a sermon preached before an audience that included Governor Shirley. "I am sure there is not a true New

England Man, whose Heart is not already engag'd in this Contest; and whose Purse, and his Arm also, if need be, is not ready to be employ'd in it; in a Cause so just in the Sight of God and Man; a Cause so necessary for our own Self defence; a Cause wherein our Liberties, our Religion, our Lives, our Bodies, our Souls, are all so nearly concern'd."[14]

Shirley's next step was to contact Charles Lawrence and begin exploring the possibility of a joint operation against Fort Beauséjour. Although their earliest surviving correspondence dates from November 1754, Shirley made reference to their communication in an August dispatch to Lord Halifax, president of the Board of Trade. "From the experience he hath had of the behaviour and spirit of the Acadians," Shirley wrote of Lawrence, "he is of sentiment with me that the refusal of the revolted Inhabitants of Chignecto to comply with the terms upon which they had permission given to return . . . is happy for the country, and even thinks it would be fortunate if a favourable opportunity should offer for ridding His Majesty's Government there of the French Inhabitants of the two districts of Minas and Annapolis River." Not only should the refugees be kept from returning; the operation Shirley and Lawrence envisioned would cleanse the province of all its Acadian inhabitants. Shirley's summary certainly corresponded with Lawrence's expression to the Board of Trade, three weeks before: "it would be much better," he had written, ". . . *that they were away.*" This would be the final resolution of the Acadian problem. "That, my Lord, would indeed be a day of Jubilee for His Majesty's northern Colonies," Shirley crowed. "And I need not repeat to your Lordship how ready I am to contribute every thing in my power towards hastening this happy event."[15]

Lawrence echoed Shirley with a letter of his own to Halifax at almost the same time. "I flatter myself I could, with Mr. Shirley's assistance, raise a Body of Men in New-England which joined to the few troops we could muster on so good an occasion would, I believe, make a pretty successful campaign." Once Fort Beauséjour was taken, "the French inhabitants on that side must either be removed to this, or driven totally away by Fire and Sword. For if all the villages beyond Beauséjour are not destroyed, and some of the Dykes cut, the French would immediately return to take possession of their habitations and rebuild their Forts." He wondered what Lord Halifax thought of those alternatives. "I should esteem myself most happy in having the least hint from your Lordship how far any attempt I should make to dispossess them would be well received at home."[16]

Lawrence sought official sanction for the removal of the Acadians from Chignecto, but he already had in hand an operational plan for the expulsion of all the Acadians from the province. It was prepared by Charles Morris, author of the 1748 survey of Acadian communities conducted on Shirley's request in anticipation of the settlement of Protestant emigrants. Largely because of that report, Morris had been appointed to the position of provincial surveyor-general in 1749, an office he would hold until his death in 1781, and that in turn would be held by his son, grandson, and great-grandson, a Morris family dynasty lasting for more than a century. Morris conducted the first comprehensive surveys of the province, drew the first accurate maps, and has been celebrated as one of North America's first field geographers. He was also deeply involved in the implementation of Acadian removal. First arriving in l'Acadie during King George's War as a junior officer in the Massachusetts militia, he was garrisoned at Grand Pré during the surprise attack by Canadien forces in the winter of 1747. With that experience he became an inveterate enemy of the Acadians, and rarely did he miss an opportunity to advocate their destruction.[17]

In a 1751 report on l'Acadie, prepared for Shirley's work on the boundary commission, Morris argued that the province would never be secure as long as the Acadians continued in possession of the "chief granary of the country [and] all the water communication." It would be impossible to settle Protestants in the province, he concluded, "without their removal." At that time he urged a military campaign against the inhabitants at Chignecto and Chipoudy Bay. "They are at all adventures to be rooted out, and the most effectual way is to destroy all these settlements by burning down all their houses, cutting the dikes, and destroying all the grain now growing." Two years later, in a policy paper submitted to Governor Hopson, Charles Morris urged the removal of the inhabitants of Cobequid, arguing that the Míkmaw war of resistance would not end until their source of supply among the inhabitants had been destroyed. By the summer of 1754 he had presented Lawrence and the council with a comprehension plan for the removal of all the Acadians.[18]

The long title of Morris's report told the tale: "Some Reflections on the Situation of the Inhabitants, commonly called Neutrals, and some methods proposed to prevent their escape out of the Colony, in case upon being acquainted with the design of removing them, they should attempt to desert over to the French neighboring settlements, as their firm attachment to them may be conjectured to raise in them a strong effort to attempt it." Morris made no attempt to argue the case for the removal of the Acadians, but only to examine the operations necessary to put it into effect. These plans had to be kept secret, he argued, for once the Acadians knew about them, it would be impossible to prevent them from fleeing the province and contributing their capacious skills as sailors and rangers to the French enemy. The British must strike them by stealth. Morris considered a variety of stratagems by which this might be accomplished. Perhaps the inhabitants could be captured while they were in church on Sunday, or surprised at dead of night while they were in their beds. But their scattered hamlets made this a difficult operation to man and coordinate.[19]

The best alternative, he concluded, was to set a trap they would fall into voluntarily and on their own accord. The men could be summoned to attend a meeting, then seized and held hostage against the surrender of their families. It would be critical to encourage them to think they were being sent to join their French brethren, he suggested. "It will much facilitate their readiness *to go* if a persuasion could obtain among them that they are to be removed to Canada." In that case, others would come in voluntarily to join their captive kindred. Nonetheless, some certainly would make an attempt to escape, so Morris drew up detailed plans for blocking "the passages by which they may desert the Colony." In its cold calculation, its weighing of various stratagems, its invention of tricks and lies, Morris's logic was diabolical. Once the Acadians were in British hands, it would be necessary to disperse them in small groups throughout the empire, as far from their homeland as possible. Morris aimed at nothing less than the complete destruction of the Acadian community.[20]

The arguments and proposals of Morris, Shirley, and Lawrence rested on the assumption that British troops and settlers were in great danger. In fact, the situation was not nearly so bleak as they made it seem. Earlier in the summer of 1754, the leaders of a Míkmaw community from the southern peninsula had come to Halifax to negotiate. They had refused to follow Le Loutre to Chignecto, the chiefs told Lawrence, and wished to be friends of the British. The council sent them food, blankets, and ammunition. Lawrence received peace feelers from other Míkmaq as well—much to the horror of the French. Although arrogance and pure diplomatic clumsiness prevented him from seizing this opportunity, the initiatives suggested serious difficulties behind the French lines. Other evidence was provided by the reapplication of refugee Acadians for return to the province. Most of the refugees balked at the requirement of an unconditional oath; but one group of exiles from Minas agreed to return on British terms, and after taking the unconditional oath was sent to Lunenburg, where they were provisioned and provided with land. They told of starvation conditions in French territory, and complained bitterly of the French regime at Chignecto, where abbé Le Loutre exercised absolute and theocratic rule. A protest organized by the "deserted inhabitants," they told Lawrence, "was little short of a mutiny."[21]

The condition of the refugees north of rivière Missaguash was growing desperate. In the spring of 1754 surging storm tides broke through the main cross-dike of Le Loutre's large-scale reclamation project at rivière Au Lac, destroying nearly everything the Acadians had accomplished in several months of intense work. "The accident served to disconcert all the inhabitants," Le Loutre wrote in his third-person autobiography, "who had only commenced this work, which they regarded as an impossibility, because the Missionary made them do so." A large group of refugees, represented by Paul Doiron and Olivier Landry, had petitioned Governor-General Duquesne for permission to return to their former homes on the peninsula. When Le Loutre saw the petition, he could barely contain his rage.[22]

He was the real source of authority at Chignecto. Claude-Antoine de Bermen de La Martinière, commandant at Fort Beauséjour through the first half of 1754, was seriously ill, and his successor, Louis Dupont Duchambon de Vergor—cousin of François Dupont Duvivier, yet another member of the ubiquitous Dupont clan of Louisbourg—was thoroughly corrupt, preoccupied with skimming the funds sent from Québec to provision the Acadian refugees. Both of them deferred to Le Loutre in the handling of the Acadians. From the altar the abbé demanded that all those who had signed the petition to Duquesne "efface their crosses with their own saliva." Otherwise, he thundered, "they cannot hope for heaven, nor for the sacrament to take them there." Anyone caught attempting to cross back into British territory, he warned, "would be shot." He would instruct the Míkmaq to "look upon them as enemies, and [the natives] would treat them as such." Duquesne reacted similarly, condemning the petitioners for their disloyalty, and proclaiming that those who attempted to return would be "considered and treated as rebels against authority, disobedient servants of the King, and even as deserters." Intimidated by threat of religious excommunication and military execution, most refugees continued to suffer through their deplorable exile, although at least one group braved the journey to the British side, where they took the unconditional oath and returned to their homes in Pisiquid.[23]

Lawrence and the council were well informed about these developments, because they had a well-placed spy at Fort Beauséjour: Thomas Pichon, chief clerk of the commissary and secretary to the commandant. Pichon was gifted with a brilliant mind, but haunted by his resentments. Betrayal and bitterness were the main themes in his own account of his life. His *petit bourgeois* Norman parents wanted him to become a priest, but at fourteen he fled to Paris hoping to study medicine. As Pichon told the story, his father withdrew his stipend and forced him to take work as a clerk. At night he read the classics, imbibed an Enlightenment sensibility, including a strong dose of anti-clericalism, and decided to pursue a career in law. He reconciled with his family and spent several years assisting them in a complicated lawsuit. But his father refused to compensate him, and once again he was forced to take work unworthy of his talents. He found employment in the hospital service of the army, where he impressed a French officer, Jean-Louis de Raymond, who hired him as his personal secretary.[24]

When Raymond was appointed governor of Ile Royale, Pichon was invited to come along, promised professional and financial advancement. But once more he was betrayed. Louisbourg turned out to be a backwater, Québec not much better, and when, after two years, Raymond returned to France, Pichon ended up at Beauséjour, which made Louisbourg look like a metropolis. He became scribner for Le Loutre as well as the fort's commandant, taking dictation, writing letters, and improving what he disdained as their crude French. He quickly concluded that de Vergor was a crook and Le Loutre a tyrant, and he came to despise them both.

Some time after Pichon's arrival at Beauséjour, Captain George Scott, commandant at Fort Lawrence, who had met Pichon during an official visit to Louisbourg the year before, invited him to dine.

The skirmishing between the two sides had long since subsided; officers and enlisted men had settled into bored indifference and there was a great deal of fraternization going on. Pont-à-Buot—a disorderly cluster of ramshackle buildings and a small French fortified outpost or *redoute*, on the north side of the main crossing of rivière Missaguash—had become a meeting place for both sides, and it was at a tavern there that Scott and Pichon rendezvoused. In the course of their conversation, Pichon later recalled, Scott "gave me to understand that he could make my fortune, that he knew of means which were very safe, and that I should have no cause for regret." Soon the Frenchman was supplying Scott with intelligence, using British supporters among the refugee Acadians (including Jacques Maurice Vigneau) as couriers. He provided detailed plans of Forts Beauséjour and Gaspereau, copies of official correspondence, and exhaustive accounts of activities on the French side. "Moses dominates and directs everything," he wrote in a typical report, using his code name for Le Loutre, "whereas M. de Vergor merely applies himself to skimming the cream off this colony."[25]

Pichon would later attempt to justify his treason by praising the British nation as "the most just and liberal of all that exist," but his principal motives were his contempt for his superiors and his desire for monetary gain and personal comfort. He insisted on being paid in gold guineas, and looked forward to retiring somewhere in the British Empire. Fort Beauséjour was prime for a British attack, he wrote in one letter in the fall of 1754. "The good Vergor, who cannot even read, but is no less arrogant on that account, would at once lose his head. The officers could give little heed to their duty. The troops are disgusted and a considerable number would desert. The inhabitants would think more of escaping to the woods than of joining the French, especially when they realized that you were the stronger." It was important that the British act soon. "I forsee all this so clearly," he concluded, "that I am already wishing that my personal effects and books were at Halifax, or rather in Philadelphia." After his work at Beauséjour was accomplished, Pichon would be supported by a British pension and spend time at both Halifax and Philadelphia, before retiring to London. There he would endure an increasingly lonely old age, and come to deeply regret his betrayal of France.[26]

A MORE open-minded leader than Charles Lawrence might have taken the mounting evidence of French weakness as an opportunity for an opening with the Acadians. But to his military mind, signs of weakness inspired thoughts of aggression. Ignoring Governor Hopson's standing order that the inhabitants were to be afforded "the protection of the Laws"—despite the fact that as lieutenant-governor he was legally bound by the governor's orders—in the summer of 1754 Lawrence reinstituted Cornwallis's policy of requisitioning provisions and labor from the inhabitants by military force. At Pisiquid, Captain Alexander Murray, commander at Fort Edward, ordered the inhabitants to provide food and fuel, as well as posts and pickets for the expansion of his facilities. Murray, another "military man" like Lawrence, spent seven years as commandant of "the Hill," his name for Fort Edward, situated on a height of land overlooking the junction of the Pisiquid and Saint-Croix rivers. He gave every indication of hating his posting and loathing the Acadians, whom he described as "poor, unlucky, obstinate, blind to their own interests, and insensible of every benefit bestowed on them by an indulgent government."[27]

The inhabitants had not forgotten Hopson's original order, and citing his guarantee of their rights, they refused to comply with the new demands. Lawrence remained adamant. "They are not to be bargained with," he instructed Murray. "If they should not immediately comply, you will assure them that the next courier will bring an order for military execution upon the delinquents." Still the Acadians resisted, even after Murray threatened to "take their houses for fuel." They served him with a remonstrance signed by eighty-six heads of household, protesting that nothing in their oath of allegiance obligated them to provision the king's troops. Murray believed they had been put up to it by their new priest, Henri Daudin, whom Le Loutre had recruited in France to lead the parishes at Pisiquid.[28]

The inhabitants were certainly capable of acting on their own—as they had many times before. Yet Daudin's letters to Le Loutre, copies of which Pichon supplied to the British, showed him to be an active agent of disaffection. "You shall have news of me which will convince you that you did not bring a man of straw from France," he boasted. The Pisiquid inhabitants, he reported, were resolved to resist British tyranny, but were divided on the best means, and he was doing his best to unite them. Once Lawrence saw Pichon's copy of this letter, he ordered Daudin and the Pisiquid deputies—Claude Broussard, Charles Leblanc, Jean-Baptiste Galerne, and Joseph Hébert—"to repair immediately to Halifax to give an account of their conduct." When they refused to go voluntarily, insisting the government had no right to treat "a people who were free as slaves," Murray had them arrested and taken to Halifax in chains. After some weeks in a cold dungeon the Acadians agreed "to return to their duty," while Daudin promised "to comport himself for the future dutifully to the government." Intimidation was freely employed by the British as well as the French.[29]

Daudin left an account of his experience that provides a rare glimpse of events from the Acadian perspective. The inhabitants, he wrote, considered Lieutenant-Governor Charles Lawrence "a self-willed man, who would like to rule with a rod of iron." Lawrence had established a regime very different from Hopson's. Acting under his instructions and orders, officials became increasingly arbitrary and hostile. "They no longer responded to inhabitants' requests, they no longer granted them justice. For a yes or a no, prison served as an answer. They only spoke to the inhabitants in order to announce to them their near and imminent destruction. They told them they would be made into slaves, that they would be dispersed like the Irish. In brief, everything announced the destruction of their nation. There was nothing but talk of burning houses and ravaging fields."

The Acadians held Lawrence personally responsible for this harsh treatment. He was, according to Daudin, "a man the inhabitants personally hated." What did it all mean? Where were they headed? Living in an increasingly authoritarian environment, Daudin wrote, the Acadians "began to suspect something sinister."[30]

IN November 1754, Lawrence and Shirley received identical dispatches from colonial minister Sir Thomas Robinson, responding to Shirley's report of the previous spring that rebel Acadians and Míkmaq had invaded the frontier of Maine. That "intelligence"—if it ever actually existed—had proven faulty, but Robinson had no way of knowing that. He had laid Shirley's alarming report before the king, he wrote, who instructed him to urge both governors to pursue such joint measures "as will frustrate the designs of the French." Shirley treated Robinson's letter as a blank check. "I construe the contents," he wrote Lawrence, "to be orders to us to act in concert for taking any advantages to drive the French of Canada out of Nova Scotia." Robinson was specifically referring to the threat of Canadien militia in Maine, not at Chignecto, but Lawrence willfully drew the same conclusion as Shirley. Emphasizing "the necessity of undertaking the Grand Project without waiting for any further sanction from England," he dispatched Lieutenant-Colonel Robert Monckton—a young officer who rose rapidly in the ranks because of family connections—to Boston with a proposal that Shirley raise two thousand volunteers and outfit an expedition for an assault on Beauséjour as early in the spring of 1755 as possible. Lawrence would pay for the entire operation "out of the money granted for this Colony," and he provided Monckton with a letter of unlimited credit made out to the merchant house of Charles Apthorp & Thomas Hancock in Boston, the firm that had provisioned the Massachusetts troops at Louisbourg and became sole suppliers for the military regime at Halifax. Unlike the Massachusetts government, which operated on revenue raised through provincial taxes levied by the

Assembly, the government of Nova Scotia was financed directly by the British treasury, and while Parliament complained of budget overruns it had continued to authorize disbursements. Lawrence's proposal was a windfall for Shirley. With another province picking up the tab, he would get his expedition and the patronage that went with it without having to win over the Assembly.[31]

Delayed by stormy weather, Monckton and Scott did not arrive in Boston until 8 December. Two days later, Shirley received another dispatch from Robinson. The cabinet had learned of the defeat of the Virginia militia by the French, and had decided that the time had come for a systematic strike against the French encroachments. Two regiments of Irish infantry were being sent to Virginia under the command of Major General Edward Braddock. Shirley and Pepperell's colonial regiments from King George's War were to be revived and recruited up to strength. Robinson was vague about the plan of operations—at the time he wrote it was still under discussion—and Shirley worried that the assault on Beauséjour he and Lawrence were planning might not be included among them. "At this time particularly I am concerting Measures with Colonel Lawrence to drive the French out of Nova Scotia next Spring," he wrote to Robinson, "and propose that my Regiment should assist in the Service, unless I am forbid by different orders." In fact, when Braddock sailed with his regiments in early January 1755, he carried instructions that included an assault on Fort Beauséjour at Chignecto, as well as expeditions to expel the French from Fort Duquesne at the Forks of the Ohio; Fort Niagara at the portage between Lakes Erie and Ontario; and Fort Saint-Frédéric on Lake Champlain.[32]

It remained, however, for London to endorse the removal of the Acadians. Early in January, Lawrence received a response from the Board of Trade to his request of the previous August for their "approbation" regarding his proposal to remove the inhabitants from Chignecto. It was thoroughly ambiguous. The board could not offer a final judgment on the question, read the letter, "until We have laid the whole State of the Case before His Majesty and received his

Directions upon it." In the meantime the members were willing to make some "provisional points." Settling New Englanders on the lands of the "deserted inhabitants" they thought an idea of "great utility." But it would be "absurd" to attempt any such thing unless and until Forts Beauséjour and Gaspereau had been destroyed and the Acadians "driven to seek such an Asylum as they can find in the barren Island of Cape Breton and St. Johns and in Canada." Yet that prospect gave them pause. "We could wish that proper Measures were pursued for carrying such Forfeiture into Execution by legal Process." By refusing to swear an unconditional oath of loyalty, had the inhabitants in fact forfeited their rights to property? That was a question, they equivocated, "which We will not take upon ourselves absolutely to determine." Instead, they recommended Lawrence consult on the matter with Nova Scotia's new chief justice, Jonathan Belcher, son of the former governor of Massachusetts, who had arrived at Halifax from London.[33]

Surely Lawrence had hoped for something more than this. Lord Halifax and the Board of Trade had received his and Shirley's recommendation that the Acadians be removed following a successful campaign against the French garrison at Beauséjour. Halifax and the board members knew that the Beauséjour operation would take place in the spring, part of the general offensive against the French encroachments. Yet they declined to issue an opinion on the issue of removal itself, despite the five or six months required for two-way communication across the Atlantic. The board raised a serious question about the legality of dispossessing the Acadians, but advised Lawrence to seek the judgment of a new chief magistrate—a man thoroughly unfamiliar with the province, its history, and its current condition. There is only one conclusion to be drawn: the board was distancing itself, providing itself with "plausable deniability," while shifting the responsibility to Lawrence. Better to let their local agents take the risk. Lawrence would have to move forward without clear authorization or approval.[34]

He immediately wrote back. The province would not be secure,

Lawrence believed, "until the fort at Beauséjour and every French settlement on the north side of the Bay of Fundy was absolutely extirpated." He was highly sensitive to the risk he would be taking in attempting an enterprise of this importance "without having previously obtained your Lordship's approbation," but it was "imperative to act." He could do no more than to keep his options open. He wrote to Colonel Monckton with instructions regarding the treatment of the refugee Acadians if and when Beauséjour was taken. Monckton was to proclaim in the king's name that all those who did not surrender their arms were "declared Rebells and may expect to be treated accordingly." In the event of their submission, under no circumstances was he to offer them an opportunity to take the oath of allegiance, "as their taking them would tye up our hands and disqualify us to extirpate them, should it be found (as I fancy it will) hereafter necessary."[35]

In Boston, Shirley and Monckton worked out the details of the operation. The Massachusetts Assembly would be asked to authorize the recruitment of two thousand men for an enlistment of twelve months. The recruits would be offered "the King's pay," a suit of clothes, a blanket, haversack, and 30 shillings bounty money. They would be organized into two battalions, one commanded by George Scott, who was brevetted lieutenant-colonel, the other by the popular militia commander, John Winslow. "He hath the best reputation as a military man of any officer in this province," Shirley wrote to Lawrence, "and his character in every respect stands high with the Government and people, and he is particularly well esteem'd and belov'd by the Soldiery, so that I greatly rely upon him for success in raising the men."[36]

Winslow, a man in his fifties, was a well-to-do farmer from the town of Marshfield in old Plymouth Colony, the scion of one of the more prominent families of New England, great-grandson of a *Mayflower* Pilgrim and first governor of Plymouth. In 1740, during the colonial conflict between Great Britain and Spain, Winslow was commissioned captain of militia and served in campaigns in the West Indies. With the outbreak of the war with France in 1744, he transferred to regular service in the 40th Regiment and was garrisoned at Annapolis Royal and later at Halifax. He participated in the conquest of Louisbourg in 1745, and commanded the company that reasserted British control at Minas in 1747. He returned home to Marshfield in 1751. In a portrait commissioned about that time, Winslow posed in his powdered wig and officer's uniform of scarlet broadcloth, edged in gold lace. Slightly stout, with ruddy complexion, he appears a man at ease with himself. "Command in the Military and Civil way in New England has often been in our Family from 1620, the year of the Country's being first Settled," he wrote. "I Flatter my Self No Man Can raise in it a Better Regiment or Sooner than it is in my Power to do."[37]

He proved to be right. When recruitment began in early February 1755, immediately after the Assembly voted to approve the Beauséjour expedition in secret session, men joined readily at Winslow's call; within six weeks the quota was filled. As a group the recruits were mostly unemployed young men from seafaring towns along the Massachusetts coast. Many had been to the eastward before, as hands on fishing vessels or merchant transports, and many of their officers had served there during the late war. The recruits were formed into companies and sent off to Boston to the accompaniment of shrill anti-Catholic cant. "Are we willing to give up our Religion, the Religion of Jesus, which we now enjoy in its Purity, and which should be more dear to us than our Lives?" Reverend Isaac Morrill of Wilmington asked the young men of Captain Phineas Osgood's company. "O! for God's sake, let us think of our Danger, and labour to prevent our Ruin. Let us determine to defend our Country though it be at the Price of our Blood. Let there not be an unwilling Mind, or a faint Heart in any son of New England. Let such as are willing, and may be called to go forth in the Defence of their Country, go out with Courage and Resolution." The French

Catholics, he concluded, must be evicted from l'Acadie "at the Muzzle of our Guns and at the Point of our Swords."[38]

In March, Shirley sailed to Virginia for a conference of governors called by General Braddock, who had arrived with his Irish regiments. Braddock laid out the plan of the general campaign. He would march with his troops on the French fortification at the Forks of the Ohio. Shirley—who had been commissioned major general—was to lead his and Pepperell's regiments in an assault on the French at Niagara. A third expedition of provincials and Mohawks would move against the French fort at Crown Point on Lake Champlain. Shirley explained the Beauséjour operation to Braddock, who sent orders by express to Monckton at Boston "to proceed with the command of it without delay." Thomas Hancock already had assembled a fleet of thirty-one schooners, sloops, and brigantines to transport the nearly two thousand men and officers, but their departure was delayed by the late arrival of the shipment of arms and ammunition from England. When Shirley returned to Boston in the second week of May, he found them still waiting. But the munitions arrived soon thereafter, and on 19 May 1755 the fleet set sail under the protection of three gunships.[39]

Fort Beauséjour, commanding the southwest summit of the ridge that separated the Missaguash from rivière Au Lac, was a classic earthwork fortification with five bastions connected by parapets, surrounded by ditchwork and glacis, and armed with twenty-six artillery pieces. Capable of accommodating up to eight hundred men, in the spring of 1755 its garrison numbered barely two hundred French marines and Canadien militia, but with ammunition and provisions sufficient to hold out against a siege. The fort was intended to defend against an attack precisely like the one that was coming, but it had a serious design flaw: an adjacent height of land some six or seven hundred yards from the bastions on the fort's northeast face. That was the logical position for any besieger to entrench. Jacau de

Fiedmont, the fort's military engineer, recognized the problem and sought to correct it with a plan for a series of redoubts in the area; but because the Acadians were engaged in Le Loutre's diking project, he had been unable to call up the necessary labor. De Fiedmont was an Acadian—the maternal grandson of Pierre Melanson dit Laverdure—but he had been raised in a military family at Louisbourg and considered himself thoroughly French. While he felt a distant kinship with the Acadians he knew at Beauséjour, he thought they were weak patriots.[40]

In April 1755, noting the absence of schooner traffic to Fort Lawrence on the south side of rivière Missaguash, and correctly surmising that Yankee merchant vessels were being held in port while preparations were made for an offensive, de Fiedmont urged de Vergor to order a crash program to shore up the defenses. The commandant brushed aside his warnings. A few weeks later, an Acadian from Annapolis Royal arrived with letters for Le Loutre detailing rumors of the New England expedition circulating there. "Moses does not believe it," Pichon informed Captain John Hussey at Fort Lawrence. On Pentecost Sunday, 11 May, at the chapel in the shadow of the fort, Pichon reported, Le Loutre preached to the Acadians that if they had truly believed in Jesus, "they would not have suffered all the misfortunes which had pursued them." Once they became dutiful Catholics, he told them, "miracles would be performed." After the service the Acadians were treated to bread and brandy and there was much conviviality; but according to Pichon, "as they were leaving the fort, some were heard to say that they would be on the side of the strongest." It was the old Acadian game.[41]

At almost that same moment the Governor's Council at Halifax was debating a change in the rules of the game, formally taking up the question of Acadian removal. "The point was much debated," Lawrence wrote to Monckton, "and it seemed to be thought the most prudent method to drive away the inhabitants and destroy the country, because that would render it very difficult for the French to reestablish themselves in case of war." The issue had not yet been resolved. "The Council have deferred coming to any determination upon this head until they have your opinion upon the matter, and by that time we may probably hear from England and be better able to judge of our own circumstances."[42]

That letter reached Monckton when he and the fleet arrived at Annapolis Royal on 26 May. Lawrence had sent several vessels from Halifax with a detachment of three hundred regulars and a company of artillery with ordnance. After further preparations, the fleet departed for Chignecto at dawn the following Sunday, 1 June. In the lingering sunlight of a late spring evening, Acadian sentinels at Cape Maringouin, the spit of land separating Beaubassin Channel from Chipoudy Bay, spied the British approach and dispatched a messenger. Awakened to receive the news early Monday morning, de Vergor immediately sent off couriers soliciting aid from Québec and Louisbourg, and drafted a proclamation ordering the Acadian militia to arm and report to the fort under penalty of death. By early afternoon, de Fiedmont had some four hundred inhabitants at work constructing a rough breastwork and positioning cannon on the vulnerable northeast face of the fort. At five that afternoon, with the turn of the tide, the first of the British vessels were seen making their way through thick fog to the Beaubassin landing. Within an hour the Yankee militia and British regulars were disembarking and beginning their march to Fort Lawrence, and by sunset they were setting up an encampment. The siege was about to begin.[43]

Early Tuesday morning, de Fiedmont took a company of marines to Pont-à-Buot, where a small redoubt with two carriage guns and four swivels defended the crossing of the Missaguash. This was the place, he believed, where the battle for control of Chignecto would be won or lost. Over the previous several years the dikes on the British side of the river had fallen into disrepair, and the trail leading from Fort Lawrence to the crossing traversed some very soggy ground. For the last five hundred yards or so the enemy would be within the range of French fire. De Fiedmont ordered the bridge destroyed. While the British attempted to lay a new one they would be exposed to shot and ball poured down on them from the height across the river. A strong detachment of regular troops at the crossing might be able to stop their progress. At least before retreating back to the fort and preparing for the siege the French could force the enemy to fight hard for position, weakening his forces.[44]

De Fiedmont presented this plan to de Vergor, but the commandant rejected it, protesting that he could not spare his regulars, that he needed them within the fort. De Fiedmont was forced to do what he could, assigning only thirty men to the redoubt and supplying them with ordnance. He also ordered the Acadians and Míkmaq to take up defensive positions along the north bank of the river, but they too refused, objecting that they would be exposed to deadly fire from the British. They preferred to remain mobile, able to strike and retreat, using irregular tactics. Consequently, de Fiedmont would blame the Acadians for the loss at Pont-à-Buot, but it seems hard to fault them for refusing an assignment the French commandant himself would not accept.[45]

As de Fiedmont attempted to mount a defense at Pont-à-Buot, Lieutenant-Colonel Monckton held a council of war to plan the assault. It would begin the next morning, he told his officers. Packing provisions for five days on their backs, the troops would march to the river, cross it, and advance on the fort. There was no thought of being stopped at the crossing. At first light on Wednesday, 4 June, the officers roused their men, and by 6 a.m. they were on the march, artillery in the lead—Yankee matrosses dragging four bronze field pieces—followed by the regulars, then the battalions of volunteers, nearly two thousand men in all. Quickly they passed over the high ground east of Fort Lawrence, but found the wetland vale of the Missaguash much tougher going. Across the river the troops could see several hundred Acadians, Míkmaq, and Maliseets running along the crest of the dike, gesturing angrily with their muskets and getting into position. Most of the Yankees were raw recruits who had never seen action, and for them it must have been a frightening moment. By the time the vanguard came within firing range, it was nearly 11 a.m. Monckton called a halt, consulted his officers, then sent sappers rushing forward to begin laying a bridge. "As our people Began to Carry the timber to Cross the River," wrote Captain Abijah Willard of Massachusetts, "the French and Indians gave a grate shout and Came Running Down to stop our pass, and Emediately they fireed their Cannon from their fort, and a large number of small arms." Monckton ordered up his artillery and within two minutes his six-pounders were responding in kind.[46]

The roar of cannon and the shouts of men filled the air. The smoke of burning powder made it difficult for anyone to see clearly what was happening. The fog of war enveloped the Missaguash. The British sappers were raked with partridge shot from the French swivels. The French gunners were blasted with lethal sprays of small iron balls from the British cannon. "The bolets," wrote Willard, "went in at one side of their fort and oute att the other." After several minutes, the redoubt fell silent. Monckton then ordered the first Yankee battalion forward, and with a deadly barrage of musket fire they drove the defenders back from the dike. The second battalion was rushed up to assist in laying the bridge, and as soon as it was serviceable the regulars scrambled across and began ascending Beauséjour ridge in skirmishing order, firing at the defenders, who pulled back to the cover of the timber and finally retreated to the fort. The entire engagement took no more than forty-five minutes or an hour.[47]

The British halted to consolidate their strength and count casualties. Five or six French dead lay on the field. One Yankee had been killed and a score of regulars and volunteers wounded, two mortally. The toll might have been much worse. "This I think to be the most Remarkable thing I Ever Saw," wrote John Thomas, Winslow's staff surgeon, "that we Should Receive So much of thare Fire, and Nothing to Cover us from it, and yet no more Kill'd and wounded. But as we ware on a marsh and the Enemy on an Emenace, thay Shot over our Heds." The troops continued their march, advancing to within a mile of the French fort before pitching their tents.[48]

Inside Fort Beauséjour, there was terrible panic. Convinced the British would prevail, many Acadians declared themselves unwilling to run the risk of being hanged as traitors and "vanished like smoke," as de Fiedmont put it. By Thursday morning, fewer than two hundred Acadian militiamen remained at the fort—but they included the group of militants led by the brothers Beausoleil, Joseph and Alexandre Broussard of Petitcodiac. There could be no doubt that the defenders faced a difficult situation. Looking out over the fort's parapet they could see the British flags flying from Butte à Roger, the height of land a mile to the southeast, and British troops constructing an encampment in the woods considerably less than a mile away. Le Loutre, a pipe stuck defiantly in his mouth, attempted to rally the Acadians' spirits. But later that day he and de Vergor made a decision that surely weakened Acadian resolve, ordering the destruction of all the structures crowding the grounds outside the fort, including dozens of refugee shanties. They were torched shortly after sunset, setting off a conflagration that roused a great deal of excitement in the British camp. "We saw a Grate Light in the west," wrote Abijah Willard, "which was the French setting their hosees round the fort on fire, which was pleasing to the army." It was an act of military necessity, designed to deny the British any cover during their assault, but it was another devastating blow for the refugees, who were given no opportunity to collect their meager possessions. For many this was the second time they had been burned out by Le Loutre, who several years before had ordered the torching of Beaubassin and its adjacent hamlets.[49]

British troops spent the next week hauling arms and ammunition across the river and up the ridge to their encampment. It was difficult work, not helped by a cold rain that began on Friday, 6 June, and continued intermittently for the next ten days. The Beausoleil brothers led stinging forays against the British lines, in one raid capturing a young ensign. Firing from the dikes they were successful in preventing British vessels from coming upriver to deliver goods at Pont-à-Buot, until they were forced back by the fire from Yankee gunships. The British could be slowed, but they could not be stopped. On Sunday, 8 June, Winslow, in command of three hundred Yankees, seized the high ground on the northeast of the fort in sharp fighting with a strong detachment of French regulars, and over the next several days the British dragged ordnance to the site, braving blasts from the fort's cannon. On Thursday, 12 June, in another "hot engagement," the Yankees turned back a French attempt to evict them from their position, and sometime after midnight they began digging entrenchments.[50]

Rain fell all that day, Friday, 13 June, which made the digging all the more difficult. But by the late afternoon the besiegers had completed a long parallel trench and a lateral extension which brought them within five hundred yards of the fort, and a second parallel where they positioned their cannon and mortar. At 6 p.m. they began the bombardment, the French replying round for round. "Nothing was to be heard but the Roaring of Cannon and the Noise of Men," an officer wrote home to Massachusetts. "But thank God, I had as composed a Temper as ever I had in my Life." On Saturday, the British deployed their "great mortar"—an iron monster that fired a cast-iron shell measuring 13 inches in diameter and weighing nearly 200 pounds when fully loaded with black powder, a bomb that could destroy substantial structures and create "disorder and mischief" with its fragments.[51]

The British bombardment created absolute terror within Beauséjour. The defenders crowded into the casements or "bombproofs," as they were known, but several men were killed, including one of the Acadian refugees. Even more disastrous for morale, however, was the news carried by a messenger from Louisbourg who arrived on Saturday. There would be no help coming from that quarter. "Preservation now depended on prompt aid from Canada," concluded de Fiedmont, and he considered that "a frail hope." At a council of war the officers urged de Vergor to keep the bad news from the Acadians. But they learned of it immediately—possibly informed by Pichon, who during the siege had insinuated himself as their friend, and had done everything he could to stir up their dissatisfaction. De Vergor "was exposing them, without any good reason, to be butchered," he told them. They could expect "either to be crushed to death under the ruins of the fort, where it was impossible for them to subsist, or to be hanged like dogs, if they fell into the hands of the English." Some of the Acadians attempted to desert through the fort's sally port, but were stopped by French guards with orders to use deadly force if necessary.[52]

The British, meanwhile, continued extending their entrenchments, and by Sunday night they had positioned their guns within two hundred yards of the fort. At 8:30 a.m. a large bomb made a direct hit on one of the French bomb-proofs, totally destroying it and killing a regular officer, two enlisted men, and the captured British ensign. Complete disorder ensued within the fort. The leaders of the Acadians went to de Vergor with the demand that he capitulate. His officers told him further resistance was futile. The British had not surrounded or blockaded the fort, and some of them advised that he blow up the fort and retreat to Baie Verte or to the North Shore, the coast of the Gulf of St. Lawrence. Instead, de Vergor decided to treat with the British for an honorable capitulation. At 9 a.m. he sent out a flag of truce requesting a cessation of arms.[53]

MONCKTON dictated moderate terms. The French and Canadien officers and soldiers of the garrison would be granted the honors of war and transported to Louisbourg without delay, on a pledge not to bear arms for a period of six months. He gave de Vergor until 2 p.m. to accept, at which point the bombardment would be resumed. There was no mention of the Acadians. De Fiedmont, in spite of his criticism of the inhabitants during the siege, was the one who zealously stood up for them at the council of war called by de Vergor, insisting that honor demanded they be protected from the British threat to deal with them as traitors. If Monckton would agree to pardon the Acadians, de Fiedmont declared, he could support a capitulation, but otherwise they must continue their resistance. In response to this principled position, Le Loutre countered with the mock-heroic declaration that it would be "far better to be buried in the Fort than to surrender it," a bit of braggadocio that took no account whatsoever of the inhabitants' interests. The council endorsed de Fiedmont's position and de Vergor sent it to Monckton, who reviewed it with his officers, and finally agreed to include a pardon for the Acadians as one of the articles in the terms of capitulation: "The Acadians, inasmuch as they were forced to take up arms under pain of death, shall be pardoned [*seront pardonné*] for the part they have played." Winslow summarized the British consensus in his journal: "That the Inhabitants be Left in the Same Scituation as they were when we arrived, and not Punished for what they had Done Since our being in the Country."[54]

The formal ceremony of capitulation took place the next morning, 17 June 1755, ten years to the day since the Yankees had taken possession of Louisbourg. The French and Canadiens marched out, flags flying and drums beating, carrying their own arms and baggage; the British regulars and their officers marched in, raised their own flags, and participated in a short ceremony in which the fort was renamed in honor of the Duke of Cumberland. The next day, the commander of Fort Gaspereau near Baie Verte gave up his small garrison without a fight. The defeated officers and troops were soon sent off. But Le Loutre was nowhere to be found. The night before the capitulation, disguised in women's clothing, he had slipped out of the fort and fled to Baie Verte, where he and another priest caught a vessel for Québec. From there Le Loutre would sail for France, only to be captured by a British man-of-war and sent to prison in England for the duration of the war, more than seven years.[55]

The Acadian militiamen returned to their families. But notwithstanding the pardon they were granted, the British immediately made it clear they had not done with them. Monckton ordered the distribution of a proclamation written in French, which Lieutenant-Governor Lawrence had prepared, addressed to the Acadians of Chignecto and the rivers of Chipoudy Bay. "In so far as the great part of the inhabitants," it read, "have not yet made their submission to the king of Great Britain but on the contrary have behaved toward their own sovereign against all order and law, this proclamation orders them to report immediately to my camp to make their submissions, bringing with them all their weapons, firearms, swords, sabres, pistols, and other instruments of war. Or, disobeying, they will be treated as rebels, with military execution." Unsure of what the British had in mind for them, feeling their way, Acadian leaders went to the Frenchman who had befriended them during the siege, the Frenchman who seemed to have established a channel of communication with the British: Thomas Pichon. He encouraged them to put their trust in the British.[56]

Over the next several days several hundred inhabitants came in to surrender their arms. Even Joseph and Alexandre Broussard dit Beausoleil—"the more warlike Acadians," as Pichon described them—presented themselves to Monckton, proposing to act as mediators in peace talks with the Míkmaq and Maliseets on the condition they be granted amnesty. Monckton agreed conditionally, on confirmation by Governor Lawrence. The Acadians were put to work clearing away rubble and repairing the fort, and instructed to stand ready for the necessary rituals of submission, which would take place at Monckton's pleasure. The inhabitants' deputies asked Pichon to help them draft an appeal to the commander. "I have been earnestly solicited by the inhabitants to prepare a petition to Mr. Monckton," Pichon wrote in his journal, "so that he may be induced to give them favourable terms, and to consider their cruel situation."[57]

Monckton had already written to Lawrence, who responded on 25 June with a letter that contained not a single note of celebration. Several days earlier he had received a message from Vice Admiral Edward Boscawen of the Royal Navy, informing him that the greater part of a large French fleet, carrying some three thousand *troupes de terre*, had escaped the British warships sent to stop it, and slipped through the spring fogs into Louisbourg. "This has greatly altered the face of our affairs," Lawrence wrote. Monckton must now take all the measures necessary to ensure that Chignecto remained in British possession. The only sure way of doing that was by "totally extirpating the French . . . [and] by the French I mean both Acadians and Canadians." The Canadien forces had already been sent off. So Monckton was now to turn to the extirpation of the Acadians. Lawrence was not at all surprised at Monckton's report that inhabitants had taken an active role in the defense of Beauséjour. "Their pretending to have been forced to take up Arms is an insult upon Common Sense," he wrote, "and as it deserves the severest treatment, I am glad to find you have carefully avoided in your articles of capitulation in granting any thing to the inhabitants that may entitle them to the future enjoyment of their Lands and Habitations." Were the Acadians to remain, "they will prove forever a sore Thorn in our Side. With their help the French may be able to do much against us, without them, I think nothing of much importance." The district could be best defended by expelling the Acadians and replacing them with settlers from New England.[58]

The Governor's Council had not yet reached a final decision as to the fate of the Acadians, but Lawrence all but ordered Monckton to prepare himself for the removal of the inhabitants at Chignecto. He was even clearer in his letters to Sir Thomas Robinson and the Board of Trade in London, informing them of the victory. Monckton had reported that "the deserted French inhabitants are delivering up their arms," Lawrence wrote. Now was the moment to strike at the Acadians. "I have given him orders to drive them out of the Country at all events."[59]

CHAPTER 11

Driven Out of the Country

The Decision to Remove the Acadians, June–July 1755

During the siege of Beauséjour, British forces on the Acadian peninsula were not idle. On 2 June 1755, as the expeditionary force was landing at Beaubassin, Lieutenant-Governor Charles Lawrence was implementing a well-laid plan to disarm the Acadians of Minas. None of the orders issued in the course of this operation appears in the official records of the province. Indeed, there is a curious dearth of documents in the public archive detailing the Acadian removal. The operation was reported, however, in the Philadelphia *Pennsylvania Gazette* for 3 July 1755. "We have letters informing that a Party of our Rangers had been at Pisguit [Pisiquid]," the paper reported, "and disarmed 3 or 400 of the French Neutrals, as they are very improperly called." Further details were provided by the recollections of Joseph Gray, a Scot merchant from Halifax who was one of the suppliers of Fort Edward and seems to have been associated with the fort's commander, Captain Alexander Murray. As the British prepared to battle the French for control of Chignecto, Gray remembered, "it was thought advisable *to Draw the Teeth* of all the Neutrals in the Province by a seizure of their arms and ammunition, which in these parts was effected with great secrecy and expedition." According to Gray, Murray—acting on orders from Lawrence—sent some two hundred regular troops and New England rangers out among the hamlets of Pisiquid, Grand Pré, and rivière-aux-Canards on the evening of 2 June with instructions to raid and ransack the inhabitants' homes simultaneously at midnight, seizing firearms and ammunition. The surprise raid netted some four hundred muskets and other arms. On 4 June, Lawrence published a proclamation that forthwith, any inhabitants found possessing firearms "should be treated as Rebells to His Majesty." Over the next few days the Acadians surrendered nearly three thousand additional muskets, fowling pieces, and pistols.[1]

The previous summer Lawrence had reinstituted the policy of forcibly requisitioning provisions and labor from the inhabitants. He followed it in the fall with an embargo on all exports from the province, punishable by fines and the confiscation of their vessels. He posted armed guards at the bridges and crossroads, isolating hamlets and preventing communication among the people. The summer confiscation of arms was the latest and most disturbing in a long train of abuses, and on 10 June twenty-five deputies from the hamlets of Minas petitioned the lieutenant-governor, in order "to make known the annoying circumstances in which we are placed, to the prejudice of the tranquility we ought to enjoy." They pleaded for the return of their firearms which, they argued, were "absolutely necessary to us, either to defend our cattle when attacked by the wild beasts, or for the protection of our children and of ourselves." The confiscation presumed that they posed a security risk to the government. "We are grieved, Sir, at seeing ourselves declared guilty without being aware of having disobeyed."[2]

The Acadians begged Lawrence to consider their past conduct. Over the years they had consistently refused to use their arms against anyone. "Besides," they noted, "the arms which have been taken from us are but a feeble guarantee of our fidelity. It is not the gun which an inhabitant possesses that will induce him to revolt, nor the privation of the same gun that will make him more faithful. But his conscience alone must induce him to maintain his oath." This remarkable statement—which the Acadians surely knew would get them into hot water—was a measure of their frustration. They included another, even more likely to infuriate Lawrence and his council. "We still entertain, Sir, the same pure and sincere disposition to prove under any circumstances our unshaken fidelity to His Majesty, provided that His Majesty shall allow us the same liberty that he has granted us."[3]

In his dispatch conveying the petition to Halifax, Murray reported that when the deputies delivered it, they "treated him with great indecency and insolence." Lawrence suspected this meant the inhabitants had heard of the arrival of the French fleet at Louisbourg, since it was "notorious that the said French inhabitants have always discovered an insolent and inimical disposition towards His Majesty's Government when they have had the least hopes of assistance from France." The petition arrived in Halifax mid-month, at the same time Lawrence received Colonel Robert Monckton's report of the French capitulation at Beauséjour. The unexpected early success of the expedition meant there were still several months of good campaigning weather. That provided Lawrence with ample opportunity to move ahead expeditiously with plans for removal of the Acadians. Lawrence immediately dispatched a courier to Murray, ordering the Minas deputies to Halifax to explain their "audacity in subscribing and presenting so impertinent a paper." As he put it in a letter to the Board of Trade, the time had come to take action, and he was determined "to begin with them."[4]

The deputies were brought to Lawrence's quarters on 3 July for a special meeting of the Governor's Council. Fifteen of the twenty-five signers answered to the reading of their names; the rest were absent, claiming illness. The original petition was read into the record, after which the deputies offered a second, signed by forty-five inhabitants. "If in the petition which they have the honor to present to your Excellency," it offered, "there shall be found any error or want of respect towards the government, it is entirely contrary to their intentions." This attempt to mollify the authorities did no good. Lawrence immediately went for the offending sentence. For their insolence in daring to suggest that they would "prove their fidelity *provided* that His Majesty would give them liberties," the Acadians deserved the most severe treatment.[5]

While the deputies stood uncomfortably before the council, the lieutenant-governor worked his way through a long harangue. They had asked him to consider their past conduct, he began. To him, their history was an indictment. They had been poor farmers, neglecting the cultivation of the soil, sitting "indolent and idle on their lands" and refusing to improve the uplands. This was patently false, and in its absolute disregard for fact it set the tone for what followed. They had refused to furnish the government with provisions, or done so only at the most exorbitant prices, all the while providing supplies and assistance to the French. They had proven themselves disloyal, refusing to take the unconditional oath required of His Majesty's subjects. They had dared to claim the pretense of neutrality, while displaying "a constant disposition to assist His Majesty's enemies and to distress his subjects." Not for one moment did Lawrence believe their argument that firearms were needed for protection and defense. He was certain they wanted them only "to insult His Majesty's Government, and to join with His Enemies, contrary to their Oath of Fidelity." In short, he concluded, the Acadians were "of no use to the province . . . but rather an obstruction to the King's intentions in the settlement." Nevertheless, in light of their ignorance of the proper functions of empire and government, he was prepared to treat them with lenity. Lawrence would give them a last and final opportunity to make their submission to the king by swearing the oath without any conditions whatsoever.[6]

Jean-Baptiste Galerne, one of the deputies from Pisiquid, provided the only Acadian account of this meeting. "We were summoned to appear before the Governor and Council at Halifax," he wrote, "where we were required to take the oath of allegiance without any exception." That was something they could not do without explicit instructions from their communities, the deputies told Lawrence. With his permission, they would return home to consult and come back with an answer. That was a "friviolous pretence," Lawrence snapped. He had no doubt "they knew the Sentiments of the Inhabitants in general, and had fully considered and determined this point with regard to themselves before now, as they had been already indulged with Six Years to form a Resolution." If they refused to speak for their communities, they must at least speak for themselves. Would they, as individuals, take the oath? The deputies requested a moment to retire and consult among themselves, which was granted; returning, they told Lawrence and the council that they could not comply. If they took the oath, they explained, "we shall be obliged to take up arms" and be compelled "to plunge our swords in the breasts of our friends and relations."[7]

Like the other deputies, Jean-Baptiste Galerne had grown up under British rule. Neutrality was the foundation of his political identity. He had defended it, he wrote, not only against the demands of the British but of the French and the Míkmaq. At the time Halifax was being settled, the Míkmaq, "by threats and blows," insisted that the inhabitants join them in waylaying and destroying the British troops and Protestant emigrants; but the Acadians resisted—the vast majority of them anyway. "I myself was six weeks before I wholly recovered of the blows received from them at that time," Galerne recalled. It was but one instance among many in which the inhabitants held steady to their "exception," their pledge *not to bear arms against anyone*. "We are still willing to take the Oath of Fidelity," the deputies declared, "and to give the strongest assurance of continuing peaceable and faithful to his Britannick Majesty, with that Exception."[8]

"His Majesty had disapproved of that manner of their taking the Oath before," Lawrence responded. "It was not consistent with his

Honour to make any conditions, nor could the Council accept their taking the Oath in any other way than as all other His Majesty's subjects were obliged by Law to do when called upon." He would give them until the next day to reconsider, he told them, and ordered them into confinement for the night. When the council reconvened on the morning of 4 July, however, the deputies had not changed their minds. They had been through this before. They had refused and the British had threatened, but in the end, there had been no consequences. So they must have been surprised this time by the council's resolve. "As they had now for their own particulars, refused to take the Oath as directed by Law, and thereby sufficiently evinced the sincerity of their inclination towards the Government, the Council could no longer look on them as subjects to His Britannick Majesty, but as subjects of the King of France, and as such they must hereafter be treated." Lawrence told them he would arrange to "send them to France by the first opportunity." Until then, they were ordered imprisoned, and were immediately conducted to George's Island in the harbor.[9]

According to the official minutes of the meeting, as well as Lawrence's summary of it to the Board of Trade, a number of the deputies immediately changed their minds and pleaded with him to be allowed to take the oath. Too late, they were told. "Persons who have once refused to take the oaths cannot be afterwards permitted to take them," since "there was no reason to hope their proposed compliance proceeded from an honest mind and could not be esteemed only the effect of compulsion and force." This was the law in regard to "Popish Recusants"—Catholics who refused to swear allegiance to the king—a crime that was punished with the loss of "lands, tenements and hereditaments."[10]

Although Galerne's account provides general corroboration for the official version of the meeting, it mentions nothing about Acadian second thoughts. In his version, the deputies told Lawrence they would not take the unconditional oath but would happily renew their oath of fidelity, with the exception of not bearing arms—"but this, in the present situation of affairs, not being satisfactory, we were made prisoners." Abbé Henri Daudin, who had moved from Pisiquid to Annapolis Royal to become parish priest at Saint-Jean-Baptiste, provided a *mémoire* of the events of 1755 which also failed to include any mention of changed minds. Indeed, according to Daudin, the deputies did not waver in their resolve, remaining "as firm as ever." He included a scene in which Lawrence confronted the deputies after their confinement to the dungeon on George's Island. In a highly threatening manner, he asked if they would persist in their refusal. "Yes, and more than ever," Daudin quoted one Acadian as responding. "We have God for us and that is enough." Lawrence flushed at this answer and angrily drew his sword, but the deputy boldly stepped forward and tore open his shirt. "Strike, Sir, if you dare," he declared. "You can kill my body, but you shall not kill my soul." Lawrence froze in his tracks. What, would they all choose death? "Yes, Sir! Yes, Sir!" they cried.[11]

The story seems implausible, not only because of its melodrama, but because it flies in the face of the Acadian instinct to negotiate. Daudin's purpose was the inflammation of French opinion, and that was served by the invention of heroic Acadians. Yet the official account of the meeting in the council minutes, while less baroque, also served the interests of its authors. While portraying the deputies as wavering and cowardly, it provided an occasion for putting on the record the only legal justification Lawrence and the council had been able to concoct for the decision they were about to announce. By refusing to swear allegiance to the king when required to do so, the deputies had committed the crime of recusancy, from which there was no turning back.

This legal justification was surely the contribution of Chief Justice Jonathan Belcher, with whom the Board of Trade had instructed Lawrence to consult on the legalities of the confiscation of Acadian property. Belcher arrived at Halifax to take up his duties in late 1754, and his first assignment was the preparation of the legal brief for the expulsion of the Acadians. A man in his mid-forties, son of the former governor of Massachusetts, and a graduate of Harvard College, Belcher had spent the previous decade as a barrister in Ireland. His brief on the question "as to the Residence or Removal of the French Inhabitants" was a political, not a legal text, its greater part devoted to expeditious arguments. It was read into the record at the council meeting of 28 July 1755, but was undoubtedly circulated among Lawrence and the councilors earlier. For forty years, Belcher wrote, the Acadians had been "Rebels to His Majesty." To allow them to remain after refusing the oath "would be contrary to the letter and spirit of His Majesty's instruction to Governor Cornwallis, and in my humble apprehension would incur the displeasure of the Crown and Parliament." Moreover, it would "defeat the intent of the expedition to Beauséjour" and "put a total stop to the progress of the settlement."[12]

Belcher's opinion was, in the words of the Canadian historian Arthur G. Doughty, "ill-founded in fact and contemptible in argument." His text, barren of references to official correspondence or even the minutes of the Governor's Council, suggests he had not bothered to examine the record. For the most part he simply mimicked the cant of Charles Lawrence and other provincial officers. Belcher's reference to the instructions issued to Governor Edward Cornwallis was curious, for not only did those instructions fail to mention the forcible removal of the Acadians, they had been superseded by the instructions prepared for Governor Peregrine Thomas Hopson, which remained in force since Hopson was still technically governor. Hopson's orders were to obtain the subjection of the inhabitants, but in the case of their resistance to ascertain "His Majesty's further directions in what manner to conduct yourself." After Hopson's departure from Halifax, Lawrence reported the Acadians' intractability, but had as yet received no positive orders from London.[13]

The single scintilla of a legal argument, in Belcher's opinion, was the charge of "recusancy." What in fact was the law regarding "Popish

Recusants"? Belcher cited 1 George I c. 13 (1715), which required all officials of church or state to take an anti-Catholic oath. It did not require an oath from Catholics themselves, however, nor did it impose any penalty on them for refusing to take one. So much for Belcher's citation. Earlier statutes, dating from Elizabethan times, did specify fines and loss of property for individuals found to be "secret Catholics." But a finding of recusancy required indictment and conviction in the king's court, as well as further legal process authorizing the state's seizure of property. Even in that event the recusant had the right to remain on his land as a "tenant for life." There was absolutely no provision in law for the "collective punishment" of a recusant's family. Wives and children could not be held responsible for the offenses of husbands and fathers. In short, the laws regarding recusancy simply did not apply to the situation at hand.[14]

Try as it might, the provincial government did not have legal process on its side. What it did have was means and opportunity. This was, in fact, Chief Justice Belcher's most telling point. After the departure of the New England troops, he wrote, when the Acadians "return to their Perfidy and Treacheries, as they unquestionably will," the government would no longer possess the power "to drive them out of their possessions." This, more than anything else, was the motivation driving Lawrence forward. He had the means at hand to remove the Acadians and he was determined to seize that opportunity. As Belcher pointedly noted, "such a juncture as the present may never occur." Lawrence was not about to let this "favourable opportunity" pass, as he made clear in a letter to the Board of Trade. "I have ordered new deputies to be elected and sent hither immediately," he wrote, "and am determined to bring the Inhabitants to a compliance, or rid the province of such perfidious subjects."[15]

ON Sunday morning, 13 July 1755, while abbé Daudin conducted mass at the church of Saint-Jean-Baptiste in Annapolis Royal, an officer and a company of soldiers from Fort Anne came to the door with a proclamation ordering "the inhabitants to carry all their arms to the fort and to meet for the nomination of thirty deputies who should immediately go to join at Halifax those of other districts." The next day, the Acadians delivered up several hundred weapons, and on Tuesday they met to choose deputies and draft a petition, which was signed by 207 male inhabitants, representing upward of two thirds of all the households along the Annapolis River.[16]

"We have unanimously consented," they wrote, "to deliver up our firearms to Mr. Handfield, our very worthy commander, although we have never had any desire to make use of them against His Majesty's government." Indeed, they noted, during the late war they had refused the French demand that they take up arms, and several of them had risked their lives delivering intelligence to the provincial government. "We have therefore nothing to reproach ourselves with, either on that subject, or on the subject of the fidelity that we owe His Majesty's government." They had selected thirty of their best men and instructed them "to do or say nothing contrary to His Majesty's Council." But on the question of the oath, they could not compromise. It was a matter of principle. "We shall charge them strictly to contract no new oath." They were resolved to adhere to the one they had previously taken, to which they had been faithful for many years. The deputies departed for Halifax the next morning, and soon afterward, according to Daudin, troops from Fort Anne confiscated and burned all seagoing vessels belonging to the inhabitants.[17]

The inhabitants of Minas also were ordered to choose deputies—some seventy of them. Three decades later, a number of grizzled old Acadians told Reverend Andrew Brown of Halifax of the meetings that took place at Grand Pré and Pisiquid to choose and instruct deputies, the last general assemblies the Acadians held in l'Acadie before their explusion. A moderator was chosen, an elder whose task was "to preserve order, to obtain attention for the different speakers, to collect the votes on the motions proposed, and to declare the sense of the majority." Men spoke passionately but reasonably, "with strong powers of reasoning and eloquence." Brown compared these assemblies to the New England town meetings he had heard about—"little Democratical Assemblies," as he phrased it. In the memory of the aged inhabitants with whom Brown spoke, those meetings represented the high point of Acadian political organization.[18]

Deputies were chosen and sent off with instructions and petitions signed by more than three hundred inhabitants. Those remarkable texts—in effect the last will and testament of the Acadian people—evidenced a subtle and nuanced understanding of their history. Their "oath of fidelity," as they referred to the agreement they had struck with Governor Philipps, they viewed as the hard-won product of struggle and compromise. Pressed by the competing demands of two sovereigns, their fathers had wisely devised a way for the Acadian people to be both loyal and neutral, an "exception" to the ordinary rules of submission that honored their heritage while at the same time recognizing the political reality under which they were required to live. "We will never prove so fickle," the inhabitants wrote, "as to take an oath which changes, ever so little, the conditions and the privileges obtained for us by our sovereigns and our fathers in the past." They had taken that oath of fidelity in good faith and had been loyal to it through good years and bad. With exactitude they cited the proclamations issued in His Majesty's name by Governor William Shirley of Massachusetts, dated 16 September 1746 and 12 October 1747, assuring them again of their rights and privileges. "We are all resolved, with one consent and voice, to take no other oath," they declared. "We all, with a unanimous voice, beg his honour to set at liberty our people, who have been detained at Halifax for some time, not even knowing their situation, which appears to us deplorable."[19]

As the Acadians chose their deputies and wrote their petitions, Lawrence and the council met to prepare for their arrival. Joining the proceedings on 15 July were Vice Admiral Edward Boscawen and Rear Admiral Savage Mostyn of the Royal Navy, who arrived at Halifax a week earlier with their squadron of warships. Although most of the French fleet had evaded their grasp, slipping into Louisbourg through heavy fog, Boscawen had succeeded in capturing two French ships of the line, netting several hundred prisoners of war, who were confined at George's Island, along with the detained Minas deputies. He had asked the naval commanders to be present, Lawrence told the council, to offer advice concerning "the security of the province." For the benefit of the admirals he summarized the confrontation that had taken place with the deputies, then asked for their opinion. Without hesitation they joined with the council in agreeing that "it was now the properest time to oblige the said inhabitants to take the oath of allegiance to His Majesty, or to quit the Country."[20]

The admirals—especially Boscawen, a national hero who sat on the Board of Admiralty and was close to the center of political power in London—gave Lawrence the cover he was looking for, and in his future correspondence he rarely neglected to include the fact that Boscawen had endorsed the council's decision to remove the Acadians. In further discussion the council agreed that the task of removing the Acadians would be assigned to the New England troops, who would be retained in the service and pay of the crown through the coming winter. On 18 July, Lawrence wrote a summary report for the Board of Trade. He was "determined to bring the Inhabitants to a compliance, or rid the province of such perfidious subjects." The faithless Acadians were to be "driven out of the country." He would not write again for three months, by which time the deed would be done.[21]

The government's resolve was strengthened when, five days later, a vessel arrived from New York City with the news that on 9 July the forces of Major General Edward Braddock had been defeated and dispersed by Canadien and native troops on the Ohio, and Braddock himself killed. Lawrence soon had in hand detailed reports of the disaster, forwarded by Spencer Phips, lieutenant-governor of Massachusetts. Nearly 1,000 of Braddock's 1,400 troops had been killed or wounded, and in addition to Braddock, 63 of the 86 officers were dead. The French suffered fewer than sixty casualties. "This is undoubtedly an heavier stroke than ever the English upon this Continent have met with before," Phips wrote. "I must on this occasion also propose to your Consideration whether the danger with which His Majesty's interest is now threatened will not remove any scruples which may heretofore have subsisted with regard to the French Neutrals, as they are termed, and render it both just and necessary that they should be removed." In fact, any scruples regarding the Acadians had long since been put aside; but the news of the British defeat, as the historian John Bartlet Brebner puts it, "would harden the hearts of their masters."[22]

The deputies from Annapolis Royal were the first to arrive in Halifax, and on Friday, 25 July, they were called before the Governor's Council. Their petition was read into the record and Lawrence subjected them to another of his harangues. They had pretended "to be in a state of neutrality between His Majesty and His enemies," he charged. The Annapolis inhabitants might have abetted the French by treachery rather than open rebellion, but that made them no less guilty than the Chignecto inhabitants, three hundred of whom had been found in arms at Beauséjour. The deputies attempted to respond, but Lawrence cut them off. "No propositions or explanations would be received," he declared. The point was only to get what was necessary onto the record before the council committed itself. A group of Acadian exiles in Philadelphia later defended themselves against Lawrence's charge in a memorial to King George III. "No consequence can be justly drawn that because those people [the Acadians of Chignecto] yielded to the threats and persuasions of the enemy, we should do the same," they argued. "We looked on their defection from Your Majesty's interest with great pain and anxiety." But Lawrence was not interested in any defense. "Affairs were now at such a crisis in America that no delay could be admitted," he insisted. "The French had obliged us to take up arms in our defense against their encroachments, and it was unknown what steps they might take further, for which reason if they, the inhabitants, would not become subjects to all intents and purposes, they could not be suffered to remain in the country." The deputies must decide whether to take the oath without any reserve or to quit their lands. He wanted nothing from them but an answer.[23]

"Their answer was not less laconic than the question," wrote abbé Daudin. "Since we are asked only for a yes or a no," the deputies replied, "we will all answer unanimously, no." They were determined, they said, "not to take any other oath than what they had done before," their oath of fidelity, "with a reserve that they should not be obliged to take up arms." If it was the king's intention "to force them to quit their lands, they hoped that they should be allowed a convenient time for their departure." As Lawrence had done with the deputies from Minas, he gave them an opportunity to reconsider. The council would reassemble the following Monday, when their final answer would be expected.[24]

On Monday, 28 July, at ten in the morning, the Annapolis deputies, joined by their counterparts from Minas, were brought before the council. They numbered about one hundred men. Never before had so many inhabitants been called to meet with the government. Their names are nowhere recorded, but they surely constituted most of the Acadian leadership. Their communities had instructed them to refuse to swear to the unconditional oath, and since they knew that the first Minas delegation had been imprisoned, they surely assumed that they too would be locked up. Lawrence's tactics had succeeded in separating them from their communities at precisely the moment when their counsel would most be needed. There were no melodramatic scenes such as Daudin imagined, yet there was something heroic in their commitment. The deputies were playing out to the end their role as neutrals, and it would mean destruction for the Acadian people.[25]

They faced Lieutenant-Governor Lawrence, Admirals Boscawen and Mostyn, and the five members of the council—Chief Justice Jonathan Belcher, Provincial Secretary William Cotterell, Treasurer

Benjamin Green, Captain John Collier of the provincial militia, and Commander John Rous, chief naval officer. The stage was set for a dramatic confrontation, but the minutes suggest an anticlimactic meeting that was over almost as soon as it began. From Lawrence's point of view, the proceedings were purely pro forma. The petitions of the Minas Acadians were read into the record and straightaway the deputies were asked for their decision. They would not take the unconditional oath, they stated, and all were peremptorily ordered into confinement. "We were all immediately made prisoners," the Philadelphia exiles later wrote, "and were told by the Governor that our estates, both real and personal, were forfeited for Your Majesty's use." Merchant Joseph Gray of Halifax, who wrote as if he had been an observer at the meeting, noted that "every man of them refused with a most contemptuous look of resentment." Little wonder. "Notwithstanding the solemn grants made to our fathers by General Philipps, and the declaration made by Governor Shirley and Mr. Mascarene in Your Majesty's name," the exiles wrote, "we found ourselves at once deprived of our estates and liberties, without any judicial process, or even without any accusers appearing against us, and this solely grounded on mistaken jealousies and false suspicions that we are inclinable to take part with Your Majesty's enemies."[26]

Once the Acadians had been dismissed, Lawrence addressed the council himself. "As it had been before determined to send all the French Inhabitants out of the Province if they refused to Take the Oaths, nothing now remained to be considered but what measures should be taken to send them away, and where they should be sent to." The expectation of the deputies was that if they were deported—and most were unconvinced that would happen—they would be sent to Louisbourg, where the British had transported the defenders of Beauséjour, or possibly to France. One group of exiles later reported that Lawrence had told them they were officially French "prisoners of war," in the same category as the troops captured by Admiral Boscawen, with whom they were incarcerated on George's Island. "And Governor Lawrence further promised us," they wrote, "that we should be carried amongst our own people." The official minutes support their contention, recording the declaration that the government would henceforth look upon the Acadians as "Subjects of the King of France" and would "send them to France by the first opportunity." According to a report in the *Pennsylvania Gazette*, Lawrence told the deputies they would be "transported to France." They had no way to confirm this, since they were immediately sent into confinement, and they took Lawrence at his word.[27]

In fact, France was never an option. In his operational plan for removal, Charles Morris made it very clear that the Acadians must not be allowed to return to the maritime region, for if they did, it would surely be as implacable enemies, determined to win back their lands. If the government sent them to France, what would prevent them from coming back to Louisbourg or Ile Saint-Jean? But Morris recommended that the Acadians be encouraged to think they would be sent among their French brethren; otherwise he seriously doubted their willingness to quit their possessions and offer themselves "to be transported they know not wither." It was one of many stratagems Lawrence took from Morris. They must "be kept in the dark as to their destination," he wrote to Murray, "for [if] they should be of the opinion privately (and I believe they certainly are) that the government will not after all remove them from their possessions, they have the less temptation to be doing mischief."[28]

The question Lawrence put to the council was "by what means we could, with the greatest security and effect, rid ourselves of a set of people who would forever have been an obstruction to the intention of settling this colony?" The "only practicable measure," he proposed, was "to divide them among the colonies, where they may be of some use, as most of them are healthy strong people. And as they cannot easily collect themselves together again, it will be out of their power to do any mischief." They would be dispersed in fragmented groups throughout the British North American empire in a deliberate attempt to destroy them as a people. And so it was that the council decided that in order "to prevent as much as possible their attempting to return and molest the settlers that may be set down on their lands, it would be most proper to send them to be distributed amongst the several colonies on the continent, and that a sufficient number of vessels should be hired with all possible expedition for that purpose."[29]

Several days later Lawrence ordered the arrest of the parish priests at Minas and Annapolis Royal. The provincial archive contains no record of this order, but abbé Daudin recounted the arrests in his *mémoire*. On 4 August, a detachment of troops from Fort Edward seized Claude-Jean-Baptiste Chauvreulx, parish priest at Saint-Charles-des-Mines at Grand Pré. At Saint-Joseph's on rivière-aux-Canards the young priest in residence, known to history only as abbé Lemaire, fled into the woods at the approach of the soldiers, but several days later he surrendered at Fort Edward, where Chauvreulx was being held. Daudin was celebrating mass on the morning of 6 August when his chapel was surrounded by troops. The officer in charge demanded admission to the sacristy and presbytery, where he seized the parish registers and papers. There may have been a general order to seize Acadian records, such as they were, although there is no trace of such an order in the provincial archive. At least one group of Acadian exiles, however, protested the theft of their papers. "The house in which we kept our contracts, records, deeds, &c.," they wrote later, "was invested with an armed force, and all our papers violently carried away, none of which have to this day been returned to us, whereby we are in a great measure deprived of means of making our innocency and justness of our complaints appear in their true light."[30]

On 9 August, Lawrence instructed Murray to send the priests to Halifax. They were escorted by a large detachment of troops who entered the town with drums beating, drawing a large crowd. They marched to the market square, where the priests were, in Daudin's words, "exposed, during three-quarters of an hour, to mockery, contempt, and insults." It was the final step in the preparation for the actual work of removal. Lawrence had placed the Acadians under military control, disarmed them, deprived them of their records, their leaders, and now their priests. Later that day the priests were conveyed to one of the warships in the harbor, confined while awaiting deportation. With the removal of the inhabitants, Lawrence later wrote to the Board of Trade, they would be "of no further use in this province. Admiral Boscawen has been so good as to take them on board his fleet and is to give them passage to England."[31]

In the two weeks following the meeting of 28 July, Lawrence issued detailed instructions regarding the expulsion of the Acadians. On 31 July he wrote to Colonel Robert Monckton:

> The Deputies of the French inhabitants of the districts of Annapolis, Mines, and Pisiquid have been called before the Council, and have refused to take the oath of allegiance to His Majesty, and have also declared this to be the sentiment of the whole people. Whereupon the Council advised, and it is accordingly determined, that they shall be removed out of the Country as soon as possible. And as to those about the Isthmus who were in arms and therefore entitled to no favour from the government, it is determined to begin with them first.

Monckton was ordered to assemble the inhabitants "in the best manner in your power, either by stratagem or force, as circumstances may require." Following Morris's plan, Lawrence suggested calling the men to a meeting of some kind, then holding them hostage against the surrender of their families. "Above all," he wrote, "I desire you would not pay the least attention to any remonstrances or memorials from any of the inhabitants whatever."[32]

"If you find that fair means will not do with them," he instructed Major John Handfield at Fort Anne on 11 August, "you must proceed by the most vigorous measures possible, not only in compelling them to embark, but in depriving those who shall escape of all means of shelter or support, by burning their houses and destroying everything that may afford them the means of subsistence in the Country." The operation must be carried out ruthlessly. Monckton was instructed to "use every method to distress, as much as can be, those who may attempt to conceal themselves in the woods." Armed patrols were to seize anyone found on the roads or at the boat landings. It was imperative that the Acadians of the different districts be prevented from communicating with each other. Murray was to "take up and put in confinement any inhabitant you expect to be an haranguer or an intriguer amongst the people." If any of them made trouble, "punish them at your discretion," and if there was any resistance, "take an Eye for an Eye, a Tooth for a Tooth, and in short a Life for a Life from the nearest Neighbours where such mischief is performed."[33]

Lawrence notified Monckton that he had ordered "a sufficient number of transports to be sent up the Bay with all possible dispatch for taking [the Acadians] on board." Ten vessels, hired at Halifax, departed in mid-August for Chignecto. Meanwhile, Lawrence sent an urgent dispatch to Thomas Hancock in Boston to arrange for two dozen additional transports to be sent to Minas and Annapolis Royal. Hancock, who had the request in hand by 18 August, responded that he would send the vessels as soon as possible. He had no qualms, he wrote, about participating in the expulsion of "them who have so long and greatly abused His Majesty's indulgence." The inhabitants were to be boarded at the rate of two persons per marine ton, which amounted to about fifty cubic feet per person. "If you should find there are more people than there is vessels provided, reckoning two persons to each tun," Lawrence wrote, "you are immediately to send an express to acquaint me therewith, but make no delay in the embarkation upon that account." To prevent the Acadians from mounting any attempt at mutiny, they were to be kept below deck as much as possible. They would be allowed to take only "ready money and household furniture," he instructed. "They must not put on board quantities of useless Rubbish to encumber the vessels."[34]

In the meantime, it was critically important that the inhabitants' herds of livestock be secured. These were substantial—by the best estimate, nearly 20,000 head of cattle, 30,000 sheep, 1,600 horses, and countless swine at Annapolis Royal, Minas, and Chignecto. "Care must be had that nobody make any bargain for purchasing them under any colour or pretense whatever," Lawrence stressed. The horses, sheep, and cattle were forfeit to the king, and would be used to provision both troops and deportees, with any excess sold and the money raised "apply'd towards a reimbursement of the expense the government will be at in transporting [the inhabitants] out of the Country." As much as possible, the operation was to be supplied and paid for using the assets of the Acadians themselves. The Acadian herds were valuable, but it was the land that was most important. "When the French inhabitants are removed," Lawrence wrote to Monckton, "you will give orders that no person presume to take possession of any of the lands until a plan of the whole has been laid before me, and terms of encouragement to English Settlers deliberately formed and made publick."[35]

Removal would accomplish the first half of Lawrence's objective, but it was to be followed immediately by the grant of the Acadian farms to soldiers and settlers from New England. Lawrence and Shirley had agreed on this plan in December 1754, with Lawrence offering "the strongest assurances on my part that I shall do everything in my power that may contribute towards the protection and support of as many as may be disposed to sit down on these valuable lands when the Great Work is done." After John Winslow's appointment as the expedition's highest-ranking New England officer, he was enlisted in this scheme as a potential agent for the recruitment of Yankee settlers. Winslow told Monckton it might be possible for him to arrange for the migration of as many as one thousand families. "If he will carry it through," Lawrence replied after Monckton forwarded this news, "he shall have all reasonable encouragement, and I should be glad you would come to a closer conversation with him on that head." Winslow wrote Lawrence of his plans to "observe the country through which I pass, that in case it should be thought convenient to settle any part of this province by people from New England, which by them is expected."[36]

The material interest of Winslow and his troops in the expulsion of the Acadians was a culmination of the critical role played by New Englanders in the history of l'Acadie. The project was conceived and expedited by Governor William Shirley of Massachusetts, the legal justification provided by Chief Justice Jonathan Belcher, son of Shirley's predecessor as governor, the operational plan written by Surveyor-General Charles Morris, Shirley's protégé, the decision made by a council that had always been dominated by men hailing from Massachusetts. The Acadians were to be transported to distant destinations in New England vessels hired by one of the most important trading houses in Boston. They were to be forced from their homes by troops and officers from New England, and it was expected that those very men would repossess and resettle the land. It was a thoroughly Yankee operation.[37]

On 9 August 1755, an anonymous correspondent in Halifax wrote to Boston announcing the decision to remove the Acadians. Over the next two months the letter would be published widely in the colonial press:

> . . . We are now upon a great and noble Scheme of sending the neutral French out of this Province, who have always been secret Enemies, and have encouraged our Savages to cut our Throats. If we effect their Expulsion, it will be one of the greatest Things that ever the English did in America; for by all Accounts, that Part of the Country they possess, is as good Land as any in the World: In case therefore we could get some good English Farmers in their Room, this Province would abound with all Kinds of Provisions. . . .

By the time this first public notice of what was happening in l'Acadie was published, the roundup of the Acadians was already well under way.[38]

CHAPTER 12

Gone, All Gone

The Expulsion, August–December 1755

On the morning of 6 August 1755, Lieutenant-Colonel John Winslow was summoned to Colonel Robert Monckton's quarters at Fort Cumberland (*née* Fort Beauséjour). A messenger had arrived from Halifax bearing a letter from Lieutenant-Governor Charles Lawrence announcing the council's decision regarding the Acadians. Monckton conveyed the news to Winslow. "It was Determined to remove all the French Inhabitants out of the Province." Vessels would soon arrive from Halifax to transport them all to distant colonies. "That they may not have it in their power to return to this Province, nor to join in strengthening the French of Canada or Louisbourg," Lawrence wrote, "it is resolved that they be dispersed among His Majesty's colonys upon the Continent of America, and that those of the Chignecto District, who have always been the most Rebellious, shall be removed to the greatest distance." The Acadians of Chignecto were destined to be dispersed to the distant southern colonies of South Carolina and Georgia; the inhabitants of Annapolis

Royal and Minas to Virginia and Maryland, Pennsylvania and New York, Massachusetts and Connecticut, in groups not to exceed one thousand persons, in order that "they cannot easily collect themselves together again." The council's intention was to fracture the community of the Acadians and destroy their identity as a distinct people. The operation to remove the Acadians would cost thousands of lives and years of suffering and wandering, and must be marked down as one of the most horrific episodes in North American history.[1]

Following the plan outlined by surveyor Charles Morris, Lawrence instructed Monckton "to fall upon some stratagem to get the men, both young and old (especially the heads of families) into your power and detain them till the transports shall arrive, so as that they may be ready to be shipped off." Once that was done, Lawrence continued, "it is not much to be feared that the women and children will attempt to go away and carry off the cattle."[2]

Monckton told Winslow he had decided to issue a summons calling all the male inhabitants of Chignecto and Chipoudy Bay to a meeting at the fort. When he had them in his grasp, he would hold them hostage against the eventual surrender of their wives and children after the transport vessels arrived. Then they would all be deported to points south. Winslow was to closely observe the operation of this plan, Monckton instructed, for afterward he was to take several hundred men to Minas where he would carry out precisely the same scheme. It must move quickly, before any word of the incarceration at Fort Cumberland found its way to Minas and caused panic and rebellion. Simultaneously, Major John Handfield, commandant at Fort Anne, would be using the garrison soldiers there to round up the Acadians of the *banlieu* and the *haute rivière*. Transports were being dispatched to Minas and Annapolis as well as Chignecto, and the Acadians were to be deported as quickly as possible, so that their lands would be ready for new settlers in the spring.[3]

Although rumors of the removal of the Acadians had been running through the British encampment for weeks, Colonel Winslow seemed genuinely surprised by what Monckton told him. "As to the

Inhabitants commonly call'd the Nutrals at Chignecto, the pointe seams to be settled with them and they are to be removed," he wrote Governor William Shirley of Massachusetts. "The Inhabitants throughout the Province it is supposed will suffer the same Fate, although not equally guilty of open violence." John Winslow accepted his assignment, but he did not relish the role he was about to play. Eight years before, in 1747, he had been dispatched to Minas to reestablish British authority in the aftermath of the Canadien attack on New England militia at Grand Pré. He was acquainted with the leaders of the Acadian community enough to know that he faced a difficult assignment. "Shall soon have our hands full of disagreeable business," he wrote Shirley, "to remove people from their antient habitations." Numerous times over the next several weeks Winslow would confess in his journal his revulsion at what he was required to do, but he successfully pushed those feelings aside. He must do the job well, for in the coming war with France he hoped to command a regiment of his own. He had penned appeals to Lord Halifax, Secretary of War Henry Fox, and other influential British officials, angling for the opportunity. "I flatter myself," he wrote, "that my unwearied endeavors to serve my King and Country will meet with the approbation of my superiors, and they out of their Great Goodness will bestow on me a regiment, and that my Friends won't be unmindfull of me."[4]

Winslow had a strong sense of his own importance and his place in history, which explains the time and attention he devoted to his "book," the journal he wrote in nearly every day. He intended it for the edification of his descendants, and into it he copied his incoming and outgoing correspondence, orders and proclamations, transcriptions of his conversations with officers and inhabitants, as well as his own observations of the things he saw and did. Providing a detailed account of the operation from the viewpoint of one of the perpetrators, Winslow's journal is the single most significant document of the Acadian removal, all the more important because it fills gaps in the public archive. It does little, however, to illuminate the point of view of the Acadians. Silencing them was one of the objectives of removal, of course. At precisely those points when their testimony is most wanted, they are voiceless. Their perspective must be pieced together from mere scraps and fragments.[5]

Later that afternoon, 6 August, the male inhabitants of Chignecto and Chipoudy Bay received Monckton's summons by word of mouth. All men over the age of sixteen were ordered to appear at Fort Cumberland the following Sunday, 10 August, "to make arrangements concerning the return of their lands." Lawrence had counseled Monckton "to fall upon some stratagem," and this particular lie played to the refugees' principal concern, the return of their home lots, fields, and meadows at Chignecto. According to abbé François Le Guerne, who had served for several years as parish priest at Beaubassin and was then living among refugees at rivière Au Lac, the inhabitants of Chipoudy Bay who were still living in their hamlets reacted with skepticism, but the refugees were far less cautious, "blindly interested in their lands." Daniel Dugas, a nineteenth-century descendant of Beaubassin Acadians, was told by his grandfather that the refugees responded because the British "promised information of a good deal," reassuring themselves that they were protected by the pardon included in the terms of Beauséjour capitulation. Lawrence, however, interpreted that pardon to mean only that "the French inhabitants found in arms in the fort should not be put to death."[6]

On the appointed day, Sunday, 10 August, four hundred men arrived at the fort, most of them refugees from Beaubassin. This amounted to less than one third of the adult men of the district, far fewer than Monckton had hoped for. The men were kept in the fort overnight while patrols went out to round up others from the distant hamlets. The officers returned to report that they all had fled into the woods. Monckton had no choice but to make his move. "This day was one extraordinary to the inhabitants," Winslow recorded in his journal on 11 August. The Acadians assembled on the parade grounds within the fort at Monckton's command and listened while he read the government's proclamation, which Winslow summarized succinctly: "They were declared rebels. Their Lands, Goods

"Acadie, the Odyssey of a People," poster (1989; revised 1993) showing the dispersion of the Acadians across the Atlantic world, published by Parks Canada. Seven thousand Acadians were deported and another eleven thousand became refugees in their own land. It is likely that some ten thousand persons —the majority infants and children—lost their lives as a direct result of the campaign of removal.

"Major General Paul Mascarene" (1729), a portrait by John Smibert. A Huguenot refugee from France, Mascarene joined the British army and was posted in Acadia from the conquest in 1710 until his retirement in 1750. He gestures toward an idealized and pacific depiction of Annapolis Royal (née Port Royal). Serving as lieutenant-governor of the province in the 1740s, Mascarene argued that the Acadians could become "good subjects" if treated with respect, but his counsel was scorned by officials in both Great Britain and New England.

"His Excellency William Shirley Esqr. Captain General & Governor in Chief &c of the Province of the Massachusetts Bay in New England" (1746), engraving based on a painting by John Smibert. The artist depicted Shirley in much the same poise as Mascarene, but he gestures toward a representation of the Yankee armada that in 1745 besieged and conquered the French fortress of Louisbourg. Shirley's political career was founded on militant opposition to the French presence in North America, and he consistently argued for the removal of the Acadians, putting him directly at odds with the more conciliatory Mascarene.

Governor Charles Lawrence, who ordered the deportation of the Acadians. From Tobias George Smollett, *Continuation of the Complete History of England* (1757).

Colonel John Winslow, who was in charge of removing the Acadians from Grand Pré. Attributed to artist Joseph Blackburn (c. 1760).

Thomas Pichon, French official who spied for the British. Copy by Henri Baud (c. 1920) of an original portrait by N. Coucourt (c. 1790).

Charles Deschamps de Boishébert et de Raffetot, who led the armed resistance of Acadian refugees. An anonymous portrait (1753).

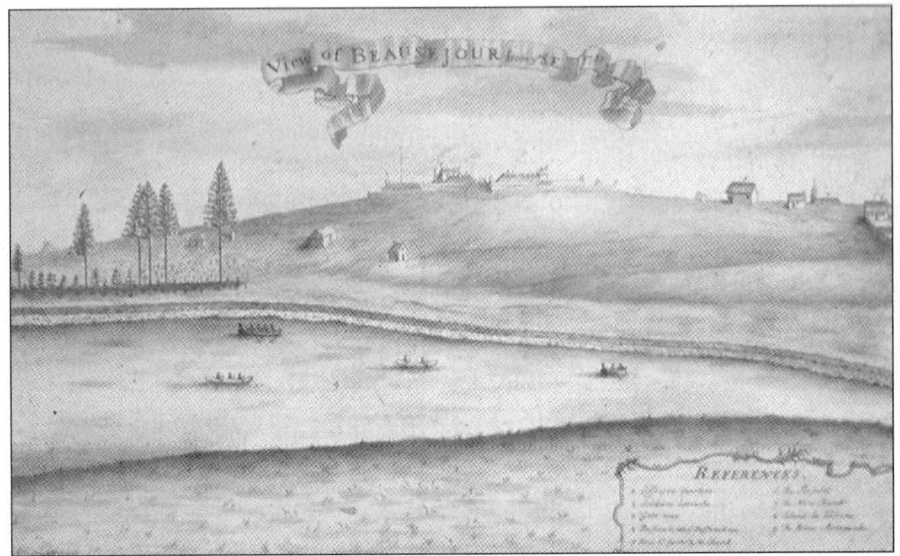

"View of Beauséjour" (1755), drawn by Captain John Hamilton. The view is from Fort Lawrence, which was situated on the ridge southeast of the Missaguash River. The June 1755 conquest of Fort Beauséjour, which resulted in the retreat of French and Canadien troops from the Acadian peninsula, opened the way for the expulsion of the Acadians.

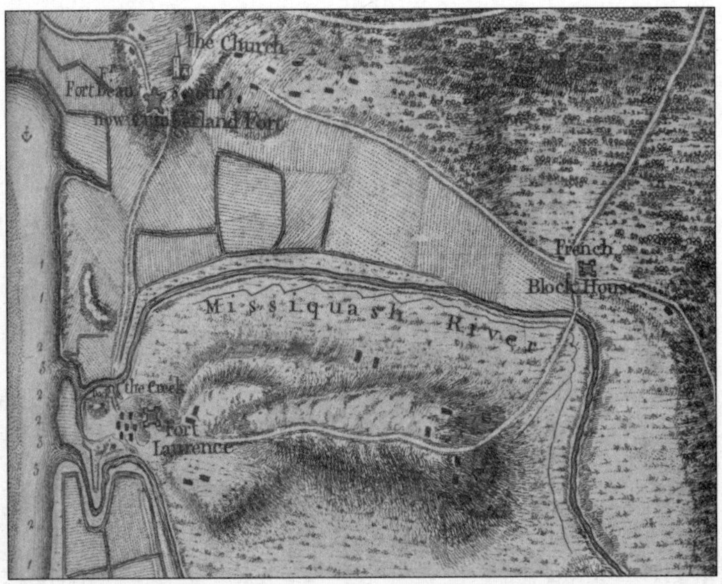

Detail from *A Large and Particular Plan of Shegnekto Bay* (1755), showing the path leading from Fort Lawrence to Fort Beauséjour, and the *redoute* ("French Block House") where Canadien and Acadian defenders failed to stop the New England advance.

"Reading the Order of Expulsion" (c. 1910), by Canadian illustrator Charles William Jefferys. The announcement by commanding officer John Winslow (see his portrait) that the Acadians were to be expelled came as a profound shock to the assembled men and boys in the church at Grand Pré. He recorded only that they were "greatly struck." There is no other evidence of their reaction, no Acadian recollections, no family stories. It is as if they had been struck dumb, and that may be close to the truth.

"Burning and Lay Waste" (1986), mural at Grand Pré National Historic Site by Claude T. Picard. After the Acadians were rounded up, their communities were torched. "You must proceed by the most vigorous measures possible," Governor Lawrence instructed his officers, "by burning their houses and destroying everything."

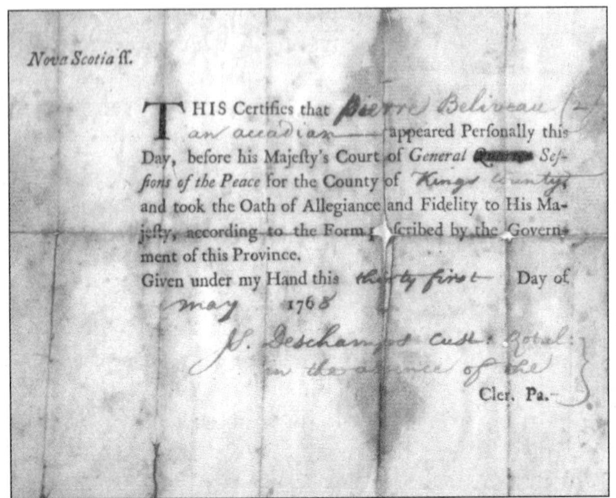

Nova Scotia ſſ.

THIS Certifies that Pierre Beliveau (2) an acadian —— appeared Perſonally this Day, before his Majeſty's Court of General [illegible] Seſſions of the Peace for the County of Kings County, and took the Oath of Allegiance and Fidelity to His Majeſty, according to the Form preſcribed by the Government of this Province.

Given under my Hand this thirty first Day of may 1768

J. Deschamps Cust. Rotul: in the abſence of the Cler. Pa.

Oath of Allegiance taken by Pierre Beliveau, 31 May 1768. Beliveau was one of several hundred Acadians who finally took the unconditional oath and were then granted the right to return to the province. It is signed by judge Isaac Deschamps, who became wealthy as the landlord of former Acadian lands at Minas.

Acadian women, frontispiece from Frederic S. Cozzens, *Acadia, or, A Month with the Blue Noses* (1859), the first published images of the Acadians.

These engravings from Longfellow's *Evangeline, with Illustrations by F. O. C. Darley* (1886) faithfully replicated Longfellow's tale, which begins with the Acadians living in an American Eden and relates the story of their forced deportation through the experience of fictional separated lovers, Evangeline and Gabriel, who after decades of searching are reunited in the last moments of their lives.

"Evangeline, Song & Chorus," sheet music (1865), by Will. S. Hays. The popularity of *Evangeline* resulted in an enormous number of spin-offs. This sheet music featured the reproduction of an image by English artist Thomas Faed, the most widely distributed nineteenth-century depiction of the Acadian heroine.

"Evangeline Statue, St. Martinville, LA," detail of a postcard (c. 1945). In southwestern Louisiana, with its large community of Acadian descendants known as Cajuns, the Evangeline story was reworked into local myth. This bronze statue of the heroine was raised in 1930, cast in the likeness of actress Dolores Del Rio, who played the Acadian maiden in a 1929 Hollywood film.

"Acadian Memorial Park, Grand Pré, Nova Scotia," glass plate (c. 1930). This Evangeline statue stands before the reconstructed chapel at the site of the historic church of St. Charles-des-Mines, where Acadians were incarcerated before they were sent into exile. Now managed by Parks Canada, the memorial is the most significant site of memory for the Acadian people.

and Chattels forfitt to the Crown and their Bodys to be Imprisoned." And then "the gates of the Forte was shut and they all confined." According to the Acadian prisoners, Monckton told them they were to be transported to Louisbourg. It was a shocking moment. In the words of Daniel Dugas, "those poor compatriots who attended as required were seized and made prisoners by the English, who treated them like *slaves!*"[7]

The leaders of the prisoners composed and delivered a memorial to Colonel Monckton. Judging from its tone, they were disoriented and confused. They were prepared to accept the sentence of the government, they wrote. "Although born here and settled here for sixty or eighty years, inhabitants cannot dwell in a country against the will of the sovereign, to which as Christians we must submit without argument." But what was a Christian to make of their treatment? They had responded to Monckton's summons in good faith, but he had imprisoned them all without warning. They were shocked by such "universal detention." They had brought no food, no blankets, no change of clothing, and Monckton had made no provision for their care. They had been crowded into damp quarters, forced to sleep on boards, were being eaten alive by vermin, and threatened with disease. Why were they being subjected to such things? It was an unendurable hardship, something a true Christian could not fail to appreciate. They had to think of the families which it pleased God to grant them. Terrified, their women and children had fled into the woods, and would perish for the want of a little milk. They prayed that Monckton inform their wives and mothers of their situation, so they would have no cause for worry. A "truly Christian and paternal heart [*d'un coeur vrayment Chretien et paternal*]," they concluded, could not refuse their prayer. Soon thereafter about half the prisoners were moved to Fort Lawrence, which relieved the crowding somewhat, and Monckton made a general announcement that the men would be kept locked up until the transports arrived, at which time their families were to report for deportation. If they failed to appear, they would be hunted down, and the men sent off without them.[8]

The ruse Monckton attempted at Fort Cumberland, Winslow perfected at Grand Pré. On 16 August, five days after the four hundred Acadians were imprisoned at Chignecto, Winslow departed for Minas in three armed vessels carrying three hundred enlisted men and officers. Late on the afternoon of the following day, his vessels dropped anchor at the mouth of rivière Pisiquid. There they remained for the night, and with the turn of the tide ascended the river to the height of land where Fort Edward stood overlooking the estuary. While his men remained on board, Winslow and several officers were rowed ashore to meet with Captain Alexander Murray, the fort's commander. After greetings, Murray handed Winslow a letter from Lieutenant-Governor Lawrence. Winslow was to be in charge of the operation at Grand Pré and western Minas, Lawrence wrote, Murray at Pisiquid. It was critically important that they encourage the Acadians to complete the harvest, for that would provide the grain to provision the transports. When the time was right, Lawrence recommended using the same stratagem used at Chignecto, calling the men together for an assembly and holding them hostage against the surrender of the women. Winslow returned to his vessel, and after another night spent aboard, sailed down the Pisiquid with the rising sun and entered the Gaspereau, arriving at Grand Pré landing in the late morning of 19 August.[9]

It must have been profoundly unsettling for the Acadians to watch as Winslow's three hundred men swept ashore, especially in the climate of fear and uncertainty that prevailed in August 1755. The inhabitants' arms had been confiscated, their leaders incarcerated, their priests arrested and taken away—and now their community was being occupied by troops. The Yankees established their encampment on the grounds of Saint-Charles-des-Mines, beneath a stand of willows on the road leading to the village center, turning the church into a barracks, the priest's house into a headquarters for their commander. An order was soon posted calling on "the Deputies and Principal Inhabitants" to meet the commander the following day. All their deputies and many of their principal inhabitants were already imprisoned at Halifax, but the next morning a number of elders made their way to the priest's house. They included François Landry from rivière Habitant, a man in his late sixties, described by Winslow as the Acadians' "principal speaker, who talks English," and René Leblanc, notary at Grand Pré, now an old man of seventy-five, who for years had been the community's most important intermediary with the provincial government. Both men had a long history of advocating accommodation with the British. Leblanc especially had suffered for those political convictions, spending two years as captive of the Míkmaq in the early 1750s, afterward retiring to his home in Grand Pré village. Both men knew Winslow from his earlier time at Minas. "I was sent here by the King's order to take command of this place," Winslow told them. It would be necessary for them to supply his troops until his provision vessel arrived. They would happily arrange it, the elders responded. They expressed concern about the "sacred things" in the church's sacristy, and Winslow gave them leave to remove the objects and cover the altar.[10]

Over the next week Winslow kept his men busy unloading supplies from the vessels and picketing the encampment. The Canadien surprise attack at Grand Pré in 1747 was very much on his mind. But from what Winslow could tell, the Acadians had no idea what was coming. "They look upon it as a settled point," he wrote, "that we are to remain with them all winter." On Friday, 29 August, Captain Murray arrived from Fort Edward in a whaleboat, and the two men cloistered themselves in Winslow's quarters going over "methods for removing the whole inhabitants." The harvest was nearly completed, and they agreed to spring the trap on the following Friday. After Murray departed, Winslow summoned his three captains—Nathan Adams, Humphrey Hobbs, and Phineas Osgood—and swearing them to an oath of secrecy, informed them for the first time of their mission at Minas. "Although it is a disagreeable part of duty we are put upon," he told them, "I am sensible it is a necessary one."[11]

The next afternoon the first of the transports arrived at Minas, three sloops from Boston, followed the next day by a schooner. A number of inhabitants were soon on board, curious about their errand. The ships' masters had instructions to say "they were come to attend me," Winslow noted. It was part of the campaign of lies intended to keep the Acadians in the dark—and must have struck the inhabitants as suspicious, since the vessels lay high in the water, obviously carrying no provisions. "I hear some vessels are arrived at Mines which I suppose are the transports," Murray wrote Winslow. "If so, I think the sooner we strike the stroke the better, therefore will be glad to see you here as soon as conveniently you can. I shall have the orders for assemblying them ready wrote for your approbation."[12]

The weather was fine—cool, dry, sunny, perfect for threshing wheat. On Sunday afternoon, Winslow made a reconnoiter of Grand Pré and sent his captains out to the settlements further west and south. It was "a fine country and full of Inhabitants, a beautiful Church and abundance of the goods of the world," they reported. "Provisions of all kinds in great plenty." Using information provided by provincial surveyor Charles Morris, they located and mapped the numerous hamlets. All the inhabitants—men, women, and children—were out working in the fields, and Winslow began making a rough estimate of the number of transports he would require for their deportation. On Tuesday morning, he took a whaleboat to Fort Edward for a final planning session with Murray. They checked over the summons to the meetings, and arranged to have them translated into French by the Huguenot trader Isaac Deschamps of Pisiquid. Winslow then returned to Grand Pré, where he arranged for another collaborator, Alexandre de Rodohan, a Flemish surgeon married to an Acadian woman, to read the summons publicly throughout the countryside. He ordered his men confined to camp and instructed them to clean and check their weapons. Winslow himself remained in his quarters, working on the statement he would read at the meeting. Late Thursday afternoon, a courier arrived from

Fort Edward. "All the people quiet and very busy at their harvest," Murray wrote. "I hope Tomorrow will Crown all our wishes."[13]

Quiet they may have appeared, but the announcement of the meeting had created a great deal of concern. Its language was frustratingly vague, and perhaps more frightening for that. It ordered all the men of the community, including boys ten years and older, "to attend at the church at Grand Pré on Friday the 5th instant at Three of the Clock in the afternoon, that we may impart to them what we are ordered to communicate." An assembly of all the men of the community, including boys, was highly unusual. Meanwhile another apparently empty sloop had arrived at the landing. Might the British actually be implementing the removal they had threatened for so many years? A group of inhabitants, fearing impending arrest, took their concerns directly to Winslow's captains. "We had the greatest assurance given us," they later wrote, "that there was no other design but to make us renew our former oath of fidelity."[14]

An unknown number of families fled in the days preceding the meeting. Augustin Leblanc, a cousin of notary René Leblanc, came home after hearing the summons with what his wife Françoise later described as a face disfigured by fear. "He remained seated for a long time in front of the hearth, his head in his hands. When he stood up, his face was entirely bathed in tears. He said not a single word, but began to collect all the objects that could be carried with them." The couple took to the woods with their two young sons. But the families most inclined to leave had already done so. Most of the Acadians who remained in September 1755 found the prospect of abandoning their homes and homeland almost unthinkable. On Thursday, dozens of them clustered in small groups, anxiously debating what they should do. At midday Friday, two large meetings took place at the homes of François Landry in western Minas and René Leblanc in Grand Pré. What else could they do, the elders counseled, but assemble as ordered? The British often appeared harsh, but cooperation usually softened their demands. That afternoon, 418 men and boys found their way to the church of Saint-Charles-des-Mines and filed into the roughhewn pews: four generations of men, bearing the names of more than seventy extended families, three quarters of them from a handful of clans—Leblanc, Landry, Hébert, Boudreau, Granger, Aucoin, Dupuis, Richard, Thériault, Gautreau, Trahan, Daigre, Melanson.[15]

Waiting until the Acadians had filled the church, Winslow entered with two of his captains, followed by the Flemish interpreter. The doors were barred and troops surrounded the building. "I ordered a table to be set in the center of the church," he wrote in his journal entry, then "delivered them by interpreter the King's orders."

> Gentlemen. I have received from his Excellency, Governor Lawrence, the King's Commission which I have in my hand and by whose orders you are convened together to manifest to you His Majesty's final resolution to the French Inhabitants of this His Province of Nova Scotia, who for almost half a century have had more indulgences granted them than any of his subjects in any part of his dominions. What use you have made of them, you yourselves best know. The Part of Duty I am now upon is what, though necessary, is very disagreeable to my natural make and temper, as I know it must be grievous to you who are of the same species. But it is not my business to animadvert, but to obey such orders as I receive. And therefore, without hesitation, I shall deliver you His Majesty's orders and instructions: That your Lands and Tenements, Cattle of all kinds, and Livestock of all sorts are forfeited to the Crown with all other [of] your Effects, saving your Money and Household Goods. And that you yourselves are to be removed from this province. Thus it is peremptorily His Majesty's order, that the whole French Inhabitants of these Districts be removed. . . . I shall do Everything in my Power that all those Goods be Secured to you, and that you are Not Molested in Carrying them off, and also that whole Families shall go in the Same Vessel, and make this remove, which I am Sensi-

> ble must give you a great Deal of Trouble, as easy as His Majesty's service will admit, and hope that in whatever part of the world you may Fall you may be Faithful Subjects, a Peaceable and Happy People. I must also inform you that it is His Majesty's Pleasure that you remain in Security under the Inspection and Direction of the troops I have the honor to command. . . .

These words, translated into French, came as a profound shock to the assembled men and boys. Winslow recorded only that they were "greatly struck." There is no other evidence of their reaction, no Acadian recollections, no family stories transcribed by genealogists or antiquarians. It is as if they had been struck dumb, and that may be close to the truth. It was impossible for most of them to accept what they heard. Years later, old Acadians who suffered through the expulsion told Reverend Andrew Brown of Halifax that "to the last hour of their confinement, they refused to believe that the government would dare to execute their threatened purpose."[16]

Winslow immediately left the church, leaving the Acadian men locked inside. It would be their prison while they awaited the arrival of sufficient transports for their deportation. The elders among them, including François Landry and René Leblanc, quickly formed a delegation and asked to see the commander. Winslow agreed, and they were admitted to his quarters. "It was a great grief to them that they had incurred His Majesty's displeasure," the men told him, but that was something they hoped to discuss later. Winslow got the impression that none of them believed they would actually be removed. Their immediate concern, the elders continued, was the welfare of the women and children left at their homes. "They were fearful that the surprise of their detention here would quite overcome their families, whom they had no means to apprise of these, their melancholy circumstances." If a number of them remained as hostages, would the commander permit the majority to return to their homes? Winslow had no intention of allowing this. The separation of men and women, and the anxiety and vulnerability it caused, was quite deliberate. Once the men were in custody, Lawrence had written, "it is not much to be feared that the women and children will attempt to go away. . . ." But Winslow assured the elders that "the women and children should be in safety in their absence," and agreed to allow twenty men to return to their hamlets that night to communicate the news. Those remaining in custody, he warned, would be "answerable" if the parolees were not back the following morning. Winslow had a good reason for making this allowance. The women were also to be told that they were responsible for feeding and clothing the prisoners, just as they were provisioning the troops. And he demanded a complete list of the Minas inhabitants, including the men who had not come in.[17]

After the delegation left, Winslow issued orders doubling the guard and detailing a patrol to continuously circle the church. He began writing in his journal but was interrupted by a courier with a note from Captain Murray: "I have succeeded finely and have got 183 men into my possession. I am hopeful you have had equal good luck." Winslow dashed off a reply: "I rejoyce at your success and also for the smiles that has attended the party here." But Winslow was not smiling. He was wracked with worry. Worry that his troops were greatly outnumbered by the Acadian prisoners, worry that most of the transports and the vessel with the provisions had not yet arrived, worry about deeds done and deeds undone. "Things are now very heavy on my heart and hands," he wrote. He began making a preliminary list of the prisoners, "but night put me off." He closed his journal with a final line: "Thus ended the Memorable fifth of September, a Day of great Fatigue & Troble."[18]

At Annapolis Royal, the roundup of the Acadians went less well. When the first of the transports arrived at the end of August, all the men of the *banlieu* fled, leaving their wives and children to bring in the harvest. Major John Handfield, commandant of Fort Anne, sent troops to the *haute rivière*, but those hamlets too were "destitute of all male heads of families who are retired into the woods, having taken their bedding etc. with them."[19]

Acadians and Britons had been living side by side at Annapolis Royal for close to half a century, and the removal operation there was complicated by the many intertwining connections between the two groups. Consider the family of Huguenot William Winniet and his Acadian wife Marie-Madeleine Maisonnat dit Baptiste, a couple with important connections in both the Acadian and the British communities. Before his death in the early 1740s, Winniett was one of the most important merchants at Annapolis Royal, for several years serving on the Governor's Council. His wife, who after Winniett's death assumed control of the family business, was related by kinship to the prominent Bourg and Leblanc families. The Winnietts raised a large family of children, and many of them married quite well—their eldest son to Lisette Robichaud, niece of the Acadian merchant Prudent Robichaud, and several of their daughters to British officers, including sixteen-year-old Elizabeth Winniett to Lieutenant John Handfield in 1730. Handfield reaped significant political and economic benefit from his Winniett connections, rising through the ranks to become commandant of Fort Anne, prospering in trade, eventually building a fine house in the English *faubourg* of Annapolis Royal, where he and his wife raised a family of seven children. They were Acadian—with numerous aunts, uncles, and cousins in the Acadian community. And they were British—the daughter marrying Lieutenant John Hamilton of the 40th Regiment, and each of the six sons serving as army officers. In 1749, eldest son William Handfield, an ensign of only seventeen, was captured by the Míkmaq while on patrol with Hamilton's party and was held captive for two years with his uncles, Lieutenant Alexander Winniett and notary René Leblanc of Grand Pré.[20]

The receipt of Lawrence's instructions for removing the Acadians surely put Handfield in a dreadful position. Alone among the British commanders, he knew his victims personally. They were extended family, friends, and neighbors. The flight of all the Acadian men at the approach of the transports suggests they were privy to the strategem of seizing the male heads of household. Handfield, it seems, was unable to keep his orders secret, not surprising in a community as pourous as Annapolis Royal. Yet he reported by courier to Winslow in early September that he had been able to convince most of the men to return to their homes. Precisely how he accomplished this is not known. Lawrence had ordered that in the face of the slightest resistance the commanders were to proceed against the Acadians by "the most vigorous measures possible . . . burning their houses and destroying everything." But Handfield seems to have used milder forms of persuasion. Inhabitants who fled Annapolis and eventually found their way to refugee camps on the North Shore reported that Handfield assured the inhabitants their removal was to be temporary and that they would be allowed to return to their farms at the conclusion of the war. In exchange for their promise to surrender voluntarily when the vessels arrived, he offered others the choice of being transported to "whichever of the colonies they pleased."[21]

Colonel Robert Monckton shared none of John Handfield's reluctance to distress the inhabitants, burn their homes, and obliterate all trace of the world they had made. A fleet of ten transports had arrived from Halifax in late August, giving him the means to deport upward of three thousand persons, and Monckton was determined to use his forces to force the surrender of those inhabitants who had refused to come in voluntarily. To prevent them from fleeing by vessel to Ile Saint-Jean or Ile Royale, he first sent a strong detachment of one hundred New Englanders under the command of Captain Abijah Willard to destroy the port village of Tatamagouche on the northern coast of Chignecto. Welcomed at the village by the unsuspecting inhabitants after several days of exhausting travel over mountain and marsh, Willard ordered the two dozen male heads of household herded together while his troops searched their homes for weapons. After confiscating a few muskets, Willard announced his mission: The men were to be conducted to Fort Cumberland to await deportation from the province, and their village was to be destroyed. The Acadians were shocked. One of their elders stepped forward. What had they done to deserve such a fate? They had sworn on the Bible before Governor Philipps that they would never take up arms against the English. They had kept their word and if necessary they were ready to swear again. His fellow Acadians shouted their agreement, but Willard cut them off. It is too late for that, he told them. By order of the government they were declared rebels. In that case, the old Acadian asked, might they be allowed to remove themselves and their families to Ile Saint-Jean? That he could not permit, Willard replied. But his orders instructed him to arrest the men only, and he would allow them to choose whether the women and children should accompany them to Fort Cumberland or remain behind. "I did not want the trouble of the women and children," Willard confessed in his journal. After deliberating, the Acadians decided the men would go alone. On Willard's order the village was torched and the men marched off, leaving the women and children "to take care of themselves." There was "great lamentation," Willard wrote. "I must confess it seemed to be sumthing shocking."[22]

While Willard was carrying the work of destruction eastward, other Yankee patrols were torching the hamlets of Au Lac, Tantramar, and Baie Verte, north of Fort Cumberland. Lawrence had urged using every method to distress the inhabitants who refused to come in, and Monckton complied with a campaign of terror. Troops plundered possessions and feasted on livestock, despite orders to keep hands off. In advance of this pillaging army, hundreds of Acadians escaped to the settlements at Chipoudy Bay, or further northwest into the woods. "Tearful women fled with their children into the forests," reported the bishop of Québec, "exposed to the ravages of the weather and disastrous consequences of a general famine, without assistance or support." Those inhabitants who remained behind were caught by the troops. At the village of Minudie, located at the water's end on Beaubassin channel, a company of New Englanders surrounded the houses of sleeping Acadians in the hours before dawn. Roused at first light by a volley of musket fire, the inhabitants rushed from their homes. Finding their escape by land cut off, many plunged into the channel and attempted to swim against the surging tide to the other shore, two miles away. The troops made targets of the struggling people. "See how I made his forked end turn up!" one Yankee shouted to another. The brutality at Minudie was intended as a lesson to other refugees.[23]

But not all the Acadians were sitting ducks. The British strategy of terror stirred the inhabitants of Chipoudy Bay to angry resistance. They appealed for assistance from the young Canadien officer Charles Deschamps de Boishébert, one of the heroes of the attack on New Englanders at Grand Pré in 1747. Boishébert had been in command of a company of several dozen Canadien militia garrisoned in a small picketed enclosure at the mouth of rivière Saint-Jean. After the surrender of Beauséjour, Monckton sent a naval squadron to evict him, and knowing he could not defend his position, Boishébert blew up the fort and fell back into the woods with his men. When he heard from the Acadians, however, he hurried his men to Chipoudy, where he helped organize the refugees as well as Míkmaq and Maliseets into a guerrilla fighting force. Boishébert acted on his own, but his course was later approved by French authorities.[24]

The guerrillas were ready to strike back when, in late August, Monckton sent Major Joseph Frye of Massachusetts in command of two hundred New Englanders in two armed sloops to lay waste to the settlements beyond Chipoudy. On the afternoon of 2 September, after burning and plundering numerous small hamlets along rivière Petitcodiac, they came upon an abandoned village just below the point where the river bends to the west, and Frye dispatched some fifty men to destroy it. The troops had burned most of the homes and were setting fire to the chapel when some three hundred armed men suddenly burst from the woods screaming their war cries and firing their muskets. The stunned New Englanders fell back to the river in panic. Hampered by the outgoing tide, Frye had difficulty in landing a force to cover their retreat, and by the time the Yankees got back to the sloops, twenty-three lay dead and another eleven were seriously wounded. As the sloops headed back downriver, the Acadians stood on the dike gesturing rudely, their "flag of defiance flying."[25]

A large number of women and children then came out of the woods to help the men harvest the crops in order to supply themselves for the winter. "I encouraged them to be patient," Boishébert wrote in his journal, "while they awaited those who could come to deliver them from the captivity under which they suffered." But there would be no deliverance. For French officials at Québec, Acadian removal had turned the neutrals into partisans, which they welcomed. They would do what they could to supply the refugees, but were too preoccupied with the defense of Canada to send troops. The Acadians were on their own. Still, their attack on the British at Petitcodiac was the harbinger of what would be an extended and violent struggle for the control of l'Acadie.[26]

The stinging defeat on the Petitcodiac, wrote abbé Le Guerne, "made the English tremble more than all the cannons of Beauséjour." Winslow and his men received the news on 7 September, two days after the imprisonment of the male inhabitants of Minas. The troops were badly frightened and on edge, for the attack made it clear that the Acadians and their Míkmaw allies were capable of fighting back. François Landry had provided Winslow with a comprehensive list of the Minas inhabitants, and it indicated that at least three dozen men remained at large. Fearing that he might at any moment be attacked, Winslow took additional precautions, directing his guards to be on the alert and ordering his men to sleep on their arms. That night he joined the guards on both watches.[27]

The next day, he sent his troops out to find and arrest the missing men, ordering them to "make examples as instructed." He hoped for an easy time of it, but Murray predicted violence. "I am afraid there will be some lives lost before they are got together," he wrote Winslow. "You know our soldiers hate them and if they can find a pretence to kill them, they will." Hatred of French Catholics was rampant in New England. In a sermon delivered in 1755, Jonathan Edwards quoted a passage from the book of Samuel: "Then David said to the Philistine . . . I will smite thee, and take thine head from thee . . . for the battle is the Lord's, and he will give you into our hands." New England's fightingmen were embarked on a religious crusade, he argued, and "how happy they are that have God on their side!"[28]

It is hardly surprising that the actions of those troops had a pronounced anti-Catholic character. Shouting epithets and oaths, the Yankees forced the families of the missing men from their homes, plundered their personal property, and threatened their lives. The soldiers "wanted to make us give up our religion and take theirs, but we did not want to," an Acadian woman remembered nearly seventy years later. "They threatened us with death, and we answered that we would prefer to die. Then they made us line up while they loaded their guns with grapeshot. We were on our knees, our faces prostrate against the ground, offering our lives to God while waiting for the firing of the guns. I was only nine years old, and I too was prostrate beside my family. But suddenly the English changed their minds; they took all our goods and effects and left us nothing to cover ourselves." The New England troops, writes one historian, "seem to have regarded the expedition as a religious duty—much the same as an Israelite raid on the uncircumcised Philistines."[29]

As the prisoners learned of the terror going on outside the church from the women who daily came in with provisions, their concern for their families mounted. Early on the morning of Wednesday, 10 September, while the prisoners were stretching their legs in the churchyard, an incident of some kind involving a number of young men took place. An attempt to overwhelm the guard perhaps, or a try at escape. Winslow's journal entry is not clear as to what happened. His soldiers quickly reestablished order, and as they pushed the Acadians back into the church, Winslow called an emergency council of his captains. There were too many prisoners for the troops to handle, he told them, so he would place all the unmarried men and boys, as well as some of the married men, aboard the five vessels anchored in Minas Basin, using them as prison ships until the remainder of the transports arrived and all the Acadians could be shipped off. He sent for François Landry. "The time was come for part of the inhabitants to embark," Winslow informed him. Landry was shocked. He and René Leblanc had been cooperative in the hope that all this talk of removal might prove, after all, only to be talk. Now, suddenly, it was upon them. Loading the young men as a group meant separating them from their fathers. What of Winslow's promise that families would be kept together? Winslow waved the questions away. "It must be done," he insisted. In only a few hours the tide would shift, and he would lose his opportunity to board prisoners that day. He gave Landry just one hour to prepare the men.[30]

It was still early morning on 11 September when approximately 450 Acadians left the church and drew up in a body along the road leading to the landing, 141 young men and boys on the left flank. Facing them were three hundred nervous Yankee troops, all shouldering arms. Winslow detailed Captain Nathan Adams to detach a company of eighty men and march the young Acadians to the waiting launches. Adams did as he was told, but the young men defiantly refused to move. "*Non!*" one of them shouted, "*pas sans nos pères*"—not without our fathers—"*Non!*" The word was taken up by the others until the air filled with their cries. Winslow stepped forward. "That is a word I do not understand," he declared, with Landry translating by his side. "The King's command is to me absolute and should be absolutely obeyed. I do not love to use harsh means but the time does not admit of parlays or delays." He turned to his troops and barked out the order to fix bayonets and advance. As the Yankees shuffled forward, steel extended, Winslow briskly walked to the young man who had first shouted, grabbed him by the shoulders, and pushed him onto the road. "He obeyed," Winslow wrote, "and the rest followed."[31]

It was a mile and a half from the church to the landing. Women and children, drawn by the clamor, were lining up along the whole distance. The young men "went off praying, singing, and crying, being met by the women and children all the way with great lamentations," Winslow wrote. Mothers, sisters, and fiancées, young sons and daughters, fearing they might never see their menfolk again, reached out for a last embrace. The troops pushed them back. According to Acadian tradition, the women began singing and the young men picked up their mournful dirge:

Let us bear the cross
Without choice, without regret, without complaint,
Let us bear the cross,
However bitter and hard.

It was a "scene of sorrow," Winslow wrote. He finally succeeded in getting the young men embarked, and before the turn of the tide a total of 230 prisoners were aboard the transports. But the affair left Winslow shaken. "Thus ended this troublesome job," he wrote in his journal.[32]

That evening, Landry and Leblanc presented Winslow with a memorial. "The evils which seem to threaten us on all sides obliges us to beg your protection," they wrote. They asked him to "intercede with His Majesty to consider those who have inviolably kept the fidelity and submission promised." Attached to the memorial were copies of several important documents from Leblanc's notarial files, including the oath of fidelity the men of Minas had sworn before Governor Philipps in 1730, and the affidavit of the parish priests attesting to Philipps's grant of an exemption from bearing arms. But Landry and Leblanc were not sanguine about Winslow's mediation. If he was unwilling to make their case, they continued, if the removal of all the inhabitants was to go forward despite their pleas, they prayed that "they may be permitted to go to such places where they will find their kindred." To Louisbourg, perhaps, or to Québec—some place where "we will be able to preserve our religion, which we have very much at heart, and for which we are content to sacrifice our estates." If only Winslow would grant them the time to make proper arrangements, they would be willing to pay the cost of transport themselves.[33]

Lawrence had explicitly instructed Winslow not to accept any remonstrances or memorials from the Acadians. But perhaps because he was still unsettled from the emotional scene earlier in the day, Winslow had the memorial and the attached documents translated and forwarded to Lawrence, and he transcribed a summary of them into his journal. That was as far as he would go, however. He refused to intercede on behalf of the Acadians and refused to make any commitment as to their ultimate destination, although he was well aware that Lawrence planned to send them to widely dispersed locations, as far away from their kindred in New France as possible. Nor would he give the Acadians more time to prepare. He would ship them off as soon as he had sufficient transports, "that at length we may get over this troublesome affair, which is more grievous to me than any service I was ever employed in." But it would be several weeks more before the transports arrived; meanwhile the Acadian men remained imprisoned at Grand Pré.[34]

At Chignecto, Monckton had more transports than he needed, and his orders were to send his extra vessels to Winslow, yet he was reluctant to release them, thinking his campaign of terror would induce more inhabitants to surrender. "The embarkation of the inhabitants here goes on but slow," he wrote, "it being very difficult to collect the women and children." Lawrence urged him not to wait any longer, but to go ahead with the deportation of the men already in his custody. "I would have you not wait for the wives and children coming in, but ship off the men without them," he wrote. Apparently this was something even Monckton was unwilling to do. For whatever reason—probably his desire to meet expectations, surely not compassion for the Acadians—he continued to delay the departure. By late September, Lawrence was at the end of his patience. "I am much surprised as well as extremely sorry and uneasy that the transports are not sailed," he wrote. "You will immediately order all the people on board which you have, whether all the women be come in or not."[35]

Monckton had yet to receive this order when, during a fierce thunderstorm in the predawn hours of 1 October 1755, eighty-six of the Acadian prisoners being held at Fort Lawrence suceeded in escaping. Using spoons, knives, and other small implements smuggled in by their wives and mothers, who were supplying them with food and clothing, they dug a tunnel under the fortress walls. According to Acadian tradition, the men passed out in order of size, from smallest to largest, each successive escapee squeezing through the passage and enlarging it for the next man. Last out was said to be René Richard dit Le Petit René—"Little René," the largest of all the prisoners. The escapees—including Joseph Broussard dit Beausoleil and several of his grown sons and nephews, but neither his son Victor nor his brother Alexandre, who remained imprisoned in Fort Cumberland—immediately joined forces with the Acadian resistance. Monckton was left with fewer than 1,100 Acadians in custody, and he resolved to get rid of them as quickly as possible. He no longer had use for the extra transports, so those he dispatched to Winslow.[36]

Once Monckton commenced the embarkation of the Acadians in his custody, hundreds of women and children began surrendering in order to be transported with their husbands. Abbé Le Guerne warned that they would be "placing themselves in a position to lose their religion," and advised instead that they flee to Canada, trusting that French authorities "would reclaim their husbands from whatever places they should be transported." It is easy to understand why so few women followed his advice; more difficult, perhaps, to understand Le Guerne's lack of empathy with their choice. "Driven by an excessive attachment to their husbands," he wrote, "and closing their ears to the voice of religion," they "threw themselves blindly and as if by despair into the English ships." His opinion was a measure of the ideological zeal of the age, precisely the kind of thinking that prepared the way for removal.[37]

After two months of waiting, the embarkation at Fort Cumberland took place in a headlong rush. Many years later Daniel Dugas heard a chilling account from his grandfather. "Families were seized and thrown pell-mell into the transports. No one was granted any grace. The least resistance meant death. Terror was everywhere. They succeeded in filling several vessels full of inhabitants. Children were separated from their parents, husbands from their wives, brothers from their sisters." Brook Watson, Monckton's assistant at the time, lamented the result. "I fear some families were divided and sent to different parts of the globe," he wrote, "notwithstanding all possible care was taken to prevent it."[38]

The convoy of eight transports departed with the morning tide on Monday, 13 October, and sailed down Chignecto Basin into the Bay of Fundy, escorted by three British men-of-war, one of which carried a contingent of twenty-one "special prisoners," the leaders of the Acadian militia, including Alexandre Broussard. Packed below the decks of the transports were 1,782 Acadians. Later that evening the vessels passed through the gut to Annapolis Basin, where they remained at anchor for the next two weeks, awaiting the arrival of the transports from Minas. Captain Thomas Proby of the escort vessel HMS *Syren* wrote Monckton to report that during the voyage down the bay, a group of Acadians on the brig *Two Brothers* had "rushed up when it was dusk and would most undoubtedly have made themselves masters of the vessel," but for the small company of troops on board. He had strengthened the guards on each transport "to frustrate any further attempts at rebellion." But the soldiers could also be troublesome. The night before the transports sailed from Chignecto, the guards had robbed the Acadians on the schooner *Jolly Phillip* of a "great deal of money" and most of their clothing, and Proby urged they be punished severely. It was the beginning of a long nightmare for the Acadians.[39]

On Saturday, 4 October, the Acadian women at Minas were instructed by Winslow "to hold themselves in readiness to embark with all their household goods." He would begin boarding those vessels that were already at anchor, expecting the other transports to arrive any day. "Even now," Winslow wrote in his journal, "I could not persuade the people I was in earnest." But at least some of the prisoners took him seriously. On Monday and Tuesday a cold, hard rain forced a postponement of embarkation, and on Tuesday evening, in the confusion of the storm, twenty-four young men managed to escape from two of the transports. Winslow was dumbfounded. In addition to the crew, eight soldiers guarded each vessel, "and how it happened they could none of them account." Discovering discarded men's clothing, it became obvious that the fugitives had escaped by disguising themselves as women and returning to shore with the boatloads of provisioning wives and mothers. Winslow was furious, and he resolved that the boarding of the women and children would begin the next morning, fair weather or foul.[40]

Wednesday, 8 October, dawned clear and cold, winter already in the air. Winslow sent his men out early, ordering them to fan out through the hamlets, driving the women, the children, the sick and infirm into the village of Grand Pré. They "went off very unwillingly," Winslow wrote, "the women in great distress, carrying off their children in their arms, others carrying their decrepit parents in their carts [with] all their goods, moving in great confusion." At midday, after several hundred inhabitants from the surrounding countryside had been assembled at the village, Winslow staged a spectacle calculated to add to their terror. His investigation of the escape the night before convinced him that the ringleader was one François Hébert, who remained in custody aboard one of the transports. He had the man bound, brought ashore, and carried to his home, where before a large throng of Acadians he was forced to witness the burning of his house, barn, and possessions. Be warned, Winslow instructed the crowd, unless the fugitives surrender themselves within the next two days, "I shall serve all their friends in the same manner." As for the young escapees themselves, if they did not give themselves up, they would be shot on sight. Then Winslow ordered the embarkation to begin, and to the accompaniment of cries and wails, the soldiers began pushing the women and children down the road toward the landing. It was "a scene of woe & Distress," Winslow wrote.[41]

At the landing all was confusion and chaos. "As many of the Inhabitants of each [village] as could be commoded should proceed in the same vessel," Winslow instructed his officers, and "whole families go together." But because the men and women had been separated, with the men further divided between those imprisoned on the transports and those in the church, attempting to unite husbands with wives and to keep families together proved terribly complicated, requiring troops and crews to shuttle prisoners from one vessel to another as families were loaded. According to Isaac Deschamps, the Huguenot trader from Pisiquid, "great pains was taken to collect families and relations that they might be together in one ship." But according to Acadian tradition, the inhabitants were packed randomly onto the transports, despite their desperate pleas to soldiers and sailors who could not understand their language. "The hurry and confusion in which we were embarked," wrote Jean-Baptiste Galerne, "was an aggravating circumstance attending our misfortunes, for thereby many who had lived in affluence found themselves deprived of every necessary, and many families were separated, parents from children, and children from parents." Anguished mothers cried out for missing children, frantic wives refused to board without their husbands, angry husbands resisted the orders of angry soldiers.[42]

The result was that, despite Winslow's orders, numerous families remained divided. Notary René Leblanc, his wife, and his two youngest children were boarded on one vessel, his other four minor children on another. Twelve adult children with their spouses and some 150 grandchildren were put on yet other transports, and the family thus scattered in colonies from Massachusetts to Virginia. This was just the "immediate" family, and since Acadians had a highly extended sense of kinship, it was inevitable that nearly all the families were fractured and dispersed. The embarkation was done "with so little regard to our necessities and the tenderest ties of nature," a group of exiles later wrote, that "parents were separated from children and husbands from wives, some of whom have not to this day met again." Deschamps vividly remembered "the phrensy" of the embarkation, and admitted that in the end it proved "absolutely impossible to keep families together, and being then late in the season every day's delay rendered it dangerous."[43]

By the evening of the first day, there were 420 persons representing 80 families aboard two of the transports; another 600 or 700 remained on shore, either in a rough encampment at the landing or imprisoned in the church. Winslow sent three vessels to Point de Boudrot, a landing midway between the mouths of the Habitant and Canards rivers, to pick up the hundreds of inhabitants from western Minas his troops had herded there.[44]

Once the inhabitants had been driven from their homes, Minas belonged to the vultures. Their abandoned property became the object of pillage and destruction. Off-duty soldiers and sailors as well as English and German colonists from Halifax, Lunenburg, and other Protestant settlements on the Atlantic coast raided homes, looted storehouses, killed chickens, butchered hogs, and dug through gardens for buried valuables. For several days, chaos reigned. On Sunday afternoon, 12 October, amid these scenes of ransack and pillage, Winslow sent several companies of soldiers out to sweep up fugitives and stragglers. One patrol discovered a number of the young escapees hiding in an abandoned hamlet. Ordered to surrender, they instead fled on horseback. The soldiers fired, killing one young man—reputedly a grandson of Pierre Melanson dit Laverdure, one of the first settlers at Minas, with a famously complicated family background—and mortally wounding another. These were the first Acadian fatalities recorded in Winslow's journal—although Acadian tradition claims many others. They were among the first of hundreds of Acadians to die violent deaths. The following day, as the boarding continued, François Landry negotiated the surrender of the other fugitives, and that evening they came in and voluntarily went aboard the transports. But Landry also complained bitterly to Winslow that in addition to plundering Acadian property, troops and colonists were abusing Acadian women in their encampment on the landing. Winslow responded by ordering a halt to the free-for-all. No troops, crews, "Englishmen or Dutchmen [Germans]," he commanded, were to "stir from their quarters without orders," and he ordered the arrest of anyone in violation, "that an end may be put to distressing this distressed people."[45]

By Monday evening, 13 October, all the Acadians of Grand Pré had been boarded onto five transports anchored in the mouth of rivière Gaspereau. These vessels, hired by Thomas Hancock in Boston, had been specially outfitted to carry human cargo, the holds divided into two or three levels about four feet high, much as they were arranged in vessels used for the slave trade. Winslow's instructions called for loading the deportees at the rate of two persons per marine ton, the equivalent of 100 cubic feet—two people sharing a space four feet high, a little over four feet wide, and six feet long. The instructions were to allow "only a small number to be on the deck at a time." Otherwise families were locked below. There was no provision for light, ventilation, heat, or sanitation. Food and water were inadequate. It was dark, damp, and suffocating. More than half of the people forced into these holds were female, and three out of five were children. As miserable as things were for the Acadians of Grand Pré, they were even worse for the Acadians of Pisiquid. Captain Murray had a total of four vessels with a maximum carrying capacity of about 650 persons. But he had 920 Acadians in custody. "They will be stowed in bulk," he wrote Winslow. "I will put them aboard, let the consequence be what it will." When his transports came downriver and joined those of Grand Pré on Monday, 20 October, they were carrying inhabitants at the rate of *three* persons per ton. A trading vessel from Maine that appeared at Minas was pressed into service, and by shifting some two hundred inhabitants, Winslow was able to ease things up a bit. But the Pisiquid transports remained badly overloaded.[46]

Winslow stretched the limits on several vessels, and greatly overloaded one, but still did not have sufficient capacity for all the inhabitants waiting at Point de Boudrot. "Although I put in more than two to a tun, and the people greatly crowded," he reported to Lawrence, "yet remains upon my hands for want of transports . . . 98 families and upwards of six hundred souls." He had those women and children marched to Grand Pré and moved into the abandoned houses in the village, while their husbands and fathers remained incarcerated in the church. On Tuesday, 21 October, this remnant watched as fourteen vessels slipped anchor and sailed into Minas Basin, carrying 2,648 inhabitants from several dozen villages and hamlets. Many years later, several Acadians provided Reverend Andrew Brown with a deckside description of the departure. As they pulled away from the shore of their homeland for the last time, gleaming streaks of late afternoon sunlight descended from the masses of rolling clouds like so many spotlights, illuminating the red mud of Minas, while in the background the pine forests faded to funereal black. The transports rounded the point of land and passed through the strait into the Bay of Fundy, and by early the next morning they had joined the vessels from Chignecto in Annapolis Basin. On 27 October 1755, after several days of preparation, the convoy carrying more than four thousand Acadians passed through the gut and sailed for points south, escorted by four men-of-war.[47]

ON 31 October, Winslow dispatched Captains Nathan Adams and Humphrey Hobbs in command of some ninety men to assist in the deportation of the inhabitants at Annapolis Royal. It took more than a month before the Acadians were embarked and the transports provisioned. At dawn on 8 December, seven vessels, escorted by a man-of-war, departed with 1,664 Acadians—251 men, 263 women, and 1,150 sons and daughters—bound for the Carolinas, New York, Connecticut, and Massachusetts. About three hundred inhabitants from the *haute rivière* had escaped, Captain Adams reported to Winslow, but "the remainder is sent off to the great mortification of some of our friends." This was surely a reference to Major John Handfield and his family, who stood by and watched as their relatives were shipped off. Years later, an old Acadian who had been deported on one of the transports recalled looking back at Annapolis Royal to see the flames and smoke of the buildings being torched by the troops.[48]

The destruction of the Acadian villages and hamlets was meant to deprive fugitive inhabitants of any place of refuge. Monckton began the burning immediately at Chignecto, and Winslow turned to it as soon as he had shipped off the majority of the Acadians. He dispatched his arson squads, and soon the Acadian prisoners still being held at Grand Pré saw clouds of black smoke rising on the southern horizon, followed later in the day by a thick fall of ash. According to Acadian tradition, the fires burned for six days, and at night the abandoned watchdogs of the exiles could be heard howling over the destruction. On 14 November, with Minas in ruins, Winslow turned the command at Grand Pré over to Captain Phineas Osgood and departed for Halifax with one hundred men. His work of destruction was finished. He made a final entry in his book: "Buildings Burnt by Lieutenant-Colonel Winslow in Districts of Minas"—255 homes, 276 barns, 11 mills, and one "mass house."[49]

Winslow's instructions to Phineas Osgood were to "make no delay in putting a finishing stroke to the removal of our friends the French." In addition to the Acadians being held at Grand Pré, there were fugitives in the woods. A few days before Winslow's departure, a notice in French was posted throughout Minas, addressed to the "*habitants réfugiés.*" They had nothing to fear from the British, it read, if they turned themselves in and submitted to His Majesty's orders, "which are none other than to embark and be consigned to the colonies of *Sa Majesté Très Chrétienne*"—His Very Christian Majesty—one of the titles of the French king. It is not known whether any of the Acadians fell for this trick, but several dozen more inhabitants either surrendered or were captured before the final contingent was sent off in mid-December when the last of the transports finally arrived. Winslow recorded that Osgood shipped 732 inhabitants to Virginia, Connecticut, and Massachusetts, which made a total of nearly 7,000 Acadians removed from their homeland during the last months of 1755.[50]

In the confusion of those final days, not only did some Acadians surrender, but others found the means to escape. One woman was able to slip away from her captors and return to her village, which had yet to be torched. Her memory of the horror she saw chronicled the destruction of a way of life. Homes plundered; household furniture and pottery smashed and strewn about the cart paths; cattle grazing in the wheat fields, pigs rooting in the gardens; oxen, still yoked to the carts that the Acadians drove to the landing, bellowing in hunger; droves of horses running madly through the wreckage. Standing before her abandoned house, she felt delirious from exhaustion and distress. The family cow came up to her, begging to be milked. She sat on her doorstep, milked it and drank, and felt refreshed. And as she sat there a Míkmaw man approached her. He pointed toward the basin. "See the smoke rise; they will burn all here tonight." He helped her gather a few things that remained. Come with me, he said. The Acadians are "gone, all gone."[51]

CHAPTER 13

REMOVED TO A STRANGE LAND

The Exiles, 1755–1758

AFTER THE LETTER TO the Board of Trade of 18 July 1755 in which he announced his intention of driving the Acadians from the province, Governor Charles Lawrence did not write again until 18 October, by which time the operation was a fait accompli. The authorities in London had given him very little instruction. Neither endorsing Acadian removal nor prohibiting it, they had left the matter for Lawrence to resolve. With the support of Governor William Shirley and Vice Admiral Edward Boscawen, he had gone ahead and accomplished what others for nearly half a century merely had talked of doing, and it seemed entirely in keeping with the spirit of the arrangement that he did not send regular reports to superiors who gave every indication of wanting to distance themselves from the deed. When he finally wrote, it was to inform them of a job completed. "The embarkation is now in great forwardness, and I am in hopes some of them are already sailed, and that there will not be one remaining by the end of the month." He was preparing for the next phase of the operation. Once the expulsion of the Acadians had been completed, it would be time to repeople the province with settlers from New England. "One of the happy effects I proposed to myself from driving the French off," he noted in a remarkably candid sentence that went to the heart of the matter, was that "it furnishes us with a large quantity of good land ready for immediate cultivation." Lawrence was proud of what he had accomplished. So it must have been terribly distressing when, three weeks later, a vessel arrived at Halifax with a letter from colonial minister Sir Thomas Robinson raising grave doubts about the wisdom of the entire project.[1]

Robinson had written in August, expecting to reach Lawrence before the expulsion got fully underway, but the vessel carrying the dispatch had been long delayed. "Use the greatest Caution and Prudence in your conduct toward these Neutrals," Sir Thomas counseled. He had no doubt, he wrote, that Lawrence had "acted upon a strict principle of immediate and indispensable security to your Government," but he hoped the lieutenant-governor had given thorough consideration to "the pernicious Consequences that may arise from any Alarm which may have been given to the whole body of the French Neutrals, and how suddenly an Insurrection may follow from Despair, or what an additional Number of useful subjects may be given, by their Flight, to the French King." These were, in fact, precisely the consequences that had ensued, which Lawrence knew all too well. Monckton, Winslow, Murray, and Handfield had supervised the forced removal of some seven thousand Acadians from the province, but five or six thousand others had escaped the nets cast at Chignecto, Minas, and Annapolis Royal and were among the Míkmaq in the interior, or in French-controlled territory extending northwest of Chipoudy Bay and along the North Shore, while others had fled to Ile Saint-Jean, where some five thousand refugees and inhabitants were living by late 1755. Many of the Acadians had already taken up arms—as evidenced by the deadly attack of early September on the New England force engaged in the destruction of the hamlets along rivière Petitcodiac.[2]

Lawrence responded with a deferential explanation of his actions. He had offered the Acadians every opportunity to become good subjects, but they had stubbornly refused and forced the confrontation. The operation had proven far more complex and difficult than expected. "The removal of the French Inhabitants has proved a Work of much more Trouble and Time than could be imagined," he explained, and "I fear a considerable part of so great a Work is yet to be accomplish'd." Some of the inhabitants had escaped and were organizing armed resistance. "I must confess," he wrote, "I am not without my apprehensions." Yet he continued to believe the outcome would be positive. "The Prospect may, I think, fairly be said to be now open that leads to Success, and no Circumstance in my Opinion, my Lord, brightens it more than that happy, tho' expensive one of extirpating those perfidious Wretches, the French Neutrals." Perhaps, he conceded, he should have kept London better informed. Criticism on that count might be justified. But the complicated operation had required his constant attention. "If on this or any other occasion either to your Lordship or the Board I have been guilty of any omission as to points that should have been wrote upon or the explanation of them, I promise myself your Lordship's goodness in consideration of the multiplicity of troublesome things I have lately on my hands will hold me in some measure excused."[3]

This tendentious defense did not reach London until February 1756. By then Robinson's concerns had been forgotten in the general anxiety over the failure of the British strategic operation against the French in North America—Braddock's army destroyed by a force of French and native irregulars near the Forks of the Ohio, and major campaigns against French positions at Niagara and Lake Champlain canceled. The taking of Beauséjour had been the only bright spot for the British, and if the questionable removal of the Acadians was an integral part of that campaign it would have to be accepted. It was deemed impolitic to raise disturbing questions about the only success Great Britain could claim. In October, Lord Halifax wrote Lawrence, not only applauding the reduction of Fort Beauséjour but generally approving his actions. "The prudence and resolution with which this important service has been planned, conducted, and executed cannot be too much commended. And we doubt not of your availing yourself of *every advantage* which this success has given you to put the province into such a state of defence and security, that it may have nothing to fear from any further attempts which may be made to disturb or distress it." After receiving Lawrence's November letter, the Board of Trade sought to reassure him further with an unequivocal endorsement. "We look upon a War between us and France to be inevitable," the members wrote. Great Britain had signed a new pact with Prussia; France soon announced an alliance with Austria; and in May 1754 the opposing alliances had declared war. The war lasted for seven years and came to be known in Europe as the Seven Years War (*La Guerre de Sept Ans*)—to the British colonists in America as the French War, or the French and Indian War. "In the present critical situation of our affairs," the board members continued, "we doubt not but that your conduct will meet with His Majesty's Approbation." Actions that the previous summer had seemed rash and unwarrantable were now considered to be in His Majesty's service. Lawrence was commended, and the board informed him he had been raised from lieutenant-governor to governor of the province. With this letter, the British government placed its imprimatur on the removal of the Acadians and assumed responsibility for the act.[4]

This exchange contained no reference to the misery of the Acadian people. The death and destruction that swept down upon them was considered part of the logic of war and conquest; yet the absence of any description of the Acadian ordeal suggests that officials felt a certain shame in the accomplishment. Accounts of the sufferings of the exiles are not to be found in official pronouncements but in obscure documents hidden in local archives, or in the few testimonies collected from survivors. One such fragment is the 1765 petition for relief addressed to Governor Francis Bernard of Massachusetts by the Acadian Pierre Pellerin, formerly of Annapolis

Royal. "A few years ago," he wrote, "I had a good farm and everything needful to make mine and my poor family's lives not only comfortable but happy, and hoped to leave a good estate to my children." Then he was torn from home and community and transported to Boston with his young wife Anne Girouard and their five children. The authorities sent them to the Massachusetts town of Pembrook, where for ten years they eked out a bare existence, Pierre and Anne working as day laborers. The family continued to grow, and by 1765, even with the two oldest boys out on their own, the couple had seven to feed and clothe. "I can, with mine and my wife's industry, get clothes to keep me and mine from suffering with cold, and victuals to prevent their perishing with hunger," Pellerin testified. But finally he had been unable to pay his rent, was sued by his landlord, and jailed when he could not pay the judgment. "Now, stripped of all that we had, removed to a strange land, and to make our misery complete, separated from my dear wife and children and shut up in a dark prison, it is impossible for me to express my troubles. Your honors will easily see that words can't express what I and my family must feel."[5]

Pellerin's ability to express himself in a foreign language seemed inadequate to him. He was among the few Acadians who could speak a little English, learned through long association with traders and soldiers. Most Acadians had great difficulty communicating with their Yankee masters. Yet Pellerin's words offered eloquent testimony of the experience of those who had been stripped of what they had and removed to strange lands. The forced migration of the Acadians began with a nightmare voyage and continued through more than a decade of wandering. The intention of Lawrence and Shirley had been to disperse them in groups so small they could never be reassembled. But with their powerful memories of *l'Acadie,* and their persistent struggle to keep connected to one another, the Acadians managed to survive as a distinct people. For Pellerin, his petition secured his release from jail. Yet for several years more he and his family continued a precarious existence as exiles, until finally, joining an exodus of other Acadians from Massachusetts, they relocated at Yamachiche, a town on the St. Lawrence River between Québec and Montréal—one of many new communities founded by refugee Acadians at the conclusion of their long journey.

THE first exile convoy of twenty-two transports sailed from Annapolis Basin into the Bay of Fundy on 27 October 1755. Almost immediately it was hit by a violent gale, the leading edge of a powerful early season nor'easter. The sea turned completely white, the air filled with foam, and huge waves and hurricane-force winds pummeled the vessels. He had never experienced a more severe storm, the captain of one of the escorts testified. His vessel sprang a leak and it took all hands working the pumps to keep her afloat. He was able to "kept company" with the convoy as far as Grand Manan Island at the mouth of the Bay of Fundy, but fearing to embark into the open ocean, he "brought too," and fought his way back to the safety of Annapolis Basin. The less seaworthy transports were not so lucky, and scattered before the winds. From their dark prisons below deck, men, women, and children cried out in terror, but they could not be heard over the roar of the tempest. Two transports—the schooner *Boscawen* and the brig *Union*, bound for Philadelphia with no fewer than 582 exiles from Chignecto—were never heard from again and presumably went down with all hands.[6]

On 5 November, after more than a week battling storm-tossed seas, six transports destined for Pennsylvania, Maryland, and Virginia straggled into Boston Harbor for repairs. An investigation by a committee of the Massachusetts Assembly found the Acadians on board suffering badly. "The vessels in general are too much crowded," read their report. The exiles on one transport were described as "sickly occasioned by being too much crowded, [with] 40 lying on deck," on another as "sickly and their water very bad." A group of Acadians exiled to Philadelphia later testified to their experience. "We were so crowded in the transport vessels, that we had not room even for all our bodies to lay down at once, and consequently were prevented from carrying with us proper necessaries, especially for the support of the aged and weak, many of whom quickly ended their misery with their lives."[7]

The mortality on two of these six transports was staggering. *Endeavour*, which had departed western Minas with 166 Acadians, arrived at Boston with only 125 alive. *Ranger*, overloaded with 263 inhabitants from Pisiquid, counted only 205 survivors. There was less loss of life on the other four that put in at Boston, but they were overcrowded and inadequately provisioned. "Their allowance of provisions is short," the Assembly report continued, "and too small a quantity to that allowance to carry them to the ports they are bound to, especially at this season of the year. And their water is very bad." This was after only ten days at sea. Declaring these conditions unconscionable, the investigators urged that a sufficient number of Acadians be disembarked to reduce the transports to the specified capacity of two exiles per ton. The ships' captains loudly protested any reduction in number, for their contracts specified payment on the basis of the number of persons delivered at their ports of destination. The authorities sought out Benjamin Green, a member of the Governor's Council of Nova Scotia who was in town on provincial business, and convinced him to agree that the province would pay for all the inhabitants counted at Boston, which cleared the way for the disembarkation of 130 Acadians on 7 November. They were sheltered temporarily in the poorhouse.[8]

Other evidence of conditions during the voyage is scattered and fragmentary. The fact is, once the vessels departed from l'Acadie, the provincial government washed its hands of them. No records were kept and no questions asked. What is known is known by chance alone. An epidemic of smallpox apparently struck the 417 Acadians from Chignecto crowded on board the *Cornwallis*, and 210 died before the vessel reached South Carolina. *Edward* and *Experience*, two of the transports in the second convoy of six that left Annapolis Basin on 8 December, were blown off course and spent six weeks beating against unfavorable winds before making landfall on the island of Antigua in the British West Indies. The exiles on the *Edward* reportedly came down with malaria, and by the time the vessel docked at New London, Connecticut, in May 1756, nearly one hundred had died. *Dove*, one of the vessels assigned to pick up the last contingent of inhabitants from Minas in December 1755, was apparently lost at sea—at least there is no record of its arrival in Connecticut. Out of the nearly seven thousand Acadians who boarded transports at Chignecto, Minas, and Annapolis Royal in 1755, the best estimate is that roughly one thousand died in transit.[9]

One shipload of Acadians failed to arrive for a quite different reason. The *Pembroke*, loaded with 226 inhabitants from the *banlieu*, departed with the rest of the convoy from Annapolis Royal on the early morning of 8 December. But separated from its escort by a fortuitous wind, the exiles somehow managed to overpower the crew and guards and head the vessel into St. Mary's Bay, where they lay for a month, then sailed the vessel across Fundy to the mouth of rivière Saint-Jean, where they delivered the British crew into the hands of Charles Deschamps de Boishébert, who had just returned from Chipoudy Bay with his small force of Canadien militia. Among those on board was Prudent Robichaud, who had been deported with the rest despite his eighty-six years and his long history of friendship with the British. Robichaud died that summer during the long trek these exiles made to Québec by the arduous overland route.

The *Pembroke* mutiny would become the stuff of Acadian legend. The vessel had arrived at Annapolis Basin with a broken mainmast, so the story was told, and the captain hired Acadian mariner Charles Belliveau to make a new one. By an irony of fate, Belliveau and his family were deported on that very same vessel. The hold was crowded with deportees, and to prevent them from suffocating, the captain announced that six at a time would be allowed on deck for a few minutes of fresh air. Choosing the strongest men, Belliveau concocted a plan. He sent six of them up first, and when their time elapsed and the hatch was opened for them to return to the hold, he and the others burst out and using nothing but their fists overwhelmed the crew. Belliveau assumed command. The wind was strong, the sails filled, and the mainmast groaned. "Stop! You are going to break it," cried the captain. "I made this mast," Belliveau shouted back, "and I know it will not break!"[10]

THE 130 Acadians who were deposited at Boston on 7 November were joined over the next few weeks by 883 more from Minas and Annapolis Royal. "About a thousand of them arrived just in the beginning of winter, crowded almost to death," wrote Thomas Hutchinson, a member of the Massachusetts Governor's Council. The government knew of their coming—informed by Thomas Hancock, who hired the transports—but had made no provision for their support. Fearing contagion, port authorities quarantined the exiles for several days on the transports before finally permitting them to land, then placed them in temporary quarters on Boston Common. Few of them had anything but the clothes on their backs, and those were in tatters. "We must acquaint your Excellency," the Massachusetts Assembly wrote to Governor Shirley, "that the livestock, the husbandry tools, and most of the household furniture of these people, were left in the Province of Nova Scotia, and that very few have brought with them any goods or estate of any kind whatsoever." Struck by their misery, Hutchinson and a few others opened their homes to some of the aged and infirm, but it was clear the government needed to do something systematic about their care.[11]

What was the legal status of the Acadian exiles and how were they to be treated? It was a perplexing problem. Lawrence and the Governor's Council took the position that by refusing the oath, they had forfeited their status as British subjects. "The Council could no longer look on them as Subjects to His Britannick Majesty, but as Subjects of the King of France, and as such they must hereafter be Treated." This was what the Acadians had been told, and Lawrence made the same point in his report to the Board of Trade: "As they refused to become English subjects we could no longer look upon them in that light." But fearing that if the Acadians were repatriated to France or one or another of France's colonies they would return in arms to reclaim their homes, the council ordered them dispersed to Great Britain's colonies. Were the colonial officials to treat them as prisoners of war, locked up and kept at government expense? Not only was that an unattractive prospect, it was a practical impossibility. Lawrence understood that, and in his letter to the colonial governors accompanying the exiles, he suggested something altogether different from what he had told the Acadians. "As most of them are healthy strong people," he wrote, "they may become profitable and it is possible, in time, faithful subjects." The implication was that they yet remained British subjects, albeit disloyal ones. This argument was more appealing to colonial officials, because it released them from absolute responsibility for the exiles' care. Yet some policy was still required for their integration into local society.[12]

The Massachusetts Assembly was not happy about assuming this responsibility, complaining: "The receiving among us of so great a number of persons whose gross bigotry [partiality] to the Roman Catholic religion is notorious, and whose loyalty to His Majesty is suspected, is a thing very disagreeable to us, but as there seems to be a necessity for it, we shall be ready to come to any reasonable acts or orders to enable and encourage them to provide for their own maintenance." On 16 November 1755, the Assembly passed an act placing the Acadians under the jurisdiction of the provincial poor laws. The exiles would be distributed in "family groups" throughout Boston and the surrounding towns. Immediate family only, however: husband, wife, and children. There was no attempt to keep extended families together, and indeed there seems to have been a deliberate attempt to break them up, to isolate the Acadians from their networks of support. Local authorities were to provide housing and food for the winter, expenses that would be reimbursed by the provincial treasury. But the law provided that the exiles must be self-supporting by the spring of 1756. If any proved unable or unwilling to work, local justices of the peace were empowered "to employ, bind out, or support said Inhabitants." Neighboring Connecticut passed a comparable law shortly after the first of approximately 630 Acadians arrived at New London. The exile families were dispersed among all the towns of the province, with local officials responsible for providing assistance to the sick and indigent and maintaining strict control over the able-bodied, preventing them from wandering from their designated locations or congregating in potentially dangerous groups.[13]

The mid-Atlantic colonies adopted a similar but significantly harsher approach. Four transports carrying 913 exiles from Minas arrived at Annapolis, Maryland, in late November 1755. "They appear very needy and quite exhausted in provisions," reported the *Maryland Gazette*. "As the Poor People have been deprived of the Settlements in Nova Scotia and sent here (for some very Political Reason) bare and destitute, Christian Charity, nay common Humanity, calls on every one, according to their ability, to lend their assistance and help to these objects of compassion." The implication was that the exiles ought to be the responsibilty of private philanthropy rather than government, and that was precisely the approach decided on by the Governor's Council, which convened in emergency session and after considerable debate voted to apportion the exiles among the several counties, where they would be expected to rely on charity for their relief.[14]

The results were disastrous. One group of exiles was forced to live for days without shelter in the snow-covered countryside, huddling together for warmth until a local minister secured housing for them. Many were reduced to begging from door to door. After complaints from local officials about Acadian vagabonds, in the spring of 1756 the Maryland Assembly passed a law authorizing local officials to jail indigent Acadians and "bind out" their children "to some person upon the best terms they can make." The Assembly of New York—the destination of two hundred exiles from Annapolis Royal—followed the same course. Most Acadians found low-paying employment as farm laborers, but still a majority of their children in both Maryland and New York were forcibly taken away and put out to service.[15]

The exiles sent to Pennsylvania had an equally rough time, but were somewhat more successful at keeping their families together. The arrival of three transports crowded with 454 exiles from Minas at Philadelphia in the third week of November caught the provincial government completely unprepared. "I am at a very great loss to know what to do with them," Governor Robert H. Morris declared. In the aftermath of the defeat of General Edward Braddock's expeditionary force, the province's western frontier had erupted in violence between settlers and natives. Pennsylvanians, wrote Morris, were "very uneasy at the thought of having a number of enemies scattered in the very bowels of the country, who may go off from time to time with intelligence, and join their countrymen now employed against us, or foment some intestine commotion in conjunction with the Irish and German Catholics in this and the neighboring Province." He ordered the Acadians kept under guard aboard the transports.[16]

They soon came down with smallpox, an endemic disease in Atlantic port towns such as Philadelphia, and doctors warned Morris that all would perish unless they were disembarked. Early in December, the exiles were allowed to land at Province Island at the mouth of the Schuylkill River, location of the city's "pest house," where immigrants were quarantined before being allowed to enter the city. But for the intervention of a number of Quaker philanthropists, among them Anthony Benezet, a descendant of Huguenots, the Acadians would have gone without provisions. But upon Benezet's appeal, the Pennsylvania Assembly authorized emergency relief.[17]

In February 1756, after lobbying by Benezet, the Assembly passed an act offering the Acadians the opportunity to assimilate into Pennsylvania society much like other immigrants. They would be provided with assistance to rent land, tools, and livestock. But no more than one family would be allowed to settle in each of the colony's townships. This was unacceptable to the Acadians, who preferred to remain together, even if it meant living in isolation on Province Island. A memorial from their leaders demonstrated they had not lost their political savvy or their will to resist. They demanded to be treated as prisoners of war. "It was contrary to common right to oblige such prisoners as we are to take engagements against their will," they wrote. When they were arrested in Halifax, "Mr. Lawrence, governor of Nova Scotia, assured us, before His Majesty's Council, that he took us prisoners of war in the same manner as the French were made prisoners . . . and further promised us that we should be carried amongst our own people." They could appreciate Pennsylvania's reluctance "to send us back to our own country or to our country people," but they appealed to the governor "to furnish us with what is necessary to keep us alive, and not to let us perish whilst we are detained here against our will." Their claim to rights as prisoners was rejected out of hand, but the Acadians remained adamant. "We shall never freely consent to settle in this Province," they declared.[18]

Refusing to support them any longer, the government released the exiles from Province Island in the spring of 1756 and allowed them to take up residence together in a squalid urban neighborhood near St. Joseph's, Philadelphia's only Catholic church. A commissioner appointed to investigate their circumstances a few months later found them in "a starving condition." The men had been unable to find work because of the prevailing prejudice against the French, and families were attempting to support themselves by the sale of traditional home crafts such as wooden shoes, for which there was little market in the city. "Many of them had neither meat nor bread for many weeks together, and were necessitated to pilfer and steal for the support of life." Disease and death were their constant attendants. The report resulted in the passage of an act very similar to Maryland's. The children of Acadians without visible means of support were to be placed in service so that "they might become reputable inhabitants entitled to the rights of British subjects."[19]

The exiles were treated much the same as other paupers, which is to say with a great deal of indifference and cruelty. François Mius petitioned the governor of Massachusetts complaining of the conditions in which he, his wife, and their ten children were forced to live. After their arrival at Boston they had been sent to the town of Tewksbury, "where they have lived ever since, if drawing breath in the depth of want and misery may be called living." They were placed in what Mius described as "the most miserable House in the world," with rotten timbers, broken glass, and a hearth that amounted to nothing more than a few stones piled up, with a hole in the roof substituting for a chimney. His family was being "smoked to death . . . add to this, that at every blast of wind they expect the House to be down upon their Heads, and think it a miracle that it has stood so long." Jean-Baptiste Guédry dit Labrador protested that "without any regard or pity" the officials of the town of Wilmington had forced his large family to stay in a house without a roof. "When it rains they are obliged to shift their bed from part of the wett to leeward, and from a melting snow there is no screening." He had complained to the town selectmen that "we were afloat in the house," and one of them responded that "I must build a boat and sail in it." He had no firewood or food, and his wife and children were barely surviving on acorns gathered in the nearby woods.[20]

Treatment like this was perhaps to be expected. But what the Acadian exiles found intolerable was the enforced separation of their children. Although the practice of putting children out to service was common among colonial Britons, it was rare among Acadians. In Massachusetts, the exiles availed themselves of the petition process to protest. Joseph Michel, formerly of Annapolis Royal but then living with his wife Marie Boudrot and their children at Marshfield, General John Winslow's hometown, wrote that during the first week of March 1756, two of the town's selectmen came to his dwelling and seized his two sons. "All your petitioner's and his wife's entreaties were in vain," he wrote. Their eldest boy was "put out" at the farm of Anthony Winslow (a cousin of John Winslow) and the other "sent to sea" on the vessel of Nathaniel Clift, Winslow's son-in-law. Daughters were also at risk. Claude Bourgeois of Annapolis Royal, who had been placed in the town of Amesbury with his wife Marie Leblanc and their six children, protested that in early April, "ten or twelve men came and took away from him two of his daughters . . . at that time employed in spinning for the family the poor remains of the flax and wool which they had saved from Annapolis." He had "fetched his daughters home again," but as a result the selectmen had withheld what little support they had been providing. In consequence, he had been unable to pay his rent and now the landlord was threatening to bind out his children in order to raise his money. In another case, town officials removed the parents in order to get at the children. Charles and Nicolas Breau, two brothers in their twenties who had grown up at Minas, were placed with their elderly parents and seven minor siblings in the town of Hanover, Massachusetts. On a Saturday morning in April, they wrote, "about twenty men came in a threatening manner to their dwelling, and several of them, with ropes in their hands, forced their father and mother, persons of seventy-seven years old, into a cart and have carried them away from there, they know not where." The brothers attempted to stop the men, but one of them attempted to strangle Nicolas while another restrained Charles. Since that time the brothers and their siblings had been bound out to service.[21]

In April 1756, nine Acadian fathers from six different towns petitioned for a change in policy. "We are in affliction on account of our children," they wrote. "The loss which we have suffered from being deprived of our farms, from being brought here, and from being separated from each other, is nothing in comparison to that which we are now bearing in having our children torn from us before our eyes. It is an outrage on nature itself. Had we the power to choose, we would prefer to give up our bodies and souls rather than be separated from our children." The Massachusetts Governor's Council drew up a new set of standards that aimed to keep children with their parents, and announced that towns "should desist binding any of them out." Unfortunately, the council's policy did not end the practice. Later that year Augustin Hébert complained that a local grandee at Watertown had come to his house, insulted his wife, and seized his nineteen-year-old son Jean-Baptiste. When Hébert attempted to intervene, he was beaten so badly he had been "scarce able to walk" for a fortnight. "It is a very hard trial for a man to see his children ravished away from him," Hébert wrote. In 1757, two of Pierre Boudrot's sons were bound out by the selectmen of Scituate, "and after two or three months hard work," Boudrot complained, paid "nothing but a few rags." He would be glad to see his sons employed if they were paid fairly, "but not understanding the English language and customs, they know not where to apply for redress, and the country people do just what they please with them." These petitions testify to the Acadians' vulnerability to exploitation, and the inability of authorities in Boston to have much direct influence on the leaders of rural towns.[22]

The Acadians in Pennsylvania protested with equal vigor, which resulted in the arrest of several of their leaders. In February 1757, a group of exiles in Philadelphia filed a memorial praying that their children no longer be bound out to service. They would be "the most unhappy people that ever appeared," they wrote, "if after having lost what God had given us for the subsistence of our families we see ourselves forced to tear our children from the arms of our tender wives. . . . What crime have these innocent creatures been guilty of that you should thus separate them from those who, after God, are the authors of their lives?" This memorial, written in French, found its way to John Campbell, Earl of Loudoun, commander in chief of British forces in North America. "I returned it," Loudoun reported a few weeks later, "and said I could receive no Memorial from the King's Subjects but in English; on which they had a general meeting at which they determined they would give no memorial but in French, and, as I am informed, they came to this resolution, from looking on themselves entirely as French Subjects."[23]

Concluding from this that the Acadians were up to no good,

Loudoun arranged for a spy to be placed among them—none other than Thomas Pichon of Beauséjour, who after his service to the British in l'Acadie had eventually found his way to Philadelphia, where he was living on a government stipend. Pichon did what he was so good at doing, ingratiating himself with the leaders of the exiles, and soon reported back to Loudoun the names of five men he claimed had "stirr'd up all the disturbances." Paul Bugeaud, Jean Landry, Charles Leblanc, Philippe Melanson, and Jean-Baptiste Galerne—all former deputies from Minas—were arrested, charged with being "suspicious and evil-minded persons," who "at divers times uttered menacing speeches against His Majesty." After spending several months incarcerated on a British prison ship anchored in the Delaware River, they were finally released in early 1758, soon after Loudoun was recalled to England to answer for a string of British military setbacks—the disastrous losses to the French of Fort Oswego on Lake Erie and Fort William Henry on Lake George, and the failure to launch an assault on the French fortress at Louisbourg.[24]

THE Acadians were even less welcome in the southern colonies, where governments took steps to quickly get rid of them. In Virginia, the mid-November arrival of the first of some twelve hundred Acadians from Minas at Hampton Roads came as a complete surprise to the authorities. "It is very disagreeable to the people to have imported to rest among us a number of French People," Governor Robert Dinwiddie complained to London, "when many of that Nation joined with Indians are now murdering and scalping our Frontier Settlers. I shall call and consult the Council what is to be done with 'em." When he suggested to a number of Acadian leaders the possibility of their settling down as peaceable subjects according to the laws of the colony, they responded that it would not be possible for them to swear allegiance to the British king. They had been declared French subjects, and insisted on their rights as prisoners of war. Dinwiddie's council was equally intransigent. "No governor had a right to send such numbers to another colony," its members argued, and they resisted the idea that such "intestine enemies" could be safely settled in the province at the same time that the French were instigating "the barbarous Murders and Robberies committed on our frontiers to the Westward."[25]

By only one vote did Dinwiddie win a motion to receive and provision the Acadians pending the meeting of the House of Burgesses in the spring. Although the government kept most of the exiles aboard the transports for the winter, apparently some were placed in quarters on land, where they aroused further suspicion by fraternizing with Negro slaves. Dinwiddie reported that one group "concerted to run away with a sloop from Hampton, which obliged me to have a guard over them for two months." Years later, Acadian storytellers told of a small number of young men who managed to escape, trekking overland through forests and across mountains until they found their way to Québec.[26]

In the spring of 1756, Dinwiddie made a halfhearted argument that the Acadians be dispersed among the eastern communities of the province on the model of Maryland, but the delegates would have none of it. "The Danger we apprehend from such a number of Neutral French Roman Catholics being suffered to continue amonst us," they resolved, made it imperative that they "be immediately shipped to Great Britain to be disposed of as His Majesty shall think proper." The council concurred and Dinwiddie went along. "I hope this step will meet with your approbation," he wrote nervously to his superiors, "as I could not shun consenting thereto from the general clamour of the whole Country." His letter accompanied the first shipment of exiles, 299 persons dispatched to Bristol, England, in May 1756. Within two weeks all the remaining exiles had been sent off: 250 bound for Falmouth on the coast of Cornwall, 340 for Southampton, and 336 for Liverpool.[27]

These Acadians arrived unannounced in England at the beginning of the summer. At Bristol, they were disembarked and left on the wharves for three days and nights before finally being put up in an old warehouse. At Liverpool, they were quartered in a cluster of abandoned workshops; at Southampton, in a dilapidated old barracks. After sending a blistering letter of criticism to Dinwiddie, the government gave orders that the exiles be maintained by the Sick and Hurt Board of the Admiralty. In practice, they were maintained hardly at all, each family allocated only a few pence per week for food and shelter. At Falmouth and Southampton some of the men found irregular employment, but all those at Liverpool and Bristol were kept in virtual imprisonment in conditions far worse than in any of the colonies. Almost as soon as they arrived, they were struck with epidemics of smallpox. At Falmouth, sixty-one Acadians were buried in a common grave. Reports of the exiles' treatment reached the French, and in the fall they filed a formal protest, charging that the Acadians were being inhumanely neglected. Admiralty officials responded that the accusation was "false, indecent, and absurd," as well as "very dishonourable to the Nation," and attributed Acadian mortality to "their long voyage, their change of climate, their habits of body, their other disorders, and their irregularity and obstinacy." The British government, the Admiralty maintained, had strictly observed "the laws of nations and the principles of justice."[28]

As punishment for taking part in the defense of Beauséjour, Charles Lawrence had ordered that the inhabitants of Chignecto "be removed to the greatest distance." Thus HMS *Syren* arrived at Charles Town harbor in South Carolina on 15 November 1755 as escort to a convoy of six transports from Fort Cumberland. Like other colonial officials, Governor James Glen had little or no warning of their coming. He received Lawrence's letter from Commander Charles Proby of the *Syren*, who informed Glen that he had been ordered to deliver some six hundred exiles on four transports, including twenty-one "special prisoners" considered so dangerous they came in shackles. That group included Alexandre Broussard dit

Beausoleil and his nephew Victor-Grégoire Broussard, one of Joseph Broussard's sons. Proby was then to proceed to Georgia with the other two transports, bearing approximately four hundred more.[29]

Governor Glen immediately called a meeting of his council. "We cannot permit these people to come ashore without the consent of the commons Assembly," he announced, "but neither can we let 'em starve to death." The council authorized him to provision the Acadians while awaiting the Assembly's decision as to their fate. In the meantime Glen summoned eight or ten of their leaders, who proved ready and able to make the case for their mistreatment at the hands of Governor Lawrence and Colonel Monckton. In support of their arguments they presented him with three documents: a copy of the articles signed by Ensign Robert Wroth in 1727, exempting them from bearing arms and permitting them to leave the province voluntarily; an order bearing the signature of Captain Jean-Baptiste-Nicolas Roch de Ramezay dated May 1747, ordering the Acadians on penalty of death to arm themselves against the return of the British; and a copy of the articles of capitulation at Fort Beauséjour, including the pardon of the Acadians, "as they have been forced to take up arms under pain of death." Clearly the will of the Acadians was far from being broken.[30]

The Acadian leaders also met with an investigative committee of the Assembly, but did not make a very favorable impression. The exiles "acknowledged that they had borne arms against His Majesty's subjects," the committee reported back; they "professed an inviolable attachment to the French Interest, with a determined resolution to continue in the public exercise of the Roman Catholic Religion, under the conduct of Priests, and obstinately refused to take an Oath of Allegiance to fight against His Majesty's Enemies." They were dangerous characters who well might conspire with slaves or natives, the committee concluded, and would surely render assistance to the French enemy in the event of an invasion. They ought to be turned away. But Glen protested that "it would be cruelty to keep these people on board the vessels till they perish," and in early December he persuaded the Assembly to allow them to be disembarked and quartered temporarily on Sullivan's Island in Charles Town harbor. A month later another vessel arrived with 343 exiles from Annapolis Royal, and after a similar struggle between Glen and the deputies that lasted nearly a month, they too were landed on Sullivan's Island. The exiles came in a weak and sickly state. The passengers on at least one vessel, the *Cornwallis*, had suffered through an epidemic of smallpox. Moreover, the provisions supplied by the government were inadequate and conditions on the island squalid. Within weeks of their landing, many more had died.[31]

During their months of confinement several groups of men escaped into the interior, including many of the "special prisoners." They were pursued by posses who recovered most of them, but a number sucessfully eluded capture. One band—which included Alexandre Broussard, described in the local press as a "general of the Indians"—broke into the house of an absent planter, took arms, clothes, and money from the terrified mistress of the plantation, and fled into the soggy woods. "Tho it was thought they would have laid their bones in the swamp they had got into," the *South Carolina Gazette* reported, they had "escaped from thence and crossed the river at Maxwell's Bluff on a bark log." The Governor's Council sent the remaining "special prisoners" to England in chains.[32]

In the meantime, Commander Proby had arrived at Savannah River with the final two transports. Governor John Reynolds of Georgia issued an order forbidding the four hundred exiles from being disembarked anywhere in his colony, but Proby ignored him and in early December 1755 landed them on Tybee Island, at the river's mouth. Reynolds in turn simply ignored the Acadians, which seems to have given their leaders—including Jacques Maurice Vigneau of Baie Verte—an opportunity to coordinate a plan of escape. Pooling their funds, they purchased several small sailing vessels, and in early March 1756 Vigneau requested permission from Reynolds to leave the province. Happy to be rid of them, Reynolds issued him a passport dated 10 March 1756:

> These are to Certify whom it may Concern that the Bearer Jacques Morrice [Vigneau] hath behaved himself very well during all the time of his Residence in His Majesty's Colony of Georgia under my Government (which hath been near four Months). I have been well informed that he always shewed great regard for the English by Saving them frequently from being scalped in Nova Scotia, where he was worth a great deal of Money before he was reduced. And he hath my leave to depart from the Province of Georgia with his Family.

Vigneau's extended family—numbering some 150 persons—departed Tybee Island a few days later. By the end of March they were in Charles Town, where Vigneau presented his passport to Governor Glen.[33]

Both Glen and the South Carolina Assembly immediately saw this as the solution to their Acadian problem. On 8 April, Glen endorsed Vigneau's passport—"Jacques Morrice with his Family came into this Province about ten days ago by virtue of the within passport and as I have not heard that he has behaved ill during his Stay here he and his Family hath by leave to depart from this Province"—and the same day the Assembly passed a resolution urging Glen to permit the Acadians in South Carolina to leave in their own vessels as soon as possible, "that no Time be lost in getting rid of this Danger." A group of exiles later recalled that the authorities provided them with "two old vessels, a small quantity of very poor provisions, and permission to go where they wished." The best estimate is that three quarters of the exiles in Georgia and about half of those in South Carolina—upward of six hundred Acadians—took this opportunity to leave, and within the month a flotilla of several dozen small vessels was coasting northward.[34]

In May, Governor Dinwiddie of Virginia reported that "many hundreds of 'em" had been seen along his coast. It appeared, he wrote to London, that the governments of South Carolina and Georgia had given them leave to go where they pleased, and he feared they would reach the Bay of Fundy. Dinwiddie said what neither Reynolds nor Glen would admit, yet he was not about to detain the boat people—Virginia was in the process of sending its own contingent of Acadian exiles off to London, and wanted no more. When one group of exiles beached their leaking vessel on the Virginia shore near the town of Hampton, Dinwiddie saw to it that they got another and were hurried on their way northward. "This ship was still less seaworthy than those they had just left," the Acadians remembered, "and they had all the difficulty in the world to run aground a second time on the coast of Maryland."[35]

By July 1756, Lawrence was in receipt of reports that hundreds of Acadians were sailing homeward, and he drafted an angry letter to his fellow governors. The exiles return, he wrote, "would great endanger the security of the Province," and he entreated them "to use your utmost endeavours to prevent the accomplishment of so pernicious an undertaking" by arresting any that appeared off their coasts. The first arrest came later that month when a party of about one hundred men, women, and children in seven vessels, under the leadership of Jacques Maurice Vigneau, beached their vessels at Sandwich on Cape Cod, much in need of repairs and provisions. After a few days under guard—"for fear of their moving away in their boats"—they were taken to Boston, where on 18 August the Massachusetts Council ordered them distributed among several towns. A few days later, a second group of seventy-eight exiles was found by New York authorities camping on a Long Island beach. They carried passports from the governors of Georgia and South Carolina, reported Governor Charles Hardy, and declared their intention "to get back to Nova Scotia." He ordered them dispersed "in the most remote and secure parts of this colony." What Hardy did not say was that just a few weeks before, Jacques Vigneau and his extended family had stopped briefly at New York City, where Vigneau had secured Hardy's endorsement of his passport.[36]

The capture and arrest of these two groups left unaccounted the fate of more than four hundred of the boat people. There is no way of knowing how many made it back to the Bay of Fundy, but many did. One group later wrote that they spent two months on a deserted island repairing their leaking vessel before finally succeeding in reaching the mouth of rivière Saint-Jean. The governor-general of New France, Pierre-François de Rigaud, marquis de Vaudreuil, reported the arrival of several groups. He recorded as well the return of a dozen men who after escaping from Sullivan's Island in South Carolina had made their way north to Fort Duquesne at the Forks of the Ohio, across the Great Lakes, and up the St. Lawrence to Québec. They included Alexandre Broussard—who later told of trekking overland 1,400 leagues "to recover his native country"—and the brothers Michel and Pierre Bastarache, who recounted to their grandchildren the story of their great escape across the interior of North America and the joy of reuniting with their wives and children.[37]

The reunification of their extended families was foremost in the minds of the Acadian exiles. Throughout the late 1750s, newspapers in Boston, New York, and Philadelphia frequently printed notices from individuals looking for parents or children:

> WHEREAS the wife and seven children of Francis Tibaudau [François Thibodeau], nine children of Germain John Petre [Germain-Jean Pitre], and Anthony Landry [Antoine Landry] and his wife, the two first of Pisiquid river, and the latter of the Inhabitants river, have been sent to some of the king's colonies, and the said Francis Tibaudau, Germain John Pitre, and some of the children of the said Anthony Landry being in the city of Philadelphia; This publick notice is given, that, if possible, intelligence may be received.

Numerous families were reunited by means of such notices. Thomas Hutchinson told of men in Philadelphia who read notices published there sent by wives, parents, or children in Massachusetts, "being till then utterly uncertain what became of their families." Travel across provincial borders required official permission and the issuance of passports. In 1758, François-Jacques Leblanc petitioned the governor and Council of Massachusetts to allow his son Jacques to take up residence in the province. During the loading of the vessels at Grand Pré, his son—then a young man of twenty-two—"begged as it had been for his life that he might be also sent with [the family], but could not obtain it." After two years of inquiries they finally located him in Maryland, and Jacques wrote "with advice that the government there are willing to give him a passport if this government will receive him." Leblanc humbly prayed that Massachusetts "will not now deny him his own son." It was agreed, and young Jacques Leblanc rejoined his family; but not before traveling to Philadelphia, where he married Anastasie Breau, his sweetheart from Grand Pré.[38]

A large number of Leblanc families were exiled to Massachusetts. One of them was placed in the town of Westboro in October 1756. The town's minister, Reverend Ebenezer Parkman, noted in his diary the arrival of a "family of Neutral French, as they were called." Three days later, he called on them. "The man's name is Simon Leblanc," Parkman wrote, "from Nova Scotia about nine leagues off from Annapolis. Has with him a Wife and 4 children. Himself Rhumatic—appears sociable. Is a Roman Catholic, but is able to read." Reverend Parkman had preached the justice of the war against the French, and he believed sincerely that the Catholic Church was doing the work of the devil. Yet he was a compassionate man, who did not let his political views keep him from establishing good personal relations. In November, he invited the Leblancs to his home for Thanksgiving. "Monsieur Leblanc was not well enough to come out," Parkman noted. It is likely that Leblanc was still suffering from the shock and exhaustion of removal. But Leblanc's wife and one of their daughters joined the Parkmans for their dinner. It was the beginning of a strong friendship between the two families.[39]

Parkman recorded many of his conversations with Jean-Simon Leblanc, a man in his mid-fifties who for many years had been a deputy at Annapolis and spoke fluent English. Parkman passed on a copy of a new book on the history of the British colonies, and after Leblanc read it, the two men shared their impressions. Leblanc offered an account of the late war from an Acadian perspective and provided a description of the Canadien attack on New Englanders at Grand Pré. The two men discussed their religious differences in ways reminiscent of the dialogue a dozen years before between Lieutenant-Governor Paul Mascarene and abbé Saint-Poncy over the relative merits of Protestantism and Catholicism. Parkman expressed his distaste for the control priests held over their faithful. He gave Leblanc a copy of the English Bible, telling him it "did not do" for priests only to know God's book. "Everybody must see for himself in the matter of religion," he argued. Leblanc was attentive but reluctant to argue about such things. "The people at Annapolis never speak to one another about religion," he told Parkman, "but are free and willing that each party should enjoy his own way. The English go to their own Church and the French to theirs." Parkman found the conversation challenging. "Can make little progress in opening his mind or convincing him of error," he wrote. "The conversation of little other avail than to promote civility and benevolences." But civility and friendship were important to both men.[40]

For most New Englanders, the Acadians in their midst were strangers and cheap day laborers. Certainly the Leblancs labored for the Parkmans. The daughters Marie-Madeleine and Marie-Josèphe, sixteen and thirteen respectively in 1757, wove and sewed and did the Parkman family laundry. The sons Pierre and Armand, twenty-three and nineteen, worked in Parkman's field and tobacco patch alongside his boys, plowing, planting, hoeing, mowing, reaping, and digging a well to water the cattle. But unlike his neighbors, Parkman cared enough about these people to get to know them. As a result his diary, perhaps more than any other surviving document, offers a glimpse of the way Acadian exiles attempted to reconstruct extended family connections.

In December 1756, only a few weeks after the Leblancs arrived in Westboro, Parkman noted that they were entertaining other exiles, and he asked about it. Leblanc explained that he and his wife Jeanne Dupuis were the parents of eight children. In addition to the four living with them in Westboro, there were four others who were married with families of their own. Two sons and a daughter, their spouses and children, had been deported to Massachusetts and were living in towns near the coast. They were the visitors. Another daughter and her husband had escaped into the woods, but Leblanc did not know of their fate—he would later learn they had safely found their way to Québec. He and his wife had siblings whose fates were unknown, but also brothers and sisters who had been deported to Massachusetts and Connecticut. Despite regulations designed to restrict Acadian movement, the extended Leblanc family did a remarkable amount of visiting. Over the two years they lived in Westboro, extended family and friends often came to visit the couple, sometimes staying for days, many times also calling on the Parkmans, who were revered for their willingness to welcome the exiles into their home and to their table.[41]

These two men, the New Englander and the Acadian, became quite intimate, and one day Leblanc confided to Parkman the story of the British side of his extended family. Leblanc's half sister, his mother's only child by a previous marriage, had not been deported, but had been permitted to remain in Annapolis Royal, living in a fine house in the English *faubourg* near Fort Anne. Her name was Marie-Madeleine Maisonnat, and she was the widow of William Winniett, formerly the most prominent trader at Annapolis. Marie's daughters—Leblanc's nieces—had married high-ranking British officers, including John Handfield, the commandant of Fort Anne. Leblanc and Handfield had known each other for years; their children had grown up together. And in the fall of 1755, Handfield had been the man charged with dispossessing the Acadians of Annapolis Royal and removing them to Massachusetts. Handfield and his wife later spent time in Boston, and Parkman went to visit him there, but in his diary there were no notations of the Handfields and the Leblancs renewing their connections in Westboro. Presumably there were some family separations that could not be overcome.[42]

CHAPTER 14

CHASSE À MORT!

The Refugees, 1756–1760

THE ANGLO-AMERICAN REMOVAL OPERATION in the fall of 1755 succeeded in deporting something less than half the Acadians living in the maritime region. Yet it shattered the world of all the inhabitants. Those who managed to avoid the roundups were forced to abandon their communities and flee to the territory northwest of Chipoudy Bay, to estuaries and bays such as Shediac, Miramichi, and Baie des Chaleurs on the North Shore, which for the next three years became places of refuge for thousands of displaced persons. There they joined with the Míkmaq, for whom the deportations were a heavy blow, for by expelling the inhabitants the British destroyed social and economic relationships on which native people had depended for a century and a half.

Although French authorities in Québec made an attempt to supply the refugees with provisions, for the most part they had to fend for themselves. Conditions in the camps were barely tolerable during summer and fall, when hunting and fishing were possible.

During winter of 1755–56, and especially during the subsequent spring—which the Míkmaq knew as "starving time"—hundreds of refugees died from exposure, hunger, and disease. "It requires an Indian's temperament to adhere to this," abbé François Le Guerne, who was living with the refugees, wrote to French authorities in March 1756. The Acadians and Mikmaq were surviving on a diet of wild game and mangy cattle, and "in truth, so poor is the meat that even the Indians reject it, carnivorous as they are." Men, women, and children were suffering from malnutrition and dysentery, and had become listless and apathetic. He recommended their immediate evacuation to Canada, but admitted that most of the Acadians expressed a reluctance to leave, "for then they must say goodbye to their country, their villages, their homes." They feared famine on Ile Saint-Jean and British attack at Louisbourg. "And they imagine, with some degree of dismay, that once in Canada they will never return from exile. Such is the way of thinking of these good people who have never yet left their country." Le Guerne offered a clear-headed description of the sentiments of the Acadians as they looked into the abyss. "To hear them talk, people everywhere else are miserable. L'Acadie, they say, until these last few years, was an earthly paradise. They still think we will soon have peace, or that l'Acadie will, perhaps, be reclaimed by a French fleet over the course of the following summer, or within two years, at most. In the meantime, they hide and wait."[1]

It was one of the Acadians' most pronounced cultural values—a reluctance to leave their homeland unless forced to do so by circumstances beyond their control. Le Guerne found it frustrating. "They assemble, they ask for advice, but then they do as they please [*on fait à sa tête*]. . . . Someone is captured, they tremble, they wish to leave, but soon they reassure themselves, and lull themselves back into a false sense of security. They live with complacent but chimerical hopes. Such is the conduct of these people rendered so unhappy by experience."[2]

With thousands of Acadians still at large, the British sent troops to scour the countryside, drive them out of hiding, and bring them in for deportation. Joined by the Míkmaq, the refugees resisted in the only way poorly equipped irregular forces can—by using stealth, ambush, and terror. Soon the British were conducting nothing but search and destroy operations, and the Acadians began to realize that they would never be able to go back to the old life. "Nothing is left to us," declared one group, "but the desire for revenge." By the summer of 1756, a full-fledged guerrilla war was producing far more violence and far more killing than the province ever had experienced before. The war years became the stuff of legend. A century later Daniel Dugas, the descendant of Acadians who fled Chignecto and eventually resettled in an exile community north of Québec, recounted some of the stories he heard as a child. "As my grandfather put it," he told a priest, "it was a true *chasse à mort*!" But the Acadians fought back. "They became active and vigorous hunters of the English."[3]

One man in particular became the focus of these tales. Dugas's grandfather told him of "an Acadian named Beausoleil, a skilled hunter, an intrepid warrior without equal, who was said to have killed not less than one thousand English." Joseph Broussard dit Beausoleil had a long history of opposing the British. In 1724, when he was a young unmarried man in his early twenties, the Governor's Council had accused him of fraternizing with the Míkmaq on the eve of their assault on Fort Anne. For the next three decades he remained a close associate of the Míkmaq and was reportedly fluent in Míkmawísimk. In 1747, Broussard was outlawed by Governor William Shirley of Massachusetts for his participation with Míkmaq and Canadiens in the attack on New Englanders at Grand Pré; and during the early 1750s, he and his elder brother Alexandre led a combined force of Acadian and Míkmaq irregulars in attacks on British patrols, in 1751 staging the raid at the village of Dartmouth on the outskirts of Halifax that thoroughly terrorized the Protestant settlers. In 1755 they jointly commanded the Acadian militia at the siege of Beauséjour. Imprisoned after the capitulation, Joseph Broussard escaped from

Fort Lawrence and assumed leadership of Acadians fighting to maintain control of the country northwest of Chipoudy Bay, which became a guerrilla stronghold. There were actually a whole clan of Broussards in arms. After his epic overland return from exile in South Carolina, Alexandre joined Joseph as a guerrilla leader and the two men had seven grown sons who acted as their lieutenants. Alexandre was Joseph's equal, and there is even some evidence that at the time he was considered the more important leader. One contemporary observer at Miramichi described him as "a great partizan" and "the most considerable person here." But legend concatenates all the Broussards into the one heroic, lonely figure of Beausoleil.[4]

By the late nineteenth century, when the French-Canadian scholar Henri Raymond Casgrain collected material for an important study of the Acadians, Beausoleil had become a figure of folklore—a mythic hero "inflamed by an excess of misfortune." According to Casgrain, before the deportation Beausoleil had been only a great huntsman, uninterested in politics. But the British determination to remove the inhabitants resulted in the destruction of his community, his home, and his family. His mother, his wife, and most of his children died in the expulsion, and a desire for revenge became his obsession. "He could not hear a Yankee name pronounced without being seized by a kind of frenzy." He continued to practice his vocation, "but this time it was not in order to hunt wild animals, but to hunt men, to hunt everyone with a Yankee or English name." Leading a group of partisans as skilful at arms as he, Beausoleil sought to visit upon his enemies all the pain and suffering he had experienced. He began to find his pleasure in taking the lives of his enemy, and every time he did so, he notched the butt of his weapon. His rifle had been preserved by his descendants, Casgrain claimed, and "one counts no less than twenty-eight notches on it."[5]

Casgrain chose a number with more apparent verisimilitude than the mythic rhetoric of "not less than one thousand English" in the version of the Beausoleil story told by Daniel Dugas. Otherwise, the two accounts are much the same. Little in either is accurate. The mythic Beausoleil dies in the final battle of the war, in Casgrain's account cut down by cannonfire from a British vessel. Myth is communal in its purposes, and killing off the ferocious fighter was perhaps a way of helping Acadians move past the violence. A man who loved to kill could not easily make peace. But the real Beausoleils, both Joseph and Alexandre Broussard, survived the war (although each lost their eldest son to the struggle), and continued to play important roles within the Acadian community.

The legend of Beausoleil conveyed an important truth about the brutality of war. The Broussards had participated in the scalping of British settlers at Dartmouth in 1751, and during the protracted resistance struggle from late 1755 to 1760 scalping became a common practice among the guerrillas. In one of the first recorded incidents, a band of Acadian and Míkmaq partisans in the early spring of 1756 ambushed a small party of New England soldiers cutting wood for Fort Cumberland, killing and mutilating nine men. Such violence provoked responses in kind. Colonel George Scott, in command of the garrison, ordered two irregular companies of rangers raised from among his New England troops, and dressed as native fighters they raided the Acadian refugee encampments in retaliation. After one attack, in which exile women and children were brutally killed, a Yankee ranger left a notice attached to a stake: "What you have begun we shall continue in the same style."[6]

During the war both French and British authorities paid for scalps. The British bounty was supposed to apply only to the scalps of native allies of the French, but there was little way to distinguish one scalp from another. Several years after the war the story was told of a group of Yankee rangers who delivered the scalps of twenty-five Acadians to the bursar at Fort Cumberland, demanding payment. Suspecting that they were the scalps of refugees, not Míkmaq, he refused. The rangers went to their commanding officer, Lieutenant-Colonel Montagu Wilmot. "According to law all the French were out of the country," Wilmot told them with a wink, and he ordered the bounty paid.[7]

The winter of 1756–57 brought the Acadian refugees to the brink of despair. Despite pleas throughout the fall, no provisions arrived from Québec, and by the new year they had been reduced to eating shoe leather, carrion, even animal dung. Many families abandoned the country, Daniel Dugas's forebears among them. "They gathered their few things and left for Québec," he wrote. "They placed their children and the little food that remained on sledges, and on their snowshoes followed a path of a thousand turns to avoid falling into the hands of the new masters of the country." The refugees who remained were starving. Many children perished. "These poor people have died in great numbers," wrote abbé Le Guerne, "from hunger and from heartbreak." Only the last-minute arrival at Miramichi of a supply vessel from Québec in March 1757 prevented complete disaster.[8]

But even this hard winter did not break the Acadian resistance. In April, a guerrilla band raided a warehouse near Fort Edward, killing thirteen British soldiers and, after taking what provisions they could carry, setting fire to the building. A few days later, Yankee troops near Fort Cumberland fought an engagement with what may have been this same group, killing and scalping two men and taking two prisoners. Under interrogation, the Acadians told commandant Wilmot that absolute want had driven them to risk the attack on a British fort. But the guerrilla war practiced by the Acadians always verged on recklessness. They seized supply vessels on the Bay of Fundy and ambushed British patrols, forcing Governor Lawrence to admit that his troops were being pinned down by the "different tribes of Indians inhabiting these countrys, and the inveterate Neutral French (our most dangerous Enemies)."[9]

In the summer of 1757, two regiments arrived from Ireland to participate in a planned assault on Louisbourg; but when faulty British planning forced the abandonment of that operation, they were assigned to relieve the New Englanders who had been at Fort Cumberland for more than two years. Among the reinforcements was

Lieutenant John Knox, an officer attached to the 43rd Regiment, whose journal of his "inglorious exile" on the shores of Fundy vividly described the guerrilla war. At Fort Cumberland, he found the enlisted men fearful and terrorized. Soon after arriving, he was ordered out on patrol with a large company. They had just camped for the night when one of the sentries heard a rustling in the brush, sounded the alarm, and opened fire. "The party immediately stood to their arms," wrote Knox, "and the men fired so furiously, some one way, and some another, that it was with difficulty their officers could restrain them." Several men were wounded, but Knox believed it was from "the impetuous firing of their own comrades," what in a later day would be known as "friendly fire." Young Gerome Noble, an ordinary soldier in Knox's regiment, wrote home that his fellow soldiers "expect every moment to be swallowed up by the French and Indians, and we dare not stray out of our lines for fear of losing our scalps. . . . What may be our fate God only knows."[10]

In late November, Knox was part of a detachment sent to Annapolis Royal to reinforce the badly undermanned garrison at Fort Anne. Within days he was out on patrol once again, scouring the countryside for Acadians. His journal described a devastated landscape. "We met with the ruins of several habitations," he wrote, "and many vestiges of industry." The company cautiously trod a footpath past carefully planted rows of spruce that once had served the inhabitants as windbreaks, but more recently had provided cover for their ambuscades. Passing an Acadian orchard, Knox admired the sweet apples still hanging on the branches. In the snow his men found moccasin tracks and half-eaten fruit, the flesh not yet browning. They cautiously followed the tracks to a small cabin in a clearing. Their scout called out in French for any persons inside to surrender, and when there was no reply, one of the men broke down the door. The floor was covered with straw "on which lay a choice collection of apples," Knox wrote, "the best we had met with since we came into the country." The soldiers filled their pockets and haversacks, set fire to the cabin, and returned to the fort by another route.[11]

A few days later, a small woodcutting party of seven men was ambushed by guerrillas. One man was killed and the others taken hostage, and the commanding office at Fort Anne ordered a large force of one hundred men and officers off in pursuit. The troops traveled only four miles against a brisk wind and freezing rain before making a cold camp. The next morning they marched another fourteen miles through the *haute rivière*, passing through a dozen half-destroyed hamlets. They crossed the river single-file on a narrow log bridge named for René Forest, one of the original Acadian settlers of the seventeenth century, which was just upriver from the mouth of Bloody Creek, where in 1711 a New England company had been ambushed by Abenakis. They made another several miles but lost the trail and could find no sign of the enemy.

After another cold night, the troops turned back on the morning of 8 December 1757. One of the scouts warned against using Forest's log bridge again, which he thought a likely spot for an ambush. But the river was high and freezing cold, nearly impossible to ford by men loaded down with heavy haversacks and weapons, so the officers decided to take the risk. Half the company was across the bridge when they were suddenly hit by what Knox described as "a dreadful shower of ball and buckshot, seconded by as horrid a yell as ever I heard." The commanding officer was killed instantly, and the men yet to cross fell back in panic. The guerrillas did not pursue them, contenting themselves with firing down on the advance guard from a fortified position high on the embankment. Eighteen British soldiers were killed before Knox and the other officers finally gained control of their men. "It was a shame to be stopped by a few peasants," one cried, and he led a charge across the bridge and up the embankment; but the Acadians had disappeared. "They knew the country," Knox wrote, "and we were strangers to it," the lament of many an occupying army fighting partisans on their own ground.[12]

Over the next several weeks the commandant at Fort Anne posted notices on trees outside the fort announcing his willingness to ransom the return of the British hostages in the hands of the guerrillas.

It was March 1758 before the Acadians responded. Knox and an armed company were providing cover for a group of woodcutters when they spied a small group of Acadian fighters at the edge of the woods. They were under a flag of truce, but several of the soldiers shouldered arms and fired nervously and ineffectively. They were quickly ordered to desist by Knox's superior officer, who placed his handkerchief on a pole to signal his peaceful intentions. One of the Acadians came forward; speaking in French, he and the officer discussed exchanging the British hostages for a number of Míkmaw prisoners being held at Fort Anne. The Acadian asked that the details be written down so he could take them back to his camp, which was a long way off, and while that was being done he requested some *eau-de-vie* and tobacco to refresh his men. The British officer supplied it, and the other guerrillas came forward to drink and smoke.

They were "a raw, hardy, active, yet mean set of fellows," wrote Knox. One of them had decorated his hat with lace taken from a British soldier's uniform, and another carried a firelock and cartouche box inscribed with the insignia of Knox's 43rd Regiment. How dare they "presume to come before us with our spoils about them?" Knox angrily inquired in French, but the Acadians "gave no answer other than an impertinent shrug." Receiving the paper with the terms, their leader gave the word to depart. When might he expect a reply? asked the British officer. "Gentlemen, we have a great way to go, and beg we may be permitted to depart," the Acadian replied in French, and "as to such of your people who have fallen into our hands, we took as much care of them as we have done of ourselves." Thanking the British for their civility, the Acadians bid adieu and quickly disappeared into the woods. Eventually the hostages were released.[13]

During the first two years of the Seven Years War—1756 and 1757—the French held the advantage in North America, turning back British offensives and winning important victories at Fort Oswego on Lake Ontario and Fort William Henry on Lake Champlain. But in 1758 the fighting turned in the British favor. The change was the consequence of a massive commitment of blood and treasure by William Pitt, the leader of the House of Commons, who became colonial minister in 1757. Pitt's first great success came at Louisbourg. In the spring of 1758, ten British ships of the line, as well as a fleet of transports carrying two regiments, assembled before the fortress for an assault under the command of Major General Jeffrey Amherst. With considerable good luck—and considerable French ineptitude—British forces led by Brigadier General James Wolfe made a successful landing on 8 June 1758 and began a siege of the fortress a few days later.

Anticipating the British assault, Governor-General Vaudreuil of New France attempted to marshal his forces, and as one part of that defense he ordered Charles Deschamps de Boishébert to Louisbourg with his irregular force of Canadiens, Acadians, and Míkmaq, to lend support in whatever way he could. Boishébert led his guerrillas in a number of harassing raids against British lines which had absolutely no impact on the outcome of the battle. But the departure of Boishébert's guerrillas left the Acadians still living west of Chipoudy Bay vulnerable to British attack. At the beginning of July, a large force of rangers from Fort Cumberland sailed up rivière Petitcodiac in an armed sloop, and near the river's bend—at the site of today's city of Moncton, New Brunswick—decoyed a company of guerrillas into an ambush. The Acadians were driven into the river. Many drowned; others were killed and scalped. One of many horrific encounters, this one was memorable because it was the first successful British foray in the area since Major Frye's defeat in September 1755, and because the defeated guerrillas were under the command of Joseph Broussard himself, who was seriously wounded in the engagement. Not long afterward, the Acadians who had been at Louisbourg with Boishébert returned with news that the French fortress had fallen and the British had refused the defenders the honors of war. The entire garrison were to be incarcerated as prisoners of war. The articles of capitulation said nothing about the fate of the inhabitants of either Ile Royale or Ile Saint-Jean, but within days it became clear that the British intended to remove all of them, civilian as well as military.[14]

The conquest of Louisbourg inaugurated a second round of removals even more brutal than those of 1755. The inhabitants of Ile Saint-Jean knew that their situation was precarious, but there was relatively little they could do about it. "We had the time to evacuate the country, had that been possible," the island's commandant Gabriel Rousseau de Villejouin reported, "but Miramichi, which is the closest port, is without food supplies. Some of our inhabitants have gone there with their small boats and were forced to come back rather than expose themselves to dying of hunger." On 8 August, British Lieutenant-Colonel Andrew Rollo was ordered to the island with five hundred troops to demand the capitulation of the small French garrison and begin the process of deporting the inhabitants to France. There was no resistance. Rolo had expected to find four or five hundred persons, but as his troops began to gather the inhabitants and refugees, it became clear there were perhaps ten times that number. The first group of 692 persons, including French officials and their families, departed in two vessels on 31 August. By 5 November, when a fleet of nine transports left the island, approximately 3,100 had been shipped off. An unknown number of Acadians—perhaps as many as fifteen hundred—succeeded in making their way to the island's northern shore, where they were picked up by French schooners and ferried to Baie des Chaleurs or Québec. Joseph Leblanc dit Le Maigre and the brothers Pierre and Joseph Gautier played important roles in assisting these Acadians to escape. Several hundred inhabitants remained in hiding in the interior, where for the next several years they lived off stray livestock and wild game on the island.[15]

The Acadians from Ile Saint-Jean began arriving at the Atlantic ports of France in November. "They are nearly naked," reported an official in Cherbourg, "the English having stripped them of everything." These exiles were the lucky ones, for the majority of those deported in 1758 failed to survive the passage. The best estimate is that of 3,100 persons who embarked from Ile Saint-Jean, at least 1,649 died en route to France. British and French registers of arriving transports record the loss of 780 persons from exposure or disease. In addition, at least three vessels wrecked or sank with deadly consequences. One hundred and thirteen Acadians drowned when the transport *Ruby* ran aground in the Azores, and two large vessels, *Duke William* and *Violet*, went down in the mid-Atlantic with the loss of an estimated 756 exiles. *Duke William* was carrying abbé Jacques Girard and many Acadians from his parish, who had fled with him from Cobequid to Ile Saint-Jean in 1753. Among those who died were several extended families, including that of the elderly Nöel Dorion and his wife Marie Henry, along with five of their married children and their spouses, more than thirty of their grandchildren, and scores of their affinal relations. Abbé Girard survived in one of the two lifeboats that carried the captain and crew to safety. "Against the maritime laws," he wrote after his return to France, the captain "abandoned the passengers to the fury of the waters." But Girard himself was scorned by clerical colleagues for the rest of his life for having saved himself and abandoned his flock.[16]

The roundup on Ile Saint-Jean was part of a general British campaign during the summer and fall of 1758 to eliminate the least possibility of resistance along the shores of the Gulf of St. Lawrence in anticipation of the assault on Québec, planned for the following year. After establishing naval control of the Gulf, General Wolfe struck the Canadien settlements of the Gaspé Peninsula, while Wolfe's subordinate, Colonel James Murray, attacked the Acadian and Míkmaq camps at Miramichi Bay. Murray's troops found few refugees, but captured stragglers reported they had fled in starving condition. The British spent several days hunting them with no success, and contented themselves with burning "provisions, wigwams and houses," as well as a handsome stone chapel at a site on the bay's northern coast, a community known ever since as Burnt Church. "I am persuaded there is not now a French man in the River Miramichi," Murray reported to Wolfe; but after he and his troops departed, the Acadians and Míkmaq returned and quickly rebuilt their encampments.[17]

Considerably more devastating were the coordinated British attacks on the Acadian hamlets along rivières Petiticodiac and Saint-Jean later that fall and winter. "Let all the Neutral French houses, barns and mass houses that escaped the flames in 1755 be burnt in 1758," advised one British intelligence agent familiar with the northern shore of Fundy. Amherst issued the orders for the assaults. "The success of these expeditions," he wrote Monckton, "will effectively secure to His Majesty's subjects of Nova Scotia a quiet possession of their settlements."[18]

In November, Major George Scott and several hundred men from Fort Cumberland sailed up the Petitcodiac in a number of armed vessels, encountering almost no resistance as they laid waste to the countryside. Like Murray, Scott had a difficult time finding Acadians, but his troops burned houses, killed livestock, and destroyed crops at dozens of hamlets, including Beausoleil, home to the Broussards. Simultaneously, Colonel Monckton, in command of two thousand men, ascended the Saint-Jean, leaving a swath of destruction on both sides of the river, although he too succeeded in capturing few inhabitants. He remedied that by returning two months later in command of a force of New England rangers with orders to "kill and give no quarter." They burned the hamlets at Sainte-Anne des Pays-Bas (near today's Fredericton, New Brunswick), killing and scalping scores of Acadians, including women and children. Even General Amherst was disgusted by the indiscriminate violence at Sainte-Anne, writing to Lawrence, "I shall always disapprove of killing women and helpless children." With these devastating raids the Acadians lost control of the districts that had played a role in providing food for the refugees, and as a result hundreds starved during the subsequent winter of 1758–59. "Here I see only the greatest distress and poverty," the missionary Pierre Maillard wrote from Miramichi. "All the families who have come over to us are starving."

The guerrillas would continue to fight in 1759, but their struggle looked increasingly hopeless. It was the beginning of the end.[19]

ANTICIPATING an end to the guerrilla resistance, in October 1758 Governor Charles Lawrence published a proclamation in Boston, New York, and Philadelphia announcing that the former lands of the Acadians would soon become available for resettlement. With "the late success of His Majesty's Arms," Lawrence declared, "the Enemy—who have formerly disturbed and harrassed the Province of Nova Scotia and much obstructed its Progress—have been compelled to retire and take Refuge in Canada." That had created "a favourable Opportunity for the peopling and cultivating [of] the Lands vacated by the French," and his government stood "ready to receive any Proposals that may hereafter be made to him for effectually settling the said vacated or other Lands in that Province."[20]

This announcement had been a long time coming, delayed not only by the deadly contest for control of the countryside going on in the province but by the absence of civil government. Immediately after the expulsion of 1755, Governor Shirley of Massachusetts put Governor Lawrence on notice that the "repeopling" of the Acadian lands by settlers from New England would not be possible until his military administration was replaced with a regular civil establishment, including an elected assembly. The Board of Trade also urged Lawrence to empower and convene an assembly, but for better than two years he resisted, unwilling to cede any of his authority. Preoccupied with the war, the board allowed Lawrence to decide the matter. In early 1758, however, the Colonial Office in London received an angry petition from a group of influential Halifax merchants who were chafing under Lawrence's tight enforcement of the maritime laws. Describing themselves as "the Slaves of Nova Scotia" and "the Creatures of Military Governors whose Will is our Law and whose Person is our God," they charged Lawrence with running a corrupt military administration and blocking their "inherent right" to an elected assembly. Their petition gained the board's attention and it ordered Lawrence to immediately execute plans for an assembly. He did as he was told, and in May 1758 the Governor's Council passed an enabling act and issued a call for elections.[21]

The first session of the Nova Scotia Assembly, which convened in October 1758, passed a series of laws intended to institutionalize Acadian dispossession. The "Act for the quieting of Possessions to Protestant grantees of the Lands formerly occupied by the French Inhabitants," declared ex post facto that from the time of the signing of the Treaty of Utrecht in 1713 until their dispossession in 1755, the Acadians had possessed no legal title to the lands they occupied, and that any rights they had supposedly acquired by prescription, transfer, or concession had been extinguished by the council's decision to remove them. The "Act for the establishment of religious public Worship" proclaimed the Church of England as the "fixed form of worship," and while providing rights for dissenting Protestants, it excluded Catholics from the franchise or public office and banned all Catholic clergy from the province. Another act prohibited Catholics from owning land, and empowered authorities to seize any and all "papist" property for the benefit of the crown. These laws—passed by a popular assembly, not enacted by military fiat—laid the foundation for the migration of the Protestant settlers Lawrence hoped to encourage with his 1758 proclamation.[22]

His announcement generated considerable interest in New England. Three months later, in January 1759, Lawrence issued a second proclamation with more specific details. The former Acadian districts of Annapolis, Minas, and Chignecto—100,000 acres of plowland and another 100,000 acres of pasture, orchard, and garden lands—were to be divided into townships, and granted in plots varying in size according to the ability of grantees to enclose and cultivate the land. Heads of families were entitled to receive up to 1,000 acres free of quitrents for the first ten years. Moreover, Lawrence added, "no Taxes have hitherto been laid upon His Majesty's subjects within this Province, nor are there any fees of office taken upon issuing Grants of Land." He believed this point would appeal especially to the residents of New England, whose taxes "are become intolerably burdensome by the War." Other details made it clear that Lawrence was particularly targeting New Englanders, with a long tradition of looking eastward. The Nova Scotia Assembly, he noted, had passed legislation providing religious freedom for all Protestants, who could build their own meetinghouses and choose their own ministers, and had created governmental institutions "constituted like those of the neighboring colonies." This last statement ignored Lawrence's long opposition to civilian government in the province, and the fact that he was at that moment in the midst of a protracted struggle with the Assembly over the extent of local self-government.[23]

The greatest interest in emigration indeed did come from southern New England, where land was in short supply and where numerous residents had direct experience in l'Acadie, either as sailors or soldiers. Numerous public meetings took place over the winter and early spring of 1759, and in April a group of leaders from New London, representing potential settlers in Connecticut and Rhode Island, sailed to Halifax to meet with Lawrence and the council. They were escorted to Minas at government expense and given a guided tour by surveyor-general Charles Morris. They spend several days studying the topography and soil at Grand Pré and Pisiquid and were delighted with what they found. The hay was growing thick and tall on the wide marshes, and around the blackened ruins of the former Acadian homesteads the apple trees were in full bloom. Returning to Halifax, they negotiated an arrangement with a council eager to move ahead. The agents agreed to settle five hundred families on three sites—on rivière Habitant in western Minas; at the "Great Marsh" (Grand Pré); and on the west side of the Pisiquid River, which the council christened as the townships of Cornwallis, Horton, and Falmouth, respectively. The government agreed to pay the cost of the emigrants' transportation from New England and provide them with subsistence for the first year. Once news of these liberal terms spread, other agents appeared in Halifax; during the spring and summer, the council made additional agreements with groups from Massachusetts and Connecticut to settle families on the Annapolis River (Annapolis and Granville townships) and at Cobequid (Truro and Onslow).[24]

Perhaps the most coveted tract in the province was the triangle of fertile marshland between the Pisiquid and Saint-Croix rivers, with Fort Edward at its apex. That was the tract nearest to Halifax, and in August the council set it aside for grants to many of the men directly involved in the removal operation of 1755. This so-called Councilors' Grant distributed more than 60,000 acres to some fifty grantees. Seven thousand acres they allotted to themselves (including large grants to surveyor-general Morris and Chief Justice Jonathan Belcher); 4,500 acres went to a group of lesser officials; and numerous smaller parcels to other favorites, including Isaac Deschamps and Moses Delesdernier, men who had assisted the removal operation at Minas. Renamed the township of Windsor, the district became the special preserve of government officers, who had the land worked by hired laborers or tenant farmers, and used it themselves as a bucolic retreat.[25]

The settlement of the "planters," as the New England settlers came to be known, was intended as the concluding chapter of the great and noble scheme of removal. By the end of the summer of 1759 the new system of land ownership was largely in place and the provincial government had in hand agreements for the settling of more than 2,500 Protestant families in nine townships. "Every acre of cleared land in the province," Lawrence wrote the Board of Trade, "will be well peopled sooner than heretofore has been conceived to be possible." The troublesome Neutral French had been dispossessed and their communities destroyed. The vacant lands were to be repossessed, parceled out to loyal Protestants in new configurations and under new names. His report was happily received in London. In a letter to the king, the Earl of Halifax, first lord commissioner of the board, offered a final judgment on the events that had taken place since 1755. The expulsion of the Acadians, he wrote to George II, had made available "vast quantities of the most fertile land in an actual state of cultivation, and in those parts of the Province the most advantageously situated for commerce." Although resettlement had been delayed by the "incursions and cruelties of the French and Indians, with which this Province has continually been harassed," he was greatly satisfied to report that "the zealous endeavours of your Governor have at length been crowned with a success greatly beyond our expectations and almost equal to our wishes."[26]

THE actual arrival of the planters was contingent on the pacification of the countryside. But in spite of the terrible defeats they suffered in 1758, Acadian and Míkmaw resistance continued into 1759, although that resistance took on an increasingly desperate character. They were forced to devote much of their attention to the theft of provisions. "These land ruffians, turned pirates, have had the hardiness to fit out shallops to cruise on our coast," Lawrence reported. "Sixteen or seventeen vessels, some of them very valuable, have already fallen into their hands." Guerrilla attacks degenerated into pure terrorism. In the winter of 1759, five British soldiers on patrol were ambushed while crossing a bridge near Fort Cumberland. They were scalped and their bodies horribly mutilated. "Never was greater or more wanton barbarity perpetrated," wrote John Knox. "Their limbs were horridly distorted, truly expressive of the agonies in which they died, and in this manner they froze, not unlike figures or statues which are variously displayed on pedestals in the gardens of the curious." The British in the maritime region would long remember "Bloody Bridge," which became a warrant for further atrocities. That spring Acadian and Míkmaw guerrillas killed several persons near Dartmouth, fired on New Englanders inspecting land near Cape Sable, and made threatening demonstrations before Fort Edward at Pisiquid. By July, the council had decided that with such "numerous and aggressive" actions, the arrival of the first planters would be best postponed until the spring of 1760.[27]

By that point British forces were already bombarding the city of Québec. Through the spring of 1759 they had assembled nine thousand troops and a fleet of ships of the line described by one correspondent as "the finest squadron of His Majesty's ships that had ever yet appeared in North America," and in June these were brought up the St. Lawrence to begin the siege. Brigadier James Wolfe launched a bloody campaign against the inhabitants on both sides of the river, spreading a reign of terror that featured not only pillage and plunder but rape, murder, and indiscriminate scalping. In mid-September, after many failed attempts to land his forces to assault the city, Wolfe and his men succeeded in scaling the cliffs upriver and deploying before Québec's walls. General Louis-Joseph de Montcalm brought his army out to engage them. A force of Acadian volunteers under Boishébert's command took part in the battle on the Plains of Abraham in which the French were defeated and both Wolfe and Montcalm killed. Following the capitulation of the city on 18 September 1759, Brigadier François-Gaston de Lévis, who succeeded to command of the French forces, sent Boishébert and his men back to Baie des Chaleurs with orders to recruit more Acadians for the final defense of Canada.[28]

Upon his return, however, Boishébert found that with the news of Québec's fall the spirit had gone out of the Acadian resistance. In October, General Edward Whitmore, British governor at Louisbourg, issued a proclamation offering the Acadian refugees an "olive branch." If they surrendered peaceably, he was "ordered by His Majesty to assure you that you will continue in the enjoyment of all your goods, the freedom of your property, with the free exercise of your religion." If they refused, however, he would "replace the white flag of peace with a red flag of war." *Guerre mortelle*—"fighting under the red flag"—was war without mercy: no quarter, no prisoners, no ransom. "I will not be responsible for the cruelties my people will unleash, once it is decided to resolve matters with the sword." There were two salient facts about this offer. Certainly the British threat was credible, as the recent campaigns at rivière Saint-Jean and the

Canadian countryside clearly demonstrated. And the offer of "the freedom of your property, with the free exercise of your religion" was a substantial concession. At Miramichi a delegation of Acadian leaders asked abbé Jacques Manach, a missionary priest ministering to the Míkmaq, to act as an intermediary for them in negotiations with the British. "We wish to surrender," they told him. "We have reached our limits." They had their doubts whether the terms of General Whitmore's offer were genuine, but they believed it would "allow us to complain if [the British] stray from what has been promised us." Had Québec not fallen, abbé Maillard wrote, the refugees might have continued for a while longer the "vagabond, miserable life" they had been living. In his opinion, Whitmore's proclamation laid out "good and reasonable" terms for a surrender.[29]

On 16 November 1759, a delegation of Acadian leaders from the Petitcodiac and Memramcook valleys appeared at Fort Cumberland under a flag of truce. Joseph and Alexandre Broussard dit Beausoleil, Jean Basque, and Simon Martin wished to accept Whitmore's terms. Their people "were in a miserable condition for want of provisions, having not more among them all than could (by most prudent use) keep more than two-thirds of their number alive till spring." They begged Commander Joseph Frye, then in command of the fort, to allow the most vulnerable of the refugees—the children and the elderly—to remain at the fort through the winter. The rest of them would come in peaceably in the spring. Frye agreed, keeping Alexandre Broussard hostage against their surrender. "There was no danger," he wrote Lawrence, "since their Canada is taken from them." Two days later another delegation of Acadian leaders came in, and surrendered in the name of several hundred refugees living in camps along the North Shore. Frye pledged to provision them and to obtain on their behalf "the best conditions permissible under the Constitution of the British Government for subjects in such situations." Mass surrenders also took place at British Fort Frederick on rivière Saint-Jean, including a group of Acadian refugees who had made their way seven hundred miles overland from Québec. Producing certificates attesting that they had taken the oath of allegiance there, they applied to the commandant for permission to return to their lands along the river.[30]

When he learned of these surrenders, Boishébert was livid. From his base at the small Canadien military post of Petit-Rochelle, situated at the mouth of the Restigouche River on Baie des Chaleurs, he sent an angry letter to abbé Manach. "I cannot imagine the reasons that have guided you," he wrote, unless "it is the independence that those of your condition wish to preserve for yourselves, or your desire to return to the despotism your predecessors enjoyed over l'Acadie." This barely veiled reference to abbé Le Loutre was made even clearer several lines later. "If we are now in a war that has made the Acadians miserable, remember that it was the priests who were the cause." Jean-François Bourdon de Dombourg, commander at Petit-Rochelle, wrote, castigating the leaders of the refugees on the North Shore. "Where is that zeal for your *patrie*, that staunch devotion to religion? What of so many years of fasting and of escapes across the woods, exposed to a thousand dangers?" He was disgusted with them. "Like stunned fools you have thrown yourselves into a bag of trickery." The British would treat them "with contempt," he warned, "and they will have reason to do so."[31]

A number of Acadian resistance leaders shared those sentiments and dissociated themselves from the leaders who had surrendered. Abbé Maillard criticized the stubbornness and obstinacy of those die-hards. "It is necessary to know how to accommodate oneself to times, to persons, and to places," he wrote one of them. He was simultaneously attempting to arrange a truce for the Míkmaq.[32]

Maillard saw no alternative to surrender; but as the date for the surrender of the guerrillas approached, abbé Manach began to have doubts about the good faith of the British. Many of the refugees had difficulty believing the assurances in General Whitmore's proclamation, he wrote Frye, and feared they would be deported when they surrendered. In retrospect, he wondered about the meaning of Frye's promise to seek the best treatment for "subjects in such situations." Were the Acadians "true subjects," Manach wanted to know, or were they "quasi-subjects"? There was good reason for his concern. Lawrence and the council soon decided that despite Whitmore's promise, all the Acadians who surrendered would be removed from the province and transported to England. Whitmore himself seems to have regarded the assurances he made to the Acadians in the king's name as nothing but a ploy. He was in favor of "sending off these incendiaries," he wrote to Lawrence, arguing that the region would never be secure "while there is a French Inhabitant in the whole Country." The present duress of the Acadians "may oblige them to temporize for a season," but he believed "they will always keep alive their old prejudices by their arts and insinuations."[33]

The deportations began in the late winter at rivière Saint-Jean, and the news soon reached the Acadian refugees along the North Shore. The British had violated "the good faith of the agreements we made," abbé Manach wrote, and he concluded that Whitmore had issued his proclamation "the better to trick us." Many of the guerrillas, including Joseph Broussard and his lieutenants, vowed to continue their resistance, moving north to Boishébert's camp at Petit-Rochelle. Manach went with them, but had little hope. "Where can we travel without provisions, and how can we escape this enemy, who will cross the ice to come remove us?" All he could do was pray for the success of French arms.[34]

That was not to be. Although Brigadier Lévis, commander of the French forces in Canada, came close to dislodging the British from Québec in the spring of 1760, British naval superiority in the Gulf of the St. Lawrence cut him off from resupply and forced him to withdraw to Montréal. In July 1760, three French provision ships attempting to sail up the St. Lawrence were discovered by a British squadron in the Gulf. They sought refuge in Baie des Chaleurs but were pursued, and in a naval battle at the mouth of the Restigouche

River the British destroyed the French vessels as well as the Canadien post at Petit-Rochelle. Several hundred Acadian refugees were captured—Joseph Broussard and his men among them—and sent to Fort Cumberland. By summer's end, more than a thousand Acadians were incarcerated there. In Canada the fighting would continue for several months more before the final capitulation of French forces at Montréal. But for the Acadians, the war was over.[35]

CHAPTER 15

THE RAYS OF THE MORNING

End of the Removal Era, 1760–1785

IN JUNE 1760 A FLOTILLA of transports carrying several hundred New Englanders rounded Cape Blomidon, entered Minas Basin, and anchored in the estuary of the Gaspereau and Pisiquid rivers. From the beginning, the plan had been to remove the Acadians and settle good New England farmers in their room. These vessels carried some of the first of ten thousand Yankee settlers who over the course of the next decade would transform l'Acadie into an eastern extension of New England. The Acadians themselves were gone. Yet the first things the New Englanders saw upon their landing was the detritus of the old Acadian world. At Point de Boudrot, the Cornwallis planters were greeted by the abandoned oxcarts in which the inhabitants had hauled their goods to the landing five years before. The ground was littered with the bleached bones of abandoned livestock, and the blackened ruins of Acadian houses and barns stood along the cart paths. Then there were the dikes, the work that had made these lands so valuable in the first place. They were in a serious state of disrepair when the planters' agents inspected the area in the spring and summer of 1759, and that fall a great nor'easter slammed into the Bay of Fundy, producing a tidal surge that breeched the dikes and inundated the fields with salt water. When the planters arrived in the spring of 1760, they were immediately confronted with the problem of reclamation. The provincial assembly passed an act empowering proprietors to choose commissioners with the authority to repair and maintain the dikes, but few planters knew the first thing about them.[1]

Dikes meant Acadians, and so to repair and work the dikes the Acadians were brought back. Not as proprietors, but as proletarians. The mass surrenders and captures of the previous months had placed nearly two thousand Acadian refugees under British control, and in the summer of 1760, Governor Lawrence devised a scheme to put them to work as laborers on lands previously their own. It would prove to be his final contribution to the complicated history of removal, for in October 1760, after catching a cold that developed into something worse, perhaps pneumonia, Lawrence died suddenly and prematurely at the age of fifty-one. The Acadian labor program was carried forward by his successor and partner in the great and noble scheme of removal, Chief Justice Jonathan Belcher, who served as lieutenant-governor for the next three years. "The dikes may be put into very good condition," Belcher wrote the Board of Trade shortly after Lawrence's death, if "the French inhabitants may be employed in different parts of the province to instruct and assist . . . the new settlers, who are come from a country in which no such works are wanting."[2]

There was terrible irony here. Or perhaps it would be more accurate to describe it as an enduring contradiction. Acadians might be feared and they might be despised, but they possessed important skills and essential knowledge about the province's agricultural system without which the planters were helpers. From the beginning, the British had been haunted by the conflict between their desire to elminate the Acadians and their dependence upon them. This resulted in a particularly intense form of fear and loathing. Removing the inhabitants and replacing them with "good English farmers" fundamentally changed the relationships of power in the province. But in the short term it did not resolve the contradiction. Moses Delesdernier, a man who knew the Acadians well, and was one of the first of the new Protestant settlers to farm the diked marshland at Windsor (formerly Pisiquid), gave expression to these sentiments. Through generations of experience, he wrote, the Acadians had "acquired the knowledge of their great production of all sorts of grain, and the facility of obtaining great crops with little labour. . . . They sold great quantities of grain and cattle and were well supplied with every common necessary of life." In his view, they had squandered that advantage. "They did not labour more than half the time, the other half being chiefly taken up by their holidays." They were too French for their own good, and their dispossession was justifiable in the name of progress. But as much as the planters might scorn Acadian values, they still had to learn the ways in which the inhabitants had made the land work for them. And to do that, Delesdernier argued, they needed the Acadians as laborers.[3]

Belcher unabashedly represented the two sides of this contradiction. In the first place he asked military authorities to assist the planters by distributing the Acadian prisoners from Halifax and Fort Cumberland at Chignecto to Fort Edward at Minas and Fort Anne at Annapolis Royal, where they could be housed under guard and put to work maintaining the dikes. "It appears extremely necessary," he wrote to the military authorities, "that the [new] inhabitants should be assisted by the Acadians in repairing the dikes for the preservation and recovery of the marshlands, particularly as the progress of this work, in which the Acadians are the most skillful people in the Country, the support and subsistence of several hundred of the inhabitants will depend." General Jeffrey Amherst approved the plan, and through the middle of the decade the British military kept several hundred Acadian families imprisoned in the province so that they might serve as a ready labor force for the New England planters.

But Belcher also sought Amherst's authorization to deport those same people when the appropriate moment arrived. Although the Acadian prisoners might be submissive, he warned, they nursed an intense bitterness and hatred as they worked the lands that once had been theirs. "They have not yet lost hopes of regaining them," Belcher wrote Amherst, and "I think it at least probable that they will disturb the beginning of these settlements." The slightest outbreak of violence might frighten the planters back to New England and delay the progressive development of the province. Belcher wanted carte blanche to deport troublemakers immediately and all the remaining Acadians once the planters had learned how to maintain and manage the dikes on their own. But Amherst would not agree. Belcher's government had nothing to fear from the Acadians, he wrote in the spring of 1761. In fact, he thought, "great Advantages might be reapt in employing them properly." No doubt the Acadians harbored resentments, but "they can hardly be mad enough to attempt anything against the Establishment of the Province at this time."[4]

Amherst had led a British army up the Hudson River–Lake Champlain corridor the year before, defeated the French at Montréal, and in September he accepted Governor-General Vaudreuil's surrender of New France. He enjoyed the confidence of a conqueror. But there had been no such stunning victory in Nova Scotia. Although the resistance had been smashed and the Acadian refugees incarcerated, the British remained dependent on the former inhabitants. The Míkmaq had signed treaties agreeing to submit peacefully to British authority "for as long as the Sun and Moon shall endure," and had retired to coastal territories in the north, guaranteed to them in perpetuity by Governor Belcher. Yet they continued to live with all of their former independence.[5]

Thus, when French naval and ground forces staged a minor counterattack in July 1762—seizing the strategically insignificant port of St. John's in Newfoundland and holding it for a few weeks before losing it again to the British—government officials at Halifax flew into panic, fearing an uprising. Belcher ordered the Míkmaq to vacate their coastal communities and relocate in the interior, away from potential contact with the French. They lost the lands they had been promised and were left with nothing more than ten small reserves. Similarly, when reports reached Halifax that Acadian laborers had "assumed fresh courage and began to be insolent to the settlers in the townships where they were at work, telling them that they should soon regain possession of their lands and cut every one of their throats," Belcher declared martial law and ordered all able-bodied male Acadians marched to Halifax under military guard. Once they were locked up on George's Island, the provincial assembly passed a resolution calling for their immediate deportation. "These people," the resolution read, "seeing the English daily in possession and enjoyment of the lands forfeited, and formerly occupied by them, will forever regret their loss, and consequently will lay hold of every favourable opportunity for regaining them, at any, even the most hazardous risk." What the expropriators feared most was their own expropriation. The resolution was endorsed by the council, which declared that the Acadian prisoners "should be transported to Boston," and on 18 August 1762—with their wives and children still imprisoned at Annapolis, Minas, and Chignecto—six hundred men were sent off in five transports.[6]

Six weeks later, the same vessels returned to Halifax with the prisoners. Massachusetts had refused to accept them, its government declaring that they had done more than their share in supporting and maintaining the Acadians sent in 1755. Belcher was outraged, and requested a ruling from the Board of Trade. It did not arrive until the spring of 1763, by which time the war in North America and Europe had formally concluded in the Peace of Paris, France ceding to Great Britain its territory in Canada and the maritime region, with the exception of the small islands of St. Pierre and Miquelon in the Gulf of St. Lawrence, which the French were allowed to keep as fishing stations. The treaty provided all inhabitants of the ceded lands—and by implication the Acadians—the right to leave British territory for "wherever they shall think proper."

In light of all this, the board declared, the expulsion of the remnant population of Acadians from Nova Scotia had been "neither necessary nor politic." Removal had been justified in 1755, the board reasoned, because the French fleet posed an immediate threat to the province. But "that danger is now over." In the aftermath of the war the task was to find a way to integrate the Acadians as useful members of provincial society, albeit as hewers of wood and drawers of water rather than as proprietors of the soil.[7]

Concluding that Belcher's handling of this and other matters had been less than sterling, the board dismissed him from his post as lieutenant-governor (although he retained the position of chief justice). Yet Belcher's successor, Montagu Wilmot, former commandant at Fort Cumberland, continued the same policy. Despite the guarantees of the Peace of Paris, the Acadians in Nova Scotia—more than seventeen hundred persons at the beginning of 1764—remained incarcerated. They continued to labor on the dikes for the planters. They were defenseless and easily exploited. They were paid low wages, which they used to provide their own subsistence. Sometimes they were not paid at all. It was hardly surprising that they were often surly and uncooperative, or that the planters were plagued by the nightmare that they would rise up in fury. Even as planters grew increasingly dependent on Acadian labor, Governor Wilmot continued to advocate their deportation to some distant location. "It cannot be expected," he wrote the Board of Trade, "that these people can submit with cheerfulness, many of whom earn their daily bread on those very lands which were formerly in their own possession."[8]

Once the treaty of peace was ratified on 10 February 1763, the French government made plans to repatriate the Acadian exiles who had spent the war years in England. The French ambassador in London, Louis-Jules Barbon Mancini Mazarani, duc de Nivernois, made contact with the leaders of the prisoners, pledging that he would "take immediate steps to remove you to France." Late in the spring, 778

Acadians were transported from prisons in England to the ports of Saint-Malo and Morlaix in Brittany, where they joined the Acadian exiles deported to France in 1758. Seven years before, 1,225 Acadians had arrived in England. That frightful decline in their number offered compelling evidence of the horrible conditions in which the prisoners had been forced to live. In fact the raw numbers considerably understate the horror. Life had gone on during exile. Young people continued to marry, couples continued to bear children, and population growth needs to be factored into the casualty figures. In the years prior to 1755, Acadian population had been growing at the annual rate of approximately 3.5 percent. Over seven years that rate of growth compounds to an increase of 27 percent, which means that under normal conditions the 1,225 Acadians shipped to England might have been expected to increase to some 1,550 by 1763. Conditions were hardly normal for prisoners at Bristol, Falmouth, Southampton, and Liverpool. Mortality rates soared, especially the mortality of infants and children, and undernourished women must have suffered many miscarriages. The English imprisonment must have cost the lives of seven or eight hundred persons.[9]

Arriving in France, the exiles from England immediately forwarded copies of Nivernois's letter to relatives in the British North American colonies, and it spread quickly through the exile communities. By the fall, French authorities had in hand reports from nearly every group of Acadians in the British colonies. "We have received a copy of the letter that you sent to our brothers who are prisoners in England," wrote the leaders of the Pennsylvania exiles, "from which we are informed that His Most Christian Majesty wishes to relieve us from our slavery which we have been held in since the beginning of the war with England." Most of them resided in Philadelphia, they reported, their numbers reduced by smallpox and other diseases, and they sent a roll with the names of 383 persons. The Acadians in Maryland provided a list of 810 persons dispersed at several locations throughout the colony, although the greatest number were concentrated in a section of Baltimore known as Frenchtown, where "the robust ones worked as laborers, and the old and sick eke out a living by begging." The exiles in South Carolina wrote to report their number at 280. They pleaded for French protection and assistance in finding their children, who had been bound out by the authorities, many not seen or heard from for years.[10]

These reports, and others like them from Georgia, New York, Connecticut, and Massachusetts, included the most precise count of the Acadians since 1755, and make it possible to assess the toll exacted by removal. Approximately 7,000 Acadians were deported in 1755, although Virginia immediately sent its contingent of 1,200 to England, and Georgia and South Carolina allowed 800 or 900 to depart by vessel, reducing the number remaining in the British colonies by the summer of 1756 to something less than 5,000. According to the reports of Acadian exiles themselves in 1763, their number had fallen to a total of 3,616 persons. Using pre-deportation growth rates, the exile population in the British colonies should have been at least 6,350 in 1763, suggesting the loss of more than 2,700 lives. For the Acadians who had remained in the maritime region—those who successfully avoided the first deportation and became refugees, suffering through seven years of warfare, exposure, and starvation, as well as a second round of deportations—the toll was even higher. During the winter of 1755–56, an estimated 11,000 refugees were living west of Chipoudy Bay, along the North Shore, or on Ile Saint-Jean. By 1763, their numbers had been reduced to approximately 4,000—6,000 if the survivors of the 1758 deportation to the Atlantic ports of France are included. That number ought to have grown to about 14,000, which would mean a loss of some 8,000 lives.[11]

Had the deportation not taken place, had the Acadian community been allowed to grow at its normal pace, the 1755 population of 18,500 would have risen to more than 23,000 by 1763. Instead, it had fallen to about 10,000. While some of the loss must have come from lowered rates of reproduction, most of it would have been from high levels of mortality. It is likely that some 10,000 Acadians—the majority of them probably infants and children—lost their lives as a direct result of the campaign of removal from 1755 to 1763.[12]

WHEN the Acadian exiles in the British colonies learned that the French had repatriated the prisoners held in England, they assumed that the offer extended to them as well. Abandoning the interior towns, they flocked to the ports on the Atlantic, hoping to arrange passage to France. "Ever since the English dispersed us from our lands," the leaders of the Philadelphia exile community wrote to French authorities, "we have desired to return to France or one of the French colonies where we again may enjoy all the liberties concerning our religion." They wished to know when the vessels would arrive. The leaders of the Acadians imprisoned at Halifax gave voice to the prevailing enthusiasm. "Your letter was for us like the rays of the morning after a stormy night," they wrote to Ambassador Nivernois. "It announced the approaching day of our delivery." They petitioned Governor Wilmot to provide them with vessels and provisions, "since peace is made, and since all prisoners, from whatever place they may be, are given up." They required passage to France, "in order that the supplicants may prove to their prince how devoted they are to his service, and how ready they are to sacrifice, not only their own lives, but the lives of their women and children, to testify their zeal and love for their country." These words seemed intended to infuriate Wilmot, and may have been written by Acadian militants associated with the Broussards. The governor reacted predictably, ordering that the leaders be confined for "traitorous practices." The Acadians, of course, were already in military custody.[13]

The British government protested what they characterized as French plans for "the seduction and secret removal of these His Majesty's Subjects." The French ambassador quickly responded that it had all been a misunderstanding, that his invitation had been intended for the exiles in England only, not those in North America, and that his government had no intention "of interfering with respect to the removal of the Acadians." Yet the incident had a lasting effect, for it convinced the Board of Trade of the need to clarify the status of the Acadians in the British Empire. Taking up the question, the Privy Council resolved that rather than forcing these potentially valuable subjects to relocate to French territory, it would be much preferable to keep them. If the Acadians, in spite of their "having taken up arms in support of France during the late war," would now take the oath of allegiance, they could "become settlers under His Majesty's government" and allowed to locate in places "agreeable to themselves." If they declined, they could exercise their right, under the terms of the peace treaty, to remove themselves "out of His Majesty's Dominions." Governor Wilmot was so instructed, and on 28 September 1764, he presented this policy to his council. For the most passionate advocates of Acadian removal, including Wilmot himself, the fact that the Acadians would be allowed to remain in the province was a bitter pill. But having no choice in the matter, he and the council took their medicine, and issued a proclamation addressed to the former inhabitants: "The King has decreed that he wishes to make it possible for French Acadians to remain in this Province, provided they take an oath of fidelity and obedience to his government." It would be another four years before the provincial government did much of anything to encourage Acadians to remain in Nova Scotia; but this proclamation marked the formal end of the campaign of removal that had begun in 1755.[14]

Outside the maritime region, nearly all the exiles chose to migrate to French territory. In 1764 most of the Acadians in Georgia and South Carolina, a total of about five hundred persons, chartered vessels and left for the colony of Saint Domingue (today's Haiti), where the French colonial governor had promised them "land and sustenance until they became self-sufficient." Soon they were joined by several hundred more from Pennsylvania, New York, Connecticut, and Massachusetts, and in 1766 by a smaller group from France. The authorities sent most of them to the settlement of Môle Saint Nicolas, on the coast about one hundred miles northwest of Port-au-Prince. Relatives and old neighbors were overjoyed at being reunited under French authority. The military commander of the settlement described a celebration that took place soon after the arrival of the first large group. Four hundred men, women, and children assembled under a makeshift arbor to consume a barbeque of wild boar. They offered toasts to the French officers, the commissary, the intendant, and the king. "They danced, the old and young alike, all dancing to a fast step," until late into the evening. But the joy was short-lived. The land was poor and the provisions inadequate. Many Acadians came down with yellow fever or malaria, and by the end of the year a third of them had perished. The French governor, who came to investigate, found them living without shelter, many too sick to work. "The worst criminal would prefer the galleys," he wrote, "rather than stay in this horrible place."[15]

Despite negative reports filtering back to North America, the idea of relocating to Saint Domingue held great attraction for the Acadians in the maritime region, largely because Governor Wilmot and the council made it as difficult as possible for them to remain. Those Acadians who took the oath, Wilmot announced, would be required to settle in the interior of the province, and in groups no larger than two or three families. In November 1764, a large group of six hundred persons, led by Joseph and Alexandre Broussard dit Beausoleil, hired vessels and departed for the West Indies. Other groups announced their intention of following once they raised sufficient funds. Although Acadians were paid very little for their labor on the dikes, they were very good at accumulating what was necessary to pay for their passage out of the province.[16]

Wilmot was delighted by this turn of events. "Thus, my Lords," he wrote the Board of Trade, "we are in the way of being relieved from these people, who have been the bane of the Province and the terror of its settlement. Their settlement in the West Indies removes them far from us, and as that Climate is mortal to the natives of the Northern countries, the French will not likely to gain any considerable advantage from them." Many planters in the old Acadian districts, however, saw things quite differently. "The French Acadians who have hitherto been station'd in this county have been of great use as labourers," a group of Minas planters wrote to Wilmot, "particularly in the repairing and making dikes, a work which they are accustomed to, and experienced in. And we find that without their further assistance many of us cannot continue our improvements, nor plough nor sowe our Lands, nor finish the dikeing still required to secure our Lands from salt water." They asked the governor to do what he could to encourage the Acadians to remain in the province by continuing to provide them with provisions, which enabled the planters to hire them "at much lower wages . . . which will tend greatly to the encouragement and success of these infant settlements." But Governor Wilmot remained unmoved.[17]

The group of six hundred Acadians from Halifax—including every living relative of Joseph and Alexandre Broussard, as well as the families of many of their associates in the Acadian resistance—arrived in Saint Domingue in January 1765. But the Broussards had no intention of remaining there. They soon hired another vessel, and with 193 Acadians continued on to New Orleans, which seems to have been their intended destination. "By the best information I can obtain of their purposes," Governor Wilmot had written a few days before the group's departure from Halifax, "they intend going directly to Cape François [in Saint Domingue], from thence to the Mississippi, and finally to the Country of the Illinois and there to make a settlement." Perhaps the Broussards indeed planned to lead their group up the Mississippi to the Illinois country, or perhaps Wilmot simply conflated Illinois with greater Louisiana, of which it was a part. Louisiana had long been a French colony. But in 1762, in exchange for Spain's entrance into the war against Great Britain, France had secretly ceded the territory to the Spanish crown, although French officials would remain in a caretaker capacity until 1766. When the Broussards and their associates arrived in New Orleans, those officials presented them with an opportunity to own land and raise cattle at Poste des Attakapas, a developing frontier station west of New Orleans on the verge of a treeless prairie. If there was ever any thought of Illinois, it was quickly forgotten. The Broussards and their associates accepted the offer.[18]

Acting Louisiana governor Charles Philippe Aubry welcomed Joseph Broussard as a French hero. "In view of the proofs of valor, fidelity, and attachment in the service of the king, which the herein named Joseph Broussard, surnamed Beausoleil, Acadian, has given on different occasions, and of the honorable testimonials which the Marquis of Vaudreuil and other Governors General of Canada have accorded him in consideration of his worth and of his character which he has given proof of in different efforts against the enemies of His Majesty," read the commission Aubry signed on 8 April 1765, "We appoint him Captain of Militia and Commandant of the Acadians who have come with him." This satisfying honor turned out to be the capstone of Broussard's life. Soon after the Acadians arrived at Attakapas, they were devasted by an epidemic of an unknown origin that claimed many lives. In September, Alexandre Broussard was struck down, and on 20 October, a Jesuit missionary recorded the death of his brother Joseph "at the camp known as Beausoleil."[19]

The two men had traveled a great distance from their birthplace along the Annapolis River early in the century. Long the leaders of the opposition to British rule, they had been unable to resist the campaign of removal. But they had successfully begun the tranplantation of a way of life from the meadows of l'Acadie to the prairies of Louisiana. By the end of the decade Attakapas was home to a growing population of Acadians, three quarters of whom had originated at Chignecto or Chipoudy Bay, where raising livestock had been an economic mainstay. It is not surprising that these people were drawn to the prairie region, and that they immediately turned to herding. The sons of Alexandre and Joseph Broussard were soon driving cattle to market in New Orleans, just as their fathers had driven cattle to ports on the northern coast of Chignecto.

Unlike the French project to settle Acadians on Saint Domingue, there was no official sponsorship of this migration to Louisiana. It was a plan developed entirely by Acadians themselves. The spark seems to have been struck by a small group of four families who preceded the Broussards by a full year. Their history tells a typical yet remarkable story of Acadian separation and reunion. In 1755, Jean-Baptiste Cormier and his wife Marie-Madeleine Richard, formerly inhabitants of Beaubassin, were deported to Georgia with their four daughters; but their unmarried son, Jean-Baptiste the younger, escaped the roundup and joined the resistance forces northwest of Chipoudy Bay, fighting under the command of the Broussards. The Cormiers went to Georgia in the company of three closely related couples and their children: Marie-Madeleine's brother Jean-Baptiste Richard and his wife Cathérine Cormier, a first cousin of Jean-Baptiste Cormier; the Richards' daughter Madeleine and her husband Jean Poirier; and Poirier's sister Cécile, with her husband Olivier Landry.

For the seven years they spent in Georgia, these interrelated families remained close, assisting one another, saving what little money they were able to make. Olivier Landry had a distant relative who was serving in a French regiment in Louisiana—Joseph des Goutin de Ville, the son of Mathieu des Goutin, who had been treasurer at Port Royal during the last years of the French regime—and from him he may have learned of an opportunity to settle in Louisiana. By 1763 this group of families had relocated to Charles Town, where in August they were listed on the register the South Carolina exiles sent to Ambassador Nivernois. Within weeks, however, they departed for New York, where they booked passage on a vessel bound for the port of Mobile on the coast of the Gulf of Mexico. Upon their arrival there in February 1764, they were greeted warmly by French officials, who provided them with lands along the Mississippi River at a place named Cabannocé, about seventy-five miles upriver from New Orleans. By the 1760s, numerous Acadians were serving as seamen on British and French ships, and it may have been by that means that the Cormiers got word back to their son, who by that time was incarcerated with the Broussards in Halifax. And it may have been through Jean-Baptiste Cormier the younger that the Broussards learned of Louisiana. This is a string of conjectures, for there is nothing but circumstantial evidence. But it is a fact that young Cormier was a member of the Broussard party, and that when he arrived in Louisiana he settled at Cabannocé, reunited with his family.[20]

A few weeks after the arrival of the Broussards, another large group left the failing settlement on Saint Domingue and sailed to New Orleans, joining the original settlers at Cabannocé. This was the pattern. The Acadians came to Louisiana in groups that they themselves organized. By the end of 1765 nearly five hundred Acadians were living at Attakapas and at Cabannocé (which became known as "the Acadian Coast"). "We do not speak of them in hundreds any more but in thousands," wrote Governor Aubry, with only a little exaggeration. "I am told that there are at least four thousand who have picked Louisiana as their destiny after an erratic ten years." At the rate they were arriving, he thought, the immigrants would "soon make Louisiana a *nouvelle l'Acadie*." When Antonio de Ulloa, the first Spanish governor, arrived in 1766, the Acadians asked for permission to recruit their friends and relations. Ulloa hesitated, but the Acadians went ahead anyway, sending letters to exile communities in Maryland and Pennsylvania. "We have seen many letters from the Acadians to their countrymen," a resident of Maryland reported, "praying them to speed themselves to partake of their good fortune in that fruitful region." In the spring of 1767, the first company of 224 exiles departed Annapolis, Maryland, on the schooner *Virgin*. Over the next several years they were followed by several more groups from Maryland and Pennsylvania—in all, another six or seven hundred Acadians, more than two thirds of all the exiles in those two provinces.[21]

Most of these Acadians had originally come from Minas, many from Grand Pré. They wanted to settle at Cabannocé, the Acadian Coast. They were mostly farmers rather than stock raisers, and they preferred the riverine environment. Already those who had preceded them were raising dikes—or *levées*—to prevent flooding from the river. Governor Ulloa agreed to let them settle on the Mississippi, but insisted they locate north of Cabannocé. He wished to use them as a line of defense against potential British encroachment. They had amply demonstrated their ability against the British, he reported to his superiors, and with their assistance he could "insure the border" against a formidable army of thousands. But Ulloa misunderstood the Acadian tradition of resistance, which was directed against not only the British but all attempts at imperial control. What the Acadians wanted was reunion with their kinsmen and independence. As it happened, Ulloa also alienated the Creole residents of New Orleans, and when they rose up in rebellion, the Acadians joined enthusiastically. Without adequate military support, Ulloa was helpless; he vacated the colony in October 1768. In a letter assessing blame, Ulloa was especially critical of the Acadians. "We had all of the trouble in the world to subject them to our arrangements," he wrote. Despite being generously supplied with provisions and offered grants of fertile land along the river, they would accept nothing but settlement on lands "contiguous to those of the other Acadians." They were a rebellious, ungrateful, and obstinate people, Ulloa concluded, and he expressed sympathy for their former governors, whom he thought must have been happy to see them go.[22]

Meanwhile the Acadians in France continued to reside in the slum districts of Saint-Malo and Morlaix, with a few hundred more clustered at the port cities of Cherbourg and Boulogne-sur-Mer.

They longed to return to l'Acadie, but the French state was determined not to lose them to another sovereign—subjects were valuable as taxpayers, soldiers, and merely as numbers, boosting the size of the population. So the government proposed a number of alternative settlement schemes. In 1763, a group of two hundred were recruited for the colony of Cayenne (French Guiana); but the venture proved as disastrous as the settlement on Saint Domingue. Later that year, Captain Louis-Antoine de Bougainville of the French navy, with the support of the crown, engaged seventy-five Acadians to join his project to settle the uninhabited Iles Malouines (Falkland Islands) in the South Atlantic, which he intended as a base from which France could explore and plant new colonies in the Pacific. Bougainville, who had been General Montcalm's aide-de-camp during the Seven Years War, thought highly of the Acadians. They were "a laborious, intelligent set of men," he declared, and they "ought to be dear to France, on account of the inviolate attachment they have shewn as honest but unfortunate citizens." After two years on the islands, however, when Spain protested that they were within its territorial sphere, the French handed the islands over, abandoning the Acadians, who were left to find their own way home, wherever that might be. Most seem to have remained on the Falklands, although a number apparently moved to Uruguay, and others made it back to France.[23]

The French government also developed a plan to establish Acadians on the windswept island of Belle-Ile-en-Mer, off the southern coast of Brittany, where they were to supplement the small native population. A delegation of Acadians who visited the island at the behest of the government in 1764 were not impressed. The climate was harsh, the soil inferior, and they feared that settling there would expose them to danger. The British had seized the island during the late war, and "in all probability we would find ourselves in a similar situation to the one that has placed us today in such painful straits." To persuade them, the government turned to abbé Louis-Joseph Le Loutre, the "incendiary" missionary priest from l'Acadie, who returned to France in 1763 after spending seven years in an English prison. Eager to assist the Acadians, he agreed to act as recruiting agent for the Belle-Ile-en-Mer project, and persuaded a number of Acadians that on the island they might reestablish their traditional way of life. He also persuaded the government to sweeten its subsidy, giving to each family not only a concession of land but a house, a horse, a cow, three sheep, a sum of 400 *livres*, and an exemption from all taxes for five years.[24]

In the fall of 1765, seventy-eight Acadian families arrived on the island. To determine their eligibility for the subsidy, the government asked that all heads of household be deposed regarding their French ancestry. Those depositions, which Le Loutre oversaw, demonstrated the Acadians' remarkable familiarity with their extended family histories, which they were able to trace back several generations in great detail. Their testimony also documented how closely the exiles in France remained in touch with relations dispersed across the Atlantic world. Typical was the deposition of Joseph Leblanc dit Le Maigre, once the largest livestock dealer in l'Acadie and a prominent partisan of the French cause, but by 1765 reduced to an impoverished supplicant of government assistance on a barren island thousands of miles from his homeland. Most of his children, Leblanc reported, were living on the French islands of St. Pierre and Miquelon in the Gulf of St. Lawrence, although two sons and their families had been transported to Maryland. He also accounted for each of his siblings. One sister, a widow, had escaped to Miquelon. Another had survived the passage to Maryland, where she lived with her husband and children. A third had been transported to Boston with her husband and children, but "all died there." A brother and his wife had escaped the roundup and become refugees, but "died in 1759 on the coasts of Miramichi," while another brother had been "taken by the English at Ile Saint-Jean, transported by them to France, and died in a shipwreck." His widow was living in Saint-Malo. Leblanc recounted a poignant and telling record of family separation.[25]

The exiles at Belle-Ile-en-Mer constituted but a broken fragment of the former community of Acadians. Yet they hoped for the best. They thanked the French officials "for all the good you have done," and the island's governor noted for the record how impressed he was with their sincerity and honesty. He was especially struck by the dignity of the women, one of whom, he wrote, "despite her rustic appearance, has the traits, the stature, the bearing, and face of a queen." Despite these mutual good intentions, trouble quickly arose. The Acadians found their plots of land disappointingly small. Raised amidst American abundance, they thought in terms of large tracts, rich soils, and abundant woodlots. They were unhappy as well with the limits the governor placed on hunting, fishing, and movement about the island. For these independent people, who had lived a relatively unrestricted life in pre-removal l'Acadie, it was difficult to adjust to the normal rules and regulations of rural France. Most of them eventually left Belle-Ile-en-Mer and returned to the port cities of Brittany, where the young men found work as seamen, allowing extended families to remain in touch with one another across the Atlantic. In 1772 the French government counted a total of 2,563 Acadians living in and around Saint-Malo and Morlaix.[26]

Gradually considerable interest developed among these Acadians in the settlements of their kinsmen in Louisiana. The French government, however, was unwilling to sponsor emigration to the territory of another crown. Relocation to Louisiana remained but a vague possibility until 1783, when the Spanish government, seeking to strengthen its colony against the newly independent United States, made an offer to subsidize the emigration of hundreds of Acadians. Leaders of the exiles petitioned the French colonial minister for permission, using some of the skills they had learned over many years of operating with the British. They had asked their fellow exiles, they wrote, "to choose between Louisiana, Mississippi, Spanish Florida, or a region of Boston to live out the rest of their days. With a unanimous voice, and of common accord, the Acadians have decided on Boston." The minister pondered this preference, which surely was calculated to raise his fears. "We provided them at first with subsistence pay, but this expense becoming too onerous, we attempted to provide them with settlements," he wrote. That attempt failed, "be it because the lands distributed among them were bad, be it because the inhabitants, accustomed to living on extensive and fertile soil were not able to provide for their subsistence upon a narrow terrain of at least mediocre quality." Other Acadians were sent to Cayenne and Saint Domingue, but those experiments turned out badly. Now this request to go either to Louisiana or Boston. "Politics," he concluded, "would perhaps advise the choice of Louisiana."[27]

In the spring and summer of 1785, seven vessels carrying 1,596 Acadians departed France for Louisiana, the largest single migration to that colony during the eighteenth century. Spanish colonial officials at New Orleans welcomed them with medical assistance and provisions, and—having learned from Ulloa's mistake—allowed them the freedom to choose where they would settle. Some joined relatives at Attakapas or along the Mississippi, the so-called Acadian Coast, but three quarters of them settled in groups in the country of Bayou Lafourche, a newly opened district west of the Mississippi River. With this mass movement from France, the Acadians established themselves as one of the largest and most distinct groups in Louisiana. By the end of the eighteenth century there were some four thousand of them in the *nouvelle l'Acadie* of the South.[28]

In 1766 James Murray, the military governor of Canada, issued a proclamation offering land there to the Acadians. "I think it will be for the good of the British Empire in General and that of this Province in particular," Murray wrote, "that these people were settled here upon the same footing with His Majesty's new Canadian subjects, and therefore I shall not hesitate to receive them." His only requirement was that they take the oath of allegiance to the British crown before entering the province. His proposal raised considerable excitement among the Acadians in New England. There were several thousand Acadian refugees already living in Canada, and they added their voice to Murray's. In Massachusetts, Acadian leaders petitioned Governor Francis Bernard for assistance and he sent their request to the Assembly with an endorsement. "It was by the exigencies of War rather than any fault of their own that they were removed from a state of ease and affluence and brought into poverty and dependence," he wrote. "You have now an opportunity at no great Expence to dispose of these People, so that instead of being a burthen to the Province and to themselves as they are like to continue whilst they remain here, they may become a fresh accession of wealth and strength to the British Empire in America."[29]

The House declined to help. But with encouragement from Governor Bernard and town officials, Acadian men representing 890 persons voluntarily took the oath of allegiance, and in the summer of 1766 there was a general exodus of Acadians, some by vessel, some on foot. Many went to Canada, settling on lands near the town of Trois-Rivières, between Montréal and Québec on the St. Lawrence River. Others joined Acadians who had already begun planting communities at Miramichi, Baie des Chaleurs, and other coastal sites on the North Shore. The following year, there was a similar exodus from Connecticut. By 1770, at least four thousand persons were living in predominantly Acadian communities in Canada with another two thousand along the North Shore, which was technically governed from Halifax, but in fact was outside the range of Nova Scotian authority.[30]

The relative welcome the Acadian exiles received in Canada was part of a sea change in British policy toward the inhabitants of what had formerly been New France. When James Murray became governor in 1763, he faced the daunting problem of governing more than seventy thousand Canadiens. Many Britons were skeptical that those French-speaking Catholics could ever become "good subjects." The objections were familiar. The Canadiens would retain their loyalty to the French crown and would remain under the domination of Catholic priests who were little more than French agents. British law excluded them from participation in the institutions of English government, and it would require permanent military rule to keep them from rebelling. No one, however, raised the prospect of removal. With tens of thousands of inhabitants that was clearly an impossibility, and moreover the removal of the Acadians had demonstrated the severe limitations of such an approach.

Faced with the practical problems of administration, Governor Murray soon decided that finding a satisfactory way of dealing with Catholicism lay at the heart of his ability to govern, and he was bold enough to breach, however slightly, the wall of Catholic exclusionism. Pointing out that there were barely two hundred Protestant subjects in the entire province, he permitted Catholics to be empaneled for jury service and to practice law. He permitted the former grand vicar of Québec to return as bishop and spiritual leader of the Catholic community. His attorney general rejected the claims of land speculators attempting to seize the estates of "popish recusants," ruling that even inhabitants who refused to take the oath of allegiance to the British crown retained title to their property. After Murray was replaced during a change of British government in 1766, his policies toward the Canadiens remained in place. As a member of the new Governor's Council put it, "to gain the affection of Canadian subjects they should be granted all possible freedom and indulgence in their religion." This became the guiding principal of the Quebec Act, passed by the British Parliament in 1774, which recognized the Catholic Church in Canada, permitted Catholics to hold public office, and established the *Coutume de Paris* to govern the day-to-day relations of the people.[31]

This approach represented a fundamental break with the pattern that had prevailed in Nova Scotia, and it had no effect on the authorities in Halifax until 1767, when Lieutenant-Governor Michael Francklin succeeded Wilmot and adopted something of Murray's approach in regard to the Acadians. Francklin published a proclamation requiring all Acadians in the province to immediately take the oath of allegiance, but he accompanied it with an announcement that he would consider proposals for grants of lands in areas of the Acadians' own choosing. Chief Justice Belcher, among others, raised the objection that provincial law prohibited Catholics from owning land; but a ruling from the Colonial Office, solicited by Francklin, declared there was "no legal obstruction to the granting of lands in fee to the Acadian subjects." In the weeks following Francklin's announcement, the heads of 165 Acadian families, representing 800 or 900 persons, came forward to take the oath and file for land grants. Tracts of land were set aside on Pubnico Harbor at Cape Sable and on St. Mary's Bay on the Fundy coast south of Annapolis Basin, and a number of Acadian settlements were planted at both locations. Meanwhile, Acadians founded fishing villages at Chezzetcook, on the Atlantic coast east of Halifax; at Chéticamp, on the west coast of Cape Breton Island; and at Isle Madame, on the Atlantic approach to the strait of Canso. By the mid-1770s, these districts counted a total of approximately two thousand Acadian residents. Lieutenant-Governor Francklin also ordered able-bodied Acadian men enrolled in the county militias, and he cautioned militia officers that they were to treat these new subjects "with all possible mildness and tenderness upon every occasion to the End that they may not have the least cause to repent of their having submitted in so ample a manner to His Majesty's Government."[32]

These were important moves, and they signaled the end of a long and painful era. But the consequences of Acadian removal were permanent. The Acadians in the maritime region long would remain a subject population. The provincial statute prohibiting Catholic landownership and banning Catholic clergy was not officially repealed until 1783, and it was not until that decade that the authorities allowed the organization of Catholic parishes with resident priests. Catholics were not granted the suffrage in Nova Scotia until 1789, and they continued to be proscribed from holding public office by the Test Oath. Acadians remained poor and many remained landless, while the planters and their descendants grew prosperous on the fertile farms protected by old Acadian dikes.

In the environs of the former village of Beaubassin, where the campaign of removal had begun, a number of Acadians returned to their old way of life on their old ground, farming the diked marshland, but as tenants rather than owners, obliged to provide up to a third of their annual produce to their landlords. In 1795, one of the largest of the landlords retained Captain John MacDonald to investigate the condition of his Acadian tenants at the hamlets of Minudie, Nappan, and Maccan in the Beaubassin vicinity—where some of the worst violence of the period had taken place. "They seem to be a harmless, inoffensive people," MacDonald reported, yet the British officials and settlers he talked with had nothing but disdain for them, seeing only their imperfections. "We are a saucy nation," he wrote, "too ready to despise others because we have happened to be the conquerors." And that was the thing—the Acadians had been conquered. If they kept to themselves and cleaved to their old-fashioned ways, if they were "suspicious of almost every one," who could blame them? It was important that their behavior be interpreted in the light of their history. "Having taken them in an early stage, we have destroyed them and the course of their progressive improvement in their own way." It would take many years, he believed, for the Acadians to recover from the damage done by dispossession and removal. "I fear," MacDonald concluded, "we have made them worse men and less happy than they have been."[33]

Few observers were so broad-minded. Certainly it was the rare Briton who could appreciate the ironies of those years. In the decade and a half before the American Revolution, a wave of migrants from southern New England resettled the lands taken from the Acadians. By 1775, planters and their children made up two thirds of the provincial population of seventeen thousand and nearly nine of every ten Acadian place names had been replaced with English toponyms. The Yankees carried with them strong attachments to kith and kin in their former communities. As revolutionary agitation began in New England, British officials worried it would spread to Nova Scotia. In 1765 there had been demonstrations in the province against the Stamp Act, and in the 1770s there were supporters of independence among the planters. But there was never really any danger that the fourteenth colony would leave the empire; the strong British military presence at Halifax ensured that.[34]

When privateers acting in support of American independence began harassing coastal settlements in 1775, the provincial government called up the local militia in defense. Some planters of loyalist sentiment answered the call. But many protested that they ought not to be pressed to take up arms against their own kindred. For "those of us who belong to New England," petitioned a group from Chignecto, "it must be the greatest piece of Cruelty and Imposition . . . to be subjected to march into different parts in arms against their Friends and Relations." They were loyal subjects of the crown, another group from Cape Sable argued in a memorial to the council, but the conflict put them in the terrible position of choosing between king and kin. "We want to know, if we may be permitted at this time to live in a peaceable State as we look on that to be the only situation in which we with our Wives and Children can be in any tolerable degree safe." The privateers had told them they would respect the lives and property of planter families "provided we do nothing against them," but "in case we take up Arms against them [they] threaten us highly." There was only one option open for them, they argued, and they professed their "desire to be neuter." If the government was unable to grant them neutral status, "we have nothing to do but retire from our habitations." The council, which included members who had received such petitions before, rejected these arguments out of hand. They "were unanimously of opinion, that the request and proposition of the memorialists cou'd neither be received or admitted a Neutrality, being utterly Absurd and Inconsistent with the duty of subjects." The players were different, but the drama remained the same.[35]

CHAPTER 16

LE GRAND DÉRANGEMENT

Memory and History

IN THE EARLY 1790S the Reverend Andrew Brown, the young pastor of St. Matthew's Presbyterian Church in Halifax, visited the Acadian village of Chezzetcook several miles east of the city, where he talked with a number of old veterans of removal. British provincial officials feared that the Acadian memory of removal would feed the fires of rebellion, making them dangerous subjects. Brown's conversations suggested something else. The Acadians he spoke with made little reference to the loss of their farms or their homeland. They struck him as indifferent to the nakedness and hunger they had suffered during their exile. Like other victims of collective trauma, they said little about their troubled past. Judging from the few traces the experience of removal left in the otherwise rich Acadian oral tradition of story and song, the response of the Chezzetcook Acadians may have been common. Silence is sometimes the only way of coping with great loss. "All their public calamities," Brown wrote, "were lost in the pregnancy of their private sorrows. . . . And life itself seemed to be prized only for the sake of the opportunity which it afforded them of recovering their families, or friends of their heart."[1]

Surely there was much for the Acadians to be bitter about—the seizure of their lands, the destruction of their communities, the deportation of their people. There was only one part of their experience, however, that they chose to talk about—the torment of family separation. "Many families were separated, parents from children, and children from parents," the exile Jean-Baptiste Galerne wrote in the first Acadian response to the deportation, published in Philadelphia in 1756. Four years later, a group of Philadelphia exiles wrote similarly of the horror of families torn apart. "Parents were separated from children, and husbands from wives, some of whom have not to this day met again." Exiles in Massachusetts petitioned authorities for the return of their children. "The loss which we have suffered from being deprived of our farms, from being brought here, and from being separated from each other, is nothing in comparison to that which we are now bearing in having our children torn from us before our eyes. . . . Had we the power to choose we would prefer to give up our bodies and souls rather than be separated from our children."[2]

These phrases and sentiments echoed in the accounts of descendants. *"Des enfants ont été séparés de leurs parents, les maris de leurs épouses, frères de leurs soeurs,"* in the words of Daniel Dugas of St-Jacques-de-L'Achigan, Québec—"children were separated from their parents, husbands from their wives, brothers from their sisters." Edouard Richard, great-grandson of Acadian exiles who settled in the Centre-du-Québec region, was raised on tales of separated families and struggles for reunion. "Sitting on my mother's knee," he wrote, "I have heard them repeated a hundred times, and the tears they often drew from me would alone suffice to perpetuate the remembrance of them." Conducting research for a path-breaking history of Acadian removal, Richard learned how common such stories were among the descendants of the exiles. "I knew . . . from fireside recitals that there had been much separation," he wrote, "but

I was far from suspecting that it was so general." As a story of separation and reunion, the message became one of *la survivance acadienne*, the survival of the Acadian people through the violent storm of 1755.[3]

The post-removal generation of Acadians referred back to those events as *le grand dérangement*—the great upheaval. The phrase suggested the profound disjuncture that would forever divide their history into eras before and after. Yet the phrase also implied something more personal, *le grand dérangement d'esprit*, the derangement of mind and spirit that drove their parents and grandparents to the edge of madness. The Acadians were accustomed to being played as pawns in the game of empire. "Inhabitants cannot dwell in a country against the will of the sovereign," the men of Chignecto had written to Colonel Monckton a few hours after their incarceration at Fort Beauséjour in August 1755. This was politics—regrettable, even tragic, but comprehensible. "As Christians we must submit without questioning." But what were Christians to make of the attack on their families? "The greatest injustice that the English were guilty of," declared the brothers Michel and Pierre Bastarache, deported to South Carolina while their wives and children huddled in cold refugee camps, "was that many families were separated and have not met to this day." The assault on their families was neither Christian nor honorable. Reverend Brown overheard Acadian mothers instructing their children. "The memory of those that wasted them would rot," they said. "A day was marked for the restoration of their possessions," and then Acadian happiness would be secured, "without the hazard of cabinets or the necessities of Kings."[4]

To justify the cruelty of removal, defenders invoked the right of the state to self-preservation. According to Thomas Hutchinson of Massachusetts—who wrote a history of the province and later served as the last colonial governor before the American Revolution—had the French made the effort to recover l'Acadie, "the whole body of the Acadians, some from inclination, others from compulsion, would join in the attempt." Even after more than four decades under British rule, Hutchinson believed, the Acadians "had no more affection for England than for Russia." He based this conclusion less on any overt evidence of Acadian rebellion than on a conviction of their cultural sympathies. "Being all Roman Catholicks and great bigots, and retaining the French language, they were better affected to the French than to the English." He admitted that removal had been a cruel business, and quoted without contradiction the exclamation of an Acadian exile that the fate of his people was "the hardest which had happened since our Savior was upon the earth." In fact, Hutchinson had done what he could to ameliorate the suffering of exiles in Boston. Nevertheless, he believed their deportation was justified by military necessity. No one was allowed to claim neutrality in the clash of empires. Everyone had to choose, or the choice would be made for them. During the Revolution Hutchinson made just such a choice, leaving the land of his birth for loyalist exile in England.[5]

Yet the formulation of "cruel necessity" did not entirely resolve the question of honorable conduct. Colonel Edward Lloyd III, longtime member of the Governor's Council of Maryland and one of the wealthiest planters on the colony's eastern shore, pondered this when faced with deciding what to do with the more than nine hundred exiles who arrived at Baltimore. In December 1755 he wrote to his half brother James Hollyday, who was in London reading law. "As, no doubt, much will be talk'd in London of this transaction, you'll from that, and the knowledge you have of the Law of Nations, form an adequate Judgment of the fitness of the measures taken." In the council's deliberation over the appropriate way to receive the exiles, Lloyd reported, he had argued they ought to be considered prisoners of war, incarcerated and maintained until an arrangement could be made for their exchange with France. The council decided otherwise, that the Acadians were not prisoners of war but "wayward subjects." To be sure, Lloyd had a material interest in the question.

Fifty exiles had been deposited at Wye House, his plantation in Talbot County, and "to prevent their starving" it was costing him £12 a week. But he was more generally interested in the implications of the decision for British honor.[6]

The "Law of Nations" to which Lloyd referred consisted of the informal conventions among European nations on the appropriate conduct of war (*jus in bello*). They specified the etiquette of siege and surrender and rules for the appropriate treatment of prisoners of war, but included few guidelines on wartime conduct toward civilians. Traditional Christian ethics, however, proscribed warring states from deliberately targeting civilian noncombatants. By what British law, international convention, or ethical principle, Lloyd wondered, was it proper to force the Acadians from their homes, dispossess them of their property, and disperse them throughout the empire? If they were not prisoners of war, what were they? "We cannot devise any other honourable way," he concluded, "of depriving those people, who were all free born, of their Liberty."[7]

Others may have shared Lloyd's reservations. But the first significant public dissent from the prevailing consensus of "cruel necessity" did not appear until 1757, in a work co-authored by the young British intellectual Edmund Burke. In this, the first of many political tracts he would publish over four decades in public life, Burke displayed the contrarian temperament for which he would later be renowned—as a brilliant orator in the House of Commons, as an advocate of conciliation with the colonists in the lead-up to the war for American independence, and as a scathing critic of Revolutionary France, notably in his *Reflections on the Revolution in France* (1790). Burke began by admitting that the Acadians had "yielded very little obedience to the crown of England." But, he argued, this was understandable, for "in truth they had from us very little protection." Great Britain had failed to provide order, which was the foundation of loyalty. Had the government supported a garrison of sufficient strength to protect the Acadians from danger, and magistrates to establish the rule of law, "we might have saved many useful people to this colony, and prevented the necessity (if it was a necessity) of using measures which, if they are not impolitic, are certainly such as an humane and generous mind is never constrained to but with regret." Removal had been the consequence of colonial irresponsibility and neglect.[8]

BURKE'S argument helped shape the thinking of a French intellectual whose account of Acadian expulsion would prove widely influential. Guillaume-Thomas-François de Raynal was a former Jesuit priest, defrocked for his liberal views and his association with the *philosophes,* who turned to a career in letters, publishing a series of popular histories under his clerical name, abbé Raynal. His short history of l'Acadie, included as one of the concluding chapters of his multivolume *Histoire philosophique et politique des établissements et du commerce des Européens dans les deux Indes* (1770), began by echoing Burke's argument about the irresponsibility of British colonial policy. "The ardour which the English had shewn for the possession of this territory," Raynal wrote, "did not manifest itself afterwards in the care they took to maintain or to improve it." Unwilling to develop l'Acadie on their own, British officials persuaded the Acadians to remain "upon a promise made them of never being compelled to bear arms against their ancient country." But "no magistrate was ever appointed to rule over them, and they were never acquainted with the laws of England. No rents or taxes of any kind were ever exacted from them. Their new sovereign seemed to have forgotten them, and they were equally strangers to him." In this condition of neglect, he argued, the Acadians continued to live as an independent people.[9]

Raynal attempted to convey something of the character of Acadian life and history by drawing on sieur de Dièreville's idyllic account of life at Port Royal in the late seventeenth century. "These people were, in a word," Raynal concluded, "a society of brethren, every individual of which was equally ready to give and to receive what he thought the common right of mankind." Conservative critics made a fuss over the naïveté of that conclusion, but their real objection was to the rhetorical use Raynal made of it. "Who will not be affected with the innocent manners and the tranquility of this fortunate colony?" he asked. "Who will not wish for the duration of its happiness? . . . But alas!" After several generations of Acadians had invested their labor and their lives in building a prosperous colony, Great Britain decided to settle their lands with Protestant settlers. The French countered by instigating the missionary priests to stir up the inhabitants against these "heretics"—a word, Raynal wrote, "which has too powerful an influence on deluded minds." The imperial deadlock was finally broken by an "act of treachery," the British expulsion and dispersion of the Acadians to other colonies, "where the greater part of them died of grief and vexation."[10]

All of which demonstrated Raynal's larger argument: the inherent corruption of the modern nation-state. "Such are the effects of national jealousies, and of the rapaciousness of government, to which men, as well as their property, become prey," he wrote. "What our enemies lose is reckoned an advantage, what they gain is looked upon as a loss. When a town cannot be taken, it is starved; when it cannot be kept, it is burnt to ashes, or its foundations razed. A ship or a fortified town is blown up, rather than the sailors or the garrison will surrender. A despotic government separates its enemies from its slaves by immense deserts, to prevent the irruptions of the one and the emigrations of the other." It was a story repeated time and again in the international competition for resources and colonies. "England destroyed the neutral French inhabitants of Acadia, to prevent their returning to France. Can it be said after this, that policy and society were instituted for the happiness of mankind? Yes, they were instituted to screen the wicked, and to secure the powerful." Acadian removal, Raynal argued, was a case study in the exercise of imperial logic, and in his judgment it stood as a condemnation of the entire system. It is difficult to fault either his facts or his logic.[11]

Condemned as sacrilegious and insurrectionary, Raynal's history was placed on the Inquisition's index of banned books. It had been published anonymously, but when Raynal's authorship was revealed, the French state issued a warrant for his arrest and he fled the country. The attention served to increase demand—the modern historian Robert Darnton describes *Histoire philosophique et politique* as "the title that stood out above all others" in the book trade of the late eighteenth century. The work went through thirty reprintings and three editions before 1789. It was translated into all the major languages of Europe, including an English edition published in Edinburgh, the center of rationalist scholarship in Great Britain. If Raynal had been influenced by Burke, Burke's perspective on the Acadian question seems in turn to have been affected by Raynal. In 1780, in a long speech in the House of Commons on the irresponsibility of British colonial administration, Burke turned to the Acadian example once again. "It seems our nation had more skill and ability in destroying than in settling a colony," he told the other members. "In the last war, we did, in my opinion, most inhumanely, and upon pretences that in the eye of an honest man are not worth a farthing, root out this poor, innocent, deserving people, whom our utter inability to govern, or to reconcile, gave us no sort of right to extirpate."[12]

Burke and Raynal are important because their strong dissenting voices broke through the comfortable consensus of "cruel necessity." Their criticism greatly discomfited the political establishment in the maritime region, which at the end of the eighteenth century yet included many of the men who had carried out and benefited from the expulsion of the Acadians. "On every appearance of a public discussion of the events of the war," wrote Reverend Brown, who took a strong interest in the Acadian question, "the old servants of the government manifested apprehensions and disquietude, particularly when the case of the Acadians was mentioned." When a Halifax publisher reprinted an excerpt from Raynal's account, Provincial Secretary Richard Bulkeley and acting Chief Justice Isaac Deschamps rushed to the defense. "The Abbé Raynal writes in the spirit of a Frenchman," they charged, "disposed to find fault with the English Government, and proud of making a historical discovery." The notion that Raynal was a spokesman for the French state would have come as news to officials of the *ancien régime*. His account was considerably more subtle than Bulkeley and Deschamps allowed. But the two men were responding, as Reverend Brown noted, "as if it had been a personal attack." As well they might. Bulkeley had been a member of the council since the early 1750s, and not only participated in the decision to remove the Acadians but issued the orders for their arrest and deportation. Deschamps, a merchant clerk at Pisiquid and translator at Fort Edward at the time of the expulsion, had in the years afterward risen to become a wealthy landowner at Windsor and a justice of the Supreme Court.[13]

THE deportations and dispersions of the Acadians from Nova Scotia created a diaspora that at the beginning of the nineteenth century included more than 24,000 persons in North American communities extending from the Gulf of the St. Lawrence to the Gulf of Mexico. A third of the exiles' descendants resided in the United States, the majority of them in the *nouvelle l'Acadie* of Louisiana, which the new American nation acquired by purchase in 1803 and admitted as one of the states of the union in 1812. Over the course of their subsequent history the Acadian people of Louisiana would have little or no contact with their northern cousins, gradually developing a culture that was distinctively their own, and would play an important role in shaping the cultural traditions of Louisiana.[14]

Louisiana Acadians more frequently married non-Acadians than their cousins in the maritime region. By the mid-twentieth century only a quarter of them bore the original Acadian surnames of the seventeenth and eighteenth centuries, as compared to three quarters of the Acadians in the north. Most of the intermarriage took place between Acadian women and non-Acadian men—French-speaking Creoles or migrants from Ireland, Germany, or elsewhere within the

United States. These men introduced new practices into the community. But the traditional extended family structure of the Acadians remained strong, and since it was traditional for wives to remain closely associated with their parents, and since mothers were the principal transmitters of cultural tradition to their children, these interethnic families continued to identify as Acadian. Meanwhile, well-to-do Acadians embraced the planter way of life and were gradually absorbed into the regional elite.

The end result of this process was the creation of new ethnic group: French-speaking small farmers, trappers, and ranchers who lived among the wooded bayous, marshes, and prairies of southwest Louisiana. They became known as the Cajuns—a name that came from the way they dropped the initial syllable when pronouncing their own name, *'Cadiens*; they were a people with strong Acadian roots but incorporating distinctive new cultural forms. Cajun cattlemen on the *vacheries* (ranches) of the Louisiana prairies incorporated the traditions of both Spanish vaqueros and Anglo-American herders, and in the process became the prototypes for the later cowboys of Texas. The popular cowboy holler "Hippy Ti Yo!" is thought to derive from a traditional Cajun song about two mangy dogs, *"Hip et Taïaut."*[15]

There was less dramatic change among the Acadians in British North America. At the beginning of the nineteenth century as many as eight thousand Acadians lived in the province of Lower Canada (Québec), scattered from Montréal to the Gaspé. Many preserved their identity in communities and parishes of their own, but the majority gradually assimilated with the dominant culture of the French-Canadians or Québecois, as they came to be known. The heart of Acadian tradition remained the maritime region, where in the first decade of the nineteenth century nearly ten thousand Acadians made up approximately 7 percent of the population of the three provinces carved out of the old domain of l'Acadie—Prince Edward Island (formerly Ile Saint-Jean); Nova Scotia; and New Brunswick, the mainland portion, which was separated from Nova Scotia in 1784.[16]

After the victory of American independence, New Brunswick was a refuge for thousands of loyalist exiles from New England, including kinsmen of Major General John Winslow, an outspoken Tory who would surely have joined the exodus but for his death in 1775. British authorities at Halifax appointed Edward Winslow, his nephew, to lay out tracts of land for loyalist officers on the St. John River (rivière Saint-Jean), and he selected the rich alluvial lands at the head of the tidal current, where the town of Fredericton would later rise. There was a problem, however, for several hundred Acadian families already inhabited the site. Without approval of the government they had "seated themselves upon the margins of the rivers," Winslow reported, "and there this improvident and slovenly race obtained with very little labor all the necessaries of life." The Acadians complained to him that they "had suffered what to them appeared like the most unmerited persecution and oppression from the British government." A number of them, in fact, had come originally from Minas, the very same families that his uncle, Major General Winslow, had deported to Massachusetts and Connecticut. And in 1783, on the recommendation of Edward Winslow, they were forcibly dispossessed once again. Most of them relocated to the northern reaches of the St. John, near the junction with the Madawaska River.[17]

Despite such setbacks, over the next century New Brunswick became the *nouvelle l'Acadie* of the North, the dynamic center of Acadian life in the Maritime Provinces, as they became known. To encourage the development of its vast territory, the provincial government offered generous land grants for which Acadians were ruled eligible. Although on average the tracts they received were considerably smaller than those issued to English-speaking Protestants, the land provided the material foundation for the growth of strong communities at Madawaska, on the Petitcodiac River, and along the North Shore. Yet the Acadians maintained their ambivalent connection to empire. The Madawaska region of northern New Brunswick and Maine was claimed by both Great Britain and the United States, and during the War of 1812 the British and Americans both pressed the Acadians to take sides. Most refused. "What is the point of making us fight?" one group replied to the bishop of Québec when he asked them to shoulder arms in defense of Canada. "In two months we may belong to the Americans." The tensions continued through the 1830s, when competition over the timber resources of the area almost led to another shooting war. Finally, in 1842, British and American commissioners agreed to split the difference between their respective claims, setting the boundary along the St. John River itself, and in the process splitting the Acadian community of Madawaska between the two nations. It was an appropriate symbol for the continued marginality of the Acadians.[18]

In general the provincial governments of the Maritimes treated the Acadians as a race apart through the nineteenth and into the twentieth century. Although they were granted the suffrage in Nova Scotia in 1789, it was not until 1810 that they were allowed to vote in New Brunswick and Prince Edward Island, and in all three provinces they were restricted from holding public office until 1829, when the British Parliament passed the Catholic Emancipation Act. The Acadians' attention was not on politics, however, but on finding new ways to subsist—by fishing, trapping, wood chopping, small-scale farming, and increasingly by working for wages. Many of them were drawn south, to New England, where they found work as fishermen, hired hands, or factory workers.[19]

Sometime around 1840, Horace Conolly, the rector of St. Matthew's Episcopal Church in Boston, heard a story from his Acadian housekeeper, "the legend," as the poet Henry Wadsworth Longfellow would later describe it, "of a girl who, in the dispersion of the Acadians, was separated from her lover, and passed her life in waiting and seeking for him, and only finding him dying in a hospital when both were old." Stories of separated lovers were among the most common of the tragic family tales told by the Acadians. It moved Conolly, and he repeated it to his friend Nathaniel

Hawthorne, who was inspired to write a historical account of the Acadian deportation that featured a touching depiction of the Acadian suffering.

> Now, a desolate wife might be heard calling for her husband. He, alas! had gone, she knew not whither, or perhaps had fled into the woods of Acadia, and had now returned to weep over the ashes of their dwelling. . . . Young men and maidens, whose hearts had been torn asunder by separation, had hoped, during the voyage, to meet their beloved ones at its close. Now, they began to feel that they were separated forever.

"Methinks, if I were an American poet," Hawthorne wrote, "I would choose Acadia for the subject of my song." It was no idle comment. His friend Longfellow, who had heard the same story from Conolly, had already announced his intention of using it as the basis for a narrative poem.[20]

There was considerable interest among Americans in the history of Acadian removal, which patriotic writers employed as an example of the oppression of the British Empire. Robert Walsh, American consul general in Paris during the administration of President Martin Van Buren, compared the deportation of the Acadian exiles to the violent shipment of slaves from Africa, writing that the Acadians had been "torn from their rustic homes, and transported in a way worthy of being compared with the 'middle passage.'" Walsh chose to ignore the fact that removal had been an Anglo-American operation designed to further both Yankee and British ends, for such an admission would seriously have undercut his point. The indictment of the British for the crime of Acadian expulsion became one of the most frequently repeated charges in the Anglophobic repertoire of nineteenth-century American patriots.[21]

Consider the 1842 essay "Exiles of Acadia" by the Victorian historian George Bancroft. He cited documents in British and French archives, included passages from abbé Raynal, and quoted from John

Winslow's journal, which he found in the collections of the Massachusetts Historical Society. Bancroft identified Winslow as an "American commander," yet was silent about the implications of this fact, and made nothing at all of New England's role in the operation. He concluded with a standard peroration: "I know not if the annals of the human race keep the record of sorrows so wantonly inflicted, so bitter and so perennial, as fell upon the French inhabitants of Acadia. The hand of the English official seemed under a spell with regard to them, and was never uplifted but to curse them."[22]

Longfellow was part of this American interpretive tradition, but he transcended it. He consulted Bancroft and other historians, and following the established American convention identified the officers and soldiers who conducted the campaign of removal as agents of "the tyrants of England." But the source of Longfellow's inspiration was the Acadian story of family separation. Although Longfellow himself had no direct contact with Acadians, the essence of his poem had come from them indirectly. He finished writing early in 1847 and *Evangeline, A Tale of Acadie* was published later that year.[23]

Evangeline began with lines that would become some of the most familiar in all American poetry:

This is the forest primeval. The murmuring pines and the hemlocks,
Bearded with moss, and in garments green, indistinct in the twilight,
Stand like Druids of eld, with voices sad and prophetic,
Stand like harpers hoar, with beards that rest on their bosoms.
Loud from its rocky caverns, the deep-voiced neighboring ocean
Speaks, and in accents disconsolate answers the wail of the forest.

This is the forest primeval; but where are the hearts that beneath it
Leaped like the roe, when he hears in the woodland the voice of the huntsman?

Where is the thatch-roofed village, the home of Acadian
farmers,—
Men whose lives glided on like rivers that water the woodlands,
Darkened by shadows of earth, but reflecting an image of
heaven?
Waste are those pleasant farms, and the farmers forever departed!
Scattered like dust and leaves, when the mighty blasts of October
Seize them, and whirl them aloft, and sprinkle them far o'er the
ocean.
Naught but tradition remains of the beautiful village of
Grand-Pré. . . .

Longfellow drew his portrait of the Acadians from the descriptions of abbé Raynal. But unlike Raynal, he avoided any historical explanation. The poem is situated outside real time ("This is the forest primeval"), and attributes the calamity of removal not to any deliberate policy but to man's inhumanity to man.

The poet tells the story of Evangeline Bellefontaine and her betrothed, Gabriel Lajeunesse, torn apart on their wedding day and sent to separate colonies.

. . . On the falling tide the freighted vessels departed,
Bearing a nation, with all its household goods, into exile,
Exile without an end, and without an example in story.
Far asunder, on separate coasts, the Acadians landed;
Scattered were they, like flakes of snow, when the wind from the
northeast
Strikes aslant through the fogs that darken the Banks of
Newfoundland.
Friendless, homeless, hopeless, they wandered from city to city,
From the cold lakes of the North to sultry Southern savannas,—
From the bleak shores of the sea to the lands where the Father of
Waters
Seizes the hills in his hands, and drags them down to the ocean. . . .

With a group of exiles, Evangeline travels through North America in search of Gabriel. After fruitless years of wandering she settles in Philadelphia, where she becomes a Sister of Mercy, ministering to the wretched and homeless. Living a life of "patience and abnegation of self, and devotion to others," she grows old. One day, making her comforting rounds, she is shocked to find Gabriel among the dying men in the almshouse. He recognizes her and they embrace, each imagining the other as they had been amidst "green Acadian meadows." Gabriel dies in her arms, Evangeline soon follows, and they are buried side by side in "nameless graves." Longfellow concluded the poem with a rhetorical return to l'Acadie:

Still stands the forest primeval; but under the shade of its branches
Dwells another race, with other customs and language.
Only along the shore of the mournful and misty Atlantic
Linger a few Acadian peasants, whose fathers from exile
Wandered back to their native land to die in its bosom.
In the fisherman's cot the wheel and the loom are still busy;
Maidens still wear their Norman caps and their kirtles of homespun,
And by the evening fire repeat Evangeline's story,
While from its rocky caverns the deep-voiced, neighboring ocean
Speaks, and in accents disconsolate answers the wail of the forest.

EVANGELINE was an extraordinary publishing success. The poem went through six printings in the first three months. Its fame spread rapidly throughout North America, Great Britain, and Europe, and within ten years it had been translated into a dozen languages, including a French version in 1853. It appealed to the sentimental conventions of the age, offering an ideal of womanhood that, as Longfellow put it, "hopes and endures and is patient." Such values, and indeed such poems, long ago fell out of fashion, and it requires some empathetic effort to understand the source of *Evangeline*'s power for Victorian readers. Nathaniel Hawthorne offered some suggestive comments in a review published a few weeks after the poem first appeared. In the hands of an ordinary poet, Hawthorne wrote, the story of separation would be all "gloom and wretchedness." But Longfellow presented "its pathos all illuminated with beauty—so that the impression of the poem is nowhere dismal or despondent, and glows with the purest sunshine where we might the least expect it, on the pauper's death-bed." Hawthorne's perspective might be extended. Other writers had depicted the Acadians as villains or as victims, but through the character of Evangeline Longfellow reimagined them as a people of culture, grievously wronged, yet enduring with dignity.[24]

The poem became enormously popular among the Acadians themselves. In its lines they heard the collective suffering of their ancestors. They had always maintained that the separation of their families was the most devastating thing about *le grand dérangement*. Longfellow did not indicate that the poem was based on an Acadian family story, but he did not need to, for it resonated deeply with the collective memory of the Acadians, evoking the pathos of removal, yet underscoring their endurance and survival. Moreover, it made reference to real places and real communities. It seemed to matter not at all that Longfellow had concocted the name "Evangeline" ("good news," from the Greek). The Acadians adopted it as their own, and as early as the 1850s parents in both l'Acadies north and south were christening daughters in honor of the heroine.[25]

In the Maritimes, the poem struck a spark igniting a cultural and political renaissance among the small Acadian middle class that began to emerge in the second half of the nineteenth century. The poem was excerpted in the first textbook designed for Acadian Catholic schools, and was incorporated into the curriculum of the first Acadian institution of higher education, the Collège de Saint-Joseph, founded in 1864 at Memramcook, New Brunswick. Pascal Poirier, an important Acadian leader of the late nineteenth century and one of the first graduates of the college, remembered reciting Longfellow's stanzas as he walked about the campus. "I carried *Evangeline* on my heart," he later wrote. The first Acadian newspaper, *Le Moniteur Acadien*, which began publishing in 1867, printed a French translation of *Evangeline* in its first numbers. The second Acadian newspaper took the name *L'Evangéline.* Acadian leaders frequently drew on the poem for messages of unity, and in 1881 succeeded in organizing the *Société Nationale l'Assomption* (later renamed *Société Nationale de l'Acadie*) to defend and promote Acadian interests.[26]

The poem also created a surge of popular interest in "the Land of Evangeline" among both Canadians and Americans. Regular steamship service opened between Boston and Yarmouth in 1855 and in 1859 the first travel guide appeared, pitched to middle-class travelers from the northeastern United States who could not afford Europe but wished to visit a country with picturesque scenery, a romantic past, and noble peasants living in harmony with nature. Soon the route from Annapolis Royal to Grand Pré was dotted with Evangeline tearooms and Gabriel gift shops. The Dominion Atlantic Railroad acquired the site of the church of Saint-Charles-des-Mines at Grand Pré, and erected a statue of Evangeline on the grounds. The Société Nationale l'Assomption raised funds and built a memorial church on the site, which opened in 1930, the 175th anniversary of the deportation.[27]

Evangeline made an impact, too, in Louisiana. Félix Voorheis, an occasional writer of fiction and poetry from St. Martinville (originally Poste des Attakapas), reworked Longfellow's tale as a novel in which the separated lovers are reunited under a great oak tree in the center of St. Martinville. But discovering that the young man has fallen in love with another, the woman goes mad and dies. Because of the detail of its local setting, and because the book was marketed as "the true story of Evangeline," it was widely accepted as historical fact. Tourists traveled to St. Martinville to stand under the Evangeline oak and weep over Evangeline's tomb. A bronze statue was raised in 1930, cast in the likeness of Dolores Del Rio, the actress who played the Acadian maiden in a Hollywood production. The myth of Evangeline served a useful function, writes the historian Carl A. Brasseaux, focusing attention on "the story of unsung survivors who stubbornly braved adversity, oppression, and separation to carve a Louisiana homeland for themselves and their progeny."[28]

Acadians were delighted with *Evangeline*, but the political establishment in Nova Scotia considered it an assault on their honor. In 1865, Beamish Murdoch, a descendant of the planters and a wealthy antiquarian of Halifax, published the first of three volumes of documents and commentary. He was motivated, he announced, "by a desire to throw the light of truth, if possible, upon the merits and demerits of the expulsion of the French Acadians from this country in 1755. The Abbé Raynal, Bancroft, Longfellow, etc., had given popularity to a view of this transaction so disgraceful to the British name and nation, that we of Nova Scotia, who knew traditionally something of the truth, were annoyed at the reiteration of such severe charges against our nation." Planter families had stories of their own, and they remembered the role that the Yankees had played. The expulsion of the Acadians, Murdoch wrote, "was a dismal affair altogether, but in reality one for which New England was more responsible than Nova Scotia." He took pains to document the long interest of Massachusetts in the maritime region, Governor William Shirley's promotion of Acadian removal, and the role of New England troops in carrying out the operation. "We Nova Scotians knew all these things," Murdoch wrote, "and we thought it hard that Bancroft and Longfellow should not only blame the act, but endeavor to fix the odium of it on the British government and people."[29]

The responsibility of New Englanders became a main theme of the Nova Scotian response to *Evangeline*. Longfellow had done for the Fundy tidelands what Sir Walter Scott had done for the Highlands of Scotland, Attorney General Adams George Archibald told a Halifax audience in 1886. But poets made poor historians. The circumstances of 1755 were more complicated than Longfellow cared to admit. The expulsion of the Acadians had been a "painful necessity," consistent with the "maintenance of British power" and the "protection of the British inhabitants." Those were the facts, and only the willfully ignorant would cast blame where praise was due. But

> if the expulsion be a stain on the annals of Nova Scotia, it is a stain from which Massachusetts, the country and the home of the poet, cannot claim to be free. It was a Massachusetts governor who devised the scheme. It was the soldiers of Massachusetts that drove the French from the encroachments on our territory beyond the Missiquash. It was Massachusetts officers, and Massachusetts soldiers, who carried out the decree of expulsion at the heart and centre of the Acadian settlements, at that very Grand Pré, which the poet has made a household word. It was Massachusetts vessels, chartered from Massachusetts merchants, officered and manned by Massachusetts captains and crews, that carried the poor Acadians into exile. It is clear therefore that if there be any escutcheon smirched by the transaction, it is specially that of the country and the home of the poet himself.[30]

EVANGELINE also inspired new histories of *le grand dérangement* from the Acadian point of view. In 1859, François-Edmé Rameau de Saint-Père, a Parisian scholar, published the first French-language history of the Acadians since the work of abbé Raynal. Rameau left no doubt about where he stood. Acadian removal, he declared, was a "*crime historique*," motivated by "public hatred and private greed." When Rameau came to North America to promote his book, he was greeted enthusiastically by dozens of young Acadian intellectuals, to whom he became something of a mentor. He also experienced firsthand the suspicion and hostility of the English-speaking establishment when he attempted to conduct research in the Nova Scotia archives. "I was forbidden to copy anything or make any extracts," he reported. "I was refused the use of paper, pen or pencil. I was placed near a table in the middle of a large room in which eight or ten clerks were at work. I was not given a chair, so that I could not sit down, and so that none of my movements could escape the notice of the clerks."[31]

Rameau's research revealed important gaps in the archives' collections. Those gaps had been noted previously by Thomas Chandler Haliburton, a descendant of planters and Nova Scotia's first historian. Most of the missing documents concerned the campaign against the Acadians. "It is very remarkable that there are no traces of this important event to be found among the records," Haliburton noted in 1829. "I could not discover, that the correspondence had been preserved, or that the orders, returns, and memorials, had ever been filed there." He suspected foul play. "The particulars of this affair seem to have been carefully concealed, although it is not now easy to assign the reason, unless the parties were, as in truth they might be, ashamed of the transaction." Nothing much was made of Haliburton's remark at the time; but revived by Rameau during the controversy over *Evangeline*, it proved explosive.[32]

Another partisan in the struggle over history was abbé Henri Raymond Casgrain, a native Québecois and a professor of literature at Université Laval in the city of Québec. Casgrain was already a distinguished scholar when he made the turn from criticism to history after reading Francis Parkman's *Montcalm and Wolfe* (1894), a history of the Seven Years War which included a long chapter on the expulsion. Parkman took a mean-spirited view of the Acadians, an interesting contrast to the goodwill of his great-grandfather, the Reverend Ebenezer Parkman, who had befriended the exiles in 1756. The "ideal picture" of the Acadians drawn by "prose and verse," Parkman complained, had conveyed a wholly false impression. In truth, they were "a simple and ignorant peasantry," wholly under the control of French priests, "enfeebled by hereditary mental subjection." Casgrain and Parkman had been friends for years, but appalled at this treatment of the Acadians, Casgrain wrote a critical letter which Parkman answered with a characteristically sharp retort. Before the abbé could "pronounce an intelligent criticism," he wrote, it would be necessary for him to "pursue a good deal more research in the archives of France and elsewhere." Casgrain took up the challenge. "Behind the Archibalds and the Parkmans hide the multitudes," he wrote a colleague at Laval. "We are only a small number; it is necessary for us to be the valiant knights charging these new Saracens with the cry, God wants it!"[33]

At the Public Record Office in London Casgrain located new evidence, Acadian memorials and British reports that documented the grant of the inhabitants' request for an exemption from bearing arms. They had not been included in the collection of documents compiled by the Public Archives of Nova Scotia. "The choice of documents published at Halifax was carefully made in order to justify the Nova Scotia government's deportation of the Acadians," Casgrain concluded, "for it systematically eliminated and left in the shadows the more compromising parts, those which best establish the rights of the Acadians." At the British Museum he examined the collection of Reverend Andrew Brown, the Halifax Presbyterian minister who in the 1790s had conducted the first real historical research on Acadian removal. Brown's papers—which were miraculously discovered in 1852 on their way to the scrap heap—included transcriptions of documents that had long since disappeared from the Nova Scotia archives, notably the operational plan for removal written by the provincial surveyor Charles Morris. The Nova Scotia Historical Society published a transcription of that critical document, but in reading Brown's transcription, Casgrain realized the printed version had been "truncated," leaving out the most incriminating portions. Casgrain proved his points by included the missing and bowdlerized documents in his own compilation drawn from the French and British archives. Nova Scotia authorities, he charged, had conspired to cover up the most damning evidence of the Acadian removal. After studying Casgrain's new material, even Parkman changed his mind. "The truth is," he admitted, "the treatment of the Acadians was a scandal on both sides."[34]

Inspired by Rameau and Casgrain, whose works were published only in French, Acadians began writing their own history. Edouard Richard left a successful career as a lawyer, politician, and businessman to devote full attention to his investigation of *le grand dérangement*, which he published to wide acclaim in 1895. Similarly, Placide Gaudet, an early graduate of Collège de Saint-Joseph, left his position as an editor at the newspaper *L'Evangéline* to become a historian. "I knew nothing of my country's history," Gaudet later wrote to Richard, "and it was indeed a disgrace." In the late 1890s both men secured positions at the Public Archives of Canada. Richard went to Paris, where he supervised the transcription of French documents, while Gaudet worked in depositories in the United States and Canada. Their compilations were published in a series of government volumes, and after Richard's premature death in 1904 Gaudet was acknowledged as the preeminent authority on Acadian history. Several years later he published his own history of removal, entitled *Le grand dérangement*.[35]

Gaudet and Richard put their emphasis on the experience of the Acadians themselves through the ordeal of expulsion and dispersion. In his collection of documents, Gaudet reprinted dozens of petitions of Acadians in Massachusetts and elsewhere, providing the exiles with a historical voice. Both men were clearly influenced by the stories they had heard in their communities. His research convinced him, Richard wrote, that "family tradition faithfully reproduced historic truth." Yet neither man was a radical. Richard considered himself a proud citizen of the Commonwealth, and he labored mightily to absolve the British of responsibility for removal, writing that "the English Government never ordered this deportation, nor ever did anything that might imply it." The operation, he argued, was solely the work of Lieutenant-Governor Charles Lawrence, whose motive had been the seizure of the inhabitants' possessions, particularly their livestock. Gaudet's research supported a considerably more general indictment of responsibility, but in his book he left it to his readers to make their own judgment. When one reviewer wrote that the evidence suggested to him that the British "had a secret understanding with Lawrence and Shirley to bring about the extinction of the Acadian race," Gaudet responded privately that the man had "perfectly grasped and interpreted what I dared not specify." As an Acadian in the employ of the Canadian government, he felt it necessary to play his hand carefully.[36]

Acadian caution was understandable, in view of the strong sentiments of the English-speaking, Protestant majority. Consider the opinion of James S. Macdonald of Halifax in 1905. By putting their emphasis on the suffering of the Acadians, he charged, Francophone historians were attempting to change the subject. The "treacherous Acadians" were nothing but "French half-breeds" who had conspired with their Míkmaw kinsmen to murder British settlers. Charles Lawrence "deserved the thanks of all British subjects" for removing them and saving the province. "Doubtless there were mistakes made," Macdonald concluded, "but we must consider how unreasonable a people [the Acadians] were to deal with, and how difficult, under the circumstances, it was to make them at all contented. The removal of nearly 6,000 people was a big undertaking, and revolutions, we know, are not made in rosewater." Acadians—a disempowered minority who continued to experience considerable discrimination because of their religion, their culture, and their language—could not avoid reading contemporary implications into such comments. The history of the past is frequently enmeshed in the politics of the present.[37]

When Gaudet felt it was necessary, however, he did not shrink from challenging the defense of "cruel necessity." In 1916 he used the occasion of an invited talk in the hall of the Nova Scotia legislature—built on the very ground where the Governor's Council had met to decide on expulsion in July 1755—to directly respond to those who defended the expulsion and dispersion of his ancestors.

> If tonight the souls of Lawrence, Belcher, Morris, Green, Collier, Cotterell, Rous, Boscawen, and Mostyn, the authors of this terri-

> ble tragedy, hover over us in this hall, they must be filled with fury to see a great-grandson of these unfortunate Acadians having the temerity to appear in this city of Halifax, before an audience made up nearly entirely of English-speaking people, who perhaps also have very little compassion, and to expose the perfidy and malicious schemes of Lawrence and his subordinates, in this crime. . . . Let me tell you here that there is in the history of Acadia, or Nova Scotia, if you wish, a stain of indelible blood. For many years now English writers have strived periodically to wipe out the stigma; but in spite of their numerous cleansings, it still remains, and nothing can make it disappear. The unspeakable tragedy of the Expulsion of the Acadians in 1755 will always remain a mark of disgrace, of cruelty, on the head of its instigators.[38]

In 1918 the literary critic and essayist Henri d'Arles (nom de plume of Henri Beaudé, an Acadian descendant and Dominican priest) offered a judicious evaluation of the contribution of these Francophone historians. They had demonstrated, he wrote, that "the deportation was no sudden storm, not an improvised piece of work, not the act of a single man, even if the gutless governor who accomplished it has long been held almost uniquely responsible in the eyes of most historians, even our own." An unbiased reading of the evidence, d'Arles believed, pointed to the critical parts played by the Yankee members of the Governor's Council of Nova Scotia, by Governor William Shirley of Massachusetts ("who must at least share equally with Lawrence responsibility for the affair"), and by Major General John Winslow, his officers and men. New Englanders had been deeply implicated in both the plan and the operation of removal.[39]

But the assessment of ultimate responsibility, d'Arles continued, had to go beyond proximate causes into the British *mentalité.* In the minds of government ministers and colonial authorities, the Acadians suffered the "double flaw" (*le double tort*) of being both French and Catholic. It marked them as alien others, as *étrangers*. Although the British kept the inhabitants within the province "by force and by trickery," they refused to integrate them within the structure of empire. The land would be developed by Acadian sweat and toil, but it would remain theirs only until the British could muster sufficient power "to harvest the fruit of their long labor." In the end it would fall to Charles Lawrence to seize "the glory of forging the last link destined to bring together the two ends of the chain with which British diplomacy had encircled the Acadians." *Le grand dérangement* was the violent climax of a long history of British double-dealing, a conclusion that came "slowly but surely." And the violent campaign of expulsion that continued for nearly a decade—"the veritable *chasse à homme* to disperse the last fragments of this unfortunate people"—was conducted with the official approval and full authority of the British government. Although others have written on the responsibility for Acadian removal, no one has improved on d'Arles's summary judgment.[40]

There was more to say, however. In the 1960s, Robert G. Leblanc, another scholar of Acadian descent, published a comprehensive study of the Acadian diaspora, and his work formed the basis for a celebrated poster issued by Parks Canada, which probably did more to educate North Americans about Acadian removal than any other publication of the twentieth century. Stimulated, perhaps, by the fact that he was raised in a Francophone section of Nashua, New Hampshire, Leblanc framed his work in international and comparative perspective, and in one of his essays he suggested the importance of a larger context for interpreting *le grand dérangement*. Cultural diversity and shifting national boundaries, he observed, had in the twentieth century led to many episodes of "forced migration." The best known examples of such violent removals and deportations were in Europe, especially the Balkans. But his study of the Acadian diaspora led him to wonder whether "the colonial history of North America provides a comparable situation." Leblanc's suggestion was considerably ahead of its time, for it was not until the early 1990s, with the violence associated with the breakup of Yugoslavia, that historians began to give serious consideration to the comparative study of what by then was being referred to as "ethnic cleansing."[41]

In 1992, the Security Council of the United Nations established a Commission of Experts to investigate the violent conflict in the Balkans, in particular the practice of ethnic cleansing (*hettoyage ethnique*), an expression that had first appeared in news reports only a year before. After a lengthy investigation, the commission issued a report in which it defined the new term:

> "Ethnic cleansing" is a purposeful policy designed by one ethnic or religious group to remove by violent and terror-inspiring means the civilian population of another ethnic or religious group from certain geographic areas. To a large extent, it is carried out in the name of misguided nationalism, historic grievances, and a powerful driving sense of revenge. This purpose appears to be the occupation of territory to the exclusion of the purged group or groups.

This definition could have been drawn from a study of the expulsion of the Acadians. The operation carried out by Anglo-American forces in 1755 included the forced deportation of civilian populations, the cruel and inhumane treatment of prisoners, and the plunder and wanton destruction of communities, practices now defined as "crimes against humanity." Although this language was unknown in the mid-eighteenth century, the concept of the "Laws of Nations" was well understood. The British Admiralty contended that the authorities in l'Acadie had strictly observed "the laws of nations and the principles of justice." The Acadians condemned the British actions as "crimes."[42]

The point is not to moralize about the past but to better understand it. Historians are in the business of asking questions, and frequently the best questions are those shaped by the times in which they live. "Each age writes the history of the past anew with reference to the conditions uppermost in its own time"—so declared the

American historian Frederick Jackson Turner at the end of the nineteenth century. "We should rework our history," he advised, "from the new points of view afforded by the present." This is what separates the work of historians from that of antiquarians. At the turn of the millennium, historians were thinking seriously about the comparative history of ethnic cleansing, and their conclusions had powerful implications for understanding Acadian removal.[43]

The twentieth century unfortunately provided many examples for comparison, not only the wars of Yugoslav succession but the Ottoman Turk operation against the Armenians during World War I, the Nazi war on the Jews, the Soviet deportation of the Chechens and Crimean Tartars at the end of World War II, and the conflict between ethnic groups in Burundi and Rwanda in the 1990s. In a number of these cases, ethnic cleansing turned to genocide, the intentional destruction of all or part of an ethnic, religious, or national group. At the extreme, as historian Norman M. Naimark puts it in *Fires of Hatred* (2001), "ethnic cleansing bleeds into genocide, as mass murder is committed in order to rid the land of a people."[44]

Mass murder was not a feature of the Acadian expulsion. It became a consistent feature in episodes of ethnic cleansing only after the introduction of industrial weaponry—compact and highly volatile explosives, automatic firearms, lethal chemical gas—in the late nineteenth century. This marks a critical difference between previous times and our own, much to our shame. Nevertheless, violence and terror were essential features of the campaign against the Acadians. People do not leave their homes voluntarily; they must be forced. Moreover, even in twentieth-century examples of ethnic cleansing, most of the deaths were not the result of murder but as the result of shock, exhaustion, dehydration, starvation, exposure, and disease. These means and methods of dying were not acts of God, however, but were invoked by the leaders, the officers, the troops who drove people from their homes to waiting transport vessels or cattle cars. The Acadian entry in the book of the dead is staggering: in July 1755 they numbered some eighteen thousand persons in the maritime region. Over the next eight years an estimated ten thousand exiles and refugees lost their lives as a direct result of the campaign of expulsion.[45]

Comparative history strongly suggests that episodes of ethnic cleansing follow long periods of ethnic stereotyping and devaluation. That was certainly the case in the relationship of l'Acadie and New England. The Acadian ethnic "other" as constructed by Anglo-Americans relied on several discourses of identity and opposition, including anti-Catholic and anti-French ideologies, as well as a systematic racial hatred of the Míkmaq, with whom the Acadians were linked. As Henri d'Arles noted, the British thought of the Acadians as alien others—*étrangers*—and refused to include them within the bounds of civil society. In 1755, the Massachusetts troops who sailed to l'Acadie both feared and hated the inhabitants and were certain of their own moral superiority, a volatile combination. "You know our soldiers hate them," Alexander Murray wrote to John Winslow, "and if they can find a pretence to kill them, they will." Ethnic hatred prepares the way and creates what one study characterizes as the "moral ambiance" that makes ethnic cleansing possible.[46]

A history of ethnic hatred and stereotyping may be a necessary precondition, but it need not determine the outcome. In all the cases historians have studied, the character of interethnic relations varied over time. Periods of conflict were punctuated by periods of accommodation. In the former Yugoslavia, ethnic groups throughout the federation—including Bosnia-Herzegovina—managed to coexist without overt violence for over a generation prior to the catastrophe of the early 1990s. In l'Acadie, during the era of merchant trader John Nelson in the late seventeenth century and during the tenure of Lieutenant-Governor Paul Mascarene in the mid-eighteenth century, Britons found ways to establish peaceful relations with Acadians. Despite the invasion of the province by French forces in the 1740s, the majority of the inhabitants kept their oath of fidelity and did what they could to assist British authorities, as Mascarene testified numerous times. As late as 1753, Governor Peregrine Thomas

Hopson wrote of his hope that "the French inhabitants will take the Oaths . . . and enjoy the benefit of English laws and Liberty." There is nothing spontaneous, nothing unavoidable about the course of history.[47]

Ethnic cleansing was never an improvisation from unfolding events. It invariably required an overt change in policy. It invariably required a plan, implemented in a deliberate and systematic manner, part of a strategy intended to achieve a political objective. It required hierarchical organization and a structure of military command. It required the resources of the state. Even though the government in mid-eighteenth-century Nova Scotia was small, the operation to remove the Acadians could not have been accomplished without the coordination it provided. Hence the great importance of Charles Morris's 1754 operational plan, which was researched, written, and delivered to the Governor's Council in Halifax months before being put into effect. That document is the smoking gun of Acadian removal, indisputable evidence of the premeditation of the operation. And that is undoubtedly why it disappeared from the provincial archives and why, after Reverend Brown's transcription of it was fortuitously discovered, it was published in a "truncated" version. It was simply too hot to handle. In the history of ethnic cleansing, such plans generally sat on the shelf until the opportunity arose to put them into operation during the first military campaigns of an anticipated or newly declared war. "War provides cover," as Norman Naimark puts it. Operations that would otherwise be condemned were found acceptable during the suspension of civility that accompanied warfare's organized violence. Similarly, military necessity was used as the justification for Acadian removal.[48]

The comparative study of episodes of ethnic cleansing reveals a remarkable set of common patterns. Tactical procedures were much the same in all cases. The confiscation of the victims' firearms in the weeks before the roundup. The isolation and arrest of community leaders, especially the clergy. The seizure and destruction of community records and registers. The separation of men from women and children. Such measures—each of them successfully employed against the Acadians—were intended to demonstrate the weakness and vulnerability of the victims and to reduce the likelihood of their resistance. The removal of the people was invariably followed by the erasure of all their cultural signs. Houses, barns, shops, and especially churches destroyed; the landscape systematically renamed. "No remnant of the language and culture of the ethnically cleansed people should be left behind," writes Naimark. Thus was the ground prepared for repossession by its new owners. In all cases that was the final objective—"the occupation of territory to the exclusion of the purged group or groups," in the words of the UN Commission of Experts of 1992—the creation of an ethnically homogeneous territory.[49]

Across the centuries, the similarities are stunning. Before 1755 there were many instances of horrible violence against innocent peoples in North America. But the removal of the Acadians was the first episode of state-sponsored ethnic cleansing in North American history.

IN 1990, Warren Perrin, a Louisiana attorney and a Cajun descendant of Acadian exiles, delivered a petition to the British government seeking from Queen Elizabeth II an official apology for what had been done to the Acadians in 1755. He took up the cause after one of his sons asked him what their ancestors had done to deserve expulsion from their homeland. "I wasn't able to tell him," Perrin later recalled. "Like most Cajuns at the time, I knew very little about our history." He began to read, and the more he read, the more incensed he became. "It is the defining event in our history," he concluded, "a precursor to what we now call ethnic cleansing."[50]

The campaign for a British acknowledgment of responsibility began as a lawyer's whim, but it attracted far more attention than might have been expected. In 1993, Perrin's petition was endorsed by a joint resolution of both houses of the Louisiana legislature and the following year by the legislature of Maine, which includes a substantial Acadian and French-speaking population in its northern counties. In 1999, the Bloc Québecois, the federal political party in Canada committed to the independence of Québec Province, proposed the introduction of a motion in the Canadian Parliament calling on the British crown for "an official apology to the Acadian people for the wrongs done to them in its name between 1755 and 1763." The same year a publication sponsored by the Société Nationale de l'Acadie, representing Acadian political and cultural groups throughout Canada, described *le grand dérangement* as "a tragic episode of ethnic cleansing *avant la lettre*," and in 2000 the Société added its support for an apology that would be offered in time for the commemoration of the 250th anniversary of the deportation in 2005.[51]

Fifty years earlier, on the eve of the celebration of the 200th anniversary of *le grand dérangement* in 1955, the politics had taken a far different form. In Louisiana, the Cajun leaders who organized the events in St. Martinville showcased the mythic Acadian image of *Evangeline*, while in the Maritimes the organizing committee of Acadian leaders did its best to produce an event that would foster no ill feeling among the majority English-speaking population. The ceremonies held on the memorial grounds at Grand Pré featured the unveiling of a bust of Longfellow, and included a speech in which the chair of the committee extended to the representative of the British government who was present "the generous offer of Christian forgiveness."[52]

But even at the time of that celebration, forces of modernization and cultural assimilation had begun to operate in earnest on previously isolated Acadian communities. During the second half of the twentieth century old ways of life were transformed. In southwestern Louisiana, the booming petroleum industry ushered in an era of prosperity. Industrialization had something of the opposite effect in the Maritimes, leaving rural Acadian communities stricken by unemployment and poverty. Thousands of young people were drawn to other, more economically developed areas of Canada or the United States. Simultaneously the proportion of French-speaking Acadians began to fall. By the end of the century fewer than three in five maritime Acadians claimed French as their primary language, while in Louisiana only half of all Cajun families spoke French at home, and a mere 8 percent of the children in those homes were fluent in the language. In part the decline in the use of French was the result of forced assimilation. Until late in the century, the public schools of both Louisiana and the Maritimes required education in the English language. But more generally language change was the consequence of the inexorable spread of a predominantly English mass culture.[53]

The loss of natal language symbolized the potential loss of cultural identity, and its retention became a potent political issue. In New Brunswick, where Acadian descendants made up a third or more of the electorate, voters elected Louis J. Robichaud as the first Acadian premier in the early 1960s. Among his considerable achievements, Robichaud made bilingualism the official policy of the province and established the first Francophone public university in the Maritimes at Moncton, a city on the Petitcodiac River—where Acadian guerrillas had once battled New England troops. It is a wonderful historical irony that the university helped turn Moncton, which was named for Robert Monckton, the British officer who conducted the brutal campaign of expulsion against the Acadians, into the educational and intellectual center of the Acadian community, the heart of a cultural renaissance in Acadian arts and letters during the last quarter of the twentieth century.

The politics of language and ethnicity were important elsewhere as well. In Nova Scotia, where Acadians were a small minority, Acadian parents pressed for French-language instruction and the incorporation of Acadian history and culture into the public school curriculum. In Louisiana, where Cajuns were considerably more integrated into mainstream society, there was also a cultural renaissance, much of it centered on the boomtown of Lafayette, where a campus of the University of Louisiana played a role similar to that of Université de Moncton in the Maritimes. In the late 1960s the state government established the Council for the Development of French in Louisiana (CODFIL) to oversee efforts to strengthen French-language instruction in the public schools. In the 1990s Warren Perrin was one of numeorus Cajun and Acadian leaders who, fearing the loss of cultural tradition, took up the politics of identity. He became a prominent cultural activist, assuming the presidency of CODFIL, establishing an Acadian museum, and pressing his campaign for a British apology.[54]

In October 2001, the motion calling for an apology came before the Canadian House of Commons. Because it was endorsed and sponsored by Bloc Québecois, the Liberal government declared the vote on the motion to be an issue of party discipline, which ensured its defeat, but not before there was a short yet serious debate. Among all the deputies who spoke on both sides the consensus was that the removal of the Acadians had been deplorable. In 2001 few were willing to argue the thesis of "cruel necessity." But there was considerable disagreement over the questions of historical culpability and guilt. Perhaps the most interesting comments came from Scott Reid of Ontario, a member of the right-wing Canadian Alliance Party. "Although we know with certainty the degree of suffering caused by the deportations," he told his colleagues, "it is much more difficult to pin down historical responsibility for them." Reid, who was something of a historian, felt certain that "governors Lawrence and Shirley were at the heart of the decision making and must bear ultimate responsibility." Yet the resolution under consideration by the House seemed to lay blame on the British exclusively. A more historically informed motion, he suggested, would demand apologies from the legislatures of the New England states, "for the harm done in their interests and with their complicity." But were such a motion proposed, he would oppose that as well. "I would do so because I do not accept the notion that an institution can maintain a heritage of collective guilt which is imposed upon successive generations."

Great wrongs of the past ought to be condemned and their consequences addressed, but the guilt for past injustices died with those who were personally responsible. "Let us vote against this motion in its present form," Reid concluded. "But let us vote for it if it is reintroduced in a form that allows us to express, without apology, our sorrow over this past wrong, and if it allows us, without condemning others, to indicate our determination that no such wrong will ever in the future be tolerated on Canadian soil."[55]

Reid made an important point. The removal of the Acadians was an early example of the ethnic cleansing that had become all too familiar in the twentieth century, and like those episodes it was perpetrated by men intent on political and material advantage. Richard Goldstone, a South African constitutional court judge, and the chief prosecutor at the International Criminal Tribunal hearing the cases of those charged in the ethnic cleansing operations in the former Yugoslavia, spoke eloquently on this point: "Specific individuals bear the major share of the responsibility, and it is they, not the group as a whole, who need to be held to account, through a fair and meticulously detailed presentation and evaluation of the evidence, precisely so that the next time around no one will be able to claim that all Serbs did this, or all Croats, or all Hutus." History records the names of the individuals responsible for the ethnic cleansing of the Acadians: William Shirley, Charles Lawrence, Jonathan Belcher, Edwin Boscawen, Savage Mostyn, the members of the Nova Scotia Council, Charles Morris, Robert Monckton, John Winslow, John Handfield.[56]

Yet the fact of individual responsibility does not relieve governments and other institutions of the responsibility to examine their histories and acknowledge the impact of past decisions and actions. The consequences of Acadian removal lived on after the fact, reproduced as prejudice, discrimination, ignorance, and poverty—as well as a profound sense of social isolation and cultural exclusion among Acadians. The parliamentary debate suggested there was considerable agreement on this legacy of ethnic cleansing, and an emerging consensus that an official acknowledgment of responsibility might be an important step toward reconciliation, including the Acadian perspective in the nation's historical narrative. Following the defeat of the motion in the Canadian Parliament the Société Nationale de l'Acadie made a subtle but significant shift away from the idea of an apology, calling instead for the government to recognize the harm that had been done to the Acadians. "We want England to accept that this was an unacceptable act," declared society president Euclide Chiasson. "It was an ethnic cleansing, and some people are still denying it."[57]

Over the next two years quiet negotiations took place, and in December 2003 the cabinet of Prime Minister Jean Chrétien announced that the queen's representative in Canada, Governor-General Adrienne Clarkson, would sign a carefully worded Royal Proclamation, an official acknowledgment of responsibility.

> Whereas on 28 July 1755, the Crown, in the course of administering the affairs of the British colony of Nova Scotia, made the decision to deport the Acadian people;
>
> Whereas the deportation of the Acadian people, commonly known as *le Grand Dérangement,* continued until 1763 and had tragic consequences, including the deaths of many thousands of Acadians—from disease, in shipwrecks, in their places of refuge and in prison camps in Nova Scotia and England as well as in the British colonies in America;
>
> Whereas We acknowledge these historical facts and the trials and suffering experienced by the Acadian people during *le Grand Dérangement*;
>
> Whereas We hope that the Acadian people can turn the page on this dark chapter of their history;
>
> . . . Now know you that we, by and with the advice of Our Privy Council for Canada, do by this Our Proclamation . . . designate

> 28 July of every year as "A Day of Commemoration of the Great Upheaval," commencing on 28 July 2005.[58]

Euclide Chiasson, speaking for the Société Nationale de l'Acadie, welcomed the proclamation enthusiastically. "We finally have a document that recognizes the events surrounding that very sad part of our history," he declared. It was something the Acadians had asked from the British in the years immediately following their deportation. In 1760, the exiles in Philadelphia appealed to King George to "let the justice of our complaints be truly and impartially enquired into." The royal response had been a long time coming. "These are the historical facts," said Chiasson, referring the proclamation's establishing clauses, and a "recognition of the wrongs that were done to our people." Those facts had been established long before by historians, but it was important that they were now acknowledged by the British and Canadian governments. "It's wonderful," Chiasson said. Now, he concluded, "it's not only Acadian history, it's Canadian history."[59]

It was also American history. Yet the acknowledgment of British responsibility in December 2003 attracted almost no attention in the United States. The expulsion of the Acadians, which Longfellow claimed as an American story, remained a part of the historical canon only so long as it told a tale of British perfidy. Once New Englanders were implicated in the chain of responsibility the story was relegated to a dimly remembered chapter in the history of Canada, about which Americans are notoriously ignorant. But *le grand dérangement* was an Acadian, French, British, Canadian, *and* American story. As Edouard Richard put it, in order to reimagine that history, "one must become, so to speak, by turns, a missionary, an Acadian peasant, an Englishman and a Frenchman, a Catholic and a Protestant. One must divest oneself of preconceived notions, narrow or broaden one's views, penetrate into the prejudices of all. This is not always easy, nor equally easy for everyone." It has not been easy for Americans. It requires recognizing the wider realms of our history and acknowledging the dark side of our past, the evil means men used to pursue the end of continental expansion. The Acadian story indeed tells a story of America. A story of frontiers and borderlands at the founding moment of American history, of a people born on the margins of empire who sought a way to live with two masters, of those who attempted to foster peace, and of those who out of hatred and fear, jealousy and greed, pursued the ways of war.[60]

NOTES

Works Cited Frequently in the Notes.
Chapter Notes begin on page 493.

Akins	Thomas B. Akins, ed., *Selections from the Public Documents of the Province of Nova Scotia* (Halifax: Charles Annand, 1869).
Arsenault (1965)	Bona Arsenault, *Histoire et généalogie des Acadiens*, 2 vols. (Quebec: Le Conseil de la vie française en Amérique, 1965).
Arsenault (1994)	Bona Arsenault, *History of the Acadians* (1966; Saint-Laurent, Quebec: Fides, 1994).
Bailey	Alfred Goldsworthy Bailey, *The Conflict of European and Eastern Algonkian Cultures, 1504–1700. A Study in Canadian Civilization*, 2nd edn. (Toronto: University of Toronto Press, 1969).
Baker and Reid	Emerson W. Baker and John G. Reid, *The New England Knight: Sir William Phips, 1651–1695* (Toronto: University of Toronto Press, 1998).
Ball	Howard Ball, *Prosecuting War Crimes and Genocide: The Twentieth-Century Experience* (Lawrence: University Press of Kansas, 1999).
Basque	Maurice Basque, *Des hommes de pouvoir: Histoire d'Otho Robichaud et de sa famille, notables Acadiens de Port-Royal et de Néguac* (Néguac, New Brunswick: Société Historique de Néguac, 1996).
Baxter	W. T. Baxter, *The House of Hancock: Business in Boston, 1724–1775* (Cambridge, MA: Harvard University Press, 1945).

Beaujeu — Daniel-Hyacinthe-Marie Liénard de Beaujeu, "Journal de la Campagne du détachement de Canada à L'Acadie et aux Mines, en 1746–47," in Casgrain (1888–90) 2:20–74.

Bell — Winthrop Pickard Bell, *The "Foreign Protestants" and the Settlement of Nova Scotia: The History of a Piece of Arrested British Colonial Policy in the Eighteenth Century* (Toronto: University of Toronto Press, 1961).

Belliveau — Pierre Belliveau, *French Neutrals in Massachusetts: The Story of Acadians Rounded Up by Soldiers from Massachusetts and Their Captivity in the Bay Province, 1755–1766* (Boston: Kirk S. Giffen, 1972).

Blanchet — J. Blanchet, ed., *Collection de manuscrits contenant lettres, mémoires, et autres documents historiques relatifs à la Nouvelle-France, recueillis aux archives de la province de Québec, ou copiés à l'étranger*, 4 vols. (Quebec: Imprimerie A. Coté et Cie, 1884).

Brasseaux (1985) — Carl A. Brasseaux, "A New Acadia: The Acadian Migrations to South Louisiana, 1764–1803," *Acadiensis* 15 (1985):123–32.

Brasseaux (1987) — Carl A. Brasseaux, *The Founding of New Acadia: The Beginnings of Acadian Life in Louisiana, 1765–1803* (Baton Rouge: Louisiana State University Press, 1987).

Brasseaux (1991) — Carl A. Brasseaux, *Scattered to the Wind: Dispersal and Wanderings of the Acadians, 1755–1809* (Lafayette, LA: Center for Louisiana Studies, 1991).

Brasseaux (1992) — Carl A. Brasseaux, *Acadian to Cajun: Transformation of a People, 1803–1877* (Jackson: University Press of Mississippi, 1992).

Brasseaux (1994) — Carl A. Brasseaux, "Phantom Letters: Acadian Correspondence, 1766–1784," *Acadiensis* 23 (Spring 1994):124–32.

Brebner (1925) — John Bartlet Brebner, "Subsidized Intermarriage with the Indians," *Canadian Historical Review* 6 (1925):233–36.

Brebner (1927) — John Bartlet Brebner, *New England's Outpost: Acadia Before the Conquest of Canada* (New York: Columbia University Press, 1927).

Brebner (1929) — John Bartlet Brebner, "Paul Mascarene of Annapolis Royal," *Dalhousie Review* 8 (1929):501–16.

Brebner (1937) — John Bartlet Brebner, *The Neutral Yankees of Nova Scotia: A Marginal Colony During the Revolutionary Years* (New York: Columbia University Press, 1937).

Brown (1815) — Andrew Brown, "Removal of the French Inhabitants of Nova Scotia by Lieutenant Governor Lawrence and His Majesty's

	Council in October 1755" (1815), 59–60, Brown Collection, Manuscripts and Archives, University of Edinburgh, in McMahon.
Brown (1881)	[Andrew Brown,] "The Acadian French," *NSHSC* 2 (1881): 129–60.
Brymner	"Calendar of Papers Relating to Nova Scotia, 1603–1801," ed. Douglas Brymner, in PAC (1895).
Buckner and Reid	Phillip A. Buckner and John G. Reid, eds., *The Atlantic Region to Confederation: A History* (Toronto: University of Toronto Press, 1994).
Casgrain (1888)	Henri Raymond Casgrain, *Un Pélerinage au pays d'Evangéline*, 2nd edn. (1887; Quebec: L. J. Demers & frère, 1888).
Casgrain (1888–90)	Henri Raymond Casgrain, ed., *Collection de documents inédits sur le Canada et l'Amérique publiés par le Canada-Français. Documents sur L'Acadie*, 3 vols. (Quebec: L. J. Demers & frère, 1888–90).
Casgrain (1897)	Henri Raymond Casgrain, *Les Sulpiciens et les prêtres des missions-étrangères en Acadie* (Quebec: Pruneau & Kirouac, 1897).
Chagnon	F. X. Chagnon, *Annales religieuses de la paroisse de St. Jacques le Majeur vulgo de l'Achigan* (Montreal: J. A. Plinguet, 1872).
Champlain	*The Works of Samuel de Champlain*, ed. H. P. Biggar, 6 vols. (Toronto: Champlain Society, 1922–36).
Chard (1975)	Donald F. Chard, "The Impact of French Privateering on New England, 1689–1713," *American Neptune* 35 (1975):153–63.
Chard (1980)	Donald F. Chard, "The Price and Profits of Accommodation: Massachusetts-Louisbourg Trade, 1713–1744," in *Seafaring in Colonial Massachusetts* (Boston: Colonial Society of Massachusetts, 1980), 131–49.
Chiasson	Anselme Chiasson, "Placide Gaudet," *CSHA* 4 (1971–73):6–23.
Choquette	Leslie Choquette, *Frenchmen into Peasants: Modernity and Tradition in the Peopling of French Canada* (Cambridge, MA: Harvard University Press, 1997).
Church	Thomas Church, *The History of the Great Indian War of 1675 and 1676, Commonly Called Philip's War. Also the Old French and Indian Wars, from 1689 to 1704*, ed. Samuel G. Drake (New York: H. Dayton, n.d. [1860]).
Cigar	Norman Cigar, *Genocide in Bosnia: The Policy of "Ethnic Cleansing"* (College Station: Texas A&M University Press, 1995).
Clark (1965)	Andrew Hill Clark, "New England's Role in the Underdevelop-

ment of Cape Breton Island During the French Regime, 1713–1758," *Canadian Geographer* 9 (1965):1–12.

Clark (1968) — Andrew Hill Clark, *Acadia: The Geography of Early Nova Scotia to 1760* (Madison: University of Wisconsin Press, 1968).

CMHS — *Collections of the Massachusetts Historical Society.*

Conrad — Margaret Conrad, ed., *Looking into Acadie: Three Illustrated Studies. Nova Scotia Museum. Curatorial Report No. 87* (Halifax: Nova Scotia Museum, n.d. [1998]).

Courville — Louis-Léonard Aumasson, Sieur de Courville, *Mémoires sur le Canada depuis 1749 jusqu'à 1760* (Quebec: La Société littéraire et historique de Québec, 1838).

CSHA — *Les Cahiers—Société historique acadienne.*

CSP — *Calendar of State Papers, Colonial Series,* 44 vols. (London: Public Record Office, 1860–1994).

Daigle (1967) — Jean Daigle, "Documents: La pêche en Acadie au 17e siècle," *CSHA* 2 (1967):227–29.

Daigle (1976) — Jean Daigle, "Nos Amis les Ennemis: Les marchands Acadiens et le Massachusetts à la fin du 17e siècle," *CSHA* 7 (1976):161–70.

Daigle (1982) — Jean Daigle, ed., *The Acadians of the Maritimes: Thematic Studies* (Moncton, New Brunswick: Centre d'études acadiennes, 1982).

Daigle (1995a) — Jean Daigle, "Acadia, 1604–1763: An Historical Synthesis," in Daigle (1995b):1–44.

Daigle (1995b) — Jean Daigle, ed., *Acadia of the Maritimes: Thematic Studies* (Moncton, New Brunswick: Chaire d'études acadiennes, Université de Moncton, 1995).

Davenport — Frances Gardiner Davenport, ed., *European Treaties Bearing on the History of the United States and Its Dependencies,* 4 vols. (Washington, DC: Carnegie Institution, 1929).

DCB — *Dictionary of Canadian Biography/Dictionnaire biographique du Canada,* 14 vols. on CD-ROM (Toronto and Quebec: University of Toronto, Université Laval, 2000).

De Fiedmont — *The Siege of Beauséjour in 1755; A Journal of the Attack on Beauséjour written by Jacau de Fiedmont, Artillery Officer and Acting Engineer at the Fort,* ed. John Clarence Webster (St. John, New Brunswick: New Brunswick Museum, 1936).

Delaney — Paul Delaney, "The Husbands and Children of Agathe de la Tour," *CSHA* 25 (1994):263–84.

Delesdernier — Moses Delesdernier, "Observations of the Situation, Customs and Manners of the Ancient Acadians" (1791), in Clarence d'Entremont, "The Golden Age of the Old Time Acadians," *YV*, 3 October 1989.

D'Entremont and Hébert — Clarence J. d'Entremont and Hector J. Hébert, "Parkman's Diary and the Acadian Exiles in Massachusetts," *French Canadian and Acadian Genealogical Review* 1 (Winter 1968):241–93.

Denys — Nicolas Denys, *The Description and Natural History of the Coasts of North America*, ed. William F. Ganong (Toronto: Champlain Society, 1908).

Dièreville — Sieur de Dièreville, *Relation of the Voyage to Port Royal in Acadia or New France*, ed. John Clarence Webster (1708; Toronto: Champlain Society, 1933).

Doughty — Arthur G. Doughty, *The Acadian Exiles: A Chronicle of the Land of Evangeline* (Toronto: Glasgow, Brook & Co., 1916).

Dunn — Brenda Dunn, "Aspects of the Lives of Women in Ancienne Acadie," in Conrad:29–51.

Eaton (1910) — Arthur Wentworth Hamilton Eaton, *The History of Kings County, Nova Scotia: Heart of the Acadian Land* (Salem, MA: Salem Press, 1910).

Eaton (1915) — Arthur Wentworth Hamilton Eaton, "Rhode Island Settlers on the French Lands in Nova Scotia in 1760 and 1761," *Americana* 10 (1915):1–43, 83–104, 179–97.

EIHC — *Essex Institute Historical Collections.*

Fergusson — Charles Bruce Fergusson, ed., *Minutes of His Majesty's Council at Annapolis Royal, 1736–1749* (Halifax: Public Archives of Nova Scotia, 1967).

Ferling — John E. Ferling, *A Wilderness of Miseries: War and Warriors in Early America* (Westport, CT: Greenwood Press, 1980).

Foote — William A. Foote, "British Regulars in Colonial America: The Independent Companies in Nova Scotia," *Journal of the New Brunswick Museum* (1980):82–91.

Frame — Elizabeth Frame, *A List of Micmac Names of Places, Rivers, etc., in Nova Scotia* (Cambridge, MA: J. Wilson, 1892).

Galerm — Jean-Baptiste Galerm [Galerne], "The Case of the French Neutrals," 12 February 1756, in *Votes and Proceedings of the House of Representatives of the Province of Pennsylvania* (Philadephia: B. Franklin, 1756).

Ganong — William F. Ganong, ed., "Report of the proceedings of the troops on the expedition up St. John's River in the Bay of Fundy under the command of Colonel Monckton [1758]," *Collections of the New Brunswick Historical Society* 5 (1904).

Gaudet — Placide Gaudet, "Acadian Genealogy and Notes," in PANS (1906), vol. 2.

Gipson (1942) — Lawrence Henry Gipson, *The Great War for the Empire: The Years of Defeat, 1754–1757*. Vol. 6 of *The British Empire Before the American Revolution* (New York: Alfred A. Knopf, 1942).

Gipson (1954) — Lawrence Henry Gipson, *The Great War for the Empire: The Culmination, 1760–1763*. Vol. 8 of *The British Empire Before the American Revolution* (New York: Alfred A. Knopf, 1954).

Godfrey — William G. Godfrey, *Pursuit of Profit and Preferment in Colonial North America: John Bradstreet's Quest* (Waterloo, Ontario: Wilfrid Laurier University Press, 1982).

Graham (1963) — Dominick Stuart Graham, "The Making of a Colonial Governor: Charles Lawrence in Nova Scotia, 1749–1760." M.A. thesis, University of New Brunswick, 1963.

Graham (1968) — Dominick Stuart Graham, "The Planning of the Beauséjour Operation and the Approaches to War in 1755," *New England Quarterly* 41 (1968):551–66.

Griffiths (1969) — Naomi E. S. Griffiths, ed., *The Acadian Deportation: Deliberate Perfidy or Cruel Necessity?* (Toronto: Copp Clark, 1969).

Griffiths (1976) — Naomi E. S. Griffiths, "Acadians in Exile: The Experiences of the Acadians in the British Seaports," *Acadiensis* 4 (1976):67–84.

Griffiths (1984) — Naomi Griffiths, "The Golden Age: Acadian Life, 1713–1748," *Histoire sociale—Social History* 17 (May 1984):21–34.

Griffiths (1992) — Naomi E. S. Griffiths, *The Contexts of Acadian History, 1686–1784* (Montreal: McGill-Queen's University Press, 1992).

Griffiths and Reid — Naomi E. S. Griffiths and John G. Reid, "New Evidence on New Scotland, 1629," *William and Mary Quarterly*, 3rd series, 49 (1992):492–508.

Gwyn — Julian Gwyn, ed., *The Royal Navy and North America: The Warren Papers, 1736–1752* (London: Navy Records Society, 1973).

Hale — "Journal of a Voyage to Nova Scotia Made in 1731 by Robert Hale of Beverly," *EIHC* 42 (1906):217–44.

Haliburton — Thomas C. Haliburton, *An Historical and Statistical Account of Nova-Scotia*, 2 vols. (Halifax: Joseph Howe, 1829).

Hamer — Marguerite B. Hamer, "The Fate of the Exiled Acadians in South Carolina," *Journal of Southern History* 4 (1938):199–208.

Hannay — James H. Hannay, *History of Acadia, From Its First Discovery to the Surrender to England, by the Treaty of Paris* (St. John, New Brunswick: J. & A. McMillan, 1879).

Harvey (1926) — D. C. Harvey, *The French Regime in Prince Edward Island* (New Haven: Yale University Press, 1926).

Harvey (1953) — D. C. Harvey, "Journal and Letters of Colonel Charles Lawrence," *Bulletin of the Public Archives of Nova Scotia* 10 (1953).

Hudnut — Ruth Allison Hudnut and Hayes Baker-Crothers, "Acadian Transients in South Carolina," *American Historical Review* 43 (1938):500–13.

Hustvedt — Eric Hustvedt, *Maritime Dykelands: The 350 Year Struggle* ([Halifax]: Province of Nova Scotia, 1987).

Hutchinson — Thomas Hutchinson, *The History of the Colony and Province of Massachusetts-Bay*, ed. Lawrence Shaw Mayo, 3 vols. (Cambridge, MA: Harvard University Press, 1936).

Hynes — Gisa Hynes, "Some Aspects of the Demography of Port Royal, 1650–1755," *Acadiensis* 3 (1973):3–17.

Innis — Harold A. Innis, ed., *Select Documents in Canadian Economic History, 1497–1783* (Toronto: University of Toronto Press, 1929).

Johnson — Richard R. Johnson, *John Nelson, Merchant Adventurer: A Life Between Empires* (New York: Oxford University Press, 1991).

Johnston — A. J. B. Johnston, "Borderland Worries: Loyalty Oaths in *Acadie*, Nova Scotia, 1654–1755," *French Colonial History* 4 (2003): 31–48.

Knox — John Knox, *An Historical Journal of the Campaigns in North America for the Years 1757, 1758, 1759, and 1760*, ed. Arthur G. Doughty, 3 vols. (Toronto: Champlain Society, 1914).

Lafrenière — Albert N. Lafrenière, "Acadian Deportation Ships," *Connecticut Maple Leaf* 6 (1993).

Lahontan — Louis-Armand de Lom d'Arce, Baron de Lahontan, *New Voyages to North America*, 2 vols. (London: H. Benwicke, 1703).

Lauvrière — Emile Lauvrière, *La tragédie d'un peuple: Histoire du peuple acadien de ses origines à nos jours*, 2 vols. (Paris: Editions Bossard, 1923).

Leblanc — Robert G. Leblanc, "The Acadian Migrations," *Cahiers de géographie de Québec* 11 (1967):523–41.

Ledet	Wilton Paul Ledet, "Acadian Exiles in Pennsylvania," *Pennsylvania History* 9 (1942):118–28.
Léger	Maurice A. Léger, "Les Missionnaires de l'ancienne Acadie (1604–1755)," *CSHA* 28 (1997):63–97.
Leonard	Kevin Leonard, "The Origin and Dispersal of Dykeland Technology," *CSHA* 22 (1991):31–59.
Lescarbot	Marc Lescarbot, *The History of New France,* trans. W. L. Grant, 3 vols. (1609; Toronto: Champlain Society, 1907–14).
Little	Otis Little, *The State of Trade in the Northern Colonies Considered; with an Account of their Produce, and a Particular Description of Nova Scotia* (1748; Boston: Thomas Fleet, 1749).
Lockerby	Earle Lockerby, "The Deportation of the Acadians from Ile Saint-Jean, 1758," *Acadiensis* 27 (1998):45–94.
Longley	R. S. Longley, "The Coming of the New England Planters to the Annapolis Valley," *NSHSC* 33 (1961).
Loudoun Papers	Loudoun Papers, Huntington Library and Art Gallery, San Marino, California.
Lowe	Richard G. Lowe, "Massachusetts and the Acadians," *William and Mary Quarterly*, 3rd series, 25 (1968):212–29.
McMahon	Nancy McMahon, "Andrew Brown and the Writing of Acadian History." Master's thesis, Queen's University, Kingston, Ontario, 1981.
MacDonald	Majorie Anne MacDonald, *Fortune and La Tour: The Civil War in Acadia* (1983; Halifax: Nimbus, 2000).
MacMechan (1900)	Archibald M. MacMechan, ed., *A Calendar of Two Letter-Books and One Commission-Book in the Possession of the Government of Nova Scotia* (Halifax: Public Archives of Nova Scotia, 1900).
MacMechan (1908)	Archibald M. MacMechan, ed., *Original Minutes of His Majesty's Council at Annapolis Royal, 1720–1739* (Halifax: [Public Archives of Nova Scotia], 1908).
Maillard	[Pierre Antoine Simon Maillard], *An Account of the Customs and Manners of the Micmakis and Maricheets, Savage Nations, Now Dependent on the Government of Cape Breton* (London: S. Hooper & A. Morley, 1758).
Maillet	Antonine Maillet, *Rabelais et les traditions populaires en Acadie* (Quebec: Presses de l'Université Laval, 1971).
Mascarene	Paul Mascarene, "A Narrative of Events at Annapolis from the Capture in October 1710 till September 1711," in G. Patterson:70–84.

Mascarene Papers	Mascarene Family Papers, Massachusetts Historical Society (microfilm).
Massignon	Geneviève Massignon, *Les parlers français d'Acadie: Enquête linguistique,* 2 vols. (Paris: C. Klincksieck, 1962).
Millard	Clifford Millard, "The Acadians in Virginia," *Virginia Magazine of History and Biography* 40 (1932):241–58.
Milling	Chapman J. Milling, *Exile Without an End* (Columbia, SC: Bostick & Thornley, 1943).
Milner	W. C. Milner, "Records of Chignecto," *NSHSC* 15 (1911):1–85.
Moody	Barry Morris Moody, "'A Just and Disinterested Man': The Nova Scotia Career of Paul Mascarene, 1710–1752." Ph.D. thesis, Queen's University, Kingston, Ontario, 1976.
Moogk	Peter Moogk, *La Nouvelle France: The Making of French Canada—A Cultural History* (East Lansing: Michigan State University Press, 2000).
Morrison	Kenneth M. Morrison, *The Embattled Northeast: The Elusive Ideal of Alliance in Abenaki-Euramerican Relations* (Berkeley: University of California Press, 1984).
Morse	William Inglis Morse, ed., *Acadiensis Nova, 1598–1779*, 2 vols. (London: Quaritch, 1935).
Munson	Gorham Munson, "St. Castin: A Legend Revised," *Dalhousie Review* 45 (1965–66):338–60.
Murdoch	Beamish Murdoch, *A History of Nova-Scotia or Acadie,* 3 vols. (Halifax: James Barnes, 1865).
Naimark	Norman M. Naimark, *Fires of Hatred: Ethnic Cleansing in Twentieth-Century Europe* (Cambridge, MA: Harvard University Press, 2001).
Nicholson	"Journal of Colonel Nicholson at the Capture of Annapolis, 1710," ed. John T. Bulmer, *NSHSC* 1 (1879):59–104.
NSHQ	*Nova Scotia Historical Quarterly.*
NSHR	*Nova Scotia Historical Review.*
NSHSC	*Nova Scotia Historical Society Collections.*
O'Callaghan	E. B. O'Callaghan, ed., *Documents Relative to the Colonial History of the State of New-York,* 15 vols. (Albany: Weed, Parsons, 1853–87).
Officer	E. Roy Officer, "Crown Land Grants to Acadians in New Brunswick, 1760–1848," *CSHA* 12 (1981):148–62.

PAC (1895) — Public Archives of Canada, *Report for 1894* (Ottawa: Queen's Printer, 1895).

PAC (1906) — Public Archives of Canada, *Report Concerning Canadian Archives Branch for the Year 1905,* 2 vols. (Ottawa: S. E. Dawson, 1906).

PAC (1913) — Public Archives of Canada, *Report of the Work of the Archives Branch for the Year 1912*, ed. Arthur G. Doughty (Ottawa: King's Printer, 1913).

PAC (1926) — Public Archives of Canada, *The Northcliffe Collection* (Ottawa: King's Printer, 1926).

PANS RG1 — Public Archives of Nova Scotia, Commissioner of Public Records Collection, RG1: selected volumes (microfilm).

Pargellis — Stanley Pargellis, ed., *Military Affairs in North America, 1748–1765: Selected Documents from the Cumberland Papers in Windsor Castle* (New York: D. Appleton-Century, 1936).

Parkman — Francis Parkman, *France and England in North America,* 2 vols. (1865–93; New York: Library of America, 1983).

G. Patterson — George Patterson, "Hon. Samuel Vetch, First English Governor of Nova Scotia," *NSHSC* 4 (1885):11–112.

S. Patterson — Stephen E. Patterson, "Indian-White Relations in Nova Scotia, 1749–61: A Study in Political Interaction," *Acadiensis* 22 (1993): 26–57.

PG — *Pennsylvania Gazette.*

Plank — Geoffrey Plank, *An Unsettled Conquest: The British Campaign Against the Peoples of Nova Scotia* (Philadelphia: University of Pennsylvania Press, 2000).

Rameau — François-Edmé Rameau de Saint-Père, *La France aux colonies* (Paris: A. Jouby, 1859).

Rawlyk — George A. Rawlyk, *Nova Scotia's Massachusetts: A Study of Massachusetts-Nova Scotia Relations, 1630 to 1784* (Montreal: McGill-Queen's University Press, 1973).

Raymond — W. O. Raymond, *Winslow Papers, A.D. 1776–1826* (St. John, New Brunswick: Sun Printing Company, 1901).

Reid (1981) — John G. Reid, *Acadia, Maine, and New Scotland: Marginal Colonies in the Seventeenth Century* (Toronto: University of Toronto Press, 1981).

Reid (1991) — John G. Reid, "Change and Continuity in Nova Scotia, 1758–1775," in Margaret Conrad, ed., *Making Adjustments: Change and*

	Continuity in Planter Nova Scotia, 1759–1800 (Fredericton, Brunswick: Acadiensis Press, 1991):45–59.
Reid (1992)	John G. Reid, "Unorthodox Warfare in the Northeast, 1703," *Canadian Historical Review* 73 (1992):211–20.
Reid (2004)	John G. Reid, et al., *The "Conquest" of Acadia, 1710* (Toronto: University of Toronto Press, 2004).
Richard	Edouard Richard, *Acadia: Missing Links of a Lost Chapter in American History,* 2 vols. (New York: Home Book Company, 1895).
Robison	Mark Powers Robison, "Maritime Frontiers: The Evolution of Empire in Nova Scotia, 1713–1758." Ph.D. thesis, University of Colorado, 2000.
Ross and Deveau	Sally Ross and Alphonse Deveau, *The Acadians of Nova Scotia: Past and Present* (Halifax: Nimbus Publishing, 1992).
Salusbury	*Expeditions of Honour: The Journal of John Salusbury in Halifax, Nova Scotia, 1749–53*, ed. Ronald Rompkey (Newark, DE: University of Delaware Press, 1982).
Sauvageau	Robert Sauvageau, *Acadie: La guerre de Cent Ans des Français d'Amérique aux Maritimes et en Louisiane* (Paris: Berger-Levrault, 1987).
Shirley	*Correspondence of William Shirley, Governor of Massachusetts and Military Commander in America, 1731–1760*, ed. Charles Henry Lincoln, 2 vols. (New York: Macmillan, 1912).
Shortt	Adam Shortt, V. K. Johnston, and Gustave Lanctot, eds., *Documents Relating to Currency, Exchange and Finance in Nova Scotia, with Prefatory Documents, 1675–1758* (Ottawa: Board of Historical Publications, 1933).
Smith	Philip H. Smith, *Acadia: A Lost Chapter in American History* (New York: the author, 1884).
Sollers	Basil Sollers, "The Acadians Transported to Maryland," *Maryland Historical Magazine* 3 (1908):1–21.
STATCAN	Canadian Department of Agriculture, *Censuses of Canada, 1665–1871. Statistics of Canada.* Vol. IV (Ottawa: I. B. Taylor, 1876), www.statcan.ca/english/freepub/98-187-XIE/acadians.htm#part1.
Taylor	M. Brook Taylor, "The Poetry and Prose of History: Evangeline and the Historians of Nova Scotia," *Journal of Canadian Studies* 23 (1988):46–67.

Léon Thériault, "Acadia from 1763 to 1990: An Historical Synthesis," in Daigle (1995b):45–88.

Diary of John Thomas," *NSHSC* 1 (1879):119–40.

ueben Gold Thwaites, ed., *Jesuit Relations and Allied Documents*, 73 vols. (Cleveland: Burrows Brothers, 1898).

Trask — Kerry A. Trask, *In the Pursuit of Shadows: Massachusetts Millenialism and the Seven Years War* (New York: Garland, 1989).

Trigger — Bruce G. Trigger, ed., *Northeast.* Vol. 15 of *Handbook of North American Indians* (Washington, DC: Smithsonian Institution Press, 1978).

Upton — L. F. S. Upton, *Micmacs and Colonists: Indian-White Relations in the Maritimes, 1713–1867* (Vancouver: University of British Columbia Press, 1979).

Webster (1930) — John Clarence Webster, ed., *The Forts of Chignecto: A Study of the Eighteenth Century Conflict Between France and Great Britain in Acadia* (Shediac, New Brunswick: privately printed, 1930).

Webster (1931) — John Clarence Webster, *Charles des Champs de Boishébert: A Canadian Soldier in Acadia* (n.p.: privately printed, 1931).

Webster (1933) — John Clarence Webster, *The Career of the Abbé Le Loutre in Nova Scotia, with a Translation of His Autobiography* (Shediac, New Brunswick: privately printed, 1933).

Webster (1934) — John Clarence Webster, ed., *Acadia at the End of the Seventeenth Century: Letters, Journals and Memoirs of Joseph Robineau de Villebon, Commandant in Acadia, 1690–1700, and Other Contemporary Documents* (St. John, New Brunswick: New Brunswick Museum, 1934).

Webster (1936) — John Clarence Webster, ed., *The Journal of Joshua Winslow, Recording His participation in the events of the year 1750, Memorable in the History of Nova Scotia* (St. John, New Brunswick: New Brunswick Museum, 1936).

Webster (1937) — John Clarence Webster, *Thomas Pichon, "The Spy of Beauséjour." An Account of His Career in Europe and America* (Sackville, New Brunswick: Public Archives of Nova Scotia, 1937).

Webster (1942) — John Clarence Webster, ed., *Memorial on Behalf of the Sieur de Boishébert, Captain, Chevalier de Saint-Louis, former Commandant in Acadia* (St. John, New Brunswick: New Brunswick Museum, 1942).

White — Stephen A. White, *Dictionnaire généalogique des familles acadiennes: Premiére partie, 1636 à 1714*, 2 vols. (Moncton, New

	Brunswick: Centre d'études acadiennes, Université de Moncton, 1999).
Wicken	William Wicken, "Re-Examining Míkmaq-Acadian Relations, 1635–1755," in *Habitants et Marchands Twenty Years Later: Reading the History of Seventeenth- and Eighteenth-Century Canada*, ed. Sylvie Dépatie, Catherine Desbaras, et al. (Montreal: McGill-Queen's University Press, 1998):93–114.
Willard	"Journal of Abijah Willard of Lancaster, Mass., An Officer in the Expedition which captured Fort Beauséjour in 1755," ed. John Clarence Webster, *Collections of the New Brunswick Historical Society* 13 (1930).
Winslow (1883)	"Journal of Colonel John Winslow, of the Provincial Troops, While Engaged in Removing the Acadian French Inhabitants from Grand Pré, and the Neighbouring Settlements, in the Autumn of the Year 1755," *NSHSC* 3 (1883):71–196.
Winslow (1885)	"Journal of Colonel John Winslow, of the Provincial Troops, while engaged in the Siege of Beausejour . . . 1755," *NSHSC* 4 (1885):113–246.
Winslow Papers	Winslow Papers, Massachusetts Historical Society (microfilm).
Winthrop	John Winthrop, *The History of New England from 1630 to 1649*, ed. James Savage, 2 vols. (Boston: Little, Brown, 1853).
Winzerling	Oscar William Winzerling, *Acadian Odyssey* (Baton Rouge: Louisiana State University Press, 1955).
Wright	Esther Clark Wright, *The Miramichi: A Study of the New Brunswick River and of the People Who Settled Along It* (Sackville, New Brunswick: Tribune Press, 1945).
YV	*Yarmouth Vanguard*, articles reprinted at the Web site of the Acadian Museum and Archives, West Pubnico, Nova Scotia, www.ccfne.ns.ca/~museum/english/archives/articles/index.htm.

Note: All Web site addresses (URLs) last verified 15 December 2003.

Chapter 1

1. From 1582 until 1752, France and England (later Great Britain) employed the Gregorian and Julian calendars, respectively, between which there was a gap of ten (later eleven) days. Following standard historical convention, when it is necessary to coordinate dating in the text, I use Gregorian (New Style), and have so indicated in the notes. Otherwise all dates are left as found without comment.

2. Lescarbot 2:209–10n; Letters patent to M. de Monts, 8 November 1603, Lescarbot 2:211–13; Huia Ryder, "Jean de Biencourt de Poutrincourt et de Saint-Just," *DCB*.
3. Champlain 1:367; Barbara M. Schmeisser, "The Port Royal Habitation: A 'Politically Correct' Reconstruction," *NSHSC* 44 (1995):41–47. The spelling and use of the names Míkmaw (singular) and Míkmaq (plural) are in accordance with the Francis-Smith Orthography, the official phonemic orthography of the Santé Mawiómi (Grand Council) of the Míkmaq Nation; see Bernard Francis, "Micmac Alphabet and Orthography," in Ruth Whitehead, *Stories from the Six Worlds* (Halifax: Nimbus, 1988).
4. Lescarbot 2:287.
5. French captain quoted in Raymond Douville and Jacques-Donat Casanova, *La vie quotidienne en Nouvelle-France* (Paris: Hachette, 1964):207; Lescarbot 2:296, 299, 306, 309.
6. William Francis Ganong, "An organization of the scientific investigation of the Indian place-nomenclature of the Maritime Provinces of Canada," *Mémoires de comptes rendus de la Société Royale du Canada*, 3rd series, 2 (1914):260–63; Cabot quoted in Samuel Eliot Morison, *The European Discovery of America: The Northern Voyages* (New York: Oxford University Press, 1971):203.
7. Marcel Trudel, *Le Comptoir, 1604–1627*, Vol. 2 of *Histoire de la Nouvelle-France* (Montreal: Fides, 1966):21; Kelsie B. Harder, ed., *Illustrated Dictionary of Place Names, United States and Canada* (New York: Van Nostrand Reinhold, 1976); Frame:12.
8. Lescarbot 1:33, 2:309, 3:157. Because of the difference in French and English meanings, I have retained the French *sauvage* in translated texts rather than rendering it as "*savage*" or "*Indian*."
9. Lescarbot 3:125. On the Basque-Algonquian trade jargon, see Peter Bakker, "The Language of the Coast Tribes Is Half Basque": A Basque-American Indian Pidgin, 1540–1640," *Anthropological Linguistics* 31 (1989):117–47.
10. Carl Sauer, *Sixteenth Century North America* (Berkeley: University of California Press, 1971):51; Lescarbot 2:339.
11. Lescarbot 2:312, 550.
12. Lescarbot, "La Conversion des Sauvages" (1610), in Thwaites 1:65–67; Lescarbot 2:312. The river was first named l'Esquille but had become Dauphin by 1609.
13. Lescarbot 2:312.
14. Lescarbot 2:312; Champlain 1:384.
15. Lescarbot 3:214.
16. Ibid. 2:354–55.
17. Champlain 1:384; Lucien Campeau, "Henri Membertou," *DCB*; Maillard:3; Lescarbot , "La Conversion des Sauvages" (1610), in Thwaites 1:73; Lescarbot 3:362.
18. Lescarbot , "La Conversion des Sauvages" (1610), in Thwaites 1:73.
19. H. P. Biggar, ed., *The Voyages of Jacques Cartier* (Ottawa: Public Archives of Canada, 1924):53.
20. Denys:440. See Calvin Martin, "The Four Lives of a Micmac Copper Pot," *Ethnohistory* 22 (1975):111–33.
21. Pierre Biard to Baltazar, 10 June 1611, and Biard, "Relation of New France" (1616), Thwaites 1:175, 3:105–09; Lescarbot 3:368–69; Virginia P. Miller, "Aboriginal Micmac

Population: A Review of the Evidence," *Ethnohistory* 23 (1976):117–27; Philip K. Bock, "Micmac," in Trigger:117.

22. Biard to Baltazar, 10 June 1611, Thwaites 1:175. On the dynamics of power within Míkmaq society in the early seventeenth century, see Daniel B. Thorp, "Equals of the King: The Balance of Power in Early Acadia," *Acadiensis* 25 (1996):3–17.

23. Champlain 1:392, 438.

24. Marc Lescarbot, *Théâtre de Neptune en la Nouvelle-France*, trans. Harriette Taber Richardson (Boston: Houghton Mifflin, 1927); Champlain 1:306–07; Lescarbot 2:342–44; Michael A. Salter, "L'Ordre de Bon Temps," *NSHQ* 5 (1975):143–54.

25. Lescarbot 2:28, 342–44, 3:252; Champlain 1:447; Maillard:4–7.

26. Lescarbot 2:342–44, 3:252.

27. Lescarbot 2:354–56; Bailey:13.

28. Lescarbot 2:351, 363–64.

29. Ibid. 2:364; Le Clercq quoted in Bailey:64.

30. Choquette:130; Champlain and Lescarbot quoted in Parkman 1:186; Parkman 1:206.

31. Lescarbot, "La Conversion des Sauvages" (1610), Thwaites 1:67–69; George MacBeath, "Claude de Saint-Etienne de La Tour," *DCB*.

32. Lescarbot 3:611.

33. Lescarbot, "La Conversion des Sauvages" (1610), Thwaites 1:67–69; Harold Prins, *The Mi'kmaq: Resistance, Accommodation, and Cultural Survival* (Orlando, FL: Harcourt Brace, 1996):82.

34. Lescarbot 3:43–44; Bertrand to sieur de la Tronchaie, 28 June 1610, Thwaites 1:129–31.

35. Lescarbot 3:48; Ryder, "Charles de Biencourt se Saint-Just," *DCB*.

36. Lescarbot 3:53; Biard to R. P. Provincial, 31 January 1612, and Biard, "Epistola ex Porturegali in Acadia," Thwaites 2:7–11, 51, 87.

37. Biard to Provincial, 31 January 1612, and Biard, "Relation of New France" (1616), Thwaites 2:7, 3:195.

38. Biard to Provincial, 31 January 1612, and Biard, "Relation of New France" (1616), Thwaites 3:163–65, 2:9, 11.

39. Lucien Campeau, *La Première Mission d'Acadie, 1602–1616* (Quebec: Les Presses de l'Université Laval, 1967):158. For helpful comments on the use of Míkmawísimk, see the language page of "The Míkmaq Portal," www.mikmaq.com/language/.

40. Biard to Baltazar, 10 June 1611, and Biard, "Relation of New France" (1616), Thwaites 1:165, 3:145.

41. Biard to Provincial, 31 January 1612, Thwaites 2:87.

42. Paul Ragueneau, "Relation of 1647–48," Thwaites 33:145–47.

43. Biard to Provincial, 31 January 1612, Thwaites 2:37.

44. Biard, "Relation of New France" (1616), Thwaites 3:143–49, 243.

45. Ibid., 3:139; Charles de Biencourt to Jean de Biencourt de Poutrincourt, 13 March 1612, Campeau, *La Première Mission d'Acadie*, 233.

46. "Expedition of Captain Samuel Argall, Afterward Governor of Virginia, Knight, &c. to the French Settlements in Acadia and to Manhattan Island, A.D. 1613," *Collections*

of the New-York Historical Society, 2nd series, 1 (1868):336; Biard, "Relation of New France" (1616), Thwaites 3:277.

47. Biard, "Relation of New France" (1616), Thwaites 4:45.

48. Biencourt quoted in Lescarbot 3:67, 70; Biard to Father Claude Aquaviva, 26 May 1614, and Biard, "Relation of New France" (1616), Thwaites 4:43, 3:10–12.

49. Champlain 4:21; Lescarbot 3:70; "Brief Intelligence from Virginia by Letters, a supplement of French-Virginian Occurants, and their supplantation by Sir Samuel Argal, in right of the English Plantation," Samuel Purchas, *Purchas his Pilgrimes*, 4 vols. (London: Henry Fetherston, 1625), 4:1808.

50. Privy Council quoted in Thwaites 2:309; Parkman 1:239.

51. Lescarbot, "Relation Dernière de ce qui s'est Passé au Voyage du Sieur de Poutrincourt" (1612), and Biard, "Relation of New France" (1616), Thwaites 2:125, 3:137–39.

52. Biard, "Relation of New France" (1616), Thwaites 3:69; MacBeath, "Claude de Saint-Etienne de La Tour," *DCB*.

Chapter 2

1. MacBeath, "Claude de Saint-Etienne de La Tour," and Ryder, "Charles de Biencourt de Saint-Just," *DCB*.

2. Champlain quoted in Bailey:23–24, 123.

3. Lescarbot 3:162–63; Bailey:16–17, 102; Biard, "Relation of New France" (1616), Thwaites 3:103; Philip K. Bock, "Micmac," Trigger:114.

4. Bailey:112; White 2:1435; MacBeath, "Charles de Saint-Etienne de La Tour," *DCB*; Naomi E. S. Griffiths, "Mating and Marriage in Early Acadia," *Renaissance and Modern Studies* 35 (1992):121; Clarence d'Entremont, "Premier Enfant Né en Acadie," *CSHA* 1 (1966–68):350–56.

5. Ryder, "Charles de Biencourt de Saint-Just,"and MacBeath, "Charles de Saint-Etienne de La Tour," *DCB*; Reid (1981):29–30; Charles de La Tour to Louis XIII and Cardinal Richelieu, 25 July 1627, Azarie Couillard-Després and L. Riboulet, *Charles de Saint-Étienne de La Tour, gouverneur, lieutenant-géneral en Acadie, 1593–1666, au tribunal de l'histoire* (St.-Hyacinthe, Canada: Le Courrier de St.-Hyacinthe, 1932):149; MacDonald:13.

6. MacBeath, "Claude de Saint-Etienne de La Tour," *DCB*.

7. Haliburton 1:324; MacBeath, "Claude de Saint-Etienne de La Tour," *DCB*.

8. Articles of agreement [between William Alexander and Claude de La Tour], 6 October 1629, Murdoch 1:74–75; MacBeath, "Claude de Saint-Etienne de La Tour," *DCB*; Reid (1981):32–33.

9. Richard Guthry, "A Relation of the Voyage and Plantation of the Scotts Colony in New Scotland under the conduct of Sir William Alexander Younger" (1629), quoted in Griffiths and Reid:503–04.

10. Griffiths and Reid:506; Murdoch 1:78; Denys:132–36.

11. Léger:70–71; La Tour quoted in MacDonald:45; MacBeath, "Claude de Saint-Etienne de La Tour," *DCB*.

12. King Charles I to Sir William Alexander, 10 July 1631, Murdoch 1:80.

13. Razilly quoted in MacDonald:59; Denys:147; Daigle (1995a):6; Reid (1981):51–53; Joan Dawson, "Colonists or Birds of Passage? A Glimpse of the Inhabitants of La Have, 1632–1636," *NSHR* 9 (1989):42–61.
14. Massignon 1:40; White 2:1125–26, 1536–37.
15. Brasseaux (1987):4–8; Choquette:17–20, 262, 317–18; Moogk:92–93, 107–08.
16. Casgrain (1888–90) 3:147–48; White 1:40–41, 57–58, 96, 184–86, 221–22, 251–53, 271–73, 289–90, 369–71, 400, 526–31, 562, 596–97, 666–67, 691, 718–19, 2:798–801, 915–18, 983–85, 1294–96, 1327, 1373–74, 1456, 1483–84, 1508–11; Nicole T. Bujold and Maurice Caillebeau, *Les origines françaises de premières familles acadiennes: Le sud loudunais* (Poitiers: Imprimerie l'Union, 1979), 1–59 *passim*; anonymous *mémoire*, 1644, quoted in Massignon 1:39.
17. White 1:41, 257, 691, 2:1126, 1130; Clarence J. d'Entremont, *Histoire du Cap-Sable de l'an mil au Traité de Paris, 1763*, 5 vols. (Eunice, LA: Hébert Publications, 1981), 3:1124; Bill Wicken, "26 August 1726: A Case Study in Mik'maq-New England Relations in the Early Eighteenth Century," *Acadiensis* 23 (1993):5–22, esp. 10–13; La Varenne quoted in Maillard:102; Fidele Theriault, "Acadian Families," St. John, New Brunswick, *Telegraph-Journal*, special supplement, 11 August 1994, reprinted at www.pinette.net/genealogy/acadian1.html; François-Edmé Rameau de Saint-Père, "Notes explicatives, sur les Déclarations des Acadiens conservées à Belle-isle-en-Mer, et sur les Etablissements des premiers colons de l'Acadie," Casgrain (1888–90) 3:140, 142–43.
18. Bailey:111–12; Lauvrière 1:22–23; Brebner (1925):233–36.
19. Reid (1981):62–79; Mathé Allain, *"Not Worth a Straw": French Colonial Policy and the Early Years of Louisiana* (Lafayette, LA: Center for Louisiana Studies, 1988):29; Champlain quoted in Paul Le Jeune, "Relation de ce qui s'est passé en Nouvelle France, en l'année 1633," Thwaites 5:211; James Axtell, *The Invasion Within: The Contest of Cultures in Colonial North America* (New York: Oxford University Press, 1985).
20. Griffiths (1992):24; Dunn:39; Bailey:122–23; Brasseaux (1987):20; Francis Jennings, *Empire of Fortune: Crowns, Colonies, and Tribes in the Seven Years War in America* (New York: W. W. Norton, 1988):176.
21. Leonard:33–44; Ross and Deveau:35; Hustvedt:19–21; E. L. Eaton, "The Dyke Lands," *NSHQ* 10 (1980):197–211; Yves Cormier, *Les Aboiteaux en Acadie: hier et aujourd'hui* (Moncton: Chaire d'études acadiennes, 1990), 19–34; Denys:123–24.
22. Joseph Robineau de Villebon, "Memoir on the Settlements and Harbors from Minas at the Head of the Bay of Fundy to Cape Breton," 27 October 1699, Webster (1934):133; Dièreville:95; Cadillac quoted in Moogk:174.
23. Hustvedt:20; Clark (1968):165; Denys:123–24.
24. Louis XIII to d'Aulnay, February 10, 1638, Murdoch 1:93; Winthrop 2:219–20.
25. New England traders quoted in Hutchinson 2:63; Clarence J. d'Entremont, "Un enfant métis de Charles d'Aulnay," *CSHA* 4 (1971):48–61, and response by Gerald M. Kelly, ibid., 236–42; d'Aulnay quoted in MacDonald:69.
26. George MacBeath, "Françoise-Marie Jacquelin," *DCB*; White 2:1435; Winthrop 2:243. For a survey of historians' treatment of Françoise-Marie Jacquelin, see Majorie Anne MacDonald, "Three Portraits from the La Tour–D'Aulnay Story: Which Are Authentic?" *Journal of the New Brunswick Museum* (1980):43–56.

27. Louis XIII to d'Aulnay, 12 February 1641, Murdoch 1:95; Denys:106.
28. Winthrop 1:184, 2:51, 106–07, 150–52, 251–52; Reid (1981):94–95.
29. Winthrop 2:128–37; Reid (1981):96.
30. Winthrop 2:162–63; Capuchins quoted in Arsenault (1994):26-27.
31. Charles de Menou d'Aulnay de Charnizay to John Endicott, 21 October 1644, quoted in MacDonald:145–47; Winthrop 2:241–43; Reid (1981):110.
32. Murdoch 1:110–11; Arsenault (1994):27–28; Denys:116; Winthrop 2:243; quoted in MacDonald:163–65. "Scalado" is the act of scaling the walls of a fortification by the use of ladders.
33. King Louis XIV, letters patent to d'Aulnay, February 1648, Murdoch 1:116; Reid (1981):128.
34. Jeanne Motin, *mémoire*, 1688, quoted in Lauvrière 1:95.
35. Articles of Marriage, 24 February 1653, Murdoch 1:120–23; Motin, *mémoire*, 1688, quoted in Lauvrière 1:95. Winthrop 2:243 mentions a child of La Tour and Jacquelin, sent to France after its mother's death, but there was no mention of such a child in the marriage agreement between La Tour and Motin (while his *métis* children were specifically provided for).
36. Madame d'Aulnay to Massachusetts General Court, 2 March 1651, and Governor John Endicott to Madame d'Aulnay, 12 July 1651, quoted in Rawlyk:20.
37. Robert Sedgwick to Oliver Cromwell, 1 July 1654, and John Leverett to Oliver Cromwell, 1 July 1654, quoted in Rawlyk:23–24; Henry Dwight Sedgwick, *Robert Sedgwick, A Sketch* (Cambridge, MA: John Wilson & Son, 1896):10; Reid (1981):129–30, 135–36.
38. Daigle (1995a):9; MacDonald:180; Reid (1981):136–38.
39. Capitulation of Port Royal, 16 August 1654, Murdoch 1:132; Emmanuel Le Borgne, "Mémoire de l'Estate present de l'Acadie pais de la nouvelle france," 28 November 1665, quoted in Johnston:35.
40. Dièreville:85–86, 96, 118; Joseph Robineau de Villebon quoted in Clark (1968):165; Brasseaux (1987):133–34; Bernard V. LeBlanc and Ronnie-Gilles LeBlanc, "Traditional Material Culture in Acadia," Daigle (1995b):617.
41. Dièreville:82, 90–91.
42. Robert Gallant, "Dièreville: Voyage à l'Acadie, 1699–1700," *CSHA* 16 (1985): 20–21.
43. Massachusetts General Court, n.d., quoted in Rawlyk:31.
44. Memorandum regarding Acadia, 1667, quoted in Reid (1981):138.
45. Hynes:7; Wicken:101–03; White 1:305–06, 763, 2:1318–19; Clark (1968):204–05; Stephen White, *Patronymes acadiens/Acadian Family Names. Odyssée acadienne/Acadian Odyssey* (Moncton: Les Editions d'Acadie, 1992):8–9. F. René Perron, "Sur la trace du pionnier acadien Laurent Granger," *CSHA* 15 (1984):40–53, offers evidence that Granger was of Huguenot background.
46. Dièreville:82, 85; David J. Christianson, *Belleisle 1983: Excavations at a Pre-Expulsion Acadian Site. Nova Scotia Museum. Curatorial Report No. 48* (Halifax: Nova Scotia Department of Education, 1984); Rameau 124–27; Lauvrière 1:185.
47. Dièreville:92; White 1:224–25, 401–02; Hynes:11–12.

48. Reid (1981):136, 164; Léger:74, 86; abbé Louis Petit to bishop of Québec, n.d., quoted in Antoine Bernard, *Le drame acadien depuis 1604* (Montreal: Les Clercs de Saint Vateur, 1936):165; Griffiths (1984):32.
49. Denys:474, 483.
50. John G. Reid, "Styles of Colonization and Social Disorders in Early Acadia and Maine: A Comparative Approach," *CSHA* 7 (1976):105–17; Joan Dawson, "The Governor's Goods: The Inventories of the Personal Property of Isaac de Razilly," *NSHR* 5 (1985):99–112; Alaric Faulkner, "Gentility on the Frontiers of Acadia, 1635–1674: An Archaeological Perspective," Dublin Seminar for New England Folklife, *Annual Proceedings* 14 (1989):82–100; Birgitta Wallace, "An Archaeologist Discovers Early Acadia," in Conrad:93; Dièreville:93. For the operation of the seigneurial system in Acadia see Joan Bourque Campbell, "The Acadian Seigneury of St.-Mathieu at Cobequid," *NSHR* 9 (1989):74–88.
51. Louis de Buade de Frontenac to Louis XIV, 6 November 1679, quoted in Reid (1981):160; Choquette:289; Rameau 124–27.
52. Hannay:212; White 1:221–31; Arseneault (1965) 1:50; Molins quoted in PAC (1906) 2, Appendix A, 1–6.
53. M. de Gargas, "Mon Séjour de l'Acadie [1687–88]," in Morse 1:168–69; Richard 1:214.
54. Dièreville:95; Reid (2004):48–63, 159. Melvin Gallant, *CSHA* 16 (1985):22, argues that Dièreville was the first commentator to recognize the Acadians as a distinct people.

Chapter 3

1. Frame:11; Samantha Rompillon, "La mobilité à Beaubassin ou la fin du mythe de l'immobilité des Acadiens," *Actes du 2e Colloque étudiant du Département d'histoire* [l'Université Laval] (Québec: CELAT, 2003):99–116; Clément Cormier, "Jacques Bourgeois," *DCB*.
2. François-Marie Perrot, "Relation de l'Acadie," 9 August, 1686, in Griffiths (1992):22; Lahontan 1:20; Gargas, "Mon Séjour de l'Acadie" (1687), Morse 1:177–80; Minister of Marine to Louis-Alexandre Desfriches, sieur de Meneval, n.d. [c. 1687], Hannay:302; Rameau 124–27.
3. Cormier, "Jacques Bourgeois," *DCB*; Wicken:96–98; Johnson:51, 74, 77; Donald F. Chard, "John Nelson," *DCB*; Jean Talon to Jean-Baptiste Colbert, 11 November 1671, quoted in Reid (1981):158.
4. Henri Brunet to M. Delagny, 4 February 1675, and Brunet to Intendant, 5 February 1675, in Louis-André Vigneras, "Letters of an Acadian Trader, 1674–1676," *New England Quarterly* 13 (1940):105–06, 109.
5. Lahontan 1:326; Perrot to M. de Seignelay, 29 August 1686, O'Callaghan 9:919; Daigle (1976):166; Daigle (1967):227–29.
6. Johnson:25; Lahontan 1:222, 223–24; Arsenault (1965) 1:60.
7. Clarence J. d'Entremont, "The Children of the Baron de St.-Castin," *French Canadian and Acadian Genealogical Review* 3 (1971):23; Daigle, (1976):167.

8. Jean Daigle, "Notes sur Michel le Neuf, Sieur de la Vallière, Seigneur de Beaubassin et Commandant à l'Acadie de 1678 à 1684," *CSHA* 1 (1966–68):252–56; J.-Roger Comeau, "Michel Leneuf de La Vallière de Beaubassin," *DCB*.
9. Mathieu des Goutin to Minister of Marine, 9 September, 1694, White 2:1489–90; Frame:10–11. Damien Rouet, "L'Acadie, du comptoir à la colonie. Migration et colonization du bassin des Mines (1680–1714)," *CSHA* 29 (1998):34–56, provides a detailed analysis of the kinship migration to Minas, although his interpretation differs somewhat from the one offered here.
10. La Vallière to Governor Bradstreet, 8 August 1684, Daigle (1967):227–29; Lahontan 1:222; Hannay:229.
11. Jacques de Meulles, "Account of a Voyage to Acadie, 1685–1686," Morse 1:104; Jacques de Meulles, "Beaubassin ou Chignectou et la Baye Verte, Mémoires originaux 1686," *CSHA* 4 (1973):381–82; Lahontan 1:224; John G. Reid, "1686–1720: Imperial Intrusions," Buckner and Reid:78; Lauvrière 1:135.
12. Casgrain (1888):457–61; Maillet:134–54, 162–68; Anselme Chiasson, "Traditions and Oral Literature in Acadia," Daigle (1982):477–512. Hynes:16 concluded from an examination of marriage certificates that 50 percent of Acadian men and 20 percent of women could sign their names. But in 1695 only seventeen of fifty-eight Acadian men (29%) signed their names rather than using marks on an oath demanded by a New England officer; "A list of the French at Port Royal to whom Capne Fleetwood Emes, Commander of the Sorlings Frigatt gave the oath of Allegiance Aug 4 1695," Laurie Ebacher, "Charles Mellanson Letters," *Memoires de la Societé Généalogique canadienne-française* 6 (1955):316–17.
13. Jean Daigle, "1650–1686: 'Un pays qui n'est pas fait,'" Buckner and Reid:71; Daigle (1976):161–70 *passim*. In a document of 1691, sixteen Acadians signed using what were described as "a rude mark apparently in imitation of the Indian totem-marks"; see "Deed of submission given by the French inhabitants of Siganecto [Chignecto] to John Nelson," 17 September 1691, *CSP* 15:444.
14. Treaty of Whitehall, 16 November 1686, Davenport 2:319–22; Max Savelle, *Origins of American Diplomacy: The International History of Angloamerica, 1492–1763* (New York: Macmillan, 1967):108; Reid (1981):99–100, 179–82.
15. Bruce T. McCully, "The New England-Acadia Fishery Dispute and the Nicholson Mission of August, 1687," *EIHC* 96 (1960):277–90; Johnson:134; Louis Alexandre des Friches de Meneval, *mémoire*, 10 September 1688, Daigle (1976):167.
16. Paul Chasse, "The d'Abbadie de Saint-Castin and the Abenakis of Maine in the Seventeenth Century," *Proceedings of the Annual Meeting of the French Colonial Historical Society* 10 (1984):59–73; Memorial of John Nèlson, 2 July 1697, Johnson:46.
17. Mather quoted in Rawlyk:56–57; Abenaki sachems to governor of Massachusetts, 1 July 1677, Morrison:110–11.
18. New England seamen quoted in Samuel G. Drake, *Biography and History of the Indians of North America* (Boston: Benjamin B. Mussey & Co., 1841):286–87; William Willis, *The History of Portland from 1632 to 1864*, 2nd edn. (Portland: Bailey & Noyes, 1865):214; Reid (1981):167–68.
19. Morrison:110–11.
20. Clarence J. d'Entremont, "They Cut off the Finger That Tipped the Scale," *YV* 18

April 1989; Wilcomb Washburn, "Seventeenth-Century Indian Wars," Trigger:95.

21. Ferling:38; Jeremy Belknap, *The History of New Hampshire* (Philadelphia: Robert Aitken, 1784):126, 284–85; Harold E. Selesky, "Colonial America," Michael Howard, et al., eds., *The Laws of War: Constraints on Warfare in the Western World* (New Haven: Yale University Press, 1994):84–85.

22. Webster (1934):199; Munson:352; Cotton Mather, "Decennium Luctuosum" (1699), Charles H. Lincoln, ed., *Narratives of the Indians Wars, 1675–1699* (New York: Charles Scribner's Sons, 1913):206, 214.

23. Massachusetts Assembly, 16 December 1689, quoted in Baker and Reid:83.

24. Johnson:59, 134.

25. "Journal of Dr. Benjamin Bullivant," *Massachusetts Historical Society Proceedings* 16 (1878):106.

26. Meneval to marquis de Seignelay, 29 May 1690, O'Callaghan 9:921.

27. Pierre-François-Xavier de Charlevoix, *Historie et description générale de la Nouvelle France*, 3 vols. (Paris: Rolin fils, 1744) 3:96–100; Daigle (1976):167; Murdoch 1:183–88; *mémoire* of Petit, Trouvé, Dubreuil, and Meneval, 27 May 1690, Blanchet 2:8. On the extension of the "Laws of War" to North America, see Ian K. Steele, "Surrendering Rites: Prisoners on Colonial North American Frontiers," Stephen Taylor, et al., eds., *Hanoverian Britain and Empire: Essays in Memory of Philip Lawson* (Rochester, NY: Boydell Press, 1998):137–57.

28. Meneval to de Seignelay, 29 May 1690, O'Callaghan 9:921; "A Journal of the Proceedings in the late Expedition to Port-Royal" (1690), PAC (1913):54–55; Johnson:64.

29. Meneval quoted in Rawlyk:67–69; James Lloyd to unknown, 8 January 1691, and Frances Nicholson to the Lords of Trade, 4 November 1690, PAC (1913):64, 76.

30. "Journal of the Proceedings in the late Expedition to Port-Royal" (1690) and "Relation de la prise du Port-Royal" (1690), PAC (1913):54–58, 70.

31. Joseph Robineau de Villebon to marquis de Chevry, n.d. [c. 1691], Webster (1934):30; Baker and Reid:149; Emerson W. Baker and John G. Reid, "Sir William Phips and the Decentring of Empire in Northeastern North America, 1690–1694," Germaine Warkentin and Carolyn Podruchny, eds., *Decentring the Renaissance: Canada and Europe in Multidisciplinary Perspective, 1500–1700* (Toronto: University of Toronto Press, 2001):292; Munson:352–53.

32. John Usher to unknown, 27 May 1690, PAC (1913):64; M. de Monseignat, "Narrative of the most remarkable Occurrences in Canada [1689–1690]" (1690), O'Callaghan 9:483, 487; Baker and Reid:102–03.

33. John Nelson to Council of Trade and Plantations, 12 April 1697, *CSP* 10:443–44.

34. Deposition of Mark Emerson, 5 November 1691, *CSP* 8:564; George Lincoln Burr, ed., *Narratives of the Witchcraft Cases, 1648–1706* (New York: Charles Scribner's Sons, 1914):353. James Kences, "Some Unexplored Relationships of Essex County Witchcraft to the Indian Wars of 1675 and 1689," *EIHC* 20 (1984):527–42, argues that what he calls "invasion neurosis" was a prominent factor in the Salem witchcraft scare.

35. Acadian memorial, 5 February 1691, Murdoch 1:206–07; Villebon to comte de Pontchartrin, n.d. [c. 1693], Webster (1934):45.

36. Villebon to comte de Pontchartrain, n.d. [c. 1693], Webster (1934):45.

37. Francis Foxcroft to Francis Nicholson, 26 October 1691, Samuel Ravenscroft to

Francis Nicholson, 5 November 1691, and David Jeffreys to John Usher, 19 November, 1691, *CSP* 8:560, 563–64, 571; Johnson:66–67.

38. "An Account of the Most Remarkable Occurrences in Canada [1690–1691]" (1691), O'Callaghan 9:526–27; Villebon to comte de Pontchartrain, n.d. [c. 1693], Webster (1934):47; Francis Foxcroft to Francis Nicholson, 26 October 1691, Samuel Ravenscroft to Francis Nicholson, 5 November 1691, and David Jeffreys to John Usher, 19 November, 1691, *CSP* 8:560, 563–64, 571.

39. John Nelson to the Council of Trade, 23 September 1696, *CSP* 10:112–13, 134–38; "An Account of the Most Remarkable Occurrences in Canada [1690–1691]" (1691), O'Callaghan 9:527; Petition of John Nelson and John Alden, 16 August 1694, and John Nelson to Board of Trade, 6 November 1696, Johnson:74, 78.

40. John Nelson to the Lords Justices, 12 April 1697, *CSP* 10:442–43; Ross and Deveau:38–39, 42–43; Phips quoted in Baker and Reid:228.

41. Joseph Robineau de Villebon, journal, 4 December 1692 and 3 June 1693, and Villebon to Jérôme Phélypeaux, comte de Pontchartrain, 20 August 1694, Webster (1934):44–45, 47, 68, 72.

42. Baker and Reid:158–59; Villebon to Pontchartrain, n.d. [c. 1692], Webster (1934):40–41, emphasis added.

43. Villebon to Pontchartrain, n.d. [c. 1692], Webster (1934):40–41.

Chapter 4

1. John G. Reid, "1686–1720: Imperial Intrusions," Buckner:83; James Axtell, *The European and the Indian: Essays in the Ethnohistory of Colonial North America* (New York: Oxford University Press, 1981):16–35, 223–24.

2. Church:228–29; Villebon, "Events in Acadia," 29 October 1696, Webster (1934):95.

3. "An Account of the Most Remarkable Occurrences in Canada [1696–1697]" (1697), O'Callaghan 9:664.

4. Church:228–29, 232–33; Reid (2004):59.

5. Governor Jacques-François de Brouillon to Pontchartrain, 6 October 1701, Murdoch 1:249–49.

6. Arsenault (1965) 1:463–67, 2:690–94; Dunn:11–12, 40–41; White 2:1146–50.

7. Melanson quoted in Clarence J. d'Entremont, "He Jumped Bail," *YV* 11 April 1989. See also d'Entremont, "Du nouveau sur les Melanson," *CSHA* 3 (1970):339–52, 363–69.

8. Melanson quoted in Clarence d'Entremont, "Les Melanson d'Acadie sont français de père et anglais de mère," *CSHA* 4 (1973):417–18; Delaney:263–64; Ross and Deveau:38–39; White 1:78–80, 2:1146–47, 1150–51.

9. "Journal of the Proceedings in the late Expedition to Port-Royal" (1690), PAC (1913):56; William Phips, "Summons sent on Shoar to Mr. Levedures," *NSHQ* 3 (1973):138.

10. Villebon to Pontchartrain, n.d. [c. 1693], Webster (1934):47; Charles Melanson to Governor William Stoughton, 5 February 1695, Laurie Ebacher, "Charles Mellanson Letters," *Mémoires de la Societé Généalogique canadienne-française* 6 (1955):315; Reid (2004):58; White 1:562.

11. Davenport 2:357; Nelson to Duke of Shrewsbury, February 1696, quoted in Johnson:90–91.
12. Nelson to Board of Trade, 23 September 1696, 2 November 1697, and 2 December 1697, *CSP* 11:112–13, 134–38, 16:6–7, 53–55.
13. Nelson to Board of Trade, 23 September 1696, *CSP* 10:135; James Vernon to Sir Joseph Williamson, 2 July 1697, and Nelson to Philippe de Rigaud de Vaudreuil, 12 January 1725, Johnson:102–03, 132.
14. Villebon to the Minister of Marine, 3 October 1698, John G. Reid, "1686–1720: Imperial Intrusions," Buckner and Reid:86; Villebon to Stoughton, 5 September 1698, *CSP* 11:545; Villebon, "Memoir . . . sent to Count Frontenac and M. de Champigny," n.d. [c. 1699], Webster (1934):140.
15. Jacques-François de Brouillon to Jérôme Phélypeaux, comte de Pontchartrain, 6 October 1701, and Touche [Trouvé] to Pontchartrain, n.d. [1702], Murdoch 1:248–49, 268; des Goutin to Pontchartrain, n.d. [1705], Hannay:264.
16. Jean-Chrysostome Loppinot to Pontchartrain, n.d. [c. 1703], Moogk:174–75; Lahontan 1:222.
17. Abenakis quoted in Reid (1992):212; Dunn:11–12.
18. Church:244, 255.
19. Church:261; d'Entremont, "The Children of the Baron de St.-Castin," *French Canadian and Acadian Genealogical Review* 3 (1971):17.
20. René Baudry, "Jacques-François de Monbeton de Brouillon," *DCB*; Dunn:43; Church:272–73, 278–79.
21. Church:269, 280–82.
22. Governor Joseph Dudley to Lords of Trade, 10 October 1704, Brymner:10; Cotton Mather to Dudley, 20 January 1707, quoted in Charles D. Mahaffie, Jr., *A Land of Discord Always: Acadia from Its Beginning to the Expulsion of Its People, 1604–1755* (Camden, ME: Down East Books, 1995):124; Little:35–36.
23. Paul Mascarene, "A Narrative of Events at Annapolis from the Capture in October 1710 till September 1711," in G. Patterson:73; "A Memorial of the Present Deplorable State of New England," *CMHS,* 5th series, 6 (1879):58.
24. Subercase to Pontchartrain, n.d. [c. December 1708], Murdoch 1:299–301; Robert Leblanc, "Un corsaire de Saint-Domingue en Acadie," *Nova Francia* 6 (1931):199–201; White 1:456.
25. J. D. Alsop, "The Age of the Projectors: British Imperial Strategy in the North Atlantic in the War of Spanish Succession," *Acadiensis* 21 (1991):49; des Goutin to Pontchartrain, 23 December 1707, Murdoch 1:295; Joseph Dudley to Fitz-John Winthrop, 10 February 1707, *CMHS,* 6th series., 3 (1889):368; General Court quoted in Chard (1975):158.
26. Simon-Pierre Denys de Bonaventure to Pontchartrain, 5 July 1707, quoted in Chard (1975):158; René Baudry, "Daniel d'Auger de Subercase," *DCB*; Reid (1992):218.
27. John Winthrop to Fitz-John Winthrop, n.d. [c. July 1707], quoted in Rawlyk:105.
28. Francis Wainwright to commissioners, 14 August 1707, Murdoch 1:292.
29. Ibid.
30. Subercase to Pontchartrain, 26 June 1707, O'Callaghan 9:925; Subercase to Pontchartrain, n.d. [1707], Arsenault (1965) 1:92; Subercase to Pontchartrain, n.d. [1708],

Murdoch 1:304; des Goutin to Pontchartrain, 23 December 1707, Ross and Deveau:39; Pontchartrain to Subercase, n.d. [c. 1707], quoted in Baudry, "Daniel d'Auger de Subercase," *DCB*.

31. Colonel Robert Quary to Board of Trade, 10 January 1708, *CSP* 18:637–38.

32. Samuel Vetch to Earl of Sunderland, 15 June 1708, quoted in James D. Alsop, "Samuel Vetch's 'Canada Survey'd': The Formation of a Colonial Strategy, 1706–1710," *Acadiensis* 12 (1982):39.

33. Samuel Vetch, "Canada Survey'd," 27 July 1708, *CSP* 19:42.

34. Vetch, "Canada Survey'd," *CSP* 19:149.

35. Webster (1930):26; William Dyre, "Some propositions concerning the ill consequence of New York being in the hands of the Dutch," 24 September 1673, and Council for Trade and Plantations, "Opinion and humble advice," 15 November 1673, *CSP* 7:525–26, 532–33; "Memoir of Instructions to Count de Frontenac Respecting the Expedition Against New-York," 7 June 1689, O'Callaghan 9:425; Bernard Ransom, "A Century of Armed Conflict in Newfoundland," *Museum Notes* [Newfoundland Museum] 10 (Winter 1982).

36. Bruce T. McCully, "The New England-Acadia Fishery Dispute and the Nicholson Mission of August, 1687," *EIHC* 96 (1960):277–90; "Address of the principal inhabitants and merchants at Boston and other adjacent places to the Queen," 25 October 1709, *CSP* 19:493.

37. Samuel Vetch, "Case for Payment of Arrears" (1714), in Shortt:68–70; Queen Anne's Instructions for Francis Nicholson, 18 March 1710, Nicholson:560–62; G. Patterson:22n.

38. Subercase to Pontchartrain, 1 October 1710, Arsenault (1965) 1:92 and Murdoch 1:311–12; Reid (2004):7. All dates for the siege and conquest of Port Royal are in New Style.

39. Nicholson to Subercase, 3 October 1710 [sic: 5 October 1710 ns], Murdoch 1:312; Nicholson:69–70, 72, 74; Subercase to Pontchartrain, 26 October 1710, O'Callaghan 9:927–28.

40. Subercase to Nicholson, n.d. [c. October 1710], Nicholson:92.

41. Proclamation of Nicholson, Vetch, and the Council of War to the Acadians, 12 October 1710, Shortt:17–18; "Instructions for Richard, Viscount Shannon," 13 July 1710, *CSP* 25:135.

42. Memorial to the Queen of the Council of War, 14 October 1710, Casgrain (1888–90) 1:149–51.

43. Council of War to Vaudreuil, 11 October 1710, Nicholson:98–99.

Chapter 5

1. Eaton (1910):19–20; *Place-Names and Places of Nova Scotia* (Halifax: Public Archives of Nova Scotia, 1967):73.

2. *Place-Names and Places of Nova Scotia,* 638.

3. "A Description of the Bay of Fundy . . . Observed by Nathaniel Blackmore . . . ,"

Herbert Moll, *Atlas Minor: or, A New and Curious Set of Sixty-Two Maps* (London: Thomas Bowles, 1736):48.

4. Mascarene to unknown, n.d., quoted in Brebner (1929):501–16.

5. Mascarene:70–71; "Proclamation to the People of Minas by Mascarene," n.d. [12 November 1710], G. Patterson:87.

6. Des Goutin quoted in Yvettte Thériault, "Pierre Terriot," *DCB*; White 2:926–28.

7. Mascarene, "A Description of Nova Scotia," 27 September 1720, Akins:41–48.

8. Mascarene:71–72; White 1:234–36, 257–59, 2:926–28, 950–52, 989–90, 1134–35, 1149–50, 1331–33. Estimate of property based on the French 1707 census of l'Acadie, National Archives of Canada, microfilm C-2572.

9. Mascarene:71–72; Vetch to Mascarene, 1 November 1710, G. Patterson:85–86.

10. Mascarene:72–73, 88.

11. Ibid.:73.

12. Mascarene, "A Description of Nova Scotia," 27 September 1720, Akins:41–48. On this point, see Griffiths (1992):43.

13. Vetch to Earl of Dartmouth, 22 January 1711, *CSP* 20:343–45.

14. Mascarene:74–75.

15. Inhabitants of Port Royal to Vaudreuil, n.d. [c. November 1710], Murdoch 1:321–22; George Vane to unknown, 5 May 1712, Shortt:42; Mascarene:78–79.

16. Mascarene:74–76.

17. Christophe Cahouet to Louis Phélypeaux, comte de Pontchartrain, 20 July 1711, Murdoch 1:322–23.

18. J. E. Belliveau: "The Acadian French and Their Language," *Canadian Geographical Journal* 95 (1977):54; Vetch to Lord Dartmouth, 14 June 1711, Casgrain (1888–90) 1:151–52; Vetch to "My Lord," 24 June 1711, G. Patterson:95; Basque:78–82.

19. Vetch to Captain David Pidgeon, 9 June 1711, G. Patterson:91; Vaudreuil to Pontchartrain, 25 October 1711, O'Callaghan 9:858–59.

20. Mascarene:83–84; Gaulin to Costebelle, 5 September 1711, and Costebelle to unknown, n.d. [c. September 1711], Murdoch 1:322–25; Vaudreuil to Pontchartrain, 25 October 1711, O'Callaghan 9:858–59.

21. Vetch to Thomas Caulfeild, n.d. [c. November 1711], and Vetch to unknown, n.d. [c. November 1711], G. Patterson:37–38; Statement of the Principal Inhabitants of Acadia, 28 November 1711, quoted in Plank:94; Vetch to Lord Dartmouth, 8 August 1712, Shortt:46; John Mulcster, memorial, 13 May 1715, and John Doucette to Richard Philipps, 5 November 1717, *CSP* 25:179–80, 29:189–90. In general on the miserable condition of the independent companies see Foote:82–91.

22. Murdoch 1:332; Fred L. Israel, ed., *Major Peace Treaties of Modern History, 1648–1967*, 5 vols. (New York: Chelsea House, 1967–80), 1:210.

23. Philippe Doucet, "Politics and the Inhabitants," Daigle (1982):228–29; Louis Cullen, "Catholics Under the Penal Laws," *Eighteenth-Century Ireland* 1 (1986):23–36.

24. Queen Anne to Francis Nicholson, 23 June 1713, Murdoch 1:333; Vetch, "Case for Payment of Arrears," n.d. [c. 1714], Shortt:68–70.

25. Costebelle to Pontchartrain, 30 November 1711, Murdoch 1:338; Pontchartrain to Costebelle, n.d. [c. March 1712], quoted in Lauvrière 1:208.

26. Inhabitants [of Beaubassin?] to Pain, 23 September 1713, Arsenault (1965) 1:103–04; Pain to Costebelle, 23 September 1713, Murdoch 1:336–37.
27. Inhabitants [of Beaubassin?] to Pain, 23 September 1713, Arsenault (1965) 1:103–04.
28. Desmond H. Brown, "Foundations of British Policy in the Acadian Expulsion: A Discussion of Land Tenure and the Oath of Allegiance," *Dalhousie Review* 57 (1977–78):709–25.
29. Emmanuel Le Borgne, "Mémoire de l'Estate present de l'Acadie pais de la nouvelle france," 28 November 1665, quoted in Johnston:7; Villebon to Pontchartrain, n.d. [c. 1692], Webster (1934):40–41; Reid (2004):156.
30. Anonymous French report, 29 August 1714, quoted in Lauvrière 1:208; Vetch to Board of Trade, 24 November 1714, Akins:5–7; Board of Trade, "Report on Nova Scotia," 17 March 1715, *CSP* 23:124–28.
31. Board of Trade, "Report on Nova Scotia," 17 March 1715, *CSP* 23:124–28; Mascarene to Governor William Shirley, 6 April 1748, Richard 1:84n.
32. Thomas Caulfeild to Vetch, 2 November 1715, Shortt:96; Major Jacques de L'Hermite to Pontchartrain, 29 August 1714, Richard 1:86; Michel Bégon to Pontchartrain, 25 September 1715, O'Callaghan 9:931–32.
33. Mémoire on the inhabitants of Acadie," 1714, Blanchet 3:8–9; Brebner (1927): 67–68; Clark (1965):4.
34. Board of Trade, "Report on Nova Scotia," 17 March 1715, *CSP* 23:124–28; Intendant Bégon to Pontchartrain, 25 September 1715, O'Callaghan 9:931–32; Inhabitants of Minas [and Chignecto] to Peter Capon and Thomas Button, 12 March 1715, Casgrain (1888–90) 1:111–12.
35. "Oath Taken by the French Inhabitants of Annapolis Royal," 22 January 1715, Casgrain (1888–90) 1:110–12.
36. Caulfeild to Board of Trade, 1 November 1715, and Caulfeild to Secretary of War, 24 October 1716, Akins:9, 12; Bernard Pothier, "Les Acadiens à Ile Royale (1713–1743)," *CSHA* 3 (1969):97–111, and "Acadian Emigration to Ile Royale after the Conquest of Acadia," *Histoire sociale—Social History* 3 (1970):116–31.
37. Pontchartrain to Saint-Castin, 8 April 1713, Upton:32; Pain to Costebelle, 23 September 1713, Murdoch 1:336–37.
38. Indians of Penobscot to Commissioners, April 1714, quoted in Upton:37–39; Moody:44; Costebelle to Conseil de Marine, 28 March 1716, Casgrain (1888) 85–86n; Cornelius J. Jaenen, *The French Relationship with the Native Peoples of New France and Acadia* (Ottawa: Indian and Northern Affairs Canada, 1984):40.
39. Costebelle to Conseil de La marine, 9 September 1715, Casgrain (1888):62–63n; S. Patterson:27.
40. Doucette to Joseph Addison, 5 November 1717, Akins:14–16; Doucette to James Craggs, 5 November 1717, MacMechan (1900):52–53; Inhabitants of Minas to Doucette, 10 February 1718, Casgrain (1888–90) 1:170. See also Naomi E. S. Griffiths, "Subjects and Citizens in the Eighteenth Century: The Question of the Acadian Oaths of Allegiance," Edouard Langille and Glenn Moulaison, eds., *Les abeilles pillotent: mélanges offerts à René LeBlanc* (Pointe-de-l'Eglise, Nova Scotia: Revue de l'Université Ste-Anne, 1998): 23–33.

41. Doucette to Addison, 5 November 1717, Akins:14–16; Richard 1:106; Doucette to Inhabitants of Minas, 12 March 1718, Casgrain (1888–90) 1:171.
42. Inhabitants of Annapolis, Minas, and Beaubassin to Governor Joseph Monbeton de Brouillon dit Saint-Ovide, [March] 1718, and Council Minutes (Ile Royale), 23 May 1719, Casgrain (1888–90) 1:128, 193–96.
43. Council Minutes (Ile Royale), 3 May 1718, 23 May 1719, and 21 October 1719, Casgrain (1888–90) 1:190–96, 2:5; Brebner (1927):68. For the French usage of *Acadien*, see Saint-Ovide, instructions, 2 June 1718, Blanchet 3:27; Saint-Ovide to Doucette, n.d. [c. June 1718], and Council Minutes (Ile Royale), 23 May 1719, Casgrain (1888–90)1:119, 193–96.
44. Clark (1965):1–12; Chard (1980):131–49.
45. [British] inhabitants and merchants of Annapolis Royal to Doucette, 5 February 1718, Shortt:111.

Chapter 6

1. Maxwell Sutherland, "Richard Philipps," *DCB*; Foote:82–91.
2. Colonel Richard Philipps to Board of Trade, 11 March 1718, Murdoch, 1:352; Harry Piers, "The Fortieth Regiment, Raised at Annapolis Royal in 1717," *NSHSC* 21 (1927): 121–23.
3. Philipps to James Craggs, 26 May 1720, Akins:31–35; Acadians of Annapolis Royal to Governor Joseph Monbeton de Brouillon dit Saint-Ovide, 17 May 1720, Casgrain (1888):84.
4. Philipps to Justinien Durand, 13 May 1720, and Philipps to Craggs, 26 May 1720, Akins:23–24, 31–35; Board of Trade to Philipps, 19 June 1719, quoted in Brebner (1927):77–78, and Brebner (1925):33–34.
5. "Proclamation by His Excellency Richard Philipps, Esquire, Captain-General and Governor-in-Chief of the Province of His Majesty, Nova Scotia or Acadia, &c.," 10 April 1720 [21 April 1720 ns], Casgrain (1888–90) 1:120–21; Reid (2004):185.
6. Acadians of Annapolis Royal to Philipps, 26 May 1720 [26 April 1720], Casgrain (1888–90) 1:125–26; Acadians of Minas to Philipps, May 1720, Akins:28–29.
7. Philipps to the Acadians of the Annapolis River, 30 April 1720, Council Minutes, 15 May 1720, and Philipps to Craggs, 26 May 1720, Akins:22, 25, 31–35; Acadians of Annapolis to Governor Philipps, 20 May 1720, Casgrain (1888–90) 1:122–24.
8. Philipps to Craggs, 6 August 1720, *CSP* 27:80; Durand to Philipps, 26 May 1720, and Council Minutes (Ile Royale), August 1720, Casgrain (1888–90) 1:121–22, 2:6–7.
9. Philipps to Craggs, 26 May 1720, Akins:31–35; Philipps to Craggs, 6 August 1720, *CSP* 27:80.
10. Brebner (1925):33–34; Philipps to Craggs, Akins:31–35; Council Minutes, 26 July 1720, Murdoch 1:373; Philipps to Craggs, 6 August 1720, *CSP* 27:80.
11. Council Minutes (Ile Royale), 21 October 1719, Casgrain (1888–90) 2:5; Upton:41; Council Minutes, 24 August 1720, Shortt:131–32; Basque:78-82; Robison:15–39, 53–61, 66–67.
12. Council Minutes, 5 September 1720 and 17 May 1721, MacMechan (1908):13, 31;

Deposition of John Alden, 14 September 1720, Shortt:133–34; John Doucette to Board of Trade, 29 June 1722, Casgrain (1888–90) 1:172–73; Philipps, "Aux quatre Deputez des Mines," 9 September 1720, MacMechan (1900):66; Robison:70–71.
13. Míkmaq of Minas to Philipps, 2 October 1720, Blanchet 3:46–47.
14. Roger B. Ray, "Eastern Indians' Letter to the Governour," *Maine Historical Society Quarterly* 13 (1974):179–81.
15. Council Minutes, 28 February 1721, MacMechan (1908):23; Philipps to William Winniett, 4 March 1721, and Council Minutes, 4 March 1721, Akins:59–60.
16. White 1:326–29; Ruth Whitehead, *The Old Man Told Us: Excerpts from Micmac History 1500–1950* (Halifax: Nimbus Publishing, 1991):78–79; Clarence J. D'Entremont, *Histoire du Cap-Sable,* 5 vols. (Eunice, LA: Hébert Publications, 1981), 3:1128–29. The *dit nom* Memcharet appears variously in the record as Momquaret, Nemecharet, Amecouret, Amquaret, Anecouaret, Annqualet, etc.
17. Paul Mascarene, "Description of Nova Scotia," 27 September 1720, Akins:41–48.
18. Ibid.
19. Philipps to James Craggs, 26 September 1720, Akins:51.
20. Board of Trade to Philipps, 28 December 1720, Murdoch 1:381; Board of Trade, "State of the British Plantations America," 8 September 1721, O'Callaghan 5:592–94; Bell:33; "Petition of Col. Samuel Vetch," 21 July 1719, "Petition of the South Sea Company," 2 January 1720, and "Memorial by Col. Samuel Vetch," 12 January 1721, *CSP* 27:174, 32:229–30, 232.
21. Philipps to inhabitants of Annapolis, 10 April 1721, MacMechan (1900):74.
22. Doucette to Board of Trade, 29 June 1722, Casgrain (1888–90) 1:172–73; Murdoch 1:400–01; Robison:76–78. For more on Míkmaw sailors, see Charles A. Martijn, ed., *Les Micmacs et la mer* (Montreal: Recherches amérindiennes au Québec, 1986).
23. Samuel Penhallow, *The History of the Wars of New-England* (Boston: Printed by T. Fleet for S. Gerrish, 1726):86–87.
24. Penhallow:86–87; Charlevoix quoted in Samuel G. Drake, *Biography and History of the Indians of North America* (Boston: Benjamin B. Mussey, 1841):311.
25. Hannay:318; Vaudreuil to Jean-Frédéric Phélypeaux, comte de Maurepas, 24 April 1724 [sic; c. July 1724], O'Callaghan 9:945; Council Minutes, 8 July 1724, MacMechan (1908):56–57.
26. Council Minutes, 16 July, 22 July, 10 August, and 12 August 1724, MacMechan (1908):58, 65–66, 68–72.
27. *Mémoire* of Vaudreuil and Bégon, 14 October 1723, Murdoch 1:405; Doucette to Board of Trade, 29 June 1722, Casgrain (1888-90) 1:172–73; Council Minutes, 26 October 1722, and 14 November 1722, MacMechan (1908):37, 39.
28. Council Minutes, 22 May 1725, MacMechan (1908):100–01; Basque: 73.
29. Doucette to unknown, 16 August 1726, Robison:86; "Treaty of 1725, Ratification at Annapolis Royal," and "Treaty of 1725, Promises By Lieutenant Governor of Nova Scotia," www.mikmaq.com/law/1725-d.html. These treaties are the foundation documents for Míkmaq aboriginal rights in Canada. For a discussion, see William C. Wicken, *Míkmaq Treaties on Trial: Histories, Land, and Donald Marshall Junior* (Toronto: University of Toronto Press, 2002).
30. Vetch to Board of Trade, 20 November 1712, Brebner (1927):60; Caulfeild to Board

of Trade, 1715, Richard 1:136; Armstrong to Board of Trade, 17 November 1725 and 2 December 1725, Casgrain (1888–90) 1:173–75; Philipps to Craggs, 15 May 1720, Akins:31–35.
31. Council Minutes, 21 September 1726 and 25 September 1726, MacMechan (1908):125, 129–30.
32. Armstrong to Thomas Pelham Holles, Duke of Newcastle, 24 November 1726 and 30 April 1727, Akins:69–71.
33. Jacques-François de Brouillon to Jérôme Phélypeaux, comte de Pontchartrain, 6 October 1701, Murdoch 1:248–49; Paul Mascarene, "A Description of Nova Scotia," 27 September 1720, Akins:41–48; Armstrong to Newcastle, 30 April 1727, Murdoch 1:443.
34. Council Minutes, 25 July, 23 August, and 30 August 1727, MacMechan (1908): 149–50, 153–55.
35. Council Minutes, 7 September, 16 September, 17 September, and 14 October, 1727, MacMechan (1908):158–60, 164; Armstrong to Newcastle, 17 November 1727, Akins:80–81; White 2:938–39.
36. Armstrong to Robert Wroth, 28 September 1727, Casgrain (1888–90) 1:175–77; Richard 1:141.
37. Wroth to Armstrong, 13 November 1727, Casgrain (1888–90) 1:180–84.
38. Ibid. I infer that the Acadians Wroth identified as "Vero" and "Ybere" were Vécot and Hébert; see White, *Dictionnaire généalogique des familles acadiennes* 2:818–20, 1558–60.
39. Wroth, "Copy of the Oath of Loyalty I have left with the Inhabitants of Chignitou and Dependencies," 31 October 1727, Casgrain (1888–90) 1:179.
40. Wroth, "Articles granted to Minas, Pisiquid, etc.," 31 October 1727, Casgrain (1888–90) 1:178.
41. Armstrong to Newcastle, 17 November 1727, Akins:80–81; Council Minutes, 13 November 1727, MacMechan (1908):168–69. My argument here follows that of Doughty:42–43.
42. Murdoch 1:449, 451; Barry M. Moody, "Alexander Cosby," Maxwell Sutherland, "Richard Philipps," and Maxwell Sutherland, "Lawrence Armstrong," *DCB*.
43. Maurepas to René-Charles Breslay, 22 May 1729, Casgrain (1897):331; Breslay to Philipps, 23 December 1729, Gaudet Appendix A, Part III, 70–72.
44. Armstrong to Board of Trade, 23 June 1729, Akins:82–83.
45. MacMechan (1908):169; Philipps to Newcastle, 30 January 1730, *CSP* 32:3–4; Council Minutes, 21 November 1729, Murdoch 1:456, 460.
46. "Petition of the Acadians [of Annapolis] to take the Oath of Allegiance," n.d. [c. September 1729], Gaudet Appendix B, 72–73; Philipps to Newcastle, 25 November 1729, Brymner:70; Philipps to Newcastle, 30 January 1730, *CSP* 32:3–4; Council Minutes, 16 May 1730, MacMechan (1908):171; Philipps to Newcastle, 2 September 1730, Akins:86–87.
47. Philipps to Newcastle, 30 January 1730, *CSP* 32:3–4; Alexandre Bourg, certificat, 25 April 1730, Gaudet Appendix B, 24–25.
48. Mascarene to Council, 8 November 1745, Fergusson:81; Ministère des Affaires Etrangers, *mémoire*, June 1778, quoted in Lauvrière 1:258.

Chapter 7

1. Lawrence Armstrong, "Representation on the State of the Province in Case of War with France," 13 July 1734, MacMechan (1900):91–92; Richard Bulkeley and Isaac Deschamps, *Nova-Scotia Magazine* (April 1790):287–89, emphasis added; Griffiths (1984):24. The first appearance in print of the term "French neutrals" or "neutral French" was during King George's War, in 1745; see Plank:104–05. Some of those references, however, suggest that the term was already in use, as when two correspondents wrote that "something should be done to keep these neutral French, as they are called, within proper bounds"; William Pepperrell and Peter Warren to Paul Mascarene, 8 March 1746, *The Pepperrell Papers* (Boston: Massachusetts Historical Society, 1899):450–51. Neutrality is a topic that deserves more historical attention. For an interesting discussion, see Donald Desserud, "Nova Scotia and the American Revolution: A Study of Neutrality and Moderation in the Eighteenth Century," in Margaret Conrad, ed., *Making Adjustments: Change and Continuity in Planter Nova Scotia, 1759–1800* (Fredericton, New Brunswick: Acadiensis Press, 1991):89–112.
2. Philipps to Thomas Pelham Holles, Duke of Newcastle, 2 September 1730, Akins: 86–87; Muriel K. Roy, "Settlement and Population Growth in Acadia," Daigle (1982):135.
3. Hynes:11–12; Delesdernier.
4. Allan E. Marble, "Epidemics and Mortality in Nova Scotia, 1749–1799," *NSHR* 8 (1988): 72–93; Philip K. Bock, "Micmac," Trigger:117; Elizabeth Anne Fenn, *Pox Americana: The Great Smallpox Epidemic of 1775–82* (New York: Hill & Wang, 2001):39–40, 43, 65, 87; Carl Bridenbaugh, *Cities in the Wilderness: Urban Life in America, 1625–1742* (New York: Ronald Press, 1938):240–41; George Burns, "Smallpox at Louisbourg, 1713–1758," *NSHR* 10 (1990):30–44.
5. Brown (1815):125; Hale:232–34; White 1:27–29, 436–38.
6. Brown (1815):130–31. For an interesting discussion of the roles of Acadian women see Maurice Basque and Josette Brun, "La neutralilté à l'épreuve: des Acadiennes à la défense de leurs intérêts en Nouvelle-Ecosse du 18e siècle," Phyllis E. LeBlanc, Monique Hébert, and Nathallie J. Kermoal, eds., *Entre le quotidien et le politique: facettes de l'histoire des femmes francophones en milieu minoritaire* (Gloucester, Ontario: Réseau national d'action education femmes, 1997): 107–22.
7. Le Conseil de la Marine, 5 June 1717, Bernard V. LeBlanc and Ronnie-Gilles LeBlanc, "Traditional Material Culture in Acadia," Daigle (1995b):615; Brown (1815):121; Hale:225, 233; Delesdernier.
8. Ross and Deveau:37–45; Andrée Crépeau and Brenda Dunn, *The Melanson Settlement: An Acadian Farming Community. Parks Canada. Research Bulletin No. 250* (Ottawa: Parks Canada, 1986); Leslie Still, "Analysis of Faunal Remains from the Belleisle Site, Nova Scotia," David J. Christianson, *Belleisle 1983: Excavations at a Pre-Expulsion Acadian Site. Nova Scotia Museum. Curatorial Report No. 48* (Halifax: Nova Scotia Department of Education, 1984):87; Council Minutes, 23 December 1732, Akins:100.
9. Hale:232; Chard (1980):148–49; Clark (1965):1–12; Hibbert Newton to Board of Trade, 1 September 1743, Shortt:223–24; Bernard Pothier, "Joseph de Saint-Ovide Monbeton de Brouillon, dit Saint-Ovide," *DCB*; Richard Philipps, "Proclamation to

Regulate Currency and Exports," 11 March 1731, and Lawrence Armstrong, "Order to Prevent Exportation of Cattle," 2 April 1735, MacMechan (1900):181–82, 204–05.

10. Brown (1815):110; Bernard Pothier, "Joseph-Nicholas Gautier, dit Bellair," *DCB*; Casgrain (1888):525; Arsenault (1994):93–94; Lauvrière 1:308; White 2:1569.

11. Andrée Crépeau and David Christianson, "Home and Hearth: An Archaeological Perspective on Acadian Domestic Architecture," *Canadian Folklore/Folklore Canadien* 17 (1995):93–109. There is a reconstructed Acadian house at Annapolis Gardens in Annapolis Royal.

12. Hale:232, 234; LeBlanc and LeBlanc, "Traditional Material Culture in Acadia," Daigle (1995b):614.

13. George Mitchell, "Map of the River of Annapolis Royal, Surveyed in the Year 1733," *Acadiensis* 3 (1909):294; Anselme Chiasson, "Traditions and Oral Literature in Acadia," in Daigle (1982):486; J. E. Belliveau: "The Acadian French and Their Language," *Canadian Geographical Journal* 95 (1977):54; Brook Watson quoted in Lauvrière 1:185–86.

14. Maurice Léger, "Les aboiteaux," *CSHA* 1 (1962):62–66; Griffiths (1992):58; Gabriel Bertrand, "La culture de marais endigués et le développement de la solidarité militante en Acadie entre 1710 et 1755," *CSHA* 24 (1993):238–49; Little:35–36; Dunn:32–33; Hugh Graham to Andrew Brown, 9 September 1791, Brown (1881):147.

15. Maillet:31–32, 43, 48, 51, 52, 102; Brown (1815):133, 136.

16. Brown (1815):136–39.

17. Hale:232–34; Maillet:54; Pierre Maillard to director of the Séminair des Missions-Etrangèrs, Paris, 29 September 1738, Casgrain (1888–90) 1:63–66; Report of the Bishop of Québec, 1742, Éloi DeGrâce, et al., eds., *Histoire d'Acadie par les textes* (Fredericton: Ministère de l'éducation du Nouveau-Brunswick, 1976) 1:19.

18. Maillet:54.

19. Delesdernier; Clark (1968):204–05.

20. White 1:157, 446, 759, 2:1236, 1466; Council Minutes, 12 May 1726, MacMechan (1900):121–23. Maurice Basque uses the Broussard paternity case as a lens to examine social tensions within the Acadian community; see "Conflits et solidarités familiales dans l'ancienne Acadie: l'affaire Broussard de 1724," *CSHA* 20 (1989):60–69, and "Genre et gestion du pouvoir communautaire à Annapolis Royal au 18e siècle," *Dalhousie Law Journal* 17 (1994):498–508.

21. Mascarene:77; Council Minutes, 20 April 1721 MacMechan (1900):28–29; Mascarene to Alexandre Bourg, 2 July 1741, MacMechan (1900):152; Basque:77.

22. Queen Anne to Francis Nicholson, 23 June 1713, Murdoch 1:333; Philipps to James Craggs, 15 May 1720, Akins:31; Bell:68, 82; Council Minutes, 10 December 1730, Murdoch 1:468.

23. Hannay:324–25; Agathe Campbell, petition and memorial, 2 April 1733, *CSP* 35:69; Murdoch 1:354; Delaney:263–84; Clarence d'Entremont, "Marie-Agathe de Saint-Etienne de La Tour," *DCB*.

24. Philipps to Newcastle, 2 September 1730, *CSP* 32:251–52.

25. Agathe Campbell, petition and memorial, 2 April 1733, *CSP* 35:69, 123–24; Mary Barton, deposition, 2 September 1733, quoted in Godfrey:4.

26. Board of Trade to Privy Council, 23 October 1733, Shortt:193–94.

27. Alured Popple to John Scrope, 22 March 1734, Shortt:197.

28. Armstrong, Order for Survey of Lands, 15 October 1731, MacMechan (1900):186; Council Minutes, 10 January 1732, 3 January 1733, and 11 August 1733, MacMechan (1908): 210–11, 260–61, 285–86; Armstrong to Alexander Bourg, 22 January 1732, Murdoch 1:478; Mascarene to unknown, n.d. [c. 1752], Brebner (1927):154.
29. Armstrong to Charles de la Goudalie, 30 August 1733, MacMechan (1900):89–90; Thomas Garden Barnes, "'The Daily Cry for Justice': The Juridical Failure of the Annapolis Royal Regime, 1713–1749," Philip Girard and Jim Phillips, eds., *Essays in the History of Canadian Law* (Toronto: University of Toronto Press, 1990):18–19; Armstrong to Board of Trade, 16 November 1731, *CSP* 33:347; Paul Mascarene to Board of Trade, 16 August 1740, Moody:149.
30. Armstrong to Board of Trade, 5 October 1731, and 15 November 1732, Akins: 91–94, 99; Board of Trade to Armstrong, 2 November 1732, *CSP* 34:242–43.
31. Bell:52–56.
32. Mascarene to [wife] Elizabeth Mascarene, 6 November 1724, and Mascarene to [daughter] Elizabeth Mascarene, 7 June, 1740, Mascarene Papers; Moody:44, 86.
33. Hale:231; Council Minutes, 11 September, 1732, MacMechan (1908):191; Armstrong and William Shirreff, advertisement for New England papers, 26 September, 1732, Murdoch 1:481; Jonathan Belcher to Thomas Coram, 6 October 1733, W. S. MacNutt, *The Atlantic Provinces: The Emergence of Colonial Society, 1712–1857* (Toronto: McClelland & Stewart, 1965):32.
34. Harvey (1926):40–60 *passim;* Esther Clark Wright, *The Petitcodiac: A Study of the New Brunswick River* (Sackville, New Brunswick: Tribune Press, n.d. [1945]):2–4; Webster (1936):41.
35. David Dunbar to Alured Popple, 4 June 1731, *CSP* 33:124; Armstrong to Board of Trade, 20 November 1733, *CSP* 35:239; Armstrong to René Leblanc, 11 May 1732, MacMechan (1900):189; Armstrong to Board of Trade, 10 June 1732, *CSP* 34:146–48; Council Minutes, 25 July 1732, and Armstrong to Board of Trade, 15 November 1732, Akins:97–99; Council Minutes, 26 July 1732, MacMechan (1908):241.
36. Council Minutes, 25 July 1732, Akins:97–98; Council Minutes, 26 July 1732, MacMechan (1908):241; Armstrong to unknown, 1 August 1732, and Armstrong to Board of Trade, 15 November 1732, Murdoch 1:481–83. Geoffrey Plank, "The Two Majors Cope: The Boundaries of Nationality in Mid-Eighteenth Century Nova Scotia," *Acadiensis* 25 (1996):27, identifies the three Míkmaq intruders as Jacques Winaguadesh, his brother Antoine, and a third unrelated man known only as Andres. René, Pierre, and François Leblanc were three of six sons of René Leblanc and Anne Bourgeois of Grand Pré; White 2:987.
37. Armstrong to Board of Trade, 15 November 1732, Akins:99; Upton:45; François Dupont Duvivier, *Mémoire* on Acadie, 1735, Murdoch 1:508–11.
38. Wicken:101, 108.
39. Maxwell Sutherland, "Lawrence Armstrong," *DCB*.
40. Council Minutes, 4 February 1724, MacMechan (1908):52; Armstrong to Saint-Ovide, 17 June 1732, Akins:96–97; Saint-Ovide to Armstrong, 19 September 1732, *CSP* 34:253–53.
41. Armstrong to Saint-Ovide, 26 July 1736, MacMechan (1900):107–08.

42. Council Minutes, 18 May 1736, MacMechan (1908):343–45.
43. Acadians of Annapolis to King Louis XV, n.d. [c. June 1736], emphasis in original, Casgrain (1888):105–07; Armstrong to Saint-Ovide, 26 July 1736, MacMechan (1900): 107–08.
44. Saint-Ovide to Armstrong, 8 October 1736, *CSP* 42:340; Armstrong to Saint-Ovide, 26 July 1736, MacMechan (1900):107–08; comte de Maurepas to Saint-Ovide, 16 April 1737, quoted in Brebner (1927):161n.
45. Armstrong to Newcastle, 22 November 1736, MacMechan (1900):111; Armstrong to Board of Trade, 23 November 1736, *CSP* 42:338.
46. Armstrong to Board of Trade, 10 June 1732, *CSP* 34:146–48; Board of Trade to Armstrong, 11 August 1734, *CSP* 41:200; Moody:115; Brebner (1927):102–03.
47. Sutherland, "Lawrence Armstrong," *DCB*; John Adams to Jonathan Belcher, n.d. [c. 8 December 1739], MacMechan (1900):129; Adams to Board of Trade, 8 December 1739, Brebner (1927):103.

Chapter 8

1. Paul Mascarene, "Proclamation," 24 March 1740, Mascarene to Alexandre Bourg dit Bellehumeur, 25 March 1740, and Mascarene to Françoise Mangeant, 25 March 1740, MacMechan (1900):131, 233; Brebner (1927):108–09.
2. Mascarene to Thomas Pelham Holles, Duke of Newcastle, 7 June 1740, Brymner:93; Mascarene to Françoise Mangeant, 25 March 1740, MacMechan (1900):131.
3. Moody:107–08.
4. John Adams to King George II, 28 July 1740, Moody:110.
5. Ibid.; Max Sutherland, "Paul Mascarene," *DCB*; Ilene Susan Fort and Michael Quick, *American Art: A Catalogue of the Los Angeles County Museum of Art Collection* (Los Angeles: Los Angeles County Museum of Art, 1991):88–90. Mascarene's appointment was as lieutenant-governor of Annapolis and Fort Anne, not the province of Nova Scotia; that office remained unfilled until 1749.
6. Mascarene to Board of Trade, n.d. [c. April 1740], Brymner:93; Mascarene to Newcastle, 1 December 1743, Akins:129; Mascarene, certificate issued to certain Acadians, 1 July 1741, and Mascarene, notes, 27 May 1740, MacMechan (1900):241, 243–44.
7. Mascarene to William Douglass, 20 August 1744, Mascarene Papers.
8. Mascarene to Saint-Poncy, 22 April 1739, and Mascarene to Jean-Baptiste de Gay Desenclaves, 18 June 1741, Moody:158, 165.
9. Mascarene to Charles de la Goudalie, 12 January 1742, MacMechan (1900):160; Mascarene to Elizabeth Mascarene, 7 June 1740, Mascarene Papers.
10. Murdoch 2:27–28; Maillard:62–70.
11. Mascarene to King Gould, 9 June 1744, Mascarene to William Shirley, April 1748, and James Wibault, "Defenses of Annapolis," n.d. [c. 1740], Moody:195, 204; Mascarene to Colonel Ladeuze, n.d. [11 November 1752], Casgrain (1888–90) 2:82.
12. Robison:141; Marc Egnal, *A Mighty Empire: The Origins of the American Revolution* (Ithaca, NY: Cornell University Press, 1988):30–44 *passim*.

13. Moody:208; Shirley to General Court of Massachusetts, 31 May 1744 [11 June 1744 ns], Shirley 1:122–23; Robison:144–45. All dates for wartime events in the text are converted to New Style.

14. Mascarene to Shirley, n.d. [c. 12/1744], Akins:141–49; Mascarene to Bourg, 18 June 1744, Murdoch 2:29.

15. Mascarene to King Gould, 2 June 1744 [13 June 1744 ns], Moody:301; Mascarene to Board of Trade, 9 June 1744 [20 June 1744 ns], Casgrain (1888–90) 2:80.

16. Mascarene to Board of Trade, 20 September 1744, and Mascarene to Shirley, n.d. [c. December 1744], Akins:131–32, 141–49. Most accounts of this attack claim it was led by the missionary Louis-Joseph Le Loutre. But according to his own statement, in which he made no disavowal of his other military activities, Le Loutre claimed he first became involved in the fighting in 1745; see Webster (1933):10, 35.

17. Mascarene to Shirley, 28 July 1744, Richard 1:207–08.

18. Casgrain (1888) 520; François Dupont Duvivier, *mémoire*, 1735, Murdoch 1:508–11.

19. Duvivier, orders to the Acadians of Minas, Pisiquid, Canard, and Cobequid, 27 August 1744, Akins:134–36; Duvivier, order to René Leblanc, 22 September 1744, Fergusson:63. In general, see Fergusson:62–67 *passim*.

20. Maillard:62–70; Rawlyk:122–24.

21. Casgrain (1897):376–77; Acadians of Grand Pré, Canard, Pisiquid, and Cobequid to Michael de Gannes de Falaise, 10 October 1744, and de Gannes to Bourg, 13 October 1744, Akins:134–36.

22. Duvivier quoted in Casgrain (1897):375; Duvivier to Maurepas, n.d., Griffiths (1969):58–60; Mascarene to Shirley, n.d. [c. December 1744], and Mascarene to Shirley, 6 April 1748, Akins:141–49, 159–60.

23. Louis Robichaud to Shirley, 10 September 1756, Gaudet Appendix I, 197–98; Mascarene to Shirley, n.d. [c. December 1744], Akins:141–49; John Henry Bastide to Shirley, 3 October 1744, Moody:248.

24. Shirley to Board of Trade, 16 October 1744, Shirley 1:150; Murdoch 2:50.

25. Mascarene to Deputies of Minas, 13 October 1744, Akins:137–38; Council Minutes, 8 December 1744, Fergusson:51.

26. Council Minutes, 4 January 1745, Akins:153–55.

27. Casgrain (1888):520; Council Minutes, 26 January 1745, Fergusson:61–63; Mascarene to Shirley, 15 March 1745, Akins:150–51.

28. Casgrain (1888):520–21; Council Minutes, 2 May 1745, Fergusson:68–70; *PG*, 23 May 1745; Council Minutes, 25 May 1745, Akins:155; Louis Dupont Duchambon to Paul Marin de la Malgue, 16 May 1745, Rawlyk:182.

29. Godfrey:19–20.

30. William Pepperrell to Newcastle, 19 June 1745, Murdoch 2:65.

31. Alfred G. Bailey, "Samuel Moody," *DCB*; John Barnard to Pepperrell, 11 March 1745, "The Pepperrell Papers," *CMHS*, 6th series, 10 (1899):116.

32. Samuel Waldo quoted in John Stewart McLennan, *Louisbourg, from Its Foundation to Its Fall, 1713–1758* (London: Macmillan, 1918):152; Louis Effengham de Forest, ed., *Louisbourg Journals, 1745* (New York: Society of Colonial Wars, 1932):15, 84–85; Ferling:22–23.

33. Thomas Prince, *Extraordinary Events the Doings of God* (Boston, 1745); Nathan O. Hatch, *The Sacred Cause of Liberty: Republican Thought and the Millennium in Revolutionary New England* (New Haven: Yale University Press, 1977):36; Shirley to Pepperrell, 25 May 1745, Shirley 1:220.
34. Moody:332; William Bollan to Newcastle, 19 August 1747, Shortt:259–60; Annapolis deputies to Mascarene, 21 June 1745, Belliveau:50–51.
35. Annapolis deputies to Mascarene, 21 June 1745, Belliveau:50–51.
36. Murdoch 2:65; Peter Warren to Thomas Corbett, 18 June 1745, Gwyn:121–22; Harvey (1926):112–14; Warren to Newcastle, 3 October 1745, Gaudet, 2, Appendix C, 39.
37. Council Minutes, 8 November 1745, Fergusson:81–84.
38. Mascarene to Shirley, 7 December 1745, Moody:336–41.
39. Ibid.; Mascarene to Newcastle, 9 December 1745, PANS RG1: 17.
40. William Shirley, Jr., to Andrew Stone, 9 March 1746, Rawlyk:186; Shirley to Newcastle, 23 December 1745, and Shirley to Newcastle, 11 February 1746, Moody:342–44; Shirley to Newcastle, 29 October 1745, and Shirley to Newcastle, 18 June 1746, Shirley 1:245, 327–28; Shirley to Newcastle, 14 December 1745 and 10 May 1746, Parkman 2: 792–93, 795–96.
41. Mascarene to Isaac Townsend, 30 June 1746, Moody:351; Shirley to Newcastle, 28 July 1746, Parkman 2:800; Rawlyk:188.
42. Shirley to General Court of Massachusetts, 9 September 1746, Shirley 1:346–50.
43. Shirley to Newcastle, 15 August 1746, and Shirley to Mascarene, 16 September 1746, Shirley 1:336–37, 354–55.
44. Shirley to Newcastle, 21 November 1746, Parkman 2:807–16.
45. Ibid.
46. Ibid.
47. Council Minutes, 29 September 1746 [9 October 1746 ns], Fergusson:91; Mascarene to Newcastle, 23 January 1747, Gaudet Appendix C, 46.
48. Shirley and Warren to Townsend, 21 September 1746, Gwyn:319; Beaujeu 2:35–36, 41, 42.
49. Beaujeu 2:41–42.
50. Ibid.:48–49, 51–52.
51. Mascarene to Warren and Shirley, 26 October 1746 [6 November 1746 ns], Gwyn:356–65; Shirley to Newcastle, 1 November 1746, Moody:285–86; *PG*, 16 December 1746.
52. Mascarene to Edward How and Erasmus Philipps, 8 December 1746, Moody: 361–62; Noble to Mascarene, 28 January 1747, PANS RG1: 13; Webster (1942):16; William Bollan to Newcastle, 19 August 1747, Shortt:259–60.
53. Noble to Mascarene, 28 January 1747, PANS RG1:13; Beaujeu 2:59.
54. Beaujeu 2:59; Murdoch 2:104–05.
55. Will R. Bird, *A Century at Chignecto: The Key to Old Acadia* (Toronto: Ryerson Press, 1928):183–84; Archibald MacMechan, *Red Snow on Grand Pré* (Toronto: McClelland & Stewart, 1931):20; Beaujeu 2:60–62, 65.
56. Chevalier de La Corne, "Relation of an Expedition Against the English in Acadia," 28 September 1747, Casgrain (1888–90) 2:12–16; Webster (1942):12; Murdoch 2:104–10.

57. Ramezay to Chignecto deputies, 31 March 1747, Chignecto deputies to Ramezay, 24 May 1747, and Ramezay to Chignecto deputies, 25 May 1747, Parkman 2:709–11; Beaujeu 2:72–74.
58. Shirley to Newcastle, 8 June 1747, Richard 1:229; Ramezay to Chignecto deputies, 25 May 1747, Parkman 2:711.
59. Newcastle to Shirley, 30 May 1747, Shirley 1:388–39.
60. Shirley to Newcastle, 8 July 1747, Parkman 2:825.
61. Newcastle to Shirley, 3 October 1747, Brebner (1927):129–30.
62. Mascarene to Acadian deputies, 21 October 1747, Richard 1:226; "A Declaration of William Shirley, Esq.," n.d. [21 October 1747], Gaudet Appendix C, 47–48.
63. Mascarene to Shirley, 6 April 1748, Akins:159–60; Mascarene to Captain Askew, 31 May 1748, Shortt:271–72.
64. Shirley to John Russell, Duke of Bedford, 18 February 1749, Brymner:135; Mascarene to "Dear Ladevèze," 11 November 1752, Casgrain (1888–90) 2:82.
65. Mascarene to "Dear Ladevèze," 11 November 1752, Casgrain (1888–90) 2:82; Brebner (1929):514–15.

Chapter 9

1. George Montagu Dunk, Earl of Halifax, to John Russell, Duke of Bedford, n.d. [1748], *Report of the Board of Trustees of the Public Archives of Nova Scotia* (Halifax: Public Archives of Nova Scotia, 1971), Appendix B, 29. See T. R. Clayton, "The Duke of Newcastle, the Earl of Halifax, and the American Origins of the Seven Years' War," *Historical Journal* 24 (1981):573–84.
2. Newcastle to Henry Pelham, 9 June 1750, Clayton, "The Duke of Newcastle," 576; William Shirley to Bedford, 18 February 1749, Shirley 1:472–76.
3. Charles Morris, "Report by Captain Morris to Governor Shirley upon his Survey of Lands in Nova Scotia Available for Protestant Settlers, 1749," PAC (1913):82–83; Shirley to Bedford, 18 February 1749, Shirley 1:472–76.
4. Little:24–26.
5. Ibid.:38.
6. Dominick Stuart Graham, "British Intervention in Defence of the American Colonies, 1748–1756," Ph.D thesis, University of London, 1965, 23; Graham (1963):4; Halifax, "Extract of a Plan . . . for Settlement of His Majesty's Colony of Nova Scotia," 3 March 1749, in Bell:39; Murdoch 2:136–38; Brebner (1927):130–32; Ronald Rompkey, Introduction to Salusbury:18–19. Shirley offered a summary of his views in his later publication, *Memoirs of the Principal Transactions of the Last War Between the English and French in North America. From the Commencement of it in 1744, to the Conclusion of the Treaty at Aix la Chapelle* (London: R. & J. Dodsley, 1757).
7. J. Murray Beck, "Edward Cornwallis," *DCB*; James S. Macdonald, "Hon. Edward Cornwallis, Founder of Halifax," *NSHSC* 12 (1905):1–17; W. A. Speck, *The Butcher: The Duke of Cumberland and the Suppression of the 45* (Oxford: Basil Blackwell, 1981):166–74.
8. Halifax, "Royal Instructions for Governor Cornwallis," 29 April 1749, Gaudet Appendix C, 49–52.

9. Cornwallis to Bedford, 22 June 1749, and Cornwallis to Bedford, 23 July 1749, Akins:560–61, 563–64. Dates in the text for 1749 and 1750 are converted to New Style.
10. James S. Macdonald, "Richard Bulkeley, 1717–1800," *NSHSC* 12 (1905):66–67; Council Minutes, 14 July 1749 [25 July 1749 ns], and Cornwallis to Bedford, 11 September 1749, Akins:166–68, 586–87.
11. "His Majesty's Declaration," 14 July 1749 [25 July 1749 ns], Council Minutes, 14 July 1749 [25 July 1749 ns], and Cornwallis to Bedford, 23 July 1749 [3 August 1749 ns], Akins:165–66, 166–67, 563–64; Salusbury:53.
12. Council Minutes, 31 July 1749 [11 August 1749 ns], Council Minutes, 1 August 1749 [12 August 1749 ns], Declaration of Cornwallis, 1 August 1749 [12 August 1749 ns], Inhabitants of Acadia to the French King, n.d. [c. 1749], Cornwallis to Board of Trade, 20 August 1749 [31 August 1749 ns], Cornwallis to Bedford, 20 August 1749 [31 August 1749 ns], Akins:168–69, 170, 171–72, 233–34, 576, 577–78; Salusbury:55; W. Peter Ward, "The Acadian Response to the Growth of British Power in North America, 1749–1755," *Dalhousie Review* 51 (1971):165–77.
13. Declaration of Cornwallis, 1 August 1749 [12 August 1749 ns], Akins:171–72.
14. Acadian deputies to Cornwallis, 18 September 1749 ns, Akins:173.
15. Cornwallis to Acadian deputies, 6 September 1749 [17 September 1749 ns], Akins:174–75.
16. Ibid.
17. Cornwallis to Board of Trade, 11 September 1749 [22 September 1749 ns], Akins:175–76.
18. George T. Bates, "The Great Exodus of 1749: or, The Cornwallis Settlers Who Didn't," *NSHSC* 38 (1973):27–62; John Wilson, 1751, Harold A. Innis, ed., *Select Documents in Canadian Economic History, 1497–1783* (Toronto: University of Toronto Press, 1929):172–73.
19. Roland-Michel Barrin de la Galissonière to Rouillé, 25 July 1749, Griffiths (1992):85; La Galissonière, "Memoir on the French Colonies in North America," December 1750, O'Callaghan 10:220–32; Patrice Louis-René Higonnet, "The Origins of the Seven Years' War," *Journal of Modern History* 40 (1968):58, emphasis in original.
20. Antoine-Louis Rouillé to the King, 29 August 1749, and Jacques-Pierre de Taffanel, marquis de La Jonquière, to Rouillé, 9 October 1749, Gaudet 2 Appendix N, 291–93, 310–11.
21. Pierre Maillard to Director of Missions-Etrangères of Paris, 29 September 1738, Henri Raymond Casgrain, "Coup d'oeil sur l'Acadie, avant la dispersion de la colonie française," *Le Canada-Français* 1 (1888):122–23; Le Loutre to unknown, 1 October 1738 and 3 October 1740, Casgrain (1888–90) 1:19–25, 25–27.
22. Le Loutre, "Autobiography," Webster (1933):37–39.
23. Courville:2–3, 32–33.
24. Cornwallis to Desherbiers, 21 September 1749, Gaudet Appendix N, 293–94; Míkmaw chiefs to Cornwallis, 24 September 1749, Casgrain (1888–90) 1:17–19; Cornwallis to Board of Trade, 11 September 1749 [22 September 1749 ns], and Cornwallis, Proclamation, 1 October 1749 [12 October 1749 ns], Akins:581–82, 583–84.
25. Salusbury:70; Cornwallis to Board of Trade, 17 October 1749 [28 October 1749 ns], Akins:592.

26. Desherbiers to Rouillé, 15 August 1749, Inhabitants of Chignecto to King of France, 12 October 1749, and Inhabitants of Annapolis to La Jonquière, December 1749, Gaudet Appendix N, 285–86, 298–300, 301–02; Pierre-François-Xavier de Charlevoix, *History and General Description of New France*, trans. and ed. John Gilmary Shea, 6 vols. (New York: Francis P. Harper, 1900), 5:296–99; *PG*, 12 October 1749; Murdoch 2:226.
27. *PG*, 30 January 1750 and 13 February 1750; Richard 1:248–49; "Petition of the Philadelphia Neutral French to the King of Great Britain," n.d. [1760], Smith:369–77; Cornwallis to Board of Trade, 7 December 1749, "Nous les Sauvages" to Acadians of Minas, 12 December 1749, and Cornwallis to Board of Trade, 19 March 1750, Brymner:149, 150, 154–55; Deposition of Honoré Gautrol, 13 December 1749 [24 December 1749 ns], and Cornwallis, orders for the arrest of Acadians, 23 December 1749 [3 January 1750 ns], Akins:177.
28. Harry Piers, *The Evolution of the Halifax Fortress: 1749–1928* (Halifax: Public Archives of Nova Scotia, 1947):2; Cornwallis to Sylvanus Cobb, 13 January 1750, and Cornwallis to Board of Trade, 19 March 1750 [30 March 1750 ns], Akins:178–79, 605–06; Cornwallis to Cobb, 13 January 1750, Brymner:151.
29. Cornwallis to Bedford, 19 March 1750 [30 March 1750 ns], Akins:184; Cornwallis to Joseph Gorham, 24 March 1750 [4 April 1750 ns], Murdoch 2:175.
30. Acadians of Cobequid to Acadians of Beaubassin, n.d. [c. April 1750], Webster (1937):61–62.
31. Cornwallis to the Acadians of Annapolis Royal, Grand Pré, Rivière Canard, and Pisiquid, 25 May 1750, Akins:198.
32. Courville:8; Cornwallis to Charles Lawrence, 4 April 1750 [15 April 1750 ns], and Lawrence, journal, 21 April 1750 [2 May 1750 ns], Webster (1936):30, 32.
33. Lawrence, journal, 22 April 1750 [3 May 1750 ns], Webster (1936):33–34; La Corne to Desherbiers, n.d. [c.1750], Gaudet Appendix N, 323–24; Eaton (1915): 179–80.
34. Cornwallis to Board of Trade, 30 April 1750 [10 May 1750 ns], Brymner:155; Louis-Philogène Brulart, marquis de Puysieulx, to William Anne Keppel, Earl of Albemarle, 15 September 1750, Gaudet Appendix N, 333; Board of Trade to Cornwallis, 8 June 1750, Akins:611.
35. Louis de La Vallière, "Journal of What Occurred at Chignecto," Webster (1930):135.
36. Jacques Prévost de la Croix to unknown, 25 October 1750, Lauvrière:344–45; Claude-Elizabeth Denys de Bonaventure to unknown, 22 July 1750, quoted in Harvey (1926):137.
37. Augustin Doucet to Madame Languedoc, 5 August 1750, Doughty:77–78; sieur de la Roque, "Census of the Settlers on Ile Saint-Jean," 5 December 1752, PAC (1906) 1:75–165.
38. François Bigot to Rouillé, 22 October 1750, Gaudet Appendix N, 317–18; sieur de la Roque, "Census of the Settlers on Ile Saint-Jean," 5 December 1752, PAC (1906) 1:150; Jacques Girard to Bonaventure, 27 October 1753, Parkman 2:919–20.
39. Charles Le Moyne, baron de Longueuil, to Rouillé, 26 April 1752, Blanchet 3:508–09; La Vallière, "Journal of What Occurred at Chignecto," Webster (1930):138; Desherbiers to Bonaventure, n.d. [c. 1752], Harvey (1926):143–44.

40. Le Loutre, "Autobiography," Webster (1933):42–44; La Jonquière to Rouillé, 1 May 1751, Gaudet Appendix N, 339–42; La Jonquière, "Ordonnance," 12 April 1751, John Bartlet Brebner, ed., "Canadian Policy Toward the Acadians in 1751," *Canadian Historical Review* 12 (1931):284–86; La Vallière, "Journal of What Occurred at Chignecto," Webster (1930):140; Plank:215–16.
41. La Jonquière to Rouillé, 1 May 1751, Gaudet Appendix N, 339–42; La Vallière, "Journal of What Occurred at Chignecto," Webster (1930):137–38, 140; Cornwallis to Board of Trade, 24 June 1751, Murdoch 2:400–01; John Wilson, "Genuine Narrative" (1751), quoted in Archibald MacMechan, *Red Snow on Grand Pré* (Toronto: McClelland & Stewart, 1931):182–83; Pierre-Roch de Saint-Ours Deschaillons to Desherbiers, 30 July 1751, Webster (1930):123–24. French and British sources disagree on casualties in the Dartmouth attack, La Vallière in his official report listing thirty killed and twelve captured, Wilson in his narrative eight killed and six captured.
42. Le Loutre, "Autobiography," Webster (1933):45–47; S. Patterson:33, 42; Gérard Finn, "Jean-Louis Le Loutre," *DCB*.
43. Wendy Cameron, "Peregrine Thomas Hopson," *DCB*.
44. Council Minutes, 14 September 1752, 22 November 1752, and 16 April 1753, Akins:673–74, 694–98; Upton:54–55; Geoffrey Plank, "The Two Majors Cope: The Boundaries of Nationality in Mid-18th Century Nova Scotia," *Acadiensis* 25 (1996): 18–40.
45. Peregrine Thomas Hopson to Board of Trade, 10 December 1752, Akins:197; Board of Trade to Hopson, 28 March 1753, Gaudet Appendix C, 56.
46. Hopson to commanders at Grand Pré and Pisiquid, 15 December 1752, Minas Acadians to Hopson, 4 July 1753, and Council Minutes, 12 September 1753, Akins: 197–203; Council Minutes, 12 December 1752, Murdoch 2:213.
47. Brebner (1927):171; Bell:339; Hopson to Board of Trade, 16 October 1752, Akins:677–78.
48. Hopson to Board of Trade, 16 October 1752, Akins:677–78; Dominick Stuart Graham, "Charles Lawrence," *DCB*; Phyllis R. Blakeley, "Charles Morris," *DCB*; Harvey (1953): vii–viii, 8–13.
49. Hopson to Board of Trade, 23 July 1753, Acadians of Megoguich to Hopson, n.d. [c. September 1753], Akins:199–201, 203–05.
50. William Cotterell to Hopson, 1 October 1753, Gaudet Appendix C, 57–58.
51. Council Minutes, 27 September 1753, Murdoch 2:224; Hopson to Board of Trade, 23 July 1753, and William Cotterell to Captain George Scott, 12 April 1754, Akins:199–201, 208–09; Hopson to Board of Trade, 1 October 1753, Gaudet Appendix C, 57.

Chapter 10

1. Lawrence to Board of Trade, 5 December 1753, Akins:206; Board of Trade to Hopson, 28 March 1753, Gaudet Appendix C, 56.
2. Board of Trade to Lawrence, 4 March 1754 [sic; 4 April 1754], Akins:207–08. The word "nice" in this context means "difficult to decide or settle."

3. Harvey (1953):13; Lawrence to Board of Trade, 29 December 1753, Brymner:196; Upton:54; Graham (1963):119.
4. Brebner (1927):190–91; James S. Macdonald, "Life and Administration of Governor Charles Lawrence, 1749–1760," *NSHSC* 12 (1905):19–22.
5. Cornwallis to Bedford, 22 September 1750, Brymner:166. Dominick Stuart Graham, "Charles Lawrence," *DCB,* offers a somewhat more positive view of Lawrence.
6. Lawrence to Board of Trade, 1 August 1754, Akins:212–14, emphasis added.
7. John A. Schutz, *William Shirley: King's Governor of Massachusetts* (Chapel Hill: University of North Carolina Press, 1961):120; Ferling:73–74. The final report of the commission was published as *The Memorials of the English and French Commissaries Concerning the Limits of Nova Scotia or Acadia,* 2 vols. (London, 1755).
8. *PG,* 7 June 1753.
9. Patrice Louis-René Higonnet, "The Origins of the Seven Years' War," *Journal of Modern History* 40 (1968):64; Robert D'Arcy, Earl of Holderness, circular letter to colonial governors, 28 August 1753, O'Callaghan 6:794–95.
10. Shirley to Holderness, 7 January 1754, O'Callaghan 6:823–25; Shirley to Holderness, 19 April 1754, Shirley 2:52–53; Shirley to General Court, 28 March 1754, Trask: 229; Shirley to Thomas Robinson, 23 May 1754, Akins:382.
11. Rawlyk: 200.
12. *Boston News-Letter* and *Post-Boy* quoted in Rawlyk:201; William Clarke, *Observations on the Late and Present Conduct of the French, with Regard to their Encroachments Upon the British Colonies in North America* (Boston: S. Kneeland, 1755):31.
13. Jonathan Mayhew, "Election Sermon," 29 May 1754, *PG,* 29 August 1754; Samuel Checkley, "The Duty of God's People When Engaged in War" (1755), quoted in Trask:258; Jonathan Edwards, sermon on Psalms 60:9–12, n.d. [c. 1755], Jonathan Edwards Papers, Yale University.
14. Mayhew, "Election Sermon," 29 May 1754, *PG,* 29 August 1754.
15. Shirley to Halifax, 20 August 1754, Pargellis:24–24.
16. Lawrence to Halifax, 23 August 1754, Pargellis:27–29.
17. Phyllis R. Blakeley, "Charles Morris," *DCB.*
18. Morris to Shirley, 25 June 1751, PANS RG1:284; Charles Morris, "Remarks Concerning the Settlement of Nova Scotia," n.d. [c. 1753], Casgrain (1888–90); Charles Morris, "Account of the Acadians, Drawn up in 1753 . . . ," *NSHSC* 2 (1881):154–57; Charles Morris, "Some Reflections on the Situation of the Inhabitants," n.d., PANS RG1:284. Because these important texts are not extant in the original, and exist as transcriptions made by Reverend Andrew Brown in the 1790s, only the first, Morris's letter to Shirley, has a firm date. The second was assigned a date of 1753 by the editors of the *NSHSC.* The dating of the last, Morris's operational plan for removal, is a matter of some question and considerable importance. The three documents appear to have been produced sequentially. In the 1751 letter to Shirley, Morris suggests the necessity of removing the inhabitants of Chignecto; in the second, from 1753, he goes farther and suggests the removal of the inhabitants of Cobequid; and in the last he discusses the tactical problems of a removal operation for all the Acadians of the Minas Basin. Brown and most subsequent commentators have assumed that last document was written on the eve of removal, in the spring or even the summer of 1755. A close reading of the text, however,

indicates that it was prepared no later than August 1754. In that report, Morris wrote that removal could be effected "only with a superior force to that which at present is in the colony." That sentence could not have been written after November 1754, when Lawrence sent Lieutenant-Colonel Robert Monckton to Boston to work out the details of the joint operation with Shirley. Morris also referred to the flight of the "several of the inhabitants of Cobequid last summer and this spring," He made no mention of this in the 1753 text, where he explicitly discussed the prospect of removing the Cobequid inhabitants. By the fall of 1753 Father Jacques Girard and his Cobequid parishioners were at Ile Saint-Jean. That suggests the later text was written after the spring and before November of 1754 (although other textual references suggest the possibility that it was written even earlier). Lawrence's letter to Lord Halifax of 23 August 1754 shares several striking similarities with Morris's report—the reference to inadequate troop strength, the insistence on the necessity of burning the inhabitants' villages and cutting their dikes—suggesting that Lawrence had it in hand at the time. Brebner (1927):197–200 argues that there is "no evidence that before the end of June, 1755, Lawrence entertained any scheme for expelling any large part of the Acadians." But the evidence presented here adds up to a compelling case that planning for the removal of all the Acadians was well underway at least a year earlier.

19. Morris, "Some Reflections on the Situation of the Inhabitants . . . ," n.d. [c. 1754], in Casgrain (1888–90) 1:130–37.

20. Ibid.; Dudley J. LeBlanc, *The True Story of the Acadians* (Lafayette, LA: privately printed, 1937):28.

21. Upton:56; Lawrence to Board of Trade, 1 August 1754, and Cotterell to Captain Patrick Sutherland, 24 August 1754, Akins:212–15.

22. Le Loutre, "Autobiography," Webster (1933):46–47.

23. Thomas Pichon to George Scott, 23 September 1754, Pichon to Scott, 14 October 1754, and Ordinance of Duquesne, n.d. [c. October 1754], Webster (1937):41–45, 67.

24. Webster (1937):2–5; T. A. Crowley, "Thomas Pichon," *DCB*.

25. Pichon to Halifax, 27 June 1756, Pichon to John Hussey, 9 November 1754, and Pichon to John Hussey, 24 December 1754, Webster (1937):8, 57, 75.

26. Pichon to Scott, 17 September 1754, and Pichon to Archibald Hinchelwood, 26 September 1755, Webster (1937):39–40, 111; T. A. Crowley, "Thomas Pichon," *DCB*.

27. Alexander Murray to his wife, 31 July 1755, Beckles Willson, "Wolfe's Men and Nova Scotia," *NSHSC* 18 (1914):8.

28. William Cotterell to Murray, 5 August 1754, and Cotterell to Murray, 1 September 1754, Haliburton 1:169n; Murray to Lawrence, 22 September 1754, Akins: 222.

29. Henri Daudin to Le Loutre, 5 August 1754, and Daudin to Le Loutre, 27 September 1754, Webster (1937):68, 70; Murray to Lawrence, n.d. [24 September 1754], Murray to Lawrence, 30 September 1754, and Cotterell to Murray, 21 October 1754, Akins: 223–24, 225–26, 235.

30. Daudin to abbé de l'Isle Dieu, 26 September 1754, Webster (1937):68–69; Daudin, *mémoire,* n.d. [c. 1756], Casgrain (1888):102–03; Murray to Lawrence, n.d. [24 September 1754], Akins:223–24.

31. Robinson to Shirley, 5 July 1754, Robinson to Lawrence, 5 July 1754, Lawrence to Shirley, 5 November 1754, Shirley to Lawrence, 7 November 1754, and Lawrence to

Robert Monckton, 7 November 1754, Akins:377–79, 380–84, 391–92; Robison:162; Lawrence to Monckton, 12 December 1754, Griffiths (1969):108; Graham (1968): 551–66.

32. Graham (1968):555; Shirley to Robinson, 14 December 1754, Shirley 2:109; Robinson, "Sketch for the Operations in North America," 16 November 1754, LO514, Loudoun Papers; Instructions to General Braddock, O'Callaghan 6:920–22.

33. Board of Trade to Lawrence, 29 October 1754, Akins:235–37.

34. Richard 1:365–66.

35. Lawrence to Board of Trade, 12 January 1755, Brymner:202; Graham (1963):55; Lawrence to Monckton, 20 January 1755, Griffiths (1969):108–09.

36. Shirley to Lawrence, 6 January 1755, Akins: 393–400.

37. Cynthia Hagar Krusell, *The Winslows of Careswell in Marshfield* (Marshfield Hills, MA: Historical Research Associates, 1992):25–27; Winslow to Halifax, 27 June 1755, Winslow (1885):179–80.

38. Shirley to Robinson, 18 February 1755, Gipson (1942):224–26; Morrill quoted in Rawlyk:207–09.

39. Braddock to Robinson, 19 April 1755, LO572, Loudoun Papers; Shirley to Lawrence, 31 May 1755, Akins:406–07; Baxter:129.

40. De Fiedmont:12–14, 18–19; George F. G. Stanley, *New France: The Last Phase, 1744–60* (Toronto: McClelland & Stewart, 1968):117.

41. Lawrence to Murray, 27 May 1755, Akins:242; Pichon to Hussey, 13 May 1755, Webster (1937):96–97.

42. Lawrence to Monckton, 1 May 1755, Geoffrey Gilbert Plank, "The Culture of Conquest: The British Colonists and Nova Scotia, 1690–1759," Ph.D. thesis, Princeton University, 1994, 366.

43. De Fiedmont:18–19. Louis-Léonard Aumasson, sieur de Courville, notary at Beauséjour, later wrote that the Acadians asked de Vergor to issue that proclamation in order to provide them with cover in the event the British were victorious; but there is no contemporary evidence to corroborate his claim, and the French had issued similar orders many times before; Courville:44.

44. De Fiedmont:21–22.

45. Ibid.

46. Winslow, journal, 3 June 1755, Winslow (1885):145; Monckton, journal, 4 June 1755, Webster (1930):111; Willard, journal, 4 June 1755, Willard:19–20.

47. *PG,* 7 July 1755 and 31 July 1755; Winslow, journal, 4 June 1755, Winslow (1885):146–47; Willard, journal, 4 June 1755, Willard:19–20.

48. Thomas, journal, 4 June 1755, Thomas:123.

49. De Fiedmont:24–25; Pichon, journal, 10 June 1755, Webster (1937):101–03; Willard, journal, 5 June 1755, Willard:20–21.

50. Willard, journal, 7 June 1755, Willard:21–22; Pichon, journal, 8 June 175, Webster (1937):103; Winslow, journal, 8 June 1755, Winslow (1885):148–49, 150–55; Thomas, journal, 8 June 1755 and 16 June 1755, Thomas:124–25; de Fiedmont:28–30; *PG,* 31 July 1755.

51. Winslow, journal, 14 June 1755, Winslow (1885):155; *PG,* 31 July 1755.

52. Pichon, journal, 13–16 June 1755, Webster (1937):103–04; de Fiedmont:28–32;

Thomas Pichon, *Genuine Letters and Memoirs, Relating to the Natural, Civil, and Commercial History of the Islands of Cape Breton, and Saint John* (London: J. Nourse, 1760):320–21.
53. M. de Joubert to M. de Surlaville, n.d. [1755], de Fiedmont:9.
54. Courville:50; de Fiedmont:32–35; Brebner (1927):202; Winslow, journal, 15 June 1755, Winslow (1885):157–58.
55. Monckton, journal, 17 June 1755, Webster (1930):113; Pichon, journal, 16 June 1755, Webster (1937):104; Winslow, journal, 19 June 1755, Winslow (1885):164.
56. Monckton to Winslow, 18 June 1755, Winslow (1885):160–61; Pichon, journal, 19 June 1755, Webster (1937):105.
57. Pichon, journal, 19 June 1755, and Pichon to Halifax, 27 June 1756, Webster (1937):105, 122.
58. Lawrence to Board of Trade, 21 June 1755, Graham (1963):86; Lawrence to Monckton, 25 June 1755, Griffiths (1969):109.
59. Lawrence to Robinson, 28 June 1755, and Lawrence to Board of Trade, 28 June 1755, Akins:243, 408–09.

Chapter 11

1. *PG,* 3 July 1755; Statement of Joseph Gray, n.d. [c. 1790], PANS RG1:363 [this text is mistakenly included with the memoirs of Isaac Deschamps in Casgrain (1888–90) 1:138–42]; Richard 2:6–9.
2. Lawrence to Alexander Murray, 27 May 1755, and Acadian deputies of Minas to Lawrence, 10 June 1755, Akins:242, 247–49.
3. Acadian deputies of Minas to Lawrence, 10 June 1755, Akins:247–49.
4. Council Minutes, 3 July 1755, and Lawrence to Board of Trade, 18 July 1755, Akins:250, 260.
5. Acadian deputies of Minas to Lawrence, 24 June1755, and Council Minutes, 3 July1755, Akins:249–55, emphasis added.
6. Council Minutes, 3 July 1755, Akins:250–55.
7. Galerm:61–62. On Galerne, see White 1:833, 2:1193; and Donald J. Hébert, *Acadians in Exile* (Cecilia, LA: Hébert Publications, 1980):144.
8. Galerm:61–62.
9. Council Minutes, 3 July and 4 July 1755, and Lawrence to Board of Trade, 18 July 1755, Akins:250–56, 260.
10. Council Minutes, 3 July and 4 July 1755, and Lawrence to Board of Trade, 18 July 1755, Akins:250–56, 260; William Cawley, *The Laws of Queen Elizabeth, King James, and King Charles the First Concerning Jesuites, Seminary Priests, Recusants, &c. and Concerning the Oaths of Supremacy and Allegiance* (London: John Wright & Richard Chiswell, 1680):252.
11. Galerm:61–62; Daudin quoted in Richard 2:53–54.
12. Belcher to Board of Trade, n.d., Gaudet Appendix C, 63–65.
13. Doughty:115–17.
14. Cawley, *The Laws of Queen Elizabeth,* 104, 252; “The Acadian Confessors of the

Faith—1755," *American Catholic Quarterly Review* 9 (1884):592–607. Belcher actually cited 1 George II c. 13 (1727–28), but since there was no such statute he must have meant 1 George I c. 13 (1715).

15. Belcher to Board of Trade, n.d., and Lawrence to Governor Arthur Dobbs of North Carolina, 11 August 1755, Gaudet Appendix C, 63–65, and Appendix B, 15–16; Lawrence to Board of Trade, 18 July 1755, Akins:260.

16. Daudin quoted in Richard 2:53–54. Daudin gave the date of the announcement of the proclamation as 6 July 1755, but since the petition from the Annapolis Acadians cites it as dated 12 July 1755, I assume he was mistaken and have corrected his dating accordingly.

17. Acadians of Annapolis Royal to His Majesty's Council, n.d. [15 July 1755], Akins:261.

18. Brown (1815):142.

19. Memorial of the Acadians of Minas Basin, River Canard, and neighboring places, n.d. [22 July 1755], and Memorial of the Acadians of Pisiquid, 22 July 1755, Akins: 263–66.

20. Council Minutes, 15 July 1755, Atkins:258–59.

21. Lawrence to Board of Trade, 18 July 1755, Akins:260.

22. Spencer Phips to Lawrence, n.d. [28 July 1755], Akins:409–10; Brebner (1927):221.

23. Council Minutes, 25 July 1755, Akins:261–62; "Petition of the Neutrals to the King of Great Britain," n.d. [c. 1760], Smith:369–77.

24. Daudin quoted in Richard 2:53–54; Council Minutes, 25 July 1755, Akins:261–62.

25. Richard 2:48–49.

26. Council Minutes, 28 July, 1755, Akins:267; Statement of Joseph Gray, PANS RG1:363; "Petition of the Neutrals to the King of Great Britain," Smith:369–77.

27. Council Minutes, 3 July 1755, Lawrence to Board of Trade, 18 July 1755, and Council Minutes, 28 July 1755, Akins:256, 260, 267; Acadians to Governor William Denny of Pennsylvania, 27 August 1756, Murdoch 2:321–32; *PG*, 24 July 1755.

28. Charles Morris, "Some Reflections on the Situation of the Inhabitants," n.d. [1754], Casgrain (1888–90) 1:130–37; Lawrence to Murray, 9 August 1755, Winslow (1885):241–43.

29. Lawrence to Dobbs, 11 August 1755, Gaudet Appendix B, 15–16; Council Minutes, 28 July, 1755, Akins:267.

30. Arsenault (1994):134; Gaudet 1:vii; Daudin, Lauvrière 1:454–55; "Petition of the Neutrals to the King of Great Britain," Smith:369–77.

31. Lawrence to Murray, 9 August 1755, Winslow (1885):241–43; Daudin, Lauvrière 1:454–55; Lawrence to Board of Trade, 18 October 1755, Akins:281–83.

32. Lawrence to Monckton, 31 July, 1755, Akins:267–69; Lawrence to Monckton, 11 August 1755, PAC (1926):85–87, and Griffiths (1969):109; Lawrence to Winslow, 11 August 1755, Winslow (1883):87.

33. Lawrence to Monckton, 8 August 1755, and Lawrence to Major John Handfield, 11 August 1755, Akins:269–70, 274–76; Thomas Hancock to unknown, 18 August 1755, Baxter:133; Lawrence to Winslow, 11 August 1755, Winslow (1883):78–81; Lawrence to Murray, 9 August 1755, Winslow (1885):241–43.

34. Lawrence to Monckton, 31 July 1755, Akins:267–69; Lawrence to Winslow, 11

August 1755, Winslow (1883):78–81; Lawrence to Monckton, 11 August 1855, Griffiths (1969):109.

35. Lawrence to Monckton, 31 July 1755 and 8 August 1755, Akins:267–70; Hustvedt:24–25.

36. Lawrence to Monckton, 24 December 1754, Griffiths (1969):108; Lawrence to Monckton, 16 July 1755, Graham (1963):86–87; Winslow to Lawrence, 23 July 1755, Winslow (1885):210.

37. Brebner (1927):222–23; Lauvrière 1:151.

38. *New York Gazette,* 25 August 1755, *PG,* 4 September 1755 (datelined Halifax), and *Maryland Gazette,* 18 September 1755. This letter has been attributed to John Winslow. Richard 2:77, who offers no supporting evidence, seems to have been the first to make the assertion, providing a transcription of the text significantly different from the one published in the colonial press (the one used here), perhaps because his book was first published in French, then translated into English. Arsenault (1994):123 also attributes the letter to Winslow, and reproduces word for word Richard's mangled text; he cites the manuscript copy of the Winslow journal in the Massachusetts Historical Society, but I could not locate it there. Arsenault is probably the source of later attributions, which include Roger Paradis, ed., *Papiers de/Papers of Prudent L. Mercure: Histoire du Madawaska* (Madawaska, ME: Madawaska Historical Society, 1998):xiii, and Jim Bradshaw, "'A Scene of Confusion, Despair, and Desolation': Acadians at Grand Pré told they will be sent away from their ancestral lands," *Lafayette Daily Advertiser,* 23 February 1999, and "UL Lafayette Acquires 1755 Letter: Historic message to friend tells of Acadian exodus from eastern Canada," *Lafayette Daily Advertiser,* October 20, 2001. Doughty:143–44, quotes Richard's version of the text, but asserts the author was Lawrence, offering no supporting evidence. Either Winslow or Lawrence could have written the letter, but in the absence of confirming evidence its author remains unknown.

Chapter 12

1. Winslow (1885):221; Lawrence to Monckton, 31 July 1755, and Lawrence, "Circular Letter from Governor Lawrence to the Governors on the Continent," Akins:267–69, 277–78; Lawrence to Monckton, 11 August 1755, PAC (1926):85–87.

2. Lawrence to Monckton, 11 August 1755, PAC (1926):85–87.

3. Winslow (1885):221.

4. Winslow to Shirley, 22 August 1755, Winslow (1883):71–72; Winslow to Lawrence, 3 July 1755, and Winslow to Thomas Lane, 26 September 1755, Winslow (1885):178, 192, 231. The Winslow journal was later donated to the Massachusetts Historical Society.

5. Winslow, journal, 14 August 1755, Winslow (1885):231.

6. François Le Guerne to Jacques Prévost de la Croix, 10 March 1756, Casgrain (1888–90) 2:149, 153–56; Pierre-François de Rigaud de Vaudreuil de Cavagnal, marquis de Vaudreuil, to Jean-Baptiste de Machault d'Arnouville, 18 October 1755, Gaudet Appendix H, 177–79; Daniel Dugas quoted in Chagnon:2–3; Lawrence to Thomas Robinson, 30 November 1755, Akins:283–85.

7. Winslow (1885):227–28; Dugas quoted in Chagnon:2–3; Acadian prisoners to Monckton, n.d. [12 August 1755], PAC (1926):33–34.
8. Acadian prisoners to Monckton, n.d. [12 August 1755], PAC (1926):33–34, original French text in Northcliffe Collection, Robert Monckton Papers, microfilm C-365, National Archives of Canada; Vaudreuil to Machault, 18 October 1755, Gaudet Appendix H, 177–79.
9. Lawrence to Murray, 9 August 1755, and Winslow to Lawrence, 18 August 1755, Winslow (1885):241–44.
10. Winslow, journal, 10 September 1755, Winslow (1883):108–10; Winslow, journal, 20 August 1755, Winslow (1885):245–46.
11. Winslow to Shirley, 22 August 1755, Winslow to Lawrence, 30 August, 1755, and Winslow, journal, 30 August 1755, Winslow (1883):71–72, 85, 87–88.
12. Winslow, journal, 1 September 1755, Murray to Winslow, 31 August 1755, and Winslow to Murray, 1 September 1755, Winslow (1883):87–89.
13. Winslow, journal, 3 September 1755, and Murray to Winslow, 4 September 1755, Winslow (1883):89–91, 92, 94; Bell:501.
14. Winslow, journal, 2 September 1755, Winslow (1883):90; "Petition of the Neutrals to the King of Great Britain," n.d. [c. 1760], Smith:369–77.
15. Casgrain (1888):493; White 2:1013; Eaton (1910):30–31; Richard 2:85–87; Smith:213n.
16. Winslow, journal, 5 September 1755, Winslow (1883):94; Brown (1815):142.
17. Winslow, journal, 5 September 1755, and Winslow to Lawrence, 17 September 1755, Winslow (1883):94–95, 108; Lawrence to Monckton, 31 July 1755, Akins:267–69.
18. Murray to Winslow, 5 September 1755, Winslow to Murray, 5 September 1755, and Winslow, journal, 5 September 1755, Winslow (1883):96–98.
19. Handfield to Winslow, 31 August 1755, Winslow (1883):96.
20. William G. Godfrey, "John Handfield," *DCB*; Murdoch 1:339; White 2:1588.
21. Lawrence to Handfield, 11 August 1755, Akins:274–76; Le Guerne to Prévost, 10 March 1756, Casgrain (1888–90) 2:153–54; James Fraser, "Notes from Tradition and Memory of the Acadian Removal" (1815), PANS RG1:363; Petition of Louis Robichaud, 10 September 1756, Gaudet Appendix I, 70–72; Winslow, journal, 7 September 1755, Winslow to Handfield, 7 September 1755, and Lawrence to Winslow, 23 September 1755, Winslow (1883):103, 145–47.
22. Lawrence to Monckton, 31 July 1755 and 8 August 1755, Akins:267–70; Robert Monckton, journal, 2 August 1755, Webster (1930):114; Willard, journal, 16 August 1755, Willard:41–42.
23. Henri-Marie Dubriel de Pontbriand, "Mandement pour des prières publiques—Dispersion des Acadiens," 15 February 1756, quoted in Léon Thériault, "The Acadianization of the Catholic Church in Acadia (1763–1953)," Daigle (1982):278; Le Guerne to Prévost, 10 March 1756, Casgrain (1888–90) 2:149; Milner:33–34; Will R. Bird, *A Century at Chignecto: The Key to Old Acadia* (Toronto: Ryerson Press, 1928):167–68.
24. Charles Deschamps de Boishébert, journal, 10 October 1755, Gaudet Appendix N, 176–77.
25. *PG*, 9 October 1755 and 16 October 1755; Webster (1942):16, 18–19.
26. Boishébert journal, 10 October 1755, Gaudet Appendix N, 176–77.

27. Le Guerne quoted in Sauvageau:263; Winslow, journal, 7 September 1755, Winslow (1883):106.
28. Winslow to Murray, 7 September 1755, and Murray to Winslow, 8 September 1755, Winslow (1883):104, 107–08; Jonathan Edwards, sermon I Samuel 17:45–47, n.d. [c. 1755], Jonathan Edwards Papers, Yale University.
29. Sister Elizabeth, C. E. Lart, "Notes on the Fate of the Acadians," *Canadian Historical Review* 5 (1924):112; Milner:30.
30. Winslow, journal, 10 September 1755, Winslow (1883):108.
31. Ibid.:108–10 (slightly modified for clarity).
32. Ibid.; Casgrain (1888):183.
33. Winslow, journal, 12 September 1755, Winslow (1883):111–12 (slightly modified for clarity).
34. Lawrence to Winslow, 11 August 1755, Winslow to Handfield, 19 September 1755, and Winslow to Lawrence, 29 September 1755, Winslow (1883):87, 134, 154–56.
35. Monckton to Winslow, 2 September 1755, Winslow (1883):99; Lawrence to Monckton, 11 September 1755 and 27 September 1755, Griffiths (1969):109–10.
36. Monckton to Winslow, 7 October 1755, Winslow (1883):177–78; Sauvageau:266; Clarence J. D'Entremont, "The Escape of the Acadians from Fort Lawrence at the Time of the Expulsion," *YV*, 8 May 1990.
37. Le Guerne to Prévost, 10 March 1756, Casgrain (1888–90) 2:156–57.
38. Dugas quoted in Chagnon:3; Brook Watson to Andrew Brown, 1 July 1791, Brown (1881):129–34.
39. *PG*, 13 November 1755; Thomas Proby to Monckton, 20 October 1755, Northcliffe Collection, Robert Monckton Papers, microfilm C-365, National Archives of Canada.
40. Winslow to Lawrence, 29 September 1755, Lawrence to Winslow 1 October 1755, and Winslow to Lawrence, 11 October 1755, Winslow (1883):154–56, 162–63, 165–66, 169.
41. Winslow, journal, 8 October 1755, Winslow (1883):166 (slightly modified for clarity).
42. Winslow, journal, 4 October 1755, Winslow (1883):156; Isaac Deschamps, "Recollections," n.d. [c. 1790], Casgrain (1888–90) 1:138–42; Galerm:61–62; Casgrain (1888):182.
43. Deschamps, "Recollections," n.d. [c. 1790] Casgrain (1888–90) 1:138–42; "Petition of the Neutrals to the King of Great Britain," Smith:369–77.
44. Winslow, journal, 8 October 1755, and Winslow to Lawrence, 27 October 1755, Winslow (1883):166, 179–80.
45. Winslow, journal, 12 October 1755 and 13 October 1755, Winslow (1883):171, 173; Casgrain (1888):173.
46. William Faulkner Rushton, *The Cajuns: From Acadia to Louisiana* (New York: Farrar, Straus & Giroux, 1979):51; Winslow to Captain Thomas Church, 13 October 1755, and Murray to Winslow, 14 October 1755, Winslow (1883):172, 173.
47. Murray to Winslow, 14 October 1755, Winslow to Shirley, 20 October 1755, and Winslow to Thomas Hancock, 23 October 1755, Winslow (1883):173, 175, 178; Brown (1815):144.
48. Knox 1:114–15; Adams to Winslow, 8 December 1755, Winslow (1883):180–83, 186–87; Haliburton 1:180–81.
49. Winslow to Lawrence, 31 October 1755, Winslow to Adams, 13 November 1755,

and Winslow, journal, n.d. [13 November 1755], Winslow (1883):182, 185; Lauvrière 1:493–501; *PG*, 8 January 1756.

50. Lieutenant Cox to Acadians, 12 November 1755, in Gaudet:x; Winslow to Osgood, 29 November 1755, Osgood to Winslow, 18 December 1755 and 20 December 1755, Winslow, journal, n.d. [13 November 1755], Winslow (1883):185, 186, 188, 192.

51. Thomas Miller, *Historical and Genealogical Record of the First Settlers of Colchester County* (Halifax: A & W. Mackinlay, 1873):7–9.

Chapter 13

1. Lawrence to Board of Trade, 18 October 1755, Akins:279–80.

2. Thomas Robinson to Governor Lawrence, 13 August 1755, Akins:281–83; Arsenault (1994):122.

3. Lawrence to Robinson, 30 November 1755, Akins:283–85; Lawrence to Halifax, 9 December 1755, Pargellis:155–57; Brebner (1927):229.

4. Shirley 2:303–04; Halifax to Lawrence, 9 October 1755, PANS RG1:363; Board of Trade to Lawrence, 25 March 1756, Akins:298; Doughty:137; Lauvrière 2:42.

5. Peter Pelerine [sic] to Governor Francis Bernard, 13 April 1765, Gaudet Appendix E, 129.

6. Nathan Adams to Winslow, 8 December 1755, Winslow (1883):186–87; Lafrenière.

7. Lowe:212–29; "Petition of the Neutrals to the King of Great Britain," n.d. [c. 1760], Smith:369–77.

8. Massachusetts House of Representatives, "Report of the committee . . . on the condition of the French deportees," 5 November 1755, Gaudet Appendix E, 81; Belliveau:4–6, 16–17.

9. Lafrenière; Griffiths (1992):93; *PG*, 4 March 1756. The estimate is my own, based on the evidence detailed.

10. Lawrence to William Shirley, 18 March 1756, Akins:296–97; *PG*, 18 March 1756; Père Labrosse to unknown, 31 July 1756, Sauvageau:270; Webster (1942):20; Placide Gaudet, "Charles Belliveau et les siens durant la Déportation et après" [1922], *CSHA* 3 (1971):389–90.

11. Lafrenière; Hutchinson 3:28–31.

12. Council Minutes, 3 July 1755, Lawrence to Board of Trade 18 July 1755, and "Circular Letter from Governor Lawrence to the Governors on the Continent," 11 August 1755, Akins:256, 260, 277–78.

13. General Court to William Shirley, 7 February 1756, Belliveau:92; Lowe:214–15; Griffiths (1976):68; Frances Manwaring Caulkins, *History of New London, Connecticut* (New London: privately printed, 1852):469–70; Brasseaux (1991):24–28.

14. Sollers (1908):1–21.

15. Brasseaux (1991):17–18; Griffiths (1992):113.

16. Robert H. Morris to Shirley, n.d. [c. 20 November 1755], and Pennsylvania Assembly report, 25 November 1755, Smith:228–29, 231, 232.

17. Council Minutes (Pennsylvania), 8 December 1755, Gaudet 1:vi; Brasseaux (1991):18–22.

18. Acadians to Governor William Denny, 2 September 1756, Murdoch 2:321–32; Gipson (1942):313.
19. Ledet:118–28; Gaudet 1:xvi.
20. Francis Miuse [sic] to Governor, 18 November 1757, John Labardor [sic] to Governor, 26 December 1757, and Francis Meuse [sic] to Governor, 6 January 1759, Gaudet Appendix E, 114–15, 117–18, 124; White 2:1207; "The Guedry-Labine Family Genealogical Database," http://freepages.genealogy.rootsweb.com/~guidryrm/Guedry-Labine/PS08/PS08_029.HTM.
21. Joseph Michelle [sic] to Shirley and the House of Representatives, 30 March 1756, Claude Bourgeois to the Council, 4 May 1756, and Charles and Nicholas Breau [sic] to the Council, 26 April 1756, Gaudet Appendix E, 100–04; Nahum Mitchell, *History of the Early Settlement of Bridgewater, in Plymouth County, Massachusetts* (1840; Bowie, MD: Heritage Books, 1983):138.
22. Jean Landry, Claude Bennois [Benoit], Claude Leblanc, Charlie Daigle, Pierre Leblanc, Augustin Leblanc, Jacques Hébert, Joseph Vincent, and Antoine Hébert to Shirley, 13 April 1756, and Augustin Hébert to Lieutenant-Governor Spencer Phips, 7 October 1756, and Peter Boudreau [sic] to Council, n.d., Gaudet Appendix E, 88–89, 107, 110–11; Belliveau:190–91.
23. Acadians to Honorable Mr. Norris of the Pennsylvania Assembly, n.d. [8 February 1757], Naomi E. S. Griffiths, "Petitions of Acadian Exiles, 1755–1785," *Histoire Sociale* 11 (May 1978):218; John Campbell, Earl of Loudoun, to William Pitt, 25 April 1757, LO3467, Loudoun Papers.
24. Ledet:123; Gipson (1942):237.
25. Dinwiddie to Robinson, 15 November 1755, Griffiths (1976):69; Gipson (1942):301; Brasseaux (1991):11.
26. Dinwiddie to Henry Fox, 9 November 1756, Millard:250–51; Arsenault (1994):169.
27. Gipson (1942):302–03; Dinwiddie to Robinson, 24 May 1756, Millard:246–47.
28. Gaudet 1:vi; Medical Department of the Sick and Hurt Board of the Admiralty to John Cleveland, 17 September 1756, Griffiths (1976):71.
29. Lawrence to Robert Monckton, 11 August 1755, PAC (1926):85–87.
30. Milling:16–17.
31. Milling:16–17; Hudnut:500–13.
32. *PG*, 4 March 1756; Milling:25–26.
33. Brasseaux (1991):12; Hamer:199–208; Jacques Morrice [sic], passport, 10 March 1756, LO903, Loudoun Papers.
34. Jacques Morrice, passport, 10 March 1756, LO903, Loudoun Papers; Hudnut:506; Acadian memorial, 1762, Richard 2:241; Hamer:199–208.
35. Dinwiddie to Fox, 24 May 1756, Gipson (1942):296; Dinwiddie to Glen, 12 June 1756, Milling:246–47; Henry Fox to Dinwiddie, 14 August 1756, LO1489, Loudoun Papers.
36. Lawrence to colonial governors, 1 July 1756, Akins:303; Belliveau:23–26; Charles Hardy to Board of Trade, 5 September 1756, O'Callaghan 7:125; Jacques Morrice, passport, 10 March 1756, LO903, Loudoun Papers.
37. Vaudreuil to Machault, 6 August 1756 and 7 August 1756, Gaudet Appendix N, 181–83; Gamaliel Smethurst, *Narrative of an Extraordinary Escape out of the Hands of*

Indians, in the Gulph of St. Lawrence (London: privately printed, 1774):17; James Fraser, "Notes from Tradition and Memory of the Acadian Removal" (c. 1815), PANS RG1:363; Corinne LaPlante, "Michel Bastarache dit Le Basque," *DCB*.
38. Winzerling:17; *PG*, 25 March 1756; Hutchinson 3:28; François-Jacques Leblanc to Governor Thomas Pownall, n.d. [c. May 1758], Gaudet Appendix E, 120; White 2:1019–20.
39. Ebenezer Parkman diary quoted in d'Entremont and Hébert:243, 265.
40. Ibid.:287–88.
41. White 1:601–02, 2:993–94ff.
42. Parkman diary quoted in d'Entremont and Hébert:249.

Chapter 14

1. François Le Guerne to Jacques Prévost de la Croix, 10 March 1756, Casgrain (1888–90) 2:157–60.
2. Ibid.
3. Acadians to Vaudreuil, n.d. [c. July 1756], Sauvageau:280–81; Daniel Dugas quoted in Chagnon:4.
4. Dugas quoted in Chagnon:4; White 1:284–88; Michael Conover, *Broussard: Descendants of François and Nicolas* (Lafayette, LA: privately printed, 1995); Kathy LaCombe Tell, Broussard genealogy, http://kandrtell.tripod.com/gen/broussard.html; Gamaliel Smethurst, *Narrative of an Extraordinary Escape out of the Hands of Indians, in the Gulph of St. Lawrence* (London: privately printed, 1774):17–18.
5. Casgrain (1888):32–36.
6. George Scott to Charles Lawrence, n.d. [c. April 1756], and Lawrence, proclamation, 14 May 1756, Murdoch 2:306, 308; François Le Guerne to Jacques Prévost de la Croix, 10 March 1756, Casgrain (1888–90) 2:158.
7. Hugh Graham to Andrew Brown, n.d. [c. March 1791], Brown (1881):141–42.
8. Le Guerne quoted in Lauvrière 2:86; Dugas quoted in Chagnon:5; Vaudreuil to Machault, 18 April 1757, Gaudet Appendix N, 185.
9. Lawrence to John Campbell, Earl of Loudoun, 24 April 1757, LO3451, Loudoun Papers.
10. Knox 1:78–81; Gerome Noble to unknown, 29 October 1757, *The White Fence* [Tantramar Heritage Trust newsletter, Sackville, New Brunswick] 16 (October 2001), http://heritage.tantramar.com/Newsletter_20.html.
11. Knox 1:104–05, 111–13.
12. Ibid.:1:122–29; Dan Dyson, affidavit, n.d. [c. December 1757], LO4957, and George Montgomery, report, n.d. [c. December 1757], LO4963, Loudoun Papers.
13. Knox 1:108, 142–44; Lockerby:45–94.
14. *PG*, 3 August 1758; Milner:32; Hugh Graham to Andrew Brown, n.d. [c. March 1791], Brown (1881):141–42; Ganong:172–73.
15. Rousseau de Villejouin to Claude-Louis, marquis de Massiac, 8 September 1758, Harvey (1926):190–94; Lockerby:48–51, 54, 78–79; Casgrain (1888):529.
16. Lauvrière 2:74–75; Lockerby:80–81; *PG*, 19 April 1759; White 1:521, 524–25; Jacques Girard to abbé de L'Isle-Dieu, 24 January 1759, Ansèlme Chiasson, "Remark-

able Voyages and Shipwrecks: Loss of the *Duke William* on the Atlantic Ocean," *CSHA* 2 (1968):298–99.

17. James Murray to James Wolfe, 15 September 1758 and 17 September 1758, Wright:15–17; Harvey (1926):194.

18. William Martin, "Description of the St. Johns River," 11 March 1758, LO6939, Loudoun Papers; Amherst to Monckton, 24 August 1758, PANS RG1:363.

19. Ganong:170–73; George Scott to Robert Monckton, November 1758, PAC (1926): 99–101; Monckton to James Delancy, 14 November 1758, Gaudet Appendix J, 41; William O. Raymond, *The River St. John: Its Physical Features, Legends and History from 1604 to 1784* (St. John, New Brunswick, 1910):96–107; Jeffrey Amherst to Lawrence, 29 May 1759, Akins:441; Pierre Maillard to abbé du Fau, n.d. [c. 1758], in Micheline D. Johnson, "Pierre Antoine-Simon Maillard," *DCB.*

20. Charles Lawrence, proclamation, n.d. [12 October 1758], *PG,* 16 November 1758.

21. Lawrence to William Shirley, 4 January 1756, Murdoch 2:303; Shirley to Lawrence, 16 February 1756, Akins:421; Fernando John Paris to Board of Trade, 26 January 1758, Brebner (1927):257; Freeholders of Halifax to Board of Trade, 27 January 1758, Casgrain (1888–90) 1:142–47; Board of Trade to Lawrence, 7 February 1758, Lawrence to Board of Trade, 9 May 1758 and 22 May 1758, Brymner:215–16; Haliburton 1:209–10; W. P. M. Kennedy, *Statutes, Treaties and Documents of the Canadian Constitution,* 1713–1929 (Toronto: Oxford University Press, 1930):18.

22. Thériault:50; Michel Bastarache, "Acadian Language and Cultural Rights from 1713 to the Present Day," Daigle (1982):349.

23. Lawrence, proclamation, 11 January 1759, Longley:87; Haliburton 1:220; Lawrence to Board of Trade, 26 December 1758, Gipson (1954):135; Brebner (1937):27–28.

24. Longley:89–90; Eaton (1910):63; Ian F. Mackinnon, *Settlements and Churches in Nova Scotia, 1749–1776* (Montreal: Walker Press, 1930):22–23; Gipson (1954):135–37; Arthur Wentworth Hamilton Eaton, "The Settling of Colchester County, Nova Scotia, by New England Puritans and Ulster Scotsmen," *Proceedings and Transactions of the Royal Society of Canada,* 3rd series, 6 (1913):222, 229–31, 248.

25. Lawrence to Board of Trade, 20 April 1759, Murdoch 2:367; Lawrence to Board of Trade, 20 September 1759, Akins:307–08; Brebner (1937):37–41; Eaton (1915):89; Haliburton 1:153.

26. Lawrence to Board of Trade, 20 September 1759, Akins:307–08; Board of Trade to the King, 20 December 1759, Eaton (1915):186–88.

27. Lawrence to Board of Trade, 20 September 1759, Akins:307–08; Knox, Webster (1930):74; Murdoch 2:366; Council Minutes, 16 July 1759, Longley:93.

28. *PG,* 10 May 1759; Webster (1931):18.

29. "Copie du manifeste d'Edward Whitmore," Centre des archives d'outre-mer (France), COL C11A 87/fol.407-407v, www.bd.archivescanadafrance.org/acf/; Henry Schomberg to Maillard, 26 October 1759, Maillard to Alexandre Leblanc, 27 November 1759, and Jacques Manach to Vaudreuil, 10 March 1760, Gaudet Appendix N, 187–88, 194; Ian K. Steele, "Surrendering Rites: Prisoners on Colonial North American Frontiers," Stephen Taylor et al., eds., *Hanoverian Britain and Empire: Essays in Memory of Philip Lawson* (Rochester: Boydell Press, 1998):147.

30. Arsenault (1994):160; Joseph Frye to Lawrence, 9 January 1760, Akins:311–12; "Articles de Soumission des Acadiens," 6 February 1760, Casgrain (1888–90) 1:53–55; John Burrell, "Diary," Gaudet Appendix J, 241–43; *PG*, 13 December 1759; Doughty: 151–52.
31. Jean-François Burdon de Dombourg to Acadians, 14 February 1760, Acadians of Richibouctou to Frye, n.d. [c. February 1760], and Boishébert to Manach, 21 February 1760, Gaudet Appendix N, 190–94.
32. Maillard to Alexandre Leblanc, 31 December 1759, Gaudet Appendix N, 189; S. Patterson:56–57.
33. Manach to Frye, 13 February 1760, Gaudet Appendix N, 191; Doughty:151–52; Council Minutes, 10 March 1760, and Edward Whitmore to Lawrence, 20 June 1760, Akins:313, 486.
34. Manach to Vaudreuil, 10 March 1760, Gaudet Appendix N, 194.
35. Council Minutes, 5 August 1760, Akins:314.

Chapter 15

1. Longley:99–100; Graeme Wynn, "A Province Too Much Dependent on New England," *Canadian Geographer* 31 (1987):100–01; John Frederic Herbin, *Grand Pré: A Sketch of the Acadien Occupation of the Shores of the Basin of Minas* (Toronto: William Briggs, 1898):113–14; Eaton (1910):30–32, 36; Brebner (1937):33; Marjory Whitelaw, *The Wellington Dyke* (Halifax: The Nova Scotia Museum, 1997):30–33; Hustvedt:42.
2. Brebner (1937):41, 44–45; Eaton (1915):32–33, 181–83; Milner:27; Jonathan Belcher to Board of Trade, 12 December 1760, Innis:192.
3. Moses Delesdernier, "Observations on the Progress of Agriculture," n.d. [c. 1785], Innis:192–94.
4. Belcher to Colonel William Forster, 18 June 1761, Jeffrey Amherst to Belcher, 22 March 1761, Belcher to Amherst, 14 April 1761, and Amherst to Belcher, 28 April 1761, Akins:319–20, 326–28; Amherst to Forster, n.d. [c. September 1761], Gaudet Appendix K, 257.
5. Treaty of 25 June 1761, S. Patterson:56–57; Upton:58–60.
6. Brebner (1937):46–48; Upton:62; J. S. Martell, "The Second Expulsion of the Acadians," *Dalhousie Review* 13 (1933–34):368; Nova Scotia Assembly to Belcher, 26 July 1762, Akins:315–18; Council Minutes, 30 July 1762, Murdoch 2:422.
7. Belliveau:39; Belcher to Board of Trade, 21 October 1762, Minutes of the Board of Trade, 3 December 1762, and Council Minutes, 5 July 1763, Akins: 335–38.
8. Montagu Wilmot to Halifax, 22 March 1764, Akins[338]; Wilmot to Halifax, 10 December 1763, Murdoch 2:436–37; Reid (1991):48–50.
9. M. de la Rochette to Acadians, 18 March 1763, Winzerling:39; Muriel K. Roy, "Settlement and Population Growth in Acadia," Daigle (1982):135; Stephen White, *Moncton Times and Transcript*, 3 November 2003.
10. Acadians of Pennsylvania to Nivernois, 20 June 1763, Acadians of Maryland to Nivernois, 2 July 1763, and Acadians of South Carolina to Nivernois, 13 August 1763, Winzerling:17, 47–48; Milling:37–38; Brasseaux (1991):13–15.

11. Leblanc:530; Winzerling:45.
12. STATCAN.
13. Belliveau:228–30; Acadians of Pennsylvania to Nivernois, 20 June 1763, and Acadians of Halifax to Nivernois, 13 August 1763, Winzerling:17, 175n; Acadian prisoners to Wilmot, 12 May 1764, Akins:347; Council Minutes, 15 May 1764, Gaudet Appendix K, 258; Leblanc:533–35.
14. Charles Wyndham, Earl of Egremont, to Montagu Wilmot, 26 November 1763, and Board of Trade to Wilmot, 16 July 1764, Brebner (1937):105–06; Halifax to Wilmot, 9 June 1764, Akins:347–48; Privy Council to the King, 11 July 1764, Wilmot to Board of Trade, 5 November 1764, and Council Minutes, 28 September 1764, Gaudet Appendix J, 210–11, 214, Appendix K, 258.
15. Gabriel Debien, "The Acadians in Santo Domingo: 1764–1789," Glenn R. Conrad, ed., *The Cajuns: Essays on Their History and Culture* (Lafayette, LA: Center for Louisiana Studies, 1978):25–70; Brasseaux (1991):44–46.
16. Council Minutes, 22 October 1764, Murdoch 2:443.
17. Wilmot to Board of Trade, 17 December 1764, Gaudet Appendix J, 216; Memorial of the Inhabitants of Kings County to Governor Wilmot, 23 March 1765, Casgrain (1888–90) 2:93–94.
18. Wilmot to Halifax, 9 November 1764, Akins:349–50.
19. Dudley J. Leblanc, *The True Story of the Acadians* (Lafayette, LA: privately printed, 1937):65, 164; Jacqueline Voorhies, "The Attakapas Post: The First Acadian Settlement," *Louisiana History* 17 (1976):91–96.
20. Brasseaux (1985):123–32; Brasseaux (1994):124–32. For genealogical information on the first group of Acadians in Louisiana, see Roger Rozendal's posts to the ACADIAN-CAJUN listserv, "First Acadians in Louisiana, 1764" and "Trek of the 1764 Acadians to Louisiana," archived at http://archiver.rootsweb.com/th/index/ACADIAN-CAJUN/2002-11. Stephen White suggests the Landry–des Goutins connection; see Tim Hebert, "The First Acadian in Louisiana: Joseph de Goutin de Ville," www.acadian-cajun.com/degoutin.htm.
21. Brasseaux (1985):124; Charles Philippe Aubry to unknown, 14 May 1765, Arsenault (1994):193; Brasseaux (1987):46–47, 77; Brasseaux (1991):68–70; Henry Jerningham to Antonio de Ulloa, 28 November 1767, Brasseaux (1994):129–30; Sollers (1908):1-21; R. E. Chandler, "End of an Odyssey: Acadians Arrive in St. Gabriel, Louisiana," *Louisiana History* 14 (1973):69–87.
22. Brasseaux (1987):78, 81, 125–31; Leonard:46-48; Ulloa, "Observations on the memorial presented by the settlers to the Superior Council," 1769, Jacqueline K. Voorhies, "The Acadians: The Search for the Promised Land," Conrad, ed., *The Cajuns,* 114n.
23. Brasseaux (1991):46–54; Lauvrière 2:201; Hutchinson 3:28–31.
24. Naomi Griffiths, "The Acadians Who Had a Problem in France," *Canadian Geographic* 101 (1981):40–45.
25. Henri Raymond Casgrain, "Registres des Acadiens de Belle-Isle-en-Mer," Casgrain (1888–90) 2:165–94, 3:5–59.
26. Jean-Marie Fonteneau, "Victimes de la Guerre de Sept Ans . . . Les Acadiens, citoyens de l'Atlantique," *CSHA* 30 (1999):52; Griffiths (1992):122–23.

27. Acadians of St. Malo to maréchal de Castries, 19 February 1784, and Castries, *mémoire*, 14 March 1784, Gaudet Appendix N, 168–70.
28. R. E. Chandler, "A Shipping Contract: Spain Brings Acadians to Louisiana," *Revue de Louisiane* 8 (1979):73–81; Brasseaux (1985):132; Henry Jacques, "From Acadien to Cajun to Cadien: Ethnic Labelization and Construction of Identity," *Journal of American Ethnic History* 17 (1998):29–62.
29. Acadians to Francis Bernard, 8 February 1766, Bernard to House of Representatives, 13 February 1766, and James Murray to Governor Francis Bernard, 28 April 1766, Gaudet Appendix E, 95–99; Acadians to Bernard, 2 June 1766, Belliveau:242–45.
30. Brasseaux (1991):24–28.
31. Philip Lawson, *The Imperial Challenge: Québec and Britain in the Age of the American Revolution* (Montreal: McGill-Queen's University Press, 1989):12, 18–19, 49, 57–58, 115, 121–23.
32. Michael Francklin to William Petty, Earl of Shelburne, 20 February 1768, Gaudet Appendix J, 219–20; Wills Hill, Earl of Hillsborough, to Francklin, June 1768, Mason Wade, "After the Grand Dérangement: The Acadians' Return to the Gulf of St. Lawrence and to Nova Scotia," *American Review of Canadian Studies* 5 (1975):61; Francklin to H. D. Denson, 4 July 1768, Akins:354–55.
33. Alan MacNeil, "The Acadian Legacy and Agricultural Development in Nova Scotia, 1760–1861," Kris Inwood, ed., *Farm, Factory and Fortune: New Studies in the Economic History of the Maritime Provinces* (Fredericton, New Brunswick: Acadiensis Press 1993); John MacDonald to J. F. W. DesBarres, 1795, in Wade, "After the Grand Dérangement," 61–62.
34. Samuel Arseneault, "Place Name Changes in the Cartography of Acadia," *CSHA* 14 (1983):95–103.
35. Inhabitants of Yarmouth to Council, 8 December 1775, and Inhabitants of Cumberland County to Council, 22 December 1775, Brebner (1937):309–11.

Chapter 16

1. Brown (1815):147–48; Maillet:6–7; Marguerite Maillet, "Acadian Literature—Bibliography," Daigle (1982):513–49.
2. Galerm:61–62; Petition of the Philadelphia Neutral French to the King of Great Britain, n.d. [1760], Smith:369–77.
3. Daniel Dugas quoted in Chagnon:2–3; Jean Landry, Claude Bennois [Benoit], Claude Leblanc, Charlie Daigle, Pierre Leblanc, Augustin Leblanc, Jacques Hébert, Joseph Vincent, and Antoine Hébert to Shirley, 13 April 1756, Gaudet Appendix E, 88–89; Richard 2:205, 211.
4. Michel and Pierre O'Bask [Bastarache] quoted in James Fraser, "Notes from Tradition and Memory of the Acadian Removal" (1815), PANS RG1:363; Brown (1815): 147–48. In the digital database "Early Canadiana Online," which contains over 1,458,000 pages in more than 8,500 volumes of early Canadian history, the earliest use of the phrase *le grand dérangement* to refer to Acadian removal is in a publication of 1877: *"Peu d'évènements ont causé des aventures aussi romanesques, aussi curieuses, que le grand*

dérangement; c'est ainsi que les Acadiens ont nommé leur expulsion de la terre le leurs pères—Few events produced romantic adventures as curious as *le grand dérangement*, as the Acadians called the dispossession of their fathers"—Jean-Baptiste-Antoine Ferland, *La Gaspésie* (Quebec, 1877):196–97. Nineteenth-century usage of the phrase included "*un grand dérangement d'esprit*," meaning "great mental derangement." See *Journaux de la Chambre d'assemblée du Bas-Canada, depuis le 21 novembre 1828 jusqu'au 14 mars 1829* (Quebec: John Neilson, n.d. [1829]):360.

5. Thomas Hutchinson, *The History of the Colony of Massachuset's Bay*, 2nd edn. (London: M. Richardson, 1765):96; Hutchinson 3:28–31. The first two volumes of Hutchinson's history initially appeared in 1764 and 1767, but the third, which included his treatment of Acadian removal, remained unpublished during his lifetime.

6. Edward Lloyd to James Hollyday, 9 December 1755, in William D. Hoyt, Jr., ed., "A Contemporary View of the Acadian Arrival in Maryland, 1755," *William and Mary Quarterly*, 3rd series, 5 (1948):571–75.

7. Lloyd to Hollyday in ibid.:575; Ian K. Steele, "Surrendering Rites: Prisoners on Colonial North American Frontiers," Stephen Taylor, et al., eds., *Hanoverian Britain and Empire: Essays in Memory of Philip Lawson* (Rochester, NY: Boydell Press, 1998):137–57; Armstrong Starkey, "War and Culture, a Case Study: The Enlightenment and the Conduct of the British Army in America, 1755–1781," *War and Society* 8 (1990):1–28.

8. Edmund Burke and William Burke, *An Account of the European Settlements in America in Six Parts*, 2 vols., 3rd edn. (1757; London: R. & J. Dodsley, 1760), 2:277–79.

9. Abbé Raynal, *A Philosophical and Political History of the Settlements and Trade of the Europeans in the East and West Indies*, 5 vols. (1770; Edinburgh: Mundell & Son, 1804), 5:313.

10. Ibid.:315.

11. Ibid.:319–20.

12. Robert Darnton, "Sounding the Literary Market in Prerevolutionary France," *Eighteenth-Century Studies* 17 (1984):481; Edmund Burke, *The Works of the Right Honorable Edmund Burke*, 12 vols. (Boston: Little, Brown, 1865–71), 2:345–46.

13. Brown (1881):150–52; Richard Bulkeley and Isaac Deschamps, *Nova-Scotia Magazine* (April 1790):287–89.

14. Leblanc:535.

15. Jacques Henry, "From Acadien to Cajun to Cadien: Ethnic Labelization and Construction of Identity," *Journal of American Ethnic History* 17 (1998):30; Harley H. Gould, "The Acadian French in Canada and in Louisiana," *American Journal of Physical Anthropology* 28 (1941):297; Brasseaux (1992) passim; Carl A. Brasseaux, "Acadian to Cajun: History of a Society Built on the Extended Family" (1999), www.lsuhsc.edu/no/centers/genetics/hereditaryhealing/keynote_brasseaux_p.htm.

16. Muriel K. Roy, "Settlement and Population Growth in Acadia," Daigle (1982):160; Leblanc:535.

17. Raymond:5–9, 503–04, 508–11.

18. Ibid.:670n; Officer:152–54.

19. Philippe Doucet, "Politics and the Acadians," Daigle (1982):219–69; Thériault:45–88; Reid (1991):48–50.

20. Nathaniel Hawthorne, *Famous Old People: Being the Second Epoch of Grandfather's*

Chair (Boston: Tappan & Dennet, 1842):122–23, 125–26, 135; Hawthorne Manning and Dana Longfellow, *Origin and Development of Longfellow's "Evangeline"* (Portland, ME: Anthoensen Press, 1947):12; H. E. Scuder, *Historical Introduction to Henry Wadsworth Longfellow, Evangeline: A Tale of Acadie* (Boston: Riverside Press, 1896):5–6. For a documented case of separated Acadian lovers, see Casgrain (1888):274–75 and Arsenault (1965) 1:778–83.

21. Robert Walsh, *An Appeal from the Judgments of Great Britain Respecting the United States of America* (London: Longman, Hurst, 1820):86–87, 91.

22. George Bancroft, "Exiles of Acadia," *The Token and Atlantic Souvenir, an Offering for Christmas and the New Year* (Boston: D. H. Williams, 1842):279–89 passim.

23. Henry Wadsworth Longfellow, *Evangeline, A Tale of Acadie* (Boston: W. D. Ticknor, 1847); all subsequent quotes are from this edition.

24. Naomi Griffiths, "Longfellow's *Evangeline:* The Birth and Acceptance of a Legend," *Acadiensis* 11 (1982):28; *Salem Advertiser*, 13 November 1747; Hubert H. Hoeltje, "Hawthorne's Review of Evangeline," *New England Quarterly* 23 (1950):232–35.

25. Barbara Leblanc, "Evangeline as Identity Myth," *Canadian Folklore/Folklore Canadien* 15 (1993):139–53 *passim*; James de Finney, "Idéologie et archétypes dans les récits du 'Grand Dérangement' acadien," *Canadian Issues* 16 (1994):9–19; Winzerling:vii.

26. Griffiths, "Longfellow's *Evangeline*," 36; Thériault:55.

27. Sharon Ingalls, "Mad About Acadians: Nineteenth-Century Americans Flocked to the Land of Evangeline," *The Beaver* 69 (June–July 1989):21–27.

28. Carl A. Brasseaux, *In Search of Evangeline: Birth and Evolution of the Evangeline Myth* (Thibodaux, LA: Blue Heron Press, 1988).

29. Beamish Murdoch to John Edwards Godfrey, 22 February 1869, Taylor:53; Murdoch, 2:286–87.

30. Sir Adams George Archibald, "The Expulsion of the Acadians," *NSHSC* 8 (1895): 13–14, 15, 86.

31. Rameau 1:59; Thériault:55; Rameau de Saint-Père to Henri Raymond Casgrain, n.d., Casgrain (1888):57. For Rameau's mentoring role among the Acadians, see P. D. Clarke, "Rameau de Saint-Père, Moïse de l'Acadie?" *Journal of Canadian Studies* 28 (1993):69–95.

32. Richard 2:145; Haliburton 1:192.

33. Parkman 2:468, 691–92, 1008–09, 1022–23; Francis Parkman to Casgrain, 4 November 1887, and Casgrain to Thomas Chapais, 18 November 1887, Taylor:58, 61.

34. Casgrain quoted in Cuthbertson, "Thomas Beamish Akins," 98; Parkman quoted in Howard Doughty, *Francis Parkman* (1962; Cambridge, MA: Harvard University Press, 1983):312.

35. P. D. Clarke, "Edouard Richard," *DCB*; Richard 1:5; Chiasson:6–23; Placide Gaudet, *Le grand dérangement, sur qui retombe la responsabilité de l'expulsion des Acadiens* (Ottawa: Ottawa Printing Company, 1922).

36. Chiasson:14.

37. James S. Macdonald, "Life and Administration of Governor Charles Lawrence, 1749–1760," *NSHSC* 12 (1905):31, 45. See also Macdonald, "Hon. Edward Cornwallis, Founder of Halifax" and "Richard Bulkeley, 1717–1800," *NSHSC* 12 (1905):1–17, 59–87.

38. Chiasson:16.
39. Henri d'Arles, *La déportation des acadiens* (Quebec: Imprimerie de l'Action Sociale, 1918):25–29 *passim.*
40. Ibid.
41. Leblanc:521; personal communication from Wayne Kerr, Senior Interpretation Specialist, Parks Canada, 13 November 2003. See also Robert G. Leblanc, "The Acadian Migrations," *Proceedings of the Minnesota Academy of Science* 30 (1962):523–41; Leblanc, "The Acadian Migrations," *Canadian Geographical Journal* 81 (1970):10–19; and Leblanc, "Les migrations acadiennes," *Cahiers de géographie de Québec* 58 (1979):99–124. A traveler and border-crosser in the great Acadian tradition, Leblanc was killed on 11 September 2001 when the plane on which he was a passenger was hijacked and crashed into the World Trade Center in New York City. For a short overview of Leblanc's life and work, see Steward Doty, "Robert G. Leblanc, 1930–2001," *Québec Studies* 33 (2002):5–7.
42. William Safire, "Ethnic Cleansing," *New York Times*, 14 March 1993; Commission of Experts, Final Report (S/1994/674), 24 May 1994, archived at www.ess.uwe.ac.uk/comexpert/report_toc.htm; Ball:86–87, 132–33; Medical Department of the Sick and Hurt Board of the Admiralty to John Cleveland, 17 September 1756, in Griffiths (1976):71.
43. John Mack Faragher, ed., *Rereading Frederick Jackson Turner: "The Significance of the Frontier in American History" and Other Essays* (1994; New Haven: Yale University Press, 1998):18, 135.
44. Naimark:3–4.
45. Ibid.:18, 187; Ball:93. See also Ervin Staub, *The Roots of Evil: The Origins of Genocide and Other Group Violence* (Cambridge: Cambridge University Press, 1989).
46. Cigar:16, 22, 79; Alexander Murray to John Winslow, 8 September 1755, Winslow (1883):107–08; John L. P. Thompson and Gail A. Quets, "Genocide and Social Conflict: A Partial Theory and a Comparison," *Research in Social Movements, Conflict and Change* 12 (1990):245–66.
47. Cigar:12–13, 21; Peregrine Thomas Hopson to Board of Trade, 1 October 1753, Gaudet Appendix C, 57.
48. Cigar:2–3, 47; Charles Morris, "Some Reflections on the Situation of the Inhabitants," n.d. [1754], *NSHSC* 2 (1881):158–60, and Casgrain (1888–90) 1:130–37, 2:107–11; Naimark:187.
49. Naimark:192; Cigar:57, 60.
50. Eric Lawlor, "The One Man Acadian Liberation Front," *Los Angeles Times Magazine*, 4 September 1994.
51. Chris Morris, "Acadians Defined by Past, Hopeful of Future," Canadian Press Wire Service, 17 November 1999, www.canoe.ca/CANOE2000/history_5.html; "La déportation des Acadiens refait surface," Radio-Canada, 29 October 1999, www.radio-canada.ca; Maurice Basque, Nicole Barrieau, and Stéphanie Côté, *L'Acadie de l'Atlantique* (Moncton, New Brunswick: Centre d'études acadiennes, 1999), 22.
52. Shane K. Bernard, "Acadian Pride, Anglo-Conformism: The Acadian Bicentennial Celebration of 1955," *Louisiana History* 41(2000):161–74; Sacha Richard, "Commémoration et Idéologie nationale en Acadie. Les Fêtes du Bicentenaire de la Déportation Acadienne," *MENS: Revue d'historie intellectuelle de l'amérique française* 3 (2002):27–59.

53. Muriel K. Roy, "Demography and Demolinguistics in Acadia, 1871–1991," Daigle (1995):168–69; Ron Thibodeaux, "Vive le français," *New Orleans Times-Picayune*, 17 July 2001; Ross and Deveau:170.

54. Joseph Yvon Thériault, "The Robichaud Period and Politics in Acadia," *The Robichaud Era, 1960–70* (Moncton, New Brunswick: Institut canadien de recherche sur le développement régional/Canadian Institute for Research on Regional Development, 2001):37–52; Morris, "Acadians Defined by Past, Hopeful of Future"; "La déportation des Acadiens refait surface," Radio-Canada; Lawlor, "The One Man Acadian Liberation Front."

55. *Ottawa Citizen,* 1 October 2001; House of Commons Debates, Vol. 137, No. 091, 1st Sess. 37th Parliament, Official Report (Hansard), Wednesday, October 3, 2001, www.parl.gc.ca/37/1/parlbus/chambus/house/debates/091_2001-10-03/han091_1740-E.htm.

56. Ball:92.

57. "Déportation: Les Acadiens réclament toujours des excuses," Radio-Canada, 25 September 2003, www.radio-canada.ca; Gérald LeBlanc, "Encore trois ans pour faire reconnaître la Déportation des Acadiens," *La presse le dimanche,* 24 February 2002; Beurmond Banville, "Acadians Seeking Queen's Apology," *Bangor Daily News*, 19 February 2002.

58. "Minister Copps Announces a Day of Commemoration of the Great Upheaval," new release, Heritage Ministry, Canadian Government, Ottawa, 10 December 2003; Royal Proclamation, 10 December 2003, Heritage Ministry, Canadian Government.

59. "Ottawa Admits Deportation of Acadians Was Wrong," CTV, 11 December 2003, www.ctv.ca/servlet/ArticleNews/story/CTVNews/1071092605650_66501805/; Chris Morris, "Acadians Celebrate Expulsion Proclamation," *Winnipeg Sun*, 3 December 2003; Petition of the Philadelphia Neutral French to the King of Great Britain, n.d. [1760], Smith:369–77; Luma Muhtadie, "Ottawa Approves Acadian Proclamation," *Toronto Globe and Mail,* 4 December 2003; Beurmond Banville, "Acadians to Get Apology from Queen Elizabeth. Proclamation Acknowledges Deportation," *Bangor Daily News*, 5 December 2003.

60. Richard 1:292–93.

PERMISSIONS

The publisher and author make grateful acknowledgment for permission to reproduce the following illustrations.

First Insert

"The Embarkation of the Acadians," engraving by French illustrator Émile Bayard from William Cullen Bryant and Sydney Howard Gay, *A Popular History of the United States* (1884). © Bettmann/CORBIS.

Petroglyph: European vessel, with stick figures. Rock carving: anonymous Mìkmaq, in situ: Kejimkujik National Park, N.S. Photography: Olive and Arthur Kelsall, 1946–1955. Nova Scotia Museum, Halifax, reference number 59.60.3. Reproduced courtesy of Nova Scotia Museum, History Collection, Halifax, Canada.

"Homme Acadien," Nova Scotia, 1788–1796, etching by Jacques Grasset de Saint-Sauveur. Published in *Tableaux des principaux peoples de l'Europe, de l'Asie, de l'Afrique, de l'Amérique et les découvertes des Capitaines Cook, La Pérouse, etc.* (Paris et Bordeaux, chez l'auteur, 1796–1798). National Archives of Canada / C-021112.

"Femme Acadienne" [recto l.c.], etching by Jacque Grasset de Saint-Sauveur. Possibly from J. G. de Saint-Sauveur, *Encyclopédie des voyages . . .* ," vol. 5 (Paris, 1795). National Archives of Canada / C-070665.

"Figure de la Terre, Neuve Grande Riviere de Canada, et Cotes de L'Ocean en la Nouvelle France" and "Figure du Port Royal en La Nouvelle France," maps from Marc Lescarbot's *Histoire de La Nouvelle France* (1609). Courtesy of Beinecke Rare Book and Manuscript Library, Yale University.

"Habitation de Port Royal," by Samuel de Champlain, engraving, copied for Publishers Association, 1914–15. Wm. Notman & Son, 1914–15, 20th century. View-14806, McCord Museum of Canadian History, Montreal.

"L'Ordre de Bon-Temps, 1606," by Charles William Jefferys, from No. 3 in a set of twelve reproductions entitled "Canadian Historical Paintings, 1534–1885" that reproduces works by C. W. Jefferys and Henry Sandham. National Archives of Canada / C-013986.

"Repairing a Dike" and "Saltmarsh Haying," painted by artist Azor Vienneau, c. 1981. © Nova Scotia Museum, History Collection, Halifax, Canada.

"PLAN TRES EXACT DV Terrain où sont sçituées les maisons du Port Royal et ou lon peut faire une Ville considerable," Jean-Baptiste-Louis Franquelin, 1686. Original in France, Bibliothèque nationale, Cartes et plans, Service hydrographique, Portefeuille 133, Division 8, Pièce 2. Reproduced from National Archives of Canada contact print BK/240/Port Royal/[1686], which shows a portion of the original. Transcript made by Baudouin in 1933.

"Plan of the River Annapolis in Royal in Nova Scotia." Surveyed in the year 1733 by Mr. George Mitchell Depty, Surveyor of the Woods, corrected and amended from other surveys etc., 1753. Holmden 2594 "M.S. 9" From MG 21 King's MSS. 209 (originally in BL). Courtesy of National Archives of Canada.

Detail from "A New and Accurate Map of the Islands of Newfoundland, Cape Breton, St. John and Anticosta; Together with the Neighbouring Countries of Nova Scotia; Canada &c.," Emanuel Bowen (1747). Reproduced courtesy of Map Collection, Sterling Memorial Library, Yale University.

Detail from "Map of Nova Scotia, or Acadia," John Montressor (1768), reproduced courtesy of Map Collection, Sterling Memorial Library, Yale University.

"Chignecto," detail of a map from J. F. W. Des Barres, *Atlantic Neptune* (1781), reproduced courtesy of Map Collection, Sterling Memorial Library, Yale University.

"Proclamation Par Son Excellence Richard Philipps Escuyer," 10 April 1720, reproduced by permission of the Archives de France, Centre des archives d'outre mer.

Second Insert

"Acadie, the Odyssey of a People," 1993 © Parks Canada.

Portrait of Major General Paul Mascarene, 1729, by John Smibert. Los Angeles County Museum of Art, Museum purchase with funds provided by Mr. and Mrs. William Preston Harrison Collection, Charles H. Quinn Bequest, Eli Harvey, and other donors. Photograph © 2004 Museum Associates/LACMA.

"His Excellency William Shirley." Reprint of engraving by P. Pelham by the Pelham Club, Boston, 1901. Courtesy of the Massachusetts Historical Society.

"General Lawrence," engraving from Tobias George Smollett, *Continuation of the Complete History of England* (1757). Courtesy of Beinecke Rare Book and Manuscript Library, Yale University.

Portrait of General John Winslow. Courtesy of Pilgrim Hall Museum, Plymouth, Massachusetts.

Portrait of Thomas Pichon. National Archives of Canada / C-010608.

Marquis de Boishébert—Charles Deschamps de Boishébert et de Raffetot (1727–1979). Anonymous, c. 1753. M967.48 McCord Museum of Canadian History, Montreal.

"View of Beausejour from ye S.E. 1755," J. Hamilton del. et fecit. By permission of the British Library/Maps CXIX 70.

Detail from *A Large and Particular Plan of Shegnekto Bay* (1755). Courtesy of Map Collection, Sterling Memorial Library, Yale University.

"Lecture de l'ordonnance d'expulsion des Acadiens dans l'église de Parish à Grand Pré, 1755," vers 1920, by Charles William Jefferys. National Archives of Canada/C-073709.

"Burning and Lay Waste," by Claude T. Picard, 1986 © Parks Canada. Reproduced by permission of Parks Canada and Claude T. Picard.

1768 Oath of Allegiance, signed by Pierre Beliveau, reproduced from the collection of the Centre d'études acadiennes, Université de Moncton.

Acadian women, frontispiece from Frederic S. Cozzens, *Acadia, or, A Month with the Blue Noses* (1859). Courtesy of Beinecke Rare Book and Manuscript Library, Yale University.

Four illustrations from *Longfellow's Evangeline, with Illustrations by F. O. C. Darley* (1886). Courtesy of Sterling Memorial Library, Yale University.

"Evangeline, Song & Chorus," by Will S. Hays (1865), courtesy of Library of Congress and Duke University Rare Book, Manuscript, and Special Collections Library.

Evangeline statue at St. Martin de Tours Catholic Church, St. Martinville, Louisiana, postcard published by Louis J. Fournet Drug Store, St. Martinville, Louisiana, n.d. [1940s] from Coll. 146 Louisiana Photographs, University Archives and Acadiana Manuscripts Collection, Edith Garland Dupre Library, University of Louisiana at Lafayette.

"Acadian Memorial Park, Grand Pré, NS, about 1923," anonymous. MP-0000.158.3 McCord Museum of Canadian History, Montreal.

INDEX